Global Copyright

Global Copyright

Three Hundred Years Since the Statute of Anne, from 1709 to Cyberspace

Edited by

Lionel Bently

Herchel Smith Professor of Intellectual Property Law, University of Cambridge, UK

Uma Suthersanen

Professor in International Intellectual Property Law, Queen Mary, University of London, UK

Paul Torremans

Professor of Intellectual Property Law, School of Law, University of Nottingham, UK

IN ASSOCIATION WITH ALAI
Published in conjunction with www.blaca.org

Edward Elgar
Cheltenham, UK • Northampton, MA, USA

Published by
Edward Elgar Publishing Limited
The Lypiatts
15 Lansdown Road
Cheltenham
Glos GL50 2JA
UK

Edward Elgar Publishing, Inc.
William Pratt House
9 Dewey Court
Northampton
Massachusetts 01060
USA

A catalogue record for this book
is available from the British Library

Library of Congress Control Number: 2009942845

Mixed Sources
Product group from well-managed
forests and other controlled sources
www.fsc.org Cert no. SA-COC-1565
© 1996 Forest Stewardship Council
FSC

ISBN 978 1 84844 766 0

Printed and bound by MPG Books Group, UK

Contents

Influence, past and present, of the Statute of Anne on civil and common law countries

Contributors

Lionel Bently, Herchel Smith Professor of Intellectual Property Law, University of Cambridge, UK

June M. Besek, Executive Director, Kernochan Center for Law, Media and the Arts, Columbia University Law School, USA

Dame Lynne J. Brindley, Chief Executive, The British Library, UK

Trevor Cook, Partner, Bird & Bird, UK

William Cornish, Herchel Smith Professor of Intellectual Property Law emeritus, University of Cambridge, UK

Ronan Deazley, Professor of Law, School of Law, University of Glasgow, UK

Joris Deene, Faculty of Law, University of Ghent, Belgium

Christophe Geiger, Associate Professor and General Director and Director of the Research Laboratory, Centre for International Intellectual Property Studies (CEIPI), University of Strasbourg, France

Ysolde Gendreau, Professor of Law, Faculty of Law, Université de Montréal, Canada

Jane C. Ginsburg, Morton L. Janklow Professor of Literary and Artistic Property Law, Columbia University School of Law, USA

Willem Grosheide, Professor of Intellectual Property Law, Center for Intellectual Property Law (CIER), Molengraaff Institute for Private Law, Law Faculty, Utrecht University, The Netherlands

Takeshi Hishinuma, Visiting Scholar, Institute of Intellectual Property (IIP) of Japan, Japan

Lord Hoffmann, Honorary Professor in Intellectual Property Law, Queen Mary, University of London, formerly Lord of Appeal in Ordinary, UK

Tarja Koskinen-Olsson, Honorary President of IFRRO, Finland

Delia Lipszyc, Professor of International Law and UNESCO Chair of Copyright and Related Rights, School of Law, University of Buenos Aires (UBA), Argentina

André Lucas, Professor of Law, Faculté de Droit, Université de Nantes, France

Pierre-Emmanuel Moyse, Assistant Professor, McGill University, Canada

Victor Nabhan, Chairman, ALAI

Harjinder Obhi, Senior Legal Counsel, Google, UK

Marybeth Peters, Register of Copyright, United States Copyright Office, USA

Gunnar Petri, Chairman of the STIM Board, Sweden

Marco Ricolfi, Professor of Law, Faculty of Law, University of Turin, Italy

Mark Rose, Prof.Em., English Department, University of California, Santa Barbara, USA

Pierre Sirinelli, Professor of Law, Université Paris-I (Panthéon – Sorbonne), France

Christian Sprang, Justiziar/Senior Legal Counsel, Börsenverein des Deutschen Buchhandels, Germany

J.A.L. Sterling, Professorial Fellow, Queen Mary Intellectual Property Institute, Centre for Commercial Law Studies, Queen Mary, University of London, UK

Michael F. Suarez, S.J., Professor of English, University Professor, & Director of the Rare Book School, University of Virginia, USA

Uma Suthersanen, Professor in International Intellectual Property Law, Queen Mary, University of London, UK

Tomasz Targosz, Institute of Intellectual Property Law, Jagiellonian University, Kraków, Poland

Paul Torremans, Professor of Intellectual Property Law, School of Law, University of Nottingham, UK

Stef van Gompel, Institute for Information Law, University of Amsterdam, The Netherlands

Martin Vogel, European Patent Office, Germany

Andreas Wiebe, Chair for Intellectual Property Law, University of Göttingen, Germany

Raquel Xalabarder, Universitat Oberta de Catalunya, Spain

Preface

The first modern copyright law was enacted by the British Parliament in 1709 and came into force in 1710. This was the Statute of Anne: an

> Act for the Encouragement of Learning, by Vesting the Copies of Printed Books in the Authors or Purchasers of such Copies. . .

The Act proved to be a catalyst and was soon followed by other copyright legislation, the most influential being the French droit d'auteur decrees passed in 1791 and 1793. For more than a century all efforts remained focussed at a national level, but increasingly this territorial approach became a problem.

Consequently, the International Literary and Artistic Association (ALAI) was founded in Paris in 1878, with Victor Hugo as its honorary chairman. Its main objective was to promote an international agreement to protect authors of literary, scientific and artistic works. The association achieved this with the adoption on 9 September 1886, of the Berne Convention for the Protection of Literary and Artistic Works. This was the culmination of 175 years of modern copyright laws. The Convention recognised and developed legal principles that were first forged under national systems. In essence this is still the copyright system as we know it.

The ALAI 2009 London Congress celebrated the tercentenary of modern copyright law. It explored the various principles set out in the Statute of Anne, such as the right of printing and publishing, the notion of libraries as repositories of knowledge, the right of authors to control the importation of books, and the question of formalities. The discussion then moved on in a second stage to the ways in which these historic issues manifest themselves in the era of Cyberspace: online digital libraries, illegal downloading and distribution of protected works, authors' contracts and the economic impact of copyright. In a third stage the current globalised context that puts fundamentally into question the basis of modern copyright, that is national systems with an international top layer based on national treatment, was examined from the angle of international exhaustion and the renewed interest in formalities.

This volume is in essence the crystalisation of these debates during the

Congress. Three stages have become the three main parts of the book. Each of these topics is analysed in depth by those who presented their papers at the Congress and those who participated in the panels. Each stage is also introduced by one of the editors to show its place in the wider picture, as well as the links between the various contributions.

We have also retained the symbolism of the Congress in this volume. The journey started at Stationers' Hall, a place with a strong historical link to copyright and the first stage of the debates of the Congress, before ending at Lincoln's Inn, a place linked to modern law as we know it. The volume opens with the opening speech of Victor Nabhan, President of ALAI, and it ends with his closing speech that rounded off the work of the Congress, followed by Lord Hoffmann's dinner speech at Lincoln's Inn. We hope that in this way not only the scientific content of the Congress, but also its atmosphere finds its way into this volume. This also emphasises the dual role of the book. On the one hand it forms the conference proceedings for those that shared these three memorable days in London in June 2009 and on the other hand it provides an in depth scientific analysis of the legacy of the Statute of Anne and modern copyright 300 years on from its origins.

This book is published in conjunction with the website of Blaca, which contains additional material. This includes the replies to the questionnaire sent in ahead of the Congress by the national groups of ALAI, as well as the original language versions of the papers that were not submitted in English and translations into French and Spanish of a number of key papers. The website, which can be found at www.blaca.org, and the book should be looked at together as a joint publication.

Professor Paul Torremans
Professor Lionel Bently
Professor Uma Suthersanen

Opening speech

Victor Nabhan*

Ladies and Gentlemen,

Dear Friends,

In 1812 a book was published, the title of which is very telling. It was called 'Calamities and Quarrels of Authors'. In this book, the author, Isaac Disraeli, draws a rather bleak picture of the situation of authors.

'In all nations of Europe, [he asserts] authors, though they have been the most honored, were nevertheless the least remunerated.'

'Authors continue poor', he goes on, 'and booksellers become opulent'. 'They are heirs to fortunes, but by a strange singularity they are disinherited at their birth; for, on the publication of their works, these cease to be their own property.'

'Most of them close their lives in apathy and despair, and too many live by means which few of them would not blush to describe.'

This dramatic description is well portrayed by a poem attributed to a mendicant author:

> Forgive me, God, although I curse my birth,
> And ban the air wherein I breathe a wretch!
> For misery hath daunted all my mirth —
> In some far land will I my griefs rehearse,
> England, adieu! the soil that brought me forth!
> Adieu, unkinde! where skill is nothing worth!

Despite this rather dramatic depiction, Disraeli finds, however, some reason for solace. In a chapter entitled 'The Suffering of Authors' he refers to 'That Act of Anne which confers on them some right of property, acknowledges that works of learned men have been carried on too often to the ruin of them and their families.'

300 years later, or rather 299, as the Statute of Anne was enacted in 1710, the chance could not be missed to reflect on the importance of this historical event and to put it in proper historical perspective as well as in

* ALAI Chairman

current context. Our friends from BLACA have wonderfully grabbed this opportunity by organizing this Congress.

In terms of history, the Statute of Anne was the first enactment ever to spell out the basic components that were to form the common structure of future copyright laws, that is providing for (1) exclusive rights to (2) authors, with respect to (3) a subject matter and (4) for a limited time. These are the backbones of any copyright legislation, anywhere in the world.

However, it would seem that not everybody agrees with this fact. Some even beg to differ. For example President Sarkozy emphatically stated last year, and I quote, that 'France has invented Copyright' ('La France a inventé le Copyright'). I must say that this somewhat puzzling statement was made in the aftermath of the European Football Games competition during which the French national team did not fare exceedingly well, and from which the English team was excluded. This might explain that, perhaps.

Put into historical perspective, the Statute of Anne was only but the beginning of an exponential development of copyright laws all over the world that were to provide for (1) more rights applying to (2) more subject matter and for (3) a longer period of time.

But we are witnessing now a time of profound turbulence. One may even refer to a backlash of sorts. Copyright is pointed at with an accusing finger. To such an extent that a political party running under the name of the Pirate Party, has succeeded in having one representative elected to the European Parliament. Its program is quite simple: free use of works on the net and a much shorter term of protection in general. On the other hand, active lobbying from developing countries and consumer groups requires that free use of works be expanded, and that compulsory exceptions be provided for in future treaties.

As we are in a country where understatement is a way of life, it would be fair to say that Copyright is at a crossroads. In the mind of many, at present, Copyright is not very likely to win a popularity contest. As a matter of fact, and for some, one wonders which, between swine flu and copyright, is perceived as the more hazardous! Never before, have the stakes been so high nor Copyright a more controversial topic.

The conference is thus highly, hugely timely. The topics that it will address are very relevant and quite inspiring. And speaking about inspiration, allow me to quote an extract from a poem by James Thomson, a Scot. It is entitled 'The Seasons'. Even though pompous at times it is one of the finest nature poems in English literature. And one of the longest too, as it runs over 200 pages. It has also given rise to a formidable and very long legal dispute and to two important well known court decisions: *Millar v.*

Taylor and *Donaldson v. Beckett*. In this poem Thomson describes creativity in the following terms:

> Come, Inspiration! from they hermit-seat, By mortal seldom found: may Fancy dare, From they fix'd serious eye, and raptured glance Shot on surrounding Heaven, to steal one look Creative of the Poet, every power Exalting to an ecstasy of soul

Drawing on this poem, I trust that this meeting will be a source of inspirational and inspired debates. And I hope that these debates will be exalting in a way that might lead to an ecstasy of our souls. Or at least, the legally inclined side of our souls!

It is thus with the utmost pleasure that I have the honor and privilege to declare open the ALAI Congress in London, to celebrate a unique and historical event: the almost tercentennial advent of the Statute of Anne.

PART I

The Statute of Anne and its role in the world of copyright

1. Introduction to Part I: the history of copyright

Lionel Bently*

The 2009 ALAI Conference was held in London in recognition of 300 years of the Statute of Anne.[1] That Act is traditionally claimed to be the world's first copyright statute,[2] and has thus become viewed as the origin of a system of national laws that today exist in virtually all countries of the world. But, while there is some truth in such a claim, it is also important that it be treated with caution, because it is apt to mislead – in at least three ways.

1 THE WORLD'S 'FIRST' COPYRIGHT ACT

First, the statement might imply that the Act represented the world's first system of regulation of the reproduction of published books. But this is not true at all. As Ronan Deazley and Willem Grosheide describe,[3] many countries had equivalent systems of Guild regulation and royal printing privileges long before 1710, with many of the print privileges schemes developed in the wake of the practices of Venice and Rome.[4]

* Prof Lionel Bently, Herchel Smith Professor of Intellectual Property Law, Faculty of Law, University of Cambridge

1 An Act for the Encouragement of Learning, by Vesting the Copies of Printed Books in the Authors or Purchasers of such Copies, During the Times therein mentioned, 1710, 8 Anne, c.19.

2 Harry Ransom, *The First Copyright Statute: An Essay on An Act for the Encouragement of Learning, 1710* (Austin: University of Texas Press, 1956); Tomás Gómez-Arostegui, 'What History Teaches Us About Copyright Injunctions And the Inadequate-Remedy-At-Law Requirement' (2008) *S. Cal. L. Rev* 1197, 1218 ('the first modern-like copyright statute').

3 See herein, Chapters 3 and 6 respectively.

4 For a sample of key documents, with commentaries, see the contribution of Joanna Kostylo to L. Bently and M. Kretschmer (eds), *Primary Sources on Copyright in Five Jurisdictions, 1450–1900*, at www.copyrighthistory.org. For a

With respect to the United Kingdom, the Act of Anne had been preceded by well over 150 years of regulation of printing, via the grant of printing privileges (some over individual works, but several important ones over categories of works), through the regulations established by the Guild of Stationers and the statutory mechanisms that gave teeth to those privileges and regulations, namely the Licensing Acts. In Lyman Ray Patterson's account of the Statute of Anne, the Act was a 'trade regulation device' that 'restored' order to the book trade that has arisen when the Licensing Act was not renewed in 1695.[5] So the Act of Anne was not, *in substance*, something that was new. The Act merely created a legislative system giving authors and publishers standardised, time-limited, privileges as of right. And, as Michael Suarez argues very little changed as a result of the Act.[6]

And if the Act of Anne did not inaugurate a substantively different system of regulation, then all that was 'new' about it was that it was an 'Act' – a public law enacted by the Crown in Parliament, rather than a regulatory system dependent on a mix of custom, privilege and law. Of course, this shift might be thought significant, because legislation represents the form of most contemporary laws. But legislation in 1710 should not be credited with the same kind of aura of legitimacy that legislation has in an era of democracy where the legislature is voted in by a free vote of all adults, whatever their wealth, property or status.

Footnote 4 (*cont.*)
specific 'contender' for the title of 'world's first copyright Act' see Venetian Decree on Author-Printer Relations (1545), in ibid., but note also Kostylo's commentary noting that although the Decree is 'often celebrated as the first European legislative act to recognise the author's "copyright". . .[i]n reality. . .it was one of a series of remedial decrees designed to regulate the printing trade and, rather than constituting an assertion of author's rights as such.'

[5] Lyman Ray Patterson, *Copyright in Historical Perspective* (Nashville: Vanderbilt University, 1968) 150; John Feather, 'From Rights in Copies to Copyright: The Recognition of Authors' Rights in English Law and Practice in the Sixteenth and Seventeenth Century', in Martha Woodmansee and Peter Jaszi (eds), *The Construction of Authorship: Textual Appropriation in Law and Literature* (Durham and London: Duke University Press, 1994) 191, 208–9 (describing the Act as 'an inadequate and inaccurate codification. . .of existing book trade practices.' But cf. Ronan Deazley's commentary, Deazley, R. (2008) 'Commentary on the *Statute of Anne* 1710', in L. Bently and M. Kretschmer (eds), *Primary Sources on Copyright (1450-1900)* www.copyrighthistory.org (describing these accounts as too reductionist).

[6] See Chapter 4 in this volume.

2 THE WORLD'S FIRST 'COPYRIGHT' ACT

Secondly, the reference to the Act of Anne being a 'copyright' Act is also misleading, for we might question whether the Act of Anne was a 'copyright' statute at all. After all, it did not use the term 'copyright' – so we cannot justify calling it a 'copyright Act' because this was how the Act described itself.[7] The rights the Act conferred were described as the rights to 'print and reprint' books, not 'copyright'. Moreover, it is unclear how widely the term 'copyright' was used in 1710. Certainly some references to such a term have been found in the Stationers Company (dating from 1678) and court records (1681/2) dating from before 1710,[8] but even then the term referred to 'rights in copies', that is manuscripts, rather than the 'right to copy'.[9] Had anyone celebrated the passage of the Act in April 1710 by declaring 'this is the world's first copyright Act', the chances are that few, if any, would have understood what that meant.

As is clear from what I have just said, to contend that the Act was the first 'copyright Act' rather begs the question as to what we mean by 'copyright'. And here, I think, we need to be careful, because the term 'copyright' is resonant with meaning (as Paul Goldstein observed in his 1989 Brace Memorial Lecture[10]). If all we mean by 'copyright' is the right to control copying, then I think there is not much harm in the statement (though, it should be noted the right was confined to published works). But, if one understands 'copyright' to mean the rights of authors, or the regime of regulation of literary and artistic works, or a regime of

---

[7] Perhaps this is one answer to Professor Cornish's inquiry, at Chapter 2, Section 1 in this volume, into why it came to be known as the 'Act of Anne': a term had yet to be generally known that would satisfactorily describe the Act's operation.

[8] Tomás Gómez-Arostegui, 'What History Teaches Us About Copyright Injunctions And the Inadequate-Remedy-At-Law Requirement' (2008) *S. Cal. L. Rev* 1197, 1225-6, referring to *Herringman v. Clerke*, C8/301/33. Indeed, at least one pamphlet preceding the 1710 Act used the term 'Copy-Right' as well as the more common phrase 'rights in copies': Reasons Humbly Offer'd for the Bill for the Encouragement of Learning (1709), L. Bently and M. Kretschmer (eds), *Primary Sources on Copyright (1450–1900)* www.copyrighthistory.org.

[9] For a typical example of such usage, see Reasons Humbly Offer'd for the Bill for the Encouragement of Learning (1709), L. Bently and M. Kretschmer (eds) *Primary Sources on Copyright (1450–1900)*, www.copyrighthistory.org (referring to the 'sole and undoubted right to *the copy* of his own book', the 'assignment of such copy' and so on).

[10] P. Goldstein, 'Copyright' (1990–1) 38 *Journal of the Copyright Society of the USA* 109.

regulation related to but distinct from laws of patents and designs, then we need to be much more wary.

For the 1710 Act was, in its inception, concerned with the regulation of published books. The Act conferred protection on *existing* works for 20 years. It was conceived as a device that would prevent other booksellers copying those published works. It was not, primarily, a mechanism for recognising 'authorship', even if it was expressly directed at 'the encouragement of learned men to compose and write useful books'. As has now been thoroughly exposed, the Act preceded the generation of ideas of authorial genius, the so-called 'romantic author',[11] and to read back such later conceptualisations into the word 'author' (or the inclusion of a reversionary term) is to commit a historical sin.

Similarly, if we think of the Act as the origin of the legal regime for the protection of literature and art, we read back into the moment a conception that simply was not present: an abstract vision of the 'creative field' – the 'fine arts' or 'les beaux arts'. But the Act was about books, and sought by booksellers. It would come to be a legislative model which was copied, and adapted, by others who sought protection for engravings against copying, and later for fabric designs and sculpture.[12] But that is not how it was conceived. And, in Britain, no legislative protection was given to an artist over his drawings and paintings until 150 years later when the Fine Art Copyright Act was passed in 1862.[13] The world's first copyright act, in this sense, was almost certainly the French decree of 1793.[14]

---

[11] M. Rose, *Authors and Owners: The Invention of Copyright* (London: Harvard University Press, 1993).

[12] An Act for the encouragement of the arts of designing, engraving, and etching historical and other prints, by vesting the properties thereof in the inventors and engravers, during the time therein mentioned, 1735, 8 Geo. II, c.13; An Act for the Encouragement of the Arts of designing and printing Linens, Cottons, Callicoes, and Muslins, by vesting the Properties thereof, in the Designers, Printers and Proprietors, for a limited time, 1787, 27 Geo.III, c.38; An Act for Encouraging the Art of Making New Models and Casts of Busts, and other things therein mentioned, 1798, 38 Geo.III, c.71.

[13] Lionel Bently, 'Art and the Making of Modern Copyright Law' in Daniel McClean and Karsten Schubert, *Dear Images: Art, Copyright and Culture* (ICA/Ridinghouse, 2002) 330; Ronan Deazley, (2008) 'Commentary on *Fine Arts Copyright Act* 1862', in L. Bently and M. Kretschmer (eds), *Primary Sources on Copyright (1450–1900)* www.copyrighthistory.org

[14] French Literary and Artistic Property Act (1793), L. Bently and M. Kretschmer (eds), *Primary Sources on Copyright (1450–1900)* www.copyrighthistory.org. However, as Frédéric Rideau explains elsewhere, even the interpretation of this Act required a considerable degree of judicial creativity: 'Nineteenth century controversies relating to the protection of artistic property in France under the 1793

Moreover, we might think of the Act as the first 'copyright' statute, in the sense of marking a differentiation from other fields of (what we now call) intellectual property, such as patents, designs and trade marks. But, as Deazley reminds us, this is hardly accurate: printing privileges continued to be granted, renewed and enforced well into the eighteenth century. The Statute of Anne was not a 'clean break' of book regulation from the patent system. Moreover, the regulation of designs was to develop through a process of legislative mimicry from the Engravers Act, which itself was an adaptation of the Act of Anne. Indeed, as Brad Sherman and I have argued elsewhere,[15] these distinct categories of intangible monopoly rights really only crystallised into their 'modern' form in the middle of the nineteenth century.

3 THE 'WORLD'S' FIRST COPYRIGHT ACT

Thirdly, the claim that this was 'the world's' first Act is also somewhat misleading, at least in so far it may be thought to suggest that it was British genius that led to the Act, the first *in* the world, which was subsequently imitated rather mechanically elsewhere. Such an image over-emphasises the distinctiveness of the British contribution, and marginalises the contributions of some other countries to the construction of today's conception(s) of 'copyright'.

It is true, of course, that the Act of Anne was influential. It became – despite its widely recognised flaws – a model within Britain on which subsequent legislation was based. Moreover, the Statute of Anne was a model for other countries. It was copied in many of the newly independent American states,[16] and doubtless came to exert some sort of influence

---

Act' in R. Deazley, M. Kretschmer and L. Bently (eds), *Privilege and Property: Essays in the History of Copyright* (OpenBook Publishers, forthcoming 2010).

[15] Brad Sherman and Lionel Bently, *The Making of Modern Intellectual Property Law: The British Experience, 1760–1911* (Cambridge: CUP, 1999) pp. 95 ff.

[16] See Oren Bracha, 'Connecticut Copyright Statute (1783)', in L. Bently and M. Kretschmer (eds), *Primary Sources on Copyright (1450–1900)* www.copyright-history.org (and other state statutes passed between 1783 and 1786). In his commentary Bracha reviews the state laws and concludes:

> The state enactments were the first time that a general copyright regime, as opposed to ad hoc privilege grants, was created in the United States. Their legislation situated the Statute of Anne as the dominant framework for such a general copyright regime and familiarised Americans, some of whom would be

over the United States federal copyright law enacted in 1790.[17] The choice of term, in multiples of 14 years, at the very least is evidence of continued influence, right up until the 1976 overhaul that preceded the decision of the United States to adhere to the Berne Convention. Moreover, the operation of the Statute of Anne was explicitly extended outside of Britain to its colonies through the 1814 Act.[18] The indirect influence of the Act in other countries of Europe is more difficult to identify, though I have little doubt that such influence did exist. Even in 1710, the British legislature did not operate in a vacuum, uninfluenced by what was going on elsewhere (with one of the petitions that preceded the Bill, specifically referring to practices in Amsterdam).[19] Ideas circulated around Europe, and indeed across the Atlantic, through books, correspondence, trade fairs, diplomatic contacts, colonisation and the movement and migration of peoples. So, it seems plausible to assume (even if the historical proof has yet to be provided), that the Act of Anne was known about in France, the German states, and elsewhere in Europe over the following century.

I have little doubt that the Act of Anne was an influential legal text in Europe for precisely the same reason that I consider it potentially misleading to call the Act 'the world's first'. This phrase fails to recognise the significant contributions of other European legal systems both before 1710 (which influenced the development of the Act) and thereafter to the idea of, and institutional reality of copyright law and practice. We need to look outside of the Statute of Anne, and beyond British shores, for other key

Footnote 16 (*cont.*)
later involved with creating the federal regime, with its details. By the time that the United States embarked on creating a national copyright system it was only natural that the Statute of Anne would provide the basic template for its creation, at least in part thanks to the Americanisation of the statute's model in the previous decade.

[17] An Act for the Encouragement of Learning, by securing copies of maps, charts, and books, to the authors and proprietors of such copies, during the times therein mentioned (1790). In his commentary on the 1790 Act, Oren Bracha observes that 'the statute of Anne served as a general inspiration, as well as a source of basic concepts and specific technical details for the 1790 Copyright Act'.

[18] An Act to amend the several Acts for the Encouragement of Learning, by securing the Copies and Copyright of Printed Books, to the Authors of such Books or their Assigns, 1814, 54 Geo.III, c.156.

[19] 'Reasons Humbly Offer'd for the Bill for the Encouragement of Learning (1709)', L. Bently and M. Kretschmer (eds), *Primary Sources on Copyright (1450–1900)* www.copyrighthistory.org ('Nor is it in England alone that this Copy-Right is observ'd, but in all other Countries whatsoever where Printing is Ecercis'd: And it is but a few Years since the Copies of Mr Henry Wetstein of Amsterdam were sold for several thousand Gilders.')

contributions, such as the development of the idea of authors' rights, of the right to control performances of work, of moral rights and contractual protection for authors, of institutions such as collecting societies, and, of course, to the development of international laws.[20]

[20] While it is appropriate in a context such as ALAI to recognise the multiple, international contributions to the development of copyright law and practice, let us at the same time be careful not to think of 'copyright' as 'the world's' in the sense of '*of* the world'. The 'copyright' that we know is not the product of, or even a symbol of, some common, consensual, global legal culture. Rather, the concept of 'copyright' that is embodied in international norms is one that was developed primarily in Europe. That concept is built on ideas and institutions, such as creativity, individualism and property, that are today widespread but are nevertheless not universally shared. And the process by which this concept of 'copyright' has been institutionalised elsewhere has involved processes that have not always been voluntary, such as colonisation and its post-colonial equivalents.

2. The Statute of Anne 1709–10: its historical setting

William Cornish*

1 QUEEN ANNE: A LIMITED MONARCH

This keynote address to the Congress should be heard in a celebratory key, a key with rich and lasting sonorities: E Flat major perhaps. The Statute of Anne has sounded many striking chords in its long history as a model for copyright. Some of them are harmonious, some discordant; but as most people have appreciated, even before the knell of post-modernism, we hear what we are disposed to hear. Whatever the impression of the Statute on each of us, it has its distinctive timbre. Hence today's act of homage.

The Statute is set out in the appendix of this Volume for easy reference in much that was discussed in the First Session of the Congress and is found in the first part of this volume.[1] Why copyright experts have come to regard this piece of Parliamentary legislation as 'the Statute of Anne' is obscure. The British do not talk of the Copyright Act 1842 as the Statute of Victoria, or the Imperial Copyright Act of 1911 as the Statute of Edward (VII). Nor in Anne's own reign do we regard the truly fundamental Act of Union joining Scotland to England as another 'Statute of Anne', though nationalist Scots may condemn it as a Statute of Anne-xation. The Act on Copy-right (9 Anne c.21) is named after the monarch in the obtuse way that some nicknames stick. Of itself the name is of no more historical significance than the question whether the Act should bear the date of 1709 or 1710 (or both, in the alternative).

This does not mean that, in surveying the history of its enactment, we should ignore the place of the Queen herself, and in particular her position in a process of constitutional evolution that has had many resonances since. Queen Anne (1665–1714) was the last of the Stuart monarchs,

* Prof. Em., University of Cambridge. A French and Spanish translation of this chapter can be found on the website of the British Literary and Artistic Copyright Association (BLACA): www.blaca.org.

1 Suggestions for further reading are found in Appendix 2 of this book.

the line which had succeeded Henry VIII's second daughter, the great Elizabeth Tudor. On her spinster death, King James of Scotland, son of the ill-fated Mary, Queen of Scots, became entitled to the English throne and ruled the two countries – as James VI of Scotland, and James I of England (1603–25). In turn he would be succeeded by his son, Charles I; and then, his grandsons, Charles II (1660–85) and James II (1685–88). But ensnared within this simple recitation of names and dates lies the bitter and tumultuous history of antagonism between the monarch and many of his propertied subjects, which reached two climaxes.

The first was the overthrow of the first Charles, executed in 1649 and replaced by the republican Commonwealth. This Puritan revolution, led for most of its dozen years by Oliver Cromwell, ended with the recall of the younger Charles from exile in France.

The second catharsis was the forced departure of James II and his replacement, by his daughters – first Queen Mary II – who brought as joint monarch, not consort, the forceful William of Orange (1689–1702); and subsequently Anne (1702–14), whose mild husband, Prince George of Denmark, remained only her consort.

The ousting of James II in the 'Glorious Revolution' of 1688 was one expression of the antagonisms between Catholics and Protestants that had run persistently through English history from the time of Henry VIII's Reformation. The earlier Stuarts had all been at least outwardly committed to their role as Head of Henry's Church of England. But James II, while still Duke of York, had in 1673 made his allegiance to Rome clear. When in 1688, his second wife, Mary of Modena, bore him a son, the recommitment of the English monarchy to Catholicism suddenly became an enduring prospect. This was a major alarum to those in and around Parliament. But it was coupled with a fear of James' penchant for ignoring elements in a rule of law, since James was beginning to use his royal prerogative to override effects of common and statute law in order to grant privileges to favorites and to put down critics, asserting the divine right of kings as the ultimate power even in a kingdom which had two assemblies, House of Lords and House of Commons, as Parliamentary institutions.

Parliament's choice of James' daughters as replacement monarchs was acceptable precisely because their uncle, Charles II, had insisted that they be brought up in France as Protestants. They stood firm in that allegiance and married Protestant princes. The Stadtholder, King William, was soon required to put down James II's attempt at insurgency in Ireland and the bloodthirsty Battle of the Boyne (1692) would leave its stain on Anglo-Irish relations to the present day. Catholic sympathisers in England remained watchful for a further chance, and eventually James' son, James Stuart, grew to be the 'Old Pretender' who led an invasive force through Scotland in 1715, the year after Anne's death; but he was defeated. Thirty years later the same fate would befall his own son, 'Bonnie Prince Charlie' – the 'Young Pretender'. Both victories sustained the position of the Georges from Hanover, who, on Anne's death in 1714, inherited the English Crown from a secondary line that stemmed from James I's daughter, Elizabeth, the Winter Queen of Bohemia.

Georgian England became a state in which a type of limited monarchy would be tested and on the whole found workable as a structure of government for its time and place. The Bill of Rights of 1689 set out the terms on which William and Mary agreed to accept the throne. It had as its foundation a doctrine of sovereignty which treated the supreme source of legal authority over the country as that of the Parliament. This gave unchallengeable force to enactments passed by both Lords and Commons and approved by the Crown – an approval that was only once withheld by Anne and never refused thereafter. The monarch retained the personal prerogative of carrying out executive government for the kingdom, but Parliament could limit that prerogative as it chose. It did so, above all, by granting taxing powers only on an annual basis, and likewise the power to maintain a standing army. Out of this was built that balance of constitutional powers that would be so enthusiastically endorsed by the Baron de Montesquieu in *L'Esprit des Loix* (1748); and enthusiastically taken up by Sir William Blackstone in his adulation of the 1689 settlement, which is strategic to the *Commentaries on the Law of England* (vol 1, 1765).

Queen Anne's reign is accordingly of great interest to political historians and theorists. Leading figures who enjoyed her favour were in some ways the precursors of a cabinet, but they came to ministerial posts and departed from them at her choice. There was not yet a dominant figure who could quite be regarded in the later sense prime minister. The three longest–remembered of these courtiers were John Churchill, who led the great English victories over Louis XIV in the War of the Spanish Succession and was made Duke of Marlborough; Robert Harley, who came closest to being first minister, became Earl of Oxford; and Henry St John, who in the end fell from grace, and was to his chagrin given the lesser title of Viscount Bolingbroke.

Anne herself was later regarded as stupid, being monumentally obese and sadly liable to gynaecological mishaps. But much of that came from a memoir by the acid, domineering Sarah Jennings, Marlborough's wife, written long after she had lost her bosom companionship with the Queen. Anne has been rescued by modern historians, who stress her skill in dealing with the most self-advancing figures among her advisers, and in overseeing the final settlements with Louis and other participants that were signed at Utrecht in the spring of 1713.

2 GOVERNMENT AND THE BOOK TRADE 1480–1700

The Statute of Anne on copyright was not a matter of high state and there is no record of the Queen's personal attitude concerning it, if indeed she had one. With the haut monde, as we shall see, there was one connection – that between Harley and Daniel Defoe – which did play a significant role. The Statute was a victory attained mainly by an entrepreneurial cartel – the leading London booksellers of the Stationers Company – who decided that the route to protection against the unfair competition of rival copyists lay in securing an Act of Parliament rather than through any measure of legal change by royal prerogative or decisions of courts. Even in that, however, it was not novel, since there were earlier enactments on which to draw as precedents. To understand this element in the Act we need to probe a little into the previous relations between governments and book producers.

By 1710 England was more than two centuries on from the first introduction of print technology into the kingdom. As the political and cultural consequences of that remarkable advance in the spread of literate culture became apparent, those who governed understood that print had great economic potential, but at the same time offered a twin-edged sword to those wielding political power. Tudor, and then Stuart, monarchs accordingly used their prerogative in two main ways. First they took to granting patents to printers which gave the grantee exclusionary rights to produce either specific works (such as the Bible) or categories of work (such as law books). This conveniently allowed for an element of political selection, while providing a source of up-front revenue – since such patents had to be paid for.

Secondly, as the book business grew, the London trade developed a powerful guild for mutual protection and 'stability', in the form of the Stationers' Company ('stationers' by the sixteenth century being those who roughly corresponded to the later booksellers and the publishers of modern times). And in 1557 Queen Mary I granted the Stationers Company a charter under which, in liaison with leading figures from State and Church, the Company would license one or more of its members to produce and sell a particular title, which it would enter in its Register. The Company not only had internal controls over its own members; it was also given powers to pursue those outside its ranks who engaged in unlicensed copying. In the seventeenth century, the licensing system came to be underpinned by Parliamentary enactment – for instance by the Licensing Act 1662, which was part of restoring monarchical powers to Charles II after his exile. However, Parliament took the precaution of requiring the Licensing Act to be renewed from time to time; and from 1679 there were lapses. After the revolution of 1688, what proved to be the final Licensing Act expired in 1695 and the powers of the Stationers' Company shrank in the face of ideas about the basic freedom to publish. These new political liberties therefore appeared to open doors to imitative book producers and the Company sought to ally their interest in regaining the lost trade protection of the licensing system with the government's ever-present concern over published attacks on its policies and its record.

Of the detailed history of the lobbying of Parliament which would produce the Statute of Anne 15 years after the disappearance of the last Licensing Act we know only a certain amount. Undoubtedly the Stationers' Company were active, though it is hard to say just what part its leaders played in the drafting of the various clauses, some of which ran against their interests. As to links with the high figures of government, there is one intriguing relationship that certainly had its influence on the position of authors in the eventual text: this concerns the connections between Robert Harley and Daniel Defoe. Defoe was son of a London tradesman and he went first into a variety of businesses. He would later become the prince of adventure-story writers with the dauntless *Robinson Crusoe* (1720), and those resilient feminist icons, *Moll Flanders* (1722) and *Roxana* (1724). In-between, he became a very early example of a journalist pungently engaged in political controversy. He published a corruscating satire on High Church Tories and others, *The Shortest Way with the Dissenters*, for which the House of Commons (led by Harley, who was then its Speaker) had him placed in the pillory and then gaoled at Newgate Prison. However, Harley then secured a pardon for him and he would become Harley's secret agent and publicist, a role that he filled for several years. During this period he produced a succession of tracts and articles in his *Weekly Review* which took John Locke's position that there must be freedom for the press to publish what it would, whatever the legal consequences after the event; and that it was primarily authors who deserved the law's protection against copying. Neither were views that the Stationers had a real will to support – particularly the latter. What they wanted restored was a means of regulating publication which they between them controlled.

3 THE STATUTE OF ANNE: HOW FAR A BEGINNING?

By way of reviewing the provisions of the Statute, I shall ask what features made it an originating text, and what were rather a reversion to what had gone before. Beginnings and ends are after all the starting points for any history, and it is as well to remember that Mary, Queen of Scots, progenetrix of the Stuart line, when imprisoned under threat of execution by her distant cousin, Elizabeth, defied her with the motto, 'En ma Fin gît mon Commencement' – 'In my End is my Beginning'.[2] With legal subject-matter the origin and abandonment of ideas are particularly tricky to identify, let alone interpret for their significance. As the years after 1695 confirmed there had been one important end: the system by which the Stationers' Company granted licences under the authority of statute had ended and the Statute of Anne did not seek directly to revive it. Let us then look first at the elements of the 1710 Act that seem distinctively novel.

3.1 A Private, 'Subjective' Right

As a constitutional starting point, the Act confers an 'entitlement' on the beneficiaries of its provisions. These beneficiaries did not depend on the Crown's grace and favour. By contrast, those who sought patents for their inventions had still to crave the sovereign's gracious condescension for the grant of market exclusivity over exploitation. In the early eighteenth century, it is hard to know how far such patents were conferred, for instance, because their potential was to benefit a whole industry; or because the Crown saw no serious threat to its interests in getting the latest armaments as cheaply as possible; or because the applicant had paid officials enough to get them to process the application. For whatever reason, policy could condition the right to protection. So far as books were concerned, only where the publication was founded on a printer's licence from the Crown did an equivalent discretion operate (and that system was preserved by the Statute of Anne, s. 9). Apart from this, the general system of licensing by the Stationers' Company had already built up an expectation that its members had an 'owner-like right' to the titles that they registered. What therefore is most novel is that the Statute was giving all holders of the copy in a book who registered it and published it the benefits of its provisions. The Act would indeed contain firm provisions requiring the Company to register a title on payment of a regular fee – in other words without bribery (see 3.3 below). Until 1852, patents were available only upon payments to the various officers of state who were involved in the granting process.

---

[2] In 'East Coker' (second of his *Four Quartets*), T.S. Eliot would start with a counterclaim, 'In my beginning is my end', only to conclude, after mysterious rumination, with Mary's own apophthegm.

3.2 A Right Rooted in Authorship

The right conferred by the Statute lay against copying by strangers and others who did not have the right-holder's licence. The copying could be by printing, reprinting, importing, selling and so on. It was a right that was given initially to the author of a 'book', who had the capacity to pass the right by formal assignment to another – typically a bookseller/publisher. Each of these persons, while they enjoyed the right, are referred to in s. 1 as 'proprietor or proprietors' of the book; so it seems that in some more or less specific sense, the enactment gave practical effect to an ideal of literary property that had an independent existence.

3.3 A Right to Forfeiture and Penalties

The remedies given to the person who had registered and published the book against third party pirates were also adapted from the former licensing system. In the Statute of Anne, these were, first, the right to demand forfeiture of unauthorised copies, and second, the entitlement to a fine from the wrongdoer of one penny for every sheet published. One-half of the fine went to Crown, one-half to any person who sued for it. The Act specified that the amounts and costs could be recovered by action in the superior courts of record (as it did also for penalties laid down in other sections). This suggests a process of enforcement embracing what in today's law would be regarded as penal, the entitlement to half the fine being a way of encouraging individual informers to set criminal processes in motion. It was a technique for encouraging private citizens to prosecute others that was widely used for minor social or economic offences in a world which lacked anything much by way of regular police to act as detectives and prosecutors.

When it came to the marketing of pirated books, a prosecutor would probably be a bookseller set on protecting his exclusive rights that grew out of the practices of the Stationers' Company. What is so striking to a lawyer looking back through the shimmer of 300 years of subsequent development, is the absence of any reference in the Statute to a civil right of action for acts of imitation which was recognised separately as a wrong either at common law or under a principle of equity. As would eventually be argued in the 'Battle of the Booksellers' half a century after 1710, if there was such a distinct basis of liability, it would be in support of the literary property in the registered and published book, and would be as indeterminate and perpetual as were property rights in tangible objects. This line of argument accordingly insisted that the limited terms of the forfeiture and fining remedies in the Statute of Anne had no effect on a private right of action, which was perpetual. Its form would be an action in a common law court for damages or a bill in equity for an injunction to prevent piratical material appearing. It was a line of argument that a majority of the judges of King's Bench, following the view of their great chief, Lord Mansfield, would accept in 1769. By that time, however, Mansfield and his allies seemed to accept it on the basis that common law would have given its own course of action and remedy before the Statute of Anne became law, if it had been called upon to do so (which it was not).

In the evolution of legal rules by reliance upon judicial precedent, it is often hard to identify the historical moment when practice has become concrete enough for a rule to be acknowledged as such. This is particularly evident in the centuries of Tudor and Stuart rule over England, when the precedents themselves were often known only from word of mouth and private record, and when much was therefore bound up in the mutual understandings of the various bands of practising lawyers and the judges drawn from the ranks of barristers. In the discussion at the Congress, Tomás Gómez-Arostegui reported on his current study of the records of the Court of Chancery at the National Archives at Kew in West London, from 1660 onwards.[3] These records are difficult to bring together so as to give a complete picture of any case, but they reveal that a practice of securing injunctive relief from Chancery, mostly in order to secure preliminary relief against book pirates, was becoming quite common through the period when the Licensing Acts were fading and well before the Statute of Anne was enacted. This exciting work will have some impact on our understanding of why the Statute was sought and what it was intended to achieve. It will also call for a re-assessment of the judgments about the place of the Statute in copyright history that waxed so eloquent in the 1760s and 70s.

3.4 Private and Public Justification

The Statute gave in its preamble a twin justification for what it was doing. One reason was that printing and publishing a book or other writing without the consent of its authors or proprietors was to 'their very great detriment, and too often to the ruin of their families'; the other was the need to encourage learned men to compose and write useful books. And so plain expression was given to the aims of securing justice to individuals

---

[3] H.T. Gómez-Arostegui, 'What History Teaches Us about Copyright Injunctions and the Inadequate Remedy-at-Law Requirement' (2008) 81 *Southern California L.R.* 1197–1280.

and fostering the culture of the society, which have thereafter been juxtaposed in the advocacy for a copyright system. What is more, for so early a piece of legislation on the subject, the Act was noteworthy for the degree to which it sought to work out in practical terms how far the law would go in its provisions towards these ends.

3.5 A Right for the Conjoined Kingdoms

The Statute twinned the two parts of the recently united Kingdom – Scotland as well as England; an approach that would be extended to Ireland, once that country was brought into the Union in 1800. In this copyright was also ahead of the patent system, where until 1852 separate patents had to be obtained for the three countries. Since in the future of British copyright there lay heated controversies between the booksellers of London, and those of Edinburgh and Dublin, first and foremost over the duration of the right, the Act set a framework of argument that had a meaning that we no longer perhaps appreciate.

3.6 A Right Based in Statute

Fifthly, because the Statute had taken its lead in relation to the copyright of 'books', it was usually necessary thereafter to secure a further enactment, if similar rights were to be conferred in other forms of cultural expression than 'books'. So it would be with rights in engravings and the like under Hogarth's Act of 1735, in designs for some types of cloth (1789, 1792), in statues (1814), in the performance of plays and music (1833, 1842) and in drawing, paintings and photographs (1862). While the courts might play some part in expanding the range of copyright, this tended to turn more or less directly on interpretation of words in existing statutes, as when Lord Mansfield treated 'books' in the Statute of Anne as including printed music.[4] It would take until 1911, for the British, at last intent on reaching a fully reciprocal copyright system within its whole Empire, to enact a harmonised legal regime in the form of a code established by statute law alone.

3.7 The Limit on Duration

Famously, the Statute of 1710 imposed a limitation of term. This did not take the form of a constriction on the general powers of the Stationers'

---

4 *Bach v. Longman* (1777) 2 Cowp. 623.

Company to operate a licensing system of the old, by then defunct, type. The new formula concerning duration operated for each book separately and set a legal pattern which would be imitated in a great many countries as they introduced copyright systems. In the Statute of Anne, for 'old' books already published by 1710, the period was 21 years from publication; for 'new' books, it was 14 years (s. 1). However, the term for new books would be extended by another 14 years if the author was alive at the end of the first term (s. 11). How exactly this provision found its way into the Act is far from clear, and it was expressed in an intriguing way. For the second 14-year period, the 'sole right of printing or disposing of copies shall return to the authors thereof'. Did 'return to the authors' confer on them a reversionary entitlement, requiring the first bookseller, or his successors as assignees, to obtain a separate licence or assignment of right from the author for the second 14 years, which could be done only when that period took effect? Whatever the basic intent, initial contracts between author and entrepreneur tended expressly to include a grant of rights for both periods; and eventually the effectiveness of this tactic was approved by court decision.[5] In an age when freedom of contract was gaining an increasing hold, the judges were not willing to read an ambiguous section of the Statute as imposing a mandatory constriction in the hope of protecting authors against the booksellers who sold their books at prices free from the direct competition of imitators.

3.8 The Public Interest: Library Deposits

One of the public interest factors that operated to impose some burden on the beneficiaries of rights under the Statute, was the requirement of public deposit. Those who printed books were obliged to deposit nine copies with the Stationers Company for distribution to the Royal Library, six Universities, Sion College in London and the Faculty of Advocates in Edinburgh; failure to do so made not only the printer but the 'proprietor' and bookseller liable to a fine of the value of the book, plus five pounds. The obligation was collateral in the sense that deposit was not an express condition of protection under the Statute. When in the nineteenth century systematic attempts were made to build up the named libraries through this measure, there would be publishers who loudly denounced it, as bearing particularly harshly on those who brought out scholarly editions at considerable cost for which there were only limited markets. But the obligation has survived in Britain, and similar institutions have been established in other countries.

---

[5] *Carnan v. Bowles* (1785) 1 Bro. C.C. 80.

3.9 The Public Interest: Abusive Pricing of Books

In its section 4, the Statute contained a highly elaborate scheme for averting the monopolistic pricing of books. A certain precedent for this could be found in the Statute of Monopolies 1624, which allowed the grant of invention patents only where they would not be 'contrary to the law or mischievous to the state, by raising prices of commodities at home, or hurt of trade, or generally inconvenient'. The criteria which might measure the acceptability or otherwise of conferring exclusive rights over the invention would remain obscure; and that was equally true of the s. 4 arrangements. These were not a mechanism that instituted a hope for more reasonable competition by refusing legal protection to a particular book or by granting others a compulsory licence to publish it on payment to the right-holder of a set royalty. Rather it was a means of directly requiring the publisher to lower his own price. As the modern history of competition law demonstrates, this is a drastic form of inhibition within a functioning market economy. Certainly no direct use was ever made of the 1710 power. As with all measures to curb the full potential of intellectual property rights, what their indirect effects on commercial behaviour are can only be a matter of speculation. The power was formally abandoned in 1739, the Stationers being hostile to the very idea that regulators rather than the market should determine what they could charge.

4 A VERDICT

This version of my talk began in up-beat style and so it should finish. The Statute of Anne, by some modern standards, is deficient in its conceptual language, its detailed drafting, its determination to give the leading booksellers much, though not all of what they sought and therefore its neglect of the broader fields in which it was situated. Daniel Defoe described the situation of authors and their associates before its enactment as 'a miserable Havock' and Ronan Deazley has chosen to transfer that grinding expression to describe the Statute itself. But before we damn it too categorically, we should recall that this was law-making at a time when the sovereignty of a legislature was a novel concept and there was very little experience of mechanisms for consulting 'public opinion' or for calling up the professional drafting skills of experts, which would later become an inherent part of that process. We must also remember that modern copyright enactments, not least in the Anglo-American traditions, tend to become a morass of verbiage when they wrestle with novel technologies, or complex business arrangements, or the inherent tensions of international exploitation.

The remedies that the Statute restored to the Stationers' Company and extended to booksellers more generally may not have been used greatly as such, because equity, and ultimately the common law, provided other outcomes that suited copyright owners better. The Statute failed to consider what the relationship between these roots of protection were to be, and so left for the future the crucial issue of whether limitations on the duration of its own remedies also truncated those under an emergent 'common law of copyright' – a problem that would in time prove both central and far-reaching in its impact. Yet for all these imperfections, the Statute would last – of course with amendment – as the basis on which the copyright law for the United Kingdom and then for the British Empire would be built until it was re-erected in the Imperial copyright structure of 1911. Above all it would implant in legal thinking the concept of the author as the person initially entitled to the exclusive right to publish, and later to perform, the protected work. It goes too far to see it as a catalyst for the development of copyright laws elsewhere, apart from its influence on the position in the independent United States. But particularly in this concrete expression of a moral ideal it gave the world a model that with time would be adopted in many parts of the globe. It is a model that has had to meet the challenge of neighbouring rights that, for the most part, exist to protect investment rather than intellectual expression. The bifurcation that resulted is not essentially different from the identification of parallel objectives set out in the Preamble to the Statute three centuries ago. There has to be recognition, on the one hand, of the inherent entitlements of authors and their commercial associates; and, on the other hand, of the public interest in fostering the culture of a society. That is why the legislation of 1710 should be honoured as a pervasive achievement that remains vital to us today.

3. What's new about the Statute of Anne? *or* Six observations in search of an act

Ronan Deazley*

1 INTRODUCTION

When I was invited to present at the ALAI Congress 2009, the broad focus of my paper had been predetermined. One of the conference organisers wrote to me asking 'whether [I] would talk about the impact of [the] Statute of Anne, and in particular whether there is anything "new" in the sense of the lessons that the Statute teaches us' in relation to contemporary copyright law. In short, my brief was to consider the following question: 'What's new about the Statute of Anne?' As the time approached for writing this paper, and while conscious of remaining within my prescribed brief, I decided to grant myself the indulgence of a subtitle: *Six Observations in Search of an Act.*

That subtitle, of course, is taken from Luigi Pirandello's *Six Characters in Search of an Author*, nor am I the first within the copyright community to draw upon Pirandello. David Nimmer, in his lengthy article on 'Copyright in the Dead Sea Scrolls', presented 'Six Case Studies in Search of an Author'.[1] More recently, Jane Ginsburg, in her comparative analysis of the concept of authorship in copyright law, elaborated 'Six Principles in Search of an Author', while at the same time alerting us to the fact that '[r]eferences in copyright scholarship to Pirandello risk becoming trite'.[2] While heedful of Prof Ginsburg's warning, I would nevertheless like to play out the use of Pirandello one more time. Indeed, I would tentatively offer a number of substantive synergies between this paper and Pirandello's play.

---

* Prof Dr Ronan Deazley, School of Law, University of Glasgow.

1 D. Nimmer, 'Copyright in the Dead Sea Scrolls: Authorship and Originality', (2001–02) *Houston Law Review* 38: 1–217, 16–23.

2 J. Ginsburg, 'The Concept of Authorship in Comparative Copyright Law', (2002–03) *DePaul L Rev* 52, 1063–92, 1071 n.34, and 1072–91.

First: Those familiar with *Six Characters* will be aware that not all of the Characters are realised with the same level of sophistication or depth, and purposefully so. The FATHER and STEPDAUGHTER are more fully realised than the MOTHER and the SON, whereas the BOY and the CHILD remain altogether more ambiguous and lacking in definition. Similarly, you will find that my six observations are not all drawn with an equal hand; one or two will almost certainly appear less fully considered than others.

Second: Even those familiar with the play may not be aware that *Six Characters* had a number of previous incarnations before its final embodiment as a dramatic work.[3] Indeed, the practice of self-plagiarism lies at the heart of much of Pirandello's writing and method. Pirandello's novel, *Suo Marito* [*Her Husband*], first published in 1911, is a work concerned with the process of artistic creation, and with notions of originality and authorship. Silvia Roncella, the novel's central character, is presented as a writer who bears all the hallmarks of the classic conceit of the romantic author. Indeed, she even insists on giving the work that she produces away for free, a practice designed to frustrate her husband's attempts to appropriate and (economically) exploit the same. However, the works that are attributed to Sylvia within the novel are actually re-cycled re-presentations of some of Pirandello's earlier texts. That is, Pirandello presents Sylvia as the author of Pirandello's own earlier work. The boundaries between quotation and original text are blurred within the novel in a manner that encapsulates and problematises the extent to which Pirandello himself confused copying and creation throughout his literary career.[4] Similarly,

---

[3] For example, in *La Tragedia d'un personaggio* [*A Character's Tragedy*], a short story first published in 1911, Pirandello (as narrator) gives audience to characters that he may wish to write about at a future date. Dr Fileno, a character from a book which the narrator had been reading the previous night, complains about the way in which he has been written and asks the narrator to re-write his story. The parallels between *A Character's Tragedy* and *Six Authors* are compounded by the fact that passages of text from the former are later repeated word for word in the latter. About *Six Characters*, Ann Caesar writes: '[T]he theatre becomes the last resort for a group of characters at loggerheads with Pirandello, who has refused to take up their case after they have been ill-served by another writer. The breakdown in their relationship is re-enacted, not only on stage, but also in three short stories that were written before the play and a twenty-page preface added later. On each of these occasions Pirandello presents the events from a different point of view'; A. Hallamore Caesar (1998), *Characters and Authors in Luigi Pirandello*, Oxford: Clarendon Press, p. 19.

[4] For a discussion as to the significance of *Suo Marito* within Pirandello's work, see C. O'Rawe (2005), *Authorial Echoes: Textuality and Self-Plagiarism in the Narrative of Luigi Pirandello*, London: Legenda, pp. 107–46.

if some of this paper appears unnervingly familiar (to some of you at least) then you should not be alarmed; that will be simply because you have probably heard or read most of it before.

Third: Pirandello's play ends in some considerable confusion, with the audience left trying to differentiate between artifice and reality: are the children actually dead?, was the action played out by the characters real or a fiction?, and so on. The bewilderment which the audience may feel about the irresolution of the play is foreshadowed within the work itself as, in the opening scene, THE MANAGER bemoans that he is reduced to 'putting on Pirandello's works, where nobody understands anything, and where the author plays the fool with us all'. Now, I certainly don't intend to play the fool with anyone who might take the time to read this paper, but I do wonder whether, by the time you have finished, you might share THE MANAGER'S sense of confusion, exasperation, and irritation.

In any event, let me turn to the first of my observations . . .

2 OBSERVATION 1

'That an absence of copyright protection can often be beneficial in promoting and facilitating the emergence of new audiences, new markets, and the production of new cultural content . . .'

The Statute of Anne 1710 provided the authors of 'any book or books already composed and not printed and published or that shall hereafter be composed' with 'the sole liberty of printing and reprinting such book and books for the term of fourteen years to commence from the first publishing the same and no longer'.[5] Moreover, the Act also provided that, if the author of the work was still alive after the expiration of that 14-year period, then he or she would be granted an additional 14-year period of protection in relation to the same.[6] Much of the copyright debate and litigation throughout the eighteenth century concerned exactly this, the duration of the copyright term – whether it was limited to the times set out in the legislation or whether it was perpetual in duration at common law. This litigation culminated in the two landmark decisions of *Millar v. Taylor* (1769) and *Donaldson v. Beckett* (1774). In *Millar*, a divided King's

---

[5] An Act for the Encouragement of Learning, by Vesting the Copies of Printed Books in the Authors or Purchasers of such Copies, During the Times therein mentioned (the Statute of Anne) 1710, 8 Anne c.19, s. 1.

[6] Ibid, s. 11.

Bench, led by Lord Mansfield, concluded that copyright was a creature of the common law and as such lasted in perpetuity. In *Donaldson*, however, the House of Lords held that, whether copyright existed at common law or not, the duration of copyright in published material was definitely limited to the periods of protection set out within the statute.[7] That is, the prospect of perpetual copyright protection for published work was laid to rest (at least for a while).

Opinions differ as to the impact which the decision had upon the book trade. William St Clair, for example, describes *Donaldson* as 'the most decisive event in the history of reading in England since the arrival of printing 300 years before';[8] it was, he writes, 'a decisive moment for the whole subsequent development of notions of intellectual property, for the price of books and of access to texts, for the progress of reading, and for the subsequent course of the national culture widely defined'.[9] After *Donaldson*, he notes, the market was characterised by a surge in published output, a rise in the annual growth of book titles, as well as a rise in the growth of provincial booksellers, book publishing, and circulating libraries.[10] At the same time, the price of works that were no longer copyright-protected dramatically decreased and a new low-cost and high-volume sales market developed, as these works became affordable, for the first time, for a new body of consumers.[11]

James Raven, on the other hand, downplays the significance of *Donaldson*. The decision has, he writes, 'gained an importance in histories of the trade quite in excess of its true worth'.[12] While not dismissing

---

7 The exact nature of the decision in *Donaldson* still remains a matter of some controversy. For relevant commentary see: H. Abrams, 'The Historic Foundation of American Copyright Law: Exploding the Myth of Common Law Copyright', (1983) *Wayne Law Review*, 29, 1119–91; R. Deazley (2004), *On the Origin of the Right to Copy: Charting the Movement of Copyright Law in Eighteenth-Century Britain (1695–1775)*, Oxford: Hart Publishing, pp. 191–220; M. Rose (1993), *Authors and Owners. The Invention of Copyright*, London: Harvard University Press, pp. 92–112; J. Whicher (1961–62), 'The Ghost of Donaldson v Beckett: An Inquiry into the Constitutional Distribution of Powers over the Law of Literary Property in the United States', *Copyright Society of the USA*, 9, 102–51, 194–229.

8 W. St Clair (2007), *The Reading Nation in the Romantic Period*, (Cambridge: Cambridge University Press, p. 109.

9 Ibid, p. 111.

10 Ibid, p. 118. The book trade, he estimates, experienced a four-fold increase in output during the last quarter of the eighteenth century; ibid.

11 St Clair also notes, however, that the price of new copyright-protected works significantly increased; ibid, pp. 120–21.

12 J. Raven (2007), *The Business of Books: Booksellers and the English Book Trade*, New Haven and London: Yale University Press, p. 231.

the relevance of the decision entirely, he nevertheless suggests that the increased output of the late eighteenth century book trade is more appropriately explained by a complex set of factors impacting upon that trade from the 1740s onwards: the rise of the middle class and an increased importance of leisure time and leisure pursuits; the arrival of the novel as a literary genre; the emergence of new markets at home and abroad; the use of new promotional strategies and the deliberate cultivation of niche markets; the expansion of a country-wide distribution network servicing what was still a predominantly metropolitan industry; and, financial and organisational restructuring and improvement within the trade itself.[13] That is, for Raven, *Donaldson* does not represent the kind of watershed moment that St Clair would have us believe. In short, the impact of the legal regime upon the operation of the market must not be overstated.

It may be that Raven is right, that changes within the market and within the organisation of the book trade itself may well account for the increased output which the book trade experienced within the latter quarter of the eighteenth century. However, *Donaldson* almost certainly did have an impact upon the type of material produced, and in particular, upon the production of new work that was explicitly concerned with, and drew upon, the existing literary canon. In this regard, it is instructive to consider the impact of the decision on the production of editions of James Thomson's *The Seasons* itself, the work at the centre of the *Donaldson* litigation.

James Thomson began publishing extracts from *The Seasons* in 1726 (*Winter, A Poem*), and a collected edition of the work in its entirety was first published in 1730 by John Millan. However, Andrew Millar, who initiated the action that would culminate in the *Donaldson* decision, first published the definitive (a revised and expanded) version of Thomson's work in 1744.[14] If we regard the publication of the 1744 edition of *The Seasons* as a new work – as I believe we should – then, as Thomson died in 1748, under the 1710 Act, the copyright in that work would have expired by the

---

13 Ibid, p. 131.

14 About the 1744 edition, Campbell writes: 'During 1743 and early 1744, Thomson worked on an elaborately revised and expanded edition of The Seasons, apparently with the assistance of his patron George Lyttleton. This enlarged edition of The Seasons was published in mid-July, 1744, in an edition of 1500 copies. Here Spring has 1173 lines; Summer has 1796 lines; Autumn has 1375 lines; and Winter has 1069 lines. Altogether, Thomson here expanded The Seasons from the 1730 edition by more than 1000 lines'. Hilbert H. Campbell (1976), *James Thomson (1700–1748): An Annotated Bibliography of Selected Editions and the Important Criticism*, New York & London: Garland Publishing, p. 13.

end of 1758. It is no coincidence that from 1758 onwards a spate of 'unauthorised editions' were published in Dublin, Glasgow and Edinburgh (one of which included Alexander Donaldson's first impression of the work in 1761).[15] The emergence of these 'unauthorised editions' almost certainly prompted Millar, in 1759, to petition for and secure a Royal licence for 'the sole printing & publishing' of a new edition of *The Whole Works of James Thomson* for an additional 14 years.[16] In fact, the new edition promised by Millar (the 'Royal Quarto Edition') did not appear until 1762, which work was edited, and contained an introduction to the life and works of Thomson, by Patrick Murdoch.

Millar himself died in 1768. Between 1744 and 1768, Millar published and republished *The Seasons* at least 19 times in various formats.[17] During this 24-year stewardship of *The Seasons* portfolio, Murdoch's essay (and his editing of the text) was the only innovation that Millar initiated in relation to the same. In the 24 years after the decision in *Donaldson*, the proliferation of competing versions of *The Seasons* was considerable. Between 1775 and 1799, at least 75 different editions were published in Britain, four times more than had been published by Millar between 1744 and 1768.[18]

---

[15] At least three unauthorised editions were published: (Dublin: 1758); (Glasgow/Dublin: 1760); (Edinburgh: Donaldson, 1761). Before 1758, the only time that *The Seasons* appears to have been published outside of London was in a two-volume edition of *The Works of James Thomson*, published by John Exshaw in Dublin in 1751, sandwiched between Millar's two four-volume editions of the same (in 1750 and 1752).

[16] The terms of the Royal Licence extended to 'forbidding and prohibiting all our subjects within our kingdoms of Great Britain & Ireland, & other Our Dominions, to reprint or abridge the same, either in the like, or any other volume or volumes whatsoever, or to import . . . any copies of the same, or any part thereof, reprinted beyond the seas, within the said term of fourteen years without the consent or approbation of the said Andrew Millar'; The National Archives (hereafter: TNA), SP/44/374, 78–80.

[17] Millar published three editions of *The Works of James Thomson, in Four Volumes* (in 1750, 1752 and 1766), as well as two two-volume editions of Thomson's collected works (in 1744 and 1762), one one-volume edition (in 1768), and at least one three-volume edition, all of which contained *The Seasons*. In addition, he published at least eleven editions of *The Seasons* as an individual work in its own right (these were published in 1744, 1746, 1752 [2], 1757, 1758 [2], 1762, 1766, 1767, and 1768). Of these single-volume editions, the last four editions (published in 1762, 1766, 1767, and 1768) each contained the introductory essay by Murdoch.

[18] Between 1800–24 another 83 editions of *The Seasons* would be printed in Britain (figures taken from R. Cohen (1964), *The Art of Discrimination. Thomson's The Seasons and the Language of Criticism*, London: Routledge & Kegan Paul, Appendix I, pp. 472–507).

Of interest is that there was considerable variation in the presentation and content of these post-1774 editions. In the first place, a number of cheap editions were published without any introductory material or any accompanying illustrations.[19] Others were published without any introductory commentary but with new illustrations.[20] New editions containing Murdoch's introductory essay were published in a number of formats: some were published as they had been in 1762,[21] some omitted Millar's original illustrations,[22] and some incorporated new illustrations.[23] Others were published with a modified (an extended) version of Murdoch's essay, which itself had been first published in Kincaid, Bell and Robertson's (unauthorised) four-volume edition of Thomson's works (in 1768). This extended version drew heavily upon Murdoch's original essay, but was expanded to include some additional biographical material largely taken from Robert Shiels' essay on Thomson in Theophilus Cibber's *The Lives of the Poets* (first published in 1753).[24] Again, as with the editions that reproduced Murdoch's essay in its original form, editions containing this expanded Introduction were published both with and without (existing and new) illustrations.[25]

More significantly, however, was the fact that a number of post-1774 editions were published with new critical commentary and explanatory notes. In 1776 John French, Thomas Hookham published an edition with 'Notes, Illustrations, and a Complete Index' by George Wright, the first edition with entirely new material (including new illustrations) to be published since the Murdoch edition in 1762. In 1779 John Murray published his own edition, again with new illustrations, and an introduction by the physician and writer John Aikin. And, between 1789 and 1793, four further new editions were published. The first was published in 1789 in Edinburgh, by P. Hill, with new illustrations, and an introductory preface by the journalist and author Robert Heron. The second was published

---

[19] See for example: (1775) Edinburgh and Glasgow: Adam and Wood; (1776), London: Oxdale.

[20] See for example: (1790), London: Wenman; (1797), Edinburgh: Imray.

[21] See for example: (1775), Edinburgh: Darling; (1792), London: For the Booksellers.

[22] See for example: (1775), Glasgow: Chapman & Duncan; (1790), London: Taylor).

[23] See for example: (1795), Edinburgh: Ross.

[24] T. Cibber (1753), *The Lives of the Poets*, 5 vols, London: Griffith, 5: pp. 190–218.

[25] For those with illustrations, see: (1776), London: J. Donaldson; Edinburgh: G. Alston; (1783), London: E. Dilly; (1791), London: William Lane. For those without any illustrations, see for example: (1786), Berwick: Phorson.

in 1792, by John Strachan, William Stewart and (again) P. Hill, boasting 'sixteen elegant engravings, designed by Charles Ansell and engraved by Alexander Birrell', and including 14 pages of new 'Notes' at the end of the work (by an unnamed contributor). Robert Heron also contributed 'an original life of the author, and a critical essay on the Seasons' to a 1793 edition published by Robert Morison in Perth. And in the same year, Alexander Hamilton published an edition in London, containing an index, glossary, and notes by the poet Percival Stockdale, as well as 'plates engraved from paintings by Thomas Stothard and Henry Singleton'.

Whatever other political or cultural forces may have contributed to the rise in Thomson's popularity during the latter part of the eighteenth century,[26] it seems relatively uncontroversial to suggest that the dramatic proliferation of Thomson's work was due, in part at least, to the decision in *Donaldson* and the enforcement of the limited term of copyright protection set out within the Statute of Anne. Had the decision in *Donaldson* come down on the side of the London monopolists, one wonders whether any of this new content might have been produced at all. Or in other words, without the competition that the decision in *Donaldson* brought to the market, would any version other than Millar's 1762 Royal Quarto edition (ever) have been produced?

3 OBSERVATION 2

'That the presence of a copyright regime need not necessarily impede the production of new, derivative, cultural goods . . .'

In his work *The Eighth Commandment* the author and playwright Charles Reade railed against a number of 'swindles' by which authors in general were deprived of their just desserts. These included: the *adaptation swindle* (concerning the publication of works in translation); the *novel-dramatising swindle*; the *drama-novelising swindle*; and the *abridgment swindle*. That an author had no legal redress against another producing a fair abridgment of his or her work was, for Reade, '[m]onstrous, idiotic, heartless, illegal, and iniquitous'.[27] In short, England was 'an author-swindling nation'.[28]

---

[26] See R. Terry (ed) (2000), *James Thomson: Essays for the Tercentenary*, Liverpool: Liverpool University Press.

[27] C. Reade (1860), *The Eighth Commandment*, Boston: Ticknor and Fields, p. 152.

[28] Ibid, p. 132.

The propriety of abridging another author's work was certainly an issue to which the public and parliament's attention had been drawn prior to the passing of the 1710 Act. Defoe touched upon the point in his *Essay on the Regulation of the Press* in 1704,[29] and returned to it the following year in the Preface to his *Second Volume of the Writings of the Author of the True-Born Englishman*.[30] The Statute of Anne, however, only prohibited the unauthorised 'printing and reprinting' of books. Read literally, the adaptation or abridgement of protected works did not seem to fall within its remit. Was this an intentional omission? Or was it simply assumed that the legislation, as drafted, would and should operate to prevent the unauthorised production of derivative works such as literary adaptations and abridgements?

The legality of abridging a copyright-protected work was considered in *Gyles v. Wilcox* (1741) in which Lord Chancellor Hardwicke concluded that '[the 1710 Act] must not be carried so far as to restrain persons from making a real and fair abridgement' of any work.[31] Over 30 years

---

[29] Defoe complained that when '[a]n Author prints a Book, whether on a Civil or Religious Subject, Philosophy, History, or any Subject, if it be a large volume, it shall be immediately abridg'd by some mercenary Bookseller, employing a Hackney-writer, who shall give such a contrary Turn to the Sense, and such a false Idea of the Design, and so huddle Matters of the greatest Consequence together in abrupt Generals, that no greater Wrong can be done to the Subject; thus the sale of a Volume of twenty Shillings is spoil'd, by perswading People that the substance of the Book is contained in the Summary of 4*s*. price, the Undertaker is ruin'd, the Reader impos'd upon, and the Author's perhaps 20 Years Labour lost and undervalued'; D. Defoe (1704), *An Essay on the Regulation of the Press*, London, p. 26. He continued: '[N]o Man has a Right to make any Abridgment of a Book, but the Proprietor of the Book; and I am sure no Man can be so well qualified for the doing it, as the Author, if alive, because no Man can be capable of knowing the true Sense of the Design, or of giving it a due Turn like him that compos'd it'; ibid, pp. 26–27.

[30] Here Defoe complained that 'Piratick Printers or Hackney Abridgers fill the World, the First with spurious and incorrect Copies, and the Latter with imperfect and absurd Representations, both in Fact, Stile, and Design', and continued that ''Tis in vain to exclaim at the Villany of these Practices, while no Law is left to punish them'; D. Defoe (1705), *A Second Volume of the Writings of the Author of the True-Born Englishman*, London, Preface. Of course, both piratical printers and hackney abridgers (to use Defoe's parlance) would, in time, set upon Defoe's most popular and enduring work: *Robinson Crusoe*. For details, see: H.C. Hutchins (1927), 'Two Hitherto unrecorded Editions of Robinson Crusoe', *The Library*, pp. 58–72; H.C. Hutchins (1925), *Robinson Crusoe and its Printing 1719–1731: A Bibliographical Study*, New York: Columbia University Press, pp. 129–40; P. Rogers, 'Classics and Chapbooks', in I. Rivers (ed) (1982), *Books and their Readers in Eighteenth Century England*, Baskerville: Leicester University Press, pp. 27–45.

[31] *Gyles v. Wilcox* (1741) 2 Atk 141, 143. Hardwicke continued: '[A]bridgements may with great propriety be called a new book, because, not only the paper

later, in *Strahan v. Newbery* (1774), Lord Chancellor Apsley agreed with Hardwicke, noting that an abridgment was 'not an act of plagiarism upon the original work, nor against any property of the author in it, but an allowable and meritorious work'.[32] Both *Gyles* and *Strahan* attracted much criticism throughout the latter part of the nineteenth century, from Curtis (in 1847),[33] from Copinger (in 1870),[34] and, of course, from Charles Reade himself. Reade considered *Strahan* to be an 'idiotic and inhuman' decision, and complained that '[t]he property of authors is governed by judges' law, not by the Acts of the realm'.[35] Reade's implication here is that, but for the intervention of the judiciary, the unauthorised abridging of copyright-protected works would (or should) have been caught by the Statute of Anne. And, this is certainly a reading of *Gyles* that many contemporary commentators would not seek to contest.[36] But, is this allegation of (unwelcome) judicial meddling fair?

One of the first printing privileges granted during Anne's reign was to William Delaune, then Vice-Chancellor of the University of Oxford, in relation to the University's three-volume edition of Clarendon's *History of the Rebellion and Civil Wars in England*. The first volume was first

---

and print, but the invention, learning and judgment of the author is shewn in them, and in many cases are extremely useful'; ibid.

32 *Strahan v. Newbery* (1774) Lofft 775, 775–76 ('[T]he act of abridgement is an act of understanding, employed in carrying a large work into a smaller compass, and rendering it less expensive, and more convenient both to the time and use of the reader').

33 Curtis rejected the jurisprudence of the English courts on this issue, contending instead that the exclusive right to print and publish a book included 'the whole book and every part of it', as well as 'the style, or language, and expression; the learning, the facts, or the narrative; the sentiment and ideas, as far as their identity can be traced; and the form, arrangement and combination which the author has given to his materials'. He continued: 'These are, or may be, all distinct objects of the right of property; and in every work of originality, likely to be abridged, they are all important aspects of that right'; G.T. Curtis (1847), *A Treatise on the Law of Copyright*, Boston: C.C. Little and J. Brown, p. 273.

34 Copinger considered the principle established in *Gyles* to be 'very unreasonable', and suggested that '[t]he law with reference to abridgements might . . . with justice receive some modification'; W.A. Copinger (1870), *The Law of Copyright in Works of Literature and Art*, London: Stevens and Haynes, pp. 36, 101–02.

35 Reade, p. 152.

36 Burrell and Coleman, for example, regard *Gyles* as an instance of judicial activism wherein it was first recognised that 'there are circumstances in which the reproduction of part of another work without the copyright owner's consent is justified' as being in the public interest; R. Burrell and A. Coleman (2005), *Copyright Exceptions: The Digital Impact*, Cambridge: Cambridge University Press, p. 254.

published in 1702, after which an abridged version of that first volume was issued by John Nutt in 1703. It seems likely that the appearance of Nutt's abridgment prompted Delaune to petition for protection and, on 24 June 1703, a 14-year privilege was granted to the University 'forbidding all our subjects to reprint *or abridge* the said history, or any part of it'.[37] However, this type of privilege was not typical. Between the Restoration and the end of the seventeenth century, the majority of privileges simply prohibited printing, selling, and importing the work in question,[38] a trend that was continued throughout Anne's reign. Indeed, of the privileges granted by Anne,[39] less than a third specifically prohibited the printing and sale of

---

[37] The privilege forbids 'all our subjects to reprint or abridge the said history, or any part of it, or to import, buy, vend, utter, or distribute any copies of the same, or any part thereof reprinted beyond the seas within the said terme, without the consent and approbation of the said University'; TNA, SP/44/350, 354–55 (emphasis added).

[38] See for example the privileges granted to: John Ogilby for his versions of Homer's *Iliad* (in 1660), Aesop's *Fables* (in 1665), and the works of Virgil (in 1665). See also: H. Bond (1676), *The Longitude Found*, London: Godbid; G. Burnet (1677), *The Memoirs of the Lives and Actions of James and William, Dukes of Hamilton and Castlehead*, London: Royston; J. Spotswood (1677), *The History of the Church and State of Scotland*, London: Royston; S. Lee (1677), *A Collection of Names of the Merchants Living in and about the City of London*, London: Lee; R. Wallis (1677), *London's Armory*, London: Wallis; E. Coles (1679), *A Dictionary, English-Latin and Latin-English*, London: Parker; J. Browne (1681), *A Complete Treatise of the Muscles as they appear in [the] Humane Body*, London: Newcombe; J.S. Weidenfeld (1684), *Secretis Adeptorum*, London: Hills; D. Newhouse (1685), *The Whole Art of Navigation*, London: Newhouse; F. Sandford (1687), *The History of the Coronation of James II*, London: Newcombe; (1694), *The History of the Famous Edict of Nantes*, London: Dunton. For examples of late seventeenth century privileges that did prohibit the abridgement of the protected work, see: E. Ashmole (1672), *The Institution, Laws & Ceremonies of the most Noble Order of the Garter*, London: Brooke (the privilege prohibits printing the book 'or any part thereof, or any Abridgment of the Laws or Ceremonies therein contained'); (1673), *Britannia, or A Geographical Description of the Kingdoms of England, Scotland, and Ireland*, London: Blome (the privilege prohibits 'epitomizing the work'); F. Sandford (1677), *A Genealogical History of the Kings of England*, London: Newcombe (the privilege prohibits printing the book 'or any Part thereof, or any Abridgement of the [work]'); G. Collins (1693), *Great Britain's Coasting Pilot*, London: Collins (the privilege prohibits the printing of the work 'or any part thereof, or to Epitomize the same . . . or any part thereof under the same, or any other Title or Name whatsoever'); J. Slezer (1693), *Theatrum Scotiæ*, London: Swalle (the privilege prohibits printing the books 'or any of them, or any Abridgment, or any part of any of them').

[39] For a complete list of the privileges granted during this period, see S. Rogers (2000), 'The Use of Royal Licences for Printing in England, 1695–1760: A Bibliography', *The Library*, pp. 133–92.

variant forms of the work in question, whether by way of abridgment or translation.[40]

The variation in the language and substance of these printing privileges provide an interesting context within which to revisit the text of the Statute of Anne. A minority of them are obviously explicit about the issue of abridgment in a way that the legislation itself is not, and that specificity may provide an insight into the intended scope of the legislation. Abridgments published prior to the Statute of Anne (as well as those published afterwards) routinely justified their existence in a number of standard ways: in meeting a need in relation to works that have become scarce in their original format;[41] in opening the work up to a new audience that might otherwise find it inaccessible whether by virtue of content or, as was more often the case, by virtue of the price of the original;[42] or, in improving the original work in excising mistakes, obsolete material, and

---

[40] In addition to the privilege granted to Delaune, six other privileges were granted as follows: to Richard Blome for *Britannick Empire* (forbidding subjects 'to epitomize the same in any volume, or in any language of speech whatsoever'), TNA, SP/44/353, 99; to Jacob Tonson for Lawrence Echard's *Complete History of England* (forbidding subjects 'to reprint or abridge the said History or any part thereof'), TNA, SP/44/353, 118; to Richard Smith for *Ezechielis Spanhemii Liberi Baronis* (forbidding subjects 'to reprint, translate, or abridge the said work or any part of it'), TNA, SP/44/354, 183; to John Chamberlayne for *Magna Britannia Notitia, or, The Present State of Great Britain* (forbidding subjects 'to reprint, translate, or abridge the said work, or any part of it', TNA, SP/44/354, 341; to William Nichols for *A Comment on the Book of Common Prayer and Administration* (forbidding subjects 'to reprint or abridge the said work or any part of it'), TNA, SP/44/353, 416; and to Egbert Sanger, Edmund Curl and John Pemberton for Sr Bulstrode Whitlocke's *Memorials of the English Affairs from the suppos'd Expedition of Brute to this Island to the End of the Reigne of King James the First* (forbidding subjects 'to reprint or abridge the same either in the like or in any other volume or volumes whatsoever'), TNA, SP/44/353, 456.

[41] The preface to (1692), *The History of Scotch-Presbytery, being an Epitome of The Hind Let Loose, by Mr Shields*, London: Hindmarsh, notes that the original book 'itself is not easily got'.

[42] The preface to (1676), *The Novum Organum of Sir Francis Bacon, Epitomiz'd for a Clearer Understanding of his Natural History*, London: Lee, suggests that the work 'might be of a singular use to such vertuosi amongst us, as are not perfectly acquainted with the Latine Tongue'. See also the prefacatory remarks in: H. Bralesford (1689), *The Poor Man's Help*, London: R. Clavell; E. Stacy (1700), *The Whole Duty of Man Epitomiz'd for the Benefit of the Poor*, London: Lawrence; (1700), *An Answer to the Dissenters Pleas for Separation, or an Abridgment of the London Cases*, Cambridge: University Press; (1701), *Camden's Britannia Abridg'd, with Improvements and Continuations to the Present Time*, London: J.B. and Joseph Wild.

long (unnecessary) digressions in the same.[43] In not explicitly extending the scope of the legislation to prohibit the production of abridgments and other derivations of protected works, can we divine an intention on the part of those drafting the legislation to encourage or facilitate the production of works of this nature? Considered in this light, the decisions of Hardwicke and Apsley may no longer smack of judicial activism or of an encroachment upon the proprietary entitlements of either authors or members of the book trade. Rather, they might read as decisions that are in tune with both the spirit and the literal language of the legislation.

4 OBSERVATION 3

'That an absence of copyright protection need not necessarily prevent the profitable exploitation of a work by the author . . .'

One obvious point to make about the Statute of Anne is that, when compared with the current copyright regime, it provided a relatively thin and narrow form of copyright protection. By contrast, copyright today is a much distended construct. This expansion has been driven, in part, by arguments to the effect that '[a] rigorous and effective system for the protection of copyright and related rights is *necessary* to provide authors and producers with a reward for their creative efforts'.[44] When we become embroiled in the rhetoric of the need for legal protection to secure financial

---

43 The preface to Lawrence Echard's (1698), *Abridgment of Sir Walter Raleigh's History of the World*, London: Gelliflower, sets out that Raleigh had 'not been without some considerable imperfections in respect to his History, which he has shewn in his too frequent and long digressions, and observations'. Echard continues that: 'All I have done, besides the expunging and shortening of some passages, is the correcting and altering of the style, which in most places was too obsolete'. John Savage, who abridged *The Turkish History* (by Richard Knolles and Paul Rycaut) in 1701, explained that 'by weeding out the superfluous embellishments of their stiles, cutting off excrescencies, and avoiding unnecessary digressions' he was able to 'couch the matter more concisely' and give the reader 'a nearer sight, and a clearer understanding of things, than when they are darkened with foreign additions, foisted in to no other purpose than to humour the author's ambition, in seeing their names in the title pages of large folios'; J. Savage (1701), *The Turkish History*, London: Cleave, Roper, Bosville, and Basset, Preface. See also: (1699), *The Works of the Learned and Valiant Josephus*, London: Roper and Basset; *An Answer to the Dissenters Pleas for Separation*; *Camden's Britannia Abridg'd*.

44 *Copyright in the Knowledge Economy*, COM(2008) 466 final, 4 (emphasis added). These sentiments, of course, echo a number of the recitals to the *Information Society Directive* 2001/29/EC.

reward, we tend to overlook that authors can, and do, exploit their works, often with great success, even in the absence of a legal regime securing *de jure* protection for the same. Here, I turn to another author who, like Defoe, was particularly interested in copyright matters: Charles Dickens.

As is well known, Dickens wrote about, and lobbied for, international copyright protection on a number of occasions, but most famously (and for the first time) during his 1842 tour of America.[45] The media backlash that Dickens endured during that tour and its impact upon him (provoked by his position on the question of international copyright) bubbles into the first novel that he wrote upon his return, *Martin Chuzzlewit*, which provided his readers with a particularly unflattering portrayal of both America and Americans.[46] It is not difficult to see in Colonel Diver and Jefferson Brick (who are responsible for the *New York Rowdy Journal*) a satirical take on the editors of the 'mammoth' newspapers that flourished in America between 1839 and 1844, which papers largely relied upon pirated material for their content.[47]

However, in 1868 when Dickens published a new postscript to *Chuzzlewit* his attitude to America had noticeably softened.[48] Having

---

[45] See: Lawrence H. Houtchens (1941), 'Charles Dickens and International Copyright', *American Literature* 13: 18–28; K.J. Fielding (1960), *The Speeches of Charles Dickens*, Oxford: Clarendon Press, pp. 22–26; Alexander Welsh (1987), *From Copyright to Copperfield: The Identity of Dickens*, Cambridge, Massachusetts: Harvard University Press; Gerhard Joseph (1994), 'Charles Dickens, International Copyright, and the Discretionary Silence of *Martin Chuzzlewit*', in Martha Woodmansee and Peter Jaszi (eds), *The Construction of Authorship: Textual Appropriation in Law and Literature*, Durham NC: Duke University Press, pp. 259–70; U. Suthersanen, '*Bleak House* or *Great Expectations*?', in H. Porsdam (ed) (2007), *Copyright and Other Fairy Tales*, Cheltenham: Edward Elgar, pp. 40–60; Larisa T. Castillo (2008), 'Natural Authority in Charles Dickens's *Martin Chuzzlewit* and the Copyright Act of 1842', *Nineteenth-Century Literature* 62: 435–64. See also Michael Slater (ed) (1979), *Dickens on America & the Americans* The Harvester Press.

[46] With the exception of the good natured Mr Bevan, the Americans that young Chuzzlewit encounters are a thoroughly dislikeable bunch who, as Castillo observes, invoke an ethic of natural right and independent self-interest to countenance 'injustice[s] as diverse as slavery, suppression of free speech, slander, fraud, and [literary] piracy'; Castillo (2008), p. 446. See also Welsh (1987), pp. 29–42.

[47] Houtchens (1941), p. 23.

[48] The postscript itself was a modified version of an address that Dickens gave at a public dinner held in his honour by the New York Press Association on 18 April 1868, at the end of his second tour of the States. That speech is reproduced in full in Slater (1979), pp. 242–45. For the postscript, see Charles Dickens, *Martin Chuzzlewit* (Margaret Cardwell (ed)), (1982) Oxford: Clarendon Press, pp. 855–56.

toured the US for a second time in late 1867 and early 1868, Dickens declared himself astounded by the changes that he had seen during that visit: 'changes moral, changes physical, changes in the amount of land subdued and peopled, changes in the rise of vast new cities, changes in the growth of older cities almost out of all recognition, changes in the graces and amenities of life, [and] changes in the Press, without whose advancement no advancement can take place anywhere'.[49] Without doubt, part of the explanation for this shift in attitude lay in the warm reception that Dickens enjoyed during this second tour (Dickens was careful to avoid any public discussion of copyright during this visit).[50] There was, however, another reason for his new-found affection for America. It was neatly captured by Dickens himself in *Chuzzlewit*, when, during young Martin Chuzzlewit's first night in New York, he finds that the conversation of his dinner companions invariably turns to one subject: 'All their cares, hopes, joys, affections, virtues, and associations, seemed to be melted down into dollars'.[51]

To put it crudely: Dickens made an enormous amount of money.

---

[49] Ibid, p. 855. Dickens continued by promising his American hosts a legacy, his personal commitment to record 'that wherever I have been, in the smallest places equally with the largest, I have been received with unsurpassable politeness, delicacy, sweet temper, hospitality, consideration, and with unsurpassable respect for [my] privacy'; ibid. Moreover, this personal testimony, he suggested, would be republished as a postscript to *Chuzzlewit* 'so long as my descendents have any legal right in my books'; ibid, p. 856. This passing reference to the 'legal right' in his works was the only time that Dickens chose to publicly broach the question of copyright during his second visit to the States. A subtle *quid pro quo* was being offered by Dickens here: so long as his estate retained control over the circulation of his work, then Dickens's personal tribute to the qualities of American life, morals, and manners would remain in public circulation. In general, see: Castillo (2008), pp. 436; Slater (1979), pp. 62–64.

[50] Slater writes that his reception was so rapturous 'it would make even the tremendous demonstrations of affection and delight he had experienced at home seem quite mild'; Slater (1979), p. 52.

[51] Dickens continues: 'Whatever the chance contributions that fell into the slow cauldron of their talk, they made the gruel thick and slab with dollars. Men were weighed by their dollars, measures gauged by their dollars; life was auctioneered, appraised, put up, and knocked down for its dollars. The next respectable thing to dollars was any venture having their attainment for its end. The more of that worthless ballast, honest and fair-dealing, which any man cast overboard from the ship of his Good Name and Good Intent, the more ample stowage-room he had for dollars. Make commerce one huge lie and mighty theft. Deface the banner of the nation for an idle rag; pollute it star by star; and cut out stripe by stripe as from the arm of a degraded soldier. Do anything for dollars! What a flag it is to *them!*' (p. 266).

Indeed, almost his entire purpose for touring the States at this time concerned money. Since April 1858, he had been giving professional Readings of his own work in Britain, an initiative that had proved to be particularly lucrative,[52] and it was clear that he thought much might be gained by giving readings in the States.[53] That intuition proved correct. During the four and a half months that Dickens was in America, he gave 76 Readings in all, accumulating nearly £20,000 in the process,[54] twice the figure that

---

[52] On Dickens's Public Readings, see: Kate Field (1868), *Pen Photographs of Charles Dickens's Readings. Taken from Life*, Boston: Loring; Charles Kent (1971), *Charles Dickens as a Reader*, reprint edition with an Introduction by Philip Collins, England: Gregg International Publishers Limited; George Dolby (1887), *Charles Dickens as I Knew Him: The Story of the Reading Tours in Great Britain and America (1866–1870)*, London: T. Fisher Unwin; Raymond Fitzsimons (1970), *The Charles Dickens Show: An Account of his Public Readings, 1858–1870*, London: Geoffrey Bles; Philip Collins (ed) (1975), *Charles Dickens: The Public Readings*, Oxford: The Clarendon Press; Robert Woodall (1979), 'The public readings of Charles Dickens', *Blackwood's Magazine*, 326, 511; Martha L. Brunson (1983), 'Novelists as Platform Readers: Dickens, Clemens, and Stowe', in David W. Thompson (ed) *Performance of Literature in Historical Perspectives*, Lanham: University Press of America, pp. 651–82; Paul Schlicke (1985), *Dickens and Popular Entertainment*, London: Allen & Unwin, pp. 226–48; Helen Small (1996), 'A pulse of 124: Charles Dickens and a pathology of the mid-Victorian reading public', in J. Raven, H. Small and N. Tadmor (eds), *The Practice and Representation of Reading in England*, Cambridge: Cambridge University Press, pp. 263–90; Malcolm Andrews (2007), *Charles Dickens and His Performing Selves: Dickens and the Public Readings*, Oxford: Oxford University Press.

[53] When he wrote to William Wills, his personal secretary, about the possibility of touring, Dickens was clear that 'there *should* be something large, to set against the objections'; 'the likelihood of making a very great addition to one's capital in half a year' was naturally 'an immense consideration'; Dickens to W.H. Wills, 6 June 1867, *Letters*, xi, 377.

[54] Dickens to John Forster, April 1867, *Letters*, xii, 101: 'We had great difficulty in getting our American accounts squared . . . my profit was within a hundred or so of £20,000. Supposing me to have got through the present engagement in good health, I shall have made by the Readings, *in two years*, £33,000: that is to say, £13,000 from the Chappells, and £20,000 from America . . . These figures are of course between ourselves; but don't you think them rather remarkable?' Dickens's earnings would have been even higher had he not insisted on exchanging dollars for gold before returning to Britain. As the tour manager George Dolby recounts: 'Supposing gold to have been at par, it will be seen from the figures named that the profits of the enterprise would have been nearly £38,000; but as Mr. Dickens had no faith in American securities at that time, he preferred to convert the currency we received into gold, paying the difference 39½ per cent., and an addition ¼ per cent. for the banker's commission'; Dolby (1887), p. 332. See also Kent (1971), pp. 78–79.

he had anticipated earning,[55] and almost half of what he earned from all of the Readings that he gave throughout the last 12 years of his life.[56]

If we take all of his Readings in the round, it is estimated that he earned something in the region of £45,000, which itself was almost half of what his estate was worth at the time of his death (£93,000).[57] Moreover, Malcolm Andrews has calculated that Dickens' income from his writings averaged around £2,900 per year during the last 25 years of his life.[58] So, during the last 12 years of his life, his earnings from the Readings he gave outstripped his earnings from the publication of his works (approx. £35,000). Focussing solely upon the money Dickens earned in the States, in four and a half months his Readings generated almost as much income as Dickens would have earned from his published output throughout the last seven years of his life.[59] In short, the time that Dickens spent on tour in America proved to be the most financially lucrative period of his long and successful career.[60]

I'm not ashamed to admit that I am a fan of Dickens, but perhaps I should be ashamed to admit that and I spend far too much of my time thinking about what Dickens might have thought about the current copyright regime. When faced with new questions or developments in copyright law, I often ask myself: *What Would Dickens Do?* No doubt, some might

---

55 Dickens wrote as follows: 'If you were to work out the question of Reading profits here [in Britain], with [George] Dolby, you would find that it would take years to get £10,000. To get that sum in a heap so soon is an immense consideration to me – my wife's income to pay – a very expensive position to hold – and my boys with the curse of limpness upon them'; Dickens to W.H. Wills, 6 June 1867, *Letters*, xi, 375–77.

56 Andrews (2007), p. 45. Between 1858 and 1870, Dickens gave 370 professional Readings throughout the United Kingdom (based upon the Schedule of Public Readings set out in the Appendix to Andrews' book (pp. 267–90)).

57 Brunson (1983), pp. 662–63.

58 As Andrews notes, in 1867, the year in which he commenced his second American tour, Dickens could exceed the amount he earned from the publication of his works in that year by giving just over 50 two-hour Readings; Andrews (2007), p. 45.

59 Nor was he unabashed about the same. Andrews relates how Dickens 'gloated in detail on [the] sensational earnings' he amassed by his Readings; Andrews (2007), p. 45. Similarly, Peter Ackroyd notes, 'his correspondence in this period is rendered almost wearisome by [Dickens's] constant emphasis on the sums acquired and the sums expected'; Peter Ackroyd (2002), *Dickens* (abridged version), London: Vintage, p. 530.

60 Kent summed up the success of Dickens's American tour as follows: 'In a single tour . . . he had appeared before upwards of 100,000 persons, earning at the same time, over 200,000 dollars within an interval of very little more than four months'; Kent (1971), p. 89.

regard my contemplation of that question as an irrelevance, or bizarre, or both. I like to think, however, that something can be gained from engaging in such thought experiments, if for no other reason than it focuses the mind on the interests and desires of the author, as opposed to those of his publisher, producer, or agent.

But Dickens provides a particularly interesting spirit to try and channel in this regard. He was an author, an entertainer, an innovator, and a raconteur of the highest order. To be sure, he was acutely preoccupied with money and the accumulation of wealth. But, he was also a social reformer, and he believed in the importance of encouraging and democratising access to culture. Everyone, he argued, had a 'right to be amused'.[61] He was an advocate of entertainment for entertainment's sake, but also believed that popular entertainment had the power to edify, to offer opportunities for self-improvement, and to enhance one's emotional well-being.[62] He was convinced in the virtues of marrying entertainment with education,[63] and was particularly interested in promoting the benefits of education for both children in poverty and the adult working class.[64] Moreover, his belief in

---

[61] C. Dickens (1850), 'The Amusements of the People (Part 2)', *Household Words*, 1, p. 58.

[62] In *Hard Times*, Dickens' work that is most overtly concerned with education and the education system, it is the performers in Mr. Sleary's circus who provide the moral core of the novel and, as Paul Schlicke observes, it is the ringmaster Sleary who extols the 'non-educational value of his entertainment as the fulfilment of an essential human need': '"People must be amuthed, Thquire, somehow," continued Sleary . . . "they can't be alwayth a working, nor yet they can't be alwayth a learning"'; Paul Schlicke (1985), *Dickens and Popular Entertainment*, London: Allen & Unwin, pp. 143, 182–83.

[63] For example, in his fictional account of the Dullborough Mechanics' Institute, Dickens gently lampooned the tendency of such institutions to offer dry and uninteresting fodder: 'On referring to lists of the courses of lectures that had been given in this thriving Hall, I fancied I detected a shyness in admitting that human nature when at leisure has any desire whatsoever to be relieved and diverted . . . Thus, I observed that it was necessary for the members to be knocked on the head with Gas, Air, Water, Food, the Solar System, the Geological periods, Criticism on Milton, the Steam-engine, John Bunyan, and Arrow-Headed Inscriptions, before they might be tickled by those unaccountable choristers, the negro singers in the court costume of the reign of George the Second. Likewise, that they must be stunned by a weighty inquiry whether there was internal evidence in Shakespeare's works, to prove that his uncle by the mother's side lived for some years at Stoke Newington, before they were brought-to by a Miscellaneous Concert'; C. Dickens (1902), 'Dullborough Town', in *The Uncommercial Traveller*, London: Chapman & Hall Ltd; and Humphrey Milford, (first published, 1861).

[64] Dickens was, throughout his life, active in supporting a number of orphanages and charity schools (or 'Ragged Schools') that provided free education (and

the role that education might play in the prevention of crime has been well documented.[65]

Without doubt, the general preoccupation which many middle class reformers had with advocating and organising different forms of 'rational recreation' for working class people,[66] when viewed from a twenty-first century perspective, appears both paternalistic and self-serving. We can certainly read such endeavours as the activities of 'an interested ideology anxious to secure a disciplined future labour force',[67] and Dickens is not immune from this critique. But, his views on the nexus between culture, education, and crime, provide an interesting set of relationships and concerns through which to explore various contemporary copyright issues.

5 OBSERVATION 4

'That one can be pro-author without being pro-Author's Rights . . .'

For some, the substance and tone of my observations thus far may not come as much of a surprise. It is sometimes the case that I am accused

---

Footnote 64 (*cont.*)
very often food and clothing) for working class and poverty-stricken children; Philip Collins (1964), *Dickens and Education*, London: MacMillan & Co, p. 3. In terms of his support for adult education, he presided as President of the Chatham Mechanics' Institution for 13 years, giving no less than six (charitable) Public Readings to generate funds for the same. Indeed, most of the charitable readings that he gave in his later career were in support of Mechanics' Institutes and similar organisations. See Philip Collins (1955), 'Dickens and Adult Education', *British Journal of Educational Studies*, 115–27 (116–17); Andrews (2007), pp. 268–69. On Dickens's attitudes to education in general, see James L. Hughes (1901), *Dickens as an Educator*, New York: D. Appleton and Company; John Manning (1959), *Dickens on Education*, Toronto: University of Toronto Press; Collins, *Dickens and Education*; Collins, 'Dickens and Adult Education'; Philip Collins (1962), *Dickens and Adult Education*, Leicester: University of Leicester.

[65] On the explicit link that Dickens made education and the prevention of crime, see Collins (1964), *Dickens and Education*, pp. v, 6, 72–73.

[66] On working class recreation, and the concept of 'rational recreation', see: P. Bailey (1978), *Leisure and Class in Victorian England: Rational recreation and the contest for control, 1830–1885*, London and New York: Methuen; James Walvin (1978), *Leisure and Society 1830–1950*, London: Longman; Brad Beaven (2005), *Leisure, citizenship and working-class men in Britain, 1850–1945*, Manchester: Manchester University Press.

[67] Walvin (1978), 50 (Walvin, however, rejects any attempt to interpret the activities of the social and moral reformers of this period in such a one-dimensional manner).

of being anti-author, and anti-copyright, or as one colleague so neatly put it, of 'wanting to tear down the copyright house'. Well, let me set the record straight: I am neither anti-author, nor am I anti-copyright. Indeed, I regard myself as being both a pro-author and a pro-copyright kind of person. And, this leads me to my fourth observation: that one can be pro-author without being pro-*Author's Rights*. Here, I'm using the term *Author's Rights* as a clumsy shorthand for the concept that authors, musicians, artists, and so on, have (and have always) enjoyed natural proprietary rights in the intangible cultural goods which they create – music, the text, and the image. That is an argument that lies at the heart of much of the debate and discussion throughout the eighteenth century as to the meaning and significance of the Statute of Anne, and it is an argument that I would reject. Absent the intervention of the legislature, no such thing as copyright exists. Copyright is no more or less than an institutional (legislative) fact. Or, to put it another way: Copyright is, and always has been, about policy.

When parliament bowed to the lobbying of the book trade in passing the Statute of Anne, I don't think they were legislating in recognition of *Author's Rights*,[68] but I do think they made some choices that were pro-author in nature and intent. With the Statute of Anne there is clear evidence of an attempt to upset certain anti-competitive conventions and practices within the book trade, just as there is evidence of an attempt to recognise and empower the author as a significant figure in the production of 'useful books'. For the first time since the incorporation of the Stationers' Company in 1557 one no longer needed to be a member of the Company to register, publish, and sell books, and at least some authors, such as John Gay, took advantage of that fact.[69] More importantly perhaps, s. 11 of

---

68 For further discussion, see Deazley (2004), *On the Origin*, pp. 40–42.

69 John Gay published *Polly* (his sequel to *The Beggar's Opera*) by subscription with the help and support of a number of his aristocratic patrons, and, in particular, Catherine Douglas, the Duchess of Queensberry. Whereas Gay had sold his copyright in both *The Beggar's Opera* and his first collection of *Fables* to the publisher Jacob Tonson and the printer John Watts for 90 guineas, the decision to publish *Polly* in his own name would prove to be far more lucrative. Burgess, for example, estimates that as a result of publishing the work, Gay amassed something in the region of £1200; cf. Burgess (ed) (1966), *The Letters of John Gay*, Oxford: Clarendon Press, p. 79, n.3. For additional commentary, see R. Deazley (2008), 'Commentary on *Baller* v. *Watson* (1737)', in L. Bently and M. Kretschmer (eds) *Primary Sources on Copyright (1450–1900)*, www.copyrighthistory.org (hereafter: *Primary Sources*). For examples of other authors who successfully published their own work during this period, see Richard B. Sher (2006), *The Enlightenment and the Book: Scottish Authors in Eighteenth-Century Britain,*

the Act provided that, after the expiration of the 14-year period of protection for new books (that is, books first published after 10 April 1710), 'the sole Right of printing or disposing of Copies shall return to the Authors thereof, if they are then living, for another Term of Fourteen years'. As we shall see, it seems entirely likely that this provision was intended to prioritise and promote the interests of the author, as opposed to those of the bookseller or the printer who might have purchased and first published the work in question.[70]

6 OBSERVATION 5

'That just because the book trade (or indeed any creative industry) suggests that they are acting in the best interests of authors, doesn't mean that they always are . . .'

When, towards the end of the seventeenth century, the book trade petitioned parliament for a reintroduction of the Licensing Act 1662, they did so with reference to the importance of securing both the State and the Church (ideologically speaking), as well as their own long-standing properties.[71] At this time, little mention was made of the interests and concerns of authors. Indeed, it was only after it became clear that parliament was unwilling to re-introduce the Licensing Act (or indeed any system of censorship that might, at the same time, also serve the economic interests of the book trade), and after Defoe had published his *Essay on the Regulation of the Press*, that the booksellers began to change their rhetorical tack.

From 1706 onwards, petitions and pamphlets prepared on behalf of the trade no longer called for a revival of the 1662 Act, but instead placed

---

Footnote 69 (*cont.*)
Ireland & America, Chicago and London: The University of Chicago Press, pp. 216–24. Moreover, in a review of 360 Scottish Enlightenment books published between 1746 and 1800, Sher has calculated that almost 40 per cent were entered at Stationers' Hall at least once, and that of those works nearly one-third (or 43 titles) were registered in the name of the author or the editor of the work, and not the publisher; Sher, p. 243.

70 For further discussion, see Deazley (2004), *On the Origin*, pp. 42–43. See also the commentary in *The Observator*, Vol.IX, No.6 (11–15 February 1710), 1, discussed in more detail below.

71 See for example *Reasons humbly offer'd to the consideration of the Honorable House of Commons, shewing the great necessity of having a Bill for the regulating of Printing and Printing-Presses*, Lincolns Inn Library, MP102 Fol.311.

the author at the centre of their arguments for new legislation.[72] Not only was it reasonable that an author 'should have all the advantages that may possibly be allowed him for his writings',[73] but, without a secure property in books, no bookseller would be able to 'give a consideration even for the most valuable copies of books: By which means, learned men will be wholly discouraged from propagating the most useful parts of knowledge and literature'.[74] In addition, there was also an author's family and dependants to consider. As one pamphlet put it: 'Regularity in Property of Printing, is equally beneficial to every body exercising the Trade; the Poor and the Weak, that happen to be favour'd by an Author, enjoy the benefit of this Order as much as the Rich and the Strong; whereby a Copy may be (and in Fact has often been) the Support of a Widow and Children'.[75]

Regardless of this rhetorical posturing on the part of the booksellers, it is important to keep in mind that the 1710 Act was, first and foremost, lobbied for and secured by the book trade in the pursuit of its own interests. Consider, for example, the discussion about the proposed

---

[72] See Rose (1993), pp. 34–36; Deazley (2004), *On the Origin*, pp. 31–34.

[73] *Reasons Humbly Offer'd for the Bill for Encouragement of Learning, and for Securing the Property of Copies of Books to the Rightful Owners thereof*, Lincolns Inn Library, MP102 Fol.100.

[74] *Reasons humbly Offer'd for a Bill for the Encouragement of Learning, and Improvement of Printing*, Lincolns Inn Library, MP102 Fol.312.

[75] *The Case of the Booksellers Right to their Copies, or sole Power of Printing their respective Books, represented to the Parliament* (1709), Lincolns Inn Library, MP102 Fol.103. See also the comments of Joseph Addison in *The Tatler*, 1 December 1709 ('The most eminent and useful Author of the Age we live in, after having laid out a Princely Revenue in Works of Charity and Beneficence . . . would have left the Person in the World who was the dearest to him in a narrow Condition, had not the Sale of his immortal Writings brought her in a very considerable Dowry'), and of Daniel Defoe in his *Review*, 6 December 1709 ('To print another Man's Copy, is much worse than robbing him on the Highway; for the Thief takes only what he finds about him, but the Pyrate Printer takes away his inheritance – An elaborate Work, a long studied Treatise, a painfully collected History; it both is and ought to be the Due, not of the Author only, but of his Family and Children').

Members of the book trade were often keen to emphasise that they had their own dependants that were reliant upon the existence of a secure property in books. For example, in *The Booksellers humble address to the Honorable House of Commons, In behalf of a Bill for Encouragement of Learning* the petitioners set out that: '[B]y refusing this Bill [the 1710 Act] innumerable inconveniences will ensue, such as the depriving many thousand mechanics and shopkeepers of their livelihood, destroying the paper manufacture in this nation, [and] reducing widows and children who at present subsist wholly by the maintenance of this Property to extreme poverty'; Bodleian, fol.w.666 (227).

reversionary copyright term (what would become s. 11) in *The Observator*, the journal founded by John Tutchin in 1702. '[D]esign'd as a Kindness to us Authors', it was suggested that the proposal might provide:

> [A] Security to Authors against being ill treated or impos'd upon by Booksellers, who run away with the Profits of their Labours, which sometimes happens to be very considerable, when Books take and become of standing use, or admit of several impressions in a little Time . . . so that Authors not being able to foresee this, because Copies are like Ships put to Sea, whose prosperous or unfortunate Voyage is not to be foreseen, they have nothing more than their first Copy-Money, let the Book sell ever so well.

The Observator, however, was not well-disposed to that point of view. The editor conceded that such a clause 'looks with a kind Aspect towards Authors', but continued that 'in the Event 'twill prove detrimental to them, as well as to Buyers'.[76] For one thing, if booksellers were to be tied to the first 14-year term, they would 'only give Copy-Money in proportion', which, the editor continued, would also result in smaller print runs and higher prices for the public. But in any event, he continued, 'if a Book happen to be of standing use, the Bookseller will print so many before his Time expire, as will make the Reversion of little or any Profit to the Author or his Assignees'.[77] Authors, the editor suggested, would be better to rely upon contractual relations rather than the suggested proviso to secure their interests in this regard.[78]

---

[76] Although it remains unclear as to who was responsible for the content and editing of *The Observator* after Tutchin's death in 1707, it appears that George Ridpath had assumed editorial control of the journal by 1709 (and continued as editor until *The Observator* ceased publication in 1712); W.R. McLeod and V.B. McLeod (1982), *A Graphical Directory of English Newspapers and Periodicals, 1702–1714*, Morgantown: West Virginia University, p. 38.

[77] *The Observator*, Vol.IX, No.6 (11–15 February 1710), 1.

[78] 'Authors may easily prevent the former Inconvenience, by agreeing for so much for every future Impression, or according to the Number of the first, which he may know by having Access to the Printers, Publishers, and Booksellers Accounts, and may make that Liberty Part of his Bargain'; ibid. Interestingly, the unsuccessful *Copyright Bill* of 1737, which proposed to grant 'the sole right of printing books' to authors (their executors, administrators, or assigns) for the duration of their life plus eleven years thereafter (Clause 1), also provided that no author would be able to sell, assign or transfer his copyright to any other person for any period longer than 10 years (except by testamentary disposition) (Clause 15). As the preamble to this clause made clear, it was intended to address the fact that 'the true worth of books and writings is, in many cases, not found out till a considerable time after the publication thereof, and authors, who are in necessity, may often be tempted absolutely to sell and alienate the right which they have to the original copies of

That the interests of the book trade might not always be in perfect alignment with the interests of authors is an obvious but an important point to reiterate. The idea that authors often suffer as a result of the unscrupulous and exploitative activities of their publishers has a currency that chimes with much contemporary scholarship upon the operation of the book trade in the eighteenth century, and in particular with the notion that authors were often very poorly paid for their work.[79] To be sure, some authors could and did retain control of their own copyright by self-publishing, by entering into profit-sharing arrangements with their publishers, or by selling the rights to a particular edition for a fixed sum in advance of publication,[80] but in general, these arrangements tended to serve the interests of the booksellers as much as they did the authors themselves. For the most part, however, booksellers would simply purchase an author's copyright outright,[81] including the author's reversionary interest set out within s. 11 of the Statute of Anne.[82]

---

the books which they have composed, before the value thereof is known, and may thereby put it out of their own power to alter and correct their compositions, upon maturer judgement and reflection'. The increased control that authors would have enjoyed over the ongoing exploitation of their work as a result of this proposal would, in terms of eighteenth century author-publisher relations, have been quite revolutionary. See *An Act for the Encouragement of Learning by the more Effectual Securing the sole Right of printing Books to the Authors thereof* (the 1737 Bill), British Library, BM 357.c.7.(41); 'Booksellers' Bill (1737)', in *Primary Sources*.

79 See for example Raven (2007), p. 230 ('Many authors were paid paltry sums for their initial surrender of rights to works which booksellers knew were very unlikely to be reprinted or to return much profit in their own right. Sometimes such cheap initial purchases proved to have a surprisingly long-term value at the auctions of reprint rights . . . but the majority of titles published did not reach a further edition.').

80 In general, see V. Bonham-Carter (1978), *Authors by Profession*, 2 vols, Los Altos, CA: William Kaufmann, 1: pp. 25–28; St Clair (2007), pp. 161–68; Sher, pp. 195–261.

81 See J. Hepburn (1968), *The Author's Empty Purse and the Rise of the Literary Agent*, London: Oxford University Press, p. 7 ('[U]ntil nearly the end of the nineteenth century, most reputable writers sold their work outright. The publisher took all the monetary risk, and above his costs, he kept all the profit for himself, whether it was meager or huge. There are recorded cases of virtuous publishers who spontaneously gave additional sums to authors of profitable books; but most such authors had to be content with fame and perhaps a better price on the next book'); Bonham-Carter (1978), 1: p. 25 ('[E]ven after the [*Statute of Anne*] the practice of selling copyright outright remained the general rule'); Raven (2007), p. 333 ('[M]ost writers in early modern and eighteenth-century England, and certainly most first-time writers, considered only outright copyright sale (even if some were able to restrict it to one edition) or full self-financing (thus acting as publishers themselves)').

82 Of course, selling all rights in a work in advance of publication, in exchange for a guaranteed fixed sum, was also an attractive option for many authors who were uncertain as to whether their work might prove successful, or who simply

For example, when James Thomson sold *Summer*, *Autumn*, and *Winter*, to John Millan in July 1729, he transferred 'the Intire Right and Property to [Millan] and his Heirs Executors and Administrators *forever*'.[83] Moreover, the legality of this practice was eventually affirmed in *Carnan v. Bowles* (1786) when the court ruled that an assignment of an author's 'interest' in his work necessarily included both the initial and the contingent 14-year terms set out in the legislation.[84]

As Richard Sher makes clear, however, we must be wary of indulging in overly broad generalisations when considering author-publisher relations at this time.[85] Indeed, *The Observator* pointed out that 'if Booksellers be generous, and Men of Substance, it seldom happens that they don't consider the Author according to the Currency of his Book, over and above the Agreement',[86] and there are sufficient examples of publishers making *ex gratia* payments to their authors whenever a publication proved to be particularly successful to support this claim.[87]

Footnote 82 (*cont.*)
wanted to avoid the trouble of having to negotiate with their publisher. As David Hume said of the sale of his first two volumes of his *History of England* to Andrew Millar in 1757: 'It is chiefly in order to avoid the Trouble and Perplexity of such Schemes that I desire at once to part with all the Property'; quoted in Sher, p. 244.

83 'Thomson's Assignment of Copyright to John Millan' (18 July 1729), in A.D. McKillop (ed) (1958), *James Thomson (1700–1748): Letters and Documents*, Lawrence: University of Kansas Press, pp. 63–64 (emphasis added). Similarly, when Millan subsequently sold the copyright in these poems to Andrew Millar, the contract re-iterated that 'John Millan now stands vested with the sole property and Right of printing publishing disposing of and assigning the said Coppys and the Right of printing and publishing the same for ever'; 'John Millan's Assignment of copyright to Andrew Millar' (16 June 1738), ibid, p. 121.

84 *Carnan v. Bowles* (1786) 2 Bro.C.R. 80, 83–84 (Lord Chancellor Thurlow: '[I]t strikes me that the contingent interest must pass by the word interest in the grant. He conveys all his interest in the copyright: the assignment must have been made upon the idea of a perpetuity; and it is probable not a syllable was said or thought of, respecting the contingent right. They merely followed the old precedents of such conveyances. It must, I think, be considered as conveying his whole right. If he had meant to convey his first term only, he should have said so').

85 'Publishers could be strikingly devious but also remarkably generous in their dealings with authors, and the terms of publication varied enormously from book to book, and sometimes from volume to volume and edition to edition'; Sher, pp. 214–15.

86 *The Observator*, Vol.IX, No.6 (11–15 February 1710), 1.

87 Hepburn (1968), 7 ('There are recorded cases of virtuous publishers who spontaneously gave additional sums to authors of profitable books; but most such authors had to be content with fame and perhaps a better price on the next book').

Andrew Millar, of course, was famously lauded by Samuel Johnson as the man who had 'raised the price of literature',[88] and, it is certainly true that some publishers, such as Millar and William Strahan, played an important role in increasing the payments received by authors for their work such that authorship became an increasingly viable profession in its own right. Moreover, in addition to the copy money that authors received for their works, publishers often supported their authors in other ways, in providing and arranging hospitality and entertainments, in brokering advantageous social or political introductions, or by underwriting major publishing projects such as Johnson's *Dictionary* or John Sinclair's *Statistical Account of Scotland* which projects might not otherwise have been undertaken.[89]

And, just as some publishers might prove to be very generous towards, and supportive of, their published authors, conversely, the behaviour and demands of authors could often prove to be troublesome and unreasonable. As Sher notes, publishers such as Millar and Strahan 'were not always comfortable in the new world they had created'.[90] In the early 1770s, for example, Strahan had encouraged his two Edinburgh co-publishers, John Balfour and William Creech, to establish a coalition which, he suggested, 'would be of great use in future Purchases, and prevent Authors from raising their Demands to the enormous Heighth they have done of late'.[91] And, to return to *The Observator*, the editor was keen to draw attention to the fact that authors often acted in ways that undermined the interests of both booksellers and the public: '[I]n Justice Booksellers ought also to be secured against the Frauds of Authors, some of whom have been known to sell the same Thing to others, under Pretence of Additions or Emandations, which makes the first Impression useless, both to Booksellers and the Buyers'. He continued that care should be taken 'to prevent such Frauds, and that Additions or Emandations should be printed separately for the Benefit of Buyers, and that the first Proprietor should have the Proffer of 'em, before others, and if they think fit to reuse them, the Author is then at liberty to do as he pleases with them'.[92]

And yet, even if we concede that sometimes publishers could be generous towards their authors, and that sometimes authors could be unscrupulous and demanding, on balance it would seem that authors, as a profession,

---

[88] J. Boswell, *Life of Johnson*, R.W. Chapman (ed) (1980), with an Introduction by Pat Rogers, Oxford: Oxford University Press, pp. 205–06.

[89] Sher, pp. 197–99, 424–28.

[90] Ibid, p. 346.

[91] Quoted in ibid, p. 344 (in general, see Sher, pp. 325–61).

[92] *The Observator*, Vol.IX, No.6 (11–15 February 1710), 1.

had plenty of reason to be resentful about the way in which booksellers, as a profession, conducted their business. As Raven writes, at the end of the eighteenth century, '[t]he unpopularity of booksellers with authors and with the public testified to the commercial success of so many manufacturers and sellers of literature – and precisely because, at least in the general perception, success too often came at the expense of writers' livelihoods and readers' purses'.[93]

7 OBSERVATION 6

'That writing the history of copyright is an important but an impossible task . . .'

At its most basic the Statute of Anne encapsulates a set of choices about who gets what legal protection for how long and why. Those same fundamental choices lie at the heart of the current copyright regime and there is, I would suggest, much to be gained from continuing to excavate and explore the substance, the contemporary impact, and the subsequent legacy of the 1710 Act. Indeed, throughout the course of this paper I have tried to do little more than begin to identify and pick at various threads of research that, in their different ways, might assist in deepening our understanding and appreciation of the Statute of Anne in this regard. That writing the history of copyright matters at all, I take to be uncontroversial. In the last 30 years, the history of copyright has been transformed from a subject of interest to a few book historians into a field of study engaging the interest and attention of scholars drawn from across the breadth of the humanities. What's more, this burgeoning interest in copyright's history has also revealed that writing the history of copyright can be a highly contested and a highly politicised activity.[94] These competing histories and interpretations of past events will no doubt continue to jumble alongside one another, vying for attention and influence, and that is as it should be. There can be no such thing as *the* history of copyright, just as there can be no definitive understanding or reading

93 Raven (2007), p. 351. See also Sher, p. 213 ('[B]ooksellers as a whole were to be regarded with suspicion because they stood on the other side of the divide separating authors from their books. / Authors usually expressed these suspicions among themselves, not wishing to alienate those responsible for putting their words into print'.)

94 K. Bowrey and N. Fowell (2009), 'Digging up fragments and building IP franchises', *Sydney Law Review*, 133–58.

of the Statute of Anne. To claim otherwise is to deceive – either oneself, or one's audience, or both.

8 BY WAY OF CONCLUSION

But to finish, let us return to Pirandello. His six characters present themselves to THE MANAGER as the subject of a compelling drama still waiting to be written. When their story is taken up by the actors, however, the actors' performances inevitably fail to capture the interior life and the immutable essence of the characters themselves. The characters quickly realise that their story can never be accurately told or presented on stage, but that it can only be approximated at best.[95] THE MANAGER puts it as follows: 'Acting is our business here. Truth up to a certain point, but no further'. So it is with writing the history of copyright: Truth up to a certain point, with conjecture and perhaps bias for the rest.

[95] Fiora A. Bassanese (1997), *Understanding Luigi Pirandello*, Columbia: The University of South Carolina Press, p. 102.

4. To what degree did the Statute of Anne (8 Anne, c.19, [1709]) affect commercial practices of the book trade in eighteenth-century England? Some provisional answers about copyright, chiefly from bibliography and book history

Michael F. Suarez, S.J.*

1 JOHN GAY'S POLLY (1729)

When *The Beggar's Opera* ran for an astonishing 62 nights in early 1728, it was said to have made its theatrical producer John Rich rather gay, and its author John Gay, quite rich. Following his enormous success on both stage and printed page, Gay quickly embarked upon a sequel. By late November of the same year, his new ballad opera, *Polly*, was in rehearsal. Notoriously, the Lord Chamberlain commanded that the play be suppressed.[1] Although it could not be performed in public it could, nevertheless, legally be sold in printed form, and Gay lost no time in preparing the book for his eager public.[2] The author published the ballad

* Professor of English, University Professor, & Director of the Rare Book School, University of Virginia (mfs3x@virginia.edu). The author wishes most especially to thank H. Tomás Gómez-Arostegui, Lewis & Clark Law School, Portland, Oregon, for his great kindness in reading a draft of this article, generously sharing some of his findings from The National Archives, and in answering several queries about particular Chancery documents. Any errors of fact or judgment are, of course, entirely my own

1 On the 1737 Licensing Act and its effects on stage censorship in eighteenth-century England, see L. W. Conolly (1976), *The Censorship of English Drama, 1737–1824*, San Marino, CA: Huntington Library Press.

2 Much of what immediately follows is based on James R. Sutherland (1942), '"Polly" among the Pirates', *Modern Language Review*, 37, 291–303. Sutherland

opera at his own expense in a handsome quarto volume, with accompanying music engraved on 31 copper plates, which he planned to sell for the considerable sum of six shillings. William Boyer printed 10,500 copies and, as far as we can tell, the book went on sale on 3 April 1729. Within a week, however, Gay was advertising in the public press that the vendors of piratical editions of his new ballad opera were 'now under prosecution' in the courts.[3] By 12 April, there were *at least* three illicit London octavo editions for sale costing 25 per cent or less of the authorized edition. Most probably, the cut-price editions had all been produced within four days. Gay quickly reduced his own price by more than half; yet, by the end of the month, a Dublin piracy was also circulating on the English market.

By my count, no fewer than 21 London booksellers were involved in the production and distribution of illegal editions. One printer alone had produced 3,000 copies. Another told the court that he had made a mere 500, the final 150 of which, he explained, he had 'made waste paper', both assertions nearly impossible to verify.

Yet, the Court of Chancery did not grant its interlocutory injunction against the booksellers until 12 June (see C33/351, f.305r), more than two months after the spurious copies were first publicly sold. Unaccountably, a surviving bill of complaint indicates that Gay did not sue in this court until 3 June (see C12/1817/67).[4] Gay's delay seems very odd indeed, especially given the widespread public notice he gave in April that he was seeking legal redress against the pirates. Did he first pursue a legal remedy elsewhere? If so, where would he have gone? Yet, Gay's friend John Arbuthnot wrote to Jonathan Swift on 8 May that Gay 'has about twenty Law suits with booksellers for pyrating his

---

wrongly indicates that a key document in the case had 'disappeared' (292), when in fact he merely was unable to locate it. Thus, his analysis is incomplete, but not incorrect.

[3] Among the newspapers carrying advertisements announcing Gay's legal prosecution against the pirates were: the *Daily Journal*, 11 April 1729 (et seq.); the *Daily Post*, 11 April 1729; and the *London Evening Post*, 12 April 1729.

[4] Cf. the further answer (10 November 1730) of the bookseller Thomas Read (C 11/1272/7(1)), indicating he thought that Gay filled his bill on 3 June 1729. The *Universal Spectator and Weekly Journal* for Saturday, 14 June, 1729 (Issue XXXVI) reports that, 'On Thursday the Counsel for Mr. *Gay* made a Motion in the Court of Chancery at *Westminster*, against several Booksellers, for vending the Pyrated Edition of *Polly* an *Opera*, and obtain'd Judgment', indicating that he was granted the injunction he sought. Further collaboration of Gay's timing comes from the bill of revivor in the case (C12/1817/15, 5 March 1732/3), which also attests to a 3 June date for the original bill of complaint.

book'.[5] Could there have been an earlier bill of complaint in Chancery? That seems most unlikely. It would be unusual – given that so much was at stake both financially and artistically (authors do not like the circulation of mangled texts) – for his newspaper advertisement to have been mere bluffing. Nevertheless, might the interval not be best explained by the possibility that Gay, via an agent in the trade, had entered into negotiations with the London pirates?

Evidence from newspaper advertisements and from title-pages reveals that this is in fact what happened. Apparently not trusting the courts to effect a satisfactory remedy, Gay had sought the assistance of the wealthy printer-turned-politician, John Barber, who had excellent connections in the London book trade and among the Livery Companies more generally; he would in a few months be elected sheriff (1729–30) and subsequently become lord mayor (1732–33).[6] Barber went to Thomas Astley, the most reputable and commercially powerful of the pirates, and negotiated a business agreement whereby Astley paid some damages, promised to sell no more pirated copies, and, in return, became a legitimate partner in Gay's publication.[7] The chief poacher thus became one of the principal gamekeepers. From the author's perspective, Barber's business solution was far from ideal, but it was eminently practical in that it preserved for Gay a greater portion of the profits from *Polly* than he would otherwise have received.

Writing Jonathan Swift two and a half years later, in December 1731, Gay revealed his frustration that the issue had yet to be definitively resolved:

> I have had an injunction for me against pyrating-booksellers, which I am sure to get nothing by, and will, I fear, in the end drain me of some mony. When I began this prosecution I fancy'd there would be some end of it, but the law still goes on, and 'tis probable that I shall some time or other see an Attorney's bill as long as the Book.[8]

In the end, Chancery finally granted a perpetual injunction in December 1737, five years after the author's death and a long, long time after *Polly* had ceased to be a hot publishing property. The opera had been duly entered into the Stationers' Register on 3 April 1729, but the Statute of

---

[5] Jonathan Swift, *The Correspondence of Jonathan Swift*, Harold Williams (ed) (1963–65), 5 vols, Oxford: The Clarendon Press, 3:232.

[6] *Oxford Dictionary of National Biography*.

[7] See James R. Sutherland, '"Polly" among the Pirates', 299–301.

[8] Alexander Pope, *The Correspondence of Alexander Pope*, George Sherburn (ed) (1956), 5 vols, Oxford: The Clarendon Press, 3:249.

Anne seems to have had very little bearing upon the ensuing actions of the many businessmen involved.

John Gay's case suggests a truth that we may not wish to hear: that for many years the Copyright Act of 1709 had only a limited practical effect on the rights of authors and, more significantly still, on actual commercial book trade practice. I shall briefly tender seven observations, chiefly of a bibliographical and book-historical nature, that help to explain why this should be so.

2 SEPTEM RATIONES

1. The booksellers seldom entered their properties in the *Stationers' Register*, as mandated by the Statute of Anne. After an initial rush in 1710, when 678 titles are registered, the average between 1711 and 1760 is a mere 65 works per year and, as Shef Rogers reminds us, 'a fair proportion of those represent multiple entries for the same work published in parts'.[9] An analysis of data from the English Short-Title Catalogue indicates that the *minimum* number of titles published annually in this period was about 1,600. Thus, at its lowest level of eighteenth-century production – even taking no account of the multiple entries for serially published books – the British book trade was registering less than 4 per cent of its output. At its highest level of production in this period (1711–60), the figure dips to less than 2.5 per cent.[10] This astonishingly low level of registration is all the more remarkable when one recalls that both the statute itself and the decisions of the law courts made it clear that registration was a necessary prerequisite for the protections and penalties for infringement specified in 8 Anne, c.19.

How could this be so? Harry Ransom explains that, 'The *Stationers' Register* was considered legally necessary only for recovery under the Act and was not held indispensable to ownership of copy'.[11] In other words, because the booksellers did not seek the penalties specified in the

[9] Shef Rogers (2000), 'The Use of Royal Licences for Printing in England, 1695–1760: A Bibliography', *Library*, 7th ser., 1, 145–92.

[10] See Suarez, 'Toward a Bibliometric Analysis of the Surviving Record, 1701–1800', in Michael F. Suarez, S.J. and Michael L. Turner (eds) (2009), *The Cambridge History of the Book in Britain, Volume 5, 1695–1830*, Cambridge: Cambridge University Press, pp. 39–65.

[11] Harry Ransom (1956), *The First Copyright Statute: An Essay on* An Act for the Encouragement of Learning, *1710*, Austin, TX: University of Texas Press, p. 101.

Act (forfeiture and destruction of existing copies or parts thereof and the payment of a penny per every sheet of the pirated work found in the offender's custody, with such monies to be divided between the Crown and the successful plaintiff), considering them as inadequate to the commercial realities of the trade, they largely disregarded the Act and its provisions. Copy-owning litigants at Court of Chancery did not seek the penalties provided for infringement under the Act (nor could they), but instead preferred injunctive relief and an award of the defendant's profits in equity – neither of which had anything to do with the provisions of the Act at all.

Indeed, for most of the history of British copyright from the 1710 to 1774, the English booksellers were far more interested in common law rights and equitable remedies than in what Parliament had provided in the Act of Anne. A thoroughgoing (though, admittedly, not exhaustive) survey of court records, legal reports, and Stationers' Company records reveals that the penalties stipulated in the Act were perhaps never imposed in the landmark interval 1710–1774.[12] This finding is corroborated by Ronan Deazley, who, commenting on the penalties awarded to Thomas Beckett in 1778 for the unauthorized publication of works by Laurence Sterne, wryly observes: 'Nearly seventy years after the passing of the *Statute of Anne*, the statutory penalties that parliament had considered sufficient for the securing of an author's copyright began to be awarded against those booksellers guilty of literary piracy'.[13]

2. Some booksellers, printers, and authors continued to seek royal licenses in order to protect their property, despite the considerable expense of £8–10 involved.[14] Although it must be admitted that sometimes these licenses functioned chiefly as endorsements or imprimaturs, my survey of some 150 licenses using the Rogers bibliography indicates that a significant number were sought for works especially likely to be pirated. It was not uncommon for a license to order that the work it was protecting be entered

---

[12] It must be admitted, however, that the state of legal reporting in this period is far from all that one might desire; neither are the Stationers' Company records complete. See J. H. Baker (2000), 'Why the History of English Law Has not been Finished', *Cambridge Law Journal* 59(1) (March), 62–84; and Robin Myers (1990), *The Stationers' Company Archive: an Account of the Records, 1554–1984*, Winchester: St Paul's Bibliographies.

[13] Ronan Deazley (2004), *On the Origin of the Right to Copy: Charting the Movement of Copyright Law in Eighteenth-Century Britain (1695–1775)*, Oxford and Portland, OR: Hart Publishing, p. 230. See also H. Tomás Gómes-Arostegui (2008), 'What History Teaches Us about Copyright Injunctions and the Inadequate-Remedy-at-Law Requirement', *Southern California Law Review* 81, 1197–1280 (1269, notes 400 and 401).

[14] Rogers (2000), 'The Use of Royal Licences', cited above.

in the *Stationers' Register*, but, oddly, many titles with licenses having such mandates as a condition of their validity were nonetheless never registered. Probably, the requirement of submitting nine copies ('upon the best paper' used for the edition if there were variant issues), a non-trivial expense, was a disincentive. Even so, in all but a few instances, the financial burden of legal deposit – especially when compared to the requisite fees already noted – seems inadequate to account for the persistent disregard of the registration requirement. In short, although one aim of the Act was to re-establish the *Stationers' Register* as the record of copyright, this intention (as a number of others) was never realized. For the most part, the book trade ignored the *Register* and, concomitantly, the Act that sought to establish registration as the central means of establishing the ownership of copy so as to afford such owners the attendant protections due to them.

3. Augustine Birrell observed more than 100 years ago that, in the eighteenth century, booksellers 'fell in love with the high court of Chancery' seeking *ex parte* injunctions to restrain the commercial activities of their rivals. Interlocutory injunctions could provide booksellers with a stop-gap remedy to restrain rival publishers before the matter had been settled fully at law.[15] Indeed, Chancery only very rarely denied plaintiffs or dissolved interlocutory injunctions.[16] We should bear in mind, however, that such interlocutory injunctions from the High Court were given in a court of equity to assist a common-law right, and not with reference to the Act. In fact, although reports do not appear to exist in many instances, a survey of cases for which we do know something about the substance of the booksellers' bills of complaint reveals that in a significant number of cases the bookseller-plaintiffs did not invoke the terms of the Statute of Anne as they resorted to the time-tested and safe haven of English property law. This behaviour should not occasion surprise: the book-trade and copyright historian, John Feather, among many others, has observed the Act was particularly favourable neither to the booksellers, nor to their longstanding financial interests.[17]

---

[15] Deazley (2004), *On the Origin of the Right to Copy*, p. 51 n.5, observes that, 'Less than 25% of the cases that came before the Court of Chancery during this period proceeded beyond [the] pleadings stage.'

[16] For a reliable survey and analysis of copyright injunctions, see Gómes-Arostegui (2008), 'What History Teaches Us about Copyright Injunctions and the Inadequate-Remedy-at-Law Requirement', 1237–41.

[17] John Feather (1994), *Publishing, Piracy and Politics: An Historical Study of Copyright in Britain*, London: Mansell, p. 62, *et infra*. See also, Ronan Deazley (2003), 'The Myth of Copyright at Common Law', *Cambridge Law Journal* 62, 106–133 (107–110, 132–33).

Remarkably, a number of cases indicate the Chancellor did not appear to consider himself bound by the Act. In 1735, for example, *Motte v. Faulkner* (C11/2249/4) resulted in the granting of an injunction to restrain publication of the Pope and Swift *Miscellanies*, which were first published in 1701–2 and 1708, and hence were beyond the protection provided by the statute. In the same year, an injunction was also issued against the bookseller Jeffrey Walker, who had the temerity to print and sell *The Whole Duty of Man*, a work first published nearly 80 years earlier (see *Eyre v. Walker* (C11/1520/29)). Legal action in *Walthoe v. Walker* (1736) (C11/1534/62) produced the same result, this time for a book originally produced in 1704. Similarly, Lord Chancellor Hardwicke, hearing *Tonson and another versus Walker* in 1739 (C12/1214/66), granted an injunction to Tonson to restrain his rival from selling an edition of *Paradise Lost*, despite the fact that statutory copyright protection had clearly expired. (Walker nevertheless completed his publication, in a dozen parts or 'numbers', of Milton's epic in defiance of Tonson and the High Court. He did the same, again in 1751–52, once more disregarding the Court's injunction (C11/1106/18), this time publishing sixteen 3*d.* numbers).[18] Indeed, these were all 'old books', losing their protection under the Act in 1731.

No wonder, then, that in the aftermath of *Donaldson v. Beckett* (1774), the booksellers complained that they 'had constantly apprehended, that the [Act] did not interfere with any copy-right that might be invested in [them] by the common law'.[19] This was no innovation, neither was it special pleading. After all, the King's Bench in *Millar v. Taylor* (1769), had formally recognized that a common-law right exists and further held that the Act of Anne in no way preempted that right. Six of the judges in *Donaldson* believed the same.[20] Clause IX of the Act seemed to indicate as much. No less an astute legal mind than William Blackstone understood in both *Tonson v. Orr* (1762) (SRO CS 16 1/111) and in the *Commentaries on the Laws of England* (vol.2, 1766) that the author's work should be understood as a property and, hence, protected under the common law. Taken together, both the granting of interlocutory injunctions by the Chancery over many years – most often without the plaintiff making reference to the Act, and sometimes with the Court operating in a manner apparently contrary to its provisions – and the successful claims made for profits in

[18] *Tonson v. Walker and Marchant* (1752); see R. C. Bald (1942), 'Early Copyright Litigation and its Bibliographical Interest', in *Papers of the Bibliographical Society* 36, 81–96.

[19] C. J. vol. 34, at p. 513, quoted in Deazley (2003), 'The Myth of Copyright at Common Law', 126.

[20] Deazley (2003), 'The Myth of Copyright at Common Law', 122.

equity – also without the plaintiff making any reference to the Act – go a long way toward explaining how and why the book trade came to operate with very little reference to the Act at all.

4. Evidence from trade-sale catalogues and related commercial records amply demonstrates that the established book trade owned, bought, and sold shares in copies without taking almost any notice of the Statute of Anne throughout the eighteenth century. Under the 1710 provisions, books already published before the Act came into effect lost their protection in 1731 at the latest, but the expiration of statutory protection seems to have had no effect whatever on the value of shares in such properties, nor on the willingness of booksellers to invest in them.[21] My scrutiny of trade-sale records in the Bodleain Library, although admittedly not an exhaustive study, reveals not a single instance in which a jointly-held literary property declined in value as a result of its statutory copyright protection expiring according to the terms of the Act of Anne.[22] In the vast majority of cases, the most valuable literary properties increased in value as they aged, regardless of their falling outside the protections and penalties of the Act. Even after *Donaldson v. Beckett*, the established London trade continued to conduct its business in many of the same ways it had in the 1680s, behaving in 1800 largely as if copyright were perpetual.[23]

5. The nature of author-publisher contracts in the 50 years following the Act was not markedly different from what it had been in the decades before 1710. As Peter Lindenbaum concludes after a detailed study of the

---

[21] Terry Belanger (1970), 'Booksellers' sales of copyright. Aspects of the London book trade: 1718–1768', unpub. thesis, Columbia University; Belanger (1975), 'Booksellers' trade sales, 1718–1768', *Library*, 5th ser., 30, 281–302; and Belanger (1975), 'Tonson, Wellington and the Shakespeare Copyrights', in R. W. Hunt, I. G. Philip, and R. J. Roberts (eds), *Studies in the Book Trade in Honour of Graham Pollard*, Oxford: The Oxford Bibliographical Society, pp. 195–209. See also Cyprian Blagden (1951), 'Booksellers' trade sales 1718–1768', *Library*, 5th ser., 5, 243–57; and Graham Pollard (1978), 'The English Market for Printed Books', *Publishing History* 4, [7]–48.

[22] The John Johnson Collection in the Bodleian includes 122 trade-sale catalogues, 1718–52. I have not consulted the collection of trade-sale catalogues, 168 in all, held by the British Library and reaching all the way to 1768. The Murrary Archive in the National Library of Scotland includes similar materials spanning (with lacunae) 1768–95.

[23] Hugh Amory's fine study (1984), '"De Facto Copyright"? Fielding's Works in Partnership, 1769–1821', *Eighteenth-Century Studies*, 17, 449–76, suggests that, while many of the wealthiest members of copy-owning trade were conducting their businesses as they had always done, Alexander Donaldson and his 'pirate' contemporaries were reprinting cheap editions, selling them in volume, and making a handsome profit.

Restoration book trade, 'many of the conditions we associate with mid- to late-eighteenth-century authorship were in fact already in place at least 40 years before the Statute of Anne was passed'.[24] In light of Lindenbaum's finding, we would do well to bear in mind that Ronan Deazley, approaching the question of copyright and authorship from the perspective of legal history, has rejected the all-too-common narratives interpreting the history of copyright in eighteenth-century Britain as the inexorable and intentional rise of the author's legal, intellectual, and financial sovereignty. In Deazley's investigation, 'The traditional analysis of the development of copyright in eighteenth-century Britain is revealed as exhibiting the character of a long-standing myth, and the centrality of the modern proprietary author as the raison d'être of the copyright regime is displaced.'[25]

The veteran literary historian and authority on eighteenth-century authorship, Dustin Griffin, also summarily rejects such a traditional view about the importance of the Act of Anne in changing authorial perception and practice:

> as any careful historian of copyright observes, eighteenth-century authors almost always immediately sold their owner's right to a bookseller, and, once it was sold, did not think of themselves as legal proprietors of their work: copyright in the eighteenth century is essentially a bookseller's exclusive right to copy (and sell) a work, and not a key to authorial self-images. . .Historians of the book trade show that very few authors would have had any bargaining power in selling copyrights.[26]

The highly calculating, shrewd, and sometimes devious business arrangements of Alexander Pope are routinely adduced to establish the rise of professional authors and their empowerment by the Statute of Anne, but Pope – who seems to have made about £5,000 each for his *Iliad* (6 vols., 1715–20) and *Odyssey* (5 vols., 1725–26) – is highly atypical in almost every respect.[27]

---

[24] Peter Lindenbaum (2002), 'Authors and Publishers in the Late Seventeenth Century, II: Brabazon Aylmer and the Mysteries of the Trade', *Library*, 7th ser., 3: 32–57 (50); see also Lindenbaum (1995), 'Authors and Publishers in the Late Seventeenth Century: New Evidence on Their Relations', *Library*, 6th ser., 17, 250–69.

[25] Deazley (2004), *On the Origin of the Right to Copy*, p. [i]; see also pp. 221–26.

[26] Dustin Griffin, 'The Rise of the Professional Author?', in Suarez and Turner (eds) (2009), *The Cambridge History of the Book in Britain, Volume 5, 1695–1830*, pp. 132–45 (at 134, 141). See also Griffin (1996), *Literary Patronage in England, 1650–1800*, Cambridge: Cambridge University Press.

[27] David Foxon, *Pope and the Early Eighteenth-Century Book Trade*, rev. and ed. James McLaverty (1991), Oxford: The Clarendon Press, 63, 101. See also John

6. Unsure of how the Act would be interpreted in the Courts, and disdainful of the remedies it provided, the booksellers repeatedly sought out commercial solutions as the means that they understood best and believed were most reliable. Among the most well-remembered instances are Tonson's ruthless undercutting of Walker's Shakespeare (1739ff.),[28] and the trade's amassing a fund of more than £3,000 in 1759 largely to win over provincial booksellers by weaning them off pirated texts. Another group of measures that should be better remembered are the inauguration of the requirement that booksellers at trade sales post a £500 bond, forfeitable if they sold any pirated works, and the exclusion from all subsequent sales of any bookseller who purchased shares for pirates.[29]

Yet, far more common than such noteworthy actions was the expedient of entering into ad-hoc trading partnerships with rivals who could not be otherwise controlled. The example of Gay and his *Polly*, noted earlier, is a good case in point: cooperation with competitors was preferable to entering into commercial combat that could not ultimately be won.[30] Nevertheless, the vast majority of these instances may perforce be unknown to us today; when relevant business records do not survive, then careful bibliographical analysis is typically required to reveal this kind of collaboration.

Much of the London-Edinburgh trade too worked by ad-hoc agreements and cross-border partnerships (also often difficult to detect, except by bibliographical scrutiny) because commercial recourse allowed booksellers to control their own fate.[31] Indeterminacy is bad for business. It is particularly bad for a commercial enterprise already fraught with

Nichols (1812–16), *Literary Anecdotes of the Eighteenth Century*, 9 vols., London, 1:77–8 n., 109–10 n. and 8:169; and James McLaverty (1993), 'The contract for Pope's translation of Homer's Iliad', *Library*, 6th ser., 15, 206–25. Foxon, *Pope and the Early Eighteenth-Century Book Trade*, pp. 51–101, is the best overall guide to Pope's highly unusual relations with the trade.

[28] See Giles E. Dawson, 'The Copyright of Shakespeare's Dramatic Works', in *Studies in Honor of A. H. R. Fairchild,* Charles T. Prouty (ed) (1946), Columbia, MO: Univ. of Missouri Press, 9–35; see also Andrew Murphy (2003), *Shakespeare in Print: A History and Chronology of Shakespeare Publishing*, Cambridge, Cambridge University Press, p. 108.

[29] Belanger (1970), 'Booksellers' sales of copyright. Aspects of the London book trade: 1718–1768', p. 158.

[30] *Vide* Sutherland, '*Polly* among the pirates', cited above.

[31] See Warren McDougall (1974), 'Gavin Hamilton, John Balfour and Patrick Neill: A Study of Publishing in Edinburgh in the 18th Century', unpub. Ph.D. thesis, Edinburgh University, pp. 149–69.

endemic problems of capitalization, high initial investments (copy, paper, composition, printing, distribution and warehousing, advertising) and slow returns, extended wholesale and retail credit arrangements, uncertain markets, and the ever-present threat of piracy.[32] For the establishment bookselling community, strength within the trade was paramount. Hence, the persistence of printing and wholesaling congers well into the eighteenth century – and the perdurance of the share-book system far into the nineteenth.[33]

7. The Statute in practice provided scant protection against piracy, either within the London trade itself, or elsewhere in Britain. More often than not, crime paid. Michael Harris wryly observes, 'the London pirates of the 1730s and 1740s can be seen as the vanguard to a flotilla which, sailing on the flood of an expanding market, finally blew the monopolists out of the water and ran up the skull and crossbones over a relatively free market in books'.[34] Moreover, there was a great deal of open textual appropriation and recycling of recently-published works: the number of extracts, abridgments (or 'epitomies'), and serializations of booksellers' properties in copyright by outside parties runs into many thousands. Indeed, as R.M. Wiles and Robert D. Mayo have variously shown, the thriving periodical trade in London and the provinces – functionally 'outside the copyright law' – was utterly dependent upon this traffic in the grey market.[35]

The Act seems in practice to have been completely ignored not only in the highly popular genres of poetic miscellanies and prose compilations (for example, 'beauties', 'sprouters', 'museums', and the like), but also in the appropriation of material for dictionaries, encyclopaedias, and other works of reference, many of which were highly lucrative publishing

---

[32] See Suarez, 'Introduction' in Suarez and Turner (eds) (2009), *The Cambridge History of the Book in Britain, Volume 5, 1695–1830*, pp. 25–35. Given these financial difficulties, it is no wonder, then, that the incidence of bankruptcies in the trade was high.

[33] See Norma Hodgson and Cyprian Blagden (1956), *The Notebook of Thomas Bennet and Henry Clements (1686–1719), with some Aspects of Book Trade Practice*, Oxford: The Oxford Bibliographical Society.

[34] Michael Harris, 'Paper pirates: the alternative book trade in London in the mid-eighteenth century', in Robin Myers and Michael Harris (eds) (1989), *Fakes and Frauds: Varieties of Deception in Print and Manuscript*, Winchester, pp. 47–69 (at 65).

[35] Robert D. Mayo (1962), *The English Novel in the Magazines, 1740–1815*, Evanston, IL: Northwestern University Press, p. 160; see especially pp. 159–272. R.M. Wiles (1957), *Serial Publication in England before 1750*, Cambridge, Cambridge University Press.

projects.[36] The same is true for popular song books and jest books; even grammars and other school books, as well as almanacs – all of which potentially constituted a genuinely profitable market – were regularly plagiarized. Scrutinizing the contents and thus tracing the lineage of such works teaches us that, for all the careful analysis of legal cases that scholars have done, we still know very little about the *de facto* culture of intellectual property as it operated in the book trade.[37] Biographical dictionaries, for instance, typically recycled information and sometimes reprinted large passages from earlier works with little or no alteration – *viz.*, the *Biographia Britannica* (1747–66) appropriated extensively from the *General Dictionary* (1734–41), and Robert Shiells's *Lives of the Poets* (1753) used material from both of these – without any known accusations of plagiarism being made, or any recourse to law.[38] As Ephraim Chambers stated in the article on 'Plagiary' in his *Cyclopaedia* (1728):

> Dictionary-Writers, at least such as meddle with Arts and Sciences, seem exempted from the common Laws of *Meum* and *Tuum* . . ..Their Works are supposed, in great Measure, Assemblages of other Peoples, and what they take from Others they do it avowedly, and in the open Sun . . .and if they rob, they don't do it any otherwise, than as the Bee does, for the publick Service. Their Occupation is not pillaging, but collecting Contributions.[39]

In some instances, the Act may have deterred authors and booksellers from the open practice of piracy in its various forms, but in many others it clearly did not.

The intellectual historian and history-of-print specialist Adrian Johns describes the world of eighteenth-century London and the provinces as 'the piratical Enlightenment', which in his view 'was lower-toned, more

---

36 See, for example, Michael F. Suarez, S.J. (2001), 'The Production and Consumption of the Eighteenth-Century Poetic Miscellany', in Isabel Rivers (ed), *Books and Their Readers in Eighteenth-Century England – Volume 2*, London: Continuum, pp. 217–51.

37 Paulina Kewes (ed) (2003), *Plagiarism in Early Modern England*, London: Palgrave Macmillan, provides useful essays on the evolution of ideas about intellectual property and its theft.

38 See Isabel Rivers, 'Biographical Dictionaries and their Uses from Bayle to Chalmers', in Isabel Rivers (ed) (2001), *Books and Their Readers in Eighteenth-Century England – Volume 2*, London: Continuum, pp. 135–69, which suggests the degree to which new dictionaries were indebted to their predecessors.

39 Ephraim Chambers (1728), *Cyclopaedia: Or, An Universal Dictionary of Arts and Sciences*, 2 vols., London: James and John Knapton, John Darby, Daniel Midwinter, Arthur Bettesworth, John Senex [and 13 others in London] 2: pp. 820–1.

commercial, more hardscrabble, more various, and altogether edgier than the world of the high Parisian *philosophes* or Scottish philosophers with which we are familiar.' Considering the ubiquity of reprinting, Johns even goes so far as to proclaim, 'No piracy. . . no Enlightenment.'[40]

3 CONCLUSION

How then are we to understand the true commercial impact of the Statute of Anne on the functioning of the book trade in the 50 years following its successful passage into law? It may seem outrageous that a mere student of eighteenth-century cultural and commercial exchange (himself no legal historian) should suggest that, for a half century or more, the Statute of Anne did relatively little in practice to alter the working routines of the vast majority of printers, booksellers, and publishers, but that is the conclusion that the available historical evidence has pressed upon me.

In the first of his Sanders Lectures at Cambridge University on 'The London Book Trade in the Later Seventeenth Century', the great bibliographer and book historian D.F. McKenzie observed 'the trade's consistent concern for profit before principle, demonstrating that government censorship of news-books was only sporadically effective because the commercial impetus of the trade was ultimately more powerful and pervasive than the actions of the government.[41] In the end, McKenzie suggested, the profit motive was more powerful than the fear of legal penalty, even when those government sanctions included physical harm and disfigurement.

Another distinguished historian of the book trade, Michael Treadwell, came to a remarkably congruent conclusion about the relationship between legislation and trade operations when he studied the causes and effects of the definitive expiration of the Licensing Act, or Printing Act, in 1695:

> when the Act finally lapsed. . . leading members of the trade were not particularly disturbed . . . ..they had made those adjustments they considered prudent to protect their businesses in the changed circumstances which seemed to be coming. A far greater concern. . .was the debased state of the coinage. . . For

[40] Adrian Johns (2010), *Piracy: The Intellectual Property Wars from Gutenberg to Gates*, Chicago: University of Chicago Press, 49, 50.

[41] D. F. McKenzie, *The London Book Trade in the Later Seventeenth Century*, The Sanders Lectures, delivered at Cambridge University, 1975–6, page 8. Distributed privately; copies deposited in the British Library; the English Faculty Library, Oxford; and the University Library, Cambridge.

> the less well established[,] the lapse might even offer new opportunities. . . when it lapsed they [all] seem, for the most part, to have gone on about their business.[42]

R.M. Wiles, in his pioneering study of serial publication in England before 1750, likewise finds an ubiquity of 'publishers with an eye to business and a hearty readiness to defy the law' in the decades following 1710.[43]

By a crude analogy with the contemporary piracy situation that many intellectual property attorneys actually contend with today, we might say that Dublin was the London trade's Far East; the Netherlands and France were their South Asia or Eastern Europe. But Scotland, London, and the Provinces were roughly equivalent to the peer-to-peer electronic networks of today – maddeningly difficult to control, yet vital to established market interests where considerable investments had long ago been made.

Mark Rose is astute as ever when he explains the significance of the 1710 Act:

> The passage of the statute was in fact epochal because, at least in principle, it marked a shift from the kind of culture of regulation represented by licensing and by the guild system to a new regime based more on enlightenment ideas of individualism, property, and civil society as a collectivity. Henceforth, matters related to literary property would be adjudicated not by royal decree or by private panels assembled within the confines of the Stationers' Company, but in the legislature and public law courts'.[44]

The fact is, however, that it took more than 60 years for the courts and the trade to figure out what the Statute of Anne actually meant in practice.

The *remedies* provided in 1710 were not what the booksellers genuinely wanted, so they sought better redress outside the Act – both in injunctions restraining continued publication and sale, and in equity damages, as well as in commercial measures sustained by the trade itself. As the (retired) bookseller William Johnston stated before a Parliamentary Committee when asked 'why it was not the custom of those who are possessed of copy-right, to enter them in the books of the Stationers' Company', he

---

[42] Michael Treadwell, 'The Stationers and the Printing Acts at the End of the Seventeenth Century', in John Barnard and D. F. McKenzie, with Maureen Bell (eds) (2002), *The Cambridge History of the Book in Britain, Volume 4, 1557–1695*, Cambridge, pp. 755–76.

[43] Wiles (1957), *Serial Publication in England before 1750*, p. 154.

[44] Mark Rose, 'Copyright, Authors and Censorship', in Suarez and Turner (eds) (2009), *The Cambridge History of the Book in Britain, Volume 5, 1695–1830*, pp. 118–131 (at 119).

replied: that he never thought the penalties prescribed by the Act of the eighth of queen Anne worth contending for, as much shorter and more complete relief might be had, by filing a bill in Chancery'.[45] One might add that seeking an *ex parte* injunction was much less expensive than pursuing legal prosecution.

For the many reasons outlined above, including the longstanding practices of the book trade, the *rights* established by statute were commonly thought by copy-owning booksellers to be anterior to and more fundamental than what was wrought (rather unsatisfactorily) by parliament in 1709.[46] Hence, the booksellers' persistent commercial conduct – both individually and in groups ranging from ad hoc trading partnerships to the Stationers' Company operating under royal charter – was rooted in the conviction that copyright was perpetual. Absent this belief, the practices of the Stationers and their close associates (such as Robert Dodsley) with respect to the ownership of copy, trading in copy, profiting from copy, and the policing of copy, make very little business sense.

The historical realities I have been outlining in this investigation – although documented in the bibliographical record, the surviving business papers of publishing concerns, and in the scholarly literature of book history – are perhaps largely unknown to a number of legal historians who concern themselves with copyright and the development of intellectual property in Britain. Yet, to this student of the eighteenth-century book trade, just as bibliographers and book historians overlook the legal record and its impressive body of attendant scholarship to their historical impoverishment,[47] so too do scholars of the law sometimes neglect the realities of the book trade in ways that might diminish the long-term usefulness of their labours. Given the manifold forms of expertise required to understand the richness and pluriformity of the surviving historical evidence, perhaps the time has come for us to work more closely together.

Some attentive readers may have wondered what ever happened to those 150 illicit copies of *Polly* supposedly made into waste paper by the man who printed them? Contrary to the testimony given in the defendant's

---

45 *The Parliamentary History of England, from the Earliest Period to the Year 1803*, Hurst, Rees, Orme, & Brown; J. Richardson; [10 others], London: Longman; and T. C. Hansard, 1813, XVII, columns 1077–1110 (1085). Johnston's answers to the Committee occupy columns 1078–86.

46 Again, the testimony of William Johnston is helpful; see *The Parliamentary History of England*, cited above.

47 On the salutary effects of legal history for bibliography and book history, see for example, R. C. Bald, 'Early Copyright Litigation and its Bibliographical Interest', cited above.

answer before the Court of Chancery, bibliographical evidence shows that they ended up on the market after all. They were not sold by their piratical printer, however. No, he passed them on to another of the original pirates, Thomas Astley, the reasonably reputable member of the established trade, who had gone into partnership with Gay to sell legitimate copies. Despite his promise not to vend any more *Polly* piracies, Astley clapped a new title page on the 150 phantom copies (now very real indeed) and sold them as a 'second edition'. In the face of legal uncertainties, a profitable commercial solution had been found.[48]

48 James R. Sutherland (1942), '"Polly" among the Pirates', 301–2.

5. The Statute of Anne and authors' rights: *Pope v. Curll* (1741)

Mark Rose*

1 INTRODUCTION

It is commonplace to note that English copyright law is, despite its stated emphasis on the public interest, essentially commercial in origin. After all, the Statute of Anne, the first English copyright act, emerged in 1709 largely as a result of the disruptions in the book trade that came about with the end of licensing in 1695. Likewise, US copyright law, which descends from the English statute, is also essentially commercial. The European civil law countries, on the other hand, give priority to the author and these laws, at least in theory, are founded on authors' rights.

What I want to do is to test or qualify the familiar contrast between the copyright tradition that descends from the Statute of Anne and the authors' rights traditions of the civil law countries. I propose to do so by discussing one of the early Statute of Anne cases – *Pope v. Curll*,[1] decided in 1741 – in order to suggest how in this lawsuit the poet, Alexander Pope was using the Statute of Anne to pursue personal as well as economic interests. Furthermore, to suggest that *Pope v. Curll* is by no means a unique or erratic case, I propose to leap some 250 years from the time of the Statute of Anne to the near present and the important American case *Salinger v. Random House*,[2] decided in 1987. The similarities between *Pope* and *Salinger* are interesting, especially given the great gap of time between them. Both involve famous authors. Both concern the unauthorized publication of personal letters. Most important, both reveal plaintiff-authors using copyright laws for purposes more related to what we would call moral rights than commerce.

* Prof.Em., English Department, University of California, Santa Barbara, mrose@english.ucsb.edu

1 2 Atk 342, 26 Eng. Rep. 608 (1741).

2 811 F. 2d 90 (2nd Cir 1987).

2 THE BACKGROUND

The Statute of Anne was largely based on the trade regulation practices of the Stationers' Company, the ancient guild of English printers and booksellers. But it departed from guild practices insofar as, among other things, the act gave formal legal standing to authors as the owners and first proprietors of their writings. Nonetheless, in the first half of the eighteenth century authorship as a profession was still at an early stage of development and copyright was generally seen as more a bookseller's than an author's concern. It is not surprising, then, that most copyright litigation in the first three decades after the passage of the statute – about 20 cases in all – involved booksellers suing booksellers. As one would expect, the issues in these cases were predominantly commercial.

Prior to *Pope v. Curll*, perhaps the most notable case in which an author figured as plaintiff was *Gay v. Read* in 1729.[3] John Gay, the author of the famous *Beggar's Opera* which featured Polly Peachum as the female lead, had composed a sequel entitled *Polly* about his heroine's adventures in the West Indies. Like *The Beggar's Opera, Polly* was understood to be a satire on the government of Sir Robert Walpole and the Lord Chamberlain refused to allow the play to be performed. But although the government could suppress a stage play, it could not censor the press and Gay decided to turn *Polly* to account by employing a printer and publishing the play for his own benefit. Perhaps the fact that Gay was neither a printer nor a bookseller but merely an author proved irresistibly tempting to the series of tradesmen who quickly brought out their own competing, cheaper editions of *Polly*. Gay responded by filing suit in Chancery and within two months he obtained an injunction against a long list of printers and booksellers who had been involved in printing the competing editions. Gay thus succeeded in protecting his copyright in *Polly*. What I want to emphasize here, however, is that Gay's purposes, like those of a bookseller, were essentially commercial. He was trying to prevent his edition from being undercut by competitors.

John Gay was a close friend of Alexander Pope, the pre-eminent literary figure in England in the first half of the eighteenth century. Pope, who made a fortune from his verse, was the first author to regularly employ the Statute of Anne to protect his literary interests, and he went to law numerous times, both in his own name and through surrogates. It is very likely that Gay consulted Pope about his lawsuit. But despite his active concern with the law and his deep involvement in the literary marketplace,

---

[3] C 33 351/305, Entry from the Court of Chancery's Book of Orders.

Pope always presented himself as a gentleman and a scholar rather than a professional author and he was almost obsessively concerned with what we would call image management. These were important factors in Pope's case against Edmund Curll in 1741.

Pope was conspicuously genteel. The bookseller Curll consistently operated on the margins of respectability. Curll was well known as a dealer in pornography and he had a reputation for unscrupulous dealings both with authors and other booksellers. Pope and Curll were in fact old antagonists. They had been at odds for a quarter of a century ever since a notorious incident in 1716 in which Pope humiliated Curll by tricking him into drinking a violent emetic. This was to punish Curll for having illicitly published poems written by Pope's friend, Lady Mary Wortley Montagu.

3 THE CASE

As I have already indicated, *Pope v. Curll* concerned private letters. The late seventeenth and early eighteenth centuries saw the emergence of a new sense of privacy together with a new interest in the private lives of prominent men and women. In this period the personal letter comes to be seen as a privileged window onto the life and opinions of an individual. This new interest is evident in the prominence of the epistolary novels of, among others, Aphra Behn and Samuel Richardson in England, as well as those of Montesquieu and Rousseau in France and Goethe in Germany. And the new interest led, too, to the publication of collections of private letters. As part of his concern with image management, an activity that included advertising his friendships with prominent men, Pope resolved to make his correspondence public. But for a gentleman to publish his letters would at this time have seemed inexcusably vain. Therefore in 1735 Pope tricked his old antagonist Curll into publishing an unauthorized collection of his correspondence, thereby creating a situation that would open the way for Pope to publish an authorized version.

But in getting Curll to print his letters in 1735 Pope evidently had a further purpose, one that illuminates his goal six years later in his lawsuit. In the spring of 1735, the London booksellers were campaigning for a bill that would extend the statutory term of copyright beyond that provided in the Statute of Anne. Pope does not appear to have been particularly concerned with the length of term, but he was concerned with authors' rights to control the ways in which their writings were presented to the public. He therefore contrived to have Curll's surreptitious edition of his letters appear while the booksellers' bill was pending. Thus Curll would serve as an example of an irresponsible bookseller in order to demonstrate the need for greater authorial control and the booksellers' bill, which did not provide the kind of protection for authors that Pope sought, would be defeated. The 1735 bill was indeed defeated, although not necessarily because of the affair of the letters as Pope claimed. Shortly after, Pope expressed the hope that if the booksellers' bill was again brought in, Parliament would not increase the copyright term without also doing something for authors and he angrily referred to the outrage of having had his private letters pirated, as he said, by Curll.

The problem, as Pope evidently saw it, was that the Statue of Anne – 'An act for the encouragement of learning' – did not clearly protect private letters. As Pope put it in the preface to the authorized edition of his correspondence that he published in 1737, the illicit printing of private letters is a form of 'betraying conversation'.

> To open Letters is esteem'd the greatest breach of honour; even to look into them already open'd or accidentally dropt, is held ungenerous, if not an immoral act. What then can be thought of the procuring them merely by Fraud, and printing them merely for Lucre? We cannot but conclude every honest man will wish, that if the Laws have as yet provided no adequate remedy, one at least may be found, to prevent so great and growing an evil.

We should observe that the issue, as Pope presents it, is a matter of personal right rather than of economic interest. Pope's complaint is not that the illicit printing of letters deprives the author of a source of income, but that it is an offence against decency.

Pope's attempt to influence Parliament in its consideration of the booksellers' bill in 1735 and his comments about the illicit printing of letters in the preface to his own edition of his correspondence in 1737 shed light on his purposes in the suit that he initiated against Curll in 1741. At issue was a volume of letters that Curll had published entitled *Dean Swift's Literary Correspondence*. This consisted of letters to and from Swift and Pope as well as letters from several other prominent men, including John Gay. Pope filed his complaint under the terms of the Statute of Anne and he claimed ownership both of the letters he wrote to Swift and the letters that Swift wrote to him. His claim to his own letters was based on his statutory copyright; his claim to Swift's letters was based on possession. Curll responded that, among other things, personal letters were not the kind of writings that were protected under the statute and, in any case, that letters actually sent to another person were no longer the property of the writer.

Lord Chancellor Hardwicke's decision was that letters were indeed significant writings and were protected by the statute. 'It is certain', he said, 'that no works have done more service to mankind, than those which have appeared in this shape, upon familiar subjects, and which perhaps were never intended to be published.' Therefore he found that Pope did indeed have a claim as to the letters he had written to Swift. But Hardwicke rejected Pope's claim so far as it concerned Swift's letters to Pope and this led him to make a crucial distinction between the copyright and the physical letter. Ownership of the physical letter, he said, did not convey a license to publish the contents to the world.

Hardwicke's decision thus represented an important moment in the development of copyright theory. Not ink and paper, but the written words themselves, apart from any material support, have become the protected property. This development is momentous, but for my present purposes what I want to emphasize is how Hardwicke's decision responded to Pope's immediate purposes. These were layered and complex. At one level Pope was probably still seeking to wound an old enemy. At another he was probably trying to protect his old friend Jonathan Swift who was in ill health at the time. Moreover, Pope may have had some financial interest that the decision secured. But as Pope's earlier comments about the indecency of printing private letters suggest, probably his central purpose was to establish that personal letters fell under the Statute of Anne. Pope was seeking to achieve in the courts what he had failed to achieve in 1735 in Parliament, a declaration that private letters were protected. Thus in his lawsuit against Curll in 1741 Pope was employing a statute that was essentially an instrument of commercial regulation in order to pursue an issue of personal right, a matter of propriety rather than profit.

4 MILLAR V. TAYLOR

Twenty-eight years later when Pope's attorney, now Lord Mansfield and the Chief Justice of the Court of King's Bench, was delivering his opinion in the great case of *Millar v. Taylor* (1769)[4] he may well have been remembering the issue of privacy with respect to personal letters that he had assisted Pope in establishing in 1741. Ruling that the author had a copyright before publication – and that therefore the Statute of Anne was supplementary to an underlying common-law right – Mansfield insisted that only the author had the right to decide how or whether to publish his writings. From what source did the author's common-law right before publication derive? From this argument among others, said Mansfield,

---

[4] 4 Burr. 2303, 98 Eng. Rep.201 (KB) (1769).

> Because it is just, that an author should reap the pecuniary profits of his own ingenuity and labour. It is just, that another should not use his name, without his consent. It is fit that he should judge when to publish, or whether he ever will publish. It is fit he should not only chose the time, but the manner of publication; how many; what volume; what print. It is fit, he should choose to whose care he will trust the accuracy and correctness of the impression; in whose honesty he will confide, not to foist in additions: with other reasonings of the same effect.

And Mansfield went on to argue that if the author had such rights before publication, he preserved them after publication as well. Thus, in this often-cited statement, Mansfield continued the process begun in *Pope v. Curll* of blending personal and property rights. The Statute of Anne may have begun as an act of trade regulation and the thrust of the enactment may have been essentially commercial, but under pressures brought by the pre-eminent author of the first half of the eighteenth century and the pre-eminent jurist of the second half, English copyright law began to acquire some of the features of a law of personal rights as well.

5 SALINGER V. RANDOM HOUSE

In 1986, some 250 years after the decision in *Pope v. Curll*, the American writer J.D. Salinger sued his biographer Ian Hamilton and Hamilton's publisher, Random House. Salinger alleged that Hamilton had illegally copied or paraphrased passages from Salinger's letters to various friends. Although they had never been published, Salinger's letters – unknown to him – had been deposited by the recipients in various university libraries and therefore were available for consultation. Salinger, who is best known as the author of *The Catcher in the* Rye, published in 1951, is a notorious recluse. He has published nothing since 1965 – publishing, he has said, would invade his privacy – and he has not allowed anyone to interview him since 1980. He was not interested in having a biography written and he was certainly not amenable to having his private letters printed or referred to.

The Salinger case turned on the question of fair use. Were Hamilton's quotations and paraphrases from Salinger's unpublished letters permissible under the doctrine of fair use? The district court judge, Pierre N. Leval, found that Hamilton's use of the letters was protected by fair use. But Leval's decision was overturned on appeal by the circuit court judge, Jon O. Newman, who issued an injunction barring Random House from publishing Hamilton's biography in its present form.

There are of course conspicuous differences between the Pope and

Salinger cases. Curll printed entire letters from Pope, Swift, and others whereas Hamilton was merely quoting or paraphrasing fragments from Salinger's letters. Moreover, in the 250 years between *Pope* and *Salinger*, the law of copyright has been vastly elaborated with doctrines such as that of fair use codified and embodied in statute law. Nonetheless, the similarities between the two famous cases are, as I have said, interesting. Once again an author was going to court to prevent publication of his letters and once again the concern was privacy. In *Salinger* as in *Pope* a famous author was using the law of copyright to pursue matters more related to personal than to commercial rights. And yet the issue between the parties was joined on a legal field largely shaped by commercial concerns.

The doctrine of fair use has roots going back to the early litigation about abridgements under the Statute of Anne. But in US law the doctrine is usually traced back to Joseph Story's famous decision in *Folsom v. Marsh* (1841),[5] a case which, incidentally, also involved personal letters. In *Folsom* the letters in question were those of George Washington, which had been published in a set entitled *The Writings of George Washington*. Selections from Washington's letters had been used by the defendant to compile a book entitled *The Life of Washington in the Form of an Autobiography*. In his decision, Justice Story articulated the principle that certain uses of a work must be considered fair, as for example citation for purposes of criticism. On the other hand, Story said, if one were to cite the most important part of a work with a view not to criticize but 'to supersede the use of the original work' that would be deemed a piracy. The test for fair use that Story articulated was thus essentially commercial. As he put it in his famous statement, 'If so much is taken, that the value of the original is sensibly diminished, or the labors of the original author are substantially to an injurious extent appropriated by another, that is sufficient, in point of law, to constitute a piracy pro tanto.'

In the statutory codification of the fair use doctrine that descends from Story's decision in *Folsom* four factors are to be taken into account to determine whether a particular use is fair: the purpose of the use; the nature of the copyrighted work; the amount and substantiality of the portion used; and the effect on the market for the copyrighted work. This last factor is precisely that noted by Justice Story when he spoke of the 'value of the original' being 'sensibly diminished' and it has been called by the US Supreme Court 'the single most important element of fair use' (*Harper & Row v. Nation*[6]). I mention this in order to emphasize

---

5 9 F Cas 342 (CCD Mass 1841).
6 471 UD 539 (SC, 1985).

the degree to which even the fair use doctrine – an aspect of copyright law concerned with use rather than protection – provides evidence of the essentially commercial thrust of copyright law.

In finding for J.D. Salinger and rejecting Hamilton's claim of fair use, Judge Newman based his decision largely on the second and third factors: the nature of the copyrighted work and the amount and substantiality of the portion used. Nonetheless, Newman recalled that the fourth and specifically commercial factor is considered the most important. He noted that Salinger had disavowed any intention of publishing his letters, but added that, whatever Salinger might say, he should have the right to change his mind. 'He is entitled to protect his *opportunity* to sell his letters.' And he noted that Salinger's literary agent had estimated the letters' commercial value as more than half a million dollars. Newman's decision was issued more than 20 years ago. Salinger, who is now 90 years old, has never changed his mind and the letters have never been published. Clearly they never will be in his lifetime. Like Alexander Pope going to law in 1741 against Edmund Curll to establish a point about privacy, so Salinger in 1986 was using copyright law not to be pre-empted by Hamilton but to defend his privacy.

6 CONCLUDING REMARKS

It is worth noting, too, that one year after issuing his opinon in *Salinger v. Random House*, Judge Newman published an essay, 'Copyright Law and the Protection of Privacy', in which he argued that courts should be explicitly allowed to weigh privacy considerations in deciding copyright issues involving unpublished materials. Indeed, in this essay Judge Newman even went so far as to suggest that one of the foundational principles of copyright law – the idea/expression dichotomy – should perhaps be altered when privacy issues are at stake. That is to say, under some circumstances, when personal rights are involved, copyright should perhaps be understood as protecting facts as well as expression. Such a change in the traditional contours of copyright would be radical.

Judge Newman has since backed off from this suggestion, but that he reached such a point in his thinking can perhaps be taken as evidence of the awkwardness sometimes involved in pressuring the copyright tradition to accommodate personal rights. But my point today is not to explore the general issue of how authors' personal rights have – or have not – been accommodated in the copyright tradition. This is, after all, a huge issue and it is one where, at least at present, the British and American copyright traditions appear to diverge. Rather my point has been to invoke the case of *Pope v. Curll* in order to suggest that even in the very early years after the passage of the Statute of Anne, the copyright statute was being invoked to pursue goals that were not strictly commercial. Moreover, as *Salinger v. Random House* and Judge Newman's subsequent essay also suggest, the impulse to use copyright law to pursue non-commercial goals continues today even in American jurisprudence. The familiar contrast between the commercial Anglo-American copyright tradition and the authors' rights based civil law tradition is certainly not incorrect. But it needs to be qualified by an understanding that even as early as 1741 the English copyright statute was being called upon to serve purposes of propriety and dignity rather than pure profit.

6. Transition from guild regulation to modern copyright law – a view from the Low Countries

Willem Grosheide*

1 INTRODUCTORY REMARKS

Since this contribution is about the transition of determining the legal status of cultural goods by guild regulation to that by modern copyright law, it appears appropriate to commence with some introductory remarks about the relation between the two legal regimes. In doing so, art production and book publishing will be taken as *pars pro toto* for the production of cultural products generally, painting and writing as the general model for authorship of cultural goods. *Cultural goods* will serve as the generic term to denominate indiscriminately any creative product. The term *author* will be used as the *terminus technicus* for those who in the course of time will be legally protected by copyright law; the term *work* respectively for the object of protection by copyright law. The term *copyright* itself is used in a legal culture-independent way in order to indicate the national and international positive law regimes which from the end of the eighteenth century and through the nineteenth century led to the establishment of the Berne Convention (BC) of 1886. In what follows the focus will be on the developments in the Low Countries during the period of reference.

It may be said then that the history of copyright law is in the end the history of the way in which creators, that is artists and writers in whatever capacity, managed to obtain a hearing in society for their claim to be socially respected and legally protected against appropriation as the producers of cultural goods. Seen in this way, the history of copyright law is

* Dr. F. Willem Grosheide is professor of intellectual property law at the Center for Intellectual Property Law ((CIER) Molengraaff Institute for Private Law, Law Faculty, Utrecht University) and solicitor at Van Doorne (Amsterdam). The author is indebted to Frans A. Janssen, David Peeperkorn and Marijke Reinsma for their valuable comments to an earlier version of the text.

also the history of the social organization and societal pressure of related and supporting groups in the successive periods of time until the establishment of the BC which may be qualified as the starting point of modern copyright law.[1] In that light, it does not come as a surprise that the rise, flourishing and decline of the guild system from the mid-thirteenth century until the late eighteenth century, and its definite fall during the nineteenth century, plays a significant role in this respect.

In what follows attention will be given first to the rise and flourishing, decline and fall of the guild system (sections 2 and 3), followed by an outline of the advent of the author, that is the relation between the producers and exploiters of cultural goods until the end of the eighteenth century (section 4), all this giving rise to the question of whether the introduction of book printing can be seen as an agent of modern copyright law (section 5). Finally, some concluding observations will be made (section 6).

The indication *the Low Countries* (also: *the Netherlands* and *les Pays Bas*) is used from the sixteenth century onwards to generally refer to the domains that today are comprising the national states of Belgium and the Netherlands.[2] So, although it is somewhat out of context to use in what follows that indication also for what in the period of time under consideration in this paper was a federation of just the seven northern provinces only, I keep using it because of its romantic connotation.

2 THE RISE AND FLOURISHING OF THE GUILD SYSTEM

From the referenced literature it becomes clear that the origins of the guilds remain obscure.[3] However, so much is clear that from the thirteenth

---

1 Comp. F.W. Grosheide (1986), *Auteursrecht op maat*, Deventer: Kluwer and F. Willem Grosheide (1994), *Paradigms in Copyright Law,* in Brad Sherman and Alain Strowel, *Of Authors and Origins*, Oxford: Oxford University Press, pp. 203–233.

2 See for the situation in Belgium Joris Deene, 'Influence of the Statute of Anne on Belgium Copyright law', elsewhere in this volume.

3 As in their medieval form the guilds appeared to combine characteristics that recall both the social solidarity of the Roman *collegium* and a concern for skilful craftsmanship that is more easily identified with Germanic societies in the early Christian centuries. In what follows the guild system is delineated in a rather generalizing way, concentrating on what is of interest in the perspective of the production of cultural products, and as a consequence leaving many peculiarities thereof outside the picture. See for a broad account of the subject S.C. Thrupp (1963), 'The Guilds', in *Cambridge Economic History of Europe*, Cambridge:

century, guilds, particularly *craft guilds*, became essential to most aspects of civic life and reflected the advance in the division of labour. Indeed, in the medieval, pre-industrial cities of the time, craftsmen tended to form exclusive associations based on their trades, such as associations of textile workers, masons, carpenters, carvers, glassworkers.[4] Guilds can be defined as *government-licensed, local organizations of industrial producers.*[5] They ensured training for their members, maintained standards of production, structured the social conditions (for example wages) of their members, and particularly controlled the secrets of traditionally imparted technology relating to their crafts.

Guilds were no less occupied as religious associations, and many of them met as devotional confraternities. According to their statutes, practical work and religious devotion were often not clearly distinguishable. Their patronage of religious confraternities often operated at a comparatively modest level, maintaining a chapel or altar.[6]

Medieval guilds were also closely involved in the production and patronage of art. Craft traditions were essential to the training of the

---

CambridgeUniversity Press; I.H. van Eeghen (1974), *De gilden: Theorie en Praktijk*, Bussum: van Dishoeck; Maarten Prak (2006), *Craft Guilds in North-Western Europe (England, France, Low Countries), The Return of the Guilds*, Utrecht: Utrecht University, 5–7 October, http://www.iisg.nl/hpw/papers/guilds.prak.pdf and Maarten Prak, Catharina Lis, Jan Lucassen, Hugo Soly (eds) (2006), *Craft Guilds in the Early Modern Low Countries: Work, Power, and Representation*, Aldershot: Ashgate. Further, I focus on craft guilds as they originated in North-Western Europe, although merchants also formed guilds to manage the local staple. See Maarten Prak (2006), *Craft Guilds in North-Western Europe (England, France, Low Countries), The Return of the Guilds*, Utrecht: Utrecht University, 5–7 October, http://www.iisg.nl/hpw/papers/guilds.prak.pdf and Maarten Prak, Catharina Lis, Jan Lucassen, Hugo Soly (eds) (2006), *Craft Guilds in the Early Modern Low Countries: Work, Power, and Representation*, Aldershot: Ashgate. It is of note, however, that according to Chris Schriks (2004), *Het Kopijrecht*, Zutphen: Walburg Pers, p. 83, the guild system did not came to flourish all over Europe at the time.

4 It is of note that the guild rules did not operate in the countryside where freedom for the entrepreneur was the order of the day.

5 Maarten Prak (2006), *Craft Guilds in North-Western Europe (England, France, Low Countries), The Return of the Guilds*, Utrecht: Utrecht University, 5–7 October, http://www.iisg.nl/hpw/papers/guilds.prak.pdf and Maarten Prak, Catharina Lis, Jan Lucassen, Hugo Soly (eds) (2006), *Craft Guilds in the Early Modern Low Countries: Work, Power, and Representation*, Aldershot: Ashgate. According to Frans A. Jansen (1986), *Zetten en Drukken in de Achtiende Eeuw*, Haarlem: Enschedé in the Low Countries guilds particularly in the seventeenth and eighteenth centuries can be qualified as organizations of labourers (the masters).

6 However, after the Middle Ages the guilds lost their religious function.

artist. To become a *master* often required the production of a *masterpiece*.[7] The place of training and production for painters and for sculptors not working on site was the workshop.[8] Renaissance and neo-classicist theories tended to view writers as being also artisans who crafted their work according to a body of rules inherited from classical rhetoric and poetics. The writer was not yet seen as the creator of an original work but as a craftsman who manipulated pre-existing forms in a manner which was pleasing to a cultivated and often courtly audience. Van Horn Melton observes that:

> (i)n cases where authors displayed extraordinary gifts, their talents were explained by reference to some external cause – the muses were often invoked, at other times divine inspiration. In both instances the writer, whether workmanlike artisan or inspired poet, was conceived more as a vessel than as an original creator. As artisans, authors were simply the vehicle of received aesthetic rules; if inspired and gifted, they were the passive instruments of superhuman or divine forces. But in neither case were they really considered the creators of their work, nor, by extension its owners.[9]

But according to Chagy this view changed in the course of time.

> By the middle of the sixteenth century, artists were no longer regarded as workmen; superior artists were greatly honoured, given titles of nobility and treated as the illustrious men they were. Individual artists were often taken to the household of a prince or the Church or a wealthy merchant.[10]

Taking into account its importance for the development of copyright law, of particular interest in this respect is the trade of book publishing. It appears that no earlier than after the invention of the printing process in

---

[7] According to Frans A. Jansen (1986), *Zetten en Drukken in de Achtiende Eeuw*, Haarlem: Enschedé, p. 48, this masterpiece requirement in fact was a fake, used to mark the inauguration of a master's son into the community of guild members.

[8] Merchant guilds were often patrons of great civic monuments, their buildings often defining the urban environment.

[9] James van Horn Melton (2001), *The Rise of the Public in Enlightenment Europe*, Cambridge: Cambridge University Press, p. 137, referring to Martha Woodmansee (1984), 'The Genius and the Copyright: Economic and Legal Conditions of the Emergence of the "Author"', *Eighteenth Century Studies* 17, pp. 425–448, at 426–427. See also Carla Hesse (2002), 'The Rise of Intellectual Property, 700 B.C.–A.D. 2000: an idea in the balance', *Daedalus*, Spring, p. 29.

[10] G. Chagy (1972), *The New Patrons of the Arts*, Minnesota: University of Minnesota, p. 25.

the fifteenth century, replacing manuscript copying by hand in monasteries first and universities later, guilds of book printers, sellers and distributors (hereafter called *publishers*) at the time operating as one and the same trade, came into the picture.[11] However, in the first years after the introduction of print and up to around 1585 nowhere in the Low Countries did any independent guild of book *printers* see the light of day. In fact, the number of publishers was too small to make such an establishment feasible. Instead, publishers usually became affiliated with other guilds, particularly those of artists such as the Guild of St Luke, present in Amsterdam, Gouda, The Hague, Haarlem, Kampen and Zwolle.[12] Contrary to what was the rule in craft guilds generally, publishers were not supposed to deliver a masterpiece, standardization at the time not being an issue.[13] No earlier than in the period between 1585 and 1685 publishers started to organize themselves in separate guilds which split from the Guild of St. Luke.[14]

Of old, guilds were founded through initiatives by either the members or the authorities, the members usually being free independent master

---

[11] According to L. Hellinga (2003), *Bibliopolis Handboek – Overzicht van de geschiedenis van het gedrukte boek in Nederland*, The Hague/Zwolle: Waanders, p. 11, the arrival of the art of printing in the Low Countries is shrouded in darkness although it is beyond doubt that from around 1455 printing branched out from Germany over Europe. From its start the trade in printed books was international, Dutch printers producing books not only in Latin and Dutch for the domestic market but also in English, French and German for foreign markets.

[12] J.T. Bodel Nijenhuis (1892), *De wetgeving op drukpers en boekhandel in de Nederlanden tot in het begin der XIXe eeuw. Vertaling van de 'Dissertatio juridica inauguralis de juribus typographorum et bibliopolarum in regno Belgico' aan de Leidsche Hoogeschool verdedigd. Met de latere bijvoegsels en verbeteringen van den schrijver.* [Vertaling door J. Soutendam en R. Jesse Jzn.], Amsterdam: P. N. van Hampen en Zoon 1892 (Bijdragen tot de geschiedenis van den Nederlandschen boekhandel, 4), p. 287.

[13] Ibid., pp. 271–314. This was generally true for St. Luke's Guild which did not require a masterpiece from any of its members nor did it impose other forms of quality control. See Maarten Prak (2006), *Craft Guilds in North-Western Europe (England, France, Low Countries), The Return of the Guilds*, Utrecht: Utrecht University, 5–7 October, http://www.iisg.nl/hpw/papers/guilds.prak.pdf, p. 7.

[14] P.G. Hoftijzer (2003), *Bibliopolis Handboek – Overzicht van de geschiedenis van het gedrukte boek in Nederland*, The Hague/Zwolle: Waanders, p. 77. See also Carla Hesse (2002), 'The Rise of Intellectual Property, 700 B.C.–A.D. 2000: an idea in the balance', *Daedalus*, Spring, p. 30: in England as early as 1577 the Crown reorganized the then already existing guild of printers and publishers known as the Stationers' Company, giving it a virtual monopoly to print and publish. Musicians (composers/performers) at the time were also organized in guilds, generally with St. Cecilia as patron. Music publishing, first done by hand and later by print, followed the general routine of publishing. See Grove Dictionary (1966); Oxford Companion (2001).

craftsmen. In addition to the internal private law regulations of the guilds, central or local authorities could issue exclusive prerogatives, for example holding trade monopolies in particular crafts, to be operated in the denominated cities.[15] The city authorities might be represented in the guild meetings which offered them a way of controlling what went on in the guild. This was important because of the fact that cities usually depended on a good reputation for the export of goods produced by the guilds. For their part, guilds used to play a major role in local politics.[16]

With respect to the book trade after the last part of the sixteenth century when publishers started establishing guilds of their own, more important than the guild's own regulatory function was the public law regulation of the book trade. Indeed, following the papal bull *Exsurge domine* of 1520, Emperor Charles V proclaimed that publishers, given the potentially subversive character of their trade, needed a publishing grant (that is, an exclusive licence) by the central or local authorities, and before that they had to have the texts that were to be printed approved by an ecclesiastical censor. Besides, it enabled the authorities for reasons of public order to monitor the book trade with an eye on the publication and distribution of subversive texts. So, in order to become accepted as a book trader it was up to the authorities which used the so-called *privilege system* which involved all sorts of formalities to be observed by the publishers, backed up by a rather harsh censorship regime. The validity of these privileges was limited to the jurisdiction of the respective authority. The term of the privileges varied from a few months to ten years or more.[17]

---

15 Carla Hesse (2002), 'The Rise of Intellectual Property, 700 B.C.–A.D. 2000: an idea in the balance', *Daedalus*, Spring, pp. 30–31. Idem Frans A. Jansen (1986), *Zetten en Drukken in de Achtiende Eeuw*, Haarlem: Enschedé. The monopoly aspect is firmly contested as a fundamentally incorrect view by Maarten Prak (2006), *Craft Guilds in North-Western Europe (England, France, Low Countries), The Return of the Guilds*, Utrecht: Utrecht University, 5–7 October, http://www.iisg.nl/hpw/papers/guilds.prak.pdf, stating that guilds *'turned out to be very 'flexible' in the ways they dealt with their 'so-called monopoly'*.

16 Maarten Prak (2006), *Craft Guilds in North-Western Europe (England, France, Low Countries), The Return of the Guilds*, Utrecht: Utrecht University, 5–7 October, http://www.iisg.nl/hpw/papers/guilds.prak.pdf, sub 3. *Guilds and politics,* speaking, among other things, of the situation in the Low Countries in the thirteenth century.

17 See Carla Hesse (2002), 'The Rise of Intellectual Property, 700 B.C.–A.D. 2000: an idea in the balance', *Daedalus*, Spring, pp. 30–31 for the situation in England, France and Germany. It is of note that the English literature on the subject also refers to *the printing patent,* the royal prerogative which was already called a copy-right but which in turn had to be distinguished from the stationer's copyright which was a private affair belonging to the Stationers' Company; see

In the Low Countries, the guild statutes differed from place to place, here and there now requiring a masterpiece to be made. Following from the licensing system which had also been introduced here, the granting of an *octroy* or *privilegie* was required. From the referenced literature it appears that it is an open question to what extent privileges were used as a form of preventive censorship.[18] In any case, the privilege system functioned primarily as regulation of the book trade, that is regulation of unfair competition. The Low Countries in fact did quite well in this respect, after 1550 taking the lead in European book publishing (for example Plantijn, Elzevier). The earliest known book privilege in the Low Countries was issued on 5 January 1512 by the Council of Brabant to the Antwerp printer Claes de Grave for the printing of new books for a period of six years.[19] In all this there were remarkable differences between the Northern and the Southern part of the Low Countries, the former being more liberal than the latter.[20]

From an economic point of view, it is held in the referenced literature that the exclusive monopolistic regulations, at least those that were implemented in the first centuries of the guilds' existence, were a form of protection for the craftsman against the risks of the market. In fact, the privilege system

---

Lyman Ray Patterson (1968), *Copyright in Historical Perspective*, Nashville: Vanderbilt University Press, pp. 4–5.

[18] According to P.G. Hoftijzer (2003), *Bibliopolis, History of the printed book in The Netherlands*, The Hague: Waanders: seldom and if so: moderately, but according to Jonathan I. Israel (2001), *Radical Enlightenment*, Oxford: Oxford University Press, pp. 97–118: usually. According to Joris van Eijnatten (2003), 'Van godsdienstvrijheid naar mensenrecht. Meningsvorming over censuur en persvrijheid in de Republiek, 1579–1795', in *Bijdragen en mededelingen betreffende de geschiedenis der Nederlanden*, The Hague: Nederlands Historisch Genootschap, p. 2, most related studies arrive *grosso modo* to the same conclusion: 'Whereas preventive censorship (execution of censorship before the respective material is printed) did not obtain a firm footing in the Republic, repressive censorship (forbidding the printed material after publication) was not absent at all.' It is of note, as Van Eijnatten underlines, that '(m)easures against individual books were taken by separate towns, provincial authorities, provincial courts as well as the Federal Assembly (Staten Generaal), in reaction to complaints by native public bodies, ambassadors and diplomats of France, England, Spain, Denmark or Prussia, and by representative bodies of Reformed and Walloon churches.' Idem J. Loewenstein (2002), The Author's Due, London: University of Chicago Press, p. 165 for England ('(. . .)the bulk of parliamentary opinion was that censorship should be sustained and that unauthorized publication should be arrested (. . .)')

[19] Bibliopolis (2003), *History of the printed book in The Netherlands*, The Hague, Waanders P.G. Hoftijzer, p. 34.

[20] Bibliopolis (2003), *History of the printed book in The Netherlands*, The Hague, Waanders P. G. Hoftijzer, pp. 36–37.

functioned primarily as a form of public competition law. It is of note that at the time the tight regulation of economic activities was also legitimized by the actual system of religious belief. For, striving to make a profit was regarded as sinful. With regard to the book trade the indicated privilege system functioned as a form of public competition law *avant la lettre.* A system of gentlemen's agreements was established to watch over unfair competition.[21]

In the referenced economic historical literature it is firmly contested whether as a consequence of the disregard of making a profit also making inventions and innovations was suppressed. Those who argue in favour of that argument refer to wording like: 'No man should think of or invent something new or use it, but everyman should follow his neighbour in brotherly love', which is often found in the guild statutes. A member gaining an economic advantage from either an invention or an innovation would have contradicted the guild's spirit. According to that view numerous documents show that innovators were severely punished for that. So these historians agree that the guilds exerted a strong pressure to preserve traditional structures and processes, and that the juxtaposition of guilds and innovation could be seen as an oxymoron.[22]

However, recent research has come to the opposite conclusion. In the words of Epstein the actual claim is 'that the impact of the (craft) guilds on the early modern economy was more positive than has so far been acknowledged by historians of the traditional, and even of the revisionist school'.[23] Indeed, also within the guild system inventing and innovating took place since some guilds were inspired to do so by courts or for other reasons occupied an exceptional position.[24] In addition, many inventions and innovations were made in monasteries due to the fact that monks were

---

21 F. Willem Grosheide (1994), 'Paradigms in Copyright Law', in Brad Sherman and Alain Strowel, *Of Authors and Origins*, Oxford: Oxford University Press, pp. 203–233, at 229.

22 Sheilagh Ogilvie (2004), 'Guilds and Countries in early modern Germany', *American Historical Review* 109, 325–359. The oxymoron analogy stems from Christine MacLeod (2008), 'Bookreview S.P. Epstein and Maarten Prak (eds), Guilds, Innovation and the European Economy, 1400–1800', http://eh.net/bookreviews/library/1379.

23 S.R. Epstein and Maarten Prak (eds) (2008), *Guilds, Innovation and the European Economy, 1400–1800*, Cambridge: Cambridge University Press, p. 2, acclaimed by MacLeod (note 22 above) but contested by Sheilagh Ogilvie (2008), 'Rehabilitating the Guilds: A Reply', *Economic History Review*, Vol. 61, Issue 1 (February), 175–182, arguing that industry flourished where guilds decayed.

24 Alfred Kieser (1989), 'Organizational, Institutional, and Societal Evolution: Medieval Craft Guilds and the Genesis of Formal Organizations', *Administrative Science Quarterly*, vol. 34, December, 540–564.

educated and learned people in a far more elevated way than craftsmen, besides their products being qualified as holy. It is an intriguing but, to my knowledge still unanswered, question how the invention of the printing press fits into this picture.

To end this section a specific aspect of the privilege system is worth mentioning: the fight against piracy. For as a correlative of the printing process which in that respect greatly differed from manuscript production, book piracy saw the light of day. Taking into account the large financial interests which were involved in the publication of printed texts, it is obvious that publishers suffered quite substantially from this aspect. At first, some practical measures were taken such as dumping one's own edition at a lower price or producing a new improved edition to undermine the pirate's market position, as well as blaming the reprinter in the foreword of a new edition. But after the introduction of the privilege system this was also used to counter piracy.[25] So reprinting another publisher's book without permission became a violation of his privilege which could lead to the confiscation of the reprints or a fine by the granting authority.

In addition, however, it is worth observing that in the referenced literature it is noted that piracy should also be seen as a response to excessively high book prices and poor book distribution, and therefore it equally functioned as an economic regulatory mechanism. However, as far as the Low Countries are concerned it seems that the privilege system was of limited importance as a way of fighting piracy. More commonly used to that aim were the so-called printer's marks.[26]

3 THE DECLINE AND FALL OF THE GUILD SYSTEM

According to the still prominent view, or so it seems, in the sixteenth and seventeenth centuries the upcoming merchant capitalism in cities that were rapidly expanding beyond the old limits of the medieval walls, operating in suburbs where guild regulation did not apply, as well as the increasing practice of putting out work to rural areas, tore down the guilds' special position. Those who would previously have been guild members were allowed to establish their own enterprises, opening up new markets and

---

[25] According to Frans A. Jansen (1986), *Zetten en Drukken in de Achtiende Euw*, Haarlem: Enschedé, fighting piracy was the one and only purpose of the privilege system in the Low Countries.

[26] The high skill of Dutch engravers (who used their engraver's marks to fight piracy) contributed to this course of things.

pushing guilds out of business. In this view, at the same time religious reformers (this was during the Reformation) began to criticize the confraternities. In addition, from the middle of the seventeenth century onwards economic interests came more to the forefront and led to a tightening of these monopolistic regulations. Further, guilds were believed to oppose free trade and to hinder technological progress. This belief was firmly expressed by such leading scholars as Jean Jacques Rousseau and Adam Smith who opposed governmental control over trade and they promoted a *laissez-faire* market system.

However, this assumed prominent view is fundamentally contested by Prak, who argues that

> (i)t has been standard fare of the guilds' image that their decline and termination was caused by economic factors. It is now more or less generally accepted that this interpretation is a mere reproduction of late eighteenth-century criticisms of the guilds, rather than a correct picture of what happened historically. On the continent at least, political rather than economic factors were the root cause of the disappearance of the guilds.[27]

This may be so, but an undisputed fact seems to be that during the indicated period the artistic importance of guilds waned as a consequence of the rise in status of the individual artist and the decline of patronage. See more on this in section 4. Courts and universities, being far removed from medieval workshops, became their successors in title. However, guilds survived in their artistic role in the seventeenth century in the Low Countries where painters in Utrecht and Leiden, for example, formed new guilds. Whereas courts and academies still commissioned paintings, sculptures and architecture, elsewhere too the luxury market was still dominated by the high-quality, expensive products of the traditional workshop, products which were much in demand among wealthy visitors in the age of the Grand Tour. In addition, the Counter-Reformation gave an enormous impetus to Catholic patronage of the arts by religious confraternities, which commissioned works to celebrate religious beliefs. However, as the economic importance of the guilds declined, so did their ability to finance great artistic creation.

In the meantime, the book trade was still regulated by the privilege system, including the monitoring of the freedom of expression. According to Israel:

---

[27] Maarten Prak (2006), *Craft Guilds in North-Western Europe (England, France, Low Countries), The Return of the Guilds*, Utrecht: Utrecht University, 5–7 October, http://www.iisg.nl/hpw/papers/guilds.prak.pdf, p. 15.

> (e)ven in Europe's two freest societies – the Dutch Republic and England – where urban culture was most prevalent, and the rigid social hierarchies of the past had become most fluid, radical writers were more profoundly influenced by censorship than is often realized.[28] [However, Israel continues,] as the eighteenth century dawned and progressed, society gradually edged towards a greater appreciation of religious toleration and intellectual freedom.[29]

This leads Israel to the following conclusion.

> The history of European censorship between 1650 and 1750 thus clearly demonstrates that the moderate Enlightenment, however far-reaching institutionally and intellectually the changes it brought about, largely rejected freedom of thought, the principle of 'libertas philosophandi' (freedom to philosophize) which Spinoza, in contrast to Hobbes, Locke, and the official stance of the *Encyclopédie*, proclaimed as one of his chief objectives.[30]

As far as book publishing in the Low Countries is concerned, in the course of the seventeenth century and up until about 1725 book production in general and the cooperation between book printers, producers

---

[28] Jonathan I. Israel (2001), *Radical Enlightenment*, Oxford: Oxford University Press, Chapter 5. *Censorship and Culture*, pp. 97–118 (97).

[29] Ibid, p. 98.

[30] Ibid, p. 117. Idem Jonathan I. Israel (2006), *Enlightenment Contested*, Oxford: Oxford University Press, p. 801, observing that '(m)ost commentators were in agreement that whatever is prejudicial to society should be prevented. (. . .) Since 'atheism' was a crime against the state, as well as God, and since Pufendorf, Barbeyrac, and all reputable Natural Lawyers agreed it should be banned, 'athées dogmatisans' like the writer of L'Homme machine [whose identity was unknown, FWG] were rightly condemned by the authorities'. See in the same sense about censorship in the Dutch Republic Joris van Eijnatten (2003), 'Van godsdienstvrijheid naar mensenrecht. Meningsvorming over censuur en persvrijheid in de Republiek, 1579–1795', in *Bijdragen en mededelingen betreffende de geschiedenis der Nederlanden*, The Hague: Nederlands Historisch Genootschap. On Hobbes and Locke see Arnold W. Green (1993), *Hobbes and Human Nature*, New Brunswick: Transaction Publishers, p. 48: 'Hobbes never rebelled against censorship. He endorsed it totally'. More nuanced on Locke are John Horton and Susan Mendus (1991), *A Letter Concerning Toleration*, London: Routledge, p. 64. On France, that is Malesherbes who was the Minister of Culture between 1750 and 1763, see D. Peeperkorn (1998), 'Malesherbes on the Rights and Duties of Authors', in Jan C. Kabel and Gerard J.H.M. Mom, *Intellectual Property and Information Law (H. Cohen Jehoram Festschrift)*, Deventer: Kluwer and Portail Litterart, 'La censure', http://www.restode.cfwb.be/francais/_ARTS/AppPeda/Encyclo/05-Censure.htm, observing that Malesherbes 'pratiquait la censure, certes, mais de manière efficace et discrete, considérant qu'íl était bon de laisser circuler les idées et aussi d'empêcher la fuite vers l'étranger des capitaux que ce commerce florissant générait'.

and distributors in particular was to change. Family relations still being important, the respective guilds transformed into professional bonds which served as a kind of trade corporation. In fact, the cooperation between different publishers became closer as time passed by. So, for instance in the case of extensive impressions various publishers shared the financial risk on the basis of rather detailed notarially advised contracts. Also international cooperation saw the light, particularly with respect to distribution.[31] However, no change had so far taken place with respect to the privilege system and the repressive censorship which it, formally at least, involved for Dutch inhabitants.[32] For the rest, publishing flourished in the Low Countries and most clandestine book production and export was concentrated there. Indeed, as has been said by many observers, the Dutch Republic became even a shelter for non-conformist intellectuals from all over Europe. The domestic liberal tradition was furthered by the strong development of the Dutch printing press in the indicated period, contributing to the rise of what can be called in modern jargon a public opinion.[33] Neither did the establishment of the Bataafse Republiek bring about any change in the piracy practice. This piracy concerned both the reprinting of foreign texts (often done under pseudonyms so as to prevent being caught) and domestic texts.[34]

The end of the eighteenth century witnessed, in the slipstream of industrialization and the modernization of trade and instigated by the freedom ideology of the French Revolution, the complete disappearance of the guild system almost Europe-wide. Accordingly, the system of privileges was considered to be contrary to the newly embraced principle of equality for all civilians and to the legal claim of every person to have his property protected. In the Low Countries the guilds were abolished by the Bataafse

---

[31] Bibliopolis Handboek (2003) – *Overzicht van de geschiedenis van het gedrukte boek in Nederland*, The Hague/Zwolle: Waanders (P. Dijstelberge).

[32] As reported by Jonathan I. Israel (2006), *Enlightenment Contested*, Oxford: Oxford University Press, p. 161, with regard to Spinoza 'the Dutch censorship posed a formidable problem as to whether, when, and how to publish his own writings (. . .)'.

[33] According to Joris van Eijnatten (2003), 'Van godsdienstvrijheid naar mensenrecht. Meningsvorming over censuur en persvrijheid in de Republiek, 1579–1795', in *Bijdragen en mededelingen betreffende de geschiedenis der Nederlanden*, The Hague: Nederlands Historisch Genootschap, p. 2, in the respective period so-called *plakkaten* (official proclamations of repression) were promulgated against the publications of Hugo de Groot, Benedictus Spinoza, Jean-Jacques Rousseau and David Hume.

[34] Bibliopolis (2003), *History of the printed book in The Netherlands*, The Hague: Waanders (P.G. Hoftijzer), pp. 79–80.

Republiek in the Staatsregeling of 1795, which was *de iure* confirmed by the Corporatiewet (Corporation Act) 1808 issued under the reign of King Lodewijk Napoleon, but which *de facto* replaced the old guilds by a system of newly created corporations.[35] Things stayed that way after the complete annexation of the Low Countries by France in 1810 and the introduction of French rule.[36] However, the end of the French occupation in 1813 did away with French rule, and contrary to general expectations, did not restore the guild system which was definitively abandoned in 1818.[37]

With regard to the book trade in the Low Countries things developed in their own way. According to the referenced literature it is difficult to say in what way it was affected by the abolition of the guilds. This is the more so, since this abolition concurred with an economic malaise in the book trade. It appears that from around 1760 the separation between bookseller and book distributor became noticeable, the role of the latter gradually adopting the modern meaning of publisher. The already mentioned Staatsregeling of 1795 also did away with the privilege system. It was held that from then on everybody had the right to freedom of expression by way of the printing press or otherwise. Printing privileges were from that time onwards considered to be contrary to the rights of man.[38] The annexation by France between 1810 and 1813 is of note in this respect. First, since it

---

35 The Bataafse Republiek (1795–1801; from 1801 onwards called Bataafs Gemenebest) was the successor of the Republiek der Zeven Verenigde Nederlanden (1588–1795) which came about after a rather peaceful, French-supported revolution in the Low Countries (urging the then stadtholder William V to flee to England and to make the Low Countries a tributary of France in order to seek assistance), in turn succeeded by the Kingdom of Holland (1806–1810), who introduced the French Emperor's brother Ludwig Napoleon who was sent to the Low Countries in 1806 in order to consolidate the French influence there, which came to an end with the complete annexation of the Low Countries by France in 1810. Article 53 Algemene Beginselen en Burgerlijke en Staatkundige Grondregels Staatsregeling 1798 prescribed that all guilds, corporations, confraternities of trades, crafts and industries were abolished, giving every *burger* (that is citizen) the right to establish an enterprise of his own; http:/www.inghist.nl/Onderzoek/Projecten/BataafsFranseBronnen/Browse/IvetProces? See also M.J. van der Burg (2007), *Nederland onder Franse invloed*, Amsterdam: Uitgeverij de Bataafsche Leeuw.

36 Bibliopolis (2003), *History of the printed book in The Netherlands*, The Hague: Waanders (H. van Goinga), p. 128. See for a somewhat different view Chris Schriks (2004), *Het Kopijrecht*, Zutphen: Walburg Pers, pp. 262–63; 342.

37 Bibliopolis (2003), *History of the printed book in The Netherlands*, The Hague: Waanders (P.J. Buijnsters; H. van Goinga), pp. 124; 128.

38 Chris Schriks (2004), *Het Kopijrecht*, Zutphen: Walburg Pers, pp. 261–265.

led to the introduction of French law *sur la propriété littéraire et artistique*. See section 5 on this. Secondly, because of the firm restrictions on the book trade which came along with it, again binding publishing and selling books to licensing (and censoring) by public authorities. However, all this came to an end when the French left the country in 1813.[39]

4 THE ADVENT OF THE AUTHOR: FROM CRAFTSMAN TO CREATOR

Thomas observes that the societal appreciation of producers of cultural goods through the ages demonstrates a varying picture. During the period under consideration here, for instance, art has not always been valued as highly as literature and music.[40] However, since the Renaissance and up to the Enlightenment

> (t)he artists came to serve the new merchant princes wherever they flourished, first in Italy, then in Burgundy, Flanders and High Germany. (. . .) With it came the rise in status of the artist and the setting up in most of the cities of Italy of studios which were at the same time universities and laboratories.[41]

This development concurred with wresting themselves from the bond of the guilds as described in section 3.[42] With respect to the *literati* it is clear that their social position from the Renaissance to the Enlightenment changed in as far as they were gradually no longer merely a part of the clergy but – according to Hauser – at the end belonged 'neither to a class-determined, nor to a culturally and professionally uniform social category', but instead

---

39 Marijke Reinsma (2006), *Auteurswet 1881 [Parlementaire Geschiedenis Wet 1881- Ontwerp 1884]*, Zutphen: Centraal Boekhuis, p. 13.

40 According to S. Thomas, *Practice and Profession of the Arts*, Encyclopaedia Britannica (15th edn), p. 93, at 100, this differentiation is due to various factors such as the relation between religion and art, the distinction between professionals and amateurs, the opposition between fine arts and applied arts and the like.

41 J.D. Bernal (1954–1971), *Science in History*, Cambridge, MA, M.I.T. Press, p. 265. See also S. Thomas, *Practice and Profession of the Arts*, Encyclopaedia Britannica (15th edn), p. 93, at 98.

42 According to Arnold Hauser (1951/1999), *The Social History of Art*, London: Routledge, pp. 301; 311–315; 319–320; 337, the guilds allowed the artists to leave without any objection because of the fact that the market for art products had reached a stage of balance, making it no longer necessary to regulate the offering of art products, i.e. to keep that offer low. Idem S. Thomas, *Practice and Profession of the Arts*, Encyclopaedia Britannica (15th edn), p. 93, at 110.

included 'clerks and laymen, rich and poor, high officials and minor notaries, merchants and schoolmasters, lawyers and scholars'.[43]

For a living, however, and if not engaged in universities or other scholarly centres, for a long time they were still entirely dependent on patrons or professional occupations other than writing.[44]

However, despite the growing appreciation of their societal contributions and the accompanying improvement of their social position, it was not until the concurrence of a number of paradigmatic and societal states of affairs: such as a dying patronage, a rising commercial market for artistic products (amongst other things because of the spread of reading) and the breakthrough of liberation philosophies, that artists and writers in the sixteenth and seventeenth centuries came to be seen as creators who deserved to be acknowledged as being authorized to determine what would be the legal status of the cultural goods they produced.

Contributing a great deal to this development is the recognition and development of the idea of personality in the eighteenth century in all spheres of law, but particularly in the domain of copyright law. Indeed, already in the preceding centuries and even though there were no explicit legal rules for the protection of producers of cultural goods, it was taken for granted that they had the right to decide over their unpublished products: whether to publish or not, whether to allow its public performance or not. However, as will be seen later in this section, these prerogatives did not concern them as the creators of their products, but rather as the owners of the physical embodiment thereof.

Also contributing to the rise of the author was an emerging definition of literary property. The notion that writers were the owners of their products, called *works,* was relatively new. According to Van Horn Melton, focussing on the position of writers,

> (i)t was not just the quantity of literary producers that made the eighteenth century, relative to previous periods, the age of the author. The modern idea of the author was itself an eighteenth-century creation. . .And only in the eighteenth century did there emerge the idea of authorship as ownership, or what we today call copyright, with authors considered the proprietors of works that

---

43 Arnold Hauser (1951/1999), *The Social History of Art*, London: Routledge, pp. 336–337.

44 Arnold Hauser (1951/1999), *The Social History of Art*, London: Routledge, pp. 338. Not much different from that of writers in this indicated period of time was the social position of composers. Pohlmann (1966), p. 30, observes for the period of ca 1400 until 1800 that composers until the end of the eighteenth century *stand unter dem bestimmenden Vorzeichen ihrer Sozialabhaengigkeit.*

> could not be published or sold without their consent. . .Authors at the same time acquired a new cultural and political identity.[45]

This new definition of literary property was already promoted by seventeenth century scholars like Locke who wrote that 'every man has a property in his own person. This nobody has any right to but himself. The labour of his body, and the work of his hands, we may say, are properly his'.[46] Intrinsic in the new definition of literary property was the concept of the writer as an original genius, shifting the basis of creative inspiration from the outside to the inside of what was now called the *creator*. By making reference to both the idea of the creator's personality as the source of his work and the genius concept particularly in the eighteenth century it began to be promoted by philosophers that the creator not only had a property right in the physical products which carried his creations, but even in the ideas contained therein. As will be seen in section 5, it would take the whole of the nineteenth century in order to finally arrive at what is called in modern copyright law jargon the idea/expression dichotomy.

As will be seen, these new proprietory claims by writers who had so far been assumed to lose all their titles after selling or licensing the physical products that carried their texts to a publisher against an outright fee, put under strain the relationship between authors and the exploiters of their works. As observed by Hesse this situation gave rise to various intriguing questions:

> Were ideas in fact a gift from God, as traditional authorities had claimed, or were they the property of those who made them manifest, as authors now asserted? Was a 'privilege' a 'grace', or was it rather the legal ratification of an anterior, natural right to property? Upon what basis could the governments of nations or cities restrict or confirm traditional privileges? Could a secular foundation be articulated for the regulation of the publication and circulation of ideas?[47]

Finally, in the course of the Age of Reason two competing, and in fact theoretically incompatible, views became prominent with respect to the

---

45 James van Horn Melton (2001), *The Rise of the Public in Enlightenment Europe*, Cambridge: Cambridge University Press, pp. 123–124. See also F.W. Grosheide (1986), Auteursrecht op maat, Deventer: Kluwer, pp. 103–104; Carla Hesse (2002), 'The Rise of Intellectual Property, 700 B.C.–A.D. 2000: an idea in the balance', *Daedalus*, Spring, pp. 31–33.

46 Locke (1690). See on that Carla Hesse (2002), 'The Rise of Intellectual Property, 700 B.C.–A.D. 2000: an idea in the balance', *Daedalus*, Spring, pp. 33–34

47 Carla Hesse (2002), 'The Rise of Intellectual Property, 700 B.C.–A.D. 2000: an idea in the balance', *Daedalus*, Spring, p. 33.

transposition of these questions into positive law: a natural rights view and a public good view. The former proposed that there was a natural right to property in ideas which only had to be confirmed by the legislator. The latter proposed that the recognition by the legislator of an exclusive right in ideas only followed from policy considerations holding that this best served the creation of new ideas. In the course of the nineteenth century the first view would become the leading one in continental Europe (*droit d'auteur; Urheberrecht; auteursrecht*); the second would be prevalent in England (*copyright*).[48] However, since neither view was ever completely enacted in any national positive law of the time, it became possible – as will be seen in section 5 – in the last part of that age to arrive at the first international legal instrument for the protection of authors' rights (the BC 1886), which from the beginning contained restrictions on and limitations to the execution of the granted prerogatives. For that aim the BC introduced the doctrine of national treatment enabling member states to impose statutory limits alongside natural law claims for protection. This state of affairs is not refuted by the fact that the BC undeniably bears a civil law stamp.[49] It is of note that from then onwards the generic legal term to refer to the creator would become *the author.*

The Low Countries followed the described developments in Europe, first by enacting their own respective regulation, later under French rule and finally in the course of the nineteenth century by again introducing their own legislation on authors' rights (*auteursrecht*). See hereafter section 5.

5 BOOK PRINTING: THE AGENT OF MODERN COPYRIGHT LAW?

Some experts seem to regard the granting of book printing privileges as the origin of authors' rights, that is copyright law as it came about in the course of the nineteenth century. However, most experts rightly seem to agree that the functions of the privileges had little to do with protecting the rights of the author. This is because they were based on quite different economic and political considerations. Economic considerations during the time of the printing privileges focussed on the exploitation of cultural

48 F.W. Grosheide (1986), *Auteursrecht op maat*, Deventer: Kluwer, pp. 125–145; Carla Hesse (2002), 'The Rise of Intellectual Property, 700 B.C.–A.D. 2000: an idea in the balance', *Daedalus*, Spring, p. 36.

49 Sam Ricketson, Jane Ginsburg (2006), *International Copyright and Neighbouring Rights: the Berne Convention and Beyond*, Oxford: Oxford University Press.

goods in the form of an exclusive guarantee, with the purpose of regulating the book trade by providing an industrial and commercial monopoly. Political considerations at the time required the monitoring of printing by requiring prior authorization by the central or local authorities, which had often initially encouraged the new invention of printing, but soon discovered its reverse side: the production of contraband, and therefore they tried to control it.[50]

However, on the eve of the coming into existence of modern copyright law economic considerations were of two kinds. First, after the abolition of the guilds, together with the waning of patronage, those working in the creative professions, now lacking the support of their trade or their patron, from then on were completely dependent upon themselves and the free market which motivated them to strive for a special legal position of their own.[51] Secondly, the concern of the then established central authorities especially addressed combating the steady spread of piracy in the book trade. This was particularly true for those countries like England, France and Germany, which were net exporters of literature and the like. In concurrence with these economic considerations political considerations came to hold that it was ethically unfair and legally unjustified to not remunerate authors, and by extension other creative professionals, for their creative contributions to society by granting them the exclusive right to determine what should be done with their works.[52]

More in particular, drawing a direct line from the time of book printing to that of modern copyright law underestimates the crucial role of both the freedom ideology in the late eighteenth century and the romantic movement of the late nineteenth century as decisive developments in this respect. For the freedom ideology and the romantic movement laid the foundation for the recognition and development of *the notion of personality* in all spheres of law, also in what would develop into intellectual property law. Although the content of the notion was disputed, it was generally agreed that under natural law there was – and ought to be according to positive

---

50 As observed by Carla Hesse (2002), 'The Rise of Intellectual Property, 700 B.C.–A.D. 2000: an idea in the balance', *Daedalus*, Spring, p. 31 ('(t)hroughout the early modern world the development of commercial printing and publishing thus first occurred through a system of state-licensed monopolies, sanctioned by religious ideologies, that made no mention at all of intellectual property rights. The prevailing theories of knowledge and of political legitimacy made such rights inconceivable.')

51 Comp. Martha Woodmansee (1994), *The Author, Art and the Market: Reading the History of Aesthetics*, New York: Columbia University Press.

52 F.W. Grosheide (1986), *Auteursrecht op maat*, Deventer: Kluwer.

law – certain human qualities and abilities connected with a person's self that were innate, non-transferable, and imprescriptible.[53]

From a positive law perspective, of special interest is the development in France where the Law of 19 July 1793 became the basis for all subsequent literary property law in France and its then satellite countries.[54] This law 'enshrined the concept of a limited property right as the best means to strike a balance between remunerating authors and protecting the public interest in the advancement of learning'.[55] It concerned authors, that is writers, composers, painters and illustrators as subjects of protection. They were granted an exclusive right to sell (and to allow the sale of) and to distribute (and to allow the distribution of) their works. The right was transferable to somebody else and could be inherited. It had a term of ten years after the death of the author. This French law was introduced in all European countries, among which were also the German states, which came under French rule. But even after the French domination had come to an end beginning with the Congress of Vienna in 1815, the French approach towards literary property remained determinant, finally leading in Germany to the adoption in 1870 of the first uniform copyright law which was rather similar to the French example.

Also in the Low Countries until 1803 it was not the producer of a text but the publisher who was legally protected on the basis of a printing privilege. However, the Copyright Act 1803 introduced a new regime under which the drafter (*opsteller*) of a text was recognized as the holder of a perpetual right to reproduce it (*copijregt*).[56] As already indicated,

---

[53] F. Willem Grosheide (1994), 'Paradigms in Copyright Law', in Brad Sherman and Alain Strowel, *Of Authors and Origins*, Oxford: Oxford University Press, pp. 203–233, at 209–213 with references.

[54] In reality things followed a more complicated course than indicated in the main text. Before arriving at the Law of 1793, and preceded by the English Statute of Queen Anne of 1709, in the run up to and in the heat of the revolutionary period in France all sorts of adaptations to the privilege system took place. See on this Carla Hesse (2002), 'The Rise of Intellectual Property, 700 B.C.–A.D. 2000: an idea in the balance', *Daedalus*, Spring, p. 38, referring to Carla Hesse (1991), *Publishing and Cultural Politics in Revolutionary Paris 1789–1810*, Berkeley: University of California Press. *Décret impérial dd 8 novembre 1810 sur la mise en activité des lois Francaises dans les départements des bouches du Rhin, et des bouches de l'Escaut et dans l'arrondissement de Breda.*

[55] Carla Hesse (2002), 'The Rise of Intellectual Property, 700 B.C.–A.D. 2000: an idea in the balance', *Daedalus*, Spring, p. 39; André Lucas and Henri-Jaques Lucas (2006), *Traité de la propriété littéraire et artistique*, Paris: Litec, pp. 9–14.

[56] According to Chris Schriks (2004), *Het Kopijrecht* (2004), Zutphen: Walburg Pers, p. 321, this regime reflects the acknowledgement of the author's contribution as the crucial factor in the publishing process.

during the French annexation that followed in 1810, the respective French legislation was introduced. But things changed once again after the French left the country. First, in the course of 1813 and 1814 French rule was withdrawn, restoring the *status quo ante*, that is introducing the *copyregt* once again, which was a publisher's right, not that of an author. Next, in 1817 legislation was enacted granting the right to reproduce to what was called from then onwards *autheurs* (authors) and their successors in title. Only they were legally authorized to reproduce and to sell (and to allow to be reproduced or sold) a protected text during a period of 20 years after the death of the author. All this subject to the condition that the text was printed by a Dutch printer and published by a Dutch publisher whose name and domicile as well as the year of publication had to be indicated in the publication. In addition, three copies of the printed text had to be given to the municipal authority of the place of publication.

The described regime would remain in force until the Auteurswet 1881. That statute – amongst other things based on an impressive study of foreign law – granted an exclusive right to the author of texts (including compilations like journals and periodicals of associations, church books and schoolbooks), geographical works, musical compositions, dramatic works and oral presentations to make them available to the public through printing. Following the example of Germany, the statute did not apply to works of art which were considered to be a different category of creative expression. A draft for a separate statute on works of art was introduced in Parliament in 1884 but never became law. A special regulation concerned translations, favouring Dutch translators above foreign original authors, which in the course of time appeared, alongside the deposit requirement, to be a main obstacle to joining the BC in 1886 (adherence did not take place until 1912). However, some of the tension between the European nations was eased as from the second half of the nineteenth century onwards many international relations were regulated by bilateral treaties.[57]

The described positive law developments should be read in light of the articulation from the late eighteenth century onwards and up until the late nineteenth century of a legal-conceptual change in view of the relationship between the author and his work. It brings back to the fore what was called, in section 4, the idea/expression dichotomy. Indeed, it took some time before legal dogmatics developed in such a way that it became

---

[57] Marijke Reinsma (2006), *Auteurswet 1881 [Parlementaire Geschiedenis Wet 1881 - Ontwerp 1884]*, Zutphen: Centraal Boekhuis, pp. 15–25. Edward W. Ploman and L. Clark Hamilton (1980), *Intellectual Property in the Information Age,* Boston: Routledge and Kegan Paul, pp. 18–21.

possible to distinguish between the idea (the content) and the expression (the form) of a work of authorship, the form again to be distinguished from the physical carrier which made it possible to communicate the expressed idea to the public.[58] Before that change neither civil law nor common law dogmatics were able to conceptualize a property right in intangible products of the mind and to legally separate the ownership of books and a legal claim to their content. Particularly German legal thinking, personified by Joseph Kohler, contributed to the development of this new concept. Kohler introduced what he called the 'Theorie vom Immaterialgueterrecht' (Theory of Intellectual Property Law) which he developed in particular with regard to the content of copyright law.[59] In his analysis he underlined what is now common knowledge, but was then the condensation of a development in legal thinking: that the work is intangible, the right to it covering the immaterial creation as it is shaped by its author, separate from the ownership of the tangible carrier such as the manuscript, and therefore requiring the acknowledgement of a *sui generis* property right.

Incited by the industrial revolution which contributed to the rise of a market for cultural goods, the growing discontent as to the conclusion of bilateral treaties, together with the indicated development in legal thinking, set in motion an *international awakening* leading to the realization that a new regime for the legal protection of cultural goods, particularly against pirating, was needed.[60] Indeed, the *mosaic of treaties* which followed from the system of bilateral treaties, based upon reciprocity, did not in fact contribute to real international protection.[61] So the notion of a common international legal framework gained ground. Interestingly, at first it was not national authorities but non-governmental organizations that were motivated to take actions of the kind that would finally lead to the establishment of the BC providing 'the cornerstones for the present

---

58 F.W. Grosheide, *Auteursrecht op maat*, Deventer: Kluwer, pp. 221–236. It is not the place here to elaborate on the idea/expression, content/form debate. See for the development of Dutch copyright law De Beaufort (1932), pp. 16–20. So for a general actual account with extensive references Maurizio Borghi (2007), 'Owing Form, Sharing Content: Natural-Right Copyright and Digital Environment', in Fiona Macmillan and Kathey Bowrey (eds), *New Directions in Copyright Law*, Volume 5, Cheltenham, UK and Northampton, MA, USA: Edward Elgar Publishing.

59 Joseph Kohler (1880), *Das Autorrecht*; and (1892) *Das literarische und artistische Kunstwerk und Sein Autorschutz*, Mannheim: Bensheimer.

60 Edward W. Ploman and L. Clark Hamilton (1980), *Intellectual Property in the Information Age*, Boston: Routledge and Kegan Paul, p. 18.

61 Ibid, p. 20.

elaborate system of international treaties and structures in the copyright field.'[62]

6 CONCLUDING OBSERVATIONS

From the preceding sections with regard to the main issue of this contribution: the transition from guild regulation to modern copyright law in the Low Countries, the following conclusions can be drawn.

1. It can be said that the guilds in the period of time under consideration here, from a legal point of view were first and foremost private commercial organizations, governed by their own private law regulations and set up to look after their own businesses. At the same time, however, public law was involved in as far as the exclusive monopolistic regulations which the central or local authorities issued on behalf of the guilds, formed a protective regime against the risks of the market for the craftsmen involved. This was so for the guilds in general as well as for those guilds that included artists and writers. So if artists and writers as members of any general or special guild were at all protected, it was because they were exploiting their own cultural goods which was seldom the case. Anyway, guilds were not introduced and were never meant to promote and protect the interests of artists and writers *per se*.
2. With regard to the book trade which is taken as a *pars pro toto* here in light of the development of modern copyright law, it appears that prior to the eighteenth century, in as far as there was already a legal regulation of the relationship between producers and publishers of texts, it was not meant to protect the interest of the former but that of the latter. According to the general custom of the day writers were to exclusively license or sell their manuscripts against an outright fee to publishers which after the introduction of the privilege system needed a public law grant to be issued by a central or local authority to publish the texts. So printing privileges were not granted to protect writers but to shore up the trade monopoly of a relatively small group of licensed publishers.
3. So, if the privilege system in the Low Countries was primarily intended to regulating the book trade and to fight unfair competition, it had at

---

[62] Edward W. Ploman and L. Clark Hamilton (1980), *Intellectual Property in the Information Age*, Boston: Routledge and Kegan Paul, p. 21.

least two what may be called note-worthy side-effects. The first side-effect was censorship. Although the impact of it in the Low Countries is contested, its influence on publishing by Dutch authors is generally agreed. At the same time – particularly during the seventeenth and eighteenth centuries – the Low Countries became internationally well-known for their freedom of expression and liberal regime towards the exchange of views by dissidents of foreign origin. A second side-effect of the privilege system should be mentioned: its function as a barrier against book piracy. However, it seems that seen from the social-economic perspective that this side-effect was of limited importance. More commonly used as a way of fighting piracy were the so-called printer's and engraver's marks.

4. From the end of the eighteenth up to the second half of the nineteenth century things will change rather dramatically. This is due to a combination of decisive factors. First, the decline and fall of the guild system as well as the waning of patronage, and in its slipstream, the abolition of the privilege regulation together with that of censorship. Secondly, the rise of the philosophy of freedom and connected to that the development of the notion of personality. Thirdly, the conceptualization in legal thinking of the distinction between idea and expression, content and form, leading to a different notion of literary property: authorship would no longer be seen as indicating the ownership of the content but as related to the way in which the content was expressed in a particular form.
5. As a consequence of all this the producers of cultural goods, who from then onwards would be called authors, were compelled to execute their professional activities in the marketplace without the support of any government-licensed organization of related industrial producers (publishers). As far as the book trade was concerned, the abolition of the privileges would also ensure that publishers had to act in free competition with those who acted in the same trade and that they lacked a specific legal protective regime which was particularly detrimental to them in light of the flourishing piracy. From the perspective of authors this gave rise to the need for a protective legal regime of their own, specifically addressed to their interest, which in the end instigated the international awakening that laid the foundation for the establishment of the Berne Convention in 1886.
6. As far as the Low Countries are concerned, in historical perspective the same applies as for the rest of Europe. However, with one notable exception, since with regard to the book trade during the whole period of time that is of interest in this contribution, the Low Countries acted as a sort of free haven for whatever could not or could hardly be

published elsewhere in Europe. In fact this free riding position was the main reason why the Dutch did not enter the Union of Berne in 1886. It took them another quarter of a century before they finally joined the family of *civilized countries*[63] in 1912.

[63] H.L. de Beaufort (1932), *Auteursrecht*, Zwolle: Tjeenk Willink.

7. Transition from guild regulation to modern copyright law (Sweden)

Gunnar Petri*

1 INTRODUCTION

When should we celebrate the birthday of authors' rights? When should we consider that the developing law of copyright starts deserving the epithet of being *modern*? A reasonable suggestion is that this is the moment when the *right to copy* transforms itself into the *right of the author*. From that moment the conditions are put in place for further development and the flowering of the whole plethora of rights which we now consider as a modern legal field *sui generis* by the name of *copyright*, *droit d'auteur* or *Urheberrecht*. This delivery is also an indispensable threshold to pass – as long as the right to copy remains a privilege and not a positive right, vested in the author, the flower beds of copyright remain barren. This transition, therefore, is the heroic and defining moment in the history of copyright, a harbinger of events to come. A study of the actual circumstances surrounding that landmark event is therefore bound to give interesting clues to the understanding of copyright law.

There are, of course, as many such birthdays as there are national legal traditions. Some of these traditions certainly have meant more for the success of the idea of copyright than others. Some are mainly recipients. In all of them, the deliveries occur during a period of roughly 150 years, from the beginning of the eighteenth century to the middle of the nineteenth. The great histories of copyright in the dominant legal traditions are well investigated, less so the receiving ones. Let us begin by inquiring into one of them in search of perspectives which could perhaps shed some light also into more well-lit quarters.

* Dr Gunnar Petri, Chairman of the STIM Board, Sweden.

2 SWEDEN

The delivery of authors' rights in Sweden took place just about 100 years after the promulgation in 1710 of the British *Statute of Anne*. On 9 March 1810, an *Act of Freedom of the Press* was enacted, abolishing censorship, defining the responsibilities of the author and including also the lapidary provision that *every script be the property of the author*. This happy event, of course, had its own pre-history.

2.1 Early Developments

Printing came late to the northern outskirts of Europe. In Sweden, only the Reformation provoked the establishment of a permanent printing office in Stockholm, under tight royal supervision. Its lonely printing press remained the only one in the country for a hundred years, excluding any risk of the appearance of a problem of reprinting. Lutheran orthodoxy, centralized government, tight control and scarce production characterized the situation.

In the early seventeenth century, printers from abroad were encouraged by general privileges, but the number of presses remained low by continental standards. Reprinting constituted no real problem, production remained scarce and individual printing privileges not asked for.

As Sweden expanded into a dominant position in the Baltic, newly conquered provinces had to be made Swedish by hook or by crook. One method was the establishment of new universities, such as the one in Lund in the recently acquired province of Scania. This, in turn, necessitated the summoning of capable competence from the continent. The best catch turned out to be Samuel Pufendorf, already a European celebrity, who was made professor in Lund and later royal historiographer.

2.2 Pufendorf

Well versed in copyright conditions in Germany and just about to publish his seminal work *De Jure Naturae et Gentium*, Pufendorf correctly assumed that this masterpiece soon would become a best-seller, prone to be pirated on a European scale. He therefore secured an individual privilege for his work, in fact the first individual printing privilege concerning a book printed in Sweden. This first privilege was issued as late as 1672 for a duration of ten years and stipulated a fine for the reprinter of 50 golden marks, a considerable sum of money. The piquancy of the matter, however, was that this privilege had no effect in Sweden. Pufendorf had not turned to his master, the King of Sweden, who up till then had felt no need to introduce the system of individual printing privileges in his lands. The issuer was Sweden's traditional enemy, the Emperor in Vienna, who had duly obliged to Pufendorf's petition. The royal chancery in Stockholm, no doubt slightly upset by this intrusion from abroad, responded by introducing the system of individual privileges also in Sweden, where they soon became ubiquitous.

2.3 The Eighteenth Century

As mercantilist ideas began to prevail in the eighteenth century, the established printers in Stockholm sought to protect their business, strengthen their hand over their journeymen and, last but not least, put an end to the problem of unfair reprinting, which was now becoming noticeable. Their ultimate aim was a perpetual protection, in their own hands, against reprinting. As regards the managing of offices and personnel, they found their inspiration in Holland. Concerning protectionism, unfair reprinting and the amalgamation of privileges and censorship, the France of Louis XIV was the model. Referring to England and the *Statute of Anne* was not possible – it was all too evident that introduction of the English system, which could otherwise be recommended, presupposed a discussion about censorship. That was not yet on the agenda.

The outcome was a statute of 1752 whereby privilege was accorded automatically for smaller publications upon registration with the Society of Printers. Provided that they were kept in stock, this protection was, in principle, perpetual. The system of individual royal privileges, limited in time, was retained for more voluminous books. Everything, of course, was on condition of censorship approval. Privilege and permission from the censor melted into one. Records were to be kept by the Society of Printers, which was transformed into a government agency with a government official as its president. Its members were given monopoly, control over the establishment of new printing shops and protection against disloyal internal competition in exchange for acting as agents of censorship. The problem of unfair reprinting, if it ever really existed, was for all practical purposes solved. The French *Regulation of Printing* of 1686 was a prototype, and the Society of Printers was given a role not unlike the English Stationers' Company in its Tudor and Stuart heyday.

In 1765, a change of government within the quasi-parliamentary system that prevailed in the Swedish so-called Era of Freedom triggered off a discussion about public accessibility to official papers and censorship in general. The notion of an independent public opinion was not yet in sway, but a number of orators in the Estates championed the advantages of letting decisions be enlightened by a public dialogue between knowledgeable men. The system of secular censorship had also proved to be all too sensitive to partisanship. The outcome was the later much vaunted Act of Freedom of the Press of 1766, abolishing secular censorship and declaring an extensive right of accessibility to public records.

Why did this act not entail a discussion on authors' rights? In effect, censorship was only abolished by halves. The important theological censorship prevailed. There had been no preceding campaign from publishers, who were satisfied with the reform of 1752, there were no Swedish writers of national renown and the writers there depended on patronage, independent means or office. In addition, the effects of the act were almost immediately severely circumscribed and censorship was ultimately restored when the monarchy soon asserted itself with Gustaf III on the throne.

2.4 The Nineteenth Century

In 1809, the situation was different. A coup had toppled the Gustavian regime in the wake of Russia's occupation of Finland, and a swift constitutional recasting was imminently necessary. The men who now got the upper hand saw freedom of the press and the establishment of public opinion as a necessary pillar and counterweight in the Montesquieu-inspired constitutional construction they envisaged. In this Constitution of 1809, concocted within a few weeks, freedom of the press was declared and defined as the absence of any restraints preceding publication. In addition, the whole system of discretionary privileges of all sorts was declared unlawful. An overhaul of the statute from 1752 duly announced itself and a committee of drafters was appointed.

With the new constitution, the two basic props to the system of regulation of printing, namely censorship and privileges, had collapsed overnight. Instead of a renewed regulation with their privileges intact the printers and their venerated society had to face a situation where the main concern of the drafters was to define the responsibilities of the now emancipated authors. The outcome was not a new regulation along the corporate lines envisaged by the printers but a solemn *Act of Freedom of the Press* of 1810, elevated to the same legal status as the Constitution, thereby signalling public opinion as a basic tenet of the new political situation. This entailed the clarification of the rights of the author. Privileges were no longer viable, and a new system had to be anchored to the author, who was duly given a perpetual property in his works.

There had been no preceding discussion about authors' rights. No publishers had waged campaigns along Lockeian lines, no authors had claimed any particular rights. This majestic gift of a perpetual right to the author was not a result of lobbying from interested parties. The influences were latent, and they came from knowledge of the campaigns by publishers in England and France, the French revolutionary decrees, reading of Kant and Blackstone and some familiarity with the English system according to the *Statute of Anne*, which could now be freely invoked. One of the framers had written a biography of Blackstone, and most of them had certainly read Kant's famous essay *Answer to the question: What is enlightenment?*, published in conjunction with his well-known dissertation of authors' rights, *On the unrighteousness of the reprinting of books*. The linkage between these two essays, coupling the freedom of expression with authors' rights, was not missed by them either.

The Swedish example is of general interest as an illustration of the connection between the abolition of censorship and the triggering of an introduction of authors' rights. The one necessitated the other. The responsibilities of the author had to be sorted out, and responsibility for one's works entailed a right to them. The old system of privileges was thus transformed into a right anchored to the author. The latent conception of authorial property made its appearance suddenly and surreptitiously as a gift from above. In addition, there were no great monopolized literary legacies, which could have woken up resistance to the perpetuity of the new right. On this point, in any case, authors and publishers had no opposite interests.

The new right was an important element when a market-oriented literature, emancipated from patronage, started to appear in the 1830s. As soon as some reticence was aired regarding its perpetuity it was, still without any discussion, circumscribed by an obligation to publish new editions within 20 years to retain the right. Finally in 1877, internationalization and the issue of translations brought about a mature, German-inspired legislation with time-limited rights, conceived in Nordic cooperation. Copyright was to last until 50 years after the death of the author.

So, the abolition of censorship and monopolies acted as the midwife to the delivery and birthday of Swedish authors' right in 1810. To apply these two perspectives, censorship and monopoly, therefore comes naturally to a Swedish observer when discussing the transition from guild regulation to modern copyright law. Are they, maybe, of interest also in the study of this transition in the great European legal traditions?

3 THE ROMAN LEGAL TRADITION

The greatest of them all, of course, is the Roman. Censorship of the written word and regulation of monopolies both have their roots there. Much ink has been spilt on the influence upon copyright of Roman Law, more often than not concentrating on the signs of a preliminary sense of respect for the value of artistic creation and the general condemnation of plagiarism. However, the important legacy from antiquity rests elsewhere, and the two aspects which merit special attention are just the ones that raised our interest concerning the Swedish case of transition from guild regulation to real authors' rights, namely monopolies and censorship.

The elaborate doctrine of justified *privilegia* on the one hand and reprehensible *monopolia* on the other was worked out in the late principate and included in *Corpus Iuris Civilis.* The Emperor had the right to grant individuals exemptions from the general law, thereby protecting certain activities from competition. But these grants had to be justified by the common good, and they should not unduly impinge upon the rights of others. In that case they were condemned as *monopolia.* Medieval commentators added the notion of justified price, adding weight to the unlawfulness of monopolies.

Also censorship is a heritage from Rome. The Emperor had, in his capacity of *pontifex maximus*, the right to control and censor the written word. This Roman prerogative was invoked with equal zeal by popes, prelates and secular rulers, reaching a high pitch in the tense atmosphere of the late medieval persecutions of heretics and forming the basis of subsequent systems of censorship.

These two legal phenomena were of basic importance when the arrival of printing made regulation of this revolutionary invention necessary. They immediately became intertwined, the needs of censorship legitimatizing obvious publishing *monopolia.* Later on, when the classical system of censorship crumbled, it dragged tolerance of these monopolies with it. Then, as a number of examples illustrate, the right to be spared reprinting had to be vested in the author.

The first of these examples regards a state where the delivery of authors' rights never took place, namely Venice, which for a period emerged as the printing centre of Europe and the breeding place for late Renaissance literary production. The deleterious effects of unfair competition between printers first became visible there. It was also in Venice that time-limited patents for inventions were first introduced and generalized by legislation, modelled on the Roman Law concepts of *privilegia* and *monopolia.* Venice is also the place which saw the first introduction of organized censorship of printing and the first framing of an *index* of forbidden books.

The Venetian government immediately recognized the necessity of a system to protect the fledgling printing industry's investments against unfair reprinting, and the new legal instrument of individual printing privileges was designed and introduced. These privileges were gradually transformed into a comprehensive system of time-limited protection against reprinting, available on request and formally and openly registered. This system offered justified *privilegia* insofar as they protected the printer against unfair competition and enabled him to reap a reasonable benefit from his investment. They never became reprehensible *monopolia* since they were strictly limited in time and in each case applied only to one particular work. The system was generalized and finalized in 1603.

For all practical purposes, this system elegantly solved the problem of unfair reprinting without creating suffocating publishers' monopolies. But there the development ended. No transition from a *right to copy* to a *right of the author* ever took place. Why, then, did Venice not become the birthplace of authors' rights?

Because censorship was part and parcel of the system, and censorship prevailed in the Republic until its demise in 1797. No abolition of censorship ever created the necessity to define the responsibility of the author and the occasion to anchor the protection against reprinting in him. The mature Venetian system can be regarded as an optimal solution to the reprinting problem in a society without freedom of the press, imitated in later times in more modern authoritarian or totalitarian states.

4 ENGLAND

In England, it took more than a century until the printing industry attained the same levels of production as in Venice. By then England had imported the printing privilege, transformed it into a generalized system of perpetuated monopolies under the auspices of the Stationers' Company and created a strict system of censorship with the Company as principal agent.

The first challenge to this tightly cemented system was the adoption of the *Statute of Monopolies* in 1624. This was the outcome of a showdown between the royal prerogative and the competence of Parliament. The struggle had been fought much in the terms of the Roman Law concepts of *privilegia* and *monopolia*. Its main thrust was to deprive the king of the possibility of bestowing lucrative monopolies on favourites. But it was also an important step in the development of the early modern concept of how to govern the state. The focus was switched from discretionary grants to generalized positive rights, from unrestrained authority to the rule of law. Only useful inventions were to have a right to protection from competition for only a limited period, that right was vested in the inventor and the system was to be transparent and objective. The statute of 1624 quickly became a pillar of parliamentary self-assertion.

But the stationers' copyrights prevailed, even though the system had degenerated into an obvious *monopolium* with perpetual rights massed in the hands of dominating London publishers or jointly administered by the same publishers through their Company. The adoption of the *Statute of Monopolies* did not, as might have been expected, trigger any discussion about these privileges, which were wholly contrary to the spirit of the statute. The reason was the important role played by the Company in the system of censorship and the tight link between entry in the stationers' register and censorship approval. And censorship was not yet put in question.

By the mid-seventeenth century this started to happen. The uncertain conditions of civil war created laxity and partisanship in censoring. Milton challenged the whole foundation of paternal censorship and linked it to papal despotism. After a relapse during the Restoration the discussion returned in the wake of the Glorious Revolution, the formation of political parties and Lockeian concepts of government. The *Licensing Act* gradually came to be regarded as a remnant of Stuart tyranny, and its lapse in 1694, sounding the knell of censorship, was a natural ingredient in the evolution towards parliamentary supremacy and the party system.

The abolition of censorship left the London publishers without arguments when their monopolies were attacked. The proud Company collapsed like a house of cards – it was no longer of public utility. But publishers, authors and public were all unanimous in their opinion that unfair reprinting was impermissible. In order to maintain their monopolies, the publishers tried to utilize Lockeian rational natural rights theories, and loosely grounded references to common law, to argue in favour of a perpetual ownership right, protecting them against reprinting. This inevitably led them to point to the author as point of attachment. Defoe, Addison and others emphasized that the author, now emancipated from censorship and fully responsible for his works, was also entitled to a right to them. The outcome was the *Statute of Anne* of 1710. This was the final victory for the principles from the *Statute of Monopolies*, which served as model. Forward stepped the emancipated author with a right of his own, limited in time to 28 years from publication. After the fall of censorship, a solution without the author was inconceivable.

The English eighteenth century saw the dwindling of patronage and the emergence of a literary market, opening up for market-orientated literary careers in mutual competition. The new statute was a powerful prop to this development. By mid-century, it also saw the beginning of the terminations of rights to important literary legacies. This initiated the lengthy campaign by publishers to return to the issue of 1710 and acquire a transferable perpetual right. The attempt, as is well known, was scuttled by the House of Lords in *Donaldson v. Beckett* in 1776. The House was in no mood to reintroduce the possibility of constructing vast literary monopolies. Thereafter, the issue was one of necessary balancing of the interest of public access on the one hand and the interest of providing incitement for creation and investment in creation on the other.

5 FRANCE

Printing privileges found their way to France via Milan. Their issuing immediately became a bone of contention between the gradually more assertive royal power and the Paris *Parlement*, versed in the tradition of adjudicating between permissible *privilegia* and pernicious *monopolia.* In the view of the *Parlement*, privileges were justified only during a limited time, long enough to enable the printer to recoup his costs. If given for categories of works or unlimited in time they became *monopolia.*

In the unruly French sixteenth century, these issues were never really sorted out. The justification of censorship, however, was not at stake, albeit used for Catholic as well as Huguenot purposes. With the consolidation of the French monarchy in the seventeenth century, the problems were dealt with more effectively. The issuing of printing privileges was concentrated firmly in royal hands and became part of a general and elaborated system of discretionary patronage. It was also altogether integrated into the impressive apparatus for censorship and literary control that was simultaneously built up. The technical terms for privilege and permission were even amalgamated into one. Literary patronage also became an acknowledged instrument for a policy of deliberate cultural mercantilism.

This great machine started to disintegrate in the century of the Enlightenment. The Jansenist debate pointed to cracks in the wall. Influences from England trickled in through the Netherlands, printed and smuggled in by Huguenots in exile. The leading *philosophes* produced a vast underground literature that dominated the *salons.* Undisputed cultural supremacy in Europe was to a large extent propped up by geniuses in exile.

In that atmosphere the provincial printers started to challenge the monopolies of their more fortunate Parisian colleagues. The latter in turn rallied to the defence of their interests. Their weapon was a persuasive argumentation of clear-cut Lockeian tenor, very similar to the campaign waged at the same time in the English courts of justice. What could be a more natural property than one's own work of the mind? And was not property always for ever and transferable, for example to a publisher?

The arguments had effect in the attempt in 1777–78, initiated by Turgot, Necker and their colleagues in the government, to reform the system along physiocratic lines. The general idea was that the author, as creator of his work, should automatically be entitled to a life-long legal protection against reprinting. This protection, however, did not come as a clear-cut positive right but as a grace from the king, albeit founded on justice, *une grâce fondée en justice.* The printer/publisher, however, was a mere manufacturer and businessman. He could demand a privilege to protect his investment during a short and limited time, not more.

The physiocrats, however, were no friends of a general freedom of expression. The public discussion between enlightened men was important, but to let in the rabble of ordinary scribblers could be dangerous. As a matter of fact, *l'ancien régime* was incapable of a conclusive reform as long as censorship prevailed. And censorship was not even openly contested by the *philosophes* themselves, soon beneficiaries of sinecures and perquisites within the generalized system of patronage. And so censorship prevailed, and the physiocratic reforms succeeded as little in saving the French monarchy as in triggering off the birth of authors' rights in France.

The opening shot for a new era was fired in 1788 by the convocation of the General Estates. The electoral councils formulated their claims and directed them to a nascent public opinion. The censorship system crumbled overnight. The self-declared National Assembly, urged by Sieyès, open-handedly abolished all privileges, echoing the principles behind the *Statute of Monopolies.* Paris was flown over by pamphlets from newly established printing shops and the venerable Association of Paris Printers went the same way as the Stationers' Company. Reprinting became ubiquitous. Ruin and anarchy threatened the thitherto dominant Paris publishers.

Something had to be done, and the two men dominating the subsequent proceedings were Sieyès and Condorcet, more cast in a Rousseauan than a Lockeian mould. To them, the freedom to form an enlightened public opinion was both a pillar of the new constitutional structure and a natural right. This freedom entailed responsibility, and responsibility, in its turn, entailed rights. Not necessarily, despite the rhetoric, a natural right to a perpetual property.

The initiating spark was the necessity to delimit the borders of the new freedom of expression and to define the consequent responsibility. The connected rights had to be weighed in a compromise between the conflicting interests of a public domain and reasonable incentives for authors and publishers. The public interest should be decisive. The outcome was the famous revolutionary decrees on copyright. In 1791, the National Assembly enacted a statutory performing right for the life of the author and five years after his death. In 1793, the Convention followed up with a right of reproduction along the same lines. As in England, what provoked the advent of authors' rights was the abolition of censorship and the urge for general codification in replacement of discretionary administration.

6 GERMAN-SPEAKING TERRITORIES

In the German lands, the printing privileges never became nearly as effective instruments to solve the problem of reprinting as in England and France. The German-speaking territory was too big, too divided and too loosely governed to allow for the erection of the same impressive constructions for regulation and censorship as in England and France. The Emperors, the Princes and the Churches (Catholic and Protestant) all fought for predominance in the system. As the religious boundaries stiffened and the principalities, bishoprics and independent cities asserted themselves as all but sovereign, a split emerged between a more expansive, protestant and national book industry centred around Leipzig and its book fair in the north and a more conservative, Catholic one in Frankfurt. The expansive Saxon printers soon took the lead, and a generalized system of printing privileges was introduced for Leipzig at an early stage. Some other cities followed suit, but so did intra-German reprinting, soon elevated to official government policy in Austria. As elsewhere, privileges were tied to censorship.

In Northern Germany, Prussia in the late eighteenth century in principle outlawed reprinting and launched the idea of reciprocal agreements as a means to create bigger markets and repressing reprinting, which was seen as an obstacle to the expansion of the printing industry. As in England and in France, publishers initiated a campaign for a perpetual literary property right, evidently constructed along Lockeian lines. In academic circles, the need for legislation against reprinting became widely acknowledged.

Fire support came from philosophical quarters. Kant, in his two connected essays, mentioned earlier, declared the supremacy of enlightened public opinion, the right to freely form that opinion and the logical necessity to regard the author as owner of his own message to the public. Fichte contributed by dissecting the intrinsic difference between form and idea, thereby dissociating the right to a text from the patent to an invention.

Fear of the revolutionary events in France, however, led to a sharpening of censorship, and for that purpose imperial prerogatives were strengthened, for the first time since the Reformation. But subsequent war also released an urge for German reassertion of which the call for the forming of German public opinion was an important element. As the French armies were leaving Germany, more liberal constitutions including freedom of the press, and, as a corollary, authors' rights, were prepared. In some cases, as in the Duchy of Nassau, they were also enacted. A sequence of events similar to those in England and France for a moment seemed possible and natural. But reaction, championed by Austria, soon got the upper hand.

The German Federation that arose in the wake of the Napoleonic wars had few real prerogatives, but censorship and authors' rights were two of them, and they were intertwined. Already at the Vienna Congress, the North German publishers tried to achieve the recognition of pan-German proprietory literary rights. Considered by the Austrian government as suspiciously connected with the high-flying hopes for real German unification under liberal auspices, this attempt was delayed.

As the political atmosphere hardened, Austrian policy retrograded to nothing less than the establishment, along the lines of Elizabethan England or the France of Louis XIV, of a pan-German government-controlled corporate regulation of literature where the publishers were asked to become instruments of censorship in exchange for monopoly and the regulation of reprinting. Since reprinting from Austria was a serious problem for the North German publishers, this was constructed as a tempting offer.

This Austrian attitude succeeded in delaying the introduction of authors' rights on a pan-German scale for three decades. There was, however, no way back to the seventeenth century. However, with authors' rights now well established in Europe and the products of the rapidly expanding and technically revolutionized printing industry flooding the market, reprinting within Germany appeared a complete anomaly. Prussia then aligned her policy on copyright along the lines of the simultaneously initiated policy of a North German Customs' Federation. Other German states were offered reciprocal agreements, and a Prussian law on authors' rights, the most advanced in the world so far, was prepared. The relinquishment of the intertwining of censorship and authors' rights finally made possible a pan-German system of time-limited authors' rights along Prussian principles.

The abortive Frankfurt Constitution of Germany of 1848 proclaimed freedom of the press, the author's responsibility and authors' rights. This Constitution proved to be short-lived, but authors' rights prevailed. As in England, France and Sweden, abolition of censorship and introduction of authors' rights were closely connected.

7 CONCLUSION

To conclude, the political systems that supported censorship were prepared to satisfy the demands from printers for perpetual monopolies and protection against reprinting in exchange for loyal participation in the system of control. For that purpose, generalized systems of privileges were efficient and sufficient. The system of classical censorship crumbled when 'man stepped out of his self-imposed minority' (Kant). The examples from Venice, England, France, Sweden and Germany support the observation that the abolition of censorship was an important releasing factor to the destruction of the guild-based monopolies and the introduction of authors' rights. When the printers' pernicious *monopolia* had to be transformed into justified *privilegia* and turned into comprehensive codification, the responsibility of the author for his words had to be clarified. Then the only conceivable point of attachment was the author, now emancipated from tutelage and responsible for his works.

It stands to reason that censorship conserves patronage and that authors' rights are a prerequisite for emancipated literature. Reintroduced censorship deprives the author of free access to the market which is an essential requisite of his rights. At best, they remain in truncated form. Patronage is then back again, and corporations with them.

The abolition of censorship functioned as a midwife to the birth of modern copyright law. But this happy event, alas, was no guarantee against a relapse into authoritarian control systems. Indeed, this is what happened in France as early as 1810, not to speak of more recent totalitarian precedents. The systems introduced simultaneously in the 1930s in Nazi Germany and the Soviet Union bore much resemblance to the earlier Venetian, English, French and Swedish systems of censorship, guild control and privilege. In its modern variants, the systems formally maintained an author's right. But the author was denied free access to his market, his words were strictly controlled and his economic remuneration set at discretion or withheld by the *Reichskulturkammer* or the *Vsesoyuznoye Upravleniye Oboroniy Avtorskih Prav, VUOAP*.

As a matter of fact, authors' rights can never come to terms with censorship, and authors' rights are a prerequisite for real freedom of expression. Some claim, maybe rightly, that history has no meaning. But historical phenomena and events can certainly be of meaningful significance. The fall of classical censorship was one, but not the only, precondition for letting the spirit of the free word out of its bottle. To this there had to be added the hope and the capacity, solidly backed by economic rights, of leaving the slavery of patronage and dependence. That is, real authors' rights.

8. From privilege to modern copyright law

Martin Vogel*

1 INTRODUCTION

When the Statute of Anne was enacted 300 years ago, England was on its way to becoming a global power. Meanwhile, the Holy Roman Empire was still wrestling with the consequences of the Thirty Years' War of 1618–1648: it had lost 30 per cent of its population and a significant proportion of its economic power. The book trade alone had been hit so hard that book production only reached pre-war levels in the middle of the eighteenth century.

The peace treaty of Münster and Osnabrück in 1648 set the seal on a remarkable reduction of the Emperor's power. It not only gave the sovereigns of the territorial states within the Empire the right to determine which religious denomination they adhered to, but also gave the law of the respective territory precedence over the law of the Empire. This had significant consequences for the book trade, since until then the printing privileges issued by the Emperor had granted protection against reprinting of books throughout the whole nation. With the peace of 1648, this changed in that the privileges granted by the Emperor lost ground in the face of territorial privileges.

2 THE LEIPZIG BOOK FAIR

Saxony – both a home to printing presses and Leipzig as a book-trade centre – exploited this situation in order to put publishing in its territory at the centre of book production in the Holy Roman Empire. Saxony achieved this by granting generous and attractive electoral privileges under Saxony's Statute of 1685 and amended in 1773. This statute

* Dr Martin Vogel, European Patent Office, Munich.

provided for a simple registration procedure combined with only light censorship. The privilege granted an industrial property right even to those who had merely had a book printed in Saxony.

At that time, in practice all booksellers needed a Saxon privilege for all their books. Only those who had applied for the protection of a privilege at the Leipzig book fair had any defence there against the economically damaging reprinting of their books. Everyone had to go to the fair twice a year, at Easter and Michaelmas. The reason for this was that the book trade in the German-speaking world was founded on the traditional barter principle. In practice, this meant that such barter could only take place at the fair, with the booksellers exchanging the books they published for those of their colleagues on the spot. This meant that each bookseller brought his books to the fair, exchanged them for the books of other publishers, and returned home with a varied selection of swaps. The barter value of a book was determined not by its content but by an estimate of its production cost. This meant that not much money changed hands.

The barter system operated successfully provided that the authors were under the patronage of the princely courts or had an income from work as officials, or in the church or in academia. Royalties were still modest at this time. From around 1750, this began to change: the proportion of church and scientific book production fell, while works intended for entertainment or practical information increased.

This was the time when writers started to work for a free market. Released from the patronage of the courts and the churches they wrote successful books of this kind to satisfy the taste of the rising middle classes and demanded a greater share of the earnings from their books from the publisher.

This meant that costs grew, particularly for those publishers in the primarily Protestant and liberal north of the Holy Roman Empire who had made the most of these more advantageous conditions for authors by paying higher royalties to the sought-after writers of secular literature under contract to them. Intellectual life in the conservative, Catholic South, where book production was still centred on traditional literature of all kinds, lacked the necessary conditions for this development.

Higher royalties for authors led to greater financial pressure on North German publishers and made them unwilling to continue to exchange their books for the (often religious) slow-selling lines from Southern booksellers. For the book trade in South Germany, this seemed tantamount to a declaration of war and threatened the very existence of the trade there. For this reason, publishers – particularly in the South – began systematically to reprint the successful works from the North and to sell them through different channels, avoiding the Leipzig fair, where the original books were protected by privilege. All this was done with the blessing of the authorities, particularly in Austria, Württemberg and Baden.

3 NATURAL LAW AS A NEW (LEGAL) BASIS

To put a stop to reprinting, North German publishers were forced to seek a sound legal basis that would protect their books from being reprinted even in places where they had not applied for a privilege. To this end, and supported by the publications of J S Pütter, professor at the University of Göttingen, publishers started to rely primarily on agreements by which the author transferred the intellectual property in his work to them.

The question of property in printed works had already been debated since the end of the seventeenth century, but this initially referred only to ownership of the printed book itself and later to an industrial property based on the economic effort made by the publisher. However, by the last third of the eighteenth century, it was the intellectual property of the author in his work, which arose as part of 'natural law' (Pütter) that had to be respected in all territories, regardless of any privilege or statute. The reasoning put forward at that time was simple: an author has ownership of his work, just as a potter has ownership of the pot he has made. The intellectual property that the publisher had rightfully acquired from the author helped to legitimise his claim against reprinters, even without the protection of a privilege.

However, intellectual property was not universally recognised. It was widely held that ownership only applied to material goods. Consequently reprinting was permitted in the absence of privileges. Furthermore, little was said about what was included in the right of intellectual property as a concept. In fact, other than ownership in objects it should be understood as comprehensive and not limited by time. Of course, this left countless questions unanswered, and these were fiercely debated well into the nineteenth century by lawyers, philosophers, publishers and authors. The concept of the similarity between the ownership of goods and intellectual property was repeatedly tested by the limits of its credibility, the more so since many considered that the reprinting of books was conducive to educating the general public.

The ongoing discussion about the nature and consequently the scope of authors' rights, from which in fact all beneficiaries derived their rights, proved progressively to erode the initial similarity between intellectual property and the ownership of material objects. Should the original publisher of a work really be authorised – as a result of his acquired intellectual property – to prevent the complete oeuvre of the author from being published in perpetuity? How could the notion of intellectual property be reconciled with recognition of the right to perform a work and with the limitation of the right in time? Did intellectual property only apply to a work in its identical form but not to an adaptation or translation?

4 THE HISTORICAL LAW SCHOOL

Under the growing influence of the so-called school of historical law, which was sceptical about natural law and harked back to the Roman and *ius commune* roots of the law, the doctrine of ownership was deemed inapplicable to immaterial goods. Numerous new theories were developed. Some considered copyright law to be merely a reaction born out of privilege or legal prohibitions on reprinting; whereas for others it had the force of a generalised privilege that only provided protection if it was established by a legislative act, as a result of cultural or economic practical considerations. Yet others understood it as a right that was based in the legal capacity of a person, which meant that reprinting was regarded as an offence against the person of the author; and another group considered that the essence of copyright lay in the authorisation held by the publisher to print a work and his ability to prohibit its being reprinted.

5 COPYRIGHT LEGISLATION

It is clear from legislation since the end of the eighteenth century that theoretical discussions had only a limited influence on practice. Two examples among others: in 1794, the Prussian Statute Book brought into force detailed regulations on publishing agreements. However, the Prussian legislation did not define the rights of the author in his role as partner to an agreement with the publisher. In 1809, during the Napoleonic occupation, the Baden Civil Code came into force widely followed by the French *Code Civil*. Unlike the French code the Baden Code added copyright provisions to the chapter of property. It determined copyright as a property right of the author, limited for the first time in Germany to lifetime pursuant to a contemporary rule saying: If the head falls into the grave, the work falls into the public domain.

The Congress of Vienna of 1815 laid the foundations for the German Confederation. Its Final Act put an obligation on the states to prohibit the reprinting of books. However, efforts to put an end to reprinting proceeded only haltingly in the Confederation. Initially, Austria wanted to link the prohibition on reprinting to censorship, but later the rivalry between Austria and Prussia made it difficult to draft a resolution quickly. This prompted Prussia to conclude individual agreements on book reprinting with more than 30 other states in the German Confederation. Only after lengthy negotiations a resolution of the Confederation in 1835 did prohibit reprinting throughout its whole territory. This happened at a time when the publication of original works was more lucrative than the reprinting of foreign books – even in the South of Germany, and Württemberg in particular.

Two years later, in 1837, Prussia enacted the most modern at that time copyright legislation in the German Confederation. It was the Law for the Protection of Property in Works of Scholarship and the Arts against Reprinting and Reproduction. Conventionally, this statute remained dominated by the topic of reprinting, but also focussed on artistic works, on personal rights and granted the author rights which were far-reaching for that time: right of reproduction, right of distribution, performing rights in unprinted dramatic and musical works, and the right to publish his work. All these rights were granted not only in respect of published but also of unpublished works for 30 years *post mortem auctoris*.

This was an important step which was followed by further measures testifying to a clearer view of the concept of author's right. In the following years several agreements were adopted by the German Confederation raising the bar of protection according to the corner stones of the Prussian legislation.

The Prussian Copyright Act inspired further laws in the various territories, such as those of Saxony (1844), Bavaria (1865) – which already took the modern approach of protecting photography – and in particular the Copyright Act of the North German Confederation (1870), which was adopted by the German Empire the following year.

6 IMPORTANT DEVELOPMENTS IN THE LATE NINETEENTH CENTURY

In the second half of the nineteenth century, three important developments set their stamp on the history of copyright in Germany. (1) From a theoretical point of view, the interpretation of author's right as a personal right became dominant. (2) Seen politically, even before the Berne Convention was established in 1886, a growing number of bilateral agreements which primarily addressed the regulation of translation and the cross-border protection of musical works came into being. (3) At national level, the invention of sound recordings meant that performing artists were replaced by sound recordings and in consequence created social problems whereas the composers were excluded from any royalties for this new form of exploitation due to unfair contracts with the music publishers. Professional associations of authors and performers were founded. The ALAI began to lobby for stronger rights for the authors. But the Copyright Act of 1901 still did not address these problems. On the contrary, the law on publishers' agreements of the same year took as its basis complete freedom of contract. It was left to the courts to ensure that agreements heavily in favour of the stronger party were settled fairly, in that the scope of the rights transferred thereby was determined by the purpose of the contract. Furthermore, the moral rights relating to recognition of the author and the integrity of his work were first accorded to him not by legislation but by the German Imperial Court.

7 THE TWENTIETH CENTURY

At the end of the 1920s – still before the Nazi-era – academics and practitioners once again presented drafts for a reform of the Copyright Act that had the aim of transforming the results of the Revisions of the Berne Convention into national law. However, no more real progress was made after 1933. Free intellectual life came to a halt. Jewish copyright holders were expropriated of their rights, and the books of democratically minded authors were burnt. Many Jewish academics specialising in IP law had – like Jewish writers – to leave Germany or were murdered.

In the post-war period, this cataclysm led legal thought in Germany to a return to the concepts of natural law. The idea of intellectual property was revived under this banner, no longer to characterise copyright law per se but simply with the aim of achieving fairness, in the form of a law that comprehensively protected constitutionally guaranteed moral and economic rights of the author. The law of 1965, which has been revised many times is based on this principle. Most of the amendments became necessary because for almost 20 years developments of copyright law in Europe have been determined centrally by the authorities of the European Union. The more copyright law in Europe is harmonised the more the individual character of national copyright law becomes cloudy.

9. The influence (past and present) of the Statute of Anne in France

Christophe Geiger*

1 INTRODUCTION

It is a difficult, almost impossible task to analyse the influence of the Statute of Anne in France from a historical point of view and from the point of view of the current legal context. This is due to several reasons.

The first reason is that it is very difficult to clearly establish a direct influence of the Statute of Anne in France. First of all, from a historical point of view, nothing indicates a direct connection with the subsequent French legislation, neither with the King's Council's rulings of 1777 and 1778, nor after the Revolution with the laws of 1791 and 1793. Certainly, as Laurent Pfister and Frédéric Rideau[1] rightly stated, the Statute of Anne was sometimes quoted by certain participants in the debates which led to the French legislation, and we may assume that the British law was known in France. The problem is that we cannot find explicit reference, neither in the preliminary works nor in the rapporteurs' statements allowing us to establish any influence. Since a direct connection seems uncertain from the very beginning, it becomes even more difficult to establish a direct relation with the current legislation. For instance, it is rather evident that the brand new French law regarding file-sharing on the Internet is not directly inspired by the British legislation elaborated in the early eighteenth century and does

* Associate Professor; General Director and Director of the Research Laboratory, Centre for International Intellectual Property Studies (CEIPI), University of Strasbourg University; Senior Researcher at the Max Planck Institute for Intellectual Property, Competition and Tax law, Munich. This contribution was originally written in French. The original version can be found on the website of the British Literary and Artistic Copyright Association (BLACA): www.blaca.org.uk.

[1] See the excellent section about history in the French national report for the ALAI Congress 2009 written by L. Pfister and F. Rideau, 'National Report, France', on the website of the British Literary and Artistic Copyright Association (BLACA): www.blaca.org.

not refer to it. In fact, it is possible that its principles might have considerably evolved in France over the past centuries.

The second difficulty in addressing this subject is that both the Statute of Anne and the first French copyright laws have been, and continue to be, the subject of an important debate and the object of very diverse, sometimes radically opposite, interpretations. It is thus very difficult to establish an influence when the principles of the hypothetical model are dramatically contested and when the interpretations of the subsequent legislations are also divergent. In spite of these doubts, it is nevertheless possible to conclude with certainty that the slightly caricatural thesis, frequently pointed up in the past, according to which there would be a radical opposition between, on the one hand, a British copyright legislation protecting only the publisher, with a purely utilitarian logic, and, on the other hand, a French legislation focusing on authors and their natural right over 'the most sacred of all properties', (to mention a passage of the rapporteur of the often quoted le Chapelier revolutionary law), is nowadays outdated; in particular since some stimulating and very elaborate works demonstrated the numerous common points shared by both systems from the very beginning.[2] In France, Frédéric Rideau clearly demonstrated in his excellent thesis on the formation of literary and artistic property laws in France and Great Britain, that there is 'a forgotten convergence'[3] between the two systems.

Thus, since we cannot clearly establish the influence of the Statute of Anne on French law, should we, as Mr Rideau did, not look for a certain *convergence*? This way, we might find a number of interesting leads, which will enable us to attempt to draw useful conclusions for the

2 See especially A. Strowel (1993), '*Droit d'auteur et copyright, Divergences et convergences*', Brussels/Paris Bruylant & LGDJ, and, by the same author (1998), 'Convergences entre droit d'auteur et copyright dans la société de l'information', in: Intergu (ed), *Schutz von Kultur und geistigem Eigentum in der Informationsgesellschaft*, Baden-Baden: Nomos, p. 59; (1994) 'Droit d'auteur and Copyright: Between History and Nature', in: B. Sherman and A. Strowel (eds), *Of Authors and Origins*, Oxford: Clarendon Press, p. 10; J. C. Ginsburg (1991), 'A Tale of Two Copyrights: Literary Property in Revolutionary France and America', 147 RIDA 125; G. Davies (1995), 'The Convergence of Copyright and Authors Rights – Reality or Chimera?', IIC 964, and, by the same author (2002), *Copyright and the Public Interest*, 2nd edn, London: Sweet & Maxwell, p. 348 et seq.; P. Goldstein (1994), *Copyright's Highway – The Law and Lore of Copyright from Gutenberg to the Celestial Jukebox*, New York: Hill and Wang, p. 170.

3 F. Rideau (2004), *La formation du droit de la propriété littéraire en France et en Grande-Bretagne: une convergence oubliée*, Aix-en-Provence: PUAM.

historical as well as the current analysis of copyright legislation, whether it is French or British, because it is not impossible conversely that an analysis of the French context might bring to light certain principles of the Statute of Anne (accordingly, it might also be interesting to study the historical influence of French legislation on the Statute of Anne and its understanding).

Indeed, it is necessary to note that the birth of copyright in Great Britain and France occurs in very similar contexts and that they share numerous similarities at multiple levels. First of all, the Statute of Anne as well as the first 'modern'[4] French copyright legislation emerged in a very similar philosophical context, with the rise of the ideas of the Enlightenment and the progressive emancipation of the minds, as opposed to a public speech controlled by the monarchy. Later on, the development of more liberal economic ideas would bring about an increasing questioning of corporatist monopolies, emphasizing the benefits of competition for the production of new goods. A growing education of the bourgeoisie follows, which entails an increasing demand for works, the knowledge becoming accessible and starting to spreading through reading and writing. And at last, throughout the eighteenth century,[5] both countries experience a similar economic structure of the publishing market with a marked supremacy of booksellers from the capital (London and Paris) over the booksellers of the provinces. This will bring about a conflict between these two actors, which will have important consequences over the legislation of both countries.[6] These ideological, philosophic and economic convergences are responsible for the existence of a number of common points between the two legislations, in spite of numerous doubts, based on the various interpretations of certain texts and on some historical uncertainties (section 2). The analysis of these similarities will allow us to extract certain hypotheses, from which we will be able to cautiously deduct a certain number of principles for the current analysis of contemporary copyright (section 3).

---

[4] There is a controversy as to whether it is the 1777 rulings of the King or the revolutionary decrees that constitute the first 'modern' legislation on copyright; a controversy to which we shall not go back to here. See L. Pfister and F. Rideau, 'National Report, France', *supra* note 1.

[5] L. Pfister and F. Rideau, 'National Report, France', *supra* note 1.

[6] This has often been called the 'Battle of the Booksellers' (M. Rose (1993), *Authors and Owners: The Invention of Copyright*, Cambridge, MA and London: Harvard University Press, p. 67) and/or la 'Bataille des Libraires' (B. Edelman (2004), *Le sacre de l'auteur*, Paris: Editions du Seuil, p. 237).

2 THE HISTORICAL ANALYSIS: COMMON POINTS BETWEEN THE STATUTE OF ANNE AND THE EIGHTEENTH CENTURY FRENCH COPYRIGHT LEGISLATION, AND RELATED DOUBTS

In spite of a certain number of convergences, there are also numerous uncertainties, which are particularly due to the fact that certain notions have not been 'clarified' yet, because they have not been clearly defined. Furthermore, at this time, legal speech was sometimes intermingled with philosophic and political speech. However, the birth of copyright in both countries occurs within a common context and the British and French laws share two characteristics: they are both aimed at the spreading of knowledge, and the position of authors is unclear within the device.

2.1 The Author's Unclear Position Within the Legislative Device

At the time, the author was the object of an utter instrumentalization. Indeed, as Bernard Edelman stated, 'copyright was born from an economic battle in which authors were, paradoxically, the big absentees'.[7] In the United Kingdom, the Statute of Anne followed upon the abrogation, in 1695, of the printing monopoly held by the Stationers' Company, the members of which were the only ones authorized to print works. In order to increase the production of books and break the monopoly the Stationers still enjoyed in practice, the crown granted authors and publishers a printing permission limited in time.[8] Likewise, in France, with most privileges in the hands of the Paris booksellers, the crown became aware of the need to create some competition in the field of publishing, in order to increase the number of works printed. Thus, starting in 1720, it stopped the systematic extension of the Paris booksellers' privileges, even cancelling some of them. It is in this context that the London and Paris booksellers, the first to escape the limited duration of the right conferred by

---

[7] B. Edelman, *Le sacre de l'auteur*, *supra* note 6, at p. 172.

[8] See L. R. Patterson (1968), *Copyright in Historical Perspective*, Nashville: Vanderbilt University Press, at p. 147, for whom the championing of the author was purely motivated by the circumstances and a desire to cut short the Stationers' Company's monopoly: 'Emphasis on the author in the Statute of Anne implying that the statutory copyright was an author's copyright was more a matter of form than of substance. The monopolies at which the statute was aimed were too long established to be attacked without some basic change. The most logical and natural basis for the changes was the author (. . .). The author was used primarily as a weapon against monopoly'.

the 1710 law[9] and the latter with the fragility of their privilege[10] in mind, have developed a rhetoric around the rights of the author, rights that the author allegedly held, not by virtue of the law, but of a higher principle of justice, which were then transferred to the publisher. In Great Britain this becomes the upholding of a 'common law copyright' as opposed to the previous legal monopoly, a debate that would continue through the eighteenth century, until it was cut short by the House of Lords in its famous 1774 *Donaldson v. Beckett* ruling.[11] This caused Mark Rose to write that 'it might be said that the London booksellers invented the modern proprietary author, constructing him as a weapon in their struggle with the booksellers of the provinces'.[12] In France, the Paris booksellers first commissioned a famous lawyer called Louis d'Héricourt,[13] and then a number of philosophers of the Enlightenment, such as Diderot, to draft texts in favour of a natural right of property of authors over their works. Thus, Diderot writes in his 1767 historical and political letter to a magistrate on the book trade: 'I repeat, either the author is master of his work or no one in society is master of his property. The bookseller owns the work as the

---

9 F. Rideau (2004), *La formation du droit de la propriété littéraire en France et en Grande-Bretagne: une convergence oubliée*, *supra* note 3, at p. 157 et seq.

10 L. Pfister (1999), 'L'auteur, propriétaire de son œuvre? La formation du droit d'auteur du XVIe siècle à la loi de 1957', Thesis of the University of Strasbourg, at p. 207.

11 *Donaldson v. Beckett* (1774), included in L. Bently and M. Kretschmer (eds) (2008), 'Primary Sources on Copyright (1450–1900)', (www.copyright history.org), with a comment by R. Deazley. See also, linking to current legal developments, R. Deazley, 'Re-reading Donaldson (1774) in the Twenty-First Century and Why it Matters', 2003 *EIPR* 273.

12 M. Rose (1994), 'The Author as Proprietor: *Donaldson v. Beckett* and the Genealogy of the Modern Authorship', in B. Sherman and A. Strowel (eds), *Of Authors and Origins*, Oxford: Clarendon Press, at p. 30: 'Putting it badly, and exaggerating for the sake of clarity, it might be said that the London booksellers invented the modern author, constructing him as a weapon in their struggle with the booksellers of the provinces'.

13 In a 1725 memoir, he writes: 'A manuscript which contains nothing against religion, nor against state laws or the interest of private individuals is, in the author's full right, a property of his own, because it is the fruit of his work, which is personally his, and he should have the freedom to dispose of it as he pleases, in pursuit of the honour for which he hopes or a profit that may satisfy his material needs, and even those of the persons related to him by blood, friendship or gratitude. . .If an author is the standing owner and consequently the sole master of his work, only he or those who represent him have the right to pass it on, granting it even above the right formerly possessed by the author', quoted by A.-C. Renouard (1838), *Traité des droits d'auteurs, dans la littérature, les sciences et les beaux arts*, Vol. 1, Paris: Jules Renouard and Co, at p. 157.

author owned it'.[14] As a reaction, the booksellers from the provinces are going to uphold, against the natural right of the author, the idea of a social contract,[15] by virtue of which the State grants the author (or the publisher) a temporary monopoly in exchange for making the work known, as a source of enrichment for the community. Within this conception, authors become a sort of worker who is remunerated for rendering a service to the community.

This ambiguity regarding the role of the author and the precise foundations of the exclusive right over literary material can be found both in the Statute of Anne[16] and in the later revolutionary legislation. The 1710 legislation grants a right to the benefit of the author, but does not give him a particular status, systematically associating him to the publisher. It creates a 21-year term for all works already in print at the time of its enactment and a renewable 14-year term for all works published subsequently. The 'proprietary' right is clearly evoked, but, as Ronan Deazley rightly emphasizes,[17] it is not defined in any way, and the scope that should be granted this de facto recognition is thus not established. This is especially true since the concept of 'property' in 'common law' countries is not necessarily identical to the civil law concept of property.[18]

---

14 D. Diderot (1876), 'Lettre historique et politique adressée à un magistrat sur le commerce de la librairie', in *Œuvres complètes de Diderot*, Vol. 18, Paris: Garnier Frères, p. 30.

15 See L. Pfister and F. Rideau, 'National report, France', *supra* note 1, who refer to the report by the lawyer Gaulthier, written for the booksellers of the provinces in 1786: 'Mémoire à consulter, Pour les Libraires et Imprimeurs de Lyon, Rouen, Toulouse, Marseille, Nismes, concernant les privilèges de Librairie, et continuations d'iceux', National Library, French Manuscripts 22073, n° 144; F. Rideau, *La formation du droit de la propriété littéraire en France et en Grande Bretagne: une convergence oubliée*, *supra* note 3, at p. 104 et seq. See also B Edelman, *Le sacre de l'auteur*, *supra* note 7, at p. 265, acccording to whom, the social contract figure was born from a 'very precise conjuncture, in a crucial phase of the struggle between the booksellers of Paris and the provinces [. . .] Literary property was a major obstacle for the rebirth of the bookstores from the provinces.'

16 On this issue, see W. Cornish, 'The History of the Statute of Anne 1709–1710', Paper presented at the ALAI 2009 Study Days, London (in this volume); F. Rideau, *La formation du droit de la propriété littéraire en France et en Grande-Bretagne: une convergence oubliée*, *supra* note 3, at p. 178; P. Drahos (1996), *A Philosophy of Intellectual Property*, Aldershot: Ashgate, p. 28.

17 R. Deazley, 'Commentary on the Statute of Anne, United Kingdom (1710)', in: L. Bently and M. Kretschmer (eds) (2008), *Primary Sources on Copyright (1450–1900)*, No. 6 (www.copyright history.org).

18 See on this issue Alain Strowel's interesting developments in his work (1993): *Droit d'auteur et copyright, Divergences et convergences*, *supra* note 2.

And then, regarding the question as to whether the law grants authors a pre-existing right or a temporary monopoly, in the context of a purely utilitarian logic, the law remains equally obscure and can be the object of divergent interpretations.[19] Certainly, the title of the law, as it was initially foreseen as a law aiming at 'securing' the property of copies in books, was then modified and became 'An Act for the Encouragement of Learning, by *vesting* the Copies of Printed Books in the Authors or purchasers of such Copies, during the Times therein mentioned', which seems to validate the monopoly-approach given by the law. However, as Ronan Deazley pointed out, the preamble of the Statute of Anne's second section goes back to the old formula, establishing that the property over books is 'secured' for the benefit of its owner.[20]

The same uncertainty about the role of the author is also found in the Revolutionary legislation. Of course, the nature of copyright as a proprietary right is sometimes greatly emphasized. This is the case of the so-often quoted statements from the rapporteur of the French decree Le Chapelier about 'the most sacred, the most indisputable, and the most personal of all properties'.[21] Notwithstanding, as certain scholars have pointed out, notably Jane Ginsburg in a famous article published by the *Revue Internationale du Droit d'Auteur*, these comments have often been accompanied by some very utilitarian considerations, which highlighted the importance of the limitation of the duration of copyright and its purpose: to serve the community's interest in the production of useful works.[22] Moreover, in that very same section, Le Chapelier continues by emphasizing that what is being dealt with is, indeed, 'a property of a different kind from all the other properties. Once the author has disclosed the work to the public, when the work is in the hands of everyone, when all educated men know it and have imbued it with happy memories, it seems that since then, the writer has affiliated the public with his property, or rather has fully transmitted his property to the public'.[23] It cannot be said that the author is actually vested with a privileged status, as the duration of the

---

19 See, regarding this matter M. Rose (1993), *Authors and Owners: The Invention of Copyright*, *supra* note 6, p. 48: 'The Statute of Anne did not settle the theoretical questions behind the notion of literary property'.

20 R. Deazley, *supra* note 17, n° 6.

21 As it was rightly noticed by Prof. Ginsburg, *supra* note 3, at p. 158, fn. 46, this passage is consistently quoted by the French doctrine outside its context, enumerating some famous reference works. From this, she concludes that these scholars wrongfully tried to emphasize that Le Chapelier's declaration furnished an apparent proof for the concept of an 'author centred' copyright legislation.

22 J. C. Ginsburg (1991), *supra* note 3.

23 See *Le Moniteur Universel*, 15 January 1791, at p. 117.

right remains short (respectively 5 and 10 years after the author's death). It would thus seem that the notion of 'property' has replaced the concept of privilege, without being in the presence of a true break. Besides, this continuity is clearly expressed by Le Chapelier: 'this is what was formerly done in France because of the privileges granted by the King, and which will now be prescribed by law, a much wiser way and the only appropriate one to be used'.[24] At this point, there are still absolutely no signs of a protective contract law for the author, nor of moral right; these will not appear until much later, during the nineteenth century.

2.2 The Will to Avoid Censorship and Disseminate Knowledge

The second common point between Great Britain and France is linked to the eighteenth century, the advent of the philosophy of the Enlightenment and the will to circumvent Royal censorship. In fact, the Enlightenment philosophers, who gradually became ardent defenders of authors' rights over their works, mostly conceived copyright as a guarantee for freedom of expression. To them, granting copyright to authors was allowing the dissemination of ideas and knowledge, the author being endowed with an educational mission, in charge of 'enlightening' the population. However, the granting of royal privileges was often preceded by a control of the works' content.[25] Hence, there was the need to find a stand-alone justification, namely, the author's proprietary right. Besides, in the eighteenth century discourse, property was closely linked to the concept of freedom and represented a guarantee of autonomy from the king.[26] The goal of the dissemination of knowledge can be found in both British and French legislations. This is explicitly established/put forward in the Statute of Anne, which is even titled 'Act for the Encouragement of Learning'. Similarly,

---

24 A Kéréver (1989) states in this sense that 'the revolutionary legislators, men of law and order, wished to provide "booksellers" (publishers) and "performers" (disseminators) with a legitimate legal framework against piracy [. . .] Hence, there was a double transposition: what was once the king's prerogative, by divine right, became henceforth the law, modern shape of sovereignty, and the natural right, i.e. the author's ability to determine the rights over his work, within the limits defined by the law. Secondarily, the replacement of privilege, a one-sided act depending on the sovereign's desires, by a contract signed between two legally *equal* persons, acting in their respective spheres of *freedom* and exchanging attributes of *property* (emphasis in the text)' ('The French Revolution and authors' rights', 141 *RIDA* 3.

25 See for example M-C. Dock (1963), *Étude sur le droit d'auteur*, Paris, *L.G.D.J.* 69.

26 For a more detailed presentation, see Ch. Geiger (2004), *Droit d'auteur et droit du public à l'information, Approche de droit compare*, Paris: Litec, p. 23 et seq.

the preamble emphasizes the need 'for the encouragement of learned men to compose and write useful books'. According to Ronan Deazley, this is the central element of the 1710 law, which primarily seeks to encourage the production and dissemination of new ideas by way of granting either the author or the publisher a legal monopoly, this being indirectly beneficial for the public and the society as a whole.[27] However, there is a doctrinal controversy about this point, because according to other scholars such as Lyman Ray Patterson, the Statute of Anne's main aim was to regulate the book trade in order to break some monopolies held by a minority of London booksellers.[28] According to this view, the Statute of Anne would have less to do with copyright than with competition law.

There is a similar controversy when it comes to the French revolutionary decrees. Though they have been long considered by many scholars as a sacralization of the author, placing him at the centre of the device, there has been over the last 20 years, as Lawrence Pfister and Frédéric Rideau noted, a serious questioning by many historians and law scholars, who 'emphasise the value attributed to public interest, the existence of a legal basis of copyright and an utilitarian inspiration'.[29] In fact, there are many points that demonstrate the legislator's will to closely bind copyright with the dissemination of knowledge. For example, it is important to recall that the second decree of 19 July 1793 was developed by the Committee of Public Instruction, which, translated to our day, would be the Ministry of Education. The social function of copyright law is also repeatedly recalled by the bill's rapporteur, Lakanal. Admittedly, he emphasizes the author's proprietary right; however, it does not deal anymore with the 'most sacred, most personal of properties', but with the 'least susceptible to contest, whose growth cannot harm republican equality, nor cast doubt upon liberty'.[30] Later in his speech, he points out several times the importance

[27] R. Deazley, 'Commentary on the Statute of Anne (1710)', *supra* note 17, No. 5.

[28] L. R. Patterson, *Copyright in Historical Perspective*, *supra* note 8, at p. 150.

[29] L. Pfister and F. Rideau, *National Report, France*, *supra* note 1.

[30] For the complete text of the Lakanal report, see *Le Moniteur Universel*, 21 July 1793, at p. 176. According to Jane Ginsburg (1991), *supra* note 3, at p. 164, 'there is in this rhetoric a lack of security in contradiction with a firm conviction about the central position given to the personal demands of the authors'. This author underlines, moreover, that following the example of the Le Chapelier report, the Lakanal report was also quoted in an incomplete way by the French classic copyright doctrine, 'leaving out the more uncertain passages/sections, namely, those which assert that copyright will not harm the Republic'. This famous Lakanal sentence recalls another famous statement by Lord Macaulay in the nine-

for the community of the granting of copyright: 'In silence, did the genius bring to life a work that pushes back the boundaries of human knowledge, literary pirates seize it immediately, and the author strides towards immortality only through the horrors of misery? [. . .] By what stroke of fate must it be that the man of genius, who devotes his waking hours to the instruction of his fellow citizens, might look forward only to a sterile glory and might not claim the legitimate tribute of such noble work?'

What can we infer from these previous developments for the theory of copyright, as well as for the current debate?

3 CONSEQUENCES OF THE HISTORICAL ANALYSIS FOR THE CURRENT DEBATE ABOUT COPYRIGHT

This historical analysis of the French and British laws allows us to draw conclusions for the current theory as well as the current practice of copyright law. We will now proceed to examine each one in their turn.

3.1 The Consequences on the Foundations of Copyright

The historical analysis of the Statute of Anne and the French laws of the eighteenth century demands caution: we must avoid using schematic reasoning, in view of the numerous uncertainties at hand. Indeed, it clearly

---

teenth century: 'Copyright is a monopoly [. . .] It is good that authors should be remunerated and the least exceptionable way of remunerating them is by a monopoly', quoted by G. Davies (2002), *Copyright and the public interest*, *supra* note 2, at p. 236. These similarities prompt us to consider, with A. Kéréver (1989) (*supra* note 24, at p. 4, that 'copyright designed by the French Revolution is little distinguished from English or American copyright law'. See also, more radical, A. Bertrand, 'Le droit d'auteur et les droits voisins', (2nd edn) (1999), Paris: Dalloz, No. 1121, which stresses that 'while we often oppose the anglo-saxon "copyright" to the French "droit d'auteur", it is undeniable that, in the beginning, French law merely copied the famous "Statute of Anne" from England'. To substantiate his remarks, the author refers to a passage/section in Le Chapelier's speech, in which he justifies the action of the revolutionary legislator: 'This is what is operating in England for authors and the public, by acts called of guardianship, this is what was done in France by means of privileges granted by the King and that will now be set by law, a much wiser way, and the only one that should be used'. Indeed Le Chapelier refers to England. He does not however expressly mention the Statute of Anne. In addition, this (somewhat vague) passage is the sole reference to Great Britain in 26 pages of speech. Therefore, inferring that the Act of 1791 is only a copy of the British legislation from this simple snippet seems too bold a conclusion.

demonstrates that it is impossible to produce clear-cut interpretations and that moderate ones are in order. The study of the first copyright laws also allows us to put the scope of certain notions into perspective, and it seems to indicate that we should not exaggerate the importance of the vocabulary used. In fact, we are in the eighteenth century, immersed in a mutating philosophical context. A large number of much quoted texts have diverse backgrounds, and we often find ourselves in front of a rhetoric, which should be contrasted with a legal reality that is not always in conformity. Furthermore, certain legal concepts are still either faultily defined or in the process of elaboration. The notion of 'property' for example, is still plagued with uncertainties when applied to immaterial assets. In any case, it seems that there was, at the time, no systematic antagonism between the proprietary right and the limited (or even very limited) duration of copyright. There was even, in the eighteenth century, a real complementarity between natural right and utilitarian justifications, between private and collective interest. This complementarity between natural right justifications and a State monopoly is also fully expressed in the preparatory work of the rulings of 1777, in which the privilege in question is defined as a 'grace founded in justice'.[31] In addition, it seems that freedom is intimately related to the concept of ownership, and vice versa. The birth of economic liberalism also plays an important role, and the issue of competition is very present in both the British and French laws. Besides, we should not forget, for example, that the Decree of 13 January 1791 'relating to performances', does not only deal with copyright, since it has the primary object of proclaiming the right of any citizen to open their own theatre and perform plays, thus terminating the monopoly previously enjoyed by the 'Comédie française'. We can find the imprint of the freedom/property dialectic in the French Declaration of Human Rights from 26 August 1789. Taking up the Enlightenment ideas, the Declaration recognizes fundamental rights, at the centre of which is freedom, in the forms of freedom of competition and freedom of expression, and property. Moreover, it is probably not a coincidence that human rights and copyright laws emerged at the same time, because they both present themselves as a synthesis between natural law and utilitarianism. Indeed, even if they are often presented as the concrete expression of natural rights, the sources of these fundamental rights are

---

[31] In a letter from 6 September 1776, prefiguring the rulings of 1777, Louis XVI expresses that the book trade privilege is a 'grace founded in justice; to the author, it is a reward for his labour; to a bookseller, it is a guarantee for his advance payments', quoted by E. Pouillet (1908) in: *Traité théorique et pratique de la propriété littéraire et artistique et du droit de représentation*, 3rd edn, Paris: Imprimerie et Librairie générale de jurisprudence, p. 11 et seq.

much more varied. Besides, their concrete formulations are 'man-made', selected and written on the basis of certain values that society intends to protect, in order to achieve a higher goal; namely, the common good.[32] We can therefore discover a certain instrumental function in the texts related to fundamental rights; a function that is also shared by intellectual property rights. If we look back at the history of copyright law, we can observe that fundamental rights may constitute an effective and particularly balanced foundation for copyright, in line with its own philosophy.[33]

In addition, the finding of these theoretical convergences between copyright 'the French way' and copyright 'the British way' can obviously have a strong symbolic relevance in the context of the future harmonization work of the Community legislator or even for the development of a common Community copyright legislation.[34]

Finally, another lesson learnt from the historical analysis is the importance, from the outset, of the dissemination of knowledge. Nowadays, we are more likely to refer to the access to information or the public's right to information, but the idea is the same. This brings us to the practical consequences.

---

[32] See, in this regard, J. J. Shestak's very stimulating chapter, 'The Philosophical Foundations of Human Rights', in J. Symonides (ed) (2002), *Human Rights: Concept and Standards*, Paris: Unesco/Ashgate publishing, at p. 31 et seq.

[33] Ch. Geiger (2004), *Droit d'auteur et droit du public à l'information, Approche de droit compare*, *supra* note 26, at p. 47 et seq; (2006), '"Constitutionalizing" Intellectual Property Law? The Influence of Fundamental Rights on Intellectual Property in Europe', *IIC* 2006, 371; (2008), 'Intérêt général, droit d'accès à l'information et droit de propriété, La propriété intellectuelle analysée à la lumière des droits fondamentaux', in M. Buydens and S. Dusollier (eds), *L'intérêt général et l'accès à l'information en propriété intellectuelle*, Bruxelles: Bruylant, p. 177.

[34] A certain number of contemporary scholars pronounce themselves in favour of the implementation, following the example of what happened with trademark and designs, of a Community copyright law, see R.M. Hilty (2004), 'Copyright in the Internal Market. Harmonization vs. Community Copyright Law', *IIC* 760; F. Gotzen (2007), 'Copyright in Europe: quo vadis?', 211 *RIDA* 2; P.B. Hugenholtz (2009), 'Copyright without frontiers: the problem of territoriality in European copyright law', in E. Derclaye (ed), *Research Handbook on the Future of EU Copyright*, Cheltenham, UK and Northampton, MA: Edward Elgar, p. 26; Ch. Geiger (2010), 'Drafting the appropriate and balanced scope of copyright protection in the European Union – What language can contribute to the debate', in: Y. Gendreau and A. Drassinower (eds), *Language and copyright/Langue et droit d'auteur*, Quebec/Brussels: Yvon Blais/Bruylant, pp. 59–94.

3.2 The Practical Consequences of Copyright Implementation

Since copyright has been implemented to bypass censorship, we can observe that freedom of expression is still not sufficiently taken into account by the current copyright laws: exceptions are often still inadequate, particularly appropriate exceptions for teaching and research purposes, as well as for informational or creative purposes are still lacking. Moreover, they are still, too often, narrowly interpreted and may be 'disabled' through technical measures.[35] These aspects have been abundantly discussed during the Barcelona ALAI study days.[36] What appears to be even more worrying today: little seems to have evolved for authors since the Statute of Anne from 300 years ago. The interests of authors continue to be put forward by producers to serve their own interests. The rhetoric of the 'poor author' still pays when it comes to expand the legal protection. The directive proposal on the extension of the term of neighbouring rights constitutes a good recent example, with the difference that, this time, it was the performers who were put forward to justify an extension of duration for the benefit of the producers.[37] But, nowadays, how many authors really fairly participate in the exploitation of their works? Contractual copyright is still often non-existent in many legislations and, where it does exist, it has not produced the desired results yet. Moreover, copyright seems totally powerless to prevent a mass digitization of works due to an agreement between a powerful

---

[35] See, in this regard, the considerations of the European Communities Commission's Green Paper, 'Copyright in the Knowledge Economy', Brussels, COM (2008) 466/3. On this text, see Ch. Geiger, F. Macrez, A. Bouvel, S. Carre, T. Hassler and J. Schmidt-Salewski (2009), 'What Limitations to Copyright in the Information Society? A Comment on the European Commission's Green Paper "Copyright in the Knowledge Economy"', *IIC* 412; R. M. Hilty, S. Krujatz, B. Bajon, A. Früh, A. Kur, J. Drexl, Ch. Geiger, N. Klaas (2009), 'European Commission Green Paper: Copyright in the Knowledge Economy, Comments by the Max Planck Institute for Intellectual Property, Competition and Tax Law', *IIC* 309.

[36] See ALADDA (ed) (2008), *Copyright and Freedom of Expression*, ALADDA: Barcelona.

[37] Proposal for a directive amending Directive 2006/116/EC of the European Parliament and of the Council on the term of protection of copyright and related rights, COM(2008) 464 final. This directive proposal started a long wave of protests, notably among University students. See especially the text by Ch. Geiger, J. Passa and M. Vivant and signed by more than 20 French speaking scholars (2009): 'La proposition de directive sur l'extension de la durée de certains droits voisins: une remise en cause injustifiée du domaine public', 31 *Propr. intell.* 146.

search engine and publishers.[38] Where do authors stand in all this? It is the task of the International Literary and Artistic Association (ALAI), whose mission is to protect authors, to finally learn a lesson from history and to rapidly imagine as soon as possible means to increasingly associate authors to the profits generated by the copyright system. Only in this case might copyright have the chance to continue to exist and shine for another 300 years.

---

[38] See the agreement signed in October 2008 by Google (the 'Google-book settlement') with a number of American publishing companies from the Association of American Publishers, with the goal of allowing the complete digitalization of numerous works (especially old and orphaned works, but not only those), in order to make them accessible online, either partially or in full/entirely. For an analysis, see Ch. Geiger (2009), 'The Future of Copyright in Europe: Striking a Fair Balance between Protection and Access to Information', Report for the Committee on Culture, Science and Education – Parliamentary Assembly, Council of Europe, Strasbourg, July 2009. For a commentary (in French) on the 'Google-book settlement', see V.-L. Benabou (2009), 32 *Propr. intell.* 284.

10. The influence of the Statute of Anne on Belgian copyright law

Joris Deene*

1 GENESIS OF THE FIRST BELGIAN COPYRIGHT LAW 1886

Researching the influence of the Statute of Anne on Belgian copyright law is by no means a simple task, as the Kingdom of Belgium as we know it today had only existed since its declaration of independence in 1830. Prior to this the areas, which are now designated as Belgium, were always subject to foreign rule. In this way, in the fifteenth century these areas fell into the hands of the Spanish and Austrian Habsburgs, until they were conquered by France in 1795. After the defeat of Napoleon in 1815 the country was absorbed into the United Kingdom of the Netherlands as a buffer state against France. With the Belgian revolution of 1830, the Kingdom of Belgium became an independent constitutional monarchy. 'Belgian' copyright regulation was therefore more a reflection of foreign regulation, such as, in particular, those of the Netherlands and France.[1]

In this way, shortly after the unification with France in 1795 under the *arrêté des représentants du peuple* of 17 Frimaire IV (19 December 1795), the French decrees of 1791 and 1793 also came into force in the Belgian provinces.[2] At the end of French oppression, the Belgian provinces came under the dominion of the Kingdom of the Netherlands. William I of

* Research Assistant – University of Ghent, Attorney – Ghent Bar.

1 For a more detailled survey of the history of Belgian copyright during the nineteenth century: A. Strowel (1993), *Droit d'auteur et copyright*, Brussels: Bruylant, pp. 39–41; J. Corbet (1986), 'La convention de Berne et la loi belge sur le droit d'auteur', *Droit d'auteur* 220–230; E. Derclaye (2009), 'A historical journey of the linguistic influences in Belgian copyright law: from united to lost in translation?', in Y. Gendreau and A. Drassinower (eds), *Language and copyright*, Brussels: Yvon Blais/Bruylant, pp. 123–147.

2 *Pasinomie: collection complète des lois, décrets, ordonnances, arrêtés et règlements généraux qui peuvent être invoqués en Belgique*, Brussels: Bruylant, série 1, vol. 7, p. L.

Orange Nassau, in the Southern Netherlands with the *arrêté concernant la liberté de presse et règlement pour l'imprimerie, la librairie et les journalistes* of 23 September 1814[3] made French copyright applicable to the Southern Netherlands (today Belgium), subject to a number of amendments. A law of 25 January 1817 enacted copyright regulation for the whole of the Netherlands,[4] (which indeed formulated the first principle of a copyright protection law for the Northern Netherlands). Just like the decree of 1814, this law only applied to works, which were printed in the Kingdom of the Netherlands, so despite protest from French authors and publishers, the Belgian printers stepped up their reprinting activities for French works.[5]

After Belgium had gained its independence, the Dutch law of 1817 as well as those stipulations of the French decree of 1793, which were not lifted by the law of 1817, remained in force. A ruling of the Provisional Government of 21 October 1830 concerning the freedom of theatres regulated the copyright of dramatic works.[6] French works, on the other hand, continued to be copied en masse, to the increasing annoyance of French writers and publishers. Finally, despite vehement protest from Belgian publishers and printers, on 22 August 1852 a treaty was drawn up with France for the protection of copyright and ratified by the Act of 12 April 1854.[7] Further treaties followed with England and the Netherlands in 1854 and 1858.[8] These international treaties on certain points even

---

3 Printed in V. Janlet (1888–1889), *De la protection des oeuvres de la pensée*, Bruxelles: Moens, vol.1, p. 52ff.

4 Wet de regten bepalende die in de Nederlanden, ten opzigte van het drukken en uitgeven van letteren kunstwerken, kunnen worden uitgeoefend van 25 januari 1817, *Staatsblad* 1817, nr. 5 (volume I, 1813–1840, pp. 246ff.); É. Romberg (1859), *Compte rendu des travaux du congrès de la propriété littéraire et artistique, suivi d'un grand nombre de documents et d'un Appendice contenant les lois de tous les pays sur les droits d'auteur, avec notices historiques*, Bruxelles/Leipzig: Emile Flatau, vol 2, p. 59ff.

5 P. Wauwermans (1894), *Le droit des auteurs en Belgique: Commentaire historique et doctrinal de la loi du 22 mars 1886*, Bruxelles: Société belge de librairie, pp. 50ff speaking of '*le règne de la contrefaçon*'.

6 'Arrêté du gouvernement provisoire of 21 October 1830, entière liberté pour élever des théâtres et y faire représenter des pièces. Droit d'auteurs', in *Bulletin usuel des lois et arrêtés concernant l'administration générale*, vol. 2 (1814–1843: Royaume de Belgique), 5.

7 Ratification law of 22 August 1852, *O.J.*. 22 April 1854. P. Wauwermans (1894), *Le droit des auteurs en Belgique : Commentaire historique et doctrinal de la loi du 22 mars 1886*, Bruxelles: Société belge de librairie, pp. 59ff.

8 É. Romberg (1859), *Compte rendu des travaux du congrès de la propriété littéraire et artistique, suivi d'un grand nombre de documents et d'un Appendice contenant les lois de tous les pays sur les droits d'auteur, avec notices historiques*, Bruxelles/Leipzig: Emile Flatau, vol 2, p. 55; *Pandectes belges*, vol. 25, 1228ff ('Contrefaçon littéraire et artistique').

favoured foreigners above Belgians. Already in around 1855, the Belgian government had a Commission draft its own national copyright law, but this draft was never seriously discussed by Parliament.

Between 1860 and 1875 academies, writers and artists associations called for a law for the protection of literary and artistic property. A fresh attempt to draft a law – taking into account developments in foreign copyright law – was begun by a legislating commission, and in 1878/1879 submitted to Parliament, likewise to no effect. A new stimulus once more came from outside: after the conclusion of the treaties with Spain in 1880, France in 1882 and the German Empire, which on certain levels offered foreigners better protection than Belgian citizens, violent protests followed from Belgian authors.

The *Association artistique et littéraire internationale*[9] at its congress in Brussels in 1884 formulated the basic principles of copyright protection. These principles formed the foundation of the Belgian government bill of 1885. This draft was presented to the *Association*, which discussed it at its Congress in Antwerp in 1885. The French copyright expert Pouillet drew up the conclusions of this congress in relation to the bill, which was then submitted to Parliament in a report by Jules De Borchgrave, and was passed subject to a few amendments on 22 March 1886.[10] The parliamentary debates mainly discussed the regulation of the performance rights for dramatic and musical works. (There were after all no stipulations foreseen in the existing regulation for the performance rights of musical works – apart from stage musicals – while the treaties with Spain of 1880 and the German Empire of 1883 did indeed protect musical performance rights). The evolutionary process of Belgian Copyright Law demonstrates particularly clearly the very profound influence which jurisprudence had over the development of this subject matter and its legislation in the second half of the nineteenth century.

Thus, copyright law – without defining this – is based on the concept of

---

9 Cf. the negotiations during the Brussels' Congress of 1858 in É. Romberg (1859), *Compte rendu des travaux du congrès de la propriété littéraire et artistique, suivi d'un grand nombre de documents et d'un Appendice contenant les lois de tous les pays sur les droits d'auteur, avec notices historiques*, Bruxelles/Leipzig: Emile Flatau, vol 1; cf. P. Wauwermans (1894), *Le droit des auteurs en Belgique: Commentaire historique et doctrinal de la loi du 22 mars 1886*, Bruxelles: Société belge de librairie, p. 64ff.

10 On the genesis of the law of 1886: P. Wauwermans (1894), *Le droit des auteurs en Belgique: Commentaire historique et doctrinal de la loi du 22 mars 1886*, Bruxelles: Société belge de librairie, p. 70ff; cf. C. Lyon-Caen in P. Delalain (1889), *Lois françaises et étrangères sur la propriété littéraire et artistique; suivies des Conventions internationales conclus par la France pour la protection des oeuvres de littérature et d'art*, Paris: Cercle de la librairie, de l'impr. et de la papeterie, vol. 1, p. 167ff.

droit intellectuel, that was developed by Edmond Picard and also adopted by Borchgrave in his report to Parliament. The draft originally mentioned the term *propriété littéraire et artistique*, however copyright law in the end adopted the neutral expression *droit d'auteur*, as in the end there was no desire to express the nature of this law.

The Belgian law took into consideration the development of the European legislations in the second half of the nineteenth century, and was welcomed as a step forward by both national and foreign critics.[11] The copyright protection was not linked to any formalities, the *dépôt légal* disappeared. The law uniformly governed the copyright over works of literature and art, without defining these individually. The law granted authors a reproduction right (Art. 1), including a translation right (Art. 12). Musical works were likewise granted a public performance right and a right to adapt (Arts. 16 and 17). A copyright protection for a period of 50 years after the author's death was introduced (Art. 2).

The protection of foreign authors regulated in Art. 38 was, moreover, far-reaching. They benefited from the same copyright law protection as the Belgian authors, even in the absence of reciprocity. One limitation to this is the fact that the protection in Belgium cannot last longer than in the relevant foreign state, a stipulation, at that time not found in most copyright laws.

2 NO DIRECT INFLUENCE OF THE STATUTE OF ANNE ON BELGIAN COPYRIGHT LAW

If Belgian copyright has experienced any influence from foreign copyright law legislation, this is mainly due to the regulation from the Netherlands and, of course, France. Proof of this is, amongst others, the influence of Pouillet (and the first Berne Convention) on the Belgian bill.

Neither, therefore, can there be any question of any direct influence of the Statute of Anne on the Belgian Copyright Act of 1886. Not only did England never have any influence at administrative law level on the Belgian areas, but a period of some two centuries stretches between the Statute of Anne and the first Belgian Copyright Law.

If there were any influence at all from English copyright law, this would mainly be from the English Copyright Law of 1842,[12] which already had

[11] E.g. J. Kohler (1909), *Urheberrecht an Schriftwerken und Verlagsrecht*, Stuttgart: Enke, p. 107.

[12] 5 & 6 Vict. c. 45.

a different approach to copyright than the Statute of Anne. By setting the protection period at seven years post mortem or 42 years as from the publication date, the utilitarian doctrine as formulated by the Statute of Anne, was indeed upheld, but it did already give way in part to the natural rights doctrine.

3 INDIRECT INFLUENCE OF ENGLISH DOCTRINE ON BELGIAN COPYRIGHT LAW

Has there been no influence at all of the Statute of Anne, or more broadly of English doctrine, on Belgian copyright law? I think there certainly was an influence at two levels (i) the protection criteria and (ii) the foundations of copyright law.

3.1 Protection Criteria

It is well-established jurisprudence in most countries of continental Europe that not just any creation is protected by copyright; only those creations that show a certain level of originality, that is those that bear the hallmark of their author.

In this respect, continental European doctrine differs from British doctrine, where the personal intellectual effort alone suffices to enjoy copyright protection.[13]

Recently, in a ruling made on 11 March 2005,[14] the Belgian Court of Cassation reiterated once more this 'originality' requirement:

> To enjoy the protection of the Copyright Act of 30 June 1994, it is necessary but sufficient to prove that the work is the expression of the intellectual effort of the maker, which is essential to give the work the required individual nature as a result of which a creation is made.

According to Belgian jurisprudence, originality is present when two conditions are met: (i) an intellectual effort, and (ii) individualisation.

These two criteria are in fact the result of two important English works, which have actually never had a major impact on English copyright doctrine at home.

---

[13] More in: J. Deene (2007), 'Originality in software: Belgian doctrine and jurisprudence remain divided', *Journal of Intellectual Law & Practice (JILP)* 692–698 and J. Deene (2005), 'Originaliteit in het auteursrecht', *Intellectuele Rechten – Droits Intellectuels (IRDI)* 223–237.

[14] Cass. 11 March 2005, AR C.03.0591.N, www.cass.be.

The criterion of intellectual effort as a basis for human appropriation of one's own creations has it's origin in John Locke's Labour Theory as described in *The Second Treatise of Government* (1690):

> Every Man has a Property in his own Person. . . The Labour of his Body, and the Work of his Hands, we may say, are properly his[15]

The individuality criterion is generally attributed to German philosophers such as Kant, Fichte and Hegel, but originally, it came from an English writer, that is the work of English poet Edward Young, *Conjectures on original composition* (1759). Young preached originality and he located the source of this essential quality in the poet's own genius. According to Young (talking about writers):

> His works will stand distinguished; his the sole property of them; which property alone can confer the noble title of an author; that is, of one who (to speak accurately) thinks and composes; while other invaders of the press, how voluminous and learned soever, (with due respect be it spoken) only read and write[16]

His essay attracted relatively little attention in England; but in Germany, it had a profound impact. German theorists like Kant and Fichte elaborated the ideas sketched out by Young in which originality was put forward as the condition to enjoy protection.

It is remarkable that both authors had little or no impact on English copyright doctrine that has a more utilitarian and pragmatic approach, while these authors had a very strong influence on continental European copyright law, and therefore on Belgian copyright law, as well.

3.2 The Foundations of Copyright Law

However, the Statute of Anne itself, and especially its juridical interpretation in *Donaldson v. Beckett*, 1774, had a certain influence on Belgian copyright law.

---

15 J. Locke (1690), *The Second Treatise of Government*, www.constitution.org/jl/2ndtr05.htm, Chap V, sec. 26.

16 E. Young (1759), 'Conjectures on original composition in a letter to the author of Sir Charles Grandison', in E.D. Jones (ed) (1975), *English Critical Essays, Sixteenth, Seventeenth and Eighteenth Centuries*, London: Oxford University Press, p. 289. More in M. Woodmansee (1984), 'The genius and the copyright: economic and legal conditions of the emergence of the "author"', *Eighteenth-Century Studies* vol. 17.4, 425–448.

In *Donaldson v. Beckett*,[17] two opposing currents clashed. On the one hand, there was the vision of a Blackstonian natural common law that considered that the Statute of Anne had a purely declarative nature and aimed at having copyright recognised as a perpetual property right. Copyright protection had to be offered on grounds of fairness and to protect the private interests of authors (and publishers).

The opposite view is put forward by the Scottish book publishers, supported by Lord Camden, who advocated a statutory copyright law, and therefore considered the Statute of Anne as purely constitutive and, to them, copyright was nothing more than a monopoly, a privilege, that had a limited duration. Copyright was developed to promote the *encouragement of learning*, and therefore the general interest.

We all know that, eventually, the House of Lords favoured the latter vision.

During the Belgian parliamentarian debates, MPs thoroughly discussed the question whether the protection of authors should be moulded into a form of property right (that had to be perpetual) or of a privilege (that was limited in time). The famous Belgian jurist Edmond Picard put forward a solution that was followed by Jules De Borchgraeve, the parliamentary reporter for the Copyright Act of 1886.

> Nous pouvons donc définir le droit d'auteur: un droit intellectuel en vertu duquel l'auteur a la faculté, à l'exclusion de tous autres d'exploiter son oeuvre pendant un temps déterminé et d'en tirer tous les profits qu'elle comporte. En adoptant cette définition, nous déclarons rompre ouvertement avec les théories anciennes de la propriété ou du privilège légal.[18]

The Belgian parliament was hesitant to rule on this issue. The discussion was closed with a statement by the government that the Copyright Act was only intended to give authors a protection system, and that its purpose was not to settle this difference of opinion in a definitive manner. Because the term '*author's right*' was preferred and not a '*(literary) property right*' and the protection period was limited in time, this can certainly not be considered as a victory for the property right in the sense of natural rights.

---

[17] *Donaldson v. Beckett*, 2 Brown's Parl. Cases 129, 1 Eng. Rep. 837; 4 Burr. 2408, 98 Eng. Rep. 257 (1774); 17 Cobbett's Parl. Hist. 953 (1813). More in: M. Rose (1988), 'The author as proprietor: *Donaldson v. Beckett* and the genealogy of modern authorship', *Representations* vol. 23, 51–85.

[18] 'Rapport fait, au nom de la section centrale par M. Jules de Borchgrave, dans la séance du 9 Juillet 1885, nr. 23', in M. Benoidt and L. Descamps (1886), *Commentaire législatif de la Loi du 22 mars 1886 sur le droit d'auteur*, Bruxelles: Ramlot, p. 59.

The related question whether the copyright was to serve the general interest or the private interest was also discussed during these debates. The opinion of the Belgian government was that both elements had to be taken into account:

> Cette propriété ne saurait être perpétuelle: ce serait créer une sorte de monopole préjudiciable à la société et dangereux pour les auteurs eux-mêmes. . .il importe surtout d'accorder dans la loi l'intérêt privé et l'intérêt social[19]

> Tous les intérêts y semblent conciliés: en garantissant aux auteurs et à leurs héritiers la jouissance des droits exclusifs pendant une durée suffisante, elle ménage ceux de la société qui est certaine de voir tomber dans la domaine public les œuvres littéraires et artistique, quelle que soit d'ailleurs leur valeur[20]

Interests were always weighed up against each other, and the general interest and the public domain were also recognised.

The Statute of Anne and *Donaldson v. Beckett* have therefore, be it indirectly, indeed contributed to the parliamentary preparations leading to the first Belgian Copyright Act.

---

[19] 'Projet présenté dans la séance du 19 février 1878, nr.1', in M. Benoidt and L. Descamps (1886), *Commentaire législatif de la Loi du 22 mars 1886 sur le droit d'auteur*, Bruxelles: Ramlot, p. 20.

[20] 'Projet présenté dans la séance du 19 février 1878, nr.3', in M. Benoidt and L. Descamps (1886), *Commentaire législatif de la Loi du 22 mars 1886 sur le droit d'auteur*, Bruxelles: Ramlot, p. 21.

11. Colonial copyright redux: 1709 *v.* 1832

Pierre-Emmanuel Moyse*

1 INTRODUCTION

This contribution is an essay on legal transplants in an historical and colonial context. Using the Statute of Anne[1] as a reference point, we will sketch the evolution of Canadian copyright law on its journey to self-determination during the eighteenth and nineteenth centuries. This exposé cannot possibly render justice to the extremely rich and somewhat under-exploited subject matter of colonial copyright.[2] Rather, as an impressionist would do, we will endeavor to project general impressions of Canadian law during the colonial period by exploring several Canadian firsts. As far as copyright law is concerned, the colonial period ended with the UK

* Assistant professor, McGill University, 2009.

[1] An Act for the Encouragement of Learning by Vesting the Copies of Printed Books in the Authors or Purchasers of Such Copies, During the Times therein Mentioned, 8 Anne c. 19 (1710) (UK). Many scholars, a fair number of whom are ALAI members, have contributed to the historical study of Copyright: M. Rose (1994), 'The Author as Proprietor: Donaldson v. Beckett and the Genealogy of Modern Authorship', in B. Sherman and A. Strowel, *Of Authors and Origins*, Oxford: Clarendon Press, at p. 32; L. R. Patterson (1968), *Copyright in an Historical Perspective*, Nashville: Vanderbilt University Press, at p. 12; J. Seignette (1994), *Challenges to The Creator Doctrine*, Boston: Kluwer; J. Feather (1988), *A History of British Publishing*, London; New York: Croom Helm; A. Birrell (1971), *Seven Lectures on the Law and History of Copyright in Books*, South Hackensack, New Jersey: Rothman Reprints; J. C. Ginsburg (1990), 'A Tale of Two Copyrights: Literary Property in Revolutionary France and America', 64 Tulane L. Rev. 991.

[2] See, P.-E. Moyse (2008), 'Canadian Colonial Copyright: The Colony Strikes Back', in Y. Gendreau (ed), *An Emerging Intellectual Property Paradigm, Perspectives from Canada*, Cheltenham, UK and Northampton, MA, USA: Edward Elgar Publishing. The last section of the present essay borrows in part from this latter contribution. Also, Catherine Seville (2006), *The Internationalisation of Copyright*, Cambridge: Cambridge University Press.

Copyright Act 1911,[3] which conferred authority upon the legislature of the self-governed dominions to repeal any enactments related to copyright passed by the Imperial Parliament. Canada, unlike Australia, for example, availed itself of this option and enacted its own copyright act in 1921 – which came into force in 1924 – an act that is therefore considered as Canada's first post-colonial copyright legislation.[4] Until this point, Canadian law was made of a complex set of statutory regulations, not always coherent and often conflicting, some pertaining to the imperial legislature (for example the UK Copyright Act 1842[5] which expressly applies to all colonies), others to the Colonial legislature for which Royal assent had to be sought and obtained, and some specifically enacted to address colonial or international issues,[6] a perfect example of which was the 1847 famous, or rather infamous UK Foreign Reprint Act[7] which shall be discussed further in this paper. In an attempt to understand the evolution of copyright legislation – colonial or imperial – in what was a developing country, we will navigate through various Canadian moments, some of them concerning the Bourbon legacy, others to British heritage. More specifically this essay will examine the influence of the 1709 Statute of Anne – and its progeny which becomes part of English heritage by effect of the 1763 conquest – on the 1832 colonial Acte pour protéger la propriété intellectuelle[8] voted by the Parliament of Lower Canada.

In the shadow of these legislative monuments lies a vibrant story about the dissemination of knowledge in the New World and the history of the international book trade. The Canadian narrative is also a concrete example of legal *métissage* in an asymmetric relation. What the study of colonialism shows us is that law often serves the needs and desires of both the Imperial power and the subjugated country. Concessions are necessary to rule a conquered population. In understanding Canadian law during the

---

3 Copyright Act 1911, 1 & 2 Geo. V, c. 46, s. 26 (UK).

4 An Act for the Protection of Copy Rights or, in French, *Loi modifiant et codifiant la législation concernant le droit d'auteur*, 11–12 Geo. V c. 24 (1921) (Ca); H. G. Fox (1944), *The Canadian Law of Copyright* (1st edn), Toronto: The University of Toronto Press, at p. 28.

5 An Act to Amend the Law of Copyright, (1842) 5 & 6 Vict., c. 45 (UK).

6 Reference shall be made to the imperial legislation constituted of the International Acts specifically enacted to address the question of protection in the United Kingdom of foreign authors. The so-called international copyright legislation did not apply to the colonies as they were not considered foreign countries.

7 An Act to Amend the Law Relating to the Protection in the Colonies of Works Entitled to Copyright in the United Kingdom, 1847 10 & 11 Vict. 95 (UK).

8 An Act for the protection of Copy Rights, 1832, 2 Will. IV, c. 53 (Can).

colonial period, and correlatively the measure of Imperial influence, one must understand the dialogue between the various legal traditions. Born European, pioneers of the New World reinvented themselves and their laws, which were not mere duplicates of those they brought with them. This transformative process is evidence of a complex form of acculturation or regeneration of existing legal formats. In the meantime, new-old, east-west, colony-empire – and in the case of Québec, common law-civil law, duets continued to supply a convenient explanation of legal regionalism, even if simplistic at times.[9] Such duets are the magnetic poles between which the discontinuous history of colonization runs – the process of re-engineering the law of the dominant power to fit the needs of the colony, to recondition it, its very nature organic. As will be explained, colonial narratives are not always found in the positive manifestation of the law, in our case in the colonial copyright legislation, but rather in the subtext where the political and social tensions lie. One must remember that every bill drafted and voted by the colonial legislature had to be validated by a Royal order to become law.

The analysis of the first English and colonial Canada statutes, the legislation of 1709 and 1832, shall be dealt with carefully as they are the products of different conjectures and belong to social and historical eras that had little in common. They ought to be understood within their respective political and regional context. Beyond their symbolic significance, they reveal little about the society itself and the conditions that preceded their adoption. In the nineteenth century, Canadian scholarship is particularly scant in the field of copyright. And indeed before the passing of and the first post-confederation Canadian copyright statute in 1875,[10] the body of case law is meagre at best. This should not be a surprise as Canadians, of all descents, spent more time farming, trading furs, cutting timber and protecting themselves against hostile elements than debating over intellectual property or even reading. The review of some highlights of Canadian history is, therefore, essential to comprehend the evolution of Canadian copyright law. We will then focus our discussion on the making and significance of Canada's first copyright legislation.

---

[9] The literature on regionalism has regained interest with the publication of Annalee Saxonian's work (1994), *Regional Advantage: Culture and Competition in Silicon Valley and Route 128* Cambridge, MA: Harvard University Press.

[10] An Act Respecting Copyrights or, in French, *Acte concernant la propriété littéraire et artistique*, 38 Vict. c. 88 (1875). The Canadian statute was immediately followed by the passing of an English act in lieu of the Royal assent: An Act to give effect to an Act of the Parliament of the Dominion of Canada respecting Copyright, 38 & 39 Vict. c. 53 (1875). The Canadian Confederation was formed in 1867.

2 BOOKS: A SUMPTUARY EXPENDITURE

The lives of the early settlers and voyageurs of New France have been much romanticized by historical writings.[11] However, the civic realities of Québec's colonial period before and after the Conquest (1763) were often fraught with battles with querulous First Nation tribes and between French and English partisans. The political context was tense and staged an ambitious, occasionally fragile, colonial project in a time where revolutions seemed to be a most-liked occupation.

2.1 *La Vie de Chateau* or Log Cabin?

In 1603, Samuel de Champlain boarded a vessel as a geographer to further explore what was known as the River of Canada (St Lawrence River), an expedition financed by merchants who obtained trade monopolies by letters patent. If lucre was the incentive behind these costly first journeys, it soon became a distraction that almost defeated French imperialistic ambitions. Individual entrepreneurs were less interested in the development of New France than in trading furs. Nevertheless, Champlain's *Voyages* (1604),[12] an account of his first expedition published soon after he returned to France, fired the imagination of many and nourished the expansionist ambitions of the King of France, Henri IV. He was determined to maintain French domination on the new continent, a project disputed by the English. In the spring of 1608, Champlain sailed again to the same destination and pushed to the actual site of Québec City. They laid the foundations of the first settlement of Europeans in the territory of New France. Champlain's account of the facts contrasts with the representation that we usually have of his accomplishment:

> From the Island of Orleans to Quebec the distance is a league. I arrived there on the 3rd of July, when I searched for a place suitable for our settlement; but I could find none more convenient or better situated than the point of Quebec, so called by the savages, which was covered with nut-trees. I at once employed a portion of our workmen in cutting them down, that we might construct our habitation there: one I set to sawing boards, another to making a cellar and

---

[11] G.M. Wrong (1928), *The Rise and Fall of New France*, Toronto: The Macmillan Co. of Canada.

[12] Samuel de Champlain (2007), 'The founding of Quebec' from '*The "Voyages" of Samuel de Champlain*', Teddington, UK: The Echo Library, available at http://canadiana.org/. See also (1830), *Voyages du Sieur de Champlain ou Journal ès découvertes de la Nouvelle France*, Paris : [s.n.].

> digging ditches, another I sent to Tadoussac with a barque to get supplies. The first thing we made was a storehouse for keeping under cover our supplies, which was promptly accomplished through the zeal of all, and my attention to the work.[13]

The small colony was slow to develop and its existence during the first two decades was fragile. Trade monopolies and concessions of large tracts of land along the mighty St Lawrence granted to merchants proved to be largely inefficient and led to a major reform under Louis XIV.[14] Early seigneuries were revoked in 1627 and Cardinal Richelieu entrusted an association of merchants, the Company of One Hundred Associates – soon to be replaced by the Company of West Indies in 1664, with the task of exploiting these new territories and of establishing a powerful French colony. The Company was imposed with the responsibility of bringing settlers and furnishing 'to each family of colonists a sufficient area of cleared land to enable it to support itself'.[15] In return, the stakeholders would enjoy a monopoly on fur trade. The French seigneurial system was also implemented for a very specific purpose: this system of land tenure supported the political project of developing Canada.[16] Claiming absolute

---

13 Ibid at p. 11. Champlain spent the winter of 1608–1609 in the settlement with 27 settlers, which produced certain 'discontent' as Champlain mildly expressed it. In fact, all but eight succumbed. Most died of the scourge. Canadian winter did not only oppose its forces to Champlain's ambitious designs. It is the invisible hand that would condition all human activities and shape the industrial landscape of Canada. It would directly impact the book trade, waterways being impracticable during winter, a situation that placed the United States at great advantage. To send publications across the Atlantic was a slow and costly business. As will later be explained, most of the English language books were soon imported from the United States. William Bennett Munro (1920), *Crusaders of New France*, New Haven: Yale University Press at p. 40.

14 See, for example, the development of Montréal and the survival of the seigneurial system, Georges-E. Baillargeon (1968), *La survivance du régime seigneurial à Montréal*, Ottawa: Le Cercle du Livre de France at p. 18: 'Au début de la colonie, l'île de Montréal avait été concédée en seigneurie à un particulier. Acquise en 1640 par une société pieuse, elle avait été donnée en 1663 au Séminaire de Saint-Sulpice de Paris. Cette donation avait été confirmée par lettres patentes du roi de France en 1677. [. . .] les choses étaient dans cet état quand survint la Conquête et elles devaient le demeurer jusque vers 1840'.

15 William Bennett Munro (1907), *The Seigniorial System in Canada*, Cambridge, MA: Harvard University Press at p. 23.

16 For example, the powers granted in 1676 and signed by Colbert to Messieurs de Frontenac and Duschesneau giving concessions in Canada, specified that 'said concessions be only given upon the condition of clearing the lands, and of bringing them into value within six immediate and consecutive years, otherwise the said concessions to be null', Also, Canada Legislative Assembly (1852), *Edicts, Ordinances,*

title on a *terra nullius*, Louis XIV granted large tracts of land in concession to those who were committed to settling the colony.[17] Feudal Canada was not feudal France. The complex code of relations based upon the holding of land known in France as the infamous seigniorial system was modified to suit the needs of the settlers. As Munro wrote, 'The development of feudalism in its later stages was therefore more uniform and consistent in New France than in Old, its working less obscured by the clouds of privilege'.[18] Illustrating the specificity of this system, the famous *Arrêts Marly* of 1711 provided that at the expiration of a year, 'all seigniors who should have shown conspicuous failure in developing and settling their seigniories should be deprived of their grants'.[19] Another anecdotic fact that says a lot about Canada during this period is that the main building of the Québec City settlement, today's site of the Château Frontenac, was

---

Declarations and decrees relative to The Seigniorial Tenure, Quebec: E.R. Fréchette at p. 29. The seigniorial system as part of French private law would remain in force after the change of sovereignty and would be abolished in 1854 by the Seigniorial Act of 1854, *An Act for the Abolition of Feudal Rights and Duties in Lower Canada*, Stats. Prov. Can. 1854, c. 3. The intention of the legislation is spelled out in the preamble: 'Whereas it is expedient to abolish all feudal rights and duties in Lower Canada, whether bearing upon the Censitaire or upon the Seignior, and to secure fair compensation to the latter for every lucrative right which is now legally his, and which he will lose by such abolition'. See John E.C. Brierley and Roderick A. Macdonald (1993), *Quebec Civil Law, An Introduction to Quebec Private Law*, Toronto: Emond Montgomery Publications Limited at p. 21. Also, Lelièvre and Angers (1856), *Lower Canada Reports, Questions seigneuriales – Compilation, Vol. A.*, Québec & Montréal: Augustin Côté & Bureau de la Minerve.

[17] Interestingly, the question of ownership over land has resurfaced in the recent debate over aboriginal rights: 'According to this historical interpretation, from the time of Champlain to 1763, French settlements within New France fell almost exclusively within the St. Lawrence Valley. At the date of Champlain's arrival in the Montreal area in 1603, the surrounding region was largely devoid of indigenous inhabitants. In one of the mysteries of the history of New France, the Iroquois people who occupied the region at the date of Jacques Cartier's visit in 1534 had simply disappeared by 1603. The French colonists thus claimed and occupied this particular area as *terra nullius*. But these historians argue that the French chose not to further encroach on the traditional lands of the aboriginal peoples surrounding the valley. [. . .] Content with occupation of the *terra nullius* of the Valley, the French thus never engaged in a pattern of surrender and purchase similar to British colonial policy. In this interpretation, it is argued that the French Crown only assumed ownership of the lands lining the St. Lawrence River which it actually occupied and organized under the Seigneurial system', *R. v. Côté*, [1996] 3 S.C.R. 139, para. 47.

[18] Munro, *supra* note 15, at p. 15.

[19] Ibid, at p. 42.

referred to as the 'Habitation' by Champlain himself. This timber building is a far cry from Chambord completed in 1547.

In this context, one may ask, who exactly was reading in New France when the Statute of Anne was enacted in 1710? The question is almost anachronical. The social and political organization of the colony is reflected in the rates of literacy which had prevailed among the population for over 50 years.[20] Although comparable to other European colonies, the majority of the population in Ville-Marie (Montréal, as it was known at the time) was illiterate. Most of the colony's trades did not require literacy, and there was very little interest in educating the population.[21] Books had to be imported, were expensive and difficult to obtain, a situation that would not improve after the Conquest (1763). Marguerite Bourgeoys, a French nun from Troyes and founder of Montréal's historical *Congrégation de Notre-Dame*, opened her first school in 1658 and through her efforts, a rudimentary literacy began to be taught in the small (primary) schools. However schooling did not truly develop before the social reforms of the second half of the nineteenth century. Until then, the clergy encouraged circulation of religious books and they were largely responsible for the importation and distribution of books in New France, and thus schooling. By contrast, the colony's elite had access to a larger and more varied collection of works than those made available by the clergy. These books were usually tied to the respective owners' professions.[22]

We ought to be reminded that the introduction of the printing press in the New World was recent and did not happen under the French regime. If historians report occurrences of discussions on the necessity to introduce

---

20 'Although by 1760, estimated literacy rates in Québec compared favourably with those in France, and unfavourably with those in the New England colonies', in P. Axelrod (1997), *The Promise of Schooling: Education in Canada, 1800–1914*, Toronto: University of Toronto Press at p. 5.

21 'Poor weather, the requirements of farming, the lure of the fur trade, the shortage of books, and the inconsistent support shown schooling by the Church and the Crown all inhibited the further development of education in New France', Ibid, at p. 5.

22 The printing press was introduced into Nova Scotia in 1751, a founding Canadian province in 1867, whose control alternated between France and England throughout several wars and treaties until it was finally left to the latter in 1713. Michel Verrette, 'Les usages de l'alphabétisation', in Patricia Lockhart Fleming, Gilles Gallichan and Yvan Lamonde, (eds) (2007), *History of the Book in Canada*, Toronto: University of Toronto Press, vol. 1–3 at p. 179. In 1840, 'c'est naturellement au sein de l'élite de la société que l'on retrouve l'essentiel du lectorat canadien de l'époque. [. . .] La masse des gens, elle, ne constitue pas un grand réservoir de lecteurs et de lectrices en raison des conditions générales de vie et de milieu', at p. 177.

the printing press into New France, notably for the promulgation of laws and regulations early in the eighteenth century, it should be known that the first press was effectively introduced into Lower Canada in Québec City in 1764 by a native of Scotland, William Brown.[23] The *Book Day* of Brown and Gilmore, Brown's associate, reveals that the first work printed in Canada was a 15-page document presumably printed the same year and entitled *Presentment to the Grand Juries* of which no copy seems to have subsisted.[24] The first book published in the English language in Lower Canada and still in existence today is the *Trial of Daniel Disney*.[25] We can also credit Brown with the printing in 1775 of a *compendium* by the jurist François Cugnet, the full title of which reminds us of the task left to those required to educate a new elite in French customary law still applicable in the newly acquired colony:

> Traité abregé des ancienes loix, coutumes et usages de la colonie du Canada, aujourd'huy province de Québec: tiré de la coutume de la prévôté et vicomté de Paris, à laquelle la dite colonie était assujétie, en consequence de l'Edit de l'établissement du Conseil souverain du mois d'avril 1663; avec l'explication de chaque titre et de chaque article, puisée dans les meilleurs autheurs qui ont écrit et comenté la dite coutume: nécessaire à toutes les personnes qui voudront avoir une teinture des dites ancienes loix, coutumes et usages, et qui pourra les faciliter dans l'étude qu'ils seront obligés d'en faire, tant comme juges, que comme avocats ou procureurs.[26]

---

23 AEgidius Fauteux (1957), *The Introduction of Printing in Canada*, Montréal: Rolland Paper Company Limited, folio 1 at p. 9. Fauteux recasts the discussion in terms of contributions made by two iconic figures in the expansion of the western civilization: Christopher Columbus and Johann Gutenberg: 'Some people will go so far as to claim that the discovery of this method of reproducing thought-symbols was fraught with more momentous results than any other discovery, even that of the New World. As inhabitants of the New World, it is not an easy thing for us to accept such a claim at its face value, [. . .] we cannot refrain from asking ourselves what our position be if America still awaited its discoverers; and this question, ever present in the back of our minds, effectively prevents us from admitting that Johann Gutenberg may have been a greater contribution to civilization than that of Christopher Columbus'. Although, this fact is from time to time disputed by historians, William Caxton is generally credited for having set up the first printing press in England, more precisely at Westminster, approximately 1475 upon his return from Europe. The first book known to have been printed in this period is an edition of Chaucer's *Canterbury Tales*.

24 Ibid, folio 1, at p. 11.

25 Ibid, folio 3, at p. 13. Fauteux also makes mention of the first book ever printed in the Abnaki language, reminding us that a rich First Nation culture existed prior to the European colonization.

26 Brown's name is given in its Gallicist form: Guillaume Brown. Available on Early Canadiana Online: http://www.canadiana.org/ECO/mtq?doc=33321.

2.2 British New France

The political context in which the first Canadian Copyright legislation was adopted was a tense one. Inhabitants of the former French colony became subjects of an unsympathetic monarch; rulers feared the threat of civil war, as revolutions seemed to be the principal occupation of modern civilizations; American troops invaded Lower Canada in 1812. Adding to the political instability was the vexing question of the legal regime to be implemented. Brierley and Macdonald wrote that 'in the 30 years following the military victory of the English (1759–1760) and the change of sovereignty to the English crown (1763), profound uncertainty reigned in respect of the status of the body of private law [. . .]'.[27] Transplants of English law could not be systematic, or always feasible, as the operation required first that the English conqueror deal with a colony composed of French-speaking subjects who had been in contact with the civil tradition for over 100 years. The 1830s were the theatre of great political dissensions between the British establishment, formed of merchants and unelected representatives of the Legislative Council and in whose hands was concentrated the executive power, and the partisans of the French Canadian project, a project which progressively gained in popularity in the Legislative Assembly and stood for the creation of a responsible government for the colony. The Legislative Assembly, endowed with little power, but lead by the charismatic Louis-Joseph Papineau, demanded unconditional control of the budget, which was refused. Tensions within the colony along the French-English divide reached a culminating point in Lower Canada during the events of 1837 known as the 'Révoltes des patriotes'.

In 1837 Lord Durham, High Commissioner for British North America, was sent to North America to investigate the circumstances surrounding the Lower Canada rebellions and to assess the situation of the colony. He released his report on the affairs of British North America in 1839 and recommended that Upper and Lower Canada be united into one province. The document contains the personal opinions of commissioner Durham, which further fueled resentments within the French community. Not always accurate and often biased, the document and its numerous

---

[27] Brierley and Macdonald, *supra* note 16, at pp. 14–15. And indeed, during this particularly unstable era, marriages, contracts and other civic arrangements were made according to the Customs of Paris with confidence that the newly established judicial system would assert their validity. Rodolphe Lemieux (1901), *Les origins du droit franco-canadien*, Montréal: C. Theoret, Librairie de droit et de jurisprudence at p. 410 and following.

appendices contain invaluable perspectives on the 'many evils of this unhappy Province'. Reporting on the hostile division of French and English, Durham came to the conclusion that assimilation was to be discouraged and conceded that the best way to deal with an old and settled country would be to preserve the rights and institutions of the occupants. Durham states what he perceives as the difficulty of governing French Canadians and had little esteem for them:

> [t]here can hardly be conceived a nationality more destitute of all that can invigorate and elevate people, than that which is exhibited by the descendants of the French in Lower Canada, owing to their retaining their peculiar language and manners. They are a people with no history, and no literature. The literature of England is written in a language which is not theirs; and the only literature which their language renders familiar to them, is that of a nation from which they have been separated by eighty years of a foreign rule, and still more by those changes which the Revolution and its consequences have wrought in the whole political, moral and social state of France, yet it is on a people whom recent history, manners, modes of thought, so entirely separate from them, that the French Canadians are wholly dependent for almost all the instruction and amusement derived from books: it is on this essentially foreign literature, which is conversant about events, opinions and habits of life, perfectly strange and unintelligible to them, that they are compelled to be dependent.[28]

Indeed, the Conquest froze French private law in a very particular form; it also severed New France from the Old; the new English possession created a rift with the Napoleonic reforms of 1804 and the first French copyright decrees of 1791 and 1793, which never reached Canada. The umbilical cord being cut, the civil law heritage grew on its own on fertile common law soil. Also noteworthy, the Canadian population of about

[28] Charles Prestwood Lucas (1912), *Lord Durham's report on the affairs of British North America*, Oxford: Clarendon Press. Durham also attributed the low level of agricultural development, 'this lamentable state of things', to the ill organized and repressive French feudal system, an institution 'calculated to repress intelligence and freedom of the great mass of the people'. See the vehement response of Papineau forced to exile in France: Louis-Joseph (May 1839), 'Histoire de la résistance du Canada au gouvernement anglais', in *La Revue du Progrès*, Paris, a version of the article is available online: http://biblio.republiquelibre.org/Histoire_de_la_r%C3%A9sistance_du_Canada_au_gouvernement_anglais#Lord_Durham (Mathieu Gauthier-Pilote). More recently, studies have shown that the conclusions of Lord Durham on the low level of agricultural development in Québec and the enduring impression they left were largely flawed, Gilles Paquet and Jean-Pierre Wallot (2007), *Un Québec moderne 1760–1840 – Essai d'histoire économique et sociale*, Montréal: Éditions Hurtubise HMH at p. 297.

60,000 inhabitants in 1760 increased to roughly 550,000 by 1842, of which 25 per cent were of British origin.[29]

In this unstable legal and political context, the passing of the first copyright legislation in Lower Canada in 1832, an overwhelmingly francophone province, seems almost accidental as the local market for books, and in particular French books, was embryonic. French literature concerned a small number of educated readers and the government did not encourage trade with France. Language was still perceived as a possible assimilation instrument. Also, the Catholic Church did not favorably view the initiatives of the government to instruct the population by creating Royal schools. These political and religious factors, coupled with the agrarian characteristic of the colony explain that literacy encountered a major step backward in the first half of the nineteenth century. A possible explanation for the enactment of the *Act of 1832* is the belief that it would foster the efforts of the government to educate its people[30] – a proposition which remains to be demonstrated, both in its origins and projected effects.

From a legal viewpoint, one can argue that there was no need for a regional copyright law, as the existing Imperial legislation was presumed to apply to all colonies *mutatis mutandis*. And indeed, for reasons that will be exposed, Canadian authors were more inclined to publish in London or Paris rather than remitting their works to independent Canadian publishers.

3 COLONIAL LEGAL TRANSPLANTS

The question of the influence of the Statute of Anne on Canadian legislation is necessarily biased, as it appears to presume a filial relation between the imperial and colonial systems. We must depart from such a presumption. Instructive anachronisms are reminders of the complex conjecture: Canadian law at the time of the Statute of Anne was under the Lys and not the Union Jack; the adoption of the copyright legislation in 1832 by the Parliament of Lower Canada was premature and borrowed heavily from the American copyright legislation of 1831. The enactment of this statute, an act dealing with intellectual property, also constituted a considerable encroachment on civil law, the system that survived the Conquest.[31]

---

29 Evelyn, Kolish (1994), *Nationalismes et conflits de droits: le débat du droit privé au Québec*, Montréal: Cahiers du Québec, Éditions Hurtubise HMH at p. 24.

30 Axelrod, *supra* note 20, at pp. 17–18.

31 A point which will be later clarified by the Constitutional Act 1867, 30 & 31 Victoria, c. 3. (UK) (s. 91.23). One can argue the attribution of *Patents of Invention*

The study of colonial law, of its formation, inevitably invites us to direct our efforts to social and political theories.[32] Hayek's theory on *grown* and *made* norms, in particular, offers an interesting model to contrast the 1709 and 1832 legislations. Following a brief presentation of Hayek's theory, we will then examine what we consider to be the most influential and significant normative production of Westminster: the Copyright Reprint Act of 1847, an Act which stigmatized the uneasy case of Canada in relation to cultural products.

3.1 On Grown and Made Norms

Central to one of Hayek's most influential – and controversial – works, *Law, Legislation and Liberty*,[33] lies the distinction between *made* and *grown* orders. Hayek argues that *grown* orders, including legal orders, are often organic in their formation; they emerge spontaneously and evolve without deliberate direction or planning. Conversely, *made* orders are artificial constructions, not based on experience, and aim at definite purposes and ends. Borrowing from Hayek's doctrinal exposition, one could argue that the Statute of Anne belongs to the category of *grown* orders, from a British Isle perspective, whereas the 1832 Canadian legislation would appear to fall under the category of *made* orders, as its existence cannot be traced to any customary law or pre-existing regulation.

Before applying the seminal Hayekian distinction to our subject, we will take a brief tour of his reflections on the notion of rules that may impact our understanding of the nature of modern copyright law. Bentham and other utilitarians' works are well-known within the copyright circle. Based upon their writings, we speak abundantly of the *utilitarian* dimension of copyright, as if its function was unitary and easily identifiable. The *function* of the law becomes a convenient metaphor to convey the idea that particular ends can be attributed and achieved by a man-made, particular rule. The ambitions of utilitarians are almost of a scientific nature, inferring from a known result a general rule which can deal with unforeseen, particular circumstances. Decisions are now replete with such ready-to-apply formulae. The Supreme Court of Canada, for example, frequently

and *Copyrights* to the federal jurisdiction has never been discussed and was presented as a *fait accompli*.

[32] For a practical application of social science theories in the realm of intellectual property, Jean-Frédéric Morin (2007), *Le bilatéralisme américain: la nouvelle frontière du droit international des brevets*, Bruxelles: Larcier.

[33] F.A. Hayek (1973), *Law Legislation and Liberty*, London: Routledge & Kegan Paul.

starts its analysis with the statement that copyright should be conceived of as 'a balance between promoting the public interest in the encouragement and dissemination of works of the arts and intellect and obtaining a just reward for the creator'.[34] In our opinion, this statement is specious. The Court confuses ends and means or, even worse, presents a general exposition of the utility society can derive from copyright rules as an end in itself. According to Hayek, the utilitarian approach 'completely eliminates the factor which makes the rules necessary, namely our ignorance'[35] and he specifies: 'Man has developed rules of conduct not because he knows but because he does not know what all the consequences of a particular action will be. And the most characteristic feature of morals and law as we know them is therefore that they consist of rules to be obeyed irrespective of the known effects of the particular action'.[36] Because omniscience is simply not accessible, rules of conduct are expressions of our relative ignorance and constitute 'equipment' for certain unknown contingencies. In Hayekian theory, rationalists as well as utilitarians work in the comfort of a closed system that has presumed the paramount power of the reason to embrace *ex ante* all particular circumstances that a rule need take into account. As for the biological evolution, rules of conduct emerge from a complex social evolution process, for which experience and accumulated knowledge play a predominant role. 'The horizon of our sight consists mostly of means, not of particular ultimate ends.'[37] Taking issue with positivism, which, in his own words is the ideology of 'socialism' and 'omnipresence of the legislative power', Hayek does not hide his preference for the *common law* or *customary law* system, which leaves more room for judicial creativity. When one revisits colonial copyright history, Hayek's caveat about false idols of positivism seems all the more pertinent. It appears also to confirm that the real designs of the law are only approximations.

In Hayek's legal cosmogony, the Statute of Anne is a 'grown norm'. It is an improved and rationalized expression of prior regulation.[38] If it transformed capricious privileges into legal rights, which in itself is a remarkable innovation as it divorced the *copy right* from any attempts to control the content of the printed matter, it forms nevertheless part of a

---

34 *Théberge v. Galerie d'Art du Petit Champlain inc.*, [2002] 2 S.C.R. 336, 2002 SCC 34.

35 Hayek, *supra* note 33, at p. 20.

36 Ibid, at pp. 20–21.

37 Ibid, at p. 23.

38 Frederick Seaton Siebert (1965), *Freedom of the Press in England 1476–1776 – The Rise and Decline of Government Control*, Urbana, IL: University of Illinois Press.

continuum, a system. The right to print was granted under license by those already engaged in the craft or by special dispensation from the Crown.[39] The registration system also predates the Statute of Anne as the Stationers' Company kept a record of the books printed. The Statute of Anne cannot be detached from the prior legal *corpus*; it is an extension. It synthesized rather than created a new, certain legal mechanism, which could be found in various royal ordinances, decrees, or customs of the printing industry during the previous century. This early regulation was also part of a more complex web of intertwined norms formed by written and unwritten customs and practices of the various guilds involved in the production of books, as well as Church prerogatives in censorship. Copyright legislation was perfected as the designs and operations of the economy of the printing industry were better comprehended and accepted. Here, the development of Canadian law contrasts starkly with the European experience, as no prior Canadian regulation existed, no Canadian debate to be found, nor submissions for or against the adoption of a colonial copyright act, no battle of the publishers. Although there are signs of an early attempt to table a copyright bill in 1827, this episode is poorly documented and no records appear to subsist. Literature is equally scarce on the topic. Hence, the 1832 Copyright Act seems to have appeared almost spontaneously, *deus ex-machina* so to speak, which creates the impression that in this country copyright law was invented or imported *prêt-à-porter*.

In our opinion, copyright law came to life when Canada became the theatre of commercial skirmishes between the United Kingdom and the United States:

> Few people foresaw in the 1840s that the Americans would gain control of the Canadian market because a British act (the *Foreign Reprint Act*, our addition) was passed in order to provide Canadians with cheap reading material; after all, one of the great liberal platforms of the nineteenth century was cheap reading for everyone. This situation led to the Canadian market becoming a battleground for American and British publishers, and skirmishes continued into the twentieth century because the British presence remained significant until the 1920s.[40]

From today's perspective, thus, the 1832 *Copyright Act* is almost an historical accident. First, it is doubtful that the economic and social preconditions of state intervention existed at the time. Secondly, even if such

[39] L. Ray Patterson and Stanley W. Lindberg (1991), *The Nature of Copyright*, Athens, Georgia: University of Georgia Press at p. 19.

[40] G.L. Parker (1985), *The Beginnings of the Book Trade in Canada*, Toronto: University of Toronto Press at p. 258.

needs are to be presumed, the Imperial legislation already provided for protection throughout the Empire to Canadian authors who first published their book in London, the preferred place of publication for authors writing in English. If the legislation is hardly justifiable from an economic standpoint, it is difficult to explain politically as well. Conditions of its adoption are murky. One possible explanation, and it has little to do with the Statute of Anne, is that it catalyzed the resentments Canadians felt *vis-à-vis* the legislative advantage given to London publishers' commercial ambitions. What the legislature intended in 1832 was to regain control over the book trade: instead of publishing in London, Canadians could avail themselves of local protection. Proximity is not a negligible advantage as the costs, direct or indirect, incurred for organizing printing in Great Britain were considerable. However, as we have seen, the literary production in the colony was almost inexistent or concerned works of a utilitarian or religious nature (maps, almanacs). The schooling system was at its infancy in Lower Canada where, as Lord Durham once said famously, two nations were warring. It seems rather unlikely that the *encouragement of reading* of the French inhabitants be the sole and unique motive of the enactment. Mystère! Two further explanations remain plausible. Firstly, the 1832 legislation was an act of silent resistance rather than an act of deference vis-à-vis the Imperial legislature. Copyright clearly constitutes an important piece of modern regulation and its reappropriation is an act of great significance for a developing country. Secondly, and this argument has not been made before, the Act of 1832 might have been designed especially as a boon to American printers and publishers, as prior to the passing of the Act of 1832 no protection could have been granted to American writers unless they undertook to first publish in London. This may be corroborated by the fact that the first Canadian Copyright legislation is almost a servile copy of the US Copyright statute voted in 1831,[41] as was the case for the first Canadian patent act of 1824, which itself was modeled after the 1793 US Patent Act. The influence derives, therefore, not where one would have thought.

Finally, political science has for many years strived to model normative movements. Research in this field is generally undertaken with the objective of explaining the flux of regulation, often in an international context, from an institutional or social perspective.[42] The phenomenon of what is called the migration of norms is explained by resorting to different social

---

41 The comparison of the first articles of both statutes is clear evidence of such affiliation.

42 In a post-colonial context: Sally Engle Merry (2000), *Colonizing Hawai'i: The Cultural Power of Law*, Princeton, NJ: Princeton University Press.

approaches. For functionalists, for example, it is the efficiency of a norm that explains its mobility and the likelihood of it being successfully adapted in a receiving jurisdiction. We submit that the functionalist approach is of little help to explain the 1832 legislation unless one wants to conclude that the decision to copy the American Act of 1831 was based upon evidence that it produced the best results there. It may just have constituted a convenient solution for the legislature of Lower Canada. Realists, on the other hand, view legal transplants as a manifestation of power. Here again, the explanation is not completely satisfactory. The process of migration is often more complex. Again, the 1832 Act was a unilateral act.[43]

3.2 The Real Influence of the Statute of Anne: the 1847 Foreign Reprints Act

The Act of 1832 was an initiative of the colonial government alone and was by no means commissioned or commanded by Westminster. Rather, as we have seen, it could be interpreted as an act of discreet resistance, as a measure of retaliation against oppressive practices used by the London publishers that prevented books from reaching Canadian readers. It had the ambition to reclaim control over the book trade in Canada. Passed unnoticed at first, it soon raised many concerns amongst British representatives on both sides of the Atlantic and, in 1842, in an effort to clarify the situation, Westminster finally intervened: if the Statute of Anne 1709[44] did not address the Colonial question, the 1842 Act makes it clear that it applied in 'all Parts of the United Kingdom of Great Britain and Ireland, the Islands of Jersey and Guernsey, all Parts of the East and West Indies, and all the Colonies, Settlements, and Possessions of the Crown which now are or hereafter may be acquired', hence relegating the Canadian legislation to a subordinate role. Westminster's ambitions were naturally to preserve the metropolitan industry and looked at the colonial market as a natural expansion or *comptoirs* of the home market. British authors were granted copyright protection in all

---

[43] Similarly, if the Royal Edict of 1663 directs that all cases civil and criminal be tried in Canada according to the 'Laws and Ordinances of the Kingdom of France, and the same manner and Form of Proceeding observed as practiced within the Jurisdiction of the Parliament of Paris', it does not explain how the legal system in New France has evolved.

[44] The 1801 *Copyright Act*, however, applied 'in the United Kingdom of Great Britain and Ireland', An Act to further Encouragement of Learning, in the United Kingdom of Great Britain and Ireland, by Securing the Copies and Copyright of printed Books, to the Authors of such Books, or their Assigns for the Time herein mentioned, 1801 (U.K.), 41 Geo. 3 c.107.

the colonies by the registration of their works in London. The reverse was not true. Canadian writers had to publish in England first to enjoy protection in all colonies, failing which they would be deprived of any protection abroad. Even though this eventuality was hypothetical, as there was very little Canadian production until the second half of the nineteenth century, it became a subject of discord. The Imperial system was considered oppressive, a state of affairs that was finally noticed in the Report of the British Royal Commission for the investigation of the subject of copyright released in 1878. It acknowledged the abuses of a system meant to benefit British publishers only. The Act of 1842 was felt as an outrageous intervention, since it placed the Canadian market in the hands of British publishers. As of 1846, representations were made to the Imperial Government to exempt from authorization the importation of reprints made in the United States, the main source of affordable books. In practice, the establishment of an effective customs control system appears to be illusory, since the Canadian border with the United States could not be rendered impermeable.[45] The British Government ultimately acceded to Canadian repeated demands and in 1847, the Imperial Parliament quietly enacted the Foreign Reprints Act.[46] Although this measure did not appear to be of great importance for the British administration, discontent and complaints were voiced by the English publishers. Not only were their expectations of lucre thwarted as far as the North American market was concerned, but reprints imported under the 1847 system could find their way into Great Britain and compete with home editions of the same works.[47]

---

[45] The Royal Copyright Commission concluded that: '[. . .] it is highly desirable that the literature of this country should be placed within easy reach of the colonies, and that with this view the Imperial Act should be modified, so as to meet the requirements of colonial readers. In this country the disadvantage arising from the custom of publishing books in the first instance at a high price, is greatly lessened by the facilities afforded by means of clubs, book societies and circulating libraries. These means are not available, and indeed are impracticable, owing to the great distances and scattered populations, in many of the colonies, and until the cheaper English editions have been published, the colonial reader can only obtain English copyright books by purchasing them at high publishing prices, increased as those prices are by the expense of carriage and other charges incidental to the importation of the books from the United Kingdom.' *Report of the Commission of 1878*, in G.H. Putnam (1896), *The Question of Copyright*, 2nd edn, New York: Putnam, at pp. 466–467, at paras. 183–186.

[46] *Supra* note 7. See Dispatch N. 47, p. 46. Letter from John Murray and Thomas Longman to Gladstone, dated March 1870 complaining about the effect of the 1847 Foreign Reprints Act and asking for its prompt repeal.

[47] Briggs notes that: 'There is a present danger to English authors that cheap reprints authorised in any particular colony by special arrangement may be imported thence to others in which the book sells at full price. In spite of customs

Although general in its terms, the Act of 1847 was a specific response to the North American problem. It removed the ban on the import of books which were printed abroad without authorization, on the condition that a minimal protection be given to British authors. 'The principle of this Act, commonly known as the Foreign Reprints Act, is to enable the colonies to take advantage of reprints of English copyright books made in foreign states, and at the same time to protect the interests of British authors.'[48] The law of 1847 does not specify in its text what was meant by the expression 'reasonable protection', and leaves the Imperial Government the discretion to reject or validate any bill that would be presented to it by the colonies.[49] With alacrity, Canada availed itself of the Foreign Reprints Act,[50] and six days later, on 28 July 1847, it voted An Act to Extend the Provincial Copyright Act to Persons Resident in the United Kingdom.[51] This was a 'marvel of subterfuge'.[52] The Canadian legislation provides that British subjects were protected in the same way as a person or persons residing in that province; provided that the work in question be *printed and published in the province*. In effect, it created an exclusive colonial market, but so little consideration was given to Canadian affairs that the Board of Trade blindly approved the Act.

officers thousands of Tauchitz and other English Books published abroad at low price find their way into England.' W. Briggs (1906), *The Law of International Copyright*, London: Stevens & Haynes, at p. 41.

48 *Report of the Commission of 1878*, in Putnam, *supra* note 45 at para. 188.

49 '[. . .] in the case Her Majesty shall be of the opinion that such act or ordinance is sufficient for the purpose, and shall be of the opinion that such act or ordinance is sufficient for the purpose of securing to British authors reasonable protection within such possession, it shall be lawful for Her Majesty [. . .] to issue an order in council declaring that so long as the provisions of such act or ordinance continue in force within such colony the prohibition [. . .] against the importing, selling, letting out to hire, exposing for Sale or Hire, or possessing Foreign Reprints of Books first composed, written, printed, or published in the United Kingdom, and entitled to Copyrights therein, shall be suspended so far as regards such Colony: [. . .]', Foreign Reprint Act, *supra* note 7, s. 1.

50 Ibid.

51 An Act to extend the Provincial Copyright Act to persons resident in the United Kingdom, (1847) (Can.), 10 Vict., c. 28. Other colonies, including Nova Scotia (1848) and New Brunswick (1848), passed a regulation pursuant to the Foreign Reprints Act. See E. J. Macgillivray (1902), *A Treatise Upon The Law of Copyright*, London: John Murray at p. 187, note 2; J. Shortt (1884), *Law of Copyright*, 2nd edn, London: Reeves and Turner, at p. 136; and W. A. Copinger (1881), *The Law of Copyright*, 2nd edn, London: Steven and Haynes, at p. 499.

52 J.J. Barnes (1974), *Authors, Publishers and Politicians – The Quest for an Anglo-American Copyright Agreement 1815–1854*, Columbus: Ohio State University Press, at p. 149.

The Canadian solution clearly conflicted with the Imperial legislation, whose central feature was the first publication in Great Britain. In other words, the Canadian government attempted to subtly elude Imperial competence in matters of copyright. The British government was late in reacting. If the Canadian Act was given assent, it is because '[n]othing in it directly alluded to the Foreign Reprints Act but instead granted copyright protection to British authors who. . .printed and published their works in the Province. Since British authors were under the impression that they already enjoyed such privilege under the Imperial Act of 1842, they took little notice.'[53]

Nonetheless, an irregularity remained. The issuance of an Order in Council was necessary to suspend the application of the importation provisions contained in the 1842 Copyright Act and to give full effect to the colonial provisions. The Governor-General at the time, Lord Elgin, requested that such formality be completed. By doing this and in the face of much resistance, the British authorities proceeded with a new examination of the Canadian statute and ultimately refused to endorse the issuing of the Order. The implementing colonial statute of the Foreign Reprints Act of 1847 attempted a 'divorce' which Imperial law would not tolerate. Canada thus found itself in a stalemate, and returned to the drawing board in order to remedy the situation and find a way to accommodate the Imperial requirement.[54] Since the Canadian law of 28 July 1847 was stillborn, the sitting Parliament of the Province of Canada adopted a new Act in 1850.[55] This second attempt satisfied the British government. Following other colonies' initiatives,[56] the Act established a compensation system by which British authors would receive an *ad valorem* royalty '. . .not to

---

53 Ibid.

54 'Canadians took the better part of two years to secure the passage of a new Act which conformed to the provisions of the Foreign Reprints Act, and in the meantime conditions became increasingly chaotic. [. . .] According to the prevailing Copyright and Customs Acts of 1842 British authors and publishers had to notify the Customs of their latest copyright works which were then incorporated into lists forwarded to the colonies every three months. Clever booksellers and publishers in Canada recognized the time-lag between the date of publication and the receipt of quarterly lists and simply imported all the American reprints they wished during the interval.' Barnes, ibid, at p. 150.

55 An Act to Impose Duty on Foreign reprints of British Copyright Works, 1850 (Can.), 13 & 14 Vict., c. 6.

56 Bermuda, for instance, adopted in 1848, an *ad valorem* duty of 15 per cent on importation, (1875) *Papers Relating to Copyright (colonies), Colonial Copyright Acts*, Ottawa, at p. 25. There is also indication that acts to the same effect were passed in Jamaica, British Guiana, Bahamas, St. Vincent, Cape, Natal, Mauritius, Barbados, St. Lucia, Antigua and St. Kitts. We learn in addition that the rates of duty imposed by these Acts varied from 15 to 25 per cent *ad valorem*.

exceed more than twenty percent on imported books in this province, upon which a literary property right exists, and which are originally composed or written in the United Kingdom.' The royalty was set at 12.5 per cent.

Canada capitulated on its very legitimate attempts to be master on its territory. Importing was still permitted and the reader could read, but at what cost? The reader barely remained the sole owner of his culture, the fruits of which belonged to others. He was deprived of the right to reprint English works and forced to import books from abroad at a prohibitive cost (British publications). Canadian printers and publishers emerged from the stalemate as big losers. By contrast, American printers greatly benefited from colonial and imperial measures. They continued with impunity to manufacture and supply Canada with new editions of English books; an exportation that was sanctioned by the Foreign Reprints Act. Excluded from this *de facto* reprinting privilege,[57] some Canadian publishers decided to do an end-run around the legislation. In order to benefit from the same Imperial regime, they installed their printing presses in the United States, and then supplied their own bookshops in Canada.[58]

4 CONCLUSION

That the Statute of Anne had an influence on Canadian legislation is hardly disputable. From a purely instrumental point of view at least, the Canadian legislation, past and present, has an 'air de famille' when one surveys Copyright legislations from other Common law jurisdictions. Concretely, as it has been indicated, the Act of 1832 passed by the Lower Canada Legislature was modeled after the US Copyright Act of 1831, which in turn directly integrated the basic policies of the Statute of Anne. Canada borrowed again in 1921 when it adopted its carbon copy of the 1911 UK Act, a puzzling move as Canada was finally given the opportunity to follow its own political and cultural agenda and adopt its own copy.

But beyond the obvious lies another story, as discreet as it is vocal. The normative process by which legal systems are exported cannot be

---

57 'They contended that although they might import and sell American reprints on paying the duty, they were not allowed to republish British works, and to have the advantage of the trade, the sole benefit of which was, in effect, secured for Americans', *Report of the Commission of 1878*, in Putnam, *supra* note 45 at p. 260, para. 195.

58 Catherine Seville (2006), *The Internationalisation of Copyright*, Cambridge: Cambridge University Press at p. 98.

understood by resorting to grammatical or literal comparisons. The texts of 1832 remain silent as to the motives of its adoption. Patterson and Lindberg perfectly captured the reasons for the lack of information regarding the first enactments:

> The nineteenth century was a formative era of American copyright law. The framers' prescience in putting the copyright clause into the Constitution had been a manifestation of wisdom, not knowledge. Indeed, so meager was the intellectual underpinning for copyright in the new nation that the First Congress merely copied the English Statute of Anne – the contents of which it may not have fully comprehended – to enact the first federal copyright act.

This reflection applies to the Canadian experience.

If one looks at the influence of the Statute of Anne as an expression of the Canadianess of Canadian copyright policy, it is not to be found in the text of 1832, but rather in the small prints of the numerous bills and amendments proposed to the English Parliament, in those provisions buried in the text which triggered an open war between Canadian, American and English publishers and stigmatized by the 1847 Foreign Reprints Act. It is in the context of the 1847 extraordinary piece that the influence of the Statute of Anne and its monopolistic or imperialistic effects can be fully grasped. This influence lives in a list of statutes long forgotten – some of which never received Royal Assent and which depict a story that needed to be told about the evolution of norms in an asymmetric context:

(French versions)

- *Acte pour protéger la propriété littéraire,* 2 Gui. IV c. 53 (1832) (Province du Bas-Canada).
- *Acte pour protéger les Droits d'Auteurs dans cette Province,* 4&5 Vict. c. 60–61 (1841).
- *Acte pour étendre l'Acte Provincial des Droits d'Auteur aux personnes résidant dans le Royaume Uni, à certaines conditions,* 10 & 11 Vict. c. 28 (1847).
- *Acte pour imposer un droit sur les impressions étrangères des ouvrages britanniques soumis au droit de propriété,* 14 Vict. c. 6. (1850).
- *Acte concernant les droits d'auteurs*, 22 Vict. C 81 (1859).
- *Acte concernant la propriété littéraire et artistique*, 31 Vict. c. 54 (1868).
- *Acte concernant la propriété littéraire et artistique,* 38 Vic. c. 88. (1875).
- *Acte concernant la propriété littéraire et artistique*, 49 Vict. c. 62 (1886).

- *Acte modifiant l'Acte concernant les droits d'auteur, chapitre soixante-deux des Statuts révisés,* 52 Vict. c. 29 (1889).
- *Acte modifiant l'Acte concernant les droits d'auteur*, 58–59 Vict. c. 37 (1895).
- *Acte modifiant l'Acte concernant les droits d'auteur*, 63–64 Victoria c. 25 (1900).

PART II

Digital libraries and online licensing

12. Introduction to Part II

Uma Suthersanen*

1 INTRODUCTION

> *Me, poor man, my library, Was dukedom large enough . . . Knowing I lov'd my books, he furnish'd me, From my own library, with volumes that I prize above my dukedom.*[1]

Thus does Shakespeare convey both power and control over the deposed Duke of Milan, Prospero, through the 'library'. The sessions in the ALAI Congress 2009 on digital libraries, collective management, online licensing and the Google book project, depict similar notions of control and power. The *zeitgeist* of this and the next centuries, however, is that the growing power of the custodians of the 'library' (which is widely defined) must be regulated, as must be the power of these custodians to grant access to works, and to remunerate the authors of such works.

2 THE FUNCTION OF DIGITAL LIBRARIES

The British Library (BL) is a good example of how the modest sixteenth century library, as private collections of books,[2] has expanded to the current role of a library as the custodian of the 'knowledge network'. BL's 'knowledge network' is accessible, apparently, through blogs, podcasts, Facebook, Twitter, Flickr, YouTube, and audioBoo. As its website announces proudly: 'It's not about "Sssh!". It's about "What do you need?"'[3]

This expanded role of the library, from being a physical, private repository of books to being a public purveyor of knowledge raises

* Professor Uma Suthersanen, School of Law, Queen Mary, University of London.

1 W. Shakespeare, Act 1/Scene II, *The Tempest*.

2 See paper by Dame Lynne Brindley, Chapter 13 in this volume. For an account of private libraries, see L. Febvre and H-J Martin (1997), *The Coming of the Book*, London: Verso, p.263.

3 Comment of Dr. Gabrielle Walker, on http://www.bl.uk/index4.shtml.

several concerns, especially when the notion of 'knowledge' and 'digital' is disparate in terms of content and format:[4] besides literary, artistic, musical and audio-visual works in both analogue and digital formats, the British Library offers a Business and Intellectual Property service for entrepreneurs in the creative industries, is committed to the building of a digital research environment, and is currently digitising 20 million pages of out-of-copyright nineteenth century printed books. Finally, part of its new remit is to be the 'leading voice and honest broker in the Intellectual Property debate'.[5] The same is true in the United States where the Library of Congress is similarly entrusted with the public function of preserving and providing access to works held within its collections.[6]

Several queries arise at this point. First, can all libraries, irrespective of definitional or statutory limits, or of public/public status, be allowed to provide access to the cultural heritage of a nation?[7] Secondly, are digital collections and libraries cloaked within a higher hierarchical legal order in terms of public interest, the right of education and cultural heritage?[8] Thirdly, should we be concerned when viable solutions arise outside copyright law?[9] Finally, what changes are required, if any, to the current copyright landscape?

3 EDUCATION AND PUBLIC INTEREST

A much highlighted public cause in the discourse surrounding digital libraries is the private individual right of education, coupled with the

---

4 See June Besek paper, Chapter 14 in this volume, on difficulties of defining 'library' and 'digital'.

5 See for example s.1, British Library Act 1972 (as amended); and the *British Library Funding Agreement 2008/09 – 2010/11*, between the UK Department for Culture, Media and Sport; UK Department for Innovation, Universities and Skills; UK Department for Business, Enterprise and Regulatory Reform; and the British Library – available at http://www.bl.uk/aboutus/foi/pubsch/funding0811.pdf

6 One function of the Library of Congress is to 'develop qualitatively the Library's universal collections, which document the history and further the creativity of the American people and which record and contribute to the advancement of civilization and knowledge throughout the world, and to acquire, organize, provide access to, maintain, secure, and preserve these collections.'

7 See papers of Brindley, Besek, Obhi and Sprang, Chapters 13, 14, 19 and 20 in this volume.

8 See papers of Xalabarder and Ricolfi, Chapters 16 and 15 respectively in this volume.

9 See papers of Gendreau and Koskinen-Olsson, Chapters 18 and 17 respectively in this volume.

needs of countries to educate, at an affordable rate, its populace. An educational exception has been, without exception, part and parcel of twentieth century copyright law, both within the international and domestic legislative frameworks. The notion of 'education' can also be similarly stretched to encompass teaching,[10] scholarship, research, and knowledge. Thus the WIPO Copyright Treaty 1996 refers in its Preamble to recognising the 'need to maintain a balance between the rights of authors, and the larger public interest, particularly education, research and access to information'.

Public libraries and commercial entrepreneurs emphasise this particular focus on education and access to information in relation to digital libraries. This focus stems from two bases: (a) education is a fundamental human right;[11] (b) copyright, as part of intellectual property,[12] has an ambiguous ranking within the human rights taxonomy, both in terms of law making and policy shaping.[13] In this sense, one should not be surprised to see a plethora of 'educational exceptions' and 'library exceptions' within national, regional and copyright laws. Is this, however, truly the case?

A 2008 WIPO Study on copyright exceptions in the area of libraries[14] showed that most WIPO members have statutory library exception; yet, the report suggests that libraries are still struggling with 'large-scaled digitization of collections and automated harvesting and collecting of Internet-based resources'. The pessimistic view is that education has been

---

[10] See, for example, Recital 14, Directive 2001/29/EC of the European Parliament and of the Council of 22 May 2001, on the harmonisation of certain aspects of copyright and related rights in the information society, 2001 O.J. L-167/10 (22.06.2001).

[11] Article 26, Universal Declaration on Human Rights (UDHR); Article 13, International Covenant on Economic, Social and Cultural Rights 1966 (ICESCR).

[12] Article 27.

[13] See Article 27, UDHR and Article 15(1), ICESCR. The two provisions balance the rights of authors to benefit from the protection of the moral and material interests in scientific, literary or artistic production, on the one hand, with the rights of cultural participation and enjoyment of benefits of scientific progress, on the other. Moreover, the recent 2005 General Comment on the interpretation of the 'intellectual property' clause in Article 15(1)(c), ICESCR emphasises that the Covenant cannot be understood as guaranteeing intellectual property rights, or else as elevating intellectual property to the human rights stratosphere. See G. Dutfield and U. Suthersanen (2008), *Global Intellectual Property Law*, Cheltenham, UK and Northampton, MA, USA: Edward Elgar Publishing, pp. 218–221.

[14] K. Crews, WIPO Study on Copyright Limitations And Exceptions For Libraries And Archives, Standing Committee On Copyright And Related Rights, 17th Session, SCCR/17/2, 26 August 2008.

ignored within copyright instruments. Many copyright exceptions are narrow, dependent on national interpretations of provision by courts or collecting societies, and are not digital-friendly. Little is being done, it is argued, within the international fora to forge a cogent and modern approach within copyright law to solve the daily dilemmas faced by digital libraries and, increasingly, online educational institutions.[15] The traditional context of usages within libraries and educational institutions fail to fall comfortably within 'photocopying' or single usage exceptions.[16]

4 LANDSCAPING COPYRIGHT

Unsurprisingly, we have witnessed initiatives both from the United States and the European Union[17] in trying to contour three separate legal-policy maps: libraries, 'access to knowledge', and copyright. Do these initiatives serve well?

Indeed, on 19 October 2009,[18] the European Commission made a clarion call to all stakeholders (the assumption being they are known to us) to 'tackle the important cultural and legal challenges of mass-scale digitisation and dissemination of books, in particular of European library collections'. The Communication appears to reiterate the concerns that have been outstanding for several years, that is researchers and consumers across Europe need to gain access to knowledge; we have the traditional dilemmas of copyright versus access and cultural heritage. Moreover, from the European perspective, cultural heritage can sometimes mean going against market forces. As Ricolfi points out, consumers may prefer English works, but EU institutions prioritise the preservation of linguistic and cultural diversity. Indeed, the ethos of European solutions is succinctly captured by this logo: europeana - think culture.[19]

In the US, the digitisation efforts of public libraries, including the

---

15 See paper by Raquel Xalabarder Chapter 16 in this volume

16 See paper by Xalabarder, at Chapter 16. This dilemma was also previously pointed by Sam Ricketson, in a magisterial study of the application of the Berne three step test in relation to educational exceptions in (2002), *The three-step test, deemed quantities, libraries and closed exceptions*, for the Australian Centre for Copyright Studies, at p. 117.

17 See papers by June Besek and Marco Ricolfi, Chapters 14 and 15 in this volume.

18 Communication From the Commission, *Copyright in the Knowledge Economy,* Brussels, 19.10.2009, COM(2009) 532 final.

19 See Ricolfi paper, Chapter 15; and Tarja Koskinen-Olsson paper, Chapter 17, in this volume.

Library of Congress, is governed by section 108, US Copyright Act which provides limited exceptions for libraries and archives for reproduction and distribution for preservation purposes. The report and recommendations of the Section 108 Study Group[20] make fascinating reading in relation to all pertinent and current controversies surrounding digitisation, Google, libraries and access. Nevertheless, what stands out starkly is that no consensus could be found on the very issues which plague us now: libraries providing remote access to library materials, and to digitised analogue materials.[21]

5 COLLECTIVE MANAGEMENT AND THE GOOGLE BOOK PROJECT

Part of the impetus behind why governments and organisations have begun to debate this matter openly (and urgently) has been the arrival of the Google Book phenomenon, accompanied by the Google Book Settlement in the United States.[22] As the 2009 EC Communication Paper (referred above) notes, part of the European impetus is to provide 'pro-competitive European solutions on books digitization' which will be more 'operational than the solutions presently envisaged under the Google Books Settlement in the United States'.

So, what now? How do we obtain solutions for 'simple and cost-efficient rights clearance covering mass-scale digitisation and the online dissemination of library collections still protected by copyright'?[23] Will we have to abandon our traditional normative legal classification of 'copyright works' in respect of digitised resources, and adopt the more 'efficient' view of the digital collections of libraries as economic goods. In which case, the next issue to be addressed is that of valuation and remuneration. Adjacent

---

20 See June Besek paper, Chapter 14 in this volume; and *Section 108 Study Group Report* (2008), available at http://www.section108.gov/docs/Sec108StudyGroupReport.pdf.

21 See June Besek paper, Chapter 14 in this volume.

22 *The Authors Guild, Inc., et al. v. Google Inc.*, Case No. 05 CV 8136 (S.D.N.Y.). The preliminary approval of the Settlement has been given by the Court; the settlement agreement Is available at: http://www.googlebooksettlement.com/r/view_settlement_agreement. For a summary of the settlement, see Harjinder Obhi and June Besek papers, Chapters 19 and 14 respectively in this volume.

23 Communication from the Commission to the European Parliament, the Council, the European Economic and Social Committee and the Committee of Regions i2010: Digital Libraries Brussels 30.9.05 COM (2005) final.

to this is the fact that all usage of digital collections will ultimately only reflect the very fictional 'market value' by means of licensing.

The Canadian perspective, for example reveals that legislative governance of digital works relies on traditional legal principles (both contract and copyright), even though more than half of journal subscriptions in university libraries were in electronic form.[24] The result, unsurprisingly, is an artificial valuation of goods via a private agreement,[25] between libraries, universities and collecting societies (as in the 2008 agreement between Bibliothèque et Archives nationales du Québec and COPIBEC, a reproduction right collecting society). The benefits, as Gendreau points out, is that such private agreements do manage to 'maintain the presence of authors in the overall process'; the disadvantages, however, as she wisely points out, is that 'the cumulative effect of private agreements that operate on the fringes of the *Act* in an educational context for the online diffusion of works reinforces the image of the free culture of the Internet.'[26] Nevertheless, can such private negotiations between two parties be the genesis of a universal solution for all authors and users?

Moreover, what differentiates such private agreements from the Google Book Search project's ethos, that is, to enable people to search the content of books in a useful way, either within or without copyright law.[27] Why should we give consideration to whether the digitisation efforts are by national institutions such as the Library of Congress or the Bibliothèque et Archives nationales du Québec, or by private corporations such as Google? One issue, obviously, is control. If a commercial corporation does have a *de facto* monopoly on out-of-print books, the pricing mechanism may be anti-competitive.[28] And yet, most pricing mechanisms of copyright works are, *de facto,* anti-competitive.

Perhaps the conclusion to Part II is neither difficult nor ambiguous. As Sterling's paper (Chapter 21) notes, changes are required in how we think of exceptions, territoriality and internet dissemination, the public interest, sustainable copyright administration and enforcement, efficient regulation of protected material in digital libraries, peer-to-peer file sharing and user generated content. Solutions exist: a global clearance system; a levy system; mandatory collective management; extended collective licensing; a global licensing system. At times, it appears that the copyright world is

---

24 See Ysolde Gendreau paper, Chapter 18 in this volume.

25 It should be noted, however, that such agreements are subject to the Canadian Copyright Board's control.

26 See Ysolde Gendreau paper, Chapter 18 in this volume.

27 See Harjinder Obhi paper, Chapter 19 in this volume.

28 See Christian Sprang paper, Chapter 20 in this volume.

undergoing a revolution of sorts, and as in all revolutions, the old institutions and guardians are resistant to change. Yet, perhaps it is time, like Shakespeare's Prospero in *The Tempest* to let go of the old world formed by the 1710 Statute of Anne, and wrought a new landscape. Change is not necessarily bad.

> *All changed, changed utterly:*
> *A terrible beauty is born.*[29]

---

29 WB Yeats, *Easter 1916*.

13. Phoenixes in the internet era – the changing role of libraries

Dame Lynne J. Brindley*

1 INTRODUCTION

In my contribution entitled phoenixes in the internet era – the changing role of libraries – I hope to address some of the key issues for libraries in the Internet Age, and how our functions are adapting to the demands of all things digital. I will suggest the need for changes to copyright regimes to ensure that great libraries can indeed continue their enduring purpose, revitalised as the digital library rapidly becomes a reality. I am not an expert in copyright, and I am thus particularly indebted to my expert colleague Ben White for his input to this contribution.

For those of you not familiar with the British Library let me start by sharing with you a little about this great institution. As well as being the UK's national library, the British Library is one of the world's great research libraries. The Library's physical collection includes some 150 million items, in most known languages. Three million new items are incorporated every year, and the print collections continue to grow at around 12.5 linear kilometres or eight miles per annum. Alongside books and journals, we hold maps, newspapers, magazines, drawings, music scores, sound recordings and patents. To get some idea of scale, were you to view five items each day, it would take you 80,000 years to see the whole collection! In addition we are now ingesting, licensing and digitising many terabytes of digital content, providing a portfolio of analogue and digital library services characterised by the description of hybrid library.

As a national library we have the statutory function of legal deposit, ensuring that we collect, preserve and make available the memory of the nation, as manifest in printed form. Primary legislation in 2003 extended this responsibility to digital materials and we are currently working with

* Chief Executive, The British Library. A French and Spanish translation of this chapter can be found on the website of the British Literary and Artistic Copyright Association (BLACA): www.blaca.org.

government and publishers to ensure the appropriate enactment through the regulatory process.

2 STRATEGIC CHALLENGES

Key strategic questions for us and for other great libraries are:

- How do we remain relevant to scholarship, education and the economy and a dynamic player in the digital age?
- How is publishing and information changing through digital innovation and in what ways is it important for us?
- What are expectations of our users and how are they changing?
- What are the changes in research and knowledge transfer that demand changes in libraries? And,
- What does it all mean for collecting policies, for provision of services and for statutory functions of all national libraries?

The British Library's doors are open to all who need access to our collection for research purposes, but the expectations of new generations of researchers are very different from those of us who got our research training in the analogue age. Research commissioned by the British Library and the Joint Information Systems Committee (JISC) into the Information Behaviour of the Researcher of the Future[1] has, however, cast doubt on the assumption that the 'Google Generation' is necessarily the most web-literate. The study showed that, while young people demonstrate an ease and familiarity with computers, they rely heavily on search engines, view rather than read, are promiscuous in their information seeking and do not possess the critical skills to assess the information they find on the web. The report also shows that the research behaviour associated with younger users is now becoming the norm for all age-groups. For many, Google is always their first port of call when they need information, and I would venture to suggest that for the majority of young people Wikipedia has replaced the Encyclopaedia Britannica (or your own non-English language equivalent) as the general reference tool of choice on any given subject.

So what does it all mean for great libraries? In principle it is simple. Libraries and information services must step up to the plate to provide services which meet the needs of this new generation, and ones which add

---

[1] http://www.bl.uk/news/pdf/googlegen.pdf.

value well beyond the search engine. Libraries must work to understand the changing needs and expectations of schoolchildren and scholars, and swiftly move their emphasis to the digital reality and future. The alternative is to risk becoming obsolete, or simply 'museums of the book'.

The British Library has taken a lead on this digital journey in addressing the challenges of collecting, preserving and providing access to the world's digital knowledge. Without such effort and investment future researchers and citizens will find a black hole in the captured and preserved knowledge base of large parts of the twentieth and the twenty-first century, and without a guaranteed long-term commitment to preservation, our content and creative industries will be inhibited in their global market success. However, alongside the obvious technological challenges, we face a range of copyright related challenges in carrying out this mission.

I would like now to speak about some of our key digital functions and the associated challenges of copyright.

3 DIGITISATION

Most libraries are engaged in digitisation programmes of differing sizes to make their historic collections more accessible through digitisation. Increasingly if library content is not found on the Web, it effectively does not exist for many potential users. Whilst historically we have concentrated on ensuring that our catalogues are online, as pointers to printed and other materials, now users demand instant access well beyond the metadata.

The default assumption becomes both to access content digitally and to assume that all content can and should be available in digital form, without the necessity of going to a physical library or requiring any less immediate forms of delivery. Mass digitisation of analogue content delivers much of this aspiration. The British Library is working on several fronts.

With Microsoft we digitised some 85,000 out of copyright books of nineteenth century English literature over the last year or so. Unfortunately this programme was brought to an early end when Microsoft decided to cease its book digitisation programme. It did, however, result in a good corpus of classics and hidden gems becoming available through our catalogue and potentially through a number of e-distribution channels.

Our current focus is on digitising our newspaper collection. A competitive dialogue procurement process is nearing completion, with the aim of creating a partnership with the private sector to digitise and provide an online service of massive scale – there are some 750 million pages of opportunity! JISC (the body which funds ICT in universities and beyond) support for the higher and further education communities has already resulted in three million pages of eighteenth and nineteenth century newspapers being made freely available online to those communities, providing a rich information source, with excellent search and interpretive possibilities.

Our hugely popular *Turning The Pages* digitised Treasures has brought global prominence, visibility and public endorsement to treasures which were once for the eyes of the privileged few. The British Library's online gallery provides access, for example, to Mozart's musical diary (complete with 75 audio clips), the Diamond Sutra (the World's oldest printed book), Leonardo's notebook, Blake's notebook, Sultan Babar's Qu'ran, to name but a few.

The BL's Archival Sound Recordings service provides free online access for UK higher and further education institutions to over 32,000 rare recordings of music, spoken word, and human and natural environments. Over 11,700 of these recordings are accessible to the general public listening online.

4 ORPHAN WORKS

Clearly our digitisation is a massive scale, long term endeavour. We have focussed initially on out of copyright material but one issue that we are very conscious of is around Orphan Works – works where the rights holders cannot be identified or traced. This is a significant issue for a large library and archive, like the British Library – we have estimated that potentially over 40 per cent of our collections may be orphan works. This figure has been corroborated by a recently released international study on Orphan Works from the UK based Collections Trust and Strategic Content Alliance. The study, 'In From the Cold'[2] not only found that up to 50 per cent of works in large archives were orphan works, but that there were in excess of 50 million Orphan Works sitting in the 503 organisations that formed part of their survey. This represents a huge amount of content effectively 'off limits' in the way that copyright law is currently constructed, providing little value or benefit to anyone.

Already on some of our JISC projects we have spent literally thousands of working hours trying to establish rights holders who often just aren't

---

[2] 'In from the Cold: An assessment of the scope of 'Orphan Works' and its impact on the delivery of services to the public', JISC, June 2009. www.jisc.ac.uk/publications/documents/infromthecold.aspx.

there to be found. For example, in one oral history project – a series of unpublished interviews in the 1960 and 1970s held at the St Mary Le Bow Church in the East End of London, 302 hours were spent by BL staff and paid contractors looking for 259 rights holders – some performers were famous like Sir John Betjeman, Germaine Greer, and Diana Rigg but many were local bankers, school teachers, clergymen and so on. Despite the time taken we were only able to locate 14 rights holders – all of whom gave us permission to use the material freely. Much of this type of material is of high educational value, but low or no commercial value – we find that once people understand the project is free and it is for universities a 'royalty fee' is the last thing on their mind.

Clearly expending so much time on a fruitless search is a waste of public resources. It is in everyone's interest to find a workable solution for Orphan Works – this will take on different hues in differing countries but we believe that legislation has a part to play and is required for Orphan Works to provide real legal and reputational certainty for libraries, archives and museums who are putting parts of their collections on the web. Whilst collective licensing is a very important mechanism for commercial purposes and collecting societies represent the interest of their members well, when it comes to putting Orphan Works on the world wide web I think there are a number of questions that we need to ask – and forgive me if this is an overly UK centric view:

- How can a de facto insurance scheme prevent publicly funded organisations from being taken to court – in your own country or in a foreign country that doesn't agree with or understand the collective licensing solution in your own country?
- To what extent can or should the public sector for non-commercial uses rely on private organisations employing best-practice licensing across borders?

Our experience tells us that when you do contact the majority of individuals who own the rights themselves, when they realise the digitisation is for non-commercial purposes they don't expect payment. As you may therefore have gathered much of the cultural sector in this country wants an exception in copyright law for Orphan Works.

5 GOOGLE

Discussion of the Orphan Works issue perhaps leads on naturally to Google itself. As part of the wide ranging Google book settlement,

Google through reaching an out of court settlement with the Association of American Publishers and the American Authors Guild on an opt-out basis has got a *de facto* licence for Orphan Works. As I am sure you are aware the case is attracting increasing amounts of controversy and it will be interesting to see where we end up. I am not entering today into the Google debate – it could take all day!

The settlement is being challenged in the US by the Internet Archive who believes there are anti-trust, or in Euro-speak Competition law issues. And of course recently the German foreign minister Frank-Walter Steinmeier has been putting pressure on the EU as he believes that Google has infringed European copyright law and this is giving them a significant advantage over European projects like Europeana – the grand project to bring online the cultural resources of European libraries, archives and museums who do respect copyright law.

6 DIGITAL PRESERVATION

A second important function for libraries like the British Library is preservation and increasingly digital preservation. This is at one level simply an extension of the long-standing core role of great libraries to preserve our collections 'in perpetuity', for long term access and to underpin research, creativity and innovation. It is an endeavour of some urgency as, for example, we have estimated that by 2020 at least 80 per cent of research journals and 50 per cent of monographs will be available in electronic formats only. The British Library is leading a major European Union co-funded project, which started in June 2006 and has a total budget of close to €15m. The Planets consortium brings together expertise across Europe from national libraries and archives, leading research universities and technology companies, and it aims to build practical services and tools to help ensure long-term access to European digital cultural and scientific assets.

In the UK the preservation exception in copyright law very much reflects analogue norms, and was a concern highlighted by libraries as part of the Gowers Review of Intellectual Property in 2006.[3]

The law only allows us to make one preservation copy (clearly no longer adequate in a world of format shifting, and the employment of mirror servers as best practice for digital preservation).

---

[3] 'Gowers Review of Intellectual Property'. November 2006. www.hm-treasury.gov.uk/d/pbr06_gowers_report_755.pdf.

In addition, the law does not allow us to make preservation copies of sound recordings, film, broadcasts or standalone artistic works. Neither does the law allow explicitly for format shifting – which is a requirement of digital preservation, to update technical formats through a process known as 'normalisation', that is to say the transformation of the original digital work from one format to another to prevent the digital object degrading or becoming obsolete as formats shift and change over time.

We also have some problems with technical protection measures that prevent digital preservation. This can be for a number of reasons such as the technical protection measure being 'fused' within the digital object itself like a CD or DVD thus preventing copying. It can also occur where external software companies like Microsoft or Adobe no longer remotely authenticate from their servers one's rights to access a certain piece of software on which the digital object is dependent. When this remote authentication stops effectively your ability to use the software and therefore the digital object also stops. For example we house a collection of digital photographs from the famous British photographer Fay Godwin – without format shifting these while the software still operates, when Adobe no longer supports Photoshop, these unique photos will be no longer accessible.

If you are particularly interested in the issue of TPMs and preservation I would recommend to you a recently issued, and in depth study by Patricia Akester from the Centre for Intellectual Property and Information Law at Cambridge University entitled 'Technological accommodation of conflicts between freedom of expression and DRM: the first empirical assessment.'[4]

7 ACCESS TO DIGITAL CONTENT

A key part of the role of libraries is to ensure that users can have good access to a full range of content – analogue and digital, in and out of copyright. So of course a major function is the licensing of digital content from publishers, aggregators and others to provide access to this material – in reading rooms, and in many cases from wherever users are. In trying to carry out this function we head straight into probably one of the biggest

---

4 'Technological accommodation of conflicts between freedom of expression and DRM: the first empirical assessment'. May 2009. Patricia Akester, Centre for Intellectual Property & Information Law, Cambridge University. www.law.cam.ac.uk.

issues for libraries in the digital world, namely the relationship between copyright and contract law.

The law of contract overrides the limitations and exceptions in copyright law that libraries and researchers so rely on. This is not just an issue here in the UK, but in the majority of EU member states also. Indeed Francis Gurrie, the newly appointed Australian Director General of WIPO in his acceptance speech stated that the interplay between copyright and contract was a fundamental issue that needs to be addressed in the digital era.

This is an important issue for the higher education sector particularly as university libraries purchase and acquire substantial amounts of electronic material using public money.

The British Library also licences large numbers of electronic journals and databases. We did a study of 100 contracts offered to us and found that over 90 per cent of them undermined the exceptions in law that relate to core library activities. For example:

- only 23 per cent allowed for preservation and archiving;
- only 2 per cent allowed for copying for the visually impaired and blind; and
- only 14 per cent allowed inter-library loan.

In total only 25 per cent referred to exceptions at all – and often this was Fair Use – not a UK legal concept at all.

Given the large volume of electronic content we and many other libraries subscribe to, it is impractical to expect one by one detailed contract negotiation, so we are left in a position where our core statutory functions are by contract disallowed, or we ignore the provisions in the contract – clearly a totally unsatisfactory position as digital content comes to be dominant in libraries.

If it is difficult enough for librarians then spare a thought for those who are trying to use the digital content. In the analogue world all the user (and the librarian) had to understand was copyright law – and really in the UK the basics around fair dealing. Now in order to understand what one can do with a particular digital database one has in principle to understand three sets of laws – copyright law, contract law and of course database law. And of course the contract doesn't sit next to the computer terminal for library users to read through – so they are not even in a position to evaluate what the licence may or may not say. This is frankly unrealistic.

This lack of clarity around use has the potential to really hamper the progress of new research methods. Computer technology has already significantly changed the way in which scientific research is conducted. Scientists increasingly do not read books or journals, but by writing computer programmes search, analyse and extract data from written sources in a technique known as 'data mining' or 'text mining'.

This area in particular brings together potentially the overly complex interplay of contract, copyright and database laws. At the British Library we are already seeing contract law preventing text mining, and the greyness around whether an extraction of data is substantive enough to attract either copyright or database rights. This lack of clarity around re-use of scientific data has a chilling effect on science – when as a society we are exactly at a time when we should be promoting science as an integral pillar of the knowledge economy.

I believe therefore the only practical solution to create clarity of use to support science is to ensure that the relatively simple 'usage guidelines' given to us by exceptions in copyright law trump individual contracts. In a global world of information providers, where one global platform, the Internet, provides us with the tools to access and share information, it is crucial that researchers can be clear how they can use data and scientific facts. And this can only be done I believe through ensuring that exceptions override individual contract terms.

8 LEGAL DEPOSIT OF DIGITAL MATERIAL

At the British Library, we are working hard with publishers, government and the other UK legal deposit libraries to make a reality of the national archive of electronic publications envisaged by the 2003 Legal Deposit Libraries Act to extend our statutory responsibilities from UK printed publications to UK digital outputs.

Our Web Archiving Programme is focusing on the Library becoming the point of first resort for a comprehensive archive of material from the UK Web domain. Since 2004, the British Library has led and participated in the UK Web Archiving Consortium initiative, and worked with other key UK organisations to build, through permissions, an archive of web resources of scholarly, cultural, political and scientific importance. However, there are approximately 8 million[5] .uk domain sites in scope currently and growing at 15–20 per cent annually, so the scale is enormous, and the value for future research and innovation vast.

[5] Report by the Web Archiving Sub-Committee, LDAP, April 2008. Figure based on 6.1 million .uk domains registered by Nominet in mid-2007, plus approximately 50,000 other domains which can be readily identified as published in the UK. It was estimated that this number would grow by 17% per annum until 2011.

Although a lot of material on the Web is freely accessible to view, that does not mean we are free to copy it for an archive, so, as already said, we currently operate our Web archiving by permission. But dealing with this can be a laborious and expensive process, both for the BL and for a Website owner, especially when their site includes material contributed by other people. It is too much for many: permission is only granted 25 per cent of the time. Legal deposit regulation could create an automatic limited exception to copyright which would enable us to capture 100 per cent of .uk websites at no cost to owners for the core purpose of archiving and long term access. It could also give protection to some website owners who unwittingly infringe copyright when they authorise an archive copy without owning rights for all of the material.

9 USER-CREATED CONTENT

From a curatorial and service perspective many of us have become quite excited by the potential of Web 2.0 and associated social networking services as they offer libraries significant opportunities to engage much more easily with those who use our services, and tap into their expertise and involvement – as well as reaching out to those who might not otherwise think that the library is for them. But blogs, wikis, twitters, web-based community databases, Facebook groups, YouTube, micro-blogging are all new kinds of digital content, and part of the rich fabric of creation – everyone is an author, a commentator and a contributor – arguably their contributions are as much a part of the nation's memory, scientific outputs, and intellectual records, as traditionally authoritative and mediated formal publications are.

From a copyright perspective all this material – formal or user contributed – is treated all the same – it attracts copyright. Yet much of this 'user created material' has little or no commercial value, nor was it was written or created with any commercial intent. For a library which hopes to web harvest this material, finding a way to give access to it legitimately and within the law is very important.

Of course creative commons licences can help – but this is only a partial and piecemeal solution. We noticed with interest that the EU Green paper, 'Copyright in the Knowledge Economy',[6] asked whether an exception for user created content should be created at a European level. This is

[6] Green Paper: Copyright in the Knowledge Economy, 2008. http://ec.europa.eu/internal_market/copyright/docs/copyright-infso/greenpaper_en.pdf.

certainly one way to look at it. Another way is to create a more differentiated copyright structure – one that can better distinguish commercial from non-commercial use, or research, educational and teaching purposes from other uses. Whatever the best way to achieve it, we believe as a library that such material is of significance to future researchers and we need to find a way through which it can ensure that it can legally and legitimately be used.

10 CONCLUSION

While I have naturally enough been looking at these issues through the lens of a UK-based library, I am encouraged that these issues are also being discussed more and more at an international level. WIPO commissioned a number of studies on copyright limitations and exceptions, and one relating to the Visually Impaired was presented in November 2008[7] – thus we can see exceptions being recognised at the highest level as important for education and learning.

At a European level we have seen not only the Green paper 'Copyright in the Knowledge Economy' that focuses on many issues that I have touched on here today, but also *i2010 – the Digital Libraries Programme*. Through a sub-group on copyright, led so ably by Professor Ricolfi, *i2010* has focused particular attention on the issues of digital preservation and orphan works. We have also heard statements that suggest the Copyright Unit in Brussels is taking seriously the need for European legislation on Orphan Works – something that we believe to be long overdue.

So there are glimmers of hope, but such hope is moving far too slowly to match the reality of the digital world.

I hope that in my contribution I have shown you some of the challenges facing great libraries in the digital age. Whether libraries can, like Phoenixes, renew ourselves and thrive in the digital age, is a profound but very exciting challenge that I believe many of us are up for! The technological complexities are large; the cultural and organisational challenges are formidable. But perhaps most significantly the adaptation of copyright to be fit for purpose in the digital age is absolutely crucial.

---

[7] www.wipo.int/pressroom/en/articles/2008/article_0059.html.

14. The development of digital libraries in the United States

June M. Besek*

1 WHAT IS A DIGITAL LIBRARY?

What is meant by the term 'digital libraries'? In assessing progress toward the creation of 'digital libraries' and considering the appropriate scope of copyright exceptions and limitations, it is worthwhile to consider whether everyone has in mind the same goal. That term likely means different things to different people.

First, what is a library?

In the United States there are special copyright exceptions for libraries and archives, as is true in many countries. But US copyright law does not define the terms 'library' and 'archives'. It was drafted when there was a common understanding of what a library is. Now, the term 'library' is used more casually than in the past, often to denote a collection of any kind.[1]

Under US law, only activities not undertaken for direct or indirect commercial advantage are eligible for the library exceptions.[2] Should that be the only threshold criterion for eligibility? In the age of the internet, the cost of making others' works available can be negligible, and some may

* Executive Director, Kernochan Center for Law, Media and the Arts, Columbia Law School

[1] Among the definitions for 'library' are 'a series or set of books issued by a publisher', 'a collection of recorded data or tapes arranged for ease of use', and 'a set of things similar to a library in appearance, function, or organization: a library of computer programs'. The Free Dictionary by Farlex, http://www.thefreedictionary.com/library (last visited 24 June 2009). See also 'Internet Public Library' at http://www.ipl.org/ (last visited 24 June 2009); http://www.webpowersoftware.com/vLibrary.aspx (last visited 24 June 2009) (re vLibrary, a digital asset management product).

[2] 17 USC § 108(a). While both libraries and archives are eligible for the section 108 exceptions, for convenience this paper will generally refer only to libraries.

do it not for financial gain, but simply to make those works more widely accessible.[3]

The Section 108 Study Group was formed in 2005 by the US Copyright Office and the Library of Congress to recommend changes to the exceptions for libraries in US copyright law.[4] As the Study Group considered whether to broaden exceptions available to libraries in the digital environment, members realized that it was important to provide greater precision to that term, in order to distinguish those institutions generally deemed deserving of special copyright exceptions from those that are not. The Study Group recommended that to be eligible for copyright exceptions, a library should meet several eligibility criteria, including:

> [P]ossessing a public service mission, employing trained library or archives staff, providing professional services normally associated with libraries and archives, and possessing a collection comprising lawfully acquired and/or licensed materials.[5]

If that is a library, then what is a digital library? It could be defined as a library whose collections are at least in part in digital form. Does a library have to make works available remotely to be a 'digital library'? And does it have to provide the public with free and open access to those works without restriction? Technically it is still a digital library if works are available only on premises, even though the aspiration may be remotely accessible digital libraries. E-Depot in the Netherlands is appropriately considered a digital library, even though access to most of the e-journals for which it serves as a preservation repository is available only on site. For purposes of this paper, however, it is assumed that implicit in the notion of a digital library is that the library makes all or part of its collections available remotely, though not necessarily to the general public.

There is no doubt that technology exists to create digital libraries that are capable of making a wide variety of resources available to remote users. But the utopian goal of universally accessible digital libraries has not yet been achieved. This paper will next address why that is, what stands in the way, and where things are now.

---

[3] See for example *US v. LaMacchia*, 871 F.Supp.535 (D.Mass.1994).

[4] See 'The Section 108 Study Group Report (March 2008)', available at http://www.section108.gov/docs/Sec108StudyGroupReport.pdf (last accessed 24 June 2009). The author was a member of the Section 108 Study Group.

[5] 'The Section 108 Study Group Report', *supra* note 4, at 34.

2 WHAT ARE THE OBSTACLES?

Digital libraries and digital resources are in various stages of development. There are a number of reasons why digital libraries have not yet been fully realized. The first group might be broadly considered in terms of resources, and the second in terms of law.

2.1 Insufficient Resources

The focus in meetings and publications directed to lawyers and academics naturally tends to be on the law. But among the most significant obstacles to digitizing analogue materials and creating digital libraries are limitations on resources – technological, economic, and curatorial.[6] To make digital libraries truly effective it is essential to have long term technological sustainability: systems that provide the necessary functionality to permit the works to be perceived (read, viewed or heard), that maintain the integrity of the works, that enable the migration of digital collections to new technologies as needed, and that interoperate with the systems of other libraries, archives and users. Libraries must be capable of ingesting digital materials efficiently, providing user friendly mechanisms for access, and converting analogue materials to digital form efficiently and effectively. Individuals with expertise to develop, understand and manage technical systems are required. So too are effective technological protection mechanisms to comply with limitations on access and to protect the integrity of the system from invasions, intentional or not. There is a great deal of research going on in these areas, and best practices are being developed.[7]

The economic obstacles to creating digital libraries are formidable. Developing these technologies is a costly undertaking, as is acquiring and maintaining digital materials. Of course, in the past libraries have

---

[6] See generally 'Preserving Our National Heritage: Plan for the National Digital Information Infrastructure and Preservation Program' 47–54 (Library of Congress, 2002), http://digitalpreservation.gov/library/resources/pubs/docs/ndiipp_plan.pdf (last visited 24 June 2009).

[7] See, for example, 'OCLC and CRL, Trustworthy Repositories Audit & Certification: Criteria and Checklist' (February 2007), available at http://www.crl.edu/PDF/trac.pdf (last accessed 24 June 2009). This project built on 'Trusted Digital Repositories: Attributes and Responsibilities' (May 2002), www.oclc.org/programs/ourwork/past/trustedrep/repositories.pdf (last accessed June 24, 2009), a collaboration between OCLC and Research Libraries Group, as well as on CRL's Auditing and Certification of Digital Archives project, work from the Nestor project (Germany), and from the Digital Curation Center in the UK.

spent significant amounts of money on hard copy informational materials – books, journals, CDs and DVDs, and so on – and many still do. But maintaining works in digital form presents challenges that maintaining analogue works does not. Digital works can degrade suddenly and without advance warning; they rapidly become obsolete so that the technological tools required to read them or play them back are no longer available.[8] They require constant monitoring and regular upgrades.

Finally, digital libraries require curatorial resources. Decisions have to be made about what an institution should collect and maintain, how it will acquire those materials, and to what extent it can rely on the collections of other libraries. No single entity can do it all, and libraries want to ensure the availability of the collections of greatest value to their users, at the same time preserving and making available to others their unique holdings. They will be able to rely on the digital collections of other libraries, but only if they are confident that those libraries are maintaining them according to established best practices.

2.2 The Law Usually Requires Right Holder Permissions

Characterizing the law as an obstacle to digital libraries is debatable; what some see as an obstacle others regard as valuable protection. But there is no question that copyright law poses significant challenges for the development of digital libraries.

Use of digital objects inevitably involves activities that implicate copyright rights. First, transmitting a work in digital form and rendering it perceivable by users involves the creation of copies. It may also involve the public display, public performance, or the making available of a work. Under US law, when a work is made available online in a manner that allows it to be downloaded, it might also be considered a distribution of the work. Consequently libraries need exceptions from the copyright law in order to undertake these activities.

Digitizing an analogue work entails the making of a reproduction. Exceptions in the US Copyright Act permit digitization of copyrighted works under certain circumstances. A library may make up to three replacement copies of a published work that is lost, stolen, damaged, deteriorating, or whose format has become obsolete, but only if the library

---

8 Besek et al., 'International Study on the Impact of Copyright Law on Digital Preservation', 1.4.3–1.4.4 (July 2008), available at http://www.digitalpreservation.gov/partners/resources/pubs/index.html (last visited 24 June 2009); 'Section 108 Study Group Report', *supra* note 4 at 43–46.

cannot find an unused copy available on the market at a fair price.[9] It may make those copies in digital form, but it may not make the digital copies available outside the library premises. It may make up to three copies of an unpublished work for preservation or deposit at another library, but the same limitation concerning on-premises use of digital copies applies.[10] Libraries may make broader use of works in the last 20 years of their copyright term – neither the three-copy limit nor the on-premises use restriction applies – but only if they have first determined that the work is not subject to normal commercial exploitation and not available at a reasonable price.[11] Under some circumstances, a library may be allowed to digitize a work pursuant to the fair use doctrine in US law.[12] But there is no exception that allows the wholesale digitization and making available of copyrighted works by libraries. Any efforts to create a comprehensive digital library by digitizing analogue works would require the consent of right holders.

'Born digital' works introduce some different considerations. Many of these works, such as scholarly journals and e-books, are obtained by libraries under license. Under US law, the terms of the license supersede the library exceptions, so these works can be made available remotely only if it is permitted by the license.[13] Works available only online pose

---

9 17 USC § 108(c). To qualify for any of the exceptions under section 108, a library must be open to the public, or at least to researchers in a specialized field; the reproduction and distribution may not be for direct or indirect commercial advantage; and the library must include a copyright notice or legend on copies made. Ibid, § 108(a).

10 17 USC § 108(b). The Section 108 Study Group Report has recommended some changes to sections 108(b) and (c), but whether its recommendations will be enacted into law is uncertain.

11 17 USC § 108(h).

12 Fair use excuses a use that would otherwise be infringing. Determining whether a use is a fair use is very fact-specific. There are four factors that must be considered in each case: (1) the purpose and character of the use; (2) the nature of the copyrighted work; (3) the amount and substantiality of the portion used in relation to the copyrighted work as a whole; and (4) the effect of the use upon the potential market for or value of the copyrighted work. 17 USC § 107.

13 17 USC § 108(f)(4). While license agreements are more common with respect to digital works, donor agreements with respect to letters, diaries and the like often restrict the ability of libraries or archives to make that material available, sometimes for a protracted period of time. Compare Directive 2001/29/EC on the harmonization of certain aspects of copyright and related rights in the information society, art.5(3)(n), 2001 OJ (L 167) 10–19 (permitting a copyright exception for 'use by communication or making available, for the purpose of research or private study, to individual members of the public by dedicated terminals on the premises [of publicly accessible libraries, educational establishments or museums, or by

additional challenges. Websites, blogs, news and social networking sites are an important window on current culture, yet often there is no easy way for libraries to collect, preserve and make these sites available to scholars. They are not available for sale. They can be acquired by copying, but the library exceptions generally do not permit copying for acquisition. In some cases, libraries rely on fair use to collect these materials. The Library of Congress, for example, has collections of web material related to US elections and other newsworthy events, like 9/11.[14] The Internet Archive crawls, copies, organizes and makes available a broad range of websites through its web archive.[15]

The Section 108 Study Group Report recommended two new exceptions to facilitate digital preservation. The first would allow qualified libraries to undertake proactive preservation of 'at risk' published works in their collections. They would be permitted to make copies as reasonably necessary for digital preservation in accordance with 'best practices', but would have to restrict access to the preservation copies to 'that which is necessary to effectively maintain and preserve the work'.[16] The second recommended new exception would permit libraries to capture, reproduce and make available publicly available online content (that is, content not restricted by registration or access controls) for preservation purposes.[17] Right holders (except for government and political websites) would be permitted to opt out.[18]

Footnote 13 (*cont.*)
archives] of works and other subject-matter not subject to purchase or licensing terms which are contained in their collections').

14 The Library sometimes relies on fair use in collecting materials (particularly those that are time-sensitive), but depending on the nature of the material, may seek permission from right holders before making the material publicly available.

15 The Internet Archive makes the web material it collects available to the public over its website, http://www.archive.org, after a delay ranging from one week to six months after collection. The Internet Archive relies on a protocol known as the 'Oakland Archive Policy' in collecting and providing access to web content. See 'Written Response to Section 4, Section 108' submitted by the Internet Archive to the Section 108 Study Group 4-6 (7 April 2006), available at http://www.section108.gov/docs/Kimpton_Internet-Archive.pdf (last accessed 24 June 2009). Website owners can opt out of having their content copied, or 'harvested'. The Internet Archive will also block access to previously collected website material upon request. The ability to opt out protects website owners that derive financial benefit from making available older material, and reduces the risk of a successful copyright infringement lawsuit against the Internet Archive.

16 'Section 108 Study Group Report', *supra* note 4 at 69.

17 The report also recommended allowing museums to take advantage of the section 108 exceptions. Ibid, at 31–33.

18 Ibid, at 80–87.

The Section 108 Study Group Report also recommended changing the three-copy limit for replacement copies to 'a limited number of copies as reasonably necessary' provided that the library did not expand the number of access copies, and permitting libraries to make replacement copies of 'fragile' originals.[19]

These recommendations, however, are focused on preservation and not on access, or at least, not on remote access. It is doubtful that remote access is 'necessary to effectively maintain and preserve' the works. And even if the three-copy limit were lifted, the statute limits use of digital replacement copies to library premises.

To sum up, the creation of a comprehensive digital library in the United States would require an amendment to the US copyright law, the agreement of right holders, or both.

3 THE ROLE OF MANDATORY DEPOSIT LAWS

If copyright laws do not provide exceptions and limitations sufficient to enable digital libraries, what about legal deposit laws? Many countries, including the United States, have some form of legal deposit law that requires the deposit of works of authorship in a national library or libraries for the public benefit.[20] Under US law, two copies of the best edition of a work published in the United States must be deposited with the Copyright Office for use by the Library of Congress.[21] The requirement is not limited to books, but extends to all categories of works, unless the Library chooses to exclude them.

The extent to which the Library of Congress – or any other national library – can serve as a national digital library depends on what national law permits it to do with the copies deposited. In the United States, the law permits the Library of Congress to use the copies itself or give them to other libraries. It does not provide the Library with specific authorization to make and distribute copies of deposited works, or to exercise the rights needed for online use, such as public performance and display. The Library must rely on fair use or implied license, neither of which is likely in most cases to permit making digital copies of the works available remotely.

The legal limitations of mandatory deposit are not the only obstacle to

---

19 Ibid, at 52–60. A similar change concerning the three-copy limit was recommended with respect to preservation copies of unpublished works. Ibid, at 61–68.

20 17 USC § 407. See, for example, Copyright Act 1968 (Cth) s 201 (Australia); Legal Deposit Libraries Act (Great Britain 2003, ss. 1, 3).

21 17 USC § 407(a).

the Library of Congress becoming a comprehensive digital library whose collections are accessible remotely by the general public. The Library does not have the infrastructure and resources to collect, organize, maintain and preserve all digital works published in the United States. As a consequence, the regulations associated with the mandatory deposit law do not, at present, generally require deposit of materials published only electronically (for example, on websites). The Library has been working on various technological issues relating to the ingest of electronic works. In July 2009 it initiated an administrative proceeding to change those regulations to require deposit of electronic works published in the United States and available only online, but only upon issuance of a specific demand for such work.[22] The proposed regulations do not appear to contemplate remote access; the notice indicates that the Library of Congress may allow the deposited copies to be accessed simultaneously by two on-site users.[23] A change to permit remote access would have to be effected through legislation, and it is doubtful that the law would be changed to authorize the Library to use copies received through mandatory deposit broadly to provide remote access to users outside Library premises.

4 TO WHAT EXTENT DO DIGITAL LIBRARIES CURRENTLY EXIST?

So far, the discussion has been primarily about how the law enables – and inhibits – the development of digital libraries. In fact, many US libraries are developing digital collections, and providing digital library services. They provide access to digital resources through subscriptions or other licenses; they digitize and make available their own collections; they provide access to digital materials through interlibrary loan, e-reserves, course websites and similar means; and they serve as gateways to publicly available digital resources from other libraries and databases.

4.1 Licensed Access to Information Sources

Many libraries, particularly research libraries, provide their users with access to a wide range of digital resources through licenses with right

---

[22] Copyright Office, 'Mandatory Deposit of Published Electronic Works Available Only Online; Notice of Proposed Rulemaking', 74 Fed.Reg.34286 (15 July 2009).

[23] Ibid, at 34288.

holders. For example, Columbia Law School students and faculty have access to a vast array of statutes, judicial opinions, journal articles, legal treatises and news and business sources from the United States and around the world through subscriptions to LexisNexis, Westlaw, HeinOnline, BNA reporters, a range of international databases, and other services. They also have access to databases and services available to the larger Columbia University community of faculty and students. Business Source Complete and Dow Jones Factiva provide business information and publications; Cambridge Journals Online, Project Muse, Sage, PsycINFO, ProQuest, SpringerLink, Elsevier's ScienceDirect and JSTOR provide a wide range of scholarly journals in the science and social science fields. Scholarly e-books can be accessed through services such as Safari Books online (IT books) and CLS Humanities E-Book. NetLibrary provides access to current electronic books from university and commercial publishers, as well as to electronic books in the public domain. Ebrary provides access to a collection of thousands of online full text books and other materials in many subject areas. These resources are available online to the Columbia academic community, whether they are working in the library, in their apartments, offices, or even in other countries during a school break or a semester abroad.

4.2 Digitizing Library Collections

Library resources for digitizing analogue materials are limited, so libraries often focus on their unique collections, materials for which they are the sole repository. Examples include Columbia University's collection of the letters and diaries of American statesman John Jay[24] or, on a much larger scale, the Library of Congress's American Memory Project, an initiative that provides open access to written material, maps, prints, sound recordings, still and moving images, and sheet music that documents American history and creativity.[25] Sometimes libraries engage in joint projects to make available materials of particular interest to scholars (such as The Digital Scriptorium,[26] an image database of medieval and renaissance manuscripts, or the new UNESCO World Digital Library project,[27] in

[24] The Papers of John Jay, http://www.columbia.edu/cu/lweb/digital/jay/ (last visited 24 June 2009).

[25] See About American Memory, http://memory.loc.gov/ammem/about/index.html (last visited 24 June 2009).

[26] Digital Scriptorium, http://www.scriptorium.columbia.edu/ (last visited 25 June 2009).

[27] World Digital Library, http://www.wdl.org.

which 32 partner institutions have collaborated on a website that provides free public access to cultural materials like books, manuscripts and maps from libraries and archives from around the world). In the United States, such collections generally comprise public domain materials, materials included with permission of right holders, and materials included in reliance on fair use, particularly where the right holder cannot be located and the potential exposure is low.

4.3 Interlibrary Loan and Electronic Reserves

In some cases, libraries (and educational institutions) may provide documents electronically to users as part of 'interlibrary loan', distance education programs, electronic reserves (or 'e-reserves'), or through course websites.

Interlibrary loan

Under certain conditions, libraries may make a copy of part of a copyrighted work, or even of a complete work, for a requesting user for the purpose of private study, scholarship or research.[28] However, the copy must become the requesting user's property (so that the library cannot use the exception to obtain copies to add to its collections).[29] These exceptions relate primarily to text-based works.[30] The most common use of these exceptions is to supply copies of scholarly journal articles to users of another library that does not subscribe to the journal. This practice is referred to as 'interlibrary loan', even though the requesting user receives

---

[28] Under 17 USC § 108(d), a library, in response to a user's request, may reproduce and provide to the user a copy of 'no more than one article or other contribution to a copyrighted collection or periodical issue', or 'a small part' of any other copyrighted work from its collection or that of another library. Under 17 USC § 108(e), a library may also make and provide to a user a copy of all or a substantial portion of a user-requested work if it determines, after reasonable investigation, that a copy cannot be obtained at a fair price.

[29] Ibid, §§ 108(d), (e). These exceptions encompass 'isolated and unrelated reproduction and distribution of a single copy . . . of the same material on separate occasions', but they do not apply to systematic reproduction. Libraries may participate in interlibrary arrangements as long as the practice does not substitute for a subscription to or purchase of the work. Ibid, § 108(g). Many libraries abide by guidelines developed when the 1976 Copyright Act was passed to help ensure that interlibrary supply of journal articles would not substitute for library subscriptions to the journals.

[30] Musical works, pictorial, graphic or sculptural works (other than illustrations or similar adjuncts to literary works), or audiovisual works (including motion pictures) generally are excluded. Ibid, § 108(i).

a copy that need not be returned. A library may copy all or a substantial part of a work for a user only if the library first determines that a copy is not available on the market at a fair price. Copying complete works has to date been less common because of the library resources it consumes; when an entire work is requested, libraries are more likely to engage in a genuine loan of the copy in their collection sought by the user.[31]

The limitation that only *a* copy may be made in response to a user request would appear to rule out electronic transmission, as it inevitably involves making multiple copies of any requested work. Nevertheless, libraries do use electronic means to provide copies to end users (for example, through e-mail attachments or by posting them to a secure website where the user can access only the article he or she requested), presumably relying on fair use.[32]

Distance education

There is an exception in US copyright law that permits an educational institution to stream or display copyrighted works in the course of distance education.[33] The copyrighted material must be relevant to the content of the course.[34] The performance or display must be made under the actual supervision of an instructor as an integral part of a class session, and limited to students enrolled in the class.[35] This exception hardly creates a digital library, but it does allow educational institutions to make works available for online classes. This exception is carefully circumscribed – too carefully, in the view of many in the library and educational community.

E-reserves and course websites

Colleges and universities in the United States often make copyrighted works assigned for a particular class available to students for viewing or downloading, through 'e-reserves' or course websites. Sometimes the material is licensed for such use pursuant to the school's subscription;

---

31 Whether that will continue to be the case once a significant portion of library collections has been digitized (thus reducing the time it takes to reproduce a work for a user) is unclear.

32 'Section 108 Study Group Report', *supra* note 4 at 96–97.

33 17 USC § 110(2). The law allows 'the performance of a nondramatic literary or musical work or reasonable and limited portions of any other work', though it excludes certain works produced primarily for distance education.

34 Ibid, § 110(2)(A),(B).

35 Ibid, The transmitting institution must apply technological measures that prevent retention of copies by recipients of the transmission for longer than the class session, and that prevent further dissemination. The exception also applies to transmissions to officers or employees of governmental bodies as part of their duties. Ibid, § 110(2)(C),(D).

sometimes the use is sufficiently limited to be a fair use. The extent to which the fair use doctrine permits these activities, and the impact of unlicensed uses on right holders, is a matter of some contention between educational institutions and right holders.[36] Colleges and universities vary in their policies and in the guidance and oversight they provide to their faculty and staff.

4.4 Gateways to Publicly Available Digital Resources

Libraries also perform a valuable role as information gateways, centralized directories not only of materials to which the library has a subscription, but also of free materials available on the internet. Some of these sites are run by libraries and consortia of libraries, some by independent not-for-profit entities, and still others by governments, individuals, trade groups or for-profit corporations.

Open access digital repositories

Digital repositories that permit free public access to scholarly articles and other materials are becoming more common. One highly respected open access site is PubMed Central (PMC), a free digital archive of biomedical and life sciences research journal literature managed by the US National Library of Medicine in the National Institutes of Health (NIH). PMC is committed to preserving the journal literature 'in a form that ensures unrestricted access to it over the longer term'.[37]

Journal publishers deposit articles in PubMed Central pursuant to voluntary agreements. Some publishers deposit their content in PMC immediately after publication. Others, however, wait for a period of time

---

[36] Whether or not use of copyrighted works for these purposes qualifies as fair use depends on the circumstances, for example, what the particular work is, how much of it is used and whether use in this manner is likely to displace sales or licenses of that work. There has not yet been a court ruling on the use of copyrighted works on course websites. There is a pending case by Oxford University Press and other publishers against Georgia State University over its electronic course reserves system. See 'Georgia State University Sued Over E-Reserves', Library Journal Academic Newswire, 17 April 2008, http://www.libraryjournal.com/info/CA6552504.html (last accessed 24 June 2009). Cf. *Princeton Univ. Press v. Michigan Document Servs.*, 99 F.3d 1381 (6th Cir.1996) (300+ page coursepack of copyrighted materials photocopied by commercial copy shop for students not excused under the fair use doctrine).

[37] See PMC Overview, http://www.pubmedcentral.nih.gov/about/intro.html (last accessed 24 June 2009). As a general matter, only journals that qualify based on the scientific quality of the journal and the technical quality of their digital files can be included, and PMC includes only peer-reviewed research.

after publication in order to avoid adversely affecting their own market. PMC strongly encourages deposit of full articles within one year of publication and other editorial content within three years.[38] Many scholarly journal publishers have not embraced PMC; they are reluctant to deposit their articles because they fear that making the journal articles available for free will reduce subscription revenue. Some private foundations that fund scientific research require that the resulting articles be published on PubMed Central.[39] A 2008 US law requires that the final, peer-reviewed manuscripts of articles that result from research funded by the National Institutes of Health be sent to PubMed Central.[40]

The Social Science Research Network is another respected open access repository.[41] SSRN is a database of abstracts, working papers and forthcoming papers on legal, financial, health, political, and other topics. It is designed to encourage communication and discussion on developing works of authorship.

Institutional repositories

Many institutions of higher education have institutional repositories in which faculty and students are encouraged, or required, to deposit their scholarly articles or theses. For example, Harvard University has created a digital repository for faculty works and instituted a policy that requires faculty members to deposit their journal articles in that repository and to allow the university to make them freely available online, unless they receive a waiver.[42] The university provides guidance to faculty on how to negotiate changes to typical publishing contracts to reserve the appropriate

---

38 See PubMed Central, Policies and Guidelines for Depositing and Providing Access to Full Text, http://www.pubmedcentral.nih.gov/about/guidelines.html (last accessed 24 June 2009).

39 See, for example, Wellcome Trust, Authors Guide and FAQ, http://www.wellcome.ac.uk/About-us/Policy/Spotlight-issues/Open-access/Guides-and-FAQ/WTD018855.htm; Howard Hughes Medical Institute Research Policies, http://www.hhmi.org/about/research/sc320.pdf (last accessed 24 June 2009).

40 Consolidated Appropriations Act, PL 110-161, Div.G, Title II, Section 218 (2008). There is a bill pending in Congress that would reverse this policy by prohibiting a federal agency from requiring a transfer of copyright as a condition of receiving funding. Fair Copyright in Research Works Act, H.R.801, 111th Cong., introduced 3 March 2009.

41 SSRN Social Science Research Network, http://www.ssrn.com. While most of the material on SSRN is freely available, there are some fee-based publications available through the site.

42 See Patricia Cohen (2008), 'At Harvard, a Proposal to Publish Free on the Web', *N. Y. Times* 12 February; Robert Mitchell (2008), 'Harvard to Collect, Disseminate Scholarly Articles for Faculty', Harvard Gazette Online, 13 February,

rights. As of yet, it is unclear whether faculty authors have been successful in negotiating rights to include their articles on the school's open access repository, or whether they have been forced to seek waivers.

Web archives

The Internet Archive is a nonprofit organization that regularly browses, copies and archives sites on the Internet to create a record of web content for use by scholars and researchers.[43] Through its Wayback Machine, a user can access the content of a particular site as it looked on a particular day in the past. Not all sites are accessible through the Internet Archive. Because it relies on fair use, it will take down a site (and refrain from 'crawling' it in the future to collect content) if so requested by the site owner. As discussed above, the Library of Congress also engages in web archiving projects, as do many other national libraries.[44]

Databases of existing and pending legislation

Many countries and international organizations maintain comprehensive sites of actual and/or pending legislation and related materials, such as government reports. For example, the United States government makes Congressional bills, reports and hearings, laws, government administrative reports and other publications available online.[45] The European Union's EUR-Lex site provides free access to European Union law, including treaties and legislation.[46]

These and other open access sites are clearly electronic resources. Some are created or managed by libraries, but whether they are databases or 'libraries' in their own right depends on how 'library' is defined. The open access databases available on the internet vary significantly in their quality, reliability and long term sustainability. They are available to everyone with internet capability, but libraries still play a useful role in directing their users to helpful, reliable sites.

Footnote 42 (*cont.*)
available at http://www.news.harvard.edu/gazette/2008/02.14/99-fasvote.html (last visited 25 June 2009).

[43] See Internet Archive, http://www.archive.org/about/about.php; 'Written Reponse of Internet Archive', *supra* note 15.

[44] Library of Congress, Web Capture, http://www.loc.gov/webcapture/ (last visited 25 June 2009).

[45] See, for example, Library of Congress, Thomas, http://www.thomas.gov; US Government Printing Office FDSys, http://www.gpo.gov/fdsys/search/home.action (last visited 25 June 2009).

[46] Access to European Law, http://eur-lex.europa.eu/en/index.htm (last visited 25 June 2009).

5 WHAT ARE THE SHORTCOMINGS OF THE CURRENT APPROACH TO DIGITAL LIBRARIES?

This paper has so far sketched a rather positive assessment of the state of digital library resources. So what is the problem? In fact, digital libraries are incomplete, expensive, and to many, inaccessible. Some fields, like scholarly journal publishing, have largely migrated to digital delivery. But e-books are only now becoming widely accepted and available, and most books originally published in hard copy form are not yet available for access or delivery in digital form.

Online subscriptions to licensed materials can be very costly. Many libraries now pay far more for scholarly journals and other reference works than in the past. Some ascribe this to excessive profits by journal publishers; whether or not this is true, there are also other factors. Subscriptions for access to new databases of scholarly journals and other electronic resources allow libraries to meet user expectations for a wider range of resources than have been available in the past, with greater functionality (for example, search capability) and greater user convenience. Nevertheless, all libraries feel the pinch, although the better funded libraries, like the large research libraries, are better able to purchase access to digital materials.[47]

Concerning accessibility, many of the licensed resources described above are available only to the Columbia University academic community. Local community libraries may provide some online information resources, but generally only a fraction of what is available through research libraries like that of Columbia. Community libraries may make additional digital resources available on site (and even large research libraries sometimes provide access to licensed materials to members of the local community who use terminals on the library premises). But many valuable information resources are not accessible remotely by most people.

---

[47] Many libraries would like to discontinue subscriptions to hard copy journals and discard back issues or put them in long-term storage due to space constraints. Some have been reluctant to do so, however, because they need continued access if they terminate their subscription to the electronic version of a journal, or the journal provider goes out of business. Different mechanisms are developing to address these concerns, such as JSTOR, http://www.jstor.org/; Portico, http://www.portico.org/; and LOCKSS, http://www.lockss.org/lockss/Home (last visited 25 June 2009).

6 THE GOOGLE BOOKS SETTLEMENT IN THE DIGITAL LIBRARY LANDSCAPE

The recent Google settlement provides a useful backdrop for discussing what legal or policy changes could be made to promote digital libraries.

6.1 Summary of Settlement Terms

In 2005 Google began scanning copyrighted books from US libraries for its Google Book Search database, without authorization from the right holders. In response to search requests by users, Google would provide a few 'snippets' (that is, a couple of lines on either side of a search term) from a book.[48] Authors and publishers of scanned books sued for copyright infringement, and the parties reached agreement to settle the lawsuit in October 2008.[49] Because the authors' suit was a class action lawsuit, the settlement must be approved by the court. A court hearing on the fairness of the settlement is scheduled for 7 October 2009.

The proposed settlement will, subject to a right holder's decision to opt out,[50] allow Google to continue to digitize books and include them in its Book Search database.[51] Google will be permitted to use the books to earn revenue through advertising online when search results are displayed, through individual sales of access to the full text of books, and through institutional licenses that allow full text display of many books (primarily those no longer commercially available). Money received by Google from these uses is divided, with 37 per cent going to Google and 63 per cent to the right holders.

The agreement authorizes Google only to make the books available on line to users in the United States. The licenses provided to Google are

---

[48] A more detailed summary of the agreement is contained in the US response to the ALAI 2009 London Questionnaire.

[49] See Settlement Agreement dated 28 October 2008, available at http://www.googlebooksettlement.com/r/view_settlement_agreement (last visited 25 June 2009) [hereinafter Settlement Agreement.]

[50] Right holders have until 4 September 2009 to opt out of the agreement completely.

[51] Periodicals and personal papers are excluded. Settlement Agreement, *supra* note 49 at 1.16. The settlement also applies to 'inserts' such as forewords, essays, poems, quotations, letters, children's book illustrations, graphs, charts and other material contained in books but independently copyrightable, where the book as a whole has a different author or is in the public domain. The definition of Inserts specifically excludes photographs and illustrations other than in children's books. Ibid, at 1.72; see also ibid, at 3.1.

non-exclusive. What Google can do with any particular book depends on whether or not the book is commercially available.[52] For works that *are* commercially available, Google may make only 'non-display uses', that is, uses that do not contain expression from the books.[53] For works that *are not* commercially available, Google can make both 'display uses' and 'non display uses'. Display uses include, inter alia, display of short 'snippets', display of 'previews' of the books which can include up to 20 per cent of the contents, and 'Access Uses', that is, access to the book pursuant to individual sales of access, the institutional licenses, and the Public Access Service described below. However, it should be emphasized that these are default rules, which can be varied by the right holder as to a particular work.[54]

The agreement creates a Book Rights Registry, a not-for-profit corporation to be managed jointly by authors and publishers. The Registry is authorized to act on behalf of right holders in connection with many aspects of the agreement. The Registry is to receive payments from Google on behalf of right holders (primarily the 63 per cent of the revenues from advertising, sales and subscriptions), and will divide them among registered right holders after taking a share for administrative expenses. The division is made according to a Plan of Allocation in the agreement.[55] The Registry will also own and maintain a rights information database and attempt to locate right holders. It will supervise the process of resolving disputes among right holders. It will work with Google in setting default pricing schemes for consumer sales, and prices for institutional licenses.[56]

---

52 Commercially available/not commercially available generally corresponds with in-print/out-of-print. Google makes the initial determination as to whether a work is commercially available, but there are procedures in the agreement for changing the classification and objecting to changes in the classification. Once the Book Rights Registry is operational, it will be responsible for working with Google to resolve disputes.

53 For example, display of bibliographic information, full text indexing without display of expression (like number or location of search matches), and internal research and development. Ibid, at 1.1, 1.48, 1.88, 1.106, 1.147.

54 Settlement Agreement, *supra* note 49 at 3.3, 3.4.

55 Ibid, Attachment C. The Registry and Google may agree over time to new revenue models, such as 'print on demand' copies of books distributed by third parties, custom publishing, downloadable pdf versions of books, or consumer subscription models.

56 The Registry is permitted to license right holders' US copyrights to third parties. However, it is prohibited from coordinating or representing subgroups of right holders in connection with matters under the settlement agreement. Settlement Agreement, *supra* note 49 at 6.2(b). There is also a provision that restricts the Registry or any similar entity that uses either data or resources that Google provides or 'of the same type that Google provides', from granting a better

There are four principal ways in which users will access the database. First, all users will get free access to the Book Search database, and in response to search queries they will be able to access (1) for public domain books, the full text, (2) for copyright protected but not commercially available books, up to 20 per cent of the text under the 'standard preview' (though there are variations in preview display for different categories of works),[57] and (3) for copyright protected, commercially available works, users will be able to view bibliographic data (but not snippets, as they currently can).[58]

Secondly, all users can purchase full text online access to a book. The right holder can set the price, but the default prices are to be worked out between the Registry and Google. A user will have perpetual online access, and limited ability to print and copy and paste (though with repeated commands could print the whole book).[59]

Thirdly, a user affiliated with an institution might get access through an institutional license, which will allow users at the subscribing institution to view full text of the works that are in copyright but not commercially available. Google and the Registry will agree on a price structure, and will submit to binding arbitration if they cannot reach agreement.[60]

Fourthly, a user might get access under a special Public Access Service provided free to public libraries and not-for-profit higher education institutions. This service will allow a user to view the full text of books in the Institutional Subscription database, and to print for a fee. A public library can get this service on one terminal per building; for college and university libraries, the number of terminals that will be provided with free access varies with the number of students.[61]

It is important to reiterate, however, that the default assumptions are that display uses will be made of works that are not commercially available, but not of commercially available works. But in either case, right holders can decide otherwise.

Footnote 56 (*cont.*)
deal to third parties than Google has. Ibid, at 3.8(a). This restriction lasts for ten years, and is operative only if the authorization includes rights from a significant portion of right holders other than those who have registered with the Registry.

57 Settlement Agreement, *supra* note 49 at 4.3(b)(i).

58 Ibid, at 3.2(b), 3.4(a).

59 Ibid, at 4.2.

60 Ibid, at 4.1.

61 Ibid, at 4.8(a).

Is Google a digital library?

It is unclear whether Google would meet the standard set out at the beginning. Does it really have a public service mission? Will it employ trained library staff, or provide the professional services normally associated with a library?[62] It appears that Google will be operating not so much as a library, but as an information resource: in part a subscription database with full text of certain works available, in part a free access site with bibliographic information and limited excerpts available (and a mechanism by which users can purchase access to the full text of individual books in its database).

6.2 Criticism of the Google Books Settlement

There have been a number of criticisms of the Google settlement, and space does not permit reviewing them all here. One of the principal criticisms is that it will give Google and the Book Rights Registry an unfair advantage with respect to the use of unclaimed works, many of which are 'orphan works', that is, works whose right holders cannot be identified or located.[63] 'Orphan works legislation', if passed, would likely require a prospective user to make a good faith search for the right holder.[64] Google, in contrast, would have the benefit of certain presumptions that would make it unnecessary to search in connection with books included in the settlement. Google would pay the Registry for use of those works, but could proceed without fear of liability.

A second and related criticism concerns possible competition issues, both with respect to Google and to the Book Rights Registry.[65] The US Department of Justice is currently investigating the proposed

---

[62] Under the terms of the agreement, Google will provide fully participating libraries with digital copies of their holdings, but those copies cannot serve as the basis for remote library services due to restrictions in the agreement. Ibid, at 7.2.

[63] See, for example, Brewster Kahle, 'A Book Grab by Google', Washington Post, 19 May 2009. In fact, unclaimed works under the Google Settlement are not the same as 'orphan works' as that term has been used in prospective legislation, but there is likely to be a good deal of overlap.

[64] See discussion in section H, infra.

[65] See, for example, Randal C.Picker, The Google Book Search Settlement: A New Orphan-Works Monopoly? (April 2009), http://papers.ssrn.com/sol3/papers.cfm?abstract_id=1387582 (last visited 25 June 2009); James Grimmelmann, Principles and Recommendations for the Google Book Search Settlement, The Laboratorium (Nov.8, 2008), http://laboratorium.net/archive/2008/11/08/principles_and_recommendations_for_the_google_book (last visited 25 June 2009).

settlement.[66] It is possible that the DOJ will seek to block the settlement or force the parties to alter some of its terms.

One distinguished commentator, Professor Robert Darnton of Harvard, has expressed concerns about Google's potential monopoly power and how it might affect the price of subscriptions to the database. Professor Darnton believes the Google settlement demonstrates a lost opportunity to build a digital library in a way that would better serve the public interest:

> Looking back over the course of digitization from the 1990s, we now can see that we missed a great opportunity. Action by Congress and the Library of Congress or a grand alliance of research libraries supported by a coalition of foundations could have done the job at a feasible cost and designed it in a manner that would have put the public interest first. By spreading the cost in various ways – a rental based on the amount of use of a database or a budget line in the National Endowment for the Humanities or the Library of Congress – we could have provided authors and publishers with a legitimate income, while maintaining an open access repository or one in which access was based on reasonable fees. We could have created a National Digital Library – the twenty-first-century equivalent of the Library of Alexandria.[67]

There are many questions about how Professor Darnton's vision could be achieved, however. There are significant rights issues to be resolved, something his essay does not attempt to address.

7 COMPETING CONCERNS OF RIGHT HOLDERS AND LIBRARIES

The notion of providing an 'open access repository' or one with access 'based on reasonable fees' suggests a compulsory licensing regime, which would not seem to pass muster under the three-step test.[68] Or perhaps Professor Darnton is optimistic that right holders will be swayed by

---

[66] Elizabeth Williamson, Jeffrey A.Trachtenberg and Jessica Vascellaro, 'Probe of Google Book Deal Heats Up', *Wall Street Journal*, 10 June 2009 at B1.

[67] Robert Darnton, 'Google and the Future of Books', *New York Review of Books*, 12 February 2009, available at http://www.nybooks.com/articles/22281 (last visited 25 June 2009). Professor Darnton is the Carl H.Pforzheimer University Professor at Harvard University and Director of the Harvard University Library.

[68] The three-step test in article 9(2) of the 1971 Paris Act of the Berne Convention allows member nations to permit the reproduction of copyrighted works 'in certain special cases, provided that such reproduction does not conflict with a normal exploitation of the work and does not unreasonably prejudice the legitimate interests of the author'. The WIPO Copyright Treaty and the Agreement

the benefits of his conception and enter into voluntary agreements, or acquiesce in a legislative initiative.

Negotiations within the Section 108 Study Group suggest that right holders (and possibly many libraries as well) would have significant misgivings about it. The Section 108 Study Group, as you recall, was set up to recommend changes to the copyright exceptions for libraries and archives in the US Copyright Act. Its members comprised a roughly equal number of right holder representatives, on the one hand, and library and archives representatives, on the other. Its recommendations were issued only on the basis of unanimous consensus, but its report explains in some detail the differing perspectives of members in areas where they were unable to reach consensus. Thus, the report is instructive on the concerns of the respective parties and the likelihood of achieving legislative consensus in this area.

It should be no surprise that some of the most vigorous debates in the Section 108 Study Group related to libraries providing remote access to library materials, and to digitizing analogue materials. Thus, for example, there was a consensus in the group to lift the three-copy limit for replacement copies, but not to make those copies remotely accessible. There was a consensus that qualified libraries should be able proactively to digitize materials for preservation, but no agreement on whether they could provide public access to those preservation copies.[69]

Why was the Study Group unable to reach consensus?

7.1 Right Holder Concerns

Right holders are concerned about competition from libraries. Historically, some users have preferred the convenience of owning their own copy, even though the cost was greater. For the user, libraries were less costly, but less convenient. But if libraries can provide instant, remote access to copyright protected materials, those users will see little advantage to purchasing their own copies, and libraries may become the primary, if not the sole, market for copyrighted works. The broader and more convenient the access that libraries can provide, the smaller the portion of the market left to the right holder.

on Trade-Related Aspects of Intellectual Property Rights (TRIPS) have made this standard applicable to other copyright rights.

[69] The Section 108 Study Group Report did recommend that remote access to web preservation materials be permitted after a specified time period had elapsed, but at the same time recommended allowing most right holders to 'opt out'. 'Section 108 Study Group Report', *supra* note 4 at 85–87.

Right holders' concerns are particularly acute with respect to works that are still commercially available. And they are felt not only by right holders of books, but also by right holders of motion pictures and other works that libraries in the United States would like to make available to scholars, but whose primary market is for entertainment.

Right holders resist exceptions permitting the digitization of analogue works by libraries and educational institutions. They often must expend considerable time and resources to obtain the rights for digital distribution. They fear that if libraries can digitize and make these works available to users without regard to rights clearance issues, libraries might effectively preempt the introduction of a digital version in the commercial marketplace, and deprive authors and other right holders of any financial return from the exploitation of their works in digital markets. Finally, right holders are concerned about the proliferation of unauthorized digital copies.

7.2 Library Concerns

Libraries face a user base that increasingly expects online access to resources. Many users' search mechanism of first resort is Google's search engine, and they have little interest in hard copy resources that require a trip to the library premises. Libraries see digital technology as a means by which they can bring under-used resources to users. More generally, they see digital technology as enabling them to serve more users at a lower cost, and to use their resources more efficiently, but often perceive copyright laws to thwart their ability to serve the public interest. There is great frustration about the extension of copyright term and the difficulty of locating right holders in order to obtain permissions for using works. Libraries are concerned about the high cost of subscriptions to digital materials, and the toll it takes on their budgets.[70] They also find the terms of the licenses unduly restrictive. As they increasingly substitute electronic access for hard copy subscriptions, they want to ensure long term preservation of and access to those materials. Many libraries also want the ability to continue to serve as a resource to a broader community and not just a defined user group of students and faculty.

Libraries in the United States are wary of conditioning exceptions on their use of technological protection or other security measures, both because they resist imposing conditions on patrons' use, and because they are skeptical as to the availability of effective, reasonable protection

---

70 Darnton, *supra* note 67.

measures that are not too costly. They do not want to keep track of what users look at, or employ any reporting system that implicates user privacy. Finally, they seek exceptions not limited to books and journals, since they serve scholars who also study movies, sound recordings, music, photographs, maps, and even video games.

This suggests a legislative stalemate, at least at present, with respect to any sweeping new exceptions to achieve digital libraries, even if those exceptions could be squared with the three-step test.

8 HOW CAN DIGITAL LIBRARIES BE ACHIEVED?

Considerable progress toward the goal of 'digital libraries' has already been made, and various public and private initiatives are likely to move libraries closer to that goal. More materials can and likely will be made more broadly available by libraries working independently, with other libraries, with private foundations, and in collaboration with right holders.

8.1 Public, Private, and Collaborative Initiatives

The availability and scope of digital resources is likely to continue to grow. The trend toward open access sites progresses, although long term institutional commitment and funding is necessary for those sites to be as 'trusted' and reliable as libraries have traditionally been regarded. Similarly, the trend on the part of federal, state, and local governments to put government information (laws, reports, statistics) and public records on the internet will also likely continue, but the tendency in some cases of governments to 'clean up' their websites and remove older materials demonstrates the need for web preservation.

There are many public domain materials that users would find valuable and that could be placed on open access sites; the obstacles to doing so are generally financial and technical rather than legal. Those obstacles may be overcome in time by committed governments, foundations, public interest organizations, and individuals.

Another means by which digital materials may become more broadly available is through increased flexibility in the terms of library subscriptions. Libraries, by working through consortia and by publicizing contract terms, have achieved progress over the last several years in negotiating more reasonable contract terms that permit wider access to licensed resources.

One promising approach, at least for some types of copyright protected materials, is that of collaborative ventures between libraries and right holders, as exemplified by JSTOR. JSTOR archives, preserves and makes available past issues of important scholarly journals pursuant to agreements with publishers and libraries.[71] Publishers give JSTOR a perpetual non-exclusive license to the material that goes into JSTOR's archives. This allows JSTOR to continue to provide libraries with access to journals to which they have already subscribed, even after a publisher ends its agreement with JSTOR and stops providing new materials,[72] so that libraries can remove hard-copy back issues of journals and be assured of continued access to these issues in the future. Participating publishers are not paid licensing fees (although there is some modest revenue sharing), but they have the benefit of JSTOR's digitization and preservation services. JSTOR attempts to balance libraries' interest in access to scholarly journals, right holders' interest in deriving revenue from the journals, and the broader societal interest in long term preservation. To allow publishers to get a return on their investment, journals are not made immediately available through JSTOR. It uses a 'moving wall' approach, generally a period of three to five years from publication, during which JSTOR may digitize the journal but not make it available. Each year, another year of older journals is made available.[73] Libraries pay fees for user access to JSTOR archives, based on their size and the specific research collections they seek to access.

8.2 Collective Management

Is collective management a viable approach to achieving comprehensive digital libraries in the United States? Perhaps, but there are hurdles to be overcome. The first is institutional. The United States does not have the kind of comprehensive reproduction rights organizations that exist in many other countries. The strongest and most effective collective rights administration organizations are ASCAP and BMI for musical compositions. Copyright Clearance Center (CCC)[74] is the relevant reproduction rights organization for books and journal articles, but it is not as widely

---

[71] See JSTOR The Archives, http://www.jstor.org/page/info/about/archives/index.jsp (last visited 25 June 2009).

[72] Roger C. Schonfeld (2003), *JSTOR: A History* p. 142.

[73] See 'JSTOR Moving Wall', http://www.jstor.org/page/info/about/archives/journals/movingWall.jsp (last visited 25 June 2009).

[74] See Copyright Clearance Center, http://www.copyright.com. The Copyright Clearance Center is a collective administration organization that licenses copying and 'sharing' of information for business and academic uses, including uses of copyrighted material for 'coursepacks', course websites, e-reserves and similar uses.

representative of right holders as are many RROs in other countries. CCC is generally perceived by authors more as a *publishers'* representative, although that could change in the future.

The second hurdle is economic/structural. Right holders want payment in some manner commensurate with use, and payment sufficient to justify future investment in works of authorship that may or may not ultimately be financially successful. At the same time, libraries in the United States are generally not accustomed to 'passing through' charges to their users based on books or other information that those users access, or for library services, other than out-of-pocket costs for photocopying interlibrary loan materials. Under copyright exceptions in the United States, libraries generally either purchase copyrighted works, or make free use pursuant to exceptions.[75] There is no public lending right.[76]

In theory, these economic issues can be addressed in at least a couple of ways. Pay-per-access may not be viable (nor desirable), but use can be limited to a library's user group, and based on the number of users who will have access to the material. This approach is common for library subscriptions for access to digital databases, particularly for libraries affiliated with higher education institutions that seek to provide access primarily to faculty and students. But restrictions to a defined user group are sometimes problematic, as these institutions often serve as resources for members of the local community. Sometimes subscriptions will allow unaffiliated researchers access to the databases to which the library subscribes, but only at on-premises terminals.

In any event, the 'defined user group' concept often does not work well for national, state and sometimes even local libraries and institutions that do not have a well-defined user base.[77] For those libraries, perhaps a limitation on the number of simultaneous remote users (rather than a requirement that the user belong to a specific user group) might be a way to provide greater access to users, and at the same time ensure that right holders will be able to earn a return in some measure proportionate to use.[78]

---

75 Where libraries provide document delivery services to businesses, they usually do pay fees to right holders, often through the Copyright Clearance Center.

76 However, libraries spend substantial amounts of money buying copyrighted works, and in some cases, institutional subscriptions cost more than individual subscriptions.

77 'Section 108 Study Group Report', *supra* note 4 at 58–59.

78 Library subscriptions to databases that allow, for example, five simultaneous remote users that need not be members of any particular user group suggest possible online services that might hunt for open library 'seats' for access to particular materials at any given time.

Whether or not the Google settlement goes forward, the agreement itself indicates a willingness on the part of right holders to permit digitization of their analogue books (under a scheme in which they will be paid); to develop a collective management mechanism; and to accept blanket licensing to libraries and other institutions that want to allow remote access to their users, with limited free on-site use at libraries that do not take institutional licenses.

The Book Rights Registry, as discussed above, will act as a collective management organization, identifying and locating right holders, and dividing among them revenues received from Google for advertising and other uses made by the general public, and from institutional licenses. It appears that the Registry for the most part will not be dealing with and licensing libraries directly; the right holders will license Google, and Google will in turn license libraries. However, the Registry's rights are non-exclusive, so one cannot predict how it might interact with libraries and other institutions in the future. It is difficult to know how the Registry will function; its operations were not fully delineated in the agreement (and it is not even certain at this point whether the settlement will be approved, and in what form). The Registry will face many complicated issues, not the least of which is how to divide up the money received from institutional licenses and other undifferentiated revenues.

What can be concluded about the Google settlement and collective management more generally as a means of promoting the development of digital libraries?

First, collective management schemes to enable digitization and blanket licensing of books are possible, but more likely to be accepted by right holders with respect to older works. This is demonstrated by the different treatment of commercially available and non commercially available works under the Google settlement agreement, and in another context, by the JSTOR 'moving wall'.

Secondly, and relatedly, right holders want to control the manner in which their works are distributed and made available. This is underscored by the fact that much of how the Google agreement provides for making books available are 'default rules' that may be changed by the right holder. It is also demonstrated by the option that right holders have to remove their works from the database.[79] It is commonly thought that most

79 Right holders' discretion is not unlimited, however. Under the 'coupling requirement' in the Settlement Agreement, a right holder that sells access to his book to individual consumers through this program must also make it available in the institutional license database. Settlement Agreement, *supra* note 49 at 3.5(b)(iii).

recently published books controlled by publishers will be removed from the database and sold or made available through other channels. The settlement does not attempt to embrace electronic books. In other words, the Google settlement is unlikely to yield a collective management scheme that makes newly introduced trade books, best-sellers or text books available from libraries for unrestricted access under a blanket license at no incremental cost to the end user.

Thirdly, the agreement and the collective management mechanism it envisions will not create a universally accessible digital library. Libraries will require institutional subscriptions for their users to have remote access to full text works; those individuals without access through an institutional subscription will have full text access to the database only if they use terminals on library premises. Otherwise, there will be free internet access only to bibliographic data and previews. Uses outside the United States are even more limited. In other words, access to the full text of copyrighted works will still be restricted in some measure, with payment based on use in some measure, and security and technological protection mechanisms will continue to play an important role.[80]

8.3 Government Initiatives

What can US federal and state governments do to further the development of digital libraries?

Funding

First, they can provide more funding for libraries, and in particular, funding to encourage collaborative projects. High quality, broadly accessible information resources provide benefits to society as a whole, and governments at all levels should make the necessary investment to support them.

Legislation

On the legislative front, the most pressing issue right now is orphan works legislation. 'Orphan works', as mentioned earlier, are works whose owners

---

[80] 'Fully participating libraries', that is, those that have allowed a significant portion of their collections to be digitized by Google and that sign an agreement providing for security and other use limitations, will receive a complete digital copy of the books in their collections. While use of the library digital copy is restricted in many respects (it cannot be used for interlibrary loan, for example), the library can use that copy for preservation and replacement, permit certain research uses by its faculty and staff, and provide special access to users with print disabilities. See generally Settlement Agreement, *supra* note 49, art.VII.

cannot be identified or located. Potential users, including libraries, are often reluctant to use such works, unwilling to incur potential liability if the copyright owner comes forward after the use commences. The US Copyright Office, concerned that the inability to locate right holders to obtain permission for use of these works is discouraging beneficial uses, has recommended amending the Copyright Act to limit the remedies available against users of orphan works who perform a diligent search but are unable to find the copyright owner.[81] It proposed limiting monetary relief to reasonable compensation for the use, and eliminating monetary recovery completely where use of the orphan work was non-commercial and the user ceases the use upon notice.[82]

Orphan works legislation came close to enactment in 2008, and will likely be reintroduced again in the future. If it is passed, it will expand the opportunities for libraries to digitize copyrighted works and make them available to users remotely. It is not a panacea, however, because in order to use a work, a library would first have to make a diligent search, which can be time-consuming. Moreover, many of the works that libraries would like to make broadly available are relatively current and unlikely to qualify as orphan works. Nevertheless, orphan works legislation, appropriately drafted, could be a valuable tool for digital libraries.

The other legislative initiative on the horizon is the Section 108 Study Group recommendations. Those recommendations are addressed more to digital preservation than to digital libraries, but in many respects could advance the goal of digital libraries. The Study Group's recommendations were at a high level, however. Many issues have still to be worked out before legislation could be enacted. Legislation has not yet been introduced; the Section 108 Study Group Report is currently under review by the Copyright Office.

Whether the federal government should do anything further to enable or encourage the development of collective management mechanisms remains to be seen.

---

[81] Report on Orphan Works pp. 96–97, 115–21 (January 2006), available at http://www.copyright.gov/orphan/orphan-report-full.pdf (last accessed 25 June, 2009).

[82] Ibid, pp.115–118. The Copyright Office report also proposed limiting injunctive relief, so that a user that created a derivative work relying on the original's orphan status could continue to use it, provided there was reasonable compensation to the copyright owner. Ibid, at 119.

Appropriate oversight of collective management organizations
For various reasons, collective management organizations present issues under US antitrust laws. ASCAP and BMI have long operated under antitrust consent decrees. The US Department of Justice is already reviewing the Google settlement, not only with respect to what it might mean for Google's position in the marketplace, but also with respect to the planned activities and operation of the Registry. It is appropriate for the government to scrutinize the Registry or any other collective management organization that might be developed in the future to ensure that it does not unfairly wield monopoly power. At the same time, it is important that government oversight does not unreasonably hamper the development or operation of such institutions, and leaves them free to respond to economic and technological developments in the marketplace.

9 CONCLUSION

The aspiration discussed at the outset – universally accessible digital libraries – is a noble goal. Who does not support the advancement of knowledge and education? But creation of works of authorship still requires an investment of time and resources, even though their dissemination may be much easier and less costly than in the past.

If universally accessible libraries are to be created, who should bear the costs? The benefits of free, widely accessible information seem obvious. The benefits of a class of vibrant, creative professional authors and a flourishing publishing industry should also be obvious. It is important to strike the right balance between rewarding creativity and enhancing access to copyright protected works. In the past, copyright exceptions and limitations have permitted free or modestly-priced library uses largely because they were thought to be collateral uses; in other words, there was another market through which the works could be sold that would provide a significant return for the author. That is unlikely to be the case for works that are universally accessible through digital libraries. This suggests that achieving digital libraries through broad new exceptions or limitations on copyright is likely to be problematic. Although targeted legislation may be useful and realistic, collaboration and cooperation between libraries and right holders may ultimately be essential to making copyrighted works in digital form more widely available.

15. Digital libraries in the current legal and educational environment: a European perspective

Marco Ricolfi*

1 THE EU DIGITAL LIBRARIES INITIATIVE: 'A FUTURE FOR THE PAST (AND FOR THE PRESENT)'

My contribution concerns the EU digital libraries initiative and the copyright issues related to it. Both the Communication by the Commission of September 2005[1] and the Commission Staff Working Document annexed to it[2] quite clearly illustrate what the i2010 strategy is about. Libraries, archives, museums were set up a long time ago in order to preserve text, music, images, audiovisual works and other materials. All this content was originally accumulated and made available in analogue format; in the last decade, however, it turned out that digitisation is appropriate and,

* Torino Law School, marco.ricolfi@studiotosetto.it, While I am a member of the High Level Group set up by the EU Commission on the Digital Libraries Initiative and Chairman of the Subgroup formed within the HLG, in this presentation I express my opinions only as an independent academic writer. I am deeply indebted to my colleagues in the Subgroup for their insights and dedication; however I am the only one to blame for whatever error of fact or judgement may be found in this writing. For additional detail see my *Copyright Policy for digital libraries in the context of the i2010 strategy* available at http://nexa.polito.it/content/copyright-policy-digital-libraries-context-i2010-strategy-aka-copyright-20-paper.

[1] Communication from the Commission to the European Parliament, the Council, the European Economic and Social Committee and the Committee of Regions i2010: Digital Libraries Brussels 30.9.05 COM(2005) 465 final.

[2] Commission Staff Working Document, *Annex* to the Communication from the Commission to the European Parliament, the Council, the European Economic and Social Committee and the Committee of Regions i2010: Digital Libraries, Brussels, 30.9.2005, SEC (2005) 1194.

to a large extent, indispensable in order to pass this content to the next generations.[3]

The difficulty in achieving this task lies in the fact that, while digitisation of text and even more so of images and audiovisual material is immensely costly, its outcome, digital preservation, entails vast external benefits. This characterisation of the structure of costs and benefits suggests that market forces, by themselves, may not be up to the task. That here we are dealing with a case of provision of a public good and specifically of the kind which often is referred to as a global public good[4] is specially clear in a European context. Just to give an example: market forces could be expected to give priority to text written in English; on the contrary, in the perspective of EU institutions the goal of preserving linguistic and cultural diversity has a clear priority.

So far we mentioned the issue of preserving past content for the future. But it would appear that the same analysis applies to giving a future to the present: to preserving digital born content in view of making it accessible in the future. Also in this regard, market forces may be unlikely to come up with the appropriate rate of preservation and accessibility.

2 THE COPYRIGHT ISSUES TAKEN UP IN THE CONTEXT OF THE INITIATIVE

To deal with the economic, legal and technological issues raised by the i2010 strategy, the EU Commission set up a High Level Expert Group (HLG) on the European Digital Libraries initiative. At the first meeting of the HLG, held in Brussels on 27 March 2006, the HLG took the decision to appoint some members to work together as the 'Copyright Subgroup' to analyse the relevant IPR issues and options. The mandate entrusted to the Subgroup was summarised in the following terms: 'What are the key IPR challenges? What different actions and arrangements could be undertaken jointly by stakeholders to reduce tensions surrounding copyrights? Is there a need to harmonise at Community level exceptions and limitations that relate to libraries, archives, museums? What are possible ways for facilitating the clearance of rights for cultural institutions?'

3 For a balanced view of the respective roles of analogue and digital copies in the libraries of the future see R. Darnton (2008), 'The Library in the New Age', *The New York Review of Books* 12 June 2008, 72 ff.

4 In accordance with the terminology adopted by K.E. Maskus and J.E. Reichman (2004), 'The Globalization of Private Knowledge Goods and the Privatization of Global Public Goods', *Journal of International Economic Law*, 279–320.

The Copyright Subgroup presented its *Final Report on Digital Preservation, Orphan Works, and Out-of-Print Works* at the meeting of the HLG of 4 June 2008.

The approach adopted by the Copyright Subgroup to deal with the mandate was in a number of ways selective rather than expansive. Even though digitisation and accessibility raise a vast number of IP issues, four key challenges were given priority: digital preservation, web harvesting, orphan works and out-of-print works. In this regard, the Subgroup followed quite literally the Commission Recommendation of 24 August 2006.[5] The Subgroup also preferred to see what could be done in these specific areas on the basis of existing EU legislation. Therefore, rather than investigating the possibility of amending the current Directives, it concentrated on two sets of tools at hand: Member States' implementing legislation and voluntary arrangements between rightholders and other stakeholders, be they collective and individual. In a similar vein, we could add that the approach selected was vertical rather than horizontal: it was preferred to look at the fine detail of implementation and deployment of each single selected issue, rather than to cover all the possible ground.

This selective approach may be appreciated in different ways. One may apply to it old Goethe's maxim, whereby *in der Beschränkung steht die Kraft,* the force resides in the limitation; or one may criticise the excess of cautiousness it may entail. Surely it is not for me to decide which of the two assessments is the most appropriate.

I will look briefly at each of the selected key issues and at the recommendations the Copyright Subgroup has come up in connection with them. In doing so, I will mention a few important developments which have taken place in the last few months which may impact on the solutions discussed in that document. In particular, I will refer to the Commission's Green Paper *Copyright in the Knowledge Economy*[6] and to what usually is referred to as 'the Google settlement'.

3 DIGITAL PRESERVATION

Digital technology evolves quickly; therefore obsolescence is built-in in any given format and platform. Those of us who are no longer in their thirties

---

[5] European Commission Recommendation of 24 August 2006 on the digitisation and online accessibility of cultural material and digital preservation (2006/585/EC), in OJ 236 of 31 August, 2006, 28 ff.

[6] Commission of the EU Communities, Green Paper *Copyright in the Knowledge Economy*, Brussels, COM (2008) 466/3.

have already experienced that the first digital files we created are now irretrievable; even the medium where they originally were stored (the floppy disk first, the diskette later) has already become – or is quickly becoming – useless, as the platforms to which it was connected have already disappeared or are about to disappear. Now, if copyright law allowed only a predefined number of digital copies, this would mean that all the digitisation efforts would probably turn out to be in vain in a quite short time. After a decade or so, these copies would become obsolete; and the initial investment would be altogether lost. This is not a theoretical scenario: as you know, the digital copy of the Book of Doomsday, a beautiful Middle-Ages manuscript, is no longer accessible, while the original still is alive and well.

However, nothing prevents copyright law from taking into account this quite obvious technological background and steering clear of posing unnecessary obstacles to digital preservation. All that is required in this regard from a legal viewpoint is that copyright law allows for the creation of an open-ended number of digital copies. Indeed, if the original creation of multiple copies and the subsequent creation of additional copies are permitted to the extent required to evolve (or 'shift') the original copies into the formats which from time to time appear on the technological horizon, then a modicum of technological foresight is required to enable gradual migration at the same pace as formats and platforms evolve.

The Copyright Subgroup noted that EU copyright law does not stand in the way of this possibility. On the contrary, Art. 5(2)(c) of the Directive 2001/29/EC of the European Parliament and the Council of 22 May 2001 on the harmonisation of certain aspects of copyright and related rights in the information society[7] states that 'Member States may provide for exceptions to the reproduction right provided for in Article 2 in the following cases: . . . (c) in respect of specific acts of reproduction made by publicly accessible libraries, educational establishments or museums, or by archives, which are not for direct or indirect economic commercial advantage'. This wording does not set a ceiling to the number of digital copies and therefore fully enables migration, subject to the stipulation that the from time to time created copies are linked to preservation only and are not used for other purposes. Migration is nevertheless prevented by Member States implementing legislation, which currently provides only for a limited and fixed number of copies.[8]

[7] In OJ L 167 of 22 June 2001, 10 ff.

[8] If it provides for them at all: Italy is a sad exception to this, providing only for analogue xerocopies. But then Italy has deliberately chosen to be the sick man of Europe in all possible regards.

Therefore, all that is required to take care of this obstacle to the ongoing adaptation of digital files to technological development is that Member States amend their own domestic rules to enable an open-ended number of copies.

This is indeed the solution recommended by the Report,[9] which goes on to note that the same digital copies can also be made available to the public at all relevant times on the premises of the same establishment by means of dedicated terminals within the limits provided for by Art. 5(3)(n) of the Directive to the extent provided, again, by Member States' implementing legislation.

The resulting solution quite nicely dovetails the corresponding US provision, Sec. 108 of Copyright Law as amended by the 1998 Digital Millennium Copyright Act (DMCA), which also provides for an exemption on behalf of non-profit libraries and archives.

What has a characteristically European flavour, both in the Directive and in all the documents referring to it, all the way down to the Report, is the kind of institutions, or 'establishments', as Art. 5(3)(n) puts it, we Europeans do have in mind when we talk about the task of digital preservation. What we have in mind are public institutions, like the Bibliotheque Nationale de France or the British Library, much more than private, not-for-profit institutions, such as the Internet Archive founded by Brewster Kahle. For sure private digitising entities, such as private for profit corporations, are out of the European landscape, except in the case they operate as partners in some public-private partnership (PPP), along with the responsible 'public' institution. We will come back to this feature later on (in § 8).

For the time being, it might be noted that the recommendation by the Report has to face a difficulty. What happens if Member States do not grab the opportunity afforded by the Directive to enable an open-ended number of copies? This is a real possibility, if one considers that countries like Italy failed to enable even a single digital copy. If this situation is not taken care of, some Member States' institutions would be cut off from the possibility of taking part in pan-European digitisation projects. Possibly the time has come to start considering that some exceptions and limitations should be mandatory, as indeed already is the case in the neighbouring field of software and as the *Green Book* quite wisely envisages.[10]

---

9 Report, § 3.

10 *Copyright in the Knowledge Economy*, 6.

4 WEB HARVESTING

The Commission's Recommendation of 24 August 2006 describes web-harvesting[11] as follows:

> Web-harvesting is a new technique for collecting material from the Internet for preservation purposes. It involves mandated institutions actively collecting material instead of waiting for it to be deposited, thus minimizing the administrative burden on producers of digital material, and national legislation should therefore make provision for it.

The reasons why the Copyright Subgroup felt there was an urgent need to address web-harvesting in addition to digital preservation of analogue material are quite obvious. Indeed, as earlier remarked, we must ensure a future not only for the past, but even more so for the present. Not only analogue material, but also digital-born material, requires preservation and deserves it; and this is even more so for the simple reason that digital material is even less stable than analogue material.

In this connection, rather than going into the details of the Report,[12] I shall confine myself to two remarks.

First, it should be noted that also in this connection the EU legislative framework does not require any innovation. Indeed, on top of Art. 5(2)(c), the text of which was quoted in the previous paragraph, the provision of Art. 9 of the Directive 29/2001 provides that 'This Directive shall be without prejudice to provisions concerning in particular . . . legal deposit requirements'. Now, in EU parlance, deposit means legislation mandating public institutions to store away new works as these are from time to time being created and made available to the public. Now, web-harvesting by mandated institutions clearly is a tool to implement deposit legislation, which in this specific case may be described as operating in pull mode (by the institution) rather than in push mode (by the content creator).

Therefore, once again, what is required – and was recommended by the Report – is action at the Member State level only, that is to implement through national legislation what EU law already permits. This task should now have become much easier, as the Copyright Subgroup noted, once two Member States, France and Finland, set an example with far reaching web harvesting legislation, which also deals with the most crucial issues in the sector (such as the retroactive effect, the connecting factors and so on).

---

[11] Recital 14 of the Recommendation.

[12] Report, § 4.

Secondly, the institutions to be entrusted with the task of web harvesting once again are ideally public bodies, even though the leeway granted by Art. 9 of the Directive would appear to be greater than the reference to Art. 5 of the same Directive only might be deemed to imply.

5 ORPHAN WORKS

Digital preservation and web harvesting may appear the easy part of the job, if compared to the much discussed issue of orphan works, that is of works whose rightholders cannot be identified or, if they can be identified, cannot be located. This may be very important content, as in the case of a great part of movies, silent or otherwise, created until the half of last century; sometimes the inclusion of the orphan content may be indispensable for the creation of a multi-component, derivative work. How is it possible to obtain a clearance when the creator is unknown? Here the Copyright Subgroup could not confine itself to noting, as it did in the two other areas we earlier mentioned, that the enabling provision is already available in the *acquis communautaire* and all that is required is Member States' implementing action, for the simple reason that such an enabling provision unfortunately is not to be found anywhere in the relevant EU Directives.

Of course, one could have envisaged specific new EU legislation concerning orphan works, to the effect that, under given conditions, the reproduction, distribution, communication to the public and the other acts concerning orphan works could be considered either altogether admissible or at least subject to what the current US bills call 'a limitation on remedies'.[13] I do not know whether this latter solution might have turned out to be questionable under the 1886 Berne Convention and under the incorporation of Berne by reference to it in Art. 9 TRIPs. For sure, the Copyright Subgroup also in this connection preferred to remain within the limits of the current EU framework and to confine its recommendation to the two sets of tools it had in principle selected, that is, contractual arrangements and Member States' domestic legislation.

This approach has an obvious difficulty: it has to deal with a missing link. Indeed, it is quite problematic to stick to a contractual approach in a situation where by definition the correct party to the contract cannot be located or even identified in the first place.

[13] Thereby meaning that reappearing rightholders may claim compensation but not damages and/or injunctions. Report § 5.2.

The way I see it, the Report deals with this difficulty, which quite closely resembles the difficulty which the Baron of Munchhausen had to face when trying to raise himself by pulling his bootstraps, by combining three steps.

First, it was assumed that a minimum of harmonisation is required between the rules concerning clearance of orphan works applicable in the 27 different Member States. This harmonisation should particularly concern the issue of establishing what are the relevant diligent search criteria for each sector.[14]

Secondly, it was noted that under EU law minimum harmonisation usually leads to mutual recognition. The essential principle which sees mutual recognition as a consequence of minimum harmonisation at the EU level[15] may have far reaching consequences also in our field. Indeed, once the basic rules to determine what is due diligence in the search for rightholders of orphan works are established, what is deemed acceptable in one Member State should in principle be held to be correspondingly acceptable in all the other Member States, or, in other words, should have cross-border effect. Therefore a search which is held diligent in one Member State should not be duplicated for the purpose of using the same orphan work in the other Member States but should be considered diligent also in the latter. Thus the solutions set in place in the various Member States could be in part different, but still interoperable, to the extent they are based on comparable due diligence guidelines.

Thirdly, the consequences of compliance with due diligence guidelines should be established at Member States' level. The mechanisms may again vary from one Member State to the other. One Member State may consider resorting to extended collective licenses (ECL).[16] In accordance with this mechanism, which is widespread in Nordic countries, rightholders' and users' collective bodies establish in advance by means of collective agreements what are the pre-requisites and the terms under which works originating from the rightholders who are members of the collective rights management organisations (CRMOs) which signed the collective agreement, which happen to have orphan status at the time of planned use, may

---

[14] Report § 5.3 and 4.

[15] Enshrined in the European Court of Justice decision of 20 February 1979, case 120/78, *Rewe Zentrale v. Bundesmonopolverwaltung für Branntwein*, in *European Court Reports* 1979, 649 ff., case 'Cassis de Dijon'.

[16] Report § 5.2. For a comprehensive treatment of ECL see T. Koskinen-Olsson (2006), 'Collective Management in the Nordic Countries', in Daniel Gervais (ed), *Collective Management of Copyright and Related Rights*, Wolters-Kluwer, 257 ff.

be exploited. This collective licensing feature would in principle apply to works created by members of the signing CRMO; except that in Nordic countries' State legislation steps in at this junction and adds a second, 'extending' feature, by expanding the effects of the collective agreement also to third parties who are not members of a CRMO, unless they do not chose to opt out. This mechanism automatically takes care of orphan works, because these are in principle included in the collective bargaining enlarged by extension legislation; to exclude them, the rightholder has to raise her hand and object, whereby the work instantly ceases to be orphan.

Of course, other Member States might adopt different mechanisms, for example providing for a clearance centre checking that due diligence search is complied with, granting licenses for orphan works, receiving fees at the applicable rate and paying out of the pool fund thus established the remuneration to the rightholders who may from time to time reappear and stake a claim to compensation. In either case, what is important is that an orphan work which gets the green light under any of these mechanisms in any Member State should also be considered cleared in all the other 26 Member States.

I am afraid that there may be a few hidden snags still to be taken care of here and there,[17] as one would expect considering that, as usual, the devil is in the detail. Nevertheless I would like to underline that the approach seems able to attain its stated purpose: to provide a solution for orphans by once again combining contractual arrangements (at the collective, rather than individual level) with Member States' domestic legislation. EU law does indeed come into the picture; but only to the extent it resorts to the time honoured 'minimum harmonisation-mutual recognition' sequence to give EU-wide interoperability to solutions in all other respects based only on a combination of contractual arrangements and Member States' legislation.

6 OUT-OF-PRINT WORKS

We earlier saw that under current EU legislation libraries may make digital copies of the texts they own and are even allowed to make them

---

[17] *Quaere*: should the rate set by the clearance centre in Member State A consider also use in the other Member States B, C and so on? In the event the rightholder eventually appears, should she obtain compensation from Member State A clearance centre also for uses in the other Member States? Should the cross-border effect be established in Member States' legislation and, if so, in which Member States' legislation? Of course, I do have my tentative replies to these questions; but I am fully aware that they are open to debate.

accessible on their premises through dedicated terminals. The investment which digitisation entails is huge; and this is bound to raise the next question. Once the investment is made, why not make the digitised work as widely available as possible? In this connection the formula 'to digitise once, to disseminate widely' has frequently surfaced in the debate.

The Copyright Subgroup did not fail to dutifully note that the precept to 'disseminate widely' does not by itself entail the liberty to disseminate *freely* under all circumstances, lest the opportunity for uncontrolled *secondary* dissemination destroy the incentives to create in the first place and to invest in what is described as *primary* exploitation of works, often undertaken by businesses risking their own capital in the venture. Indeed, in many contexts creators and publishers may not be expected to engage in the difficult and risky task of creating and marketing a new work, if the initial digital copy were to be available without limits immediately after it is first made.

There are cases, however, in which dissemination of already digitised material would appear to be a win-win solution for all the interested parties. Once an old, rare book is digitised by an institution, there is no reason for a sister institution to duplicate the cost by engaging in the same task. If the digitised copy is made available to the sister institution, this fact should normally not have a material adverse impact on commercial exploitation, as also the additional use would be restricted to on-the-premises-consultation. Moreover, when a book is out of print, it may be that the rightholders are not interested in its further commercial exploitation; therefore they may well be prepared to consent to an even wider dissemination, beyond the restricted networks of public institutions.

The main hurdle to the adoption of these win-win solutions would appear to consist of transaction costs. It would appear that transaction costs can be mitigated by standardisation of contractual arrangements; if they are subject to the scrutiny of the different stakeholders' associations, members may well assume that a balanced solution has been worked out. Therefore, the Copyright Subgroup engaged in an exercise of drafting two model contracts, one intended for use in secure networks (for users who are members of the digitising institution or of an institution linked to it), the other intended for online use over open networks. The idea was to provide an incentive to wider dissemination of digitised material, by facilitating the consensual arrangements between the two main players: rightholders and institutions who invested in digitisation of out-of-print works.

If I may add a personal note, I would indicate that I was surprised that the second model contract, intended for online use over open networks, could be adopted at all. I was even more surprised to find that the publishers themselves foresee that there will be a quite large number of works for which adoption of this second model is possible and even likely. Which certainly is good news: if the Digital Libraries initiative is about preservation of European heritage and accessibility of the same, then it does make a lot of sense that this accessibility is not reserved to the few EU citizens living in the neighbourhood of the physical location where the digitised resource is available in analogue format. Access from any interested person in any part of the globe is indeed most welcome.[18]

Of course, only the future may tell us whether these opportunities will in fact be exploited; and to what extent. What I can add, however, is that the Copyright Subgroup once again tried to be 'vertical' in going into the details of deployment. Again databases and clearance centres for out-of-print works should reduce transaction costs; test beds and 'champions' interested in having the projects up and running should provide the necessary critical mass; coordination with the EU and national initiatives already in place and, last but not least, endorsement by European institutions should contribute to this. Therefore let us wait and see, hoping that this quite promising tool is widely resorted to.

7 WHERE DO WE GO FROM HERE?

Whatever the assessment of the contributions made by the Report, surely it may prompt us to ask several groups of questions which, to a varying extent, go beyond it. (i) What are the other crucial copyright issues which digital libraries have to face which the Report chose not to address? (ii) What are the assumptions on which EU i2010 strategy is based, which have an impact on digitisation by libraries, archives and museums? Are they sound? (iii) Finally, is copyright as we know it still an appropriate tool in the current digital context; or should we move on to another mechanism? If so, what would be the impact of the move on the costs and benefits of digital libraries? Elsewhere I looked at the 'second basket' of open issues, under (i), and at the – admittedly visionary – possibility of moving from the current form of copyright, as we know it today (Copyright 1.0, we might say), to a new copyright (Copyright 2.0, we might say), or, possibly, to some sort of flexible combination of Copyright 1.0 and Copyright 2.0. So I will not deal again with these issues here.

---

[18] To this extent the Report has paid heed to the – quite sweeping – remarks made by F. Stasse, 'Rapport au ministre de la culture et de la communication su l'accès aux œuvres numériques conservées par les bibliothèques publiques', April 2005.

A few words may be in place in connection with item (ii), as the process which is leading to the Google settlement forces us to consider the issue again.

8 DIRIGISM AND LASSEZ-FAIRE IN DIGITAL PRESERVATION

So far, I did not question the basic assumptions on which the i2010 strategy and EU copyright law are based. However, I should confess once again that I have misgivings on one important feature which we Europeans tend to take for granted, in spite of the fact that it always puzzles and disquiets our brethren living on the other side of the Atlantic.

I refer to the dominant role played by public institutions in the preservation and dissemination of protected content. This may make sense, to a certain extent. After all, we seem to be talking here about the provision of global public goods, and it would therefore seem that a crucial role for public institutions within the i2010 strategy may well be warranted.

It should be questioned, however, whether there is a strand of this choice which could come under the heading of 'the European reply to the Google challenge' and, if this is the case, whether this would be the right approach.[19] We can take for granted that the goal of the European project goes beyond the market-based approach of Google and other private players.[20] These entities seem to work on an advertising-led model; in this perspective, digitisation and access to digitisation is seen not as a goal in itself, but as a means to attract the widest possible audience ('billions of eyeballs') to platforms simultaneously offering goods and services for a charge.

In the vision of European institutions, the goal of digitisation, to the extent it may be seen as a case of provision of global public goods, should be quite different and consist in maximising access to European cultural heritage and fostering long term societal goals, such as the preservation of linguistic diversity. Thereby, market objectives are not ignored; rather, they should be incidental to the broader objectives of the European polity. This is the context in which also public-private partnership are to

---

[19] In this context it should be remarked that a representative of Google was present in the HLG and that Ms Moll and Mr Aubert took part in the Subgroup on behalf of Google.

[20] For a characteristically European view of the issue see J.N. Jeanneney (2007), *Google and the Myth of Universal Knowledge. A View From Europe*, The University of Chicago Press.

be considered. Indeed, the deployment of market-based business models should be promoted rather than discouraged, but only to the extent they are compatible with the broader goals underlying the initiative.

Still, I do have misgivings about the paramount role of public institutions. A factor to consider is that public institutions may distort markets. This is not a moot issue. Once digitisation has taken place, there is a strong reason to favour all kinds of secondary dissemination of digitised material, including through commercialisation.[21] If this is the case, then there are reasons to say that commercialisation of (digital) works by cultural, not-for-profit institutions may in some circumstances turn out to be risky. Indeed, in a competitive environment, it may also be dangerous to have new markets entered by public institutions, because these enjoy the competitive edge granted by public funding; moreover experience shows they can cross-subsidise one sector with moneys derived from others. Initiatives adding value to digitised text, images and audiovisual content require a level playing field.

In a broader perspective, I would like to point out that we in Europe, and specially so in continental Europe, do have a *dirigiste* streak and an interventionist tradition which may turn out to be dangerous, as we should be well aware, considering all the bad, bad things which went along with it, from the economic inefficiency caused by corporatism all the way down to active contribution to two world wars.

A few years ago, Roger Shattuck remarked that 'most Americans believe that their culture should grow out of the free marketplace of ideas, fashions, and institutions, not out of a state command system'.[22] We Europeans have a rather different attitude. We are very quick in spotting market inadequacies and market failures; and possibly we are right in doing so, particularly in the field of culture. After all, this was the starting point of this very presentation.[23] However, this is not the end of the story: we should be at least as cautious in handling regulatory tools.

Maybe this is particularly so at this point in time. Indeed, at this very moment there may be a renewed impetus, in the context of the current financial and economic crisis, to have public institutions engaged in anti-cyclical spending to revive the sputtering economic machine. I am not sure, however, that this is a good reason to forget all the cautions which should surround the expansion of governmental activity. There is no point

---

[21] To the extent, of course, this does not destroy creators' and business's incentives to primary exploitation: see above, Section 6.

[22] Roger Shattuck (2005), 'In the Thick of Things', *The New York Review of Books,* 26 May, 19.

[23] See above, Section 1.

in replacing the unlimited trust in markets which characterised the last 25 years with an equally misplaced trust in the wisdom of government intervention. What we have to get right is the mix of decentralised market choices and of collective choices, in general, and in particular in the area we have been considering here.

In the present context, I submit that we should pause to reflect on the implications of the Google settlement under way. This would appear to be creating a framework under which digitisation and dissemination led by private investment may play a much greater role than originally envisaged. In this context, it may well be that the optimal mix of private and public contribution to the task ahead requires careful re-consideration of the issue whether the public contribution to the process should not be re-directed to the areas where private activity is insufficient or distortive. After all, this is what the principle of subsidiarity suggests; and the principle of subsidiarity is after all one of the basic rules of the European legal framework.

16. Digital libraries in the current legal and educational environment: towards a remunerated compulsory license or limitation?

Raquel Xalabarder*

1 INTRODUCTION

All copyright instruments mention education as a public interest that justifies an exception or limitation to the authors' exclusive rights. Educational purposes have always been present in the the Berne Convention since its very origins in 1886.[1] 'Teaching, scholarship or research' purposes are also envisioned in the Universal Copyright Convention of 1966 (Art. V*ter*). And the WIPO Copyright Treaty of 1996[2] expressly referred to education in its Preamble, when 'Recognizing the need to maintain a balance between the rights of authors and the larger public interest, particularly *education, research and access to information*, as reflected in the Berne Convention'. More recently, the EU Directive on Copyright in the Information Society[3] stressed its goal '*to promote learning and culture* by protecting works and other subject-matter while permitting exceptions or limitations in the public interest *for the purpose of education and teaching*' (Recital 14).

* Dra. Raquel Xalabarder, Universitat Oberta de Catalunya.

1 See Berne Convention for the Protection of Literary and Artistic Works, of 9 September 1886, as revised at Paris on 24 July 1971 and amended in 1979 [hereinafter, Berne Convention or BC].

2 See WIPO Copyright Treaty of 20 December 1996 [hereinafter, WCT]. A parallel clause can be found in the Preamble of the WIPO Performances and Phonograms Treaty of 20 December 1996 [hereinafter, WPPT].

3 See Directive 2001/29/EC of the European Parliament and of the Council of 22 May 2001, on the harmonization of certain aspects of copyright and related rights in the information society, 2001 O.J. L-167/10 (22.06.2001) [hereinafter, EUCD].

Education is paramount to copyright laws: it is recognized as a fundamental right that deserves to be balanced against the authors' exclusive rights.[4] Unfortunately, after the preambles and declarations, education is far from getting the preferential treatment it deserves in copyright instruments. A lot of work is to be done, especially to cover the needs of digital libraries and online education. First, because the exempted use of works for education and library purposes remains mostly a matter for domestic laws, resulting in a variety of different solutions which freeze the progress of online learning (students located all over the world). Secondly because domestic laws fail to grant educational purposes and libraries (especially on digital environments) the preferential treatment they deserve and are far from the scope of limitation allowed under international instruments such as the Berne Convention and, in Europe, the EUCD.

Domestic laws fail to grant a uniform and complete treatment of education as a copyright exception or limitation.[5] The extent and conditions of the exceptions provided for educational purposes vary, sometimes widely, among domestic laws, the lack of normative consensus being far more acute when we consider digital formats.

Most domestic exceptions and limitations tend to benefit only 'traditional' libraries and educational establishments, by referring to photocopying or use 'in classrooms', which fail to cover digital and online activities.

We will not get into a comparative law study but simply make some general remarks as to the current exceptions and limitations for education and libraries, using the Berne Convention as the starting point and referring, as necessary, to the EUCD and some national laws. After visiting the current legal scenario, we will focus on some possible solutions to the obstacles faced by digital libraries and educational establishments.

---

4 And it should not be otherwise, since the 1948 UN Universal Declaration of Human Rights acknowledged education (Art. 26.1) and access culture (Art. 27.1) as fundamental rights of all people, together with the authors' rights (Art. 27.2). See *Universal Declaration of Human Rights, General Assembly of the United Nations*, Resolution 217 A (III) of 10 December 1948.

5 Usually, a distinction is made between 'limitation' to refer to non-voluntary (usually statutory) remunerated licenses, and 'exception' to refer to free uses allowed by the law. We will not make such a distinction here, and will use the term exception or limitation without distinguishing between free or remunerated uses.

2 THE CURRENT LEGAL SCENARIO FOR TEACHING AND LIBRARY EXCEPTIONS

Despite relying on domestic laws to deal with exceptions and limitations to the exclusive rights of authors,[6] the Berne Convention provides for two limitations that may be applicable to digital education: quotations (art.10.1 BC) and illustration for teaching (art.10.2 BC). Instead, no specific exception exists in the BC (nor in the WCT or WPPT) in favor of libraries.

In addition, teaching uses and research are specially relevant in Art. 21 BC and the Annex to the Berne Convention which allows Governments in developing countries to use and translate foreign works for teaching and research purposes subject to a compulsory license, for a limited term. Unfortunately, very few countries have chosen to apply it and the Annex is far from being effective.[7]

2.1 Educational Purposes. Art. 10.2 Berne Convention and Art. 5.3(a) EUCD

2.1.1 Article 10.2 Berne Convention

The teaching exception in the Berne Convention may be traced back to the Berne Act of 1886. Its art. 8 reserved to national legislation 'the liberty of extracting portions from literary or artistic works for use in publications destined for educational or scientific purposes'. The Brussels Act of 1948 changed it, under Art. 10.2, to 'the right to include excerpts from literary or artistic works in educational or scientific publications'. At the 1976 Stockholm Revision, what started as a simple proposal for a minor amendment to replace 'excerpts' with 'borrowings'[8] (which only affected

---

[6] The BC brings a minimum of protection of exclusive rights at an international level, but does not ensure a counterpart of limitations (that is, a maximum to the exclusive rights, except for the imperative quotation exception in art. 10.1 BC).

[7] Only 15 countries have invoked the Appendix when joining the BC: http://www.wipo.int/treaties/. In 1967, a Protocol for Developing Countries was adopted at the Stockholm Conference in an attempt to meet the needs of the developing countries (education being fundamental for their development). All sorts of teaching uses were allowed, subject to compensation, not limited to classroom or library, but also distance learning and what we now call life-long learning. This Protocol never became part of Berne (most countries failed to ratify it) and in 1971, the Appendix was enacted providing for a narrower – yet more complex – compulsory licensing system.

[8] It was thought to correspond better to the French text 'emprunts'. See WIPO (1971), 'Preparatory Document s/1', *Records of the Intellectual Property Conference of Stockholm, 11 June – 14 July 1967*, p. 48.

the English text), opened up an important debate[9] that resulted in the current Art.10.2:[10]

> It shall be a matter for legislation in the countries of the Union, and for special agreements existing or to be concluded between them, to permit the utilization, to the extent justified by the purpose, of literary or artistic works by way of illustration in publications, broadcasts or sound or visual recordings for teaching, provided such utilization is compatible with fair practice.'

This is an open and flexible exception for teaching purposes which, instead of any specific quantitative or qualitative restrictions, allows the use of all kinds of works, both literary and artistic, in full[11] or in part, and in any number of copies,[12] provided that it is compatible 'with fair practice' and 'to the extent justified by the purpose' and, ultimately, in accordance with the three-step-test. Therefore, we need to consider the kind and the amount of work used, the purpose of the use, the quantity of copies made and the specific implications of the technology, in order to find *in casu* the right balance between the public interest (education) and that of the author.

The exception is technology-neutral. Since its introduction in 1886, it was always agreed that, as long as it lead to an 'official' degree, this

---

[9] See WIPO (1976), *Reports on the Work of the Five Main Committees of the Intellectual Property Conference of Stockholm 1967, WIPO Publication 309(E), # 93–94.*

[10] The final text proposed by the Working Group (document S/185) to amend art. 10(2) read : 'It shall be a matter for legislation in the countries of the Union, and for special agreements existing or to be concluded between them, to permit the utilization, to the extent justified by the purpose, of literary or artistic works by way of illustration in publications [broadcasts or recordings] for teaching, provided such utilization is compatible with fair practice.' See Stockholm Records, *op.cit.supra.*, Document S/185, p. 708.

[11] See Ricketson, Sam (1987), *The Berne Convention for the Protection of Literary and Artistic Works: 1886–1986*, London, Kluwer § 9.27 n. 2 p. 496: 'The words 'by way of illustration' impose some limitation, but would not exclude the use of the whole of a work in appropriate circumstances.' See Ricketson, Sam and Ginsburg, Jane C. (2006), *The Berne Convention for the Protection of Literary and Artistic Works: 1886–1986*, Oxford, Oxford University Press, §13.45, p. 791.

[12] See Ricketson (1987), *op.cit. supra*, § 9.27 n. 8; See also Ricketson/Ginsburg (2006), *op.cit.supra*, §13.45, p. 794: 'Just as no limitation is imposed in respect of the public which is reached by a broadcast intended for teaching purposes, so there can be no limitation on the number of copies that can be made for the same purpose. The only further qualification applied here is that the making of multiple copies must be compatible with 'fair practice'. Obviously, if this competes with the author's normal exploitation of his work and unreasonably prejudices his legitimate interests, article 10(2) should not apply.'

exception comprised both elementary and university teaching, in either private or public institutions, as well as distance teaching.[13] There is no reason to conclude that online teaching (or any other means of distance learning, such as *pod-casting*) should be left out.[14] On the one hand, the word 'utilization' is neutral enough to cover not only reproduction but also communication to the public (and the making available to the public -*ex* art. 8 WCT). And on the other, the BC revisions[15] show that, far from constituting an exhaustive list of specific means allowed, it is specifically intended to accommodate any new technology.[16]

The core of the exception is found in the language 'by way of illustration . . . for teaching'. Despite the specific terms used, the scope of this exception is neither different from nor narrower than the '*educational purposes*' previously stated in Art. 8 of the Berne Act and in Art. 10(2) of the Brussels Act. The Stockholm Conference documents show that the current wording responded exclusively to a concern about the amount of a work used (and the accuracy of the English version, that ignited the revision), rather than to an objective to modify or reduce the scope of the 'educational purposes'. In other words, 'by way of illustration for teaching' and 'educational purposes' are equivalent in terms of the specific purposes exempted.

Last but not least, Art. 10(2) BC is not a mandatory exception; it simply sets the limits within which an exception for teaching purposes may be carried out by national laws.[17] No matter how broad and flexible the BC

---

[13] See Ricketson (1987), *op.cit. supra*, §9.25 and §9.27 n. 3; See also Ricketson/Ginsburg (2006), *op.cit.supra*, §13.45.

[14] See Ricketson/Ginsburg (2006), *op.cit.supra*, §13.44 and §13.45. According to the Agreed Statement concerning Art.10 WCT, Member States may 'appropriately extend into the digital environment limitations and exceptions in their national laws which have been considered acceptable under the Berne Convention. . . . [and] devise new exceptions and limitations that are appropriate in the digital networked environment'. Digital teaching uses pose far greater risks for the author's interest, than face-to-face teaching; therefore, the exception may be subject to different conditions depending on the technology used.

[15] From 'publications destined for educational or scientific purposes' (as in the Berne Act), to 'educational or scientific publications' (as in the Brussels Act), and to 'publications intended for teaching or having a scientific character or in chrestomathies' (as proposed in the Stockholm Program), until the current text approved at Stockholm (which added recordings and broadcasts).

[16] The reason behind such wording was to enable educators 'to take full advantage of the new means of dissemination provided by modern technology. . . and there is no reason today to argue that it should not extend to digital fixations of works.' See Ricketson/Ginsburg (2006), *op.cit.supra* §13.45.

[17] See Ricketson (1987), *op.cit.supra*, §9.27 n.1; see Ricketson/Ginsburg (2006), *op.cit.supra*, §13.45, p. 791.

exception is, the exempted use of works for teaching purposes remains a matter for national law.

2.1.2 Art. 5.3(a) EUCD: Illustration for teaching or scientific research

Article 5.3(a) EUCD uses similar language to provide for teaching purposes. Member States may exempt any:

> use for the sole purpose of illustration for teaching or scientific research, as long as the source, including the author's name, is indicated, unless this turns out to be impossible and to the extent justified by the non-commercial purpose to be achieved.

Once again, the exception is technology-neutral and clearly intended to apply to both face-to-face and distance education, including by digital means.[18] Accordingly, it covers both rights of reproduction and communication to the public (including, *ex* Art. 3.1 EUCD, the right of making available to the public) and domestic laws may extend the exception to the right of distribution (Art. 5.4 EUCD). It may cover any acts of reproduction which are necessary to carry on such teaching use:[19] upload, transmission and reception, as well as permanent downloads by students; Any technical copies which are necessary to carry that out are exempted under the temporary copies exception of Art. 5.1 EUCD.

Article 5(3)(a) poses no limitation as to the extent and nature of the works used; thus, it allows for the use of fragments but also of entire works (of any kind), provided that – as the EUCD Proposal explains – 'only the part of the use which is justified by its non-commercial purpose may be exempted from the exclusive right'. The exception is also designed to cover the making of teaching anthologies (compilations).[20]

---

18 Recital 42 of the EUCD expressly includes 'distance learning' within that exception, and the Commission's Explanatory Memorandum accompanying the initial proposal of 10 December 1997 (COM(97) 628 final) further confirms that the teaching exception is intended to apply to 'the new electronic environment'.

19 The act of uploading the work on a server, in order to make it available to the public (students), entails both a reproduction and a communication to the public (also when recipients have restricted access). Temporary reproductions that enable the digital transmission and reception of the work are covered by the mandatory temporary copies exception of Art. 5.1 EUCD. The same may hold true for RAM copies that enable display of the work on the computer screen (*ex, mutatis mutandis,* Recital 33 EUCD); Or, more sensibly, they may be deemed part of the 'communication to the public' and be, consequently, exempted under Art. 5.3(a) EUCD. Permanent downloads (in any format: print-outs or digital files may be covered by the private use exception of Art. 5.2(b) EUCD or under the same teaching exception.

20 In the 1997 Explanatory Memorandum, the Commission expressly mentioned the 'compilation of an anthology' as an example of teaching uses that may

According to Recital 42 EUCD, 'the organizational structure and the means of funding of the establishment concerned are not the decisive factors' to ascertain the 'non-commercial' purpose of the educational activity. Therefore, private teaching establishments – as well as public ones – may benefit from the exception – albeit perhaps different compensation regimes will apply depending, for instance, on the nature of the establishment and the registration fees paid by their students, and on the particular nature of each teaching activity.

It is apparent that 'for the sole purpose of illustration for teaching' stems from the BC language of Art. 10.2 BC. And although it should not define *per se* the scope of this exception, it may be helpful to revisit the finding that 'illustration for teaching' was not intended to limit or reduce the 'educational' purpose itself.[21]

Furthermore, the fact that the transformation right is not included within the exceptions listed in Art. 5 EUCD[22] does not preclude domestic laws from expressly including it;[23] otherwise the work used for teaching purposes cannot be translated under the exception (can only be used in its original language!).

No fair compensation is expressly required by Art. 5.3(a) EUCD (although the EU Parliament did propose so),[24] but nothing prevents national legislators from setting compensation for teaching uses (Recital 36 EUCD). In fact, the three-step-test of Art. 5.5 EUCD may require it for some acts.

Footnote 20 (*cont.*)
fall under Art. 5.3(a) EUCD. This all-encompassing solution makes perfect sense since it is very difficult to distinguish between material that is 'used as part of the teaching' and a 'teaching anthology' in digital contexts.

21 Somehow similar to what may be inferred from the US TEACH Act of 2 November 2002 (amending the US Copyright Act of 1976, available at http://www.copyright.gov/title17 – accessed 1 August 2009): the work used must be 'directly related and of material assistance to the teaching content', not 'for the mere entertainment of the students or as unrelated background material'.

22 The main 'formal' difference between the two exceptions resides in the making of translations: implicitly included in Art. 10.2 BC – by referring to 'use' – but not mentioned in Art. 5 EUCD.

23 Unfortunately, most domestic 'illustration for teaching' exceptions fail to include (or at least, implicitly allow) the making of translations. For a comparative law study of domestic teaching exceptions, see Xalabarder, Raquel (2008), 'Los límites a los derechos de propiedad intelectual para fines educativos en Internet', *Revista pe. i.* num.29, pp. 13–110, at pp. 43–49: Malta, Netherlands, Poland, as well as (implicitly) Switzerland, Liechtenstein, Bulgaria, Estonia, Latvia and the Czech Republic.

24 See European Parliament Opinion (1st Reading) of 10 February 1999, A4/1999/26, O.J. C-150/171 (28.05.1999).

In short, member countries have a lot of discretion to shape the scope of the teaching exception. A survey of national laws[25] shows that although some sort of exception for teaching uses may be found in all European copyright laws, their scope and conditions vary widely and many of them clearly fail to cover online teaching uses.

2.2 Quotations. Art. 10.1 BC. Art. 5.3(d) EUCD

Both the Berne Convention and the EUCD provide for quotation exceptions which remain fundamental to complement narrow (or inexistent) teaching exceptions.

The quotation exception in Art. 10.1 BC[26] is a mandatory exception (thus proving its fundamental status):[27]

> It shall be permissible to make quotations from a work which has already been lawfully available to the public, provided that their making is compatible with fair practice, and their extent does not exceed that justified by the purpose, including quotations from newspaper articles and periodicals in the form of press summaries.

Art.5.3.(d) EUCD uses similar terms, when merely *allowing*[28] Member States to exempt:

---

[25] See Ernst, Silke and Haeusermann, Daniel M. (2006), 'EUCD Teaching Exceptions in selected EU Member States – A Rough Overview': http://papers.ssrn.com/sol3/papers.cfm?abstract_id=925950, accessed 1 August 2009. See also Xalabarder, Raquel (2007), 'On-line teaching and Copyright: Any hopes for an EU harmonized playground?,' in P. Torremans (ed), *Copyright Law – A Handbook of Contemporary Research*, Cheltenham, UK and Northampton, MA, USA, Edward Elgar Publishing, pp. 373–401.

[26] The exception was first introduced in 1928, at the Rome Conference, 'for the purposes of criticism, polemical discussion or teaching'. The present wording was introduced at the Stockholm Conference.

[27] It is one of the few instances of 'maximum protection' under the BC which must be enforced by Member States: to allow quotations (under Art. 10.1 BC) when protecting foreign Berne Union authors and works.

[28] It is regrettable that the EUCD completely forgot about the mandatory character of the quotation exception under the BC, especially if we take into account that domestic laws quotation exceptions tend to be less generous. This may pose interesting (and difficult) legal issues concerning the direct applicability of Art. 10(1) BC to compulsorily limit the protection of foreign authors' rights in Berne members, which go far beyond the scope of our presentation. See Xalabarder (2007), *op.cit.supra*, at pp. 397–398. In general, see Ricketson (1987), *op.cit.supra*, §§12.17–18 and Ricketson/Ginsburg (2006), *op.cit.supra*, §§6.110–111 and 130.

> Quotations for purposes such as criticism or review, provided that they relate to a work or other subject matter which has already been lawfully made available to the public, that, unless this turns out to be impossible, the source, including the author's name, is indicated, and that their use is in accordance with fair practice, and to the extent required by the specific purpose.

Both quotation exceptions are neither restricted to any specific uses or purposes,[29] nor to the reproduction right or any particular means of exploitation; therefore, applying to digital and networked environments. They exempt the quotation of all kind of works (provided they have been 'lawfully made available to the public') with no restriction as to the amount that may be quoted[30] other than 'fair practice' and to the 'extent justified [required] by the purpose'. No compensation is required.

2.3 Exceptions in Favor of Libraries

Libraries play a fundamental role with regard to teaching activities: they supply the material used for teaching purposes.

As we pointed out, the BC has never had a specific limitation in favor of libraries.[31] At the Stockholm Conference, it was expressly accepted that Art. 9.2 BC (the three-step-test) allowed the reproduction by libraries for preservation purposes (as enshrined in most domestic copyright laws). Current jurisprudence agrees that domestic limitations in favor of libraries, for preservation purposes but also for research and study purposes, are fully compatible with the BC.[32]

---

[29] The original Rome Act of 1928 referred to 'analyses or short textual quotations of published literary works for the purposes of criticism, polemical discussion or teaching'. No list of purposes was ever adopted (because such list could not hope to be exhaustive), but it is clear that quotations for 'scientific, critical, informatory or educational purposes' are within the scope of Art. 10(1) of the BC. See Ricketson (1987), *op.cit.supra*, §9.22 n.3, at pp. 492–493. See Ricketson/Ginsburg (2006), *op.cit.supra*, §13.41, p. 786. Similarly, the wording 'such as' in Art. 5(3)(d) EUCD confirms that criticism and review are not the only legitimate purposes of quotations; quotations may be made for other purposes, for instance teaching.

[30] The concept of *quotation* already implies some limitation as to extent, but a work could be quoted in its entirety if 'the specific purpose' requires it and provided that it was done 'in accordance with fair practice'.

[31] The fact that the oldest existing exception or limitation in a copyright statute failed to be included in the Berne Convention may be easily explained since – as we already pointed out – limitations and exceptions have not historically been a major concern for the Berne constituency.

[32] See Ricketson (1987), *op.cit.supra*, §9.11. See also, Ricketson/Ginsburg (2006), *op.cit.supra*, §13.45. See also C. Masouyé, *Guide to the Berne Convention for the Protection of Literary and Artistic Works (Paris Act, 1971)*, OMPI (1978), §9.10.

Instead, the EUCD does provide for two exceptions in favor of libraries under Art. 5.2(c) and Art. 5.3(n), both showing – as we will see – a blatant discrimination of digital libraries

> in respect of specific acts of reproduction made by publicly accessible libraries, educational establishments or museums, or by archives, which are not for direct or indirect economic or commercial advantage, (Art. 5.2(c))[33]

The exception contains no restrictions as to nature and extent of works or as to specific purposes of the use (be it teaching purposes, research or private study).[34] However, domestic library exceptions tend to refer to specific purposes such as research and private study, which – as we shall see – may end up generating loopholes as to other intended uses (specifically, teaching purposes).

The exception is not subject to fair compensation, although Member States may require it when implementing it; the only conditions being that the establishment is 'publicly accessible'[35] and that no economic or commercial advantage is pursued.[36]

Some domestic laws contain very detailed exceptions and limitations regarding the free reproduction and further use of works by libraries, archives and museums. However, the impact of these exceptions on digital libraries[37] is far from solved. It is generally accepted that this reproduction

---

33 The initial Commission Proposal only referred to 'establishments accessible to the public'. The Parliament (in its first reading) introduced both the condition that it be 'for archiving or conservation purposes' and the wording 'such as libraries and archives and other teaching, educational or cultural establishments'. The Council modified both issues: dropping the 'archiving and conservation purposes' in favor of a more flexible formulation (that would allow any acts of reproduction – also in digital means – as long as without economic or commercial advantage), and setting – instead – an exhaustive list of establishments benefiting from the exception (instead of all establishments accessible to the public, in general).

34 This may prove to be a sensible decision since, *de facto*, libraries are reluctant to distinguish among the specific use of the copy made.

35 What is '*publicly accessible*'? Is it equivalent to public libraries or to non-profit libraries? How publicly accessible is an online library? When is a virtual library publicly accessible: when no password is required? When no membership fee is paid?

36 It may be applicable here, by analogy, the criteria set by Recital 42 EUCD, in the sense that 'the organizational structure and the means of funding of the establishment concerned are not the decisive factors' to ascertain the 'non-commercial' purpose of the reproduction.

37 On this subject, see Laura Gasaway (2000), 'Values Conflict in the Digital Environment: Librarians Versus Copyright Holders', 24 *Colum.-Vla J.L. & ARTS* 115.

may be in any format (analog or digital), still digital libraries tend to be discriminated on several other grounds:

(i) Library exceptions tend to cover only the act of 'reproduction' (sometimes, analog or digital) provided that no economic gain is pursued (that is, Art. 5.2(c) EUCD), but nothing is said as to communication to the public.

In other words, the digital copy made upon request by a researcher or student can only be delivered to him by means of a printed copy or a USB or any other tangible digital device, but it can not be transmitted to him by e-mail?[38] Recital 40 EUCD is clear about it: 'such an exception or limitation should not cover uses made in the context of online delivery of protected works or other subject-matter'. According to Art. 5.4 EUCD, domestic laws may extend the exception to the right of distribution, but nothing is said as to communication to the public. This means that, *de facto*, electronic libraries are being discriminated (as compared to physical libraries) since they cannot offer their users/students the same services that the physical library does (at least, not without a license).

(ii) The same discrimination against digital libraries may be found in Art.5.3(n) EUCD when providing for an exception to the right of communication to the public (or making available) 'for the purpose of research or private study', which only applies to 'by dedicated terminals on the premises of establishments referred to in paragraph 2(c)'. Once again, we will have to wait for an interpretation as to whether the establishments in Art. 5.2(c) are only those with physical premises or while Art. 5.2(c) covers both physical and virtual libraries, Art. 5.3(n) only covers the former.

(iii) Library exceptions often refer to preservation, research and study purposes, but not always to teaching purposes.[39] This discrepancy is especially important for digital libraries because – as we mentioned –

[38] One might argue that despite not expressly exempted, libraries are allowed to distribute the tangible copy of the work done for research purposes; likewise, they should also be allowed to 'send' that copy to the researcher – as if concluding that any means of delivery of the copy were implicitly covered under the exception. Unfortunately, this seems to be what Recital 40 EUCD is preventing.

[39] See, for example Spain Art. 37(1): 'The owners of copyright may not object to reproductions of works where they are made without gainful intent by museums, libraries, record libraries, film libraries, newspaper libraries or archives which are in public ownership or form part of institutions of cultural or scientific character, and where the reproduction is effected solely for research purposes.'

they are the ones to provide the copies used for teaching purposes.[40] In other words, copies done by libraries for teaching purposes may end up falling in no man's land: neither exempted under the teaching exception nor under the library exception. As a result of this, licensing is required.

By failing to cover one step of the process, the whole system of teaching and library exceptions becomes useless: a work that may be reproduced for teaching purposes without authorization will still need a license to be obtained from the library.[41] The full integration of library and teaching exceptions, especially as far as online teaching, is paramount. They should leave no gaps in-between and exempt – in combination – all the acts of reproduction and delivery necessary to make the teaching use possible.

As we pointed out Art. 5.2(c) EUCD refers to 'educational establishments' and the parliamentary works of this exception focused precisely on the issue of eligibility[42] to avoid a possible gap between library exceptions and the subsequent teaching use.

Although most domestic laws tend to keep teaching purposes and library privileges separated, some hope exists. A good example is Art. 53a German Copyright Act: after a 2007 amendment, public libraries are allowed to make and deliver by any means (analog, fax and digital) copies upon request by professors and researchers (for teaching purposes and research, respectively), in exchange of an equitable compensation subject to collective management. Such an exception in favor of public libraries is perfectly aligned with Art. 5.3(a) EUCD (illustration for teaching and research) and proves how important it

---

40 No need to point out the inherent incoherence: why should a professor be allowed to obtain an exempted reproduction from the Library for research purposes (or for private use), but not for teaching purposes?

41 In the analog world, the transition between both uses (library / teaching) is smoother, but in the digital world the issue becomes very sensitive. A restrictive reading of current library exceptions would not allow the making of copies that can, instead, be lawfully used for teaching purposes.

42 The initial Commission Proposal only referred to 'establishments accessible to the public'. The Parliament (in its first reading) introduced both the condition that it be 'for archiving or conservation purposes' and the wording 'such as libraries and archives and other teaching, educational or cultural establishments'. The Council modified both issues: dropping the 'archiving and conservation purposes' in favor of a more flexible formulation (that would allow any acts of reproduction – also in digital means – as long as without economic or commercial advantage), and setting – instead – an exhaustive list of establishments benefiting from the exception (instead of all establishments accessible to the public, in general).

is to design a complete and coherent system of exceptions that takes due account of the public interests at stake. One can only hope that other laws will follow and bridge the existing gaps.

(iv) Finally, what do we do with the copies done for research, private study and preservation purposes? May these digital copies be stored and later re-used? For what purposes?[43] There is no doubt that storage and subsequent re-use makes the library more efficient. One may conclude that, as long as the subsequent re-use is itself exempted, there should be no need to 'make the reproduction' again.[44] As long as the database is not used for profit, as long as it is only used as a tool to provide the services the library is allowed to provide under the existing exceptions, it does not conflict with copyright.[45]

As a summary, digital libraries and teaching uses receive a better treatment under the BC and the EUCD than in domestic laws. Member States have ample discretion to provide for these exceptions in domestic laws, but the needs of digital libraries and digital teaching platforms remain insufficiently addressed.

---

43 For instance, can the copy done be later used for inter-library-loan purposes? Only a few library exceptions do cover both preservation and lending purposes (including inter-library loans); see, for example Hungary art. 40 or Greece art. 22: 'It shall be permissible, without the consent of the author and without payment, for a nonprofit-making library or archive to reproduce one additional copy from a copy of the work already in their permanent collection, for the purpose of retaining that additional copy or of transferring it to another nonprofit-making library or archive. The reproduction shall be permissible only if an additional copy cannot be obtained in the market promptly, and on reasonable terms.'

44 It is uncontested that Libraries are not allowed to digitize all the works in their collections and either post them on a webpage (even with restricted access) or have them for consultation in its premises. But, can they build e-reserves of works (either from their collections or received by inter-library loan), and keep them to be delivered upon request by a professor or student? The simple storage of copies of works in digital form does not *per se* cause a prejudice to the copyright owner, and as long as no commercial use is made of the works in storage (and are only used in cases clearly covered by some other exception: private use, research . . .), it simply helps the Library fulfill its duty and make a more efficient use of their resources. Notice that the Library is not making these copies available; it simply stores them to be later furnished on an individual basis to the library customers as covered under the library exception (the Library will function as a Digital Delivery Service although only for internal purposes and interlibrary loans).

45 However, a very thin line separates 'making available online' from keeping an internal-use database (that is, crossed by simply allowing customers to search it themselves).

3 LICENSING AS THE ONLY ALTERNATIVE?

As a result of the uneven and insufficient legal scenario, libraries and educational establishments must turn to licensing to cover most of their digital uses, to the extent that in some cases licenses are sought for specific uses that are already covered under the existing exceptions.

Licensing for digital library and educational uses involves practical difficulties as well as normative considerations.

3.1 Practical Difficulties

The difficulties in clearing copyright for digital library and educational uses[46] derive mostly from the legal uncertainty and from the ability to set any prices and conditions for any of the uses not formally covered under an exception: it brings extra-cautious educational establishments to seek unnecessary licenses and empowers copyright owners to unreasonably deny[47] licenses for online uses or simply to set unreasonable prices and conditions, thus damaging the freedom and quality of education. Additional difficulties exist in locating the owner[48] and obtaining timely responses, and collecting societies cannot always help because they may not have a mandate for digital exploitation in the works they manage. Furthermore, leaving educational and library uses to the exclusive management of private licensing leaves the door open to eventual abuse of right (of copyright) by means of disproportionate pricing or other unfair terms and conditions.

It is true that licensing systems are steadily developing and that technology will eventually allow the granting of individual licenses for every specific use of a work. It is true that if digital licensing was further evolved, exceptions could be less important for educators and libraries. One may also argue that no exceptions would be necessary if a solid licensing system was available, and that efforts should be devoted to building such system instead of to the 'old-fashioned' legal technique of exceptions and limitations.

---

[46] For a study on this topic, see Harvard University – Berkman Center (2006), 'The Digital Learning Challenge: Obstacles to Educational Uses of Copyrighted Material in the Digital Age', cyber.law.harvard.edu/media/files/copyrightand-education.html, accessed 1 August 2009; see also Crews, Kenneth D. and Ramos, Jacque (2004), 'Comparative Analysis of International Copyright: Law Applicable to University Scholarship', www.surf.nl/copyright, accessed 1 August 2009.

[47] Let us never forget that the exclusivity grants the copyright owner the power to authorize but also to prohibit.

[48] In many cases, aggravated by the growing problem of the so-called 'orphan works'.

In my view, these arguments miss a fundamental step: that exclusive rights granted to authors should not be unlimited and that education and culture deserve to act as a limitation to these exclusive rights, also in digital contexts; that the exclusive rights granted to authors cannot be all-encompassing just because technology allows so.[49] Technology and licensing capabilities should not be the only issues deciding how to draw the balance between public and private interests within the copyright law; the public policy rationale existing under each exception should not be forgotten. Copyright does not live in a vacuum and must be balanced against other fundamental rights. Licensing alone cannot be trusted to find the right balance when departing from an unbalanced ground. Only when a balanced system of exceptions/limitations that duly satisfy the protection of the fundamental rights of education and access to culture is established by law, will fair licensing evolve.

Prompted by similar concerns, public licenses (such as *Creative Commons*) of academic works have been gaining acceptance as an alternative means to ensure the development of e-learning and access to culture, and somehow counterbalance what is considered a 'too restrictive' copyright regime, by allowing authors to 'give back to society' what the law is granting them exclusively. Public (open) licensing is proving to be a flexible solution to promote e-learning and, in general, restore the public interest in the use of copyrighted works, but it will only take us so far. In addition to the perverse effects public licensing may have for some authors and works, and to the eventual (unexpected but likely) dangers of promoting the 'commons' by means of private legal instruments (licenses) based on exclusive rights (copyright),[50] by only focusing on 'open licensing practices' we may end up in a more complex 'licensed' world that remains as unbalanced as before. It is only within the copyright law that the balance can be restored (through the statutory exceptions). It would be wise to

---

[49] '(b)ilateral contract will be ubiquitous in cyberspace, but it is unlikely to displace completely state-backed property rights for two reasons. First . . . the 'safety net' of a property right may still be necessary to protect adequately investment by creators of digital content. Second, certain limits on the rights of intellectual property owners are best seen as immutable, i.e. outside the ability of contracting parties to waive or wary.' See Robert Merges (1997), 'The end of friction? Property Rights and Contract in the 'Newtonian' World of On-line Commerce', 12 Berkeley Technology Law Journal 115, at 136.

[50] Some voices have arisen pointing out that CC's legal strategy (based on property and licensing) will not only fail to create an alternative to copyright but may also lead to some unintended consequences (contrary to the project's worthy pursuit of promoting the free use of creative works). See Elkin-Koren, N. (2005). 'What contracts cannot do: The Limits of Private Ordering in Facilitating a Creative Commons', 74 *Fordham Law Review* 375.

take advantage of the 'thrust' of the open licensing movement to initiate some legal amendments in our copyright laws and instruments.

3.2 Normative Considerations

The normative considerations deal with DRM enforcement and licensing terms and, in general, with the underlying and unsolved question of the mandatory nature of the (some?) exceptions.

Library and educational exceptions have been loosing ground in favor of licensing schemes (often, non-negotiated) and DRMs enforcement. Within the EU, both the library and illustration for teaching exceptions are included in Art. 6.4 EUCD among the list of exceptions where, in the absence of voluntary measures taken by right holders, Member States are obliged to take appropriate measures to ensure that right holders make available the means of benefiting from that exception or limitation, as long as the beneficiary has legal access to the protected work or subject-matter concerned. Unfortunately, the effectiveness of these provisions remains to be seen – since most national laws simply choose to turn to courts as the mechanism to ensure the exception; a solution that is proving to be too slow and far too expensive for beneficiaries.

Furthermore, according to Art. 6.4(4) EUCD, this provision will not apply to works or other subject-matter contracted online: these works will remain subject to the agreed contractual terms (pricing included) and DRMs set by the copyright owner, also when used for purposes of teaching and library uses. As more and more works become available in digital formats and are contracted online, DRMs and contractual terms may drastically reduce the scope of works that can be freely – and I don't necessarily mean 'for free' – used for teaching purposes by virtue of Art. 6.4(4) EUCD. Such a restriction on the scope of works available for teaching purposes may be in detriment of two other fundamental rights: education and culture.

Not all digital exploitation acts should be subject to a license just because technology makes it possible. Public interest is part of the copyright laws. Rights granted to authors and exceptions are two sides of one same coin. Exceptions/limitations to copyright should not be considered a tolerated departure from the monopoly of the author, but rather as a necessary part of its design.[51]

[51] 'Indeed, the grant of exclusive exploitation rights under copyright law, including the limitations imposed on their exercise, is thought to reflect a balance carefully drawn by the legislator. . .'. See Guibault, Lucie (2000), 'Contracts and Copyright Exemptions', in P.B. Hugenholtz (ed), *Copyright and Electronic Commerce Legal Aspects of Electronic Copyright Management*, The Hague: Kluwer, at p. 125.

Closely related to the technology issue is the contractual one and whether contracts should be allowed to override exceptions and limitations statutorily granted. In fact, steps have already been taken precisely to prevent that some copyright exceptions be overridden by contract.[52] However, the issue of whether the exceptions to copyright are imperative or default rules that can be overridden (waived or limited) by contract[53] remains unsolved and will be decided *in casu* at a domestic level.

We can all agree that not all exceptions deserve the same treatment; that public interest must prevail in some instances but not in others. One may conclude that while educational uses should neither be subject to DRMs nor to licensing terms, library exceptions could be overridden by contracts.[54] Or that, at least, a distinction should be done between works acquired by libraries in tangible copies (which should be freely – not necessarily for free – used for teaching purposes) and works accessed by means of an electronic database (which would remain subject to licensing terms and DRMs – provided that teaching uses were always allowed).

4 ANY OTHER ALTERNATIVES?

The only alternative to voluntary licensing is to revisit the regime of exceptions and limitations and complete the job by either:

1. a flexible interpretation of the existing exceptions, or

Footnote 51 (*cont.*)

'L'economie actuelle de la propriété littéraire et artistique est un compromis visant à assurer un équilibre entre trois finalités sociales: une recompense accordée à l'auteur, la protection des investissements, la satisfaction des besoins des utilizateurs.' See Sirinelli, Pieree (1999), *Exceptions and Limitations to Copyright and Neighboring Rights*, WIPO Doc. WCT-WPPT/IMP/1, at p. 42: http://www.wipo.int/edocs/mdocs/copyright/en/sccr_9/sccr_9_7.pdf (accessed 1 August 2009).

[52] See the Directive 91/250/EEC on computer programs (Art. 5) and the Directive 96/9/EC on databases (Art. 6).

[53] See for instance, article 23bis of the Belgian Copyright Act of 1994 (last amended in 2005) stating the imperative nature of some exceptions. On that issue, see Guibault (2000), *op.cit.supra*, at p. 151 et seq.

[54] In similar terms, see Guibault (2000), *op.cit.supra*, at pp. 155–156: 'limitations based on universally recognized fundamental rights and freedoms such as . . . study, research, criticism, news reporting and parody undeniably constitute imperative rules of copyright law whose application cannot be waived by parties to a contract . . . (i)n contrast, limitations favoring schools, libraries, archives and museums should not be immune to contractual override.'

2. the introduction of a compulsory (statutory) licensing for educational digital uses

4.1 The Interpretation of the Existing Exceptions

It is true that both digital distance education and digital library services are new, growing and potentially lucrative markets. And that a flat application of the current educational exceptions (usually non-remunerated) to digital and online uses might result in the loss of an important economic market for some works. But this does not mean that educational and library exceptions should be banned from the digital world; they must be applied with extreme caution, and taking into account in each case what is the potential damage for the authors' and copyright owners' interests.

Within Europe, the introduction of any new exception is ruled out (at least, as long as the EUCD exhaustive list of exceptions remains in place). Yet, there is room for amendments: to the extent that domestic laws exceptions are far from the whole scope allowed under Art. 5 EUCD and Art. 10.2 BC (the BC and EU texts tend to be more generous than their national counterparts) domestic library and teaching exceptions could be 'enlarged' to make sure that digital and online uses for teaching and library purposes are covered.

In addition, the interpretation of the existing exceptions is paramount to ensure public interest in digital networked environments. This can be done by means of flexible reading of the three-step-test (Art. 9.2 BC, Art. 10 WCT) as proposed by some scholars[55] and already chosen by courts.[56] The three-step-test was drafted in the Stockholm Act to vest in domestic laws the ability to introduce (and maintain) exceptions to copyright; Accordingly, the test was designed as a restrictive tool to guide legislators, through a cumulative succession of steps. More recently (after Art. 10.2 WCT and Art. 5.5 EUCD) the test has found a new meaning as an interpretation rule to guide judges (and parties) in the application of

[55] See *Declaration: A Balanced Interpretation of the Three-Step-Test in Copyright Law*: http://www.ip.mpg.de/ww/en/pub/news/declaration_on_the_three_step_.cfm (accessed 1 August 2009).

[56] Domestic courts are already applying the three-step-test as a hermeneutic mechanism to 'close' the copyright system and help compensate the lack of flexibility within it (perhaps more acute in *droit d'auteur* than in *copyright* systems), sometimes resulting in an 'extensive' interpretation of the applicable exception. See, among others, Geiger, Christophe, 'From Berne to National Law, via the Copyright Directive: The Dangerous Mutations of the Three-Step-Test' (2007) *EIPR* 486, at 491 (fn. 43).

the statutory exceptions; for this purpose, the restrictive and cumulative criteria that guided the 'original' test may – when applied to interpret the statutory language of an exception – lead to unfair results (even at the expense of forsaking the normative justification of the exception). The three-step-test is destined to function now as an escape-valve of the copyright system and help judges find the solution within the copyright system instead of turning elsewhere, beyond copyright law, to find the reasonable grounds to adjudicate a specific case.

4.2 A Remunerated Compulsory (Statutory) License for Teaching Uses

Which brings us to compulsory (statutory) licensing, remunerated and subject to collective management, as probably the best solution for digital education and libraries.[57] Not only because voluntary licensing grants the author (and the publisher) absolute freedom to set any conditions and prices or even to directly prohibit the use of the work for teaching purposes, thus perverting the statutory exceptions and forfeiting the public interest behind them; but also because as more and more works are delivered in digital formats, subject to DRM and licensing terms and conditions, the scope of the library and teaching exceptions is consistently shrinking – thus diminishing the effectiveness of these exceptions and ultimately forsaking the public interest at stake.

The advantages of such a remunerated compulsory licensing scheme for digital teaching and library uses are many:

- It would ensure that all works (also those accessed by means of electronic databases) can be used for educational purposes, subject to fair terms and conditions; instead of teaching uses being subject to the will of authors and owners who are free to prohibit them (directly or by means of unfair terms and prices). In other words, the exercise of copyright will not jeopardize the fundamental rights to education and access to culture.

---

57 In fact, this is the solution adopted by the German Federal Supreme Court (*GPA v. TIB*, 25 February 1999). GPA (German Publisher's Association) sued the German State of Lower Saxony as responsible for the Hanover Technical Information Library which collected several publications in the area of civil engineering, chemistry, mathematics and physics, so that third parties could order photocopies of articles published in them (delivered by fax or mail). The court concluded that TIB only reproduced the articles requested by the user, thus providing a mere technical assistance rather than exploiting the work, and mandated an equitable compensation subject to collective management. See Roger Mann (2000), 'New Aspects of the Right of Reproduction and the Use of Archives in Germany,' *EIPR* 93.

- It would simplify the licensing process, to the benefit of all parties involved: libraries and educational establishments, on one side, as well as collective societies and authors, on the other.
- And, in general, it would ensure that more authors and copyright owners will be compensated for the teaching uses of their works, and that more works can be used for teaching and library purposes.

Both the BC and the EUCD allow for such a scheme for teaching purposes, consequently we only need to consider the parameters of the three-step-test to shape its boundaries. The result will resemble the following:

Lawfully disclosed works may be used for teaching purposes in any means and formats, including making them available online so that they can be accessed and downloaded by registered students, under the following conditions:

- works primarily intended for teaching are excluded (so that the normal exploitation is not affected);
- works accessed by means of an electronic database will remain subject to its own terms and conditions, as long as any teaching uses are allowed;
- the work is used only to the extent necessary for the teaching purpose;
- reasonable efforts (including DRMs) are undertaken to restrict access to registered students[58] and to prevent misuse or, at least, minimize downstream infringement;
- authors are duly credited (including the source),
- and receive fair compensation – which will take into account the nature of the teaching use (not all teaching uses should be compensated and compensated equally),[59] the nature of the educational establishment and/or program,[60] and the existence of technological protection measures implemented.
- All educational establishments (be it public or private, for-profit or non-profit) should benefit from the exception (provided the remaining conditions are met), albeit they may be subject to different compensation regimes.

---

[58] Passwords and other access control measures are critical to ensure that solely the students officially enrolled in the course will have access to the works.

[59] For instance, we may agree that the use of works for comment or criticism in the course of instruction does not need to be compensated (after all, it amounts to a quotation); and higher fees could apply for works that can be downloaded and retained by students, than for works that are only streamed to students.

[60] For instance, a private for-profit school should pay higher fees than a public school.

Such a limitation (compulsory statutory license) would not unreasonably prejudice the author's legitimate interests, because – as long as the specific use does not conflict with the normal exploitation of the work[61] – a strong public interest such as education and access to culture counterbalances the legitimate interests of the author, especially when served together with a fair compensation and the author's moral rights are duly preserved.

5 CONCLUSION

Education and access to culture deserve strong and clear limitations and exceptions that remain effective also in digital networked environments. The distinction between face-to-face and online education and library uses will soon be obsolete. The potential damage that digital reproduction of works may cause justifies special conditions and limitations for digital libraries and teaching purposes, but the public interest that justifies educational copyright exceptions is the same regardless of the means used to conduct that teaching.

Copyright must be enforced also in digital contexts, but it should not be at the expense of education and culture. Authors should not have a right to refuse permission (directly or indirectly – by means of setting unreasonable prices and conditions) for his or her work to be used for digital (and online) teaching purposes. Education and access to culture deserve to be directly enforced by law (under mandatory exceptions and limitations), DRM and voluntary licensing practices only in place once the teaching purposes are ensured.

In face-to-face educational contexts, the use of works is 'self-contained' – within the walls of a physical classroom or library – and does not have a major economic significance. In a digital world, this holds no longer true. Instead, there is no room for *de minimis* uses in a digital environment. The strengthening of the exclusive rights[62] required to ensure copyright subsistence in digital contexts, has shifted all the pressure to the boundaries of copyright: limitations and exceptions, rather than 'exceptional' become fundamental to copyright laws. Unfortunately, reinforcement of the authors' exclusive rights has not been balanced with an equal

---

[61] That is, text-books are excluded and digital databases must be subject to different terms and conditions as long as allowing for teaching uses.

[62] We have moved from definitions of exclusive rights based on public exploitation to definitions based on use. The concept of public, which used to be inherent to the concept of exploitation, is less important in current copyright law.

reinforcement of the applicable exceptions and limitations.[63] The job of transporting copyright into the digital world is only half-done. Digital libraries and online education are in the front line. As they were 300 years ago, when the Statute of Anne ensured that all published works could be used for educational purposes.

Unlike other exceptions, this is not a question of 'user's rights', but of public policy. It is not my 'right' as a teacher to use works of others, but my obligation, my duty towards society; and the copyright law should not be shy to state so: authors and owners should not have an exclusive right to decide what works are used for teaching. A balanced protection of educational purposes and access to culture within our copyright laws will only benefit the advance of creativity and, ultimately, benefit the authors.

International instruments have never adopted a strong policy in the field of exceptions and limitations: instead, they have proceeded on the assumption that countries will take due care of the public interest. But in the digital networked-world national solutions are no longer effective: borders blur, especially among communities sharing a same language, and domestic laws discrepancies and licensing complexities may end up stalling the development of online education. International instruments, such as the Berne Convention, are in a privileged position to envision some solution.

Libraries and educational establishments have always been the allies of the authors. Current copyright laws may not correctly address their needs. We should be ready to learn from history and revise our laws to strengthen the public interests and, thus, regain the public trust.

---

63 Art. 6.4 EUCD is a clear example of the legislator's caution (shyness?) to enforce exceptions and limitations in digital contexts.

17. Digital libraries: collective administration for online libraries – a rightsholders' dream or an outdated illusion?

Tarja Koskinen-Olsson*

1 INTRODUCTION

Starting in 2005 as a vision called the European Digital Library (EDL), Europeana[1] is now a reality. Since late 2008 it has functioned in pilot form as a common portal to digitised collections in various European libraries, archives and museums.

Permissions are needed for online exploitation of works protected by copyright and related rights by libraries. Such permissions can be given by rights holders themselves or by their representatives, such as collective management organisations (CMOs). The primary goal is to clear the necessary rights for online exploitation effectively. Whether it takes place by way of individual exercise or collective management is a subordinate issue. In the following, I explain the state-of-play by way of concrete initiatives and examples from various European countries. I leave it for the reader to judge whether the scenario is a dream or an illusion.

* Tarja Koskinen-Olsson is an international expert in intellectual property rights with management of copyright and related rights as special focus. She is a member of the High Level Expert Group of the European Commission on the European Digital Library Initiative. She was elected as Honorary President of IFRRO (the International Federation of Reproduction Rights Organisations) in 2001, having served as the Chair from 1993 to 1999. She worked as the CEO of KOPIOSTO, the Joint Finnish Collective Management Organization, from 1987 to 2003. Her career started with the Finnish Composers' International Copyright Society, TEOSTO.

[1] europeana – think culture at http://www.europeana.eu/portal/.

2 THE WAY TO THE EUROPEAN PORTAL

In April 2005, the Heads of State and Government of France, Germany, Hungary, Italy, Poland and Spain sent a letter to the President of the European Commission. They advocated for the creation of a European virtual library, to make Europe's cultural and scientific heritage accessible to all.

The European Digital Libraries Initiative soon became a flagship project of the Commission's overall plan to boost the digital economy, the so called i2010 Strategy.

The European Digital Library[2] is defined as a multilingual common access point to digital material in various collections in the Member States. Different types of material are at stake: books, films, music, photographs, manuscripts and archival objects. They need to be selected from very large volumes: there are for example 2.5 billion books and bound periodicals in European libraries, and millions of hours of film and video in audiovisual archives. Some of the materials are protected by copyright and related rights; some are in the public domain, and thus outside the focus of this paper.

In February 2006, a High Level Expert Group[3] on digital libraries was nominated to assist the Commission on how to best address the identified challenges at the European level. The first challenges related to copyright and related rights and in particular to rights clearance for online exploitation.

On 24 August 2006, the Commission issued a Recommendation[4] on the Digitisation and Online Accessibility of Cultural Material, and Digital Preservation. Council Conclusions[5] indicated full support from the Member States. The initiative also received strong support from the European Parliament.[6] A progress report was published in August 2008 in

---

[2] Communication from the Commission to the European Parliament, the Council, the European Economic and Social Committee and the Committee of Regions i2010: Digital Libraries Brussels 30.9.05 COM (2005) final.

[3] The High Level Expert Group was first nominated for 2007–2008; the term was then extended to cover 2009.

[4] European Commission Recommendation of 24 August 2006 on the digitisation and online accessibility of cultural material and digital preservation (2006/585/EC).

[5] Council Conclusions of 13 November 2006, OJ C297, 7.12.2006, p.1.

[6] Resolution on 'i2010, towards a European Digital Library' of 27 September 2007.

the form of a Communication[7] from the Commission, entitled 'Europe's cultural heritage at the click of the mouse'.

Finally the great day came and Europeana was launched on 20 November 2008. The portal showed the potential of a common access point to Europe's distributed cultural heritage. It became the victim of its own success as the service collapsed technically when 10 million people wanted to study some items in collections during its first hour of existence. The service has been up and running as a pilot version since late 2008.

The logo of the service states the essence: europeana - think culture. At the time of the launching, most collection items were works in the public domain. Now it is time for material protected by copyright and related rights.

3 TECHNOLOGY AND FINANCING RESOLVED ALONG THE WAY

Europeana has several ancestors. Progress on technical issues has been a prerequisite for the development of digital libraries in general and the improvement of the services of Europeana in particular.

A great number of EU funded projects have carried the plan forward. One of the earliest foundations was *T*he *E*uropean *L*ibrary (TEL) project during the years 1998–2002. The continuation project 'Tell Me More' incorporated participation of organisations from the new Member States of the European Union.

One important step towards the realisation of the initiative was the establishment of the European Digital Library (EDL) Foundation[8] in November 2007. The technical platform – the EDLnet – had as its aim to provide a cross-domain access to Europe's cultural heritage. The first target was two million books, films, photographs, manuscripts and other cultural works accessible through the portal by the end of the year 2008.

Financing of digitisation is a key issue. Over the last few years, several Member States have allocated considerable resources to digitisation and this has led to the digitisation of millions of new objects. One way of funding digitisation can be through sponsoring or public-private

---

[7] Communication from the Commission to the Council, the European Parliament, the European Economic and Social Committee and the Committee of the Regions, Europe's cultural heritage at the click of a mouse. Progress on the digitisation and online accessibility of cultural material and digital preservation across the EU, Brussels, 11.8.2008 COM (2008) 513 final.

[8] http://dev.europeana.eu/edlnet/edl_foundation.

partnerships. There are examples of public-private partnerships and private sponsoring, for example with technology firms, banks and telecom companies.

Large-scale digitisation projects necessitate effective technical facilities. Digitisation centres have been set up in different shapes and sizes. They have been linked up to a university, national library (as in Finland), archive, audiovisual archive, ministry or private company (as in Hungary).

4 KEY IPR ISSUES ADDRESSED BY THE HIGH LEVEL EXPERT GROUP

The High Level Expert Group (HLG) of the Commission established in its first meeting a Copyright Subgroup to deal with challenges posed by copyright and related rights, under the chairmanship of Professor Marco Ricolfi from the Turin Law School.[9]

At the outset, rightsholders and cultural institutions agreed on a set of high level principles that govern the work. They can be summarised as follows:

- For rights holders respect for copyright and related rights is the most important issue, and this includes rights clearance either individually or collectively.
- For cultural institutions it is important to have access with legal certainty. This includes large-scale digitisation and access to analogue material as well as access to already digitised material.

The solutions presented by the HLG are based on current European legal framework[10] and minimal or no changes in legislation are foreseen, depending on the legislation of a given Member State. In the following, I will deal only by way of summary with those recommendations that are directly linked to rights management. These issues relate to orphan works and out-of-print works. Issues relating to digital preservation and web-harvesting are described in the contribution written by Professor Ricolfi.[11]

[9] A separate article by Professor Ricolfi called 'Digital Libraries in the current legal and educational environment: a European perspective' highlights the work of the HLG in general; see Chapter 15 in this volume.

[10] Mainly the Directive 2001/29/EC of the European Parliament and the Council of 22 May 2001 on the harmonisation of certain aspects of copyright and related rights in the information society (Copyright Directive of 2001).

[11] See footnote 9.

4.1 Orphan Works

Clarification and transparency in the copyright status of a work is an essential element in the European Digital Library Initiative. Works are called orphan when rights holders cannot be identified or, if they are identified, they cannot be located in order to ask the necessary permissions. Among very old materials there may be many such works, and their digitisation and use would be inhibited without a feasible copyright solution.

In some countries there exists already a solution to make the use of orphan works possible.[12] These can be summarised as follows:

- *The Canadian regime for non-locatable copyright owners*: Pursuant to section 77 of the Canadian Copyright Act, the Copyright Board of Canada[13] may grant licenses authorising the use of published works, fixed performances, published sound recordings and fixed communication signals, if the copyright owner cannot be located.
- *Other regimes where a public body may issue the license*: There are specific provisions in the UK (s. 190 of the Copyright Act) and Fiji (s. 190 of the Act) on the Copyright Tribunal's powers; in Japan (s. 67 of the Act) concerning the role of the Agency for Cultural Affairs; and in South Korea (s. 47 of the Act) concerning the Minister of Culture.
- *The French model for audiovisual works*: The National Audiovisual Institute (INA) has concluded general and collective agreements with various categories of rightsholders through collective management organisations or trade unions.
- *Extended collective licenses*: the Nordic countries and Hungary apply a legislative technique called extended collective license (ECL) to certain mass use situations. Whereas an ECL is not tailored for orphan works, to a large extent it can eliminate the issue of unknown or non-locatable rights holders in the designated area. The license for represented rights holders is by law extended to cover all works of a given category, including orphan works.
- *US pending legislation on orphan works*: According to a draft bill, a user would be allowed to use an orphan work without authorisation, based on a concept of limited liability (limitation on remedies) whereby, once the threshold requirement of a reasonably diligent search to find a copyright owner is met, liability would be limited.

---

[12] Different solutions are described in detail in the Copyright Subgroup's Interim Report of 16 October 2006.

[13] http://www.cb-cda.gc.ca – Unlocatable copyright owners.

The HLG recommended that Member States analyse the feasibility of different solutions and make their own choice. Provided that Member States have different solutions to facilitate the use of orphan works, mutual recognition of solutions in other countries may be needed, to achieve a European-wide solution.

This is under the assumption that there exists a commonly accepted criterion on what constitutes a 'diligent search' that needs to be performed prior to the use of a work. To achieve such search criteria by way of voluntary cooperation, representatives of different creative sectors – text, music/sound, audiovisual and visual/photography – discussed the diligent search criteria under the auspices of the European Commission. In June 2008 the result was presented and endorsed. Due diligence guidelines constitute common understanding on what measures have to be taken before a work can be considered to be orphan. A Memorandum of Understanding[14] (MoU) to confirm the agreed solution has been signed by 27 organisations representing cultural institutions and rights holders.

The main principles for identifying and/or locating the right holder are:

- the search is done prior to the use of the work;
- the search is done title by title or work by work;
- the relevant resources would usually be those of the country of the work's origin.

The guidelines define an orphan work and describe the procedure that the search should follow. It further describes resources that are available for research, both common resources and specific resources for various categories of works.

The due diligence guidelines do not as such solve all the issues relating to the use of orphan works, but they are a necessary prerequisite in all options.

4.2 Out-of-Print Works

Perhaps the most important issue measured in volume concerns works that are out-of-print or out of commercial distribution, which is the correct term in the digital environment. These works are still protected by copyright, but it may be difficult to ask for permission to digitise and make such works available. Where to find the relevant rights holders and how to negotiate the license?

---

14 http://ec.europa.eu/information_society/activities/digital_libraries/doc/hleg/orphan/mou.pdf.

As a practical solution,[15] two Model Licenses for digitisation and availability of out-of-print works were negotiated among stakeholders. The first Model License concerns distribution in closed networks. After having successfully negotiated a Model License for out-of-print works in close network environment, negotiations continued to address online accessibility, and the second Model License covers online exploitation.

Naturally, implementation and adaptation of these Model Licenses to national circumstances are needed. Both Model Licenses show, however, that representatives of cultural institutions and rights holders can negotiate among themselves practicable solutions.

5 PRACTICAL IMPLEMENTATION OF THE RECOMMENDATIONS

The overriding aim is to facilitate access in a legal manner. This can take place by way of individual exercise or collective management, or combination thereof.

Rights clearance is a practical issue and rights holders and cultural institutions need to have mechanisms in place that facilitate and automate, to the extent possible, the transactions.

5.1 Rights Clearance Mechanisms and Databases

Rights clearance centres are logical access points to permissions. Almost all European countries have specialised collective management organisations for reprography. They are called Reproduction Rights Organisations (RROs) and they represent authors of text and images and publishers of different publications. They are members of IFRRO (the International Federation of Reproduction Rights Organisations).[16]

These RROs can be operative as access points for mass-scale rights clearances for text- and image-based works. In some cases they are directly mandated by rights holders to grant the necessary permissions to cultural institutions, in some cases RROs can facilitate contacts with rights holders. The examples in Section 6 highlight both cases.

Databases including information on out-of-print works and orphan works can greatly facilitate contacts between cultural institutions and authors and publishers. Like the European Digital Library, these databases will be

15 Report of the Copyright Subgroup, April 2007.

16 http://www.ifrro.org/show.aspx?pageid=members/rrodb&culture=.

decentralised, working together virtually. For that purpose, it is important that there exist certain common principles, which are accepted by the stakeholders. Such principles were agreed upon during the work of the HLG.[17]

5.2 ARROW: Accessible Registries of Rights Information and Orphan Works

A direct follow-up of the recommendations of the HLG is taking place in a project called ARROW[18] (Accessible Registries of Rights Information and Orphan Works), funded by the European Commission under its eContent*plus* Programme. The project involves a broad range of European national libraries, publishers and collective management organisations. The project was launched in November 2008 and will last for 30 months.

ARROW is a public-private partnership among 16 stakeholders in the book value net in 10 European countries. ARROW aims in particular to support the EC's i2010 Digital Library Initiative by finding ways to clarify the rights status of orphan and out-of-print works, so that they can be cleared for digitisation and inclusion in the Digital Library. The project also seeks to enhance the interoperability of rights information between rights holders, agents, libraries and users.

The envisaged solutions include, among others, the creation of a registry of orphan works and a network of rights clearance centres. ARROW is in all its aspects a test-base for the solutions proposed by the HLG.

6 CURRENT RIGHTS CLEARANCE INITIATIVES IN EUROPE

Rights clearance can take place either individually, for instance by the publisher, or collectively by a collective management organisation (CMO). Different types of works are customarily cleared by different mechanisms. We can differentiate the following three cases:

- works in copyright and in commerce;
- works in copyright, but out of commercial distribution, so called out-of-print works;
- orphan works.

[17] Key principles for orphan works and out-of-print works databases and rights clearance centres.

[18] http://www.arrow-net.eu.

The first group – works still in commerce – is of course of most crucial interest for authors and publishers. Europe has a vivid publishing industry and some 600,000 new titles are published yearly. Many interesting new initiatives and business models have been launched to offer online exploitation to these works.

In the work of the Commission much focus has been given to out-of-print works and orphan works. Negotiations concerning in copyright and in print works falls naturally for the stakeholders to carry on among parties. In the following, a panorama of different initiatives and examples[19] are explained to offer a window to the grand variety of possible solutions.

6.1 Private Initiative in Germany

In Germany, Libreka![20] is an example of new business models. It is a central full-text online book search platform allowing libraries to provide access to online works in different ways. There are more than 104,000 titles available. Libreka allows users to access the content either directly from the Libreka Platform or through bookshops.

In both cases, books can be browsed, read and searched in full text. The titles are indexable by search engines and can be integrated in many other book-websites, such as those from libraries. Libreka is running a pilot project with the Library of Hessen (HeBIS-Hessischen BiblioteksInformationsSystem)[21] in order to allow the library users to browse and search books in the Libreka platform.

6.2 Public-Private Initiative in France

In France, Gallica 2[22] is a business model that is based on a public-private partnership. Gallica 2 is the French brand of the European Digital Library. The French National Library is playing the role of information mediator and the portal provides information to the users about information sources; users are reoriented towards a commercial website from where the book can be accessed.

For instance, Numilog[23] is one of the companies attached to the service of the French National Library. It has electronic books of several publishers

---

19 The list is not exhaustive, rather exemplary by its nature.
20 http://www.libreka.de.
21 http://www.hebis.de.
22 http://gallica.bnf.fr.
23 http://www.numilog.com.

on its technical platform. Numilog digitises books, distributes them and ensures the safety of content through a digital rights management system.

6.3 Collective Agreements for Audiovisual Works in France

INA (the French National Audiovisual Institute) is considered to be the world's largest library for audiovisual programs produced by public television companies. Its operation is made possible through five agreements with different collective management organisations (SACEM, SACD, SCAM, SDRM and SESAM). They authorise INA to use works belonging to their repertoire, including dissemination on the internet.

However, the works of some rights holders may not be represented by a collective management organisation. Therefore the French intellectual property code (Article L122-9 and 211-2 for related rights) includes a provision dealing with the risks of blockage by allowing a judge to make various arrangements in view of the purpose of exploiting the work.[24]

6.4 Collective Agreement for Out-of-Print Works in the Netherlands

A major collective agreement on digitisation and accessibility was concluded in the Netherlands at the beginning of 2009. The organisations representing the libraries (FOBID) and the rightsholders (VOI©E) reached an agreement with the Committee dealing with digitisation of cultural heritage.

The essence of the agreement is that participating libraries receive permission, on certain conditions, from virtually all rights holders to digitise their collections and make them publicly available on their own premises for teaching or research purposes. The works concerned must be part of the Dutch cultural heritage and no longer commercially available. The libraries do not need to pay the rightsholders as long as the works are only made available on their own premises.

Separate consent is required, if the digitised works are made more widely available, for example, by means of remote access or via the internet. In this case, an agreed payment will be made to the Digitisation Committee. The library does not need to search for the rights holders, because this is done by the collective management organisations.[25] Individual rights holders can object to their works being digitised and made accessible, but in practice very few use this opportunity.

---

24 HLG – Copyright Subgroup Interim Report (16.10.2006), page 10.

25 For example LIRA and Pictorecht.

6.5 Collective Agreement and the Extended Collective License in Norway

The Norwegian Reproduction Rights Organisation, KOPINOR, signed an agreement[26] with the National Library of Norway regarding a pilot project for digital books on the internet. KOPINOR represents in the agreement the members of 21 member organisations.

Through the project, called 'Bookshelf' (Bokhylla.no), the library will make all Norwegian books from the 1790s, 1890s and 1990s available on the internet. All titles from the 1990s and some titles from the 1890s – together approximately 50,000 books – are under copyright. These books will not be made for print or download, but will be made available to Norwegian IP-addresses. The licensing agreement is supported by the extended collective license (ECL) in the Norwegian copyright law.

The Bookshelf project was launched in May 2009, with 10,000 titles under copyright. More books will be included in 2009–10, and the project will continue until the end of 2011.

6.6 Scientific Articles on the Net in Finland

The National Library of Finland and the Joint Copyright Organisation KOPIOSTO[27] had begun a pilot project called ELEKTRA as early as 1999 with the aim of safeguarding the availability of Finnish scientific articles on the net. The pilot was based on a voluntary licensing scheme and mandates from all participating rights holders. This agreement can now get the safety net of an ECL stipulation in the law, subject to the approval of the Ministry of Education and Culture.

Access to the material has been available to universities and higher education institutions, but is now offered also to companies interested in the service. For smaller countries and languages the availability of national material on the net is vital.

6.7 License to Use Orphan Works in Hungary

In Hungary,[28] new provisions concerning the use of orphan works entered into force on 1 April 2009.[29] Under the new Article 57/A of the Copyright

---

26 See the text of this at http://www.kopinor.no/layout/set/print/content/view/full/3833.

27 www.kopiosto.fi.

28 Information based on ALAI 2009 London Questionnaire – HUNGARY report.

29 ACT CXII of 2008 amending the 1999 Copyright Act.

Act, the stipulation covers any work in case of which the person who intends to use it 'has made all those measures to find the author which, in view of the nature of the work and manner of its use, are justified, and still has not succeeded to locate him' ('a diligent search').

The Hungarian Patent Office (HPO) has the right to grant a non-exclusive license for the use of such works. The license is valid for five years. The HPO also fixes the amount of remuneration, taking into account the nature and extent of the use.

The law contains provisions for the case where the rights holder appears and for the use of remuneration not claimed. After the five-year period, the HPO transfers the remuneration deposited at it to the collective management organisation which is authorised to manage the rights of the owners of copyright in respect of other uses of his work, and in the absence of such an organisation, to the National Cultural Fund.

The procedure is not applicable in cases where a collective management organisation has the right to authorise the use of orphan works or collect remuneration for them on the basis of obligatory or extended collective management.

6.8 Solution for Orphan Works in Germany

The German National Library,[30] the publishers association[31] and two collective management organisations (VG WORT for textual works[32] and VG BILD-KUNST for visual works[33]) have been working on a practical solution to clear the status and facilitate the use of orphan works.[34]

Before declaring a work as orphan and carrying out a diligent search for the rights holder, certain prerequisites must exist:

- the book is not in sale anymore (there are services to facilitate search);
- the book is still protected by copyright;
- a publisher does not exist or cannot be found to conclude an agreement.

If the library does not find the rights holder, the next in the row for identification is the collective management organisation. If there is no positive

30 Deutsche Nationalbibliotek at http://www.d-nb.de

31 Boersenverain des Deutschen Buchhandels.

32 http://www.vgwort.de.

33 http://www.bildkunst.de.

34 Memorandum of Understanding concerning orphan works, Report – Appendix on Case Studies.

response, the collective management organisation takes the responsibility to issue a license, with withdrawal provisions, should the rights holder appear. The library is exempted from financial claims.

7 CONCLUSIONS

To become viable, Europeana needs a good number of works protected by copyright added to the service. There are a large number of projects underway funded by the European Commission, such as the ARROW,[35] with the aim of facilitating online-exploitation of protected works. These projects are collaborative efforts by cultural institutions and rights holders and aim at practical results.

Apart from implementation of the HLG recommendation and test projects, real-life negotiations and deals are needed. In this, the willingness of stakeholders – cultural institutions and rights holders – will be tested on the marketplace. Current initiatives show a great variety of licensing options, both individual and collective.

Are there any lessons learnt from the above initiatives and examples? Are collective management organisations a rights holders' dream or an outdated illusion?

Most of the solutions are hybrid in their nature. They incorporate a multi-partner arrangement. Many of them include a collective management organisation in some role. It ranges from an active licensor to being a last resort. New variations come up with again new forms of partnerships. There is no one size fits all solution, but there are many viable options.

[35] See paragraph 5.2 above.

18. Towards a contextual copyright?

Ysolde Gendreau*

1 INTRODUCTION

To enquire whether the collective administration for online libraries is a right holder's dream or an outdated illusion is a most relevant question at the present point in time of the evolution of copyright law. From a Canadian perspective, which is probably representative of events elsewhere too, the growth of collective management that accompanies the expansion of mass uses of copyright protected works leads inevitably to the issue of its adaptation to the digital environment. While attention has mostly been focused on the digital diffusion of music, the print world has also been undergoing important changes that have not, however, attracted as much public consideration. It might thus prove to be refreshing and informative to examine the digital evolution of copyright through another industry – the publishing industry – in a specific environment – the educational world. The lessons to be drawn from this exercise should thus enrich our understanding of the contemporary copyright scene.

The present paper will attempt to answer the question that has been put to this panel on the basis of the Canadian experience. It must be understood, however, that two factual considerations may influence this analysis. The first one is that the Canadian Parliament has so far avoided legislating on Internet issues.[1] The last major amendments to the Copyright Act were made in 1997 as part of Phase II of the revision process of the Act.[2]

---

* Professor, Faculty of Law, Researcher, Centre de recherché en droit public, Université de Montréal; President, ALAI Canada. The author wishes to thank Messrs. Olivier Charbonneau, librarian at Concordia University, and François Senécal, LL.M. 2009 (Université de Montréal), for their help in the research that was necessary to prepare this text.

[1] A small exception would be an amendment to the retransmission regime that was designed to ensure that it did not apply to 'new media retransmitters'. See An Act to amend the Copyright Act, S.C. 2002, c. 26, s. 2

[2] An Act to amend the Copyright Act, S.C. 1997, c. 24, See D. Vaver (1997), 'The Copyright Amendments of 1997: An Overview', 12 I.P.J. 53; Y. Gendreau (1997),

Undertaken around the time of the WIPO treaties of 1996, the government chose to delay the implementation of these two agreements to a later date so as not to upset the balance that had been struck to achieve the Phase II process. Since then, two bills have been introduced in Parliament.[3] Both were highly criticised and never went beyond first reading because elections were called shortly after each tabling. Consequently, any Internet related issue must be resolved through the interpretation of the current statute. A second factor that acts as a background for the present analysis is the fact that the academic year 2002–2003 marked a turning point for Canadian university libraries: more than 50 per cent of journal subscriptions were in electronic form. This growing trend is, of course, at the heart of the present debate.

Library collections are not just made up of journals and electronic ones at that. Analogue documents remain important. However, it is quite obvious that one is moving towards a world where one wants everything to be accessible online. Such a goal requires the digitisation of current analogue holdings. Because it is a familiar issue, the digitisation of existing materials will be dealt with just before examining the issue of the acquisition of online materials as such. Both situations will provide the elements for some comments on the evolution that is taking place in libraries and which is affecting the development of copyright law.

2 DIGITISATION OF ANALOGUE MATERIALS

The constitution of a digital database of works that were originally in analogue format raises basic reproduction rights issues that need not be examined here. Instead, it is more to the point to highlight a recent development that is mentioned in the Canadian national report to this congress which deals more particularly with the digitisation of materials by a public library, that is the agreement between Bibliothèque et Archives nationales du Québec (BAnQ) and COPIBEC, a reproduction right collecting society. In order to appreciate the impact of this agreement, one must first

---

Footnote 2 (*cont.*)
'Nouveau visage pour la loi canadienne sur le droit d'auteur', 76 Can. Bar Rev. 384. Since Phase I in 1988, other amendments had been introduced to ensure compliance with new international obligations such as NAFTA and TRIPs.

[3] Bill C-60, An Act to amend the Copyright Act, House of Commons, First Session, 38th Parliament, 53–54 Elizabeth II, 2004–2005, First reading: 20 June 2005; Bill C-61, An Act to amend the Copyright Act, House of Commons, Second Session, 39th Parliament, 56–57 Elizabeth II, 2007–2008, First reading: 12 June 2008.

be aware of two factors whose combination provided the background for its negotiation.

The first element is the decision by the Supreme Court of Canada, in 2006, concerning the digital reproduction of newspapers. In *Robertson v. Thomson Corp.*,[4] the Court distinguished the reproduction of a newspaper as a whole from that of its individual articles. The newspaper as a whole, with its layout of articles, photographs, advertisements and overall visual presentation, corresponds to a collective work[5] and, as such, its reproduction is controlled by the newspaper publisher. When the reproduction of the articles within the newspaper individualises them and strips them from their presentation context, however, it is the copyright owners of the articles who must give permission for their reproduction in another medium. In those circumstances, the issue of the ownership must be resolved, that is whether the article is the work of an employee or of an independent contractor.

The other element that has helped BAnQ and COPIBEC to come to an agreement is the existence of a provision in the Copyright Act on orphan works. Introduced with Phase I of the revision process in 1988, s. 77 of the Act, on 'Owners who cannot be located', allows a person who wishes to use a work but is unable to find its copyright owner, to seek a licence from the Copyright Board. Upon examination of the request, the Board may issue a non-exclusive licence and set a royalty payment that is usually held in trust by a collecting society for five years. Resort to this procedure is fairly common.

It is in this context that the agreement between BAnQ and COPIBEC came into being in March 2008. Because it wants the public to have online access to old newspapers and magazines, the library has embarked on a digitisation project that inevitably runs into the problem of unlocatable copyright owners. The solution was an agreement with COPIBEC whereby it pays a certain amount to the collecting society, which is then held in trust for the authors of the articles that are digitised. Twice a year, BAnQ publishes in major daily newspapers a list of the works and of their authors who have thus become disseminated on its portal. The authors or their heirs are thereby invited to come forward and claim the royalties that COPIBEC holds for them.

At first glance, two remarks can be made concerning this agreement. First, one immediately notices that it is a contract that involves a collecting society. Such a structure helps to maintain the presence of authors in

---

4 (2006) 52 C.P.R. (4th) 417 (S.C.C.).

5 Copyright Act, R.S.C. 1985, c. C-42, s.2.

the overall process. At the same time, however, one cannot fail to observe that, while it seems to be inspired by the statutory regime for unlocatable copyright owners, the agreement clearly bypasses the mechanism that calls for a licence to be issued by the Copyright Board. It is true that the language of the provision seems more to have been designed for one-off situations rather than for mass uses such as the ones that the BAnQ project calls for. Yet, it would have been interesting to have it tested before the Board – and presumably before the courts – in order to see its potential for adaptability to different contexts. For the moment, the agreement must be given time to be implemented and appraised by its parties . . . and the copyright owners.[6]

3 ACQUISITION OF ONLINE MATERIALS

Like the BAnQ, university libraries are particularly aware of the challenges of online availability of materials. It has already been mentioned that over 50 per cent of journal subscriptions in Canadian university libraries are in electronic format since 2002–2003. Such acquisitions are made possible by an institution that was formally created in 2004 for this purpose in the wake of this phenomenon, the Canadian Research Knowledge Network.[7]

The Canadian Research Knowledge Network is a consortium of 72 Canadian universities and colleges. It organises subscriptions to over 2,200 journals that are thus made available to over 650,000 researchers and students. To achieve this, it has embarked on a licensing programme whereby it forms a consortium that acts as a negotiator with 'contracted publishers'. The list of these publishers keeps growing, of course, and includes for the moment various publishing associations such as the American Chemical Society, The Economic Intelligence Unit, Elsevier, Springer, Thomson Scientific, CSA-SAGE, the Royal Society of Chemistry, and so forth.

The core of the agreements that are thus negotiated is to be found in clause 2.1 of the model licence contract:

> The Publisher hereby grants to the Consortium and the Members the non-exclusive and non-transferable right to permit Authorized Users wherever located to access the Licensed Materials via a Secure Network and using the

---

[6] The agreement has already given rise to the publication of two lists of titles of publications (in June and in October 2008) in a major Montreal newspaper. The agreement has a one-year term and is automatically renewable for similar terms.

[7] http://www.researchknowledge.ca/.

> access methods specified in Schedule 3 for the purposes of research, teaching, private study, and administrative use associated with the normal practices and activities of the Consortium and the Members, subject to the terms and conditions of this Agreement. The Consortium agrees to pay the Fee and abide by the Payment Schedule as specified in Schedule 2.

Other clauses of this contract define usage rights which include interlibrary loans. The agreement basically covers the normal expected use of materials in a university context. Its overall tone seems to indicate that its original focus may have been 'traditional' scientific, technical, and medical (STM) publications.

Recently however, the Consortium has sought to expand the scope of the materials to which members may have access. Since February 2007, the Digital Content Infrastructure for the Human and Social Sciences Project has been the rallying ground for extending the negotiation of similar licences in the social sciences and humanities. It includes eight Canadian provinces and 67 participating universities. Because of the scientific fields to which it pertains, the project leads to the licensing of materials that can be identified beyond the traditional scholarly journals: musical scores, theatre in video, visual arts pictures and so on. The fact that it is a more recent initiative also means that it is willing to envisage the licensing of e-books. Standard text remains important, of course, but the openness towards other communication media is here a significant factor that may herald future developments.

4 MUSINGS ON THE PRECEDING PROCESSES

Because we are living in times where the majority of library collections are still in analogue format and new materials are increasingly made available in digital form, libraries that want to offer online access to their holdings must both convert their collections to digital form and be on the lookout for existing digital materials. If one remains optimistic, the phase of digital conversion (with its own inherent conservation problems) should come to an end in a medium-term future. The acquisition of materials in digital form, however, still has a future that is not fully mapped out. The processes that have been identified in the two preceding sections give us an indication of the difficulties that libraries and copyright owners face in adapting copyright law to an environment which is at the crossroads of technologies. While energies are mostly focused in that context on finding solutions with respect to literary works, it is immediately apparent that these solutions are destined to be extended to other types of works. Here are thus five observations on what the current library environment seems to reflect on the state of copyright law today and on where it may be heading.

4.1 Relevance of Statutory Scheme

Both the digitisation and the acquisition processes betray a distancing from the statutory scheme. The Copyright Act is not clearly irrelevant (!), but it is not necessarily the linchpin around which the transactions are structured. For instance, the provision on unlocatable copyright owners, which has up to now offered a tried and true mechanism for orphan work cases, has inspired the agreement between BAnQ and COPIBEC, but it has not been used by the parties to meet the challenge of mass requests.

The model licence agreement of the Canadian Research Knowledge Network is even further removed from the Copyright Act. Its business model no longer relies on the sale of copies of works to libraries that thereafter struggle to manage the exceptions for educational purposes and for private copying. Instead, its contract internalises the exception context and presumes that it can operate on that basis. Another indication of the distancing from the traditional copyright structure in this agreement is that the author's interests in the negotiation process are only represented by the publishers.

4.2 Presence / Absence of Authors

Authors take part in the digitisation project of the BAnQ in that a collecting society has negotiated the reproduction of their works on their behalf. In the overall activities of libraries, this kind of process is destined to have less importance because it is more concerned with past materials than with newly created works. It should therefore exert less influence on the future operations of copyright law. It is much more troubling to notice the absence of authors in the more forward-looking model licence agreement of the Canadian Research Knowledge Network. Instead of being represented by a collecting society, the authors' interests are, at best, represented by publishers whose standing is then usually derived from licences or assignment by the authors.

In this particular context, the role of the publishers remains ambiguous. They are receiving payment from the universities in exchange for the provision of the published materials. Yet, the licences or assignments which they have received from the authors in order to publish the materials are very often acquired for free. In some circumstances, authors pay the publishers in order to get published. However, nothing is ever mentioned about a trickle of royalties that would flow from the university payments through the publishers onto the authors. The structure of this scheme is sending a message about the nature of the right that is being negotiated: it is not a right for authors, but rather a right for the publishers disguised as an authors' right.

4.3 Educational Context

It is not surprising that such an agreement has been achieved in the world of education, a world where the scope of the copyright exceptions remains unclear (perhaps like that of many other exceptions, though). Both the educational and the private copying exceptions, in their various forms, can be invoked at some point in this environment. Arguments for royalties for authors, even in the form of compulsory licences, are therefore more difficult to make in this context than if one were in an entertainment context.

The university world is also a battleground for another copyright controversy: the issue of the copyright ownership of works produced by academics. For example, as a law that is rooted in the copyright tradition, the Canadian Copyright Act confers copyright ownership in works made by employees to the employers unless there is an agreement to the contrary.[8] Despite very clear wording, however, various courts and tribunals have in recent years awarded academics the copyright ownership of the works they have produced.[9] The situation is thus fairly murky and it is easy to surmise that universities, as a group, may be wary of paying for the acquisition of works which their employees, as a group, have created. With this argument in mind, it would be interesting to know the impact of the presence of non-scholarly productions in the negotiation of the payments that the universities make.

4.4 Governance

Information about the actual contents of such contracts is of course difficult to obtain. Contracts are private agreements between parties and it is in their nature not to be readily available to the public. However, the examples of the agreements undertaken by both BAnQ and the Canadian universities seem to betray a growing privatisation of copyright related transactions that occur at the edges of the statutory environment. If these

---

[8] Copyright Act, s. 13 (3).

[9] See *Dolmage v. Erskine*, (2003) 23 C.P.R. (4th) 495 (Ont.S.C.); *University of British Columbia Faculty Association v. University of British Columbia*, 2004 Carswell BC 1623 (B.C. Arbitration Bd); *Wiebe v. Saskatchewan Institute of Applied Science and Technology*, 2007 SKQB 60.

agreements are to herald a trend, the tendency is definitely a move away from the more open environment in which collective management operates in Canada. For instance, the oldest regulated scheme of collective management – for the public performance of musical works – calls for tariff proposals to be filed with the Copyright Board which holds a public hearing before certifying them and having them published in the *Canada Gazette*.[10] Not all collective management is as closely supervised as that one, but the model has been applied to a growing number of situations. The control that is exercised by the Board fulfils a competition purpose and its public nature as such can also be said to exert some influence on the general governance of collective administration.[11] A move away from a more open and public process is bound to have some serious impacts on the development of copyright law.

One category of persons who would necessarily have to deal with the consequences of this trend is the copyright academic community. With an increase in private transactions in areas of growing use of copyright works, the phenomena become more difficult to study. It becomes harder to have access to the information from which one can infer future developments in those precise areas of copyright implementation and, by the same token, it becomes more complicated to behold a global picture of the law.

Of greater concern, of course, is the impact on the general public. The cumulative effect of private agreements that operate on the fringes of the Act in an educational context for the online diffusion of works reinforces the image of the free culture of the Internet. The ultimate users of these works are placed in a situation where the material that is made available to them is provided without payment: when students receive the bill for their tuition fees, Internet access for materials is rarely an item. The transactions that have been identified clearly demonstrate however that the Internet world is *not* free; but the users of the Internet (and in particular the younger generations that download music and films liberally) are once again disconnected from the economic process and shielded from liability for any payment. In the name of education, whether scholarly or at large, these agreements help to promote a culture of free entitlement to

---

[10] Copyright Act, ss. 67 and ff.

[11] See in general M. Bouchard, 'Collective Management in Commonwealth Jurisdiction : Comparing Canada with Australia' in D. Gervais (ed.) (2006), *Collective Management of Copyright and Related Rights,* Alphen aan den Rijn: Kluwer Law International, p. 283; J. Robert, 'An Evaluation of Collective Copyright Management in Canada' in M. Boyer, M. Trebilcock and D. Vaver (eds) (2009), *Competition Policy and Intellectual Property*, Toronto: Irwin Law, p. 403.

anything which is made available on the Internet. When it is put together with the previously mentioned issue of the disappearance of authors from the process, such a consequence should raise serious concerns about the governance of copyright law. Nobody seems to be answerable to anyone. It is no wonder so many people are questioning the legitimacy of copyright law.

4.5 Drafting Language

When one starts to pay closer attention to the language that is used in the main clause of the model license to which the Canadian university libraries are agreeing, one is struck by the fact that the rights that are granted to the libraries are not expressed in the technical terms of copyright law ('reproduction', 'communication', 'making available'), but rather as a right of access to use works, coupled with various descriptions in everyday language of the uses that are contemplated. What drives the 'rights' that are granted here is the social context in which the works are used, not the technical transaction of copyright rights as envisaged in the statutes. Such an observation leads to a general reflection on the drafting of copyright laws.

Traditionally, copyright rights are mainly identified through set technical or business processes: reproduction, public performance, communication by telecommunication, distribution, rental and so on. Exceptions, however, are principally tied to social context: education, public debate, religious worship, criticism, news reporting, privacy and so on. These contexts offer broader framework than the technical descriptions of the rights. Indeed, several technical methods may be required for the use of a work in a single context. The diffusion of works over the Internet actually offers a good example of the combination of reproduction, performance, display and so on.

The discrepancy between technology-driven rights and context-based exceptions becomes apparent when copyright laws are updated: new rights are formulated according to the new technology while the contexts have remained unchanged. Are agreements, such as the one between the Canadian Research Knowledge Network and the university libraries, pointing towards an evolution where the rights are instead defined by context? Immediately, one sees the need to add at least one context that is not traditionally featured in the exceptions, that is the entertainment context. With such an approach, the topic of debate would openly be the value of copyright, rather than the technical definition of the use mechanisms, and the solution would depend on the context of the use. One can envisage a spectrum of uses that would go from, say, 'pure entertainment' to 'reporting political speech'. There is a difference between featuring a film in movie theatres and reporting a government study on climate change. Such a structure, just like today, offers many possibilities for overlaps. Why should reading Harry Potter for an English literature class be free when it requires full payment if it is read on the beach? Is access to a work through a library necessarily for educational purposes only?

To construe copyright in terms of contexts could become another way to understand what is truly at stake: remuneration for all participants in the delivery of creative materials instead of on-going battles between right holders and users over definitions of rights in light of sought-after exceptions. Another advantage would be the realisation that the decried expansion of copyright law does not really come from technological advances. Technological progress merely fleshes out existing contexts where one recognises that authors and distributors of works ought to receive remuneration. This constant fine-tuning of the law is different from the extension of the term of copyright, for instance. Technology has driven the start and the evolution of copyright law since the Statute of Anne. When this initial statute is re-evaluated 50 years from now, it will be interesting to see if the increasing speed of technological development, which already hurts the adaptation and relevance of ever lagging copyright statutes, will not have given rise to a context-based approach that could offer greater stability and legitimacy to copyright protection.

19. Google Book Search

Harjinder Obhi*

1 INTRODUCTION

The Google Book Search project is perhaps the archetypal paradigm of a modern digitization initiative. This paper, based on a presentation given by the author in June 2009 at the ALAI Congress, London, will examine and discuss two aspects of it: the Google Book Search project in Europe; and the proposed settlement agreement in the USA relating to the class action proceedings concerning Google Book Search. Readers should note that this paper was written in September 2009 and by the time it is published some of the information in it may have been superseded.

2 GOOGLE AND BOOKS: WHY?

It is worth starting off by asking a couple of questions:

- Why is Google interested in books?
- What is Google's philosophy about Book Search?

To answer these, it is necessary to go back in time to around the mid 1990s, before Google existed. At that time, Larry Page and Sergey Brin (who both later became co-founders of Google) were conducting PhD research in computer science at Stanford University, California. Part of their work was on research supported by the Stanford Digital Library Technologies Project. The dream was to devise technology that would enable people to search the content of books in a useful way: for instance, to enable a reader to identify a specific, interesting and relevant book out of a huge number of books. The technology that Larry Page and Sergey Brin created for books inspired them to produce an internet search engine, which they later named the 'Google' search engine. The word 'Google' is

* Dr Harjinder Obhi, Senior Legal Counsel, Google, London.

a play on the word 'googol', a numerical term that means 1 followed by 100 zeros. In 1998, the company Google Inc. was formed and of course, the Google web search engine was a spectacular success. Larry Page and Sergey Brin never lost sight of their dream for books and began work to create what later became known as Google Book Search. A milestone inspirational event occurred in 2004, when members of the Google Book Search team met people who managed the Bodleian Library, Oxford. An agreement was reached between the library and Google to scan and digitize public domain books held in the library's amazing collection. Google's interest in books is not new – it has always been there in the vision of the founders.

Google's corporate mission is to:

> Organize the world's information and make it universally accessible and useful.

Books are fundamental to this mission. Books contain a huge amount of cultural heritage and knowledge. They tend to indicate a certain level of learning and effort. They have gravitas. Nowadays, there is a huge amount of information and reading material available over the internet, but in my view, books are here to stay. Many people prefer to read actual books as opposed to the same content on an electronic display screen. It seems that there is an innate human need for physical books. My children spend much time on computers and on the internet. However, they both enjoy sitting down together to read books. They like to touch them, turn the pages and hold them. Parents like me, enjoy reading books with their children. People want to buy books – good bookshops are prospering and libraries continue to be busy.

3 GOOGLE'S OBJECTIVES FOR BOOK SEARCH

With that background in mind, what are Google's aims for Book Search? In essence, Google has two main goals for the project, as follows:

- make books as easy to find as webpages;
- improve users' ability to discover and access books in ways that respect copyright and create opportunities for authors and publishers.

These goals resonate with Google's corporate mission mentioned above. The second goal emphasizes that compliance with copyright law is fundamental and that authors and publishers should benefit – from for example, improved access to and visibility of their works.

4 GOOGLE BOOK SEARCH IN EUROPE

Google has two sources of books.

'Partners' are rights holders who enter into an agreement with Google. There are more than 20,000 such partners in approximately 100 countries. Although the majority are publishers, there is nothing to stop authors being partners. Many libraries around the world have entered into agreements with Google in relation to the digitization of certain books in their collections, including around half a dozen in Europe. In both the partner program and the library program, there are written terms and conditions in place with Google. Through these programs, Google digitizes books for free. Under the library agreements in Europe, Google is only authorized to digitize works that are out of copyright (although where the library is the rights holder it may have given permission to scan in-copyright works). Under the partner program, Google's activities, including digitization and display, are with the rights holder's authority. Many millions of books have been digitized.

It is submitted that Google Book Search, with the library and partner programs, represents a win-win situation for all stakeholders. It is good for Google: it progresses the company's fundamental mission, Book Search increases the comprehensiveness of Google's search offerings, it is likely to increase numbers of users of our products and therefore generate more advertising revenue. It is good for users and readers: they are able to search for books, search for words within books, access

Figure 19.1 One service, two sources of books

information about books from anywhere and download copies of out of copyright works. It is good for partners (mainly publishers and some authors): they are able to advertise their stock for free, breathe new life into their back lists (some publishers reported a 20 per cent increase in back-catalogue sales after joining the Google Book Search partner program), benefit from a new advertising revenue stream and importantly, attract targeted customers to their sites via links from the Google Book Search pages. Authors and rights holders who are not partners benefit from greater visibility of their work and more sales. Booksellers benefit because interested users can visit their online stores to buy the book via links from Google Book Search webpages. The project is good for libraries, for example, to increase their readership, preserve collections and further their charitable goals. The Bavarian State Library put it as follows:

> We are opening our library to the world and bringing the true purpose of libraries – the discovery of books and knowledge – a decisive step further into the digital era. This is an exciting effort to help readers around the world discover and access Germany's rich literary tradition online – whenever and wherever they want.

5 THE 'UNIVERSE' OF BOOKS AND ORPHAN WORKS

Consider for a moment the 'universe' of books.

This is in essence what a huge library, such as a deposit library, stores in its vaults and on its shelves. There are estimates (see references in the notes to Figure 19.2, figures relate to North American library collections) that around ~20 per cent of all books are public domain, meaning that their copyright term has expired (left hand side of Figure 19.2). A separate ~5 per cent of all books are in print, meaning that they are in copyright and available for purchase (right hand side of Figure 19.2). The remaining ~75 per cent of all books are in what some people refer to as the 'twilight zone' (middle part of Figure 19.2). These are books that are in copyright but out of print. They include 'orphan works', which are books for which the copyright owner cannot be found.

It is worth spending some time thinking about orphan works. No one really knows how many orphan works there are. How do they come about and why do they raise a challenge? Let us take an example. One may consider that books older than a certain year are probably out of copyright. For argument's sake, let that year be 1870, which is simply an estimate of the copyright term of the life of the author plus 70 years. Then, let us think

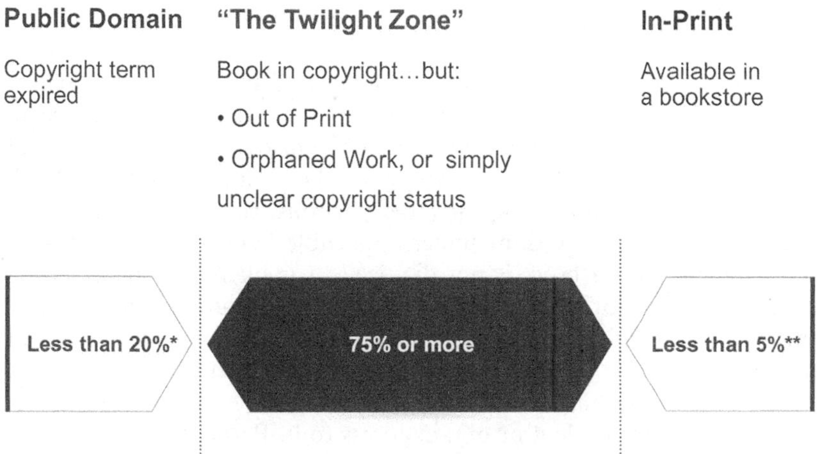

Notes:

* OCLC analysis of the Google Books Library Project http://www.dlib.org/dlib/september05/lavoie/09lavoie.html

** O'Reilly Rader: http://rader.oreilly.com/archives/2005/11/oops_only_4_of_titles_are_bein.html

Figure 19.2 A typical library collection

about more recent books. We certainly know who owns copyright for in-print books, but information becomes less clear for older books. Why? There are many reasons. For example, copyright agreements between publisher and author may expire, rights may revert from publisher to original author (and remember these agreements may contain complex terms, geographical restraints, time period limitations), publishers may go out of business, the copyright holder may die, heirs and successors in title may not know about their rights, other law (for example succession, insolvency) may apply and intervene in the chain of ownership, there may be other changes in the law that need to be considered, and so on. The net effect is that identifying and contacting the copyright holder of an older book (especially a less popular one) that is more than about half a century old may be very difficult. Commercially, potential rights holders of older books lack incentives to clarify old contract positions or face other transaction costs in order to 'clear title' to these neglected works. Thus, both the truly orphaned works (those for which no owner could ever be found) and the merely neglected works (those for which no owner is found on account of transaction costs) alike remain locked up and inaccessible to readers. Solutions such as the settlement, which both creates financial incentives for rights holders to come forward and funds a registry charged with finding absent rights holders, can greatly reduce the scope of this problem.

Orphan works represent a real challenge and not just in the field of books. If a person in Europe wants to use an extract, scan or digitize an orphan work, then by definition, the copyright owner cannot be found to obtain permission. If that person goes ahead and digitizes the book and displays the whole thing or large portions, then (subject to available defences and exclusions under applicable law) they are at risk of infringement. If the book is not digitized, it is likely to remain sitting on a dusty shelf or in the vaults of a library. Should we characterize this as a failure of the copyright system? Indeed, for orphan works that are not digitized, the copyright holder gets no benefit and the general public receives nothing useful either – they cannot easily find out about the book, search inside it or obtain access to it. Perhaps only a handful of researchers may be able to find and read it, for instance, in a private library collection.

One of the themes of this conference is the eighteenth century Statute of Anne and whether there are things in it that may guide us today. It is interesting to speculate whether there would be any challenge for orphan work books at all if the copyright term was now as it was then – that is, up to 28 years. However, this is a rather academic debate, because under international treaties (Agreement on Trade-Related Aspects of Intellectual Property Rights (TRIPS) Art. 12) we are committed to a term of at least 50 years. Nevertheless, avoiding orphan works is another reason why setting the term of copyright protection at an appropriate time period is a crucial policy consideration – not just for books, but for all types of work.

6 THE PROPOSED GOOGLE BOOK SEARCH SETTLEMENT AGREEMENT IN THE USA

There are important preliminary remarks to make before embarking on a description of the Google Book Search settlement proposed in the USA. There may be authors and publishers in the audience and they are potential class members in relation to the US litigation proceedings. I am neither addressing them in their capacity as potential class members nor advising them about the settlement. Authors and publishers have other sources of information and advice, including their respective class counsel and the settlement administrator. Contact details are available from the settlement administration websites available to the public, including the homepage for Google Book Search.

7 INTRODUCTION TO THE PROPOSAL

The agreement would settle the class action copyright infringement litigation in the USA which was commenced by authors and publishers including The Authors Guild and the Association of American Publishers. The agreement is between Google and a class, essentially, holders of US copyright interests (owner, exclusive licensee) in books and certain other works published on or before 5 January 2009. The class includes the author and publisher sub-classes. The agreement does not cover certain categories of work, such as newspapers, magazines, journals and sheet music.

It is a groundbreaking agreement that:

- opens access to millions of books in the USA;
- creates entirely new avenues for authors and publishers to sell their books;
- provides new opportunities for libraries, academics and researchers.

The agreement would enable Google to do much more than it could have done either alone, or after a court ruling on the merits. It pertains only to uses of books within the USA. Google is authorized to scan, index and make non-display uses (for example display of bibliographic information) for all books covered under the settlement. An extensive effort was made to notify potential class members of the class action settlement proposal. Notices were widely distributed, including electronically and via paper media.

8 DISPLAY AND ACCESS

It is important to understand that rights holders have choice as to their participation. They may:

- direct Google not to scan particular books;
- select desired access models (see further below);
- choose to opt out completely (the deadline for that is in September 2009).

On the second bullet point, the agreement defines a set of economic models for providing user access to the content of books. These (discussed further below) create a new opportunity for authors and publishers to sell access to their books. In addition, rights holders will receive a cash payment from Google of at least US$60 per book.

In the agreement, books are divided into two groups: those that are determined by Google (through various searches) to be 'commercially available', and those that are determined to be not commercially available. It is important to note that the rights holder (that is, a member of the class who has not opted out) is able to change Google's initial determination. Where a book is commercially available it is by default classified as 'No Display' and where it is not commercially available it is classified as 'Display'. The consequence of this is that for Display books certain text within a book may be shown to the public in accordance with the terms of the agreement, for example, previews and access uses. In contrast, text may not be shown for No Display books although the display of bibliographic information and other limited uses would be allowed. Again, the rights holder is able to override whether Display and access uses are allowed or not. Indeed, rightsholders have the right to completely remove their books from the project if they so wish.

9 THE BOOK RIGHTS REGISTRY

A new non-profit organization called the Book Rights Registry is created through the agreement. It would be entitled to act on behalf of authors and publishers and jointly managed by them. Its main purpose is to record rights holders' interests and distribute revenue to them. Google would contribute US$34.5 million towards the establishment of the Book Rights Registry, the notice procedure and other administrative costs. However, the Book Rights Registry's management is independent of Google and Google has no control over it. It is anticipated that a major benefit of the Book Rights Registry would be to encourage more and more rights holders to step forward to register their interests, including owners of copyright in out-of-print books, because they would be incentivized by the potential benefits, for example, through the access models. It is hoped that this will significantly reduce the number of orphan works.

The Book Rights Registry enables rights holders to work with Google. It provides a way for rights holders to request inclusion or removal of their works from the project and define how they want their rights to be handled. The Book Rights Registry would collect and pay out revenue from use of rights holders' works. It would enable competition and efficient licensing because it would locate rights holders and maintain an accurate database of contact information, making it cheaper and easier for people to make licensing arrangements. The Book Rights Registry will represent the interests of the rights holders, both in connection with the settlement and, to the extent authorized by rights holders, in other commercial arrangements (for example licensing deals). This may include deals with companies other than Google, subject to the express approval of the rights holders of the books involved in such other commercial arrangements.

It is important to understand that the agreement is non-exclusive in nature.

10 COMMERCIAL AND OTHER BENEFITS

Subject to the rights holder's ability under the agreement to exercise choice, Google would be able to make certain commercial uses of Display books in the USA. Google will channel 63 per cent of revenue to the Books Rights Registry who would be responsible for distributing the money to the relevant rights holders. The commercial uses include online consumer access to individual books, institutional subscriptions and revenue from advertisements displayed on webpages that show books. For the consumer access model, the user is able to buy online access in the USA to a single work. The default pricing is set by Google using an algorithmic pricing model to maximize revenue for each individual work, although the rights holder is able to set the price if desired. The institutional subscription allows access to the database to be purchased by higher education institutions, government bodies and corporations. There will be provision for public access in public libraries and non-profit higher education establishments: Google would provide a limited public access service for a terminal in such library buildings free of charge, while printing fees would be payable.

Other revenue models are possible in the future, such as print on demand, custom publishing, consumer subscription, .pdf downloads and so on, but each would require authorization from the Books Rights Registry or the rightsholder.

Further benefits include the provisions that allow Google to ensure that display and access uses are suitable for users with print disabilities and the visually impaired. This is a bold step forward to make the user experience for such people substantially similar to that for users who do not have those difficulties. Not surprisingly, the settlement has been met with a great deal of enthusiasm from organizations that represent the blind and visually impaired. Another benefit is the 'research corpus', which is the collection of books digitized by Google from libraries, hosted in the USA. Qualified users, effectively researchers, may request permission to use the research corpus for certain types of research, for example, linguistics research, translation research and computational analysis.

11 THE FUTURE

The agreement is subject to the court's approval and there will be a hearing at which the court will consider whether the proposal is fair, adequate and reasonable. At the time of writing, the court had decided that the date for this will be rescheduled to a date after 7 October 2009.

While the proposed settlement agreement is necessarily US focussed, Google is seeking ways to bring similar benefits to users in Europe. Of course, under the partner program in Europe (described above) there is the potential for partners to authorize specific commercial uses in countries where they hold relevant rights and thereby obtain financial benefit. However, when one considers the 'universe' of books (see above), it seems unlikely that commercial arrangements like that would be enough to bring the full set of in-copyright out-of-print books to the user, as it is hoped that the proposed US settlement agreement should. Despite EU harmonizing legislation, the territorial nature of copyright represents a significant challenge as do orphan works. Google supports the European digital libraries initiative and work being done in that field in the EU. Google's ears are open to hear ideas for book search initiatives in Europe.

20. Problem or solution? Mass digitisation of library stocks and the Google Book Settlement

Christian Sprang*

1 INTRODUCTION

Opening up complete library stocks for online uses is one of the greatest challenges presented to the book industry by the nascent twenty-first century – not only from a technical viewpoint, but from a legal viewpoint as well. There is hardly a better time for the ALAI to deal with this issue than a few months before the decision of the District Court in New York on a final approval of the Google Book Settlement.

In this contribution, I would like to investigate the question of whether it is recommendable, from the viewpoint of Copyright Law, to expand the concept of mass digitisation and online inclusion of books developed by the parties to the Google Book Settlement, which is currently limited to the United States, to the rest of the world. In this discussion, I will be addressing the following aspects:

- Does it make sense, when digitising books protected by copyright, to distinguish according to whether the books are commercially available or not?
- Should the author of an out-of-print book be entitled to copyright as an exclusive right (opt-in solution), or is it sufficient if the owner of the copyright can prevent the digitisation of the out-of-print book (opt-out solution)?
- Is the solution for the online embedment of 'orphan books' offered by Google appropriate from an objective standpoint?

* Dr Christian Sprang, Justiziar/Senior Legal Counsel, Börsenverein des Deutschen Buchhandels.

- Is the planned Book Rights Registry helpful or dangerous, from the viewpoint of copyright owners, for comprehensive licensing of online uses concerning books protected under copyright?

The answers I will be providing to these questions are not the official opinion of Börsenverein as the Association of German Publishers and Booksellers, but are my personal opinions.

2 DOES IT MAKE SENSE, WHEN DIGITISING BOOKS PROTECTED BY COPYRIGHT, TO DISTINGUISH ACCORDING TO WHETHER THE BOOKS ARE COMMERCIALLY AVAILABLE OR NOT?

I would like to give a somewhat differentiated answer to this question. First of all, I do not believe that it makes sense today to distinguish between in-print and out-of-print books. Today, books are generally produced from digital print files. Even the oldest works can be made re-printable in a comparatively easy and straightforward manner by digitising a copy. Modern production techniques such as print-to-order have become so widespread and sophisticated that books no longer have to be physically maintained on stock in print editions to ensure ubiquitous availability. Rather, today's merchandise management software makes it possible to satisfy the demand for books at any moment. If demand rises rapidly, a book can be printed in a large print run in several printing facilities at the same time if necessary. Where the need is only temporary, book production will not start up until booksellers receive customer orders, without meaning, however, that the delivered final product will be of inferior quality. Similarly, in future, publishing companies will increasingly offer books in electronic form only, and it could be left up to the customer or booksellers to decide whether and how they would like them to be printed out.

We will thus have to say farewell – and not without regret – over the next few years to criteria such as 'in-print/out-of-print' or 'print run' – criteria which have defined Publishing Law since the Statute of Anne. They will be replaced by the general criterion, which is difficult to pin down, of whether a publisher is still making use in a reasonable manner of the rights an author has entrusted to him, or not. The availability of a book in a tangible form will only be one of several supporting arguments.

The Google Book Settlement quite wisely does not differentiate between 'in-print' or 'out-of-print', but distinguishes only according to 'commercially available' or 'not commercially available'. The way in which this distinction is executed casts serious doubts, however, on whether it is actually suitable for justifying the differing legal consequences arising from it. As you know, a book Google classifies as being 'not commercially available' may be used comprehensively online under the Settlement without the permission of the rights owner. By contrast, the use of books allocated to the category of 'commercially available' requires the purchase of an individual licence through Google.

The database currently available under the scope of the Settlement has approximately 80 million entries of book titles. Random checks have shown that the basis of the data is corrupt to the core. For instance, three-quarters of the books in the 'Verzeichnis lieferbarer Bücher' – that is, the German counterpart to the Books in Print Database – are listed as being 'not commercially available'. There is justified reason to doubt that it will ever be possible to improve the Settlement database so substantially that a reliability quota of significantly more than 90 per cent will be reached.

This means, de facto, that even a rights owner who actively manages a book and keeps it available cannot be sure that no unwanted and unauthorised competition through Google will be created in a core area of his exploitation activities. In order to be certain to rule this out, he must register his book in the Book Rights Registry and constantly check whether Google is complying with its contractual obligations. The Settlement thus ultimately imposes a registration obligation on the rights owner with respect to the activities of a private company – Google – which is unparalleled in most countries even in relation to the government and has been eliminated from international copyright treaties for good reasons. I do not believe that this is in the least desirable.

3 SHOULD THE AUTHOR OF AN OUT-OF-PRINT BOOK BE ENTITLED TO COPYRIGHT AS AN EXCLUSIVE RIGHT (OPT-IN SOLUTION), OR IS IT SUFFICIENT IF THE OWNER OF THE COPYRIGHT CAN PREVENT THE DIGITISATION OF THE OUT-OF-PRINT BOOK (OPT-OUT SOLUTION)?

As we have just heard, the classification of a book under the Google Settlement as being 'not commercially available' is a de facto removal of the exclusivity right of the author and transforms this right into the mere right to opt out. This is a pragmatic way of making it possible for Google to put millions of books online. In general terms, the idea behind this is that the public interest in online access overrides the interest of the author of no longer actively commercially available books in the unimpaired continued existence of his copyright in his works.

It appears to me that the origin of this concept is more likely to be found in the world of Anglo-American copyrights than in the environment of the Continental European droit d'auteur, for it ignores that, in many cases, the non-availability of a work is a conscious decision by the author and the publisher based on, and an expression of, the negative publication right of the person entitled to the work [Werkberechtigter]. A midwife who was a proponent of bottle feeding in the 1970s will probably be very concerned to ensure that certain books she published at that time should remain out of print, and will not want them to be searchable in full text on the Internet. This not only applies to those areas for which the saying goes 'Die wissenschaftliche Erkenntnis von heute ist der Wahnsinn von morgen.' ('The academic findings of today are the madness of tomorrow'). A look at the history of literature, music and art shows that this applies to artistic and intellectual works in general. It is no coincidence that most copyright laws in continental Europe expressly respect the expression of the changing personality of an artist by granting him the right to recall his work due to a change in his artistic convictions.

The assumption that the disappearance of a book from the scope of commercial availability simultaneously indicates the dying interest of the person entitled to the work appears quite reckless to me. On the contrary: when weighing the opposing interests, I would give the interest of the creator of the work in an unmitigated continuation of his exclusivity right for the work precedence over the interest of the general public in having access to out-of-print books. In stating this, I am not unaware of the phenomenal potential contained in the Google digitisation project, particularly for historians. However, the digitisation of works should always require the express consent of an author, at least during his lifetime.

4 IS THE SOLUTION FOR THE ONLINE EMBEDMENT OF 'ORPHAN BOOKS' OFFERED BY GOOGLE APPROPRIATE FROM AN OBJECTIVE STANDPOINT?

The problem of so-called 'orphan books', whose rights owners cannot be located, is solved in a pragmatic manner by the Google Settlement. Each rights owner who has not registered with the Book Rights Registry must anticipate that his books will be digitised by Google and exploited on the Internet because they are deemed to be 'not commercially available'.

I will refrain from addressing the criticism that in this way Google is acquiring an exploitation monopoly for millions of books protected under copyright, which is highly questionable under Antitrust Law. Similarly, I won't discuss the question of whether the establishment of a central Book Rights Registry for all global rights owners is meaningful, until later on. What primarily interests me at this point is the provision in the Settlement for a waiver of a 'reasonable diligent search' in order to establish the existence of a person entitled to the work embodied in a book. I do not consider this waiver to be justified from an objective standpoint. For certain, the human resources and thus the financial input required for a search which is not limited to merely comparing information on a work with the existing databases, will exceed the commercial interest in access to the work for the great majority of out-of-print works. But this fact cannot justify a reliance on extremely inaccurate databases of metadata and the failure to make other efforts to identify the rights owner. The fact that such activities are supposed to be legalised de facto in the United States would appear to have less to do with Copyright Law considerations than with the use of the opportunities offered by the legal institution of class actions.

5 IS THE PLANNED BOOK RIGHTS REGISTRY HELPFUL OR DANGEROUS, FROM THE VIEWPOINT OF COPYRIGHT OWNERS, FOR COMPREHENSIVE LICENSING OF ONLINE USES CONCERNING BOOKS PROTECTED UNDER COPYRIGHT?

The implementation of the Google Settlement will hinge upon the instrument of the Book Rights Registry. This facility, which is supposed to be jointly set up and operated by American authors' and publishers' associations, will be granting licences to Google and interested third parties and is supposed to monitor usage as it takes place. Due to the specific design of the Settlement, the Registry administers the rights of authors and publishers from all over the world like a reprographic rights organisation. This also applies expressly for rights owners who do not have their works registered there, be this because they had not learned of the existence of the Registry, or because they were overwhelmed by the registration requirements. Criticism of the setup of the Book Rights Registry is growing louder because the current approach to its management indicates a virtually closed shop for the representation of American authors and publishers. All eight board members are supposed to be Americans – even though less than half of the books to be digitised by Google originate from American authors and publishers.

The setup of the Book Rights Registry is reminiscent of an international reprographic rights organisation for the provision of online rights. One difference in comparison to other reprographic rights organisations is that it does not acquire its powers through the execution of individual contracts with authors and publishers, but through the Settlement in combination with registration in a database.

This type of collective/individual licensing of mass-use processes under Copyright Law does exude a certain charm. One can only hope that it will prove to be an important impetus with respect to the needs of the users of works – such as Google – to trigger changes in the existing reciprocity system of reprographic rights organisations. It has been my experience, however, that the establishment of a single, centralised reprographic rights organisation in a particular location clearly puts authors and publishers in other countries at a serious disadvantage in terms of access. After half a year of intensive information and communication in all conceivable media, I am convinced, on the basis of many conversations, that less than 10 per cent of all German publishers, and less than 3 per cent of all German authors, have even an approximate idea of what the Book Rights Registry is and what it does.

6 CONCLUSION

For this reason, I do not believe that the selected centralised licensing approach helps rights owners. What we need for licensing such a gigantic digitisation project like the Google project is certainly the swift creation of a large database with accurate information on works and their rights owners. However, it appears better to me for this to be executed on a national level on the basis of uniform open standards, because this would be more understandable and controllable for authors than the central licensing system of the Google Book Settlement.

21. Online exploitation and licensing: General Reporter's summary and proposals for discussion

J.A.L. Sterling*

1 INTRODUCTION

In today's fascinating survey of the problems involved in the context of the internet and digital libraries, education and related questions of administration and licensing, and the use of orphan material,[1] we have been made aware of gaps in national, regional and international copyright law. One of the reasons for the problems is that we are using the copyright law of the Gutenberg era of hard copies and territorial rights to deal with the challenges of borderless communication in the electronic environment.

We have heard of a number of solutions or proposed solutions in the European Community, US and Canada. These are specifically related to the areas concerned. In the world of global communication, however, I suggest that we need to seek global solutions which are not subject to territorial restrictions.

2 THE BLACK HOLE IN THE COPYRIGHT CONSTELLATION

There is in this area what may be called the black hole in the copyright constellation. Rights of reproduction and communication to the public as well as distribution of copies are in general assigned and exploited on a territorial basis, according to traditional practices of the publishing industry,

* Professorial Fellow, Queen Mary Intellectual Property Institute, Centre for Commercial Law Studies, Queen Mary, University of London. j.a.l.sterling@qmul.ac.uk. A French and Spanish translation of this chapter can be found on the website of the British Literary and Artistic Copyright Association (BLACA): www.blaca.org.

[1] These became the papers in Part II of this book.

and hence of those who represent the owners of these rights for administration purposes (agents and collecting societies). The same applies to the online making available right (which is, for brevity's sake, here called the internet right). If a protected work is, without the necessary permission, uploaded in Country A and downloaded in Country B, the right owner must in general go to Country B to claim remedies for such download. Of course there may, through reciprocal arrangements of collecting societies, be the possibility for the local society in country B to take action. But what if in Country B there is no such agreement or no relevant collecting society or a collecting society without the necessary reciprocal arrangements? Where no licensing has been effected, the right owner is faced with the necessity of taking prior action in Country B and any other country in a similar situation where there has been an infringement.

As regards the online availability of protected material, there is on the one hand the case of material in respect of which the right owner or right owner's representative is known and is in a position to issue a global or (as is more often the case) a territorially limited licence. On the other hand, there is the case of orphan material where the relevant right owner or right owner's representative is unknown, either generally, or as regards particular territories, or where such right owner cannot be located. An additional problem concerns material in respect of which the protection criteria cannot be ascertained, for example as regards fulfilment of criteria of nationality or place of publication, or duration of protection. Such 'criteria status unknown' material may or may not be orphan.

There may in a particular country be a system legally established for obtaining permission to use orphan material. But such a system, as regards exercise of the internet right, will under national law only cover acts taking place in the country concerned: for transborder communication there will still be the need to obtain permission or be covered by legislative provision in every other access country of relevant right ownership, so that, generally, on the basis that the internet right is recognised in the countries bound by the WIPO Treaties 1996, or having implemented the EC Information Society Directive, there will, in the case where a protected work is to be legitimately placed online in Country A for legitimate global access, be the need for legitimation of the copying and making available of the work in some 90 or more countries.

Is the noble project of bringing the contents of the world's great library collections to the computers of everyone throughout the world to be impeded by the difficulties of tracing and receiving permission from every right owner of every item of protected material in every library collection? What of items with multiple rights in multiple contributions, such as films and sound recordings? Does the fact that right ownership may change from territory to territory, and even from time to time, mean that we must acknowledge defeat and consign traditional copyright to the dustbin of legal history? I do not believe so.

The right to make protected material available on the internet is of a global nature, since unless technologically restricted, material so made available is accessible everywhere. Yet collecting societies do not at present offer licenses permitting online availability of their respective repertoires throughout the world.

The consequences of the non-availability of global licences include the following:

(1) Unauthorised peer-to-peer file sharing is rampant.
(2) Accessibility of digitised library collections is impeded.
(3) Control of user-generated content cannot be effected on a global basis.
(4) Large amounts of orphan material are not available for legitimate public access.

3 TOWARDS A SOLUTION

In general, it is suggested that a new approach in licensing procedures should now take place, if these consequences are to become a thing of the past, namely, that right owners, be they authors, performers, producers or other right owners should license the exercise of their respective internet rights on a global basis.

I suggest two proposals for discussion which I believe may assist in arriving at solutions to these problems.

First, I suggest that collecting societies should establish a central licensing agency for the issuing of licences with global coverage of the internet right.[2]

Secondly, with regard to the specific problem of the licensing of use of orphan works and other orphan material, I draw attention to the British Copyright Council proposal in this connection, such proposal being based on the extended collective licensing system, in conjunction with application to the Copyright Tribunal for consent to use the required orphan material where no collecting society administers the right concerned.[3]

---

[2] For the Reporter's proposal in this connection see Annex I to this Report.

[3] See Annex II to this Report. For a description of the ECL system, see T. Koskinen-Olsson (2006), 'Collective management in Nordic countries' in Gervais (ed), *Collective Management of Copyright and Related Rights*, Kluwer at pp. 264 ff. See also G.W.G. Karnell (2004), 'Extended collective licence systems . . . a Nordic

The establishment of a global licensing system should also provide the means of licensing in the areas of accessibility to digitised libraries, and user-generated content. As to file sharing, many cases have been taken against persons engaged in unauthorised acts in this area, and some legislation, or proposed legislation, envisages the cutting of access to the internet by persons who persistently engage in unlawful sharing activities. I do not believe that such measures of prohibition and punishment will eradicate unauthorised file sharing. Like the Hydra, the decapitation of one source is immediately followed by the springing up of other sources; *vide* the experience of right owners in the USA and the *Pirate Bay*[4] case in Sweden, which shows that repressive measures do not eradicate the problem.

The operation of collecting societies and licensing schemes over the last 100 years shows that in general users prefer to take out licences where these are easily available on a reasonable basis, rather than face the risk of legal action. There has been a similar experience with lawful download sites. Such is the technological sophistication of the BitTorrent system that it can be envisaged that, through a central licensing agency, file sharing programs could be available which permit the file sharer to obtain, in regard to the file proposed to be shared, a licence to legitimate the proposed activity.

In reply to a question from the floor concerning my proposal for the necessity of a central internet licensing agency, I would like to suggest that we should bear in mind that communication between members of the human species is not now limited to the world but, increasingly, occurs in extraterritorial areas including Space. Consequently, we should plan for rules that regulate the use of protected material in such areas, for we shall soon see large numbers of humans inhabiting areas on the Moon and other Space locations, and those humans will wish to communicate with each other and send to and receive communications from Earth.[5]

Footnote 3 (*cont.*)
copyright invention with an international future?' in S. Georgiades et al (eds), *Essays in honour of George Koumantos (Symmeikta Georgiou Koumantou)*, Athens: Ekdoseis Ant. N. Sakkoula, p. 391, and 'Sweden' in (2006) *RIDA* at p. 208 (discussing ECL in respect of transposition of the EC Information Society Directive). For a legislative example, see the Swedish Author's Right and Neighbouring Rights Law, 1962, as amended July 1, 2005, s.42(a) (search 'Swedish Copyright Act'). See also the Danish Law LBK nr 586, 2008, providing for issue of licences for use of orphan works under an ECL system. See generally J.A.L. Sterling (2008), *World Copyright Law* (3rd edn), London: Sweet & Maxwell, paras 12.24, 12.32–12.37.

[4] Stockholm District Court, 17 April 2009.

[5] For survey of this aspect, with proposed Space Copyright Treaty, see J.A.L. Sterling (2007), 'Space Copyright Law: the new dimension' 54 *Journal of Copyright Society of USA* 345 and at www.qmipri.org/research.

4 CONCLUSION

It is suggested that the reality of modern communication methods shows increased public demand for global online availability of all types of material protected by copyright and related rights (and, in some countries, *sui generis* rights), and that right owners need to accede to this demand by offering fair and reasonable licensing terms to permit such availability, rather than solely relying on a policy of legal actions against infringers, with accompanying sanctions. In the global environment, the right owner's motto, it is suggested, should be 'Easy access, easy licensing.'[6]

Some years ago, a play broadcast in London concerned a number of Venetian professors who met every Saturday evening to discuss means for prevention of the flooding of Venice by rising waters from the sea. One Saturday evening they looked down and saw that the water had reached their knees.

We must not be like those Venetian professors, but should now institute the means to control the flood.

ANNEX I: GLOBAL INTERNET LICENSING SYSTEM: SYNOPSIS OF PROPOSAL[7]

1. *Establishment of a global internet licensing agency (GILA)* by existing collecting societies, the agency to administer the licensing of use of protected material on demand on the internet ('the internet right'), without territorial restriction.
2. *The structure of the system*: the right owner or right owner's representative globally mandates a collecting society (which then accordingly mandates GILA) or GILA directly with the administration of the internet right for the material concerned.
3. *Material mandated to GILA* forms part of the GILA repertoire. Every item in the GILA repertoire has a GILA Identification Number (GIN) permitting administration of rights in and tracing of online use of such item.

---

[6] See generally the undersigned's paper 'The Future of Copyright: approaches for the new era', available at http://www.blaca.org/meeting.htm, also at http://www.qmipri.org/research.html.

[7] Further further details concerning the system and its application concerning global licensing of use of orphan material are available at www.qmipri.org/research.

4. *The GILA home site* contains details of all items of the GILA repertoire and of the various categories of available licence.
5. *Prospective users* (including digital libraries, filesharers and user generated content uploaders) apply online for the required licence. If a global licence is required, this is issued by GILA. If a territorial licence is required, the applicant is referred to the relevant right owner or right owner's representative or collecting society, where this information is available to GILA.
6. *Royalties paid to GILA* are distributed to the right owner, right owner's representative or collecting society concerned.
7. *Structure, administrative procedures and licence conditions* conform to competition rules, possibly implemented under the aegis of WIPO.

ANNEX II: BRITISH COPYRIGHT COUNCIL PROPOSAL FOR LICENSING OF USE OF ORPHAN MATERIAL: SYNOPSIS[8]

1. *System for legitimation of use of orphan material* (that is material where the relevant right owner is (following reasonable enquiry) unknown or untraceable).
2. *System covers all categories of protected material* (authors' works, performances, films and sound recordings, broadcasts and so on).
3. *Statutory provisions* establishing (a) that a licence of a recognised collecting society covers use of non-members' material, and relevant conditions in connection with terms of such licence, and (b) that where no collecting society administers the right concerned, consent to use protected material may, subject to prescribed conditions, be given following application as provided by statute (application to Copyright Tribunal in UK).
4. *Revenant right owners* receive equal treatment to that accorded to collecting society members, or as provided in accordance with statutory consent procedure.

[8] For further details see http://www.britishcopyright.org/pdfs/policy/2009_014.pdf.

PART III

The borderless era: international exhaustion, global administration and formalities

22. Introduction to Part III

Paul Torremans*

Modern copyright, that developed from the Statute of Anne onwards, is essentially territorial in nature and based on national law. This should not surprise. In those days copyright works were exploited on a national basis and very few copies of works were traded internationally. Only single copy works such as sculptures and paintings crossed borders, but books were printed and exploited on a country by country basis. One (copy-)right per country, based on national law, and coupled with national treatment was therefore a very acceptable model.

1 (INTERNATIONAL) EXHAUSTION

That economic reality has changed. More and more copies of books, CDs, DVDs, and so on are manufactured in one place and exploited globally, across borders. Does it then still make sense to argue that an imported copy, sold abroad by the right holder, is an infringing copy? This is where exhaustion arises. In fact the oldest case in which the exhaustion doctrine was applied was a case relating to records. In *Deutsche Grammophon v. Metro*[1] the Court was faced with the following issue. Deutsche Grammophon sold the same records in Germany and in France, but its French subsidiary, Polydor, could only charge a lower price due to market conditions. Metro bought the records in France for resale in Germany at a price below the price Deutsche Grammophon charged. Deutsche Grammophon invoked its copyright in the records to stop this practice. The European Court of Justice ruled that Deutsche Grammophon had exhausted its copyright in the records by putting

* Professor of Intellectual Property Law, School of Law, University of Nottingham.

1 Case 78/70 *Deutsche Grammophon GmbH v. Metro-SB-Grossmarkte GmbH & Co KG* [1971] ECR 487, [1971] CMLR 631.

them on the market in France with its consent and could not oppose the importation of the records by Metro.[2]

The case law of the Court has now also been reflected in the information society Directive.[3] Article 4(2) stipulates that:

> the distribution right shall not be exhausted within the Community in respect of the original or copies of the work, except where the first sale or other transfer of ownership in the Community of that object is made by the rightholder or with his consent.

But traditionally films are not exploited through the distribution right, that is the sale of hard copies, but through the right of communication to the public, that is people go out to watch a movie. The exploitation of these works takes place therefore through public exhibitions which can be repeated an indefinite number of times. The European Court of Justice was confronted with this problem in the *Coditel* case.[4] This case made the French film *Le Boucher*, the copyright in which was owned by the French company 'Les Films la Boétie', famous. A seven-year exclusive licence to exhibit the film in Belgium had been given to Ciné Vog. One of the clauses of the licence stipulated that Ciné Vog could only allow the film to be broadcast on Belgian television 40 months after its first cinema showing. A different exclusive licensee was appointed for Germany and that licence contract did not restrict the showing of the film on television. The film was shown on German television before it could have been shown on Belgian television and the Belgian cable company Coditel picked up the German signal and retransmitted it on its cable network. This required the authorisation of the Belgian licensee under Belgian copyright law because it was held to be a communication to the public. Because no authorisation had been applied for and because they feared loss of revenue because the Belgian television stations would be less interested in acquiring the right to broadcast a film that many of their viewers had already seen in the German version, Ciné Vog sued Coditel for infringement of copyright. Coditel based its defence inter alia on the freedom to provide services and argued that as the film had been shown with the consent of the owner of the copyright all copyright in it had been exhausted.

---

[2] Case 78/70 *Deutsche Grammophon GmbH v. Metro-SB-Grossmarkte GmbH & Co KG* [1971] ECR 487 at 500.

[3] Directive 2001/29/EC of the European Parliament and the Council on the harmonisation of certain aspects of copyright and related rights in the information society [2001] OJ L167/10.

[4] Case 62/79 *Coditel SA v. Ciné Vog Films SA* [1980] ECR 881, [1981] 2 CMLR 362.

The European Court of Justice started its analysis on a traditional basis:

> Whilst Article 49 of the Treaty prohibits restrictions upon the freedom to provide services, it does not hereby encompass limits upon the exercise of certain economic activities which have their origin in the application of national legislation for the protection of intellectual property, save where such application constitutes a means of arbitrary discrimination or a disguised restriction on trade between member states. Such would be the case if that application enabled parties to create artificial barriers to trade between member states.[5]

In a next step the specific subject matter of the performing right in a film was defined as the right of authorities to forbid each and every performance of the film, including the right of it being televised. As the retransmission of the film by Coditel amounted to a new performance, the performing right in the film had not been exhausted and Ciné Vog could rely on it. The restriction on the showing of the film which Ciné Vog claimed was necessary, in order to guarantee it the benefit of the essence of the exclusive performing right. The remaining issue was whether the practice to have one exclusive licensee per member state was an example of the artificial barriers to trade to which the Court objected. The Court did not see it as such an example and accepted that such an approach was objectively justifiable because at that time all television services were organised on the national basis of a legal broadcasting monopoly.[6] Its conclusion was

> that the provisions of the Treaty relating to the freedom to provide services did not preclude an assignee of the performing right in a cinematographic film in a member state from relying upon his right to prohibit the exhibition of that film in that State, without its authority, by means of cable diffusion if the film so exhibited is picked up and transmitted after being broadcast in another member state by a third party with the consent of the original owner of the right.[7]

In other words, the exhaustion principle does not apply to the right of communication to the public in the same way it applies to the distribution

---

5 Case 62/79 *Coditel SA v. Ciné Vog Films SA* [1980] ECR 881 at 903.

6 Arguably this is no longer the case now that Directive 93/83 on copyright and neighbouring rights relating to satellite broadcasting and cable retransmission has been adopted ((1993) OJ L248/15, see above). For example Art 7(3) on co-production agreements shows that licences may have to be granted on a Community scale, thereby excluding territorial licensing. See Ph Kern (1993) 'The EC "Common Position" on Copyright Applicable to Satellite Broadcasting and Cable Retransmission' 8 *EIPR* 276 at 280.

7 Case 62/79 *Coditel SA v. Ciné Vog Films SA* [1980] ECR 881 at 904.

right. The information society Directive[8] takes this into account and stipulates in its Article 3(3) that the communication to the public right and the making available to the public right will 'not be exhausted by any act of communication to the public or making available to the public as set out in this Article'.

That decision needs to be seen in its own economic context though. What we are essentially told is that exhaustion is the rule, as most works were exploited through the distribution right and the distribution of hard copies, whereas exploitation through communication to the public was rather the exception. That latter model was in the *Coditel* scenario also strictly based on a country by country exploitation with different forms of exploitation happening at different times and non-simultaneous repeat exploitation of the work.

Our current economic model is different. First of all exploitation through communication to the public has become the norm. We access databases and various other copyright works online each time we need them rather than acquire a hard copy; video on demand and music streaming have taken over. That means that what was a small exception to the common market has now become the norm. At EU level this may not be desirable, but also at global level this approach contrasts sharply with free trade ideas.

Secondly, even in terms of broadcasting and communication to the public, the idea of repeat performance as the only business model is losing its dominant position. Live broadcasts of football matches for example are watched in real time and operate differently from the *Coditel* idea of movie theatres.

In addition all these questions also arise at global level and not just inside the common market. International exhaustion is even more important than regional exhaustion.

The time has therefore come to reconsider *Coditel* and to ask whether international exhaustion should become the norm in the digital online environment. Do the reasons that justified the *Coditel* approach still apply? Are there other reasons to either keep or change copyright's peculiar approach to exhaustion?

These are also not purely academic questions. English courts have referred questions to the European Court of Justice on this very point.[9] The use of foreign decoder cards to watch live football matches that have

---

[8] Directive 2001/29/EC of the European Parliament and the Council on the harmonisation of certain aspects of copyright and related rights in the information society [2001] OJ L167/10.

[9] *Murphy v. Media Protection Services* [2008] FSR 33; *Football Association PremierLeague v. QC Leisure* [2008] 3 CMLR 12, [2008] FSR 32.

been licensed per country on an exclusive basis is an infringement of copyright under national law. But as goods the cards are in free circulation and exhaustion applies. And the exploitation model is very different from that in *Coditel*. Can the exhaustion doctrine therefore be used in this kind of case as a defence to copyright infringement? In other words is *Coditel* still good law and does it apply to this case?

Against this background Part III looks again in detail at international exhaustion, this time in a digital environment and both in legal and in economic terms.

2 FORMALITIES

The traditional statement is that copyright arises without formalities. Modern copyright saw the end of formalities, at least at the international level. But in a digital online environment works can be changed and transformed with incredible ease. How does one prove what exactly the original work looked like, for example in an infringement scenario, and how does one prove title? Formalities and specifically a register of some kind could be useful. But as soon as one re-opens the discussion on formalities questions as to how formal or informal such a system should be and whether or not it should be obligatory arise. Passions run high on this point. Should the system apply across the board or should it be limited to the internet or to digital works? All these issues warrant a fundamental debate, grounded in history and in the use of formalities in countries such as the US where they were never abandoned. And from there the debate can move on to the internet and digital works. Part III also looks in detail at all these issues and not simply from the angle whether or not the old demons that modern copyright seemed to have put to rest awake again.

3 GLOBAL ADMINISTRATION OF COPYRIGHT

To an extent international exhaustion and formalities both fit into the broader framework of the global administration of copyright. A key problem in that context is peer-to-peer file sharing and the illegal downloading of music and films by internet users. A key measure that has been proposed to allow right holders to regain control is the gradual cut-off. After a series of warnings infringing users would see their internet access cut off and internet service providers would be obliged or encouraged to play an increasing role in the administration and enforcement of copyright. The final paper in Part III deals with that very issue and strings the whole debate together.

23. International exhaustion

André Lucas*

1 INTRODUCTION

At first, the topic looks quite arduous, and to be frank even fairly unattractive. It is, however, very interesting and the organizers should be praised for bringing it back onto the table, more than 20 years after the ALAI Study Days in Munich (where it was first discussed).

It is very interesting, if not fascinating, on a strictly legal level. This is true, primarily, from a technical point of view. The distribution right (or its variants) forces, for example, one to think of its articulation in terms of other prerogatives granted to authors, such as the making available right when it exists, which calls for a systemic analysis of the proprietary rights structure. The concept of exhaustion still holds some mysteries, in so far as one doubts its base (or rather basis) and scope. As for the international dimension of such exhaustion, it involves, as is often said, the famous principle of copyright's territoriality, on which Georges Koumantos appropriately commented that it is always brought into debates, although without ever accurately defining it, and which is not easily reconciled with the globalization of the transfer of works. Beyond the technical aspects, it is, of course, the philosophy of the copyright system that is at stake, hence the decisive importance in this field of comparative law, not only to take into account the diversity of substantive law solutions, but also to assess, which is probably more important, the differences of approach in concepts and reasoning modes.

The economic, and therefore political stakes, are essential too. As always, behind the principles there are strategies. International exhaustion serves some interests and impacts others. It is therefore natural that it causes strong lobbying.

* Professor, University of Nantes, France. This contribution was originally written in French. The original version, as well as a Spanish translation, can be found on the website of the British Literary and Artistic Copyright Association (BLACA): www.blaca.org.

Although the topic concerns only international exhaustion, it is thus necessary, in order to address its full breadth, to step back and start by analyzing the distribution right itself, in an attempt to cover its scope and future in the digital age,[1] before addressing the territorial extent of its exhaustion, that is international and regional exhaustion.

2 THE DISTRIBUTION RIGHT AND ITS EXHAUSTION ON AN INTERNAL LEVEL

Evidently it is out of the question to address all questions raised by the distribution right in this presentation. What was well done in Munich should not be redone in London. Nonetheless, before focusing our attention on a possible digital distribution right, some important points need to be recalled.

2.1 A Reminder of the Basic Points

We shall merely indicate that most legal systems admit the existence, to the author's benefit, of a distribution right understood as the exclusive right to market copies of the work. We should say 'most systems', because certain domestic laws do not subscribe to this approach. In France, while Article 1 of the law of 1793 was limiting the authors' right to the 'exclusive right to sell, have someone selling, and distribute their works across the Republic territory', therefore seemingly including the reproduction right in a kind of distribution right, the law of 11 March 1957 remained silent on this point, and it was preferred to construct, from a very broad understanding of copyright, a 'destination right' going much further than the distribution right in allowing the author to control, beyond the material distribution of copies, certain uses of said copies. Such theory has also been adopted in Belgian law. It was also in Belgium that it was best conceptualized based on the thesis of Professor Frank Gotzen.[2] But, apart from the uncertain future of this theory considering the evolution of Community law, one may consider that the destination right includes the distribution right strictly speaking, so that the latter may actually be considered as a standard, even though it is

---

[1] The questionnaire proposes to interview national groups on whether the 'exhaustion regime' as such (meaning not limited to international aspects) makes a distinction between 'analogue works' and 'digital works'.

[2] (1975) *Het Bestemmingsrecht van de Auteur*, Brussels: Larcier, publication with a summary in French under the title *Le droit de destination de l'auteur* (The author's destination right).

sometimes called otherwise (publication rights, the right to put into circulation, rights to issue copies of the work to the public). It is therefore not surprising to find it in the WIPO Copyright Treaty of 1996 (Art. 6) and in the European Union Directive of 2001 on the information society (Art. 4).

Exhaustion is also part of the landscape. One can even say that it evolved from the nature of the distribution right. The theory owes much, as we all know, to German law, and notably to the systematic presentation, across any intellectual property, that Josef Kohler made of it in the very early twentieth century. There again, legal systems may vary on terminology. In the United States, for example, one talks about first-sale doctrine. The essential point is that the distribution right is, in this analysis, a single shot pistol and not a machine gun. The author who agreed to market copies of his work has no rights to control the future circulation of these copies, and notably to forbid their resale.

The principle is clearly acquired. It is generally justified by three series of considerations, which tend to show that none is decisive, and therefore denote some blurring. The first consideration rests on the idea of reward. It was featured in the United States, for example, in a 2nd Circuit Court ruling of 1963[3] basing the '*first-sale doctrine*' on the idea of allowing the copyright holder to make a 'fair profit' on the first sale of a copy of his 'productive investments'.[4] The second is that the exhaustion, understood in that way, allows reconciliation of author's copyright and buyer's property rights of the movable property consisting of the copy.[5] We shall recall this consideration when we consider the prospect of a digital distribution. The third one is that exhaustion will make the circulation of copies 'flow' by privileging freedom of trade, which will encourage an increase in the offer of cultural assets.

But the exhaustion doctrine of the distribution right does not have limits that are as clear as one would wish for legal safety's sake. Leaving aside, for now, the complications born of the French–Belgian theory of the destination right (which, in itself, escapes any exhaustion, subject to what will be said later regarding 'community exhaustion') and from the exhaustion's international dimension, two main difficulties emerge.

---

3 *Platt & Munk Co. v. Republic Graphics, Inc.*, 315 F. 2d 847, 854.

4 See also in Germany, in similar terms, BGH, Feb. 27, 1981, *Schallplattenimport I* : *GRUR* 1981, p.587.

5 See for example H. Cohen Jehoram (1988), L'épuisement en droit d'auteur aux Pays-Bas', in *Journées d'études* ALAI, pp. 129–135, at p. 130 ('The exhaustion is therefore a sort of borderline between the various intellectual property rights of the author/inventor and movable property rights in the sense of article 625 of the Dutch Civil Code'). See also BGH, *Schallplattenimport I*, above.

First, there is a point of debate about what acts may cause exhaustion. Under the American law, this act seems to consist in a property transfer of the copy,[6] justifying the name 'first-sale doctrine',[7] but it has been ruled that the transfer of the simple possession should be considered as sufficient under the said doctrine.[8] In the European Community, a narrower concept is considered. In particular, Article 4.2 of the aforementioned 2001 Directive derives the exhaustion from the 'first sale' or the 'first other transfer of property'. This limited view has been criticized for its motivation. It should be recognized that it permits the escape from exhaustion by resorting to the gimmick of renting the supports.[9] Nevertheless, it has been affirmed by the Court of Justice in a recent decision.[10] It is also noted in the same sense, that in Japanese copyright law, the equivalent of the distribution right ('*hampu*' in Japanese) is translated in the official English version as 'right of ownership transfer'.

Then, and this question is even more delicate, one often hesitates on the point regarding whether contractual restrictions can paralyze, at least partially, exhaustion, which implies that they would be effective against the world. It is in German law in particular that the debate has been conducted. As early as 1906, in a famous ruling, the *Reichsgericht*[11] affirmed, in order to quash the claim filed by the author-publisher of railroad signs against a trader who was reselling at a low price copies legally acquired on the market, that 'an agreement that would have as its effect to exclude or

---

[6] See C. Joyce, M. Leaffer, P. Jaszi and T. Ochoa (2006), *Copyright Law*, New York: LexisNexis, (7th edn), p. 486.

[7] Even though this may be a gratuitous act. See *Walt Disney Productions v. Basmajian*, 600 F. Supp. 439 (S.D.N.Y. 1984).

[8] *United States v. Atherton*, 561 F.2d 747 (9e Cir. 1977). See also *London Sire Records v. Does*, 542 F. Supp. 2d 153 (D. Mass. 2008), affirming that the expression 'transfer of property' does not imply copy divestment. Compare, applying the presumption of property in favour of the possessor as provided by Article 2006 of BGB, BGH, 3 March 2005: *GRUR* 2005, p. 505.

[9] B. Castell, *L'épuisement du droit intellectuel en droit allemand, français et communautaire*, PUF, 1989, n°329, p. 192. (exhaustion of intellectual property rights in German, French, and Community laws). About the objection, see also, V.-L. Benabou (1997), *Droits d'auteur, droits voisins et droit communautaire*, Bruylant, n°425.

[10] 17 April 2008, case C-456/06, *Peek & Cloppenburg KG v. Cassina SPCA*, pronouncing as law that 'the notion of distribution to the public, otherwise than by sale, of a work original or copy, under article 4, paragraph 1, of Directive 2001/29/EC of the European Parliament and of the Council of 22 May 2001 on the harmonization of certain aspects of copyright and related rights in the information society, implies exclusively a property transfer of this object'.

[11] 16 June 1906, Königskursbuch,: *Dr.* author 1907, p. 84.

restrict this owner's faculty of free disposition would not create an actual right but a simple obligation for the parties', and that the author therefore cannot 'proclaim a general defence that would have the same effect as an actual right would have with regard to any third party either becoming or later becoming owner of lawfully marketed copies of the work'.[12] Later on, the analysis was refined to specify that the author can impose certain restrictions on the circulation of copies effective against the world, however, provided that such restrictions concern the distribution processes, for example limiting it to sales through book clubs.[13] One finds here an application of the traditionally accepted rule in German law, under which the contractual licenses can limit the scope of the rights granted but not their enforcement procedures.[14] Actually, the limit seems quite vague,[15] which demonstrates that the distribution right system subject to exhaustion does not necessarily provide sharper solutions than the French–Belgian destination right doctrine.

Marginal hypotheses are still to be taken into account, such as those subjected to the Dutch *Hoge Raad* in the famous *Poortvliet* case.[16] In this case, the author had transferred his reproduction right on his work for the purpose of publishing calendars, and he was opposed to third party marketing of such reproductions as framed works. The Court agreed with him, noting that he had not transferred the right to market separately reproductions to which he had agreed. The case was not so different from the one ruled on by the Supreme Court of Canada in the *Théberge* case,[17] about 'canvassing' posters bought in trade, a process consisting in collecting the used inks and transferring them onto a canvas, except that the debate was confined to a reproduction right (not violated by the initiative in dispute, decided the Court, by a small majority), the distribution right

---

[12] BIRPI translation.

[13] BGH 21 November 1958, *Heiligenhof*: *GRUR* 1959, p. 200.

[14] V. Already on Reichsgericht distinction, 30 November 1908: *Dr. auteur* 1911, p. 35. For a general presentation, see D. Reimer, 'Le droit de mise en circulation, en particulier la location et le prêt des livres et des disques', ALAI Workshop of 1972, Paris, pp. 76–87, also published in *Dr. auteur* 1973, pp. 56–62. (The right to bring out, in particular renting and loaning of books and disks.)

[15] F. Pollaud-Dulian (1989), *Le droit de destination, Le sort des exemplaires en droit d'auteur*, LGDJ, n°476. ('this distinction leaves me a little perplexed'). [The destination right, The fate of copies in copyrights] – J. Spoor (1980), *Copies in Copyright*, Sijthoff & Noordhoff, p. 63 ('the distinction (. . .) will often be a subtle one').

[16] 19 January 1979: *Auteursrecht AMR* 1979, p. 50, note J. Spoor.

[17] *Théberge v. Galerie d'Art du Petit Champlain,* 2002 *SCC* 34 ; *Intell. propr.* 2002, n°4, p. 53, obs. A. Lucas, and n°5, p. 124, obs. Y. Gendreau.

not being in cause, and the theory of destination right being evoked only to be dismissed, because it is not recognized in Canadian law.

But once more, it is mostly digital works that are rekindling the problem.

2.2 Impact of Digital Works

The developments above show that distribution right and its exhaustion generate many controversies. The following discussion will confirm this opinion. All the more reason not to refrain from the satisfaction of bringing forward certainties when they exist. And precisely, there is one regarding the question asked of the national groups, to work out whether the exhaustion regime implemented in their country distinguishes 'analogue works' from 'digital works'. If this distinction refers to the support, obviously the regime is identical. This is what the German report and the Dutch report expressly specify. True, the formulation might refer, in the mind of the questionnaire writers, to the distinction between 'online' and 'off line' transmissions. In this reading, one thus leaves the domain of certainties to again enter a path of controversies.

Since the distribution right was designed in reference to distributing material supports (books, disks), we need to consider whether it is possible to transpose it to online diffusion, which is like considering the problem of the existence of an immaterial distribution right. Reasoning in the affirmative, we would then wonder about the possibility of submitting this form of distribution to exhaustion.

2.2.1 The existence of an immaterial distribution right

Could a digital distribution right covering remote transmission be imagined? Generally, national laws do not include it, but they do not forbid it either. That gave rise to the idea of a transposition. The question was discussed in the 1990s within the European Union (at the same time as the discussion on the correlative existence of an immaterial rental right). It is in this sense that the Commission ruled for computer programs.[18] The debate, actually, quickly stopped for a very simple reason. Directly from the 1996 WIPO Copyright Treaty, in which Article 8 provides for authors

---

[18] Report of the Commission to the Council, to the European Parliament, and to the economic and social Committee on the implementation and effects of Directive 91/250/CEE concerning the legal protection of computer programs, COM (2000) 199 final, p. 18. For British law, see also S. John (1996), 'What Rights Do Record Companies Have on the Information Superhighway?', 2 *EIPR* 74–78, at 76.

the 'exclusive right to authorize to the public any communication of their work, through wire or wireless, including making it available to the public in such a way that anyone can have access to their work from the place and at the time they choose to in an individualized way', the idea arose and was imposed on Member States to deal with this new form of exploitation through the making available right. From this fact, the path to an immaterial distribution right was closed. This is how the wording of Article 4.1 of the Directive on the information society concerning the 'original' and the 'copies' of works should be understood, limiting the distribution right to circulating tangible supports. Should there remain the slightest ambiguity, it would be lifted by the 28th recital evoking 'the exclusive right to control the distribution of a work built into a material property'. Certain transposition laws expressly restated that. An example is the French law of 2006 referring to 'material copies'. This approach has been criticized.[19] But it is out of the question to reassess it. All national reports of the European Union countries make, in this respect, the same observation.

The situation is not different in countries, like Australia, Brazil, and India, which kept a synthetic concept of the right of communication to the public including a making available right or those, like China and Japan, who made of this right an autonomous prerogative.

The United States, on the other hand, constitute an excellent case study. It is known, indeed, that this country sided, during the diplomatic Conference of Geneva in 1996, against recognizing a making available right. It is even because of this opposition that the 'umbrella solution' was imagined, leaving total freedom for the States to transpose the aforementioned Article 8.[20] It was then logical to expect to see the courts looking for a solution in the extension of the distribution right for transmitting digital files, a perspective that was not dismissed in a report from the Copyright Office in 2001.[21] In fact, recently the question was repeatedly asked, most often with regards to peer-to-peer networks. Unfortunately, this case law, currently coming from trial courts, is not very encouraging, in the sense that it shows the reticence of the judges, faithful in that to the American copyright tradition, to show audacity in interpreting the existing texts in

---

19 See for example E. Tjong Tjin Tai (2003), 'Exhaustion and Online Delivery of Digital Works', *EIPR* 207–211.

20 M. Ficsor (2002), *The Law of Copyright and the Internet*, Oxford: Oxford University Press, p. 496.

21 US Copyright Office, DMCA Section 104 Report. See *Intellectual Property and the National Information Infrastructure*, The Report of the Working Group on Intellectual Property Rights, Information Infrastructure Task Force, September 1995, p. 213.

order to efficiently complete the palette of rights granted to authors. We can only refer, in examining these various matters, to the extensive report written by the group from the United States. The text in question is Article 106(3) of the Copyright Law, that grants the author the exclusive right to 'distribute to the public copies or phonograms of the work protected through sales or other means of property transfer, or through lease, rent, or loan'. Thus the question now is whether such distribution can include the actual transmission of digital files, as well as 'making these files available' when it is not established that they have been received by recipients.

The first question faces a tremendous burden of proof, since it is normally for the author, who alleges that his distribution right has been violated, to demonstrate that the offer to distribute was followed up. Some decisions remained tied to this principle[22] dismissing the precedent of a 4th Circuit Court decision, which alleviated this burden of proof by setting a presumption in favour of the copyright holder for the reason that the lack of proof of reception by the public was due to the deficiency of the defendant libraries.[23]

As for the possibility of having the distribution right playing the role of the making available right while being content with just a potential public, it has sometimes been accepted without discussion, but also been rejected based on a literal analysis of the law, which is more a postulate than a real demonstration.

In short, the distribution right umbrella is not very effective, and one may wonder, therefore, whether the United States fulfil their international obligations. The argument, in fact, has not impressed certain courts who have observed that the obligation to interpret the American law in light of international conventions (here the WIPO Copyright Treaty) was only as valuable as the disposition was ambiguous, which, according to them, was not the case for Article 106(3).[24]

The main argument in favour of immaterial distribution is based on the assessment that a single memory-resident 'original' can produce an

---

[22] See for example the ruling of the district court of Arizona of 28 April 2008 in the case *Atlantic Recording Corp. v. Howell*, specifying that the notion of distribution implies 'an actual dissemination of either copies or phonorecords', and citing to that effect Professor Paul Goldstein, for whom 'a mere offer for sale will not infringe the right'.

[23] *Hotaling v. Church of Jesus Christ of Latter-Day*, 118 F. 3d 199, 1997. Compare *London Sire Records v. Does*, above, note 8, limited to reporting that it is statistically certain that at least one work has been downloaded.

[24] *Elektra Entertainment Group, Inc. v. Barker*, 551 F. Supp. 2d 234 (SDNY 2008). *Capitol Records v. Thomas*, 2008 U.S. Dist. LEXIS 84155 (D. Minn.2008).

incalculable number of copies that will be physically found in the memory of recipient systems. Digital transmission thus scatters copies remotely. Therefore the situation is not so different from that in which copies are manufactured in number and then distributed. To avoid any discrimination between both categories of operators, reason and fairness would dictate the vesting in them all of a distribution right.[25] It is tempting to add, in this sense, that the discrimination appears indeed artificial when the tangible support, which justifies the application of the distribution right, represents only a fraction of the cost of the content, as is often the case for software.

Nonetheless, the refusal of an immaterial distribution fits perfectly the materialistic approach that has always been retained in this field. It has never been disputed until now that the distribution right concerns copies of the work such as tangible personal property and the common declaration concerning Articles 6 and 7 of the WIPO Copyright Treaty came to restate it by specifying that the terms 'copies' and 'original and copies' should be understood as exclusively designating 'fixed copies that can be distributed as tangible objects'. This is why, as I said earlier, traditionally the author's distribution right and the owner's proprietary right of the tangible support have been weighted against each other.

However, in case of digital file dissemination, the supposed distribution does not circulate copies susceptible to being a tangible property. From that point of view, the term 'copy', always used in texts written in English, is not without ambiguity, since it equally refers, in French, as dictionaries tell us,[26] to 'reproduction' and 'copy'. But the distribution right concerns only the fate of copies, considered as tangible objects whose manufacture has been authorized by the author, not that of all reproductions to which such copies may be subjected to. In other words, there is no difficulty in admitting that the transmission of a digital file produces a reproduction in the recipient's computer memory, but in no way does it mean that the latter thereby became the owner of a copy as defined above.

2.2.2 The exhaustion of immaterial distribution right

Let us admit, for the sake of argument, the existence of an immaterial distribution right. Is it then subject to exhaustion? The difficulty that has just been brought up, and which relates to the lack of transfer of a tangible property of a support on which the work is found, appears then in full

---

25 E. Tjong Tjin Tai, 'Exhaustion and Online Delivery of Digital Works', above, note 19, p. 210.

26 See for example Robert and Collins.

light. What causes the exhaustion, is, as we saw, the putting into circulation that materializes into such transfer. Correlatively, what the exhaustion makes possible is the circulation of this same copy whose property has been transferred.

However, the scheme does not fit the situation created by the digital dissemination of copies. The recipient does not become owner of a copy in the sense of an identifiable tangible object, and if he himself sends a copy to another recipient, the latter cannot also pretend to have acquired, from this fact, the property title in a copy subjected to exhaustion. For an actual assimilation with the distribution of copies in a material sense, a transfer of property should be 'mimicked'. It was suggested, supporting the idea that exhaustion could be activated should the recipient of the first copy, as he himself transmits a copy, moves to delete the one in his computer memory.[27] But, apart from the fact that this deletion is difficult to prove and that it is not sufficient to annihilate the risk of a violation of the work's normal use, it is easy to see the artificial character of the suggestion.

That is why the partisans of an immaterial distribution right most often prefer to consider that such a prerogative is not subject to exhaustion.[28] But, since the exhaustion, as we said, belongs to the nature of the distribution right, then the question becomes: what sense would it make to plead for the existence of a distribution right escaping all forms of exhaustion?

This is what led Community law to choose to submit on-demand digital transmissions to the making available right, for which Article 3.3 of the 2001 Directive on the information society expressly provides that it is not subjected to exhaustion. The confirmation, in fact, was not necessary. Contrary to what is sometimes held, exhaustion does not concern the reproduction right but only the distribution right (or the destination right component that stands for it). To say that the right of communication to the public, or the making available right it includes, cannot be exhausted is therefore opening a door that is already open.[29] This awkwardness is explained, it seems, by the fact that in Community Law exhaustion is traditionally based on the principle of free circulation of goods. It is thus natural that its dismissal for cause of the immaterial nature of the distribution is justified by being classified as a provision of services, especially since

[27] E. Tjong Tjin Tai, Exhaustion and Online Delivery of Digital Works, prev., note 19, p.210.

[28] For the first-sale doctrine in American laws see in this sense *Intellectual Property and the National Information Infrastructure*, prev., note 21, p.95

[29] See in this sense H. Cohen Jehoram, European Copyright Law – Ever More Horizontal, 32 *IIC* 532-545 (2001), at p.541, considering Article 3.3 of Directive 2001 as a '*curious superfluous provision*'.

Community case law retains a very broad acceptance of services, at least concerning the application of rules governing free service provision.[30]

3 THE DISTRIBUTION RIGHT AND ITS EXHAUSTION AT THE INTERNATIONAL AND REGIONAL LEVEL

The questionnaire sent to the national groups concerns the question of international distribution right exhaustion. All reports provide an explanation on this point. Those written by the groups from European Union countries provide, again, the same answer, dictated by Community law. The others, on the other hand, provide various and often prudent answers, accounting for fluctuations and vague jurisprudence. Therefore, a review is required before drawing a few perspectives in this domain which is very controversial, including within the European Union.

3.1 The Review

The exhaustion, whose territorial scope we are attempting to define, essentially concerns the classic distribution right, relating to material copies of the work, since the contention of an immaterial distribution right is generally not accepted. It is also necessary to specify that, by hypothesis, we are dealing with copies distributed by the right holder or with his consent, without which the import of such copies would evidently be illegal.[31] We

[30] In a recent decision (23 April 2009, Case C-533/07, *Falco Privatstiftung, Thomas Rabitsch v. Gisela Weller-Lindhorst*), the Court of Justice distanced itself from extensive acceptance, by refusing to consider the license contract of an intellectual property right as a service performance under Article 5, item 1, under b), second dash, of the 22 December 2000 regulation concerning jurisdiction, recognition, and execution of the decisions in civil and commercial matters, but it confirmed at the same time that the reasoning should not be transposed on the ground of the free service performance, noting (item 35) that 'if this domain generates, should the case arise, liberal interpretations of the notion of services, this approach is motivated from the concern that since most economic activities do not arise from free circulation of goods, funds, or people, they do not escape in as much to the application of the EC treaty'.

[31] See, for example Article 27(1) of the Canadian law, cited in the national report, or Article 113.1 (i) of the Japanese law (which consider as a violation 'the act of the importing, for the purpose of distribution in this country, objects made by an act which would have constituted an infringement on the moral rights of author, copyrights, rights of publication, moral rights of performer or neighbouring rights had it occurred in this country at the time of importation').

need to know whether the holder who has agreed to circulation outside the country in question can oppose the import into said country or not. This is why the problem is often addressed in terms of 'importation right'.[32]

The answers to the questionnaire can be classified in three categories.

A first category comprises national reports indicating that the question was not addressed by any express legislative provision nor by any judicial decision. That is the case of Colombia and Uruguay.

The second category consists of responses provided by national groups of the European Union countries. All these reports recognize the solution imposed by the Community background. The Directives from 1991 on computer programs,[33] from 1992 on the right to rental and lending, from 1996 on databases, and from 2001 on the information society, indeed impose on the Member States duty to provide an exhaustion extended to the European Community (and, beyond, to the European Economic Area), but forbid them to put in place an international exhaustion. The 2001 Directive is particularly clear. Not only does the negative formula used in Article 4.2 ('is exhausted only in case of first sale (. . .) within the Community') express clearly this interdiction, but the 28th recital drives the nail further into the wood by specifying that the distribution right 'should not be exhausted by selling the original or copies thereof outside the Community'. It is thus consistent with the solution retained by the Court of Justice regarding trademarks.[34] And recently, the Court had the opportunity, in the *Laserdisken* case,[35] to uphold the solution in the copyright domain by noting that Article 4.2 of the 2001 Directive indicates that the WIPO copyright Treaty 'does not undermine the faculty for contracting parties to determine possible conditions under which said exhaustion takes place after the first sale',[36] and that the first recital of the 2001 Directive entails that 'the harmonization of Member States legislative provisions on copyright and related rights contributes to establishing the internal market and a system fit to prevent competition distortions therein', so that the provision in question cannot be criticized on the basis of competition law.[37]

---

32 See for example WIPO International Office memorandum submitted to the Expert Committee on a possible protocol relative to the Berne Convention: *Copyright* 1992, p. 81, n°121 and following.

33 Consolidated by Directive 2009/24 of 23 April 2009.

34 CJCE, 16 July 1998, *Silhouette International Schmied GmbH & Co KG v. Hartlauer Handelsgesellschaft GmbH*, aff. C-355/96: *Rec. CJCE* 1998, I, p. 4799.

35 *Laserdisken ApS v. Kulturministeriet*, Case C-479/04, 12 September 2006: *Intell. propr.* 2007, p. 211, obs. A. Lucas ; *JCP E* 2008, 1144, n°13, obs. A. Zollinger.

36 Item 42.

37 Items 48 to 51.

This solution does not present any difficulty in Member States that had already denied international exhaustion, such as Germany[38] or France,[39] but it forced others, like the Netherlands or the Scandinavian countries, favourable to such exhaustion, into a spectacular turnaround.

Concretely, anyway, the Member States have to exercise a community exhaustion, but must consider illicit the import of supports circulated by the right holder or with his consent in a country outside the Community.[40]

The third category consists of answers to the questionnaire communicated by groups from states outside the European Community, and asked about the international exhaustion issue. It is, in fact, rather heterogeneous.

We start with the simplest, or the clearest. This is a judgement by the Swiss Federal Court from 20 July 1998, carefully written, concerning a case of parallel import of video games.[41] The Swiss national report recalls that Article 12 of the copyright law, concerning exhaustion, is silent on the question, whereas the bill clearly provided the principle of international exhaustion. Such silence, however, is not very meaningful since it has its roots in the legislator's desire to leave the question open at a time when Switzerland was considering to align itself with the Community background. In any event, the Federal Court dissipated the uncertainty by being in favour of international exhaustion, arguing notably that free trade could only be limited by an express legal provision, and that public interest required placing the least obstacles possible to access cultural assets. It is not possible to say more about it in this report, but one should refer to the critical observations of the Swiss report to see that the problem was considered from all points of view.

---

38 On opposability in German laws of the clauses organizing territorial division of distribution right, v. BGH, *Schallplattenimport I*, 27 February 1981: *GRUR* 1981, p. 587 and BGH, *Schallplattenimport II*, 21 March 1985: *GRUR* 1985, p. 824.

39 Although the French legislator performed a strange exercise consisting in foreseeing the Community exhaustion of a prerogative (distribution right) about which he says nothing in the copyright definition.

40 See for illustration concerning a circulation in Portugal (before this country joined the Community), CJCE, 9 February 1982, Case 270/80, *Polydor v. Harlequin*: *RIDA* 3/1982, p. 134; *Rec.*, p. 329. See also for software import to France from Canada, TPICE, 16 December 1999, Case T-198/98 *Micro Leader Business v. Commission: JCP G* 2000, II, 10370, note M.-C. Boutard-Labarde and P.-Y. Gautier.

41 *Nintendo v. Wahl Eximpo, ATF* 124 III 321; [1999] *EIPR* N-63. See B. Lindner (1999), a critical commentary about this ruling, [1999] *EIPR* 373–377.

The Canadian Supreme Court ruling in *Euro-Excellence Inc v. Kraft Canada Inc.*[42] should also be mentioned, although, according to the national reporter, it brings more confusion than clarity to the debate. With a small majority, the Court considered as illegal, under Article 27(2) of the Canadian Copyright Law, the parallel import of chocolate-flavoured products whose package included logos protected by both trademark and copyrights, while dismissing, based on a strict interpretation of the text, the objection according to which the use of the works here only had an 'incidental' character, as well as the objection drawn from the existence of an abuse of right.

It is still on this basis, in the United States, that the discussion is the most animated (not necessarily good news for legal certainty. . .). Four decisions are worth mentioning. The first decision is from the Court of Appeals for 3rd Circuit, which in 1984 dismissed the first-sale doctrine in the case of parallel import of products legally made outside the United States, but for which the copyright holder had not expressly granted the right to import into the United States.[43] The second one was pronounced ten years later under the same hypothesis and in the same way, by the 9th Circuit Court.[44] In this reading, the form of Copyright Law Article 109(a) allowing the owner of a copy or phonogram 'lawfully made under this title' to sell it or divest it without the consent of the rights holder (which sustains the first-sale doctrine), had to be understood, as noted in the American report, as referring to a copy both made and sold on United States territory: a reading the report finds daring. The Supreme Court ruled in favour of international exhaustion, in the case *Quality King Distributors v. Anza Research International, Inc.*[45] although this case concerned products legally manufactured in the United States with the consent of the right holder and to be sold outside the American territory. Finally, the decision of the 9th Circuit Court in the case *Omega SA v. Costco Wholesale Corp.*[46] dismissed international exhaustion. But the hypothesis was still different. It concerned copyrighted watches, made in Switzerland, that a discount seller wanted to distribute in the United States after buying them from third parties who themselves had obtained them from authorized distributors outside the United States.

---

42 2007 SCC 37.

43 *Columbia Broadcasting Sys., Inc. v. Scorpio Music Distributors*, 738 F.2d 424.

44 *Parfums Givenchy, Inc. v. Drug Emporium, Inc.*, 38 F.3d 477; [1995] 2 *EIPR* D-52.

45 523 U.S. 135 (1998).

46 541 F.3d 982 (2008); [2009] *EIPR* N-31, obs. R.H. Stern.

Although not contradictory, it is difficult, from these precedents, to have a precise idea of the territorial range of the exhaustion under American law.

3.2 The Perspectives

The uncertainties just mentioned and the diversity of national solutions can impact, considering the importance of intellectual property rights in world trade, the circulation of cultural assets. From this aspect, the silence on this point of the TRIPS agreement[47] and of the WIPO Treaties,[48] resulting from a lack of consensus, is undoubtedly an admission of failure.

The prohibition on exercising international exhaustion as imposed by Community law was and continues to be the object of harsh critics. The Swedish report notes, in a very diplomatic understatement, that the solution was received with little enthusiasm in its country. The Dutch report indicates that, in 2000, when the Copyright Committee was consulted on some essential points of the Directive, it ruled in favour of international exhaustion for 'economic and diplomatic' reasons, and that Denmark, Ireland, Luxemburg, the Netherlands, Finland and Sweden had written a common communiqué in the same sense. One will also note that in the *Laserdisken* case decided by the Court of Justice,[49] the Polish government disputed the exhaustion regime imposed by the 2001 Directive, arguing that the rule 'would prevent the promotion of a broader competition and would grant holders of copyrights and other related rights a protection of their interests, beyond the objective of such rights'.[50]

Beyond these basic oppositions, the traditional transversal approach to exhaustion (notably in German law), that puts patents, trademarks and copyright on the same footing, raised objections. In the Nintendo case,[51] the Swiss Federal Court did not hesitate in front of the amalgam. Noting that international exhaustion had already been admitted concerning trademarks, and it saw there an argument in favour of the same solution being adopted for copyright, even adding that one should not overestimate the differences

---

[47] See Article 6 ('no disposition of this agreement will be used to deal with the question of intellectual property right exhaustion').

[48] See Article 6.2 of the Copyright Treaty ('no disposition of this treaty undermines the faculty that contracting Parties have to determine possible conditions under which exhaustion of the right provided under paragraph 1) applies after a first sale or another property transfer operation of the work original or copy thereof, realized with the author's authorization').

[49] Above, note 35.

[50] Item 45.

[51] *Nintendo v. Wahl Eximpo*, above, note 41.

between the functions of copyrights and trademarks. The Swiss reporter understandably criticizes this observation, estimating that the distinctive sign is not affected by parallel imports, when the concern for better protection of the author could well lead to allow him to maximize his profits while hindering such imports. In the same frame of mind, one cannot approve the ruling of the Court of Justice,[52] which from the trademark exhaustion implied exhaustion of the exclusive reproduction right recognized based on copyrights, for reason that 'the protection granted by copyright with regard to work reproduction protected in the dealer's advertisements, may in no way be extended beyond that conferred under the same conditions to the trademark holder'.[53] One does understand the care to avoid that the exercise of copyright comes to paralyze the trademark exhaustion,[54] but the reasoning by the Court of Justice does not withstand scrutiny. It is indeed impossible to admit that the rule of free circulation of goods implies simple exhaustion of the author's reproduction right.[55]

One is obliged to note though that international exhaustion is, even more than internal exhaustion, based on opportunity considerations, which explains the lobbying efforts to reverse (or hold) the adopted rule. It is not the 'judicial strategies' which guide the behaviours of the persons concerned, as the questionnaire implies (no national group followed this point up), it is rather the 'legislative strategies'. Thus, no one will be surprised to see libraries pleading for international exhaustion[56] while video producers argue for the opposite solution.[57]

---

[52] 4 November1997, *Parfums Christian Dior SA and Parfums Christian Dior BV v. Evora*, Case C-337/95: *Rec. CJCE*, p.I-6013, concl. Jacobs.

[53] Item 58.

[54] Compare, in the case *Omega SA v. Costco Wholesale Corp.*, above, note 46, R. H. Stern comment ([2009] *EIPR* N-31), blaming the Court for diverging from the first-sale doctrine to copyright domain, for drawings playing the role of special signs, hence permitting to escape to trademark exhaustion. See also in the Canadian case *Euro-Excellence Inc v. Kraft Canada Inc.*, above, note 42 the minority opinion, evoking a function diversion.

[55] In this sense see J.-S. Bergé (1999), 'Paradoxes et droit communautaire: Observations sur l'interaction des catégories juridiques à partir de données récentes tirées des droits intellectuels et du droit de la concurrence': *JDI* 1999, pp. 85–114, n°29.

[56] Copyrights exhaustion through the first sale theory in a digital environment, the position of the Libraries Associations in the debate in the USA: *Bull. dr. auteur*, vol XXXVI, 2002, n°4. The associations fear that contractual agreements may paralyze the effects (beneficial in their opinion) of the first-sale doctrine.

[57] International Video Federation, Submission in response to the Commisson's consultation on an issues paper on 'Opportunities in online goods and services', 15 October, 2008.

The legislator himself does not hesitate to enact specific rules for a given market. Often thus, one finds clear rules concerning parallel imports of books in national laws. Such is the case, for example, in Canada.[58] It is also interesting to note that Article 113 (5) of the Japanese law makes parallel imports of phonograms published outside Japan illicit when they are likely to impact unreasonably on the profits expected by the Japanese producer from the same phonograms distributed by him across the national territory. The Swiss report gives another example of this very pragmatic attitude, indicating that a law of 14 December 2001, came to modify Article 12 of the copyright law to submit the copies of audiovisual works to a national exhaustion regime limited in time.[59]

One may see there the appearance of political stakes. The territoriality of copyright is sometimes invoked in opposition to copyright exhaustion. In the *Omega* case,[60] the US 9th Circuit Appeal Court noted in this sense that to accept international exhaustion in a specific case would amount to the American law producing a extra-territorial effect, which Congress did not expressly provide for. So formulated, the argument cannot convince because it proceeds from an archaic vision of territoriality. To say that the decision of the holder of the right to market copies of his work in a given country cannot entail the exhaustion of the distribution right in another country is by no means equal to conferring an extra-territorial effect to the law of said country, but is merely drawing the consequences from the voluntary act of distribution.[61] The truth of the matter is that, behind the territoriality objection, emerges the concern (actually a legitimate concern) for each State to ensure the best possible protection of the national beneficiaries while providing for the interests of the local cultural industries.

All that leads to accepting as plausible, and also to wishing, that the question of international exhaustion will be re-examined in the near future.

---

[58] Art. 27.1 of the copyright law.

[59] The disposition is written as follows: 'copies of an audiovisual work can only be resold or rented from the moment the exercise of the author's public performance right is no longer hindered'. Therefore it is meant, the reporter indicates, 'to avoid that DVD or other new film supports be imported during the duration of the first performance in cinemas for each linguistic region'. See, deciding that computer games cannot be, in this respect, considered as audiovisual works, TF, 1 March 2007: Intell. prop. 2007, p.379, obs. J. de Werra.

[60] *Omega SA v. Costco Wholesale Corp.*, above, note 46.

[61] See in this sense BGH, *Schallplattenimport I*, February 27, 1981: *GRUR* 1981, p. 587.

24. The economic perspective: exhaustion in the digital age

Andreas Wiebe*

1 INTRODUCTION

Today, there is a lot of talk about crisis. The crisis I will talk about today has been around for some time. It is the crisis of the exhaustion principle, the source of which lies in the way digital technology changed production and distribution of immaterial goods. This crisis will not go away within a year. Moreover, it brings up the question of whether the exhaustion principle still makes sense in the information age and if so in what specific form.

2 INTRODUCTORY CASE[1] – SECONDHAND SOFTWARE AS AN EXAMPLE

I would like to take a case as an example that has kept German courts quite busy over the last three years. It is about so-called 'secondhand software'.

The first licensees of software download the software from the internet or receive it on a master copy that can be accessed in a local network in the company. The underlying standard contracts exclude the transfer of the software or the license without consent of the right holder.

Now, sometimes it happens that the licensee does not need the software any more, be it because of new software or even bankruptcy. Then he may be interested in reselling the software. This is the business of an intermediary who buys the software from the first licensee and resells it to a second licensee with a rebate of 30–50 per cent. No physical copy is part of the

* Prof. Dr. Andreas Wiebe, LL.M. University of Göttingen, Germany. Chair for Intellectual Property Law.

1 District Court of Munich I, CR 2007, 356; *Haines/Scholz*, CR 2006, 161.

deal so the second licensee either has it running on his computers already or downloads it from the website of the producer. In case of a master copy this copy is transferred and any remaining copies with the first licensee are erased.

In legal terms the case hinges upon the application of the exhaustion principle. If it applies any contract clauses prohibiting distribution of copies are void. The question thus turns to whether in the first transaction between licensor and licensee exhaustion applies. While this is no question in the case of transfer of physical copies there has been heavy dispute in cases of transfer of a master copy or even online transmission.

3 RATIONALE AND THEORY OF THE EXHAUSTION PRINCIPLE

So we turn to the basics. The exhaustion principle is a legal instrument to establish a balance between the interests of right holders and the interests of market participants in unhampered trade in goods. Long before European law took over, the exhaustion principle was in force already. However, primary European law gave it a special twist. The execution of national intellectual property rights may encroach upon the freedom of movement of goods and services (Art. 28, 49 EC), and this limitation cannot be warranted if the goods incorporating it have been marketed with the consent of the right holder.

If you look for theoretical foundations you run into three theories on which the exhaustion theory may be based:[2]

- property theory – the right of redistribution accompanies title to the copy;
- marketability theory – avoid inappropriate hampering of trade in copies;
- remuneration theory – first marketing provides sufficient opportunity for amortisation.

I would like to draw your attention to the economic background of the problem. Intellectual property rights are supposed to work efficiently if viewed against the background of a dynamic competition theory. For a limited time they secure innovation by granting an exclusive legal right

[2] Joos (1991), *Die Erschöpfungslehre im Urheberrecht*, Munich: C.H. Beck, p. 51 et seq.

and provide for the incentive function that is indispensible for dynamic competition. They channel a competition purely on price into a dynamic quality competition.[3]

Certainly we have to keep in mind the differences between the different intellectual property schemes. Trademark law is an instrument of quality control. Patent law provides for an exclusive right on an innovative idea and its exploitation. Copyright is more of a protection against copying creative efforts. The economic function of intellectual property rights may not be neglected in the discussion. However, in brackets it may be noted that there is no convincing empirical evidence of this incentive functioning except in research results for over 100 years.

The exhaustion principle enables the acquirer of a copy the unlimited distribution of this copy. He exposes the right holder to full price competition. This may be warranted in light of the function of intellectual property rights only if strictly limited as an exception to the marketability of goods and only under the precondition that the right holder may still be compensated appropriately. In this sense I would put the marketability theory and the remuneration theory as the basis for the exhaustion principle.

From an economic point of view exhaustion makes sense when the costs of control that accrue for market participants with respect to the legality of copies are higher than the innovation included in the goods traded. This leads to a rough conclusion that internationally markets are more separated which alleviates control while national markets are more difficult to control. This may be seen as a justification to distinguish exhaustion on a national level from that in international trade. The European common market now seems to be clearly on the side of national markets.

4 DIGITISATION CHANGED THE EQUATION

Copyright was always closely related to the technology that was used for production and distribution of works. Digital technology has brought fundadmental changes that irrevocably changed the balance of interests inherent in copyright. Copying on paper included loss of quality, copying costs and was a bit awesome. With digital technology copying costs tend towards zero, the quality does not deteriorate and it is easy to distribute. Nearly all costs now shift to the production phase of the immaterial good.

---

3 *Ganea*, GRUR Int. 2005, 102.

At the same time control costs for the right holder rise as in digital networks it is hardly discernable whether a copy is legal or illegal. From what I said before this would suggest the application of the exhaustion principle to digital networks as transaction costs may become very high. This would neglect the second part of the equation, which is the incentive function of copyright. If all copies on the internet were free this function would be seriously affected. If copies with the same quality as the original were freely on the market the remuneration of the author on first sale would be diminished. The assumption that the author can obtain appropriate remuneration on first sale was at the basis of the exhaustion principle as I pointed out before. So we have a dilemma.

So looking at the function of the exhaustion principle the remuneration function is in danger. The reseller can offer equivalent quality than the first seller on the *same* market, so there is pure price competition. This will also have repercussions on the price upon first sale.[4]

As to the marketability theory, suggesting online exhaustion would at first glance diminish control costs. However, at second glance this is not the case. Exhaustion is still limited to cases where the first sale took place with the consent of the right holder. So the right holder still has to screen the market for illegal copies. As for the copy itself you cannot discern whether it was stemming from a transaction under exhaustion that these costs may even arise. On the other hand, if you limit exhaustion to distribution of physical carriers the user may present the original data carrier.

5 WAYS AHEAD

5.1 Limiting Exhaustion to Distribution Right

All of this warrants the conclusion that the exhaustion principle should be limited to the distribution of physical copies. Of course, there are some good arguments for the contrary position. The transaction is directed at providing the possibility of using the software and in this respect it does not make a difference whether the transfer is made online or by physical carrier. Digital technology allows for control and usage without physical transfer.

While this is true from the viewpoint of contract law for copyright other factors come into play. Exhaustion is not so much about the economic

---

4 *Ganea*, GRUR Int. 2005, 102, 104.

interest of the first acquirer in re-distribution but about interest in securing tradeability and protecting the market participants.[5] It is limited to tradeability of a copy already on the market, not of a copy that is produced by the acquirer. In this sense visibility plays a role in creating trust comparable to the law of tangible goods or to Rechtsscheinstatbestände in the law of cheques.[6] As a consequence the interest in protecting trade is diminishing in the course of digitisation.

In this sense it may have been a mistake to just define the copyright concept of a 'copy' broadly to encompass also digital copies. The different characteristics of digital storage are being neglected. This problem will come back in different contexts.

Digital technology separates information from any carrier and displays it more and more in its pure form. If you want to hold up exhaustion with force then you have to take recourse to treating the license itself as a copy to which exhaustion applies as did courts in Hamburg and Munich.[7,8] From the position of the exhaustion followers this is consequent. But it is clearly against the law that makes transfer of a license dependent upon consent of the right holder.[9] Licenses are not freely marketable and there is a fundamental difference between the law of tangible goods and immaterial goods. You cannot acquire intellectual property rights in good faith. All this works in favour of keeping the connection between exhaustion and a physical copy.

A narrow construction is also in line with European law. In its decision of 17 April 2008 the ECJ has limited the distribution right on such a distribution that is connected with a transfer of title. In the continental tradition this means transfer of a tangible copy. This construction also has consequences for the exhaustion that is limited to the right of distribution.[10]

I may also point to the discussion as to Art. 3(3) and recital 29 of the InfoSocDir which state clearly that exhaustion does not apply to online transmission.[11] Recital 33 of the Database Dir states that exhaustion does not apply even as to copies of the database that are produced by the user. Even more general Recital 43 of the Database Dir states:

---

5 Very clear D.Ct. Munich, CR 2007, 356, 360.

6 See *Spindler*, GRUR 2008, 69, 74.

7 MMR 2006, 827, 828.

8 D.Ct. München I, CR 2008.

9 See *Heydn/Schmidl*, MMR 2006, 830.

10 ECJ C-456/06 *Peek & Cloppenburg KG / Cassina SpA*.

11 See *Heydn/Schmidl*, K&R 2006, 74, 76. Contra *Hoeren*, MMR 2001, 515, 517; *Berger*, GRUR 2002, 198, 200 ff; *Spindler*, GRUR 2002, 105, 110.

> The distribution right shall not be exhausted within the Community in respect of the original or copies of the work, except where the first sale or other transfer of ownership in the Community of that object is made by the rightholder or with his consent.[12]

Moreover, the European legislator always distinguished goods from services and classified online transmission as part of the services area.[13] The main argument was that the right holder is not remunerated on first transaction because of the possibility of permanently repeating the process. Now it may be questionable to connect the exhaustion principle to the goods/services-distinction. However, in general the European legislator realised from the beginning that the rationale of the exhaustion principle, to secure the marketability of goods, is not valid in the online context any more.

5.2 Technical Equivalents and Fee Solutions

The answer to the machine may be the machine . . . If digital technology dissolves what used to be a copy for exhaustion purposes why not try to fix the problem by using technology to create a functional equivalent to conventional copies. DRM may help to vest digital files with characteristics similar to physical carriers. It may contain the information in a 'box' and make it identifiable, possibly even more secure against piracy than conventional carriers. Added could be rights information. Trust and market protection could be delegated to and implemented in technical systems.

However, DRM systems have their own market failures, especially information asymmetry, . . . and lock-in effects. Moreover, they are not accepted by the market, which is the users. Hence, many companies got rid of these systems again. It is also a sign that the market is functioning in the sense that user preferences prevail in the end.

Another idea would be to establish more individualised DRM systems that take into account the specific copyright limitation present in each situation in order not to unduly hamper the user in access to the information.

Other ideas to solve copyright crisis work more in the direction of fee models. Instead of an exclusive right the coypright owner just gets a fee

---

12 This was also emphasised by the ECJ, Rs C-203/02, *The British Horseracing Board Ltd. v. William Hill Organization Ltd*, Rz 59. 'Für eine Einschränkung aus Gründen der Warenverkehrsfreiheit' *Dreier*, § 87b Rz. 18; *Berger*, GRUR 1997, 169, 178.

13 See *Wiebe*, GRUR Int. 2009, 114.

appropriate to the intensity of usage. This could be a system comparable to the existing levy system. This may be appropriate for the music and film industry. However, in other areas feasibility is more doubtful, as in the software case.

6 CONCLUSION

In practice exhaustion is a phase-out-model in the digital word. The trend goes towards on-demand services. We can observe this now in the software field as well. 'SaaS' (Software as a Service) is developing as a successful business model. Software is offered to the user for temporary use. No copy is transferred to the user's computer any more.

The remuneration of the right holder is adapted to this rental model. No question of exhaustion is present in this case any more. Of course, you may ask whether this is good for the market participants. For the right holder it may be economically favourable to switch to a services model. This discretion is given to him by copyright law. In my view it is only a sign that information goods are gradually being detached from physical carriers and increasingly displaying their character as immaterial goods. In light of this development the discussion on the application of the exhaustion principle will be only an interlude.

Let me summarise the paper:

- Intellectual property rights seek to secure dynamic quality competition.
- The principle of exhaustion establishes a narrow limitation in favour of the interests of market participants in free circulation of a good incorporating the intellectual property and implies appropriate remuneration of the creator on first sale
- Consequences of digital technology encroach upon the incentive function while at the same time enhancing control costs of right holders.
- Applying exhaustion to online distribution endangers remunreation upon first sale.
- The main rationale for exhaustion is promoting marketability and is directed at a copy already put on the market, not the work or information as such.
- Limiting exhaustion to the distribution of physical copies is in line with primary and secondary European legislation.
- Technically implemented functional equivalents of containment and designation (DRM) may warrant treating online distribution of files equivalent to physical copies with respect to exhaustion.

- 'Secondhand'-software may only be re-distributed without consent of the producer if the original data carrier is transmitted; no exhaustion will take place in case of online delivery or transfer of a master copy.
- 'Software as a Service' as a new trend may show that the exhaustion principle will be a phase-out model in the digital age.

25. The legal perspective on exhaustion in the borderless era: consideration of a digital first sale doctrine for online transmissions of digital works in the United States

Marybeth Peters*

1 INTRODUCTION

In the era of the Statute of Anne, practical economic and geographic barriers limited the scope of 'the importation . . . or selling of any books . . . printed beyond the seas . . .' as permitted under the statute.[1] Today, digital works are transmitted online in what is effectively a borderless era, at least in comparison with the barriers that existed 300 years ago.

The current ease of reproduction and online transmission of perfect copies of digital works is one of the fundamental characteristics of the borderless era that led the United States to be cautious when considering the application of the principle of exhaustion – or what is generally referred to in the United States as the first sale doctrine – to online transmissions of digital works. The first sale doctrine does not currently apply to these transmissions under United States copyright law, but the question was the subject of an extensive study by the United States Copyright Office[2] and is raised again on occasion as new online technologies and delivery mechanisms emerge.[3] This paper briefly examines the background and reasons

* Register of Copyrights, United States Copyright Office.

1 Statute of Anne § 7 (1709).

2 DMCA Section 104 Report: A Report of the Register of Copyrights Pursuant to § 104 of the Digital Millennium Copyright Act (2001), available at http://www.copyright.gov/reports/studies/dmca/dmca_study.html ('Section 104 Report').

3 Although the context is somewhat different given the difference in exclusive rights involved, similar questions have been raised in Europe regarding the possible

for the United States policy decision to forgo expansion of the first sale doctrine to online transmissions of digital works.

2 THE UNITED STATES FIRST SALE DOCTRINE

The first sale doctrine in the United States is embodied in Section 109 of the Copyright Act, which provides that 'the owner of a particular copy or phonorecord lawfully made under this title, or any person authorized by such owner, is entitled, without the authority of the copyright owner, to sell or otherwise dispose of the possession of that copy or phonorecord'.[4] Thus, after a lawful sale of a copy of a work, the copyright owner does not retain the legal right to control the further distribution of that particular copy.

The first sale doctrine was initially set forth by the United States Supreme Court in 1908 in the *Bobbs-Merrill Co. v. Straus* decision.[5] The Court in *Bobbs-Merrill* held that the exclusive right to 'vend' did not permit the copyright owner to control the price charged by future retail sellers with which the copyright owner did not have a contractual agreement.[6] The Court expressed doubt that by establishing the right to vend Congress intended to abrogate the common-law principle of avoidance of restraints on the alienation of tangible property.[7]

The first sale doctrine was codified the following year in the Copyright Act of 1909,[8] and carried forward in Section 109(a) of the Copyright Act of 1976 ('Section 109').[9] Application of the doctrine limits the copyright holder's exclusive right of distribution by cutting off the distribution right for a particular copy of a work once there has been an initial sale or transfer of ownership of that copy. The first sale doctrine does not limit

---

Footnote 3 (*cont.*)
application of the doctrine of exhaustion to the online transmission of services. See, for example, Andreas Wiebe, *The Principle of* 'Exhaustion in European Copyright Law and the Distinction Between Digital Goods and Services' (*Gewerblicher Rechtsschutz und Urheberrecht Internationaler Teil*), 114 *GRUR Int.* 2009.

4 17 U.S.C. § 109 (a).

5 *Bobbs-Merrill Co. v. Straus*, 210 U.S. 339 (1908).

6 Ibid, at 350–51.

7 Ibid, at 349–50. See also The Rental Record Amendment of 1983, S. Rep. No. 98-162, at 4 (1983) ('The first sale doctrine was originally adopted by the courts to give effect to the early common law rule against restraints on the alienation of tangible property.').

8 17 U.S.C. § 27 (1977).

9 17 U.S.C. § 109 (a).

other exclusive rights of the copyright holder that may be implicated in online transmissions of digital works, including reproduction or public performance.[10]

Section 109 does not distinguish between analog and digital technologies, and the first sale doctrine applies to analog and digital works.[11] For example, the doctrine applies to tangible physical copies of works in a digital format (for example a CD-Rom or DVD). It does not, however, apply to digital transmission of works over the internet.[12] The first sale doctrine applies to *lawfully made* copies that are fixed in tangible form,[13] even if creation of a lawful copy involves the reproduction of a digital work transmitted online, for instance by downloading it onto a disk or placing it in a folder on a computer hard drive.[14]

Unlike certain other countries or regions, such as the European Union, application of the first sale doctrine to digital works in the United States does not focus on the distinction between goods and services. Sometimes the different analytical frameworks can lead to different results. For example, as noted above, in the United States the first sale doctrine would apply to a lawful copy of an online digital transmission burned onto a CD, but the principle of exhaustion would not apply to the same CD under the European Union's Information Society Directive, because it would be treated as an aspect of an online service that is not subject to the distribution right.[15]

The United States Congress has occasionally modified the application of the first sale doctrine with respect to particular classes of copyrightable works. For example, Congress has chosen not to apply the first sale doctrine to commercial rental of phonorecords (sound recordings) and

---

10 See Melville B. Nimmer and David Nimmer, *Nimmer on Copyright* § 8.12 [D].

11 Section 104 Report at 23.

12 Ibid, at 80, 97.

13 17 U.S.C. § 109 (a). See also *Quality King Distrib. v. L'Anza Research Int'l Inc.*, 523 U.S. 135, 152–53 (1998) (copy lawfully made in US and sold abroad may be reimported to the US despite right of copyright holder to exclude imports).

14 Section 104 Report at 78.

15 See Directive 2001/29/EC of the European Parliament and of the Council of 22 May 2001, on the harmonization of certain aspects of copyright and related rights in the information society (OJ L 167/10 2001). Art. 4 (1) (provides authors '[t]he exclusive right to authorize or prohibit any form of distribution to the public'); para. 28 ('Copyright protection . . . includes the exclusive right to control distribution of the work incorporated in a tangible article.'); para. 29 ('the question of exhaustion does not arise in the case of services and on-line services . . .[including] a material copy of a work').

computer software, where there are concerns that the result would be widespread uncompensated copying of the works.[16] (The United States does not have a public lending right system with remuneration for the right holder.)

3 THE WIPO INTERNET TREATIES AND IMPLEMENTATION IN THE UNITED STATES

The 1996 WIPO Copyright Treaty ('WCT') and WIPO Performances and Phonograms Treaty ('WPPT') (collectively the 'Internet Treaties') update international norms for copyright and related rights in the internet environment. The Internet Treaties address both the transfer of physical goods and the transmission of digital works, and provide for the application of the principle of exhaustion to the former category.

For physical goods, the Internet Treaties provide authors, performers and producers the exclusive right of distribution for tangible physical copies of works by granting 'the exclusive right of authorizing the making available to the public of the original and copies' of works or performances.[17] The Internet Treaties permit, but do not require, member countries to limit the making available right applicable to tangible copies by 'determin[ing] the conditions, if any, under which the exhaustion of the right . . . applies after the first sale or other transfer of ownership of the original or a copy of the work with [ ] authorization . . . '[18] Agreed statements for these provisions clarify that distribution applies to tangible physical objects by stating that 'the expressions "copies" and "original and copies", being subject to the right of distribution and the right of rental . . . refer exclusively to fixed copies that can be put into circulation as tangible objects.'[19]

For the online transmission of works, the Internet Treaties provide authors 'the exclusive right of authorizing any communication to the public of their works', and grant authors, performers and producers the exclusive right of 'making available to the public'.[20] There is no Internet

---

16 See, for example Record Rental Amendment of 1984, Pub. L. No. 98-450, 98 Stat. 1727 (1984) (codified at 17 U.S.C. § 109 (b)); Title VIII of the Judicial Improvements Act of 1990, Pub. L. No. 101-650, 104 Stat. 5089, 5134 (1990) (codified at 17 U.S.C. § 109 (b)).

17 WIPO Copyright Treaty, Art. 6 (1) (1996) ('WCT'); WIPO Performances and Phonograms Treaty, Arts. 8 (1), 12 (1) (1996) ('WPPT').

18 WCT, Art. 6 (2); WPPT, Arts. 8 (2), 12 (2).

19 WCT Art. 6 (Agreed Statement); WPPT Arts. 8, 12 (Agreed Statements).

20 WCT, Art. 8; WPPT, Arts. 10, 14.

Treaty provision for application of the exhaustion principle to the communication to the public or making available rights applicable to online transmissions. This absence is not surprising given the traditional application of the principle of exhaustion to the distribution of tangible works.

In general, the United States concluded that minimal revisions to existing United States copyright law were necessary in order to implement its obligations based on the Internet Treaties.[21] To the extent necessary, the United States implemented additional protection for online transmissions of digital works in the Digital Millennium Copyright Act of 1998.[22]

The United States implementation approach was unique because the exclusive right of making available to the public online transmissions was implemented through a combination of the exclusive rights of distribution, reproduction, public performance and public display.[23] Other countries implementing the making available right for online transmissions have generally done so through the right of communication to the public.[24] Implementation of Internet Treaty protections for online transmissions using the distribution right in the United States implicates the first sale doctrine, while implementation in other countries through the communication to the public right does not implicate the principle of exhaustion.

4 SECTION 104 REPORT ON APPLICATION OF FIRST SALE TO ONLINE TRANSMISSIONS OF DIGITAL WORKS

In the DMCA,[25] the United States Congress included a requirement to study the application of the first sale doctrine in Section 109 of the

---

21 *WIPO Copyright Treaties Implementation Act; and Online Copyright Liability Limitation Act: Hearing on H.R. 2281 and H.R. 2280 Before the Subcomm. on Courts and Intellectual Prop. of the H. Comm. on the Judiciary*, 105th Cong. 43 (statement of Marybeth Peters, Register of Copyrights), 37 (statement of Bruce A. Lehman, Assistant Secretary of Commerce and Commissioner of Patents and Trademarks) (1977).

22 Digital Millennium Copyright Act of 1998, Pub. L. No. 105-304, 112 Stat. 2860, 2876 (1998) ('DMCA').

23 Section 104 Report at 94–95.

24 Ibid.

25 DMCA, 17 U.S.C. § 104 (a)–(b) (1998). The study mandate with respect to the first sale doctrine was to examine 'the effects [of title I of the DMCA] and the development of electronic commerce and associated technology on the operation of sections 109 . . . of title 17, United States Code; and the relationship between existing and emergent technology and the operation of section 109.'

Copyright Act to online transmissions. The United States Copyright Office issued the resulting Section 104 Report,[26] which described an extensive, year-long study that examined whether a 'digital first sale doctrine' should apply to the transmission of digital works over the internet.[27] Developing a digital first sale doctrine would require reasoning by analogy from the distribution of a tangible physical copy of a work, because the exclusive right implicated in an online transmission is the reproduction right, which is not subject to the limitation of the first sale doctrine.[28] The Copyright Office looked carefully at proposals to make online transmissions more similar to distribution of physical works by implementing a 'forward-and-delete' requirement, so that the sender's copy of the work that was reproduced would be deleted following the transmission.[29] After its study, the Copyright Office recommended that Congress *not* adopt a digital first sale doctrine applicable to online transmissions of digital works.[30]

The Copyright Office recommendation was based on interrelated economic and practical considerations. One concern was the impact of a digital first sale doctrine on the ability of right holders to exploit their works. Works in digital format can be reproduced without any degradation in quality and transmitted rapidly with little cost.[31] Thus digital transmissions, and the ease of pirating perfect copies, are likely to affect adversely the market for copies of a work to a greater degree than transfers of physical copies.[32] At the time of the Section 104 study in 2001, it was

---

[26] In the House Manager's Report, the staff of the House Judiciary Committee explained the reasons for studying Section 109 in the provision that was enacted as Section 104 of the DMCA:

> The first sale doctrine does not readily apply in the digital networked environment because the owner of a particular digital copy usually does not sell or otherwise dispose of the possession of that copy. Rather, 'disposition' of a digital copy by its owner normally entails reproduction and transmission of that reproduction to another person. The original copy may then be retained or destroyed. The appropriate application of this doctrine to the digital environment merits further evaluation and this section therefore calls for such an evaluation and report.

Staff of House Committee on the Judiciary, 105th Cong., Section-by-Section Analysis of H.R. 2281 as Passed by the United States House of Representatives on 4 August 1998, at 24 (Comm. Print 1998) (Serial No. 6).

[27] Section 104 Report at 79, n. 272.

[28] Ibid, at 79–81.

[29] Ibid, at 80–85.

[30] Ibid, at 97.

[31] Ibid, at 82–83.

[32] Ibid, at 99.

not clear that reliable technology was available to delete automatically the sender's copy in a forward-and-delete system, and in any case such technology would lead to increased costs.[33] In the years since the Section 104 Report was issued, there has been no widespread movement to develop and implement technological systems with this capability.

Another pragmatic concern with adopting a digital first sale doctrine was the likely reaction of users to the concept of incorporating deletion of the original file into the system. The forward-and-delete process that would be required to make online transmissions of digital works function more like distributions is not the typical way people use digital works online.[34] Instead, the usual practice is to create and transmit a new copy of the work while often retaining the original copy. It is unlikely that senders would voluntarily delete works on a routine basis, and it would be difficult to verify compliance with a voluntary or automatic deletion requirement.[35]

The balance of interests between copyright holders and users under Section 109 did not support the extension of the first sale doctrine to online transmissions of digital works.[36] The detrimental effect of the first sale doctrine on markets – and ultimately on the incentive to create – increases in the online environment, where sales would very likely be reduced and infringement would very likely be encouraged.[37] In addition, the first sale doctrine was developed to protect users from restraints against alienation of tangible property.[38] Those interests are not implicated when a work is transmitted in digital form through the exercise of the right of reproduction.[39] These factors outweighed any pro-competitive effect favoring users that would result from the application of the first sale doctrine to online transmissions of digital works.[40]

5 CONCLUSION

While the issue of applying the first sale doctrine to online digital transmissions in the United States has been raised again at various times over

---

33 Ibid, at 98–99.
34 Ibid, at 83–85.
35 Ibid, at n. 280, 83, 97–98.
36 Ibid, at 100.
37 Ibid, at 85, 91.
38 Ibid, at 86–87.
39 Ibid, at 87–88.
40 Ibid, at 100–101.

the years since the 2001 Copyright Office Section 104 Report, no dramatic change in conditions has prompted a re-examination of the conclusion of the Report. It is possible that at some point in the future a compelling case based on marketplace or technological conditions will be made for applying the first sale doctrine to such transmissions. At present, the online marketplace, right holders, and consumers in the United States all seem to have adjusted to the absence of a first sale doctrine for online digital transmissions.

26. Exhaustion in digital products and the 'accidental' impact on the balance of interests in copyright law

Tomasz Targosz*

1 EXHAUSTION OF THE DISTRIBUTION RIGHT IN DIGITAL COPIES

The problem of exhaustion with regard to digital products is an example of a legal matter that may at first glance appear unequivocal but because of the alleged 'unfairness' tends to be questioned by some legal scholars and sometimes even courts. In Poland the legal situation of exhaustion of distribution rights in digital products seems to correspond to the European average – it is rather generally assumed that exhaustion may only apply to material copies of copyright works. Consequently, exhaustion may of course apply to digital products if they have been recorded on a tangible medium (for example a CD or DVD); however if the same copyrighted work is made available online without a tangible copy being transferred, no exhaustion occurs.[1] Thus it is not a digital or analogue

* Dr Tomasz Targosz, Institute of Intellectual Property Law, Jagiellonian University, Kraków.

[1] J. Barta and R. Markiewicz (2005), *Prawo autorskie i prawa pokrewne. Komentarz [Copyright and related rights. Commentary]*, Kraków: Wolters Kluwer, p. 453; E.Traple (2007), (in) Barta J. (ed) *System prawa prywatnego. T. 13. Prawo autorskie, [System of private law. Vol. 13. Copyright]*, Warszawa, pp. 163, 168; E. Traple (2002), 'Znaczenie wyczerpania prawa wprowadzania do obrotu we współczesnym prawie autorskim' *[Significance of exhaustion of the distribution right in the present copyright law]* in *Wyczerpanie praw własności intelektualnej [Exhaustion of intellectual property rights]*, Warszawa, pp. 107–108; Z. Okoń and P. Podrecki (2004), in P. Podrecki (ed), *Prawo internetu [Internet law]*, Warszawa, pp. 351–355.; A. Matlak, 'Handel elektroniczny a prawo autorskie' *[E-commerce and copyright law]* in J. Barta and R. Markiewicz (2005), *Handel elektroniczy. Prawne problemy. [E-commerce. Legal issues]*, Kraków, pp. 569–570, 573. Different

method of reproduction that counts, but a simple question whether the ownership of a material copy of a work is transferred. Polish copyright law is therefore deemed to be in compliance with the Directive 2001/29/EC, which, it is believed, provides for a clear solution to the problem of digital exhaustion.

At the same time very often commentators point out that this solution, although in their opinion binding, is questionable.[2] They observe that transactions 'transferring' copies of works using technologies not requiring to transfer material copies are in almost every aspect equivalent to 'traditional' sales of material objects incorporating works such as music pieces, books or films.[3] The lack of exhaustion leads to a discrimination against such buyers as they acquire fewer rights than those who choose to buy material copies. Of course, this is not only about convenience – especially in the case of software the transaction may constitute a serious investment on the part of the buyer and if no exhaustion applies, the costs are 'sunk' since the purchaser has not acquired a transferable asset. Additional controversies that arise with regard to works in a digital form stem from the fact that the acquisition of a material copy must often be accompanied by a relevant authorisation (license) to use the work, which makes it possible

---

Footnote 1 (*cont.*)
view, although not explicitly expressed, by P. Ślęzak (2007), 'Obieg egzemplarzy utworów w świetle prawa wspólnotowego' *[Circulation of copyright works under Community law], Przegląd Prawa Handlowego* (Review of Commercial Law) 3/2007, 23.

[2] P. Podrecki (2002), *Konstrukcja wyczerpania prawa w PrAut i możliwość jej zastosowania w obrocie utworami w Internecie, [Exhaustion of rights in copyright law and the possibility of its application in online distribution],* Dodatek MoP 24/2002 (supplement Legal Monitor 24/2002), 5–8; P. Podrecki (2002), 'Wprowadzenie utworów do sieci internet a konstrukcja wyczerpania prawa – uwagi na tle prawa europejskiego' *[Making copyrighted works available in the internet and exhaustion – remarks against the background of European law]* in *Wyczerpanie praw własności intelektualnej [Exhaustion of intellectual property rights],* Warszawa, pp. 117–118; M. Król (2007), 'Wprowadzenie utworu do obrotu w internecie' *[Putting a work into circulation in internet], Przegląd Prawa Handlowego* (Review of Commercial Law) 6/2007, 35–36; A. Matlak (2005), *Handel elektroniczny a prawo autorskie [E-commerce and copyright law]* in J. Barta and R. Markiewicz (2005), *Handel elektroniczy. Prawne problemy. [E-commerce. Legal issues],* Kraków, pp. 571, 573.

[3] This is just another example of the asymmetry between flexible provisions granting rights, and narrowly defined and interpreted limitations of copyright: Ansgar, Ohly (2009) 'Economic Rights' in Estelle Derclaye (ed), *Research Handbook on the Future of EU Copyright,* Cheltenham, UK and Northampton, MA, USA: Edward Elgar, p. 236 (exhaustion may be regarded as a sort of limitation as it restricts the scope of copyright).

for rights holders to further limit or even exclude the effects of exhaustion by means of contractual terms.[4]

These considerations must have been rather convincing[5] for cases have been reported (especially in Germany), in which not only academics,[6] but also courts depart from the above described axioms.[7] It is even argued that the supposedly clear wording of the Copyright Directive (including its preamble) in reality leaves this question open so that an analogy to the general principles of exhaustion could be justified.[8]

---

4 Whether such attempts prove successful depends to a large extent on how the exhaustion principle is understood by courts. In a very well known decision of the German Federal Supreme Court concerning OEM software (BGH 6.7.2000 – I ZR 244/97 ZUM 2000, p. 1079, comment Till Jaeger, 'Die Erschöpfung des Verbreitungsrechts bei OEM-Software. Anmerkung zu den Urteilen des BGH vom 6.7.2000 – I ZR 244/97 (ZUM 2000, 1079) und des OLG Frankfurt am Main vom 18.5.2000 – 6 U 63/99 (ZUM 2000, 763)', ZUM 2000 p. 1070) it was held that exhaustion of the distribution right was 'complete' meaning that once the product has been put on the market by the right holder or with his consent the right of distribution of this particular copy is exhausted regardless of the limitations the right holder wanted to introduce. The consequence of this is that even acknowledged 'propietary' limitations cannot override exhaustion – for example if a book is authorised to be sold to book clubs only, it may be then further distributed through other channels and not only in other book clubs (see Niethammer, Alexander (2005), *Erschöpfungsgrundsatz und Verbraucherschutz im Urheberrecht*, Nomos Verlag, pp. 103–130). Even the very consent granted by the right holder to a distributor not vested with the right of distribution cannot be limited as to its scope for this would adversely affect legal certainty and run counter to the goals of exhaustion (BGH ZUM 1986, p. 678 *Schallplatenvermietung*, where it was held that the 'No rental' disclaimer on copies did not limit exhaustion with regard to rental – the case had been decided before rental right was introduced into German law).

5 Most of the arguments have been listed by Eric Tjong Tjin Tai (2003), 'Exhaustion and Online Delivery of Digital Works' *EIPR*, 207 ff.

6 See for example Hoeren, T. (2007) *Ergänzungsgutachten in Sachen UsedSoft ./. Oracle*, available at: http://www.usedsoft.com/pdf/Rechtsgrundlagen/ergaenzungsgutachten_hoeren_wg_oracle_2007_04_12.pdf; T. Hoeren (2006), 'Der urheberrechtliche Erschöpfunsgrundsatz bei der Online-Übertragung von Computerprogrammen', *CR*, 573 ff.

7 District Court Hamburg, MMR 2006, p. 827; Appeals Court Hamburg, CR 2007, p. 355. Courts in Munich have chosen a different approach: Appeals Court Munich, CR 2008, 551; District Court of Munich I, CR 2007, 356; Appeals Court Munich, CR 2006, 655. Recently LG Dusseldorf in its decision of 26 November 2007, in case Az 12 O 431/08 (EIPR 2009, N48-50) joined with the Hamburg line of cases.

8 See in particular Recital 29 of the Copyright Directive and also recital 33 of the Directive 96/9/EC of the European Parliament and of the Council of 11 March 1996 on the legal protection of databases.

Since the debate has been opened, it is therefore not only possible to ask about the future developments of copyright law in this area (in particular on the European level), but it also seems not totally unfounded to ask questions about the current state of affairs. Although European copyright law has been implemented in all EC Member States by national legislation, the details (for example exact wording) of which may vary to a considerable extent, it is rather safe to assume that literal interpretation will not be of much help. The German example demonstrates that if need be, statutory construction can be quite ingenious, and besides such discussion would always be very specific to a particular legal system.[9] As a result, only a functional approach may provide assistance. Under a functional approach I would understand an argumentative process in which exhaustion of rights is looked at from different perspectives. It should be established what the purpose of exhaustion is and how this relates to digital distribution, and further, whether it would be desirable for the exhaustion principle to apply to immaterial copies as well.

2 THE PURPOSE OF EXHAUSTION

The very purpose of exhaustion is not identically understood by everyone. The most popular explanations are the following (they may be referred to as, respectively,: Property Theory, Remuneration Theory, Legal Certainty Theory, Circulation Theory):

(1) Exhaustion lessens the conflict between rights in a material object (especially property) and rights in the immaterial subject-matter incorporated in the material object (for example copyright, but this of course applies in the case of trademarks, patents and so on).[10]

---

[9] However, sometimes the wording of provisions concerning exhaustion may render it very difficult to accommodate digital copies. For example the Polish Copyright Act (Art. 51.3) uses the expression 'put into circulation' which has been defined elsewhere in the same Act as 'making publicly available the original or copies of the work through transfer of ownership' (Art. 6.1.6). Since under Polish civil law property is a concept reserved to things (material objects: movables and immovables), literal interpretation speaks clearly in favour of the 'traditional' view excluding exhaustion.

[10] This theory seems to be less popular nowadays but some commentators try to revive it. For example Christian Berger, 'Die Erschöpfung des urheberrechtlichen Verbreitungsrechts als Ausprägung der Eigentumstheorie des BGB', AcP 2001, pp. 411–450, especially pp. 418–423 sees the purpose of exhaustion in protecting the abstract property law model reflected in the German Civil Code

(2) Exhaustion is justified by the fact that the right holder has the opportunity to safeguard adequate remuneration when putting the copy into circulation for the first time. Once this has been achieved, there are no compelling reasons to allow the right holder to further control the distribution of copies.[11]
(3) Exhaustion is indispensable for legal certainty – without it the legal status of any copy of a copyrighted work would be unclear, what would greatly hamper the exchange of goods (the functioning of the market).[12]
(4) Exhaustion is necessary to enable circulation of copies[13] on the market.[14]

These traditional explanations are in my opinion supplementary, that is, they do not cancel one another out. None of them on their own is entirely satisfactory.

Since the Copyright Directive introduces Community exhaustion, at the same time excluding international exhaustion,[15] and since national copyright law provisions on exhaustion must be regarded as implementing EC law, the concept of exhaustion takes on an additional element or maybe an

---

(property rights must enable the owner to dispose of the subject-matter of his right). The opponents of this view point out that according to § 903 BGB property right is restricted by rights of third parties and copyright is exactly such a third party right (Alexander Niethammer, *supra* n. 4, pp. 43–46) but this argument is not entirely convincing, since without exhaustion copyright would *always* trump civil law property effectively depriving the owner of almost all civil law rights. Thus it is not easily comparable to for example lease or other third party rights covered by § 903 BGB and its equivalents in civil law countries.

11 It is a very common justification, albeit raising many doubts after closer scrutiny. It has also been argued that the remuneration theory is economically unsound: Peter Ganea (2005), 'Ökonomische Aspekte der urheberrechtlichen Erschöpfung' *GRUR Int*, p. 105.

12 Andreas Wiebe (2009), 'The Principle of Exhaustion in European Copyright Law and the Distinction Between Digital Goods and Digital Services', *GRUR Int*, p. 114.

13 Séverine Dusollier (2005), *Droit d'auteur et protection des oeuvres dans l'univers numerique*, Bruxelles: Larcier, p. 353; Heinz Stefan (2006), *Urheberrechtliche Gleichbehandlung von alten und neuen Medien,* München: Beck, p. 78; Phillip Koehler (2000), *Der Erschöpfungsgrundsatz des Urheberrechts im Online-Bereich,* München: Beck, p. 53.

14 Referred to as 'Verkehrssicherungstheorie' in German legal literature. This argument may be put forward regardless of Community law. Circulation of copies should be also fostered on a purely national level.

15 Lewinski, Silke von, 'International Exhaustion of the Distribution Right under EC Copyright Law', *EIPR*, pp. 233–236.

additional explanation – it should serve the purpose of the common market.[16] The ECJ's case-law on exhaustion (in this context also cases concerning industrial property rights may be relevant) conveys a slightly different meaning of exhaustion than traditionally admitted. If the aim of exhaustion is to resolve the immanent conflict between intellectual property rights and the free movement of goods, how exhaustion actually works cannot be determined only by using copyright law concepts. This can be perhaps best explained on the basis of the *Dior/Evora* case (Case C-337/95), where the ECJ allowed the reproduction of trademarks in advertising ('the reseller (. . .) is also free to make use of the trade mark in order to bring to the public's attention the further commercialization of those goods'), adding that the same reasoning must apply to copyright.[17] Consequently, if goods in packaging protected by copyright have been put into circulation in any of the EEA member states by the right holder or with his consent, exhaustion will not only affect the narrowly understood distribution right (the right to sell or resell products, that is material objects) but will also cover the right of reproduction, when necessary to stimulate distribution. This clearly goes beyond the purpose of resolving the potential conflict between property in things and intellectual property. Driven by the *effet utile* reasoning, the ECJ shapes the concept of exhaustion in an autonomous way, as a tool to ensure *effective* circulation of goods and when needed, acknowledges exhaustion of other rights than the purely 'material' right of distribution.[18] Of course this part of the *Dior/Evora* judgment may be criticised, although few would disagree with the result.[19] However it is also rather difficult to come up with an entirely different and more elegant alternative. The BGH

---

16 It is sometimes described as one of the cornerstones of the common market: David I. Bainbridge *Intellectual Property,* (6th edn), London: Pearson/Longman, pp. 150–151.

17 Case C-337/95, para. 58.

18 Other examples of extending the concept of exhaustion beyond the right of distribution are also known. For example BGH in its decision from 7 November 1980, BGHZ 79, 350 applied the doctrine of exhaustion to the broadcasting right.

19 It is rather the abuse of copyright in packaging or logos in order to stop parallel importation that justifies questions about the current state and logic of copyright law. Interestingly many court decisions concerning exhaustion have arisen precisely out of such cases: recently *Omega SA v Costco Wholesale Corp* 541 F.3d 932 (2008), case comment by Richard H. Stern (2009), 'USA: Copyright Transnational Exhaustion of Rights', *EIPR*, pp. N 31–32. This begs the question whether at least some problems with exhaustion could not be solved by adhering to stricter standards of copyright protection (see also Alexander Niethammer, *supra* n. 4 pp. 157–159).

has tried it in its *Parfumflakon* decision,[20] explicitly rejecting exhaustion, but only on a verbal level. Instead of exhaustion the BGH referred to the 'general principle', according to which copyright, just as other intellectual property rights, must yield to the interest in circulation of goods put on the market by the right holder or with his consent. This 'general principle' however is either a new name for exhaustion, or its modified and enhanced sibling with a (possibly) wider scope.

If so, it is doubtful whether the reasoning, according to which exhaustion of rights[21] in digital products may never occur in lack of material copies is unassailable. True, reproduction authorised to 'bring to the public's attention the further commercialization of the goods' is accessory to the reselling of these material goods, but what is important here is that the pair: exhaustion – material object has been separated and that as far as the result (not its justification) is concerned, this solution has found approval.

It has been noticed that sometimes the principle of exhaustion is perceived as a principle of public interest.[22] It is not the same as the function of legal certainty referred to above. Exhaustion may also be understood as an instrument of guarding the public interest in copyright law, whereas, in turn, the copyright law may be rightly regarded as a regulation the main purpose of which is to strike a balance between the interests of the authors (or more generally right holders) and the interests of the public.[23] Exhaustion thus becomes something more than a technical solution – it allows to protect the interests of users, not only economic, but also ideal. It could perhaps be claimed that because of exhaustion a 'second-hand market of ideas' comes into existence. Without exhaustion right holders could exercise control over works for the whole duration of the copyright term. Because of exhaustion an alternative chain of distribution challenges this monopoly.

Different rationales of exhaustion would have different impact on

---

[20] Decision from 4 May 2000, BGH ZUM 2000, 1082, note by Gerhard Schricker (2001), JZ, p. 463.

[21] Or the application of a 'general principle', fostering circulation of market products.

[22] Guido, Westkamp (2008), 'The limits of open source: lawful user rights, exhaustion and co-existence with copyright law', *I.P.Q.*, p. 55.; *The exhaustion of copyrights and the first sale doctrine in the digital environment.* The Position of the Library Associations in the Debate in the United States of America, Copyright Bulletin, Vol. XXXVI, No. 4, October–December 2002, pp. 5–6, 15.

[23] Recital 31 of the Directive 2001/29/EC: 'fair balance of rights and interests between the different categories of rightholders, as well as between the different categories of rightholders and users of protected subject-matter must be safeguarded'.

exhaustion of rights in digital copies made available without transferring material media. The explanation referring to the conflict of properties would not be pertinent for the cause of 'digital exhaustion' as there would be no conflict to solve.[24] The explanation based on the adequate remuneration is first of all insufficient. According to its logic the whole idea of splitting copyright into a number of specific rights (distribution, rental, reproduction, broadcasting and so on) would be called into question. More correctly, the possibility of ensuring remuneration may be regarded as a defence of exhaustion, that is a circumstance explaining why exhaustion, necessary for some other reason, does not deprive the author of an unproportionally large chunk of his or her rights. In other words, why exhaustion, necessary for some other purpose, is objectively *acceptable* for the right holder (in fact this is what the ECJ calls the specific subject-matter of intellectual property rights). The third explanation (legal certainty) can be sufficient on its own, but it does not accord to exhaustion any further-reaching purpose and in fact disguises another question that should have been asked beforehand, that is why the conflict between property and intellectual property should be solved in favour of the former.[25] Thus it is not fully compatible with the rationale behind the Community exhaustion, let alone the broader idea of exhaustion as a principle of public interest in the meaning described above. However, it should be observed that the third explanation (legal certainty) could actually speak against exhaustion of rights, since legal certainty could be strengthened if the default rule were: any re-transfer of copies (including tangible copies) is illegal.[26] The fourth explanation (*Verkehrssicherungstheorie*) is the most promising but at the same time deceptive because the real interest here is not the free circulation of tangible objects (as they have themselves no noticeable value), but the free circulation of works recorded or otherwise incorporated in those

---

24 However, there is maybe another way to look at this. Séverine Dusollier (*supra* n. 13, p. 382) commenting on the *princpe d'independence* between property and intellectual property, observes that this principle is not out of date in the digital environment since one should differentiate between the creation of the mind (always incorporeal) and the matter (vehicle) incorporating it, be it material or immaterial: 'Il importe, en définitive, de percevoir, dans le traitement juridique de la conjugation d'une oeuvre et de son support, la coexistence du régime relatif á la distribution ou a la propriété du support et de celui gouvernant l'exploitation de l'oeuvre. Sous cette nuance, la règle de l'independence de la propriété corporelle et de la propriété intellectualle est parfaitement transposable á l'environnement numérique'.

25 See Séverine Dusollier, (*supra* n. 13), p. 353.

26 The rule would be far-reaching but simple.

material objects.[27] Bearing in mind the various rationales of exhaustion it could be argued that they all could contribute to the final solution although some of them (especially the remuneration theory) cannot be properly understood as explanations of this legal concept. To start with, it is true, but insufficient that exhaustion makes free circulation of copies possible because there must be a reason why free circulation is considered to be more important than copyright. The answer to this question may be found in the public interest in free circulation of *works*,[28] no longer controlled by the right holder.[29] I would argue that there is some inherent value in having copies instead of just being allowed to access works[30] and that shifting from having copies in the analogue world to being authorised to access works in the digital world (once the process has been completed) would bring about the change of the balance of interests in copyright law that goes way beyond the purely technical aspect. As to the remuneration theory, the opportunity of the right holder to be rewarded for putting the work on the market for the first time reconciles the public interest in the sense described above and the basic interests of the right holder.

The first conclusion is therefore the following: under some explanations of exhaustion there would be no compelling arguments to depart from the view that exhaustion may only apply to material copies. The 'Circulation theory', when properly understood, and the concept of treating exhaustion as a copyright mandatory rule in favour of the public interest make it on the other hand possible (or even desirable) to include 'immaterial' copies.

---

[27] Stefan Heinz, (*supra* n. 13), p. 78, correctly stresses: '[D]enn von Interesse ist lediglich das Werk selbst, wie auch immer es verkörpert oder transportiert werden mag. Im Kern muss es der richtig verstandenen Verkehrssicherungstheorie daher darum gehen, im Interesse des Rechtsverkehrs zu verhindern, dass der Urheber auf alle Zeit beliebig über die Verwendung der – wie auch immer durch ihn in Verkehr gebrachten – *Werke* bestimmen kann.'

[28] Of course this view departs from rationales of the doctrine of exhaustion one could apply to other intellectual property rights. On the other hand it is sometimes claimed (I think with good reason) that 'Wholesale rules on exhaustion of intellectual property rights, equally applicable to all fields of technology, or to different forms of intellectual property rights will thus be a thing of the past. This approach will be equally supported by constitutional law.': Thomas Cottier (2008), 'The Exhaustion of Intellectual Property Rights – A Fresh Look', *IIC*, 757.

[29] In this sense exhaustion could be understood as an instrument helping to cut the 'umbilical cord' connecting the author and the work.

[30] Or experience them, as it was phrased by Jane C. Ginsburg (2003), 'From Having Copies to Experiencing Works: the Development of an Access Right in U.S. Copyright Law', *Journal of the Copyright Society of the USA*, Vol. 50, p. 113.

3 CONSEQUENCES OF EXHAUSTION IN DIGITAL PRODUCTS

Whether exhaustion should encompass also immaterial copies depends on the desirability of such a solution. One should therefore try to find out what the consequences of both variants could be. If there were no exhaustion by online downloads or other comparable transactions, the right holders would have the incentive to forgo the traditional sales of copyright works in tangible media. As a result, second-hand markets could be eliminated and exhaustion in copyright would cease to be important. It is useful to notice at this point that unlike patents or trademarks, where it is difficult to imagine a world without tangible, material products, many kinds of subject-matter protected by copyright can be distributed without using any material carriers and such distribution has been rapidly gaining ground (music files, software). If the sales model shifts to a purely 'immaterial' one and if the exhaustion concept does not apply, the current balance of interests will be disturbed. If we assume for example that online distribution is functionally equivalent to distribution of tangible media, then the purely technological difference would bring about a major change: exclusion of exhaustion would redefine the business model and might potentially affect the system of economic rights. It is worth noting that works in a digital form may be generally made available to users in two ways: by granting access (for example to online databases or by streaming), which resembles providing services and by authorising to make copies, (for example music files or software downloads), which resemble sales. In the first case the right holder controls access; in the second case any normal use of the work requires actions that must be authorised by the right holder (unlike for example reading a book). Thus the lack of exhaustion in digital products strengthens the legal position of right holders. It is entirely another matter that because of the very same features of digital technologies infringements are common and hard to prevent.

If exhaustion should apply in the digital environment, legally the 'traditional' balance of interests would be preserved. Technologies would be different but functionally distribution could still take place and would be treated in a comparable way to the distribution of tangible copies. The question is of course whether this is the right answer – it is possible that the technological change has rendered the old model obsolete. However, frankly speaking, it has not been convincingly shown, let alone consciously decided by national or Community legislators. The preamble to the Copyright Directive, which attempts to 'solve' the problem of exhaustion by way of a simple statement that in the online world making the works available is a service and thus no exhaustion can apply,[31] seems to be plainly incorrect.[32] While some business models should be rightly qualified as providing services, there are also important models that do not fit the service pattern since the copy of the work is left permanently under the control of the user. With regard to the *abstractly* carried out balance of interests, there is no noticeable difference when compared to transactions with tangible media. The functional arguments against exhaustion concentrate on purely 'practical' issues – it is namely assumed that the participants in the second-hand market would not comply with copyright law, for example by not deleting software or e-books that were re-transferred and because of this the economic interests of right holders would suffer. Sometimes it is added that the answer could be different if technologies were applied (for example TPMs), the use of which would make this type of infringements impossible.[33]

However, the next question arises: supposing exhaustion applies to digital copies not delivered on any tangible medium but made by the user (like in the case of downloads), how would the right holders react? If the right holders were hostile to exhaustion, they could, generally speaking, bypass it by relying on business models limited to providing services. This should be not underestimated, although currently it seems that rather the belief in service-based models is excessively strong, for consumers still

---

31 Recital 29 of the preamble: 'The question of exhaustion does not arise in the case of services and on-line services in particular. This also applies with regard to a material copy of a work or other subject-matter made by a user of such a service with the consent of the right holder. Therefore, the same applies to rental and lending of the original and copies of works or other subject-matter which are services by nature. Unlike CD-ROM or CD-I, where the intellectual property is incorporated in a material medium, namely an item of goods, every on-line service is in fact an act which should be subject to authorisation where the copyright or related right so provides.' It is also rather inappropriate for any legislative acts to decide what questions concerning the regulated subject-matter may 'arise'. Some authors suggest that the Commission is itself not fully satisfied with recital 29: Bernhard Knies (2002), 'Erschöpfung Online? – Die aktuelle Problematik beim On-Demand-Vertrieb von Tonträgern im Lichte der Richtlinie zur Informationsgesellschaft', *GRUR Int*, p. 316.

32 See also A. Wiebe (*supra* n. 12), p. 115, who however agrees with the result. Another reason why this recital may be rightly criticised is because it 'cuts off the discussion', although the drafters of the Directive could not foresee all the developments to come in the future – in this sense Ansgar Ohly, (*supra* n. 3) p. 237. Other authors however still adhere to the opinion that if there is no transfer of ownership of the material object there can be no sale but only a service – Séverine Dusollier (*supra* n. 13), p. 398, who however stresses that as a result of performing a service a *product* may be acquired by the receiving party (p. 399).

33 A. Wiebe (*supra* n. 12), pp. 117–118.

seem to prefer models where they can download the work (preferably without any DRM restrictions) and have full control of the copy. The consumer preference for 'durable' copies can be a circumstance a proper balance of interests in copyright law should take into account. Copies that are controlled by users and may be transferred to other media (for example a music file from the hard drive to a music player) are preferred not only because they are still easier to use (for example off-line), but also because it feels 'natural' to be able to enjoy the acquired works without further involvement of the seller. It is therefore questionable whether copyright law should encourage business models, the aim of which is exactly the opposite. However vague this observation may seem, it may be argued that the proper balance of interests (of right holders and of the public) in copyright requires that at some point the work has to be 'disconnected' from the right holder, so that its normal use did not demand recurring authorisations. The concept of exhaustion helps to achieve this aim,[34] whereas limiting exhaustion makes it harder. From this perspective lack of exhaustion in absence of material copies and its consequences are in a certain way similar to the consequences of the protection of technological protection measures. Under the Copyright Directive the protection of effective TPMs is not harmonised with the scope of copyright limitations and exceptions, in that circumvention of TPMs is illegal even when the resulting use would be lawful.[35] This result has been aptly described as the privatisation of law because right holders have been supplied with an instrument allowing them to practically shape the scope of lawful use of works, regardless of the statutory template (limitations and exceptions).[36] Lack of exhaustion in 'immaterial copies' makes it easier for the right holder to control the work and its use, since it binds the user permanently to the access granting party.[37]

Exhaustion plays also an important part in competition law.[38] It may be argued that lack of exhaustion would have some negative consequences.

---

34 The main role is left to copyright exceptions and limitations.

35 Directive 2001/29/EC, Art. 6.

36 Matt Jackson (2001), 'Using Technology to Circumvent the Law: The DMCA's Push to Privatize Copyright', 23 *Hastings Comm. & Ent. L.J.* 607; Nicola Lucchi (2007) 'The Supremacy of Techno-Governance: Privatization of Digital Content and Consumer Protection in the Globalized Information Society', *J Law Info Tech* 194.

37 Exhaustion and copyright exceptions overlap: see Y. Gaubiac (2002), *The exhaustion of rights in the analogue and digital environment,* Copyright Bulletin Vol. XXXVI , No. 4, October–December 2002, p. 13.

38 M. Grützmacher (2006), '"Gebrauchtsoftware" und Erschöpfungslehre: Zu den Rahmenbedingungen eines Second-Hand-Marktes für Software', *ZUM* 305.

First, it would prevent second-hand markets from coming into existence (at least as far as lawful markets are concerned). Secondly, the lack of second-hand markets may distort competition on the primary market. This can be relevant for such copyright works as professional software, constituting an investment (asset) to the user. Without the possibility of reselling the products it would be much more difficult for the competitors of the right holder to try to woo away the user by offering better conditions. The user would be stuck with products (for example software) that would simply have no market value. In other words, it would be impossible to sell the software the user already has and purchase new software, whereby the sale of the previously used software would enable the user to at least partially recoup some costs of the investment. The irony here is that these consequences mostly affect legitimate users, that is those who use copyright works legally and have paid for it (on average software piracy is more common among private than business users).

What are, then, the results of the analysis concerning the desirability of exhaustion in digital products acquired without the transfer of a material copy of a work? I would argue that when one takes into consideration the abstract picture, much more speaks in favour of exhaustion. By 'abstract picture' I understand an analysis that presupposes lawfulness of all relevant actors. In other words, it means leaving for the moment aside the question whether the immaterial character of digital copies does not render any control of their circulation so difficult that the privilege of the right holder (no exhaustion) would be well warranted. The arguments in favour of exhaustion are the following:

- Functionally, transactions may be identical.[39]
- Excluding exhaustion discriminates a category of users who do not need material copies. For many reasons (even environmental) this would not be reasonable.
- Lack of exhaustion would shift the balance of interests in copyright law for the benefit of the right holders without compelling

[39] In fact it seems that sometimes too much weight is attached to the distinction material/immaterial in copyright law, including the context of exhaustion, what may be also observed when comparing the rationale of certain court decisions. Thus it is not unjustified when William Cornish and David Llewelyn (2003), *Intellectual property: Patents, Copyright, Trade Marks and Applied Marks* (5th edn), London: Sweet & Maxwell, p. 248, discussing *Coditel v. Ciné Vog* [1980] ECR 881, in which the ECJ did not allow the principle of the free movement of services to override territorial restrictions of the communication to the public right, ask the following question: '[i]s the movement of goods between Member States really so different?'.

justification. The reason for this is that because of the technological developments more and more transactions will not involve material copies. Thus a technological change in the mere method of making the copy available to the user 'accidentally' puts the right holders in a much better position, although the change of the method does not entail any change of the previous abstract assessment of the interests worthy of protection.[40]

- Lack of exhaustion may restrict competition as it eliminates second-hand markets and makes it more difficult for businesses to switch to new competitors.

Having dealt with this abstract analysis, there remains the 'practical' side of the problem. Is it true that the control of circulation of digital copies poses insurmountable difficulties? First of all, the difference between digital copies sold on material media and digital copies made available without transferring tangible objects is not as acute as it may seem.[41] The risk of copying stems from the digital technology itself and does not necessarily depend on the fact of whether a digital copy is transferred on a tangible carrier or not. Control of circulation of copies is easier when copies are recorded on tangible media but the control itself is not decisive – the question is whether circulation aggravates the risks of infringements and threatens legal certainty. As regards the first problem the answer is positive but the increase in risk is not of unacceptable dimensions. Real difficulties lurk in the second issue. Digital copies do not have any 'presumption of legality', which in the case of tangible copies may be provided for example by original packaging.[42] Legal certainty may be therefore especially affected, primarily because most legal systems do not recognise acquisition of *rights* in good faith. It is worth noting, however, that these concerns may be alleviated by adequate technologies, for example using information managements systems allowing to check the legality

---

[40] Many authors regard exhaustion as a problem of a diminishing practical importance (a phase-out model) due to increasing use of access based models, in which no permanent copies are made, for example A. Wiebe (*supra* n. 12), p. 118.

[41] Eric Tjong Tjin Tai, (*supra* n. 5), pp. 209–210 correctly observes: 'Although online distributed copies are typically easy to copy and distribute illegally, tangible copies of digital works (e.g. software on CD-ROM) are no less prone to illegal copying. This does not justify a differentiation between online sale resulting in the postal delivery of a tangible copy, and a sale resulting in an electronic transmission of a digital copy.'

[42] However, this could be to a certain extent replaced by 'certificates' issued by the right holder: Christian Berger (2002), 'Urheberrechtliche Erschöpfungslehre und digitale Informationstechnologie', *GRUR* p. 202.

of copies.[43] Another (or complementary) solution could be a clear rule placing the burden of proof of the legality of the transaction on the parties to it, who would be obligated to provide evidence confirming that they complied with all the requirements necessary for digital exhaustion.[44]

To summarise this part: there are many functional arguments favouring exhaustion and one major counter-argument: legal certainty. The risks to legal certainty can be, however, to a large extent neutralised by right holders and there are also possibly less radical measures available than the unconditional rejection of the exhaustion doctrine. But the problem remains that even accepting exhaustion in digital transactions might not matter too much in the end. The exhaustion principle may be stretched in the digital environment to accommodate some forms of transactions but there are limits to expending this concept to the reproduction or making available rights.[45] The question of exhaustion in the digital environment should be therefore treated rather as a manifestation of a much wider problem: the impact of digital technologies on economic rights.

4 IMPACT ON ECONOMIC RIGHTS

Exhaustion in digital, intangible copies, if allowed, could pose some problems with regard to the current structure of economic rights copyright law vests with the right holder, but it is the lack of exhaustion, or more precisely the trend the lack of exhaustion only epitomises, that is responsible for a much more troubling disturbance. As already mentioned, digital technology requires that in order to use the work in the normal way the user, having acquired a copy (regardless how it was made available), must engage in actions falling under copyright law, the most common of which are further reproductions. The scope of protection granted by copyright law is nowadays more extensive than any time in history and this is not only the consequence of conscious legislative decisions, but partly of digital technology and the process referred to above. On the other hand, the same characteristics of digital technologies are responsible for widespread infringements. Simplifying one could say that the 'legal' public

43 M. Grützmacher (*supra,* n. 38), p. 305.

44 For example that the copy was lawfully acquired, that it was deleted from the computer of the seller and so on. However, some authors are of the opinion that deleting should not be required for exhaustion, although using the transferred copy would constitute copyright infringement: Christian Berger (*supra,* n. 42), p. 202.

45 Detailed analysis by Stefan Heinz, (*supra* n. 12), pp. 269–281.

domain has been shrinking while the 'factual' public domain (free access to works regardless of its legality) has been constantly growing. This trend is extremely worrying and should be reversed. A small contribution would be to look more favourably at legal concepts such as exhaustion in an attempt to extract their core meaning and try to apply it in the digital environment.

Just as some of copyright exceptions were deemed necessary (for example temporary reproductions of a transient or incidental nature;[46] back-up copies of software[47]) to adjust the use of digital copies to the 'normal' copyright standards or to take account of the specific features of the protected subject-matter, exhaustion in digital, intangible copies would have to be extended to other rights than the right of distribution, most crucially to the right of reproduction. As I have tried to show, the very idea is not entirely strange even to the law currently in force,[48] but exhaustion in digital copies would take it one step further. The real question is however, whether this constant tension between the existing legal regime and the very nature of digital uses should not justify a more general change of approach.

5 CONCLUSION

Controversies about the application of the exhaustion principle to digital intangible copies revolve around two more general problems: (1) digital uses may be functionally equivalent to traditional uses but because of technological reasons they are treated differently, whereby this difference almost always favours the right holder; (2) exhaustion in digital intangible copies could adversely affect legal certainty of transactions and increase the risk of infringements, although this may not be a permanent state.

Rejecting exhaustion (or its equivalents, should we be able to invent them) in digital intangible copies would in the longer run contribute to changing the balance of interests reflected by copyright law. This raises serious concerns since the obsoleteness of the current balance of interests has not been convincingly proven so far. It appears that some directions copyright law has taken are motivated by one important misunderstanding, that is regarding the factual huge scope of infringements as a proof

---

46 Directive 2001/29/EC, Art. 5(1).

47 Directive 91/250/EEC, Art. 5 (2).

48 Case C-337/95 *Dior/Evora.*

that the balance of interests in copyright should be shifted towards the right holders. However, the scope of infringements is primarily the problem of enforcement and it speaks little of the *abstractly* considered compromise between private and public interest in copyright law.

27. Exhaustion – a casualty of the borderless digital era

Trevor Cook*

1 THE EARLY YEARS

Some have suggested that the origins of the Statute of Anne may have lain in part in the efforts of London publishers to reassert control over the parallel trade in books from Scotland that had been lost by virtue of the Act of Union between Scotland and England in 1707.[1] Certainly those drafting the Statute were alive to the risk of imports from outside Great Britain, but though its first clause conferred on its beneficiaries a monopoly, inter alia, over the import of the books to which it applied (its application to 'any books in Greek, Latin or any other foreign language printed beyond the seas' being expressly excluded by the seventh clause) the penalties for import were found to be inadequate to discourage cheap imports from countries outside the nascent 'common market' of England and Scotland – notably at that time Ireland and the Netherlands. Accordingly, 30 years later, it proved necessary to pass in 1739 'An Act for Prohibiting the Importation of Books reprinted abroad and first composed or written and printed in Great Britain and for limiting the Prices of Books'. This increased the penalties for such import and clause 1 of this expressly prohibited importing for sale those works 'first printed, composed or written or published in Great Britain'.[2] The following century also saw numerous legislative attempts, notably through a series of Customs Acts, to deal with the increasing problems caused by the import of cheap reprints of English books into Britain.[3]

* Partner, Bird & Bird LLP, London.

[1] See Peter Prescott, 'The Origins of Copyright: A Debunking View' [1989] *EIPR* 453.

[2] For the background to this measure see pp. 94–110 of Ronan Deazley (2004), *On the Origin of the Right to Copy*, Oxford: Hart Publishing.

[3] See pp. 134–135 of John Feather (2006), *A History of British Publishing* (2nd edn), London: Routledge and p. 345 of James Raven (2007), *The Business*

Against such a background, and given the way in which copyright law developed in the UK, even as treaties were being made and copyright laws introduced elsewhere that gave protection abroad to British authors,[4] there was never, in UK copyright law, any suggestion that books could lawfully be imported into the UK (which by virtue of the Copyright Act 1842 for this purpose came to include the British Empire) simply because the rights owner had consented to and been paid for their works to be printed and published abroad.[5] This can be contrasted with the UK law of patents, which at the time was entirely judge made as to matters of infringement, and started from the premise that one could deal in a patentee's goods without infringing his patent where he had put them on the market himself, a premise that was founded on an implied licence theory, and that for such purpose it mattered not whether the patentee had put them on the market in the UK or abroad.[6] Thus for copyright, with the implied licence approach denied it, at least for imports from abroad, the law in the UK took a different approach to that adopted for patents (and subsequently trade marks[7]), to the phenomenon that has come to be

of Books; Booksellers and the English Book Trade, New Haven: Yale University Press, both citing Simon Nowell-Smith (1968), *International Copyright Law and the Publisher in the Reign of Queen Victoria*, Oxford: Oxford University Press.

4 The first such measure was an agreement with Prussia in 1846, whereby each country's books were fully protected under the terms of the other country's domestic copyright legislation

5 See the discussion at paragraph 18.27, and in particular footnote 3 to this, in Laddie, Prescott and Vittoria (2000), *The Modern Law of Copyright and Designs* (3rd edn), London: Butterworths. Some British rights holders were so paid even though they had no rights locally – the Leipzig publisher Tauchnitz paid British authors for the right to reprint their books abroad in paper-bound editions and to sell them there for English speaking travellers, although, as he made clear when he visited Britain in 1843, he had at that time no obligation to make any such payments.

6 *Betts v. Wilmot* [1871] 6 Ch App 239, in which the import in issue was from France, and in which it was said that 'when a man has purchased an article he expects to have the control of it, and there must be some clear and explicit agreement to the contrary to justify the vendor in saying that he had not given the purchaser his licence to sell the article, or to use it wherever he please as against himself'. This still remains UK law – see *Roussel Uclaf v. Hockley* [1996] RPC 441, which also emphasises the difficulty in practice of demonstrating 'a clear and explicit agreement to the contrary' by the practice of labelling products with restrictions on resale.

7 See *Revlon Inc v. Cripps & Lee Ltd* [1980] FSR 85. The law was subsequently changed to preclude parallel importation from outside the European Economic Area, without the express consent of the rights owner, as a result of Directive 89/104/EEC of 21 December 1988 to approximate the laws of Member States relating to trade marks.

known as parallel importation, namely the importation of goods placed on the market abroad by or with the consent of the rights owner. Where express (albeit latterly obscure) language such as that found in the UK copyright statutes precluded parallel importation, implied licence theories had no application.[8] Neither would there have been any great pressure to consider implied licence theories in copyright law in a domestic context – distribution was not a restricted act in UK law until the 1988 Act, thereby allowing Bill Cornish to observe in 1980 that 'United Kingdom copyright law has little coherent to contribute to a comparative discussion of rights over the distribution and subsequent use of copies'.[9]

Against the backgrounds of their differing legal frameworks other countries sought to restrict attempts to use copyright to control the subsequent sale of goods the subject of such rights and that had been put on either the domestic or the foreign market. The United States, initially in a purely domestic context, developed the 'first sale doctrine' as a way of preventing copyright owners from seeking to impose conditions, for example as to resale pricing, that would run with the goods.[10] The German Reichsgericht developed the similar concept of 'exhaustion of rights' in the early years of the twentieth century, and applied it to all intellectual property rights.[11] The doctrine of exhaustion took root in other civil law jurisdictions in Europe, and although it was initially applied in a domestic context to establish so called 'national exhaustion', for some intellectual property rights (notably, trade marks and to some extent copyright) the

---

[8] Although see the discussion at paragraphs 18.27 through 18.49 in Laddie, Prescott and Vittoria, *The Modern Law of Copyright and Designs*, concluding that the implied licence approach would have produced a more satisfactory and consistent result than the twentieth century case law of English, Australian and New Zealand courts that had sought to construe obscure language the origin of which lay in the Copyright Act 1911 as to what constituted a deemed 'infringing copy' in the context of parallel imports.

[9] See page 167 of Spoor, Cornish and Nolan (1980), *Copies in Copyright* (1980) quoted in Bently and Phillips, *Copyright Issues: the Mysteries of Section 18* [1999] *EIPR* 133.

[10] *Bobbs-Merrill Co v. Straus* ([1908] 210 US 339), rejecting analogies with patent law, but coming to a somewhat similar result. The 'first sale' principle there established is now set out in Section 109 Copyright Act, although the degree to which this applies to parallel imports of works the subject of copyright from outside the USA remains controversial – see for example *Omega v. Costco* (9th Circuit, 3 September 2008).

[11] For trade marks *Kölnisch Wasser* (RG, 28 February 1902, RGZ 50, 229) and *Mariani* (RG, 2 May 1902, 51, RGZ 263); for patents *Guajokol-Karbonat* (RG, 26 March 1902, RGZ 51, 139); and for copyright *Koenigs Kursbuch* (RG, 16 June 1906, RGZ 63, 394).

German and other national courts in Europe subsequently extended it to establish so called 'international exhaustion' and thereby permit parallel imports.[12]

The difference between these theories of exhaustion and that of implied licence as applied (primarily in other areas of intellectual property) in the UK 'is that an implied licence may be excluded by express contrary agreement or made subject to conditions while the exhaustion doctrine leaves no . . . rights to be enforced'.[13] The exhaustion doctrine, as subsequently developed in a European Community context to become one of the foundations for the single European market, has been grafted onto these disparate European national approaches, be they based on exhaustion or implied licence, and to the extent that it differs from them overrides them.

2 THE DEVELOPMENT BY THE ECJ OF THE COMMUNITY LAW ON EXHAUSTION AS APPLIED TO IMMATERIAL DISTRIBUTION

The European Court of Justice (ECJ) appropriated the doctrine of exhaustion of rights, or at least its name, to develop a means to limit the degree to which national intellectual property rights could be used to impede cross border trade within Europe in physical goods the subject of such rights and so partition the single market.[14] As interpreted by the ECJ the 'specific subject matter' of the intellectual property right in such cases, and that Community law allowed to be enforced, was limited to the right to place the product on the market for the first time in the Community. However, unlike other types of intellectual property, copyright and related rights can be exploited in ways other than by the distribution of physical goods which incorporate material the subject of such rights – namely by

---

12 For example, as to trade marks see in the Netherlands *Grundig* (Supreme Court 14 February 1956) and in Germany *Maja* (BGH 22 January 1964, GRUR Int 1964, 202) and as to copyright see the discussion in Herman Cohen Jehoram (1996), 'International exhaustion versus importation right: a murky area of intellectual property law' (*GRUR International* 1996-4, pp. 280–284) suggesting at the time that for both Germany and the Netherlands international exhaustion applied if in both the countries of export and import the copyright in issue was in the same hands.

13 Lord Hoffmann in *United Wire v. Screen Repair Services (Scotland)* [2001] FSR 365.

14 The first such decision in the field of copyright was Case 78/70 *Deutsche Grammophon v. Metro* [1971] ECR 0487.

traditional restricted acts such as by performance, broadcasting or cable diffusion, and today, online dissemination over the internet.

In Case 62/79 *Coditel v. Ciné Vog*,[15] the ECJ held that just as the EC Treaty by Article 28 and 30 EC (ex Article 30 and 36) mandates the free movement of goods, it also by Article 49 EC (ex Article 59) mandates the free movement of services and that in the context of so doing it limits the extent to which intellectual property rights can be exercised to the specific subject matter of such rights. However the ECJ then went on to find that the right of a copyright owner and his assigns to require fees for any and all showings of a film was part of the specific subject matter of copyright in this case because:

> 12 A cinematographic film belongs to the category of literary and artistic works made available to the public by performances which may be infinitely repeated. In this respect the problems involved in the observance of copyright in relation to the requirements of the Treaty are not the same as those which arise in connexion with literary and artistic works the placing of which at the disposal of the public is inseparable from the circulation of the material form of the works, as in the case of books or records.

Thus it was consistent with Community law for the rights owner to exercise his copyright to prevent the retransmission of a work in one Member State notwithstanding that the work in question had been picked up and retransmitted after first having been lawfully broadcast in another Member State.

The distinction in the copyright exhaustion context between the restricted act of distribution in relation to physical articles and other restricted acts, such as those of rental and of performance, was emphasised in Case 158/86 *Warner Brothers v. Christiansen*[16] and in Case 395/87 *Ministère Public v.*

---

[15] [1980] ECR 00881. Ciné Vog owned the exclusive distribution and exhibition rights in a film for Belgium. The German copyright owner gave permission for a television broadcast of the film in Germany, which broadcast was picked up by a cable diffusion service operated in Belgium by the *Coditel* companies who then relayed the film to their subscribers in Belgium. Ciné Vog sued the *Coditel* companies for infringement of the rights conferred on them by their exclusive licence.

[16] [1988] ECR 02605. Mr Christiansen ran a video hire shop in Denmark and purchased a video-cassette of a film in the UK that was sold with Warner's consent and imported it into Denmark with a view to hiring it out there. However, Danish law, unlike at the time that in the UK, gave the rights owner the exclusive right to hire such work out to the public. The ECJ, disagreeing with the Advocate General, held that Warner could enforce its rental rights consistently with Community law because by authorising the collection of royalties only on sales to private individuals and to persons hiring out video-cassettes, it is impossible to guarantee to

Tournier.[17] In Case 158/86 the ECJ held that the restricted act of rental was not exhausted by the sale of a carrier and so the rights owner in the country of import could assert its rights to prevent rental of a film on a carrier that had lawfully been purchased elsewhere in the Community, even though it could not use its rights to prevent the mere distribution of the carrier. In Case 395/87 the ECJ held that a rights owner could demand payment for public performance of music recorded on a sound recording carrier imported from another Member State even though the distribution of that carrier could not give rise to any further liability to royalties since the distribution right had been exhausted.[18]

3 IMMATERIAL DISTRIBUTION AND EXHAUSTION IN THE CONTEXT OF THE HARMONISATION OF COMMUNITY COPYRIGHT LAWS

As so developed by the ECJ, Community exhaustion was a flexible doctrine which took account of the economic realities of the particular restricted act in issue. Although this seemed in practice in copyright to limit the application of exhaustion to the restricted act of distribution, it is also fair to say, and as Bernt Hugenholtz has done, having first noted that in arriving at its decision in *Coditel* 'the Court expressly considered that the partitioning of markets along national borderlines in this specific case was legitimate because television broadcasting in the Member States was (then) traditionally organised on the basis of national monopolies' that 'to infer from the *Coditel* decision a general rule of non-exhaustion of performance or communication rights would therefore be unwarranted'.[19]

However, legislation should ideally draw clear lines which are justified

makers of films a remuneration which reflects the number of occasions on which the video-cassettes are actually hired out and which secures for them a satisfactory share of the rental market.

[17] [1989] ECR 02521.

[18] In Cases 55/80 and 57/80 *Musik-Vertrieb Membran v. GEMA* [1981] ECR 0147, the ECJ had held that exhaustion of the distribution right precluded a collecting society in the country of import from claiming a royalty on the basis that the royalty rate it charged was higher than that levied in the country of export.

[19] See p. 24 of Bernt Hugenholz et al. (2006), *The Recasting of Copyright and Related Rights for the Knowledge Economy*, Institute for Information Law, (IViR).

on policy grounds, and in the next stage in the development of Community copyright law, the introduction of harmonising Directives, decisions had to be taken as to how best to deal with the question of exhaustion. In so doing approaches have been adopted which are consistent with ECJ case law, but have gone further, most controversially by precluding Member States from applying international exhaustion[20] but also in where to draw the line between those restricted acts to which exhaustion applies and those to which it does not.

Thus, as to rental, as to computer programs Article 4(c) of Directive 91/250/EEC,[21] and as to copyright works other than computer programs or databases, as well as other subject matter, Article 1(4) of Directive 92/100/EEC[22] make it clear that the rental right is not to be exhausted by any sale or other act of distribution of originals and copies of copyright works or other subject matter. Other Directives adopt a policy that goes further than *Coditel* in making it clear that the delivery by the rights owner of works or other subject matter by means of online transmissions does not exhaust the rights in those works or other subject matter. Thus for copyright (other than that in computer programs or databases) and related rights Recital 29 of the Directive 2001/29/EC[23] asserts:

> 29 The question of exhaustion does not arise in the cases of services and on-line services in particular. This also applies with regard to a material copy of a work or other subject matter made by a user of such a service with the consent of the right holder. Therefore, the same applies to rental and lending of the original and copies of works or other subject-matter which are services by nature. Unlike CD-ROM or CD-I, where the intellectual property is incorporated in a material medium, namely items of goods, every on-line service is in fact an act which should be subject to authorisation where the copyright or related right so provides.

---

20 By virtue of providing for Community exhaustion of the restricted act of distribution as one of the limited list of exceptions, as confirmed by the ECJ in Case C-479/04 *Laserdisken ApS v. Kulturministeriet* [2006] ECR I-8089.

21 Directive 91/250/EEC of 14 May 1991 on the legal protection of computer programs, now replaced by Directive 2009/24/EC of the same name, but where the text formerly in Article 4(c) has been split between Articles 4(1)(c) and 4(2).

22 Directive 92/100/EEC of 19 November 1992 on the rental right and lending right and on certain rights related to copyright in the field of intellectual property, now replaced by Directive 2006/115/EC of the same name.

23 Directive 2001/29/EC of 22 May 2001 on the harmonisation of certain aspects of copyright and related rights in the information society.

This repeats, almost verbatim, Recital 33 of Directive 96/9/EC,[24] adopted five years previously, which had made it clear that exhaustion does not arise in the case of online databases and reflects a policy choice clearly set out in the *travaux preparatoires* for Directive 2001/29/EC,[25] although not one that makes its way into the Articles of the Directive. In contrast Article 3(3) of the Directive, referring to the restricted act of communication to the public of works (Article 3(1)) and the right of making available to the public other subject matter (Article 3(2)), expressly states that these rights 'shall not be exhausted by any act of communication to the public or making available to the public as set out in this Article'.[26]

Both recitals state that exhaustion does not arise in the case of material copies made by the user of the online service with the consent of the rights owner. Some commentators, questioning the practical difference between buying a physical carrier with a copyright work on it, and downloading such work and recording it onto an identical physical carrier, criticise the distinction drawn by these recitals as arbitrary.[27] One compelling response[28] starts by noting that 'even the supporters of the reward theory admit that amongst all possible transaction forms, online exhaustion

---

[24] Directive 96/9/EC of 11 March 1996 on the legal protection of databases. See also Recital 43, as to the *sui generis* database right providing that 'Whereas, in the case of on-line transmission, the right to prohibit re-utilisation is not exhausted either as regards the database or as regards a material copy of the database or a part thereof made by the addressee of the transmission with the consent of the right holder.' However, in Case I ZR 1/02 *Market Surveys* BGH 21 April 2005, [2005] GRUR 940, [2006] 37 IIC 489 the Federal German Supreme Court appears to have taken the view that although downloading a database did not exhaust the restricted acts of extraction or re-utilisation, it could exhaust the restricted act of distribution in that copy of the database.

[25] See the Commission Green Paper *Copyright and Related Rights in the Information Society* (COM (95) 382) and the Commission's follow up to the Green Paper (COM (96) 568), pp. 18–19.

[26] The 1996 WIPO Treaties that established these rights had no such provision, although in relation to the restricted act of distribution that they also established they expressly left open the issue of exhaustion, which is hardly surprising given that Article 6 of the TRIPs Agreement of 1994 expressly also disavows adopting any position on exhaustion. However, the agreed statements at the Diplomatic Conference, note that 'the expressions "copies" and "original and copies" being subject to the right of distribution . . ., refer exclusively to fixed copies that can be put into circulation as tangible objects'.

[27] For example Eric Tjong Tjin Tai (2003), 'Exhaustion and Online Delivery of Digital Works' *EIPR* 207.

[28] Peter Ganea (2006), *Exhaustion of IP Rights: Reflections from Economic Theory* IIR Working Paper WP #06-02.

rules can only be applied to cases which are analogous to purchase at the sales counter', and concludes:

> Exhaustion rules that apply only to a part of the possible online transactions, however, are likely to cause further confusion among online purchasers who are already exposed to a high degree of legal insecurity on the virtual market. What forms of resale should be allowed by the exhaustion rule and what not? May the purchaser of a virtual album resell single music pieces or, in analogy to sale in the CD shop, only the whole album? Which manner of resale should be allowed, sale of tangible CD-R copies, sale through re-transmission etc.? In sum, online exhaustion would raise insecurity and therefore run counter to the basic intention behind exhaustion rules, which is to safeguard smooth market transactions. . . .

It may also be noted that the policy enshrined in these recitals is to a large extent consistent with the situation as it exists, against a different framework of copyright law, in the United States.[29] Neither should it be thought that the harmonisation process has entirely removed the scope for the ECJ to use its discretion in interpreting the EC Treaty to extend exhaustion to apply in a limited way to restricted acts other than distribution of physical articles, such as reproduction, but then only to the extent to which such other restricted acts are strictly ancillary to distribution as permitted under Community law.[30]

4 OPEN ASPECTS OF EXHAUSTION IN COMMUNITY COPYRIGHT LAWS

Despite the extensive treatment of exhaustion both by the ECJ, and in the subsequent network of Directives that have harmonised much of copyright

---

[29] See for example Keith Kupferschmid (1998), 'Lost in Cyberspace: The Digital Demise of the First Sale Doctrine, 16 *J Marshall J Computer & Info* L 825, explaining why, under US law, 'the first-sale exception does not apply to transmissions over the Internet' and recommending that 'Congress should not amend Section 109 so as to include computer-to-computer transmissions within the first-sale exception because broadening the exception in this manner would be extremely harmful to the legitimate interest of copyright owners and would not serve the long-term interests of the public.' See also Justin Graham (2002), 'Preserving the Aftermarket in Copyrighted Works: Adapting the First Sale Doctrine to the Emerging Technological Landscape, *Stan. Tech. L. Rev.* 1, recommending amendment of Section 109 to take account of 'forward and delete' technology.

[30] As in Case C-337/95 *Parfums Christian Dior SA v. Evora BV* [1997] ECR I-6013 and Case E-2/97 *Norway v. Astra Norge* [1999] 1 CMLR 860. See also the German Federal Supreme Court in Case I ZR 256/97 *Perfume Flacon* [2001] IIC Vol. 32, p. 717.

and related rights in the Community, there remain some open issues as to the border between the restricted act of distribution as it applies to physical articles, and to which the doctrine of exhaustion applies, and other forms of distribution or making available, to which it does not.

One such area is that of computer programs, to which, in this and most other respects, Directive 2001/29/EC does not apply. Although Directive 91/250/EEC (now 2009/24/EC) addresses the issue of rental for computer programs it is silent, in view of its age, as to the question of online delivery. It is also not apparent on the face of it, again not surprisingly given its age, how it provides for the restricted act of making available to the public, as mandated by the 1996 WIPO Copyright Treaty. The answer to this, according to the Commission[31] is to interpret the restricted act of distribution in this Directive broadly, so that it is not limited, as in other harmonising Directives, to physical distribution, but also covers online distribution, in a similar way to US law. This means that it can mislead in the context of this Directive to speak of the distribution right being exhausted without qualifying this as applying only to the distribution of physical articles. Also, reflecting its specific sector focus this Directive also has a much more limited list of 'exceptions' than the later copyright Directives – indeed these are hardly exceptions at all in the sense commonly understood in copyright, in that they are only for the benefit of a 'lawful acquirer' (Article 5(1)) or someone 'with the right to use' (Article 5(2) and (3)) and Article 6). This approach reflects the widespread use of licensing in this sector, including 'shrink-wrap' or 'click-wrap' licences for computer programs that are 'sold'.

The widespread association of physical distribution with licensing for computer programs has had an impact on the issue of exhaustion,[32] although the case law here seems to have been exclusively German, and no matters under this (or any other) aspect of this Directive have ever been considered by the ECJ, and no references under it are pending. The leading case is the decision of the German Federal Supreme Court in Case I ZR 244/97 *OEM-Version*[33] in which Microsoft provided its operating systems

---

31 Report from the Commission on the implementation and effects of Directive 91/250/EEC on the legal protection of computer programs (COM (2000) 199) at p. 17, also expressing the Commission's view that the online supply of computer programs does not give rise to exhaustion.

32 Originally set out in Article 4(c) of Directive 91/250/EEC but now separated out into Article 4(2) of Directive 2009/24/EC.

33 BGH 6 July 2000 [2001] GRUR 153, discussed in Christopher Stothers (2007), *Parallel Trade in Europe*, Oxford: Hart Publishing, at p. 52, where it is suggested that if the licence were other than fully paid up the result might differ.

to an intermediate dealer under a contract that required such dealer only to 'distribute and license' such programs with computers and required the imposition of like restrictions down the chain of distribution. The intermediate dealer distributed them to a retailer who in breach of such terms sold the programs on their own to end users. Microsoft's action for copyright infringement against the retailer failed because Microsoft's rights had been exhausted on the sale to the intermediate dealer. A subsequent spate of cases in 2006 in the lower courts considered the status of 'second hand' software, the Munich courts holding that where the computer programs in issue had lawfully been downloaded the rights were not exhausted and so such sales infringed[34] and the Hamburg Court holding that where the computer programs had lawfully been copied from a master disk provided to the distributor the rights had been exhausted and they did not.[35] More recently, however, the Dusseldorf court, noting that most updates to computer programs are downloaded, has taken the view that rights can be exhausted even in physical copies of lawfully downloaded computer programs and in the back-ups that the Directive by Article 5(2) permits to be made of these, provided that no physical copy of any sort is retained by the party 'selling' the software.[36]

An area where the scope of exhaustion under Community copyright laws has only recently arisen is that of encrypted broadcasting. References were made from the English courts in 2008 to the ECJ in Case C-403/08 *Football Association Premier League Ltd v. QC Leisure*[37] and Case C-429/08 *Karen Murphy v. Media Protection Services Ltd*[38] in relation to actions taken to preserve the exclusivity of BSkyB in Premier League football matches in the UK and Ireland, which exclusivity was being undermined by the import into the UK from elsewhere in Europe of decoders and decoder cards that allowed broadcasts of the same matches by broadcasters from elsewhere in Europe to be decrypted. The decoder cards had been issued by the provider of broadcasting services in another Member State on the condition that the cards were only authorised for use in that

[34] Case 7 O 23237/05 LG Munich 19 January 2006 and on appeal OLG Munich 3 August 2006. For a discussion of this and the Hamburg case see Flemming Moos (2006), *The Copyright Minefield of Second-hand Software* 165 *Managing Intellectual Property* 38.

[35] Case Az 315 O 343/06 LG Hamburg 29 June 2006 – copyright was not in issue in the appeal OLG Hamburg 7 February 2007.

[36] Case Az 12 O 431/08 LG Dusseldorf 26 November 2008, discussed in [2009] *EIPR* N48-50.

[37] Referring judgment at [2008] EWHC 1411.

[38] Referring judgment at [2008] EWHC 1666.

other Member State. Although the main questions referred relate to the construction of Directive 98/84/EC[39] (and in particular what actually is meant in it by the expression 'illicit device') other questions referred relate to Directives 2001/29/EC and 93/83/EEC[40] and to Articles 28, 30 and 49 EC. These Articles, the defendants assert, are breached by impeding the free circulation of lawful decoder equipment and cards. They also assert that Article 49 EC is breached by restricting the freedom of customers to receive broadcasts from other Member States, thereby inviting the ECJ to revisit its decision in *Coditel.* The questions referred as to exhaustion will only however arise if those relating to the construction of the Directives are answered in certain ways, and so it is possible that the ECJ may be able to avoid revisiting the issue of exhaustion in these references.

5 CONCLUSIONS

As the degree to which physical carriers are used to deliver content continues to plummet and as online delivery of content increases, exhaustion in a copyright context, in the light of the decisions originally taken by the ECJ and the policy choices subsequently made by the Community legislature, has become ever less important, a trend which can only continue. Indeed even 'downloading' itself in the sense of making a full physical copy of the content starts to seem dated in an era of streaming. Controversies at the edges of the subject, such as that of downloaded computer software, will no doubt continue to exercise lawyers for some time to come, but even they, with the promise, or threat, of 'cloud computing' seem destined for the footnotes of future works that trace the rise and fall of the doctrine of exhaustion in a copyright context. In contrast, in other areas of intellectual property, exhaustion retains its relevance as a policy tool and seems set to do so in the future.[41]

---

[39] Directive 98/84/EC of 20 November 1998 on the legal protection of services based on, or consisting of, conditional access.

[40] Directive 93/83/EEC of 27 September 1993 on coordination of certain rules concerning copyright and rights related to copyright applicable to satellite broadcasting and cable retransmission, which had sought to deal with the problem of broadcasts which could be received outside their intended area by means, within the Community, of a 'country of origin' principle for such broadcasts, allied to harmonisation of the relevant law.

[41] One can contrast this with its use as policy tool in the field of trade marks, in precluding in Europe international exhaustion, where its use has proved much more controversial than in copyright, and as a possible policy tool in patents, where most European countries apart from the UK already have it as part of their

Although the demise of exhaustion in a copyright context would seem to be a worldwide trend its consequences within Europe will be particularly strongly felt. Exhaustion in an era of content delivery by physical carriers facilitated the single European market in copyright works. Its increasing irrelevance is removing one of the policy levers that could have driven this. Its limitations, even in an era of physical carriers, have already driven the process of harmonisation of copyright and related rights,[42] but even this has its limitations, especially when the 'country of origin' principle in a copyright context has been limited to satellite broadcasting and even there has been undermined by the growth of encrypted services. Again as observed by Bernt Hugenholz:[43]

> While EC (case) law has tackled the problem of territoriality head-on for the distribution of physical goods, by establishing a rule of Community exhaustion incorporating intellectual property, policies in respect of online services, as reflected mainly in the Information Society Directive, have been retrograde by leaving the territorial nature of rights of communication basically intact.

The consequences of the territorial nature of the rights of communication are seen in the current controversy over the online licensing of music throughout Europe where, lacking policy levers in copyright law, it has been necessary to bring those of competition policy under Articles 81 and 82 EC into play. If as copyright lawyers we feel uncomfortable with this, we have only ourselves to blame.

Footnote 41 (*cont.*)
national laws, and where US decisions on exhaustion of patent rights and its effect on licensing practices, most notably that of the US Supreme Court in *LG v Quanta*, may have resonance.

[42] Ironically it can be seen in retrospect that it was in part the limitations of exhaustion as a tool for advancing the single market in copyright goods and services that led to the programme of Community harmonisation in this field. For example, exhaustion did not apply to the import of goods from another Community Member State in which they were lawfully on the market not because of the consent of the rights owner but because of shorter term of protection in that State, as established in Case 341/87 *EMI Electrola GmbH v. Patricia Im-und Export* [1989] ECR 0079, a situation which led to Directive 93/98/EEC of 29 October 1993 harmonising the term of protection of copyright and certain related rights, now replaced by Directive 2006/116/EC of the same name. See also the 9th Recital of Directive 92/100/EEC, observing that 'Whereas, to the extent that these activities principally consist of services, their provision must equally be facilitated by the establishment in the Community of a harmonised legal framework.'

[43] See p. 30 of Bernt Hugenholz et al (2006), *The Recasting of Copyright and Related Rights for the Knowledge Economy*, Institute for Information Law, (IViR).

28. Historical appearances and disappearances of formalities: from Berne to national laws

Delia Lipszyc*

1 THE BERNE CONVENTION

The Berne Convention played a substantial role, the results of which are clearly visible in practice, in getting the principle of the absence of formalities as a condition for the grant of copyright protection from the moment during the 1908 Berlin revision when the following provision, that has remained unchanged since, was introduced in Article 5.2: 'the enjoyment and the exercise of those rights shall not be subject to any formality'.

But the situation was different in the original version of the Berne Convention in 1886. That text established the dependence of the protection on the protection established in the country of origin of the work (the subordination of the principle of national treatment to compliance with the conditions and formalities of the lex originis). Thus the right of enjoyment of the rights granted to its nationals by the law of the place of protection was subordinated to compliance with the conditions and formalities prescribed by the legislation of the country of origin of the work.

It was not until the Berlin revision of 1908 that the criterion reverted in favor of the application of the territorial law. On one hand, every condition relating to compliance with formalities was abolished and, on the other hand, the principle of protection independence was consolidated, establishing that the enjoyment and exercise of the rights acknowledged by the territorial law are independent from the existence of protection in the country of origin of the work, except if it is related to duration.

* Professor of Private International Law and UNESCO Chair of Copyright and Related Rights, School of Law, University of Buenos Aires (UBA). This contribution was originally written in Spanish. The original version and the questionnaires referred to in it can be found on the website of the British Literary and Artistic Copyright Association (BLACA): www.blaca.org.

2 FORMALITIES OF NATIONAL LAWS

2.1 The Criterion of a Lack of Formalities was Gradually Imposed in the Doctrine and in the Legislative Evolution

The criterion of a lack of formalities was gradually imposed through doctrine and legislative evolution, leaving behind records inherent in rights originating in the older system of privileges that made possible the censorship of the written word by the government power or, as in the case of England, the Stationers' Company.[1]

The requirement for recording in public registries disappeared from national legislations as a necessary requirement for the existence, maintenance or exercise of copyrights, because it corresponded to an obsolete conception: that of an exceptional protection, destined to avoid that, once disclosed, the work would end up in the public domain, namely that the public would own it and use it in any manner, except when a right was acquired over it through compliance with the formalities enshrined in the law. This notion was displaced by the modern conception of copyright according to which it derives fully in favor of the creator at the very time of creation.

In England, as from the Statute of 1911 no registration or any other formality is required as a requirement for the existence of copyright or for exercising the right in the event of infringement.[2]

In Germany, after the German Empire was founded in 1871, modern legislation adopted at the beginning of the twentieth century (law dated June 19, 1901 regarding literary and musical works and law dated January 9, 1907 relating to artistic and photographic works) did not establish the obligation to fulfill formalities.

---

[1] As a result of a Royal Privilege from 1557, the Stationers' Company had ensured its privilege of censorship of writings and, with it, the monopoly of book publications in the country.

In a detailed study on comparative jurisprudence about the formalities in various countries of Europe, during the nineteenth century, Stef van Gompel considers that, in contrast to the privileges that were merely governmental, the stationers' copyright had a public-private character ('Les formalités sont mortes, vive les formalités! 'The formalities are dead, let the formalities live!' Copyright formalities in nineteenth century Europe and their significance for current discourse', London, conference on Primary Sources on Copyright (1450–1900), 19–20 March, 2008, p. 11).

[2] Cornish, W.R. (1989), *Intellectual Property: Patents, Copyright, Trade Marks and Allied Rights*, London: Sweet & Maxwell, second edition, p. 277.

In the Netherlands, all formalities were suppressed in law dated September 23, 1912, adopted when they signed to the Berne Convention.[3]

2.2 France

In France, the institution of the legal deposit (*dêpot légal*) can be traced back to the sixteenth century, but its functionality went through different stages, in some of which it was a formality to *constitute* rights upon the work, until it was reorganized through law 19 of May, 1925, which suppresses its conditioning effect for an effective exercise of copyrights and to act due to infringements.[4] This law was modified by the law dated June 21, 1943 and, subsequently, by the law of June 20, 1992, although without changing its conservation purposes.

The expression 'legal deposit' – utilized in France when an institution had a constitutive function of the rights over the work as well as the periods when it did not have such a characteristic – is currently used to designate the obligation established by national laws upon publishers of printed works, and in general, upon the producers of the counterparts of works, to deliver one or more counterparts to certain libraries or archives with the main purpose of gathering and preserving the results of intellectual protection developed in the country, to nourish certain libraries or main archives and make them available for the community. Later, I shall return to the difference between the legal deposit and the formalities (registered or non-registered) because

[3] In the response by the Netherlands group to item ten of the questionnaire, it is recalled that in the past the Netherlands copyright system imposed several formalities. The copyright law of 1817 demanded the deposit of three counterparts and a printed mention of the publisher's name, as well as of the place and date of publication, as requirements regarding the origin of the right over literary works. Likewise, the copyright law of 1881 threatened loss of protection if two counterparts of the work were not deposited within a month following publication. Moreover, in order to maintain translation rights, public representation of drama and musical-drama works or the reproduction rights of newspaper articles, the law of 1881 required that all the counterparts carry the clause reserving those rights.

[4] Under the ancient regime of printing privileges, in France the legal deposit had a constitutive character of rights over the work. It was established by virtue of the royal patents established in 1537 by Francis I, as a formality compliance with which was a condition for the granting of protection. In 1790, it was abolished in the interests of press freedom, but it was re-established through law 19 of July, 1793 relating to 'ownership rights' of authors, although as an optional institution. Again it became obligatory by virtue of a decree dated 1810, before being reorganized, particularly by the aforementioned law of May 19, 1925 (see the answers of Laurent Pfister and Frédéric Rideau to the questionnaire about the copyrights history in France, and particularly, of the legal deposit).

this relates to two different institutions that coexist in many countries and are regulated under the same law, but whose purpose and effects are different.

2.3 Other European Countries

In other countries such as Austria, Belgium, Canada, Croatia, Denmark, Finland, Greece, Hungary, Italy, Norway, Sweden and Switzerland, and also in Japan, the legislation never established the obligation of fulfilling formalities as a condition for the enjoyment and exercise of the copyrights, even when the laws foresaw some registrations with different purposes.[5]

Spain, despite the fact that it had been one of the countries that allowed the ratification of the Berlin review to be in force as from September 9, 1910, maintained unaltered the rigor of the formalities established under its copyright law of January 10, 1789, whose Article 36 established: 'In order to enjoy the benefits of this law it is necessary to register the right in the Intellectual Property Registry pursuant to the provisions set forth in the foregoing articles [. . .] The term to verify the registration shall be one year, counted as from the publication date of the work, but the benefits of this law shall be enjoyed by the owner as from the date of publication, and these will be lost if the requirements are not complied with within the year granted for registration'. The lack of registration shall be sanctioned with the provisional or final loss of the right (Article 38: 'Any work not registered in the Intellectual Property Registry may be published again, reprinted by the State, by the scientific corporations or by individuals within the following ten years counted as from the date when the right to register it expired', and Article 39: 'If another year elapses following the ten days without the author or the right holder having registered the work in the Registry, it shall finally and absolutely enter the public domain').

The influence of the Spanish law of 1879 – in force for 108 years[6] – was felt strongly in the Spanish-speaking countries of Latin America, wherein the system of formalities compliance as a condition, in different measures,

---

[5] See *infra*, as well as the answers by the respective national groups to the questionnaire, especially regarding the subject of formalities.

[6] The regime of law 10 of January, 1879 was only superseded by the law dated November 11, 1987, where, although the institution of the general registry of intellectual property continued, the constitutive effect disappeared, as did mandatory registration.

Nevertheless, the force still borne by the registration is manifest for instance in Article 145.3 providing that 'It shall be assumed, except as otherwise evidenced, that the rights registered exist and belong to its owner as determined in the respective registry'.

for the protection or for the exercise of copyright, established deep roots in the national legislations and, in general, was enforceable until relatively recent times.

The assimilation of a copyright to an ownership right over the work, similar to the proprietary rights over material things (real and personal property), the purpose – and value – of which had been to satisfy the just expectations of the creators, providing them with a fundamental right, clear and unequivocal, determined that the registrations constitutive of enjoyment of the exercise or the subsisting of the copyright would be inherent and that the courts and the civil doctrine would analyze them predominantly from the perspective of the civil right.

Likewise, a wrongful assimilation of industrial property rights has existed, which, as we shall see later, was evidenced in the inter-American conventions.

3 DIFFERENT TYPES OF REGISTRATIONS AND FORMALITIES

The registrations, and generally the formalities, are not necessarily contrary to the basic rule of Article 5.2 of the Berne Convention, but always provided they do not constitute a condition for the enjoyment of copyrights, as set forth in Article 154 of the Dominican law: 'the registration is not a substantial condition for the procedural admissibility, or for the enjoyment or exercise of the same'.

Some registrations are useful for the author and its rightholders, but often we find, as in the Dominican provision described above and in other similar ones, that it is worth observing the administrative act, as it gives rise to a presumption *juris tantum* for the details registered and it can therefore be opposed to third parties. It is to be noted in this respect that it is the administrative act that is presumed to be valid as a result of the presumption created by the register. In other words, the assumption deriving from the registration is the validity of the administrative act and not of the contents, because the latter are not subject to examination, in contrast to what happens in the field of patents.

3.1 The Registration as an Assumption of the Constitution and Existence of the Right or of its Survival

This type of registration originates in those established during the time of privileges, when the governmental power granted a temporary exploitation monopoly to printers and booksellers, subject to the condition of having obtained the approval of censorship and registration of the published work.

The registration, as a necessary assumption for the survival and full enforcement of the right, was adopted in Spain during the term of enforceability of the previous law of 1879[7] and in all Latin American legislations that *mutatis mutandis* adopted the principles: Argentina (law 7.092 of 1910, Article 7);[8] Bolivia (law of 1909, Articles 10 to 12); Colombia (law of 1946, Article 88); Costa Rica (law of 1896, Article 53); Cuba (which adopted the Spanish law); Chile (decree-law of 1925 and amendment law of 1949, Article 1); Ecuador (law of 1927, Article 25); El Salvador (law of 1963, Article 77); Nicaragua (Civil Code of 1904, Article 831); Panama (Administrative Code of 1916, Article 1912); Paraguay (law of 1951, Article 58); Uruguay (law of 1937, Article 6); and so on.

And although currently all these countries are members of the Berne Convention, it is worth highlighting that in Uruguay the formalities referring to compulsory registration were recently repealed in 2003 (law 17.616 of January 10, of that year) and in Argentina they are still in force with regard to works published for the first time in the country, despite the fact that both countries ratified the Berne Convention in 1967 through the Minutes of Brussels (1948).

3.2 The Registration as a Requirement for Exercising the Right

This requirement shares the characteristics set out above, because the author has ownership of the title, but in order to exercise it he has to proceed to register the work. This requirement was in force in El Salvador, whose law of 1963 – repealed in 1993 while adopting the law currently

---

7 See Marco Molina, Juana (1997), 'The Registry of Intellectual Property' in Rodrigo Bercovitz Rodríguez-Cano (ed.), *Comments to the Intellectual Property Law*, second edition, Madrid: Tecnos, p. 1840.

8 Law 7.092 of 1910 – first to regulate the matter in Argentina – established that in order for the authors to exercise their rights, the work should be registered within a year following its publication. Non-compliance with the registration obligation within the aforementioned year implied the permanent loss of the rights. Publishers of works published should deposit two counterparts of the work with the National Library, up to 15 days after its publication in the city of Buenos Aires and 30 days after its publication elsewhere in the country. Non-compliance with the deposit within the mentioned term would cause the suspension of the copyright and, in the event that the obligation was not complied with during the following two years, the work would come into the public domain.

This provision was softened in Article 63 of law 11.723 of 1933, suppressing the effect of the work entering the public domain due to lack of registration.

in force – established in Article 77 that 'owners of the copyrights shall justify, for exercising the corresponding civil and criminal actions, except the legal exceptions, having registered the work with the Registry of the Office of Manufacturing Trademarks, Patents of Invention and Literary Ownership'.[9]

3.3 The Registration as a Requirement to Exploit the Published Works in an Exclusive Manner

This is another variation of the foregoing. Even when the author is the owner of the rights, in the event that the publisher does not comply with the registration requirement, exploitation rights will be deprived of their most relevant characteristic, the opposable exclusivity *erga omnes*.

This registry remains in force in Argentina, whose law 11.723 provides in Article 57 that: 'The publisher of works included under art. 1 shall deposit with the National Registry of Intellectual Property three counterparts of all published works, within the three following months'. And Article 63 adds: 'Lack of registration shall bear the consequence of suspension of the copyright until the moment it is carried out, recovering said rights at the time of its registration for the corresponding term and conditions, without prejudice of the validity of reproductions, editions and any other publication performed during the time in which the work was not under registration.'

It is worth reiterating that this registration only refers to proprietary rights and to *published works* and that the obligation is placed upon the publisher. On the other hand, *the registration of unpublished works is optional* (Article 62: 'Relating to unpublished works not published the author or its assignees *may* deposit a copy of the document').

Suspension of the exclusive character of the proprietary right established in Article 63 of law 11.723 if, within three months following its appearance, the registration of the first edition is omitted, when it is carried out in the country, authorizes only exploitation of the work by third parties *as it was* created by the author.[10]

---

9 Also in the United States of America, but as far as possible I shall omit reference to the American system, since this topic is covered by Professor Jane C. Ginsburg in Chapter 30 of this volume.

10 Transformations of the work without authorization by the author are not allowed (translations, adaptations, summaries, etc.), since the effect of the omission of the registration foreseen in Article 63 of law 11.723 is not the entrance into the public domain, not even temporarily. In *Ruiz Vigil, Encarnación v. Producciones Publiexpress*, the National Chamber D of appeals regarding civil matters (October

Such suspension only operates in connection with *national works*[11] and with respect to the author's proprietary rights, namely, it does not have any effect in connection with its personality rights (moral rights), in such a way that if any third party, without the authorization of the author or holder of a right over a work *edited for the first time in Argentina*, reproduces it within the term between the three months following the appearance of that first edition and the day when the registration is carried out, the third party performs an act authorized by Article 63 of law 11.723.[12]

On the other hand, if the third party takes advantage of the situation and introduces any modification to the work or its authorship, or omits the author's name or pseudonym or does not respect the anonymous nature of the work, it engages in the conduct set out in Article 72 (c) of the law and in these circumstance the omission of registration does not produce the consequences foreseen in Article 63 of law 11.723 *when relating to injuries to the moral right*, as it has been repeatedly and peacefully

---

Footnote 10 (*cont.*)
9, 2003, Iuris) highlighted that 'The effect of the suspension of the economic right, authorizes the free utilization without authorization and without payment obligation, namely, to perform reproductions, editions, executions, and any other publication of the work, within the term in which it was not registered. The suspension of the right is produced after the three months granted by the law to carry out the registration have elapsed; the suspension does not authorize third parties to carry out any modification of the work or to omit the name of the author, since it does not affect the powers that constitute its moral right. In this manner the registration does not have the character to constitute copyright but, pursuant to Art. 63, it is a requirement for its exercise in an exclusive way.'

[11] Article 14 of law 11.723, enforceable in absence of treaties with the country of origin of the work, establishes that 'In order to ensure protection by Argentinean law, the author of a foreign work solely needs to accredit compliance of the formalities established for its protection by the laws of the country wherein the publication was made, [. . .]'. It is a regulation similar to that in Article 2.2. of the minutes which originated the Berne Convention.

[12] In some cases, the criminal courts clarified the application of Article 63 as in *Fernández, Rodolfo Ramón v. Procesamiento* (CNCrim. and Correc. Chamber VI, April 24, 2003, cause no. 19.962, Iuris), a decision in which it was recalled that, with regard to the registration of the work with the National Copyright Registry, in a previous cause it was expressed that 'The author of a work – whichever type – has Rights over it as from the very same moment of its creation, this is when it is born. The registration, as it has been stated, is merely declarative and not attributive and consequently it does not condition whatsoever the existence of the individual right aforementioned which is obviously inherent to the act of creation of the work. . .. (Criminal Cassation. Chamber II, cause n° 3105 "*Blaustein, D.*" May 23-2001. In the same sense, see CNCrim. and Corr., Chamber IV, cause n° 18.862 "*Lecouna, R.*", June 11-2002 and Chamber VI, cause n° 27.953 "*González A.*", October 21-1997)'.

expressed in the jurisprudence based on decision *Carchano Oscar E. and another*, (CNCrim. and Correc., October 20, 1961, LL 109-633).[13]

3.4 Voluntary Registrations and other Formalities Not Contrary to the Berne Convention

3.4.1 Registrations with a declarative or evidentiary purpose

Registration with a declaratory or evidentiary purpose do not contradict the principles of copyright and they can be useful for both the author and for third parties.

---

[13] The court made clear that the suspension of the exercise of the right established in Article 63 of law 11.723 does not have any incidence with respect of the protection of the moral right, 'since such prescription evidently cannot refer to the subsequent validity of works published under the conditions of art. 72 (c), namely, works without title or author's name, or with the same changed, nor the validity of works whose text has been vexatiously altered'. The decision also highlights: 'the registration in the Intellectual Property Registry is not, within the system of law 11.723 a "condition sine qua non" for the application of criminal protection. [. . .] The concept of intellectual property covers more than the pecuniary value, and thus it is the right to paternity and harmlessness of the works of the spirit, deserving as much or greater protection than the former. Thus the principle of art. 63 of law 11.723 according to which the lack of registration has the consequence of the suspension of copyright until the time it is done, shall be interpreted referred exclusively, which is also sustained by Mouchet and Radaelli, to the suspension of the pecuniary rights'.

Id. Cresseri, Artidorio, suc. v. SADAIC', CNCiv., Chamber B, May 16, 1977, ED 75-557: 'It is well known that the moral copyright does not originate or caused in the Registration, but in the work, and the sanction due to lack of registration does not reach the loss of the right but only the "suspension" contemplated in art. 63 of law 11.723 in defense of third parties that would have acted in good faith [. . .]. In effect, the work of ingenuity belongs originally to whom created the work independently to the compliance of its registration in the Registry (art. 4°, (1°) and art. 52, law 11.723)'.

Likewise, in *Fernández, Rodolfo Ramon v. Procesamiento* (CNCrim. and Correc. Chamber VI, April 24, 2003, cause no. 19.962, Iuris) the court recalled that 'It fits prima facie in the offense described in item (a) of art. 72 law 11.723, the conduct of who commercialized photostatic copies of books (. . .). The simple partial copy of the work constitutes an anti-juridical behavior. . .' (CNCrim. and Correc. Chamber IV, cause no. 15.044 *Copymar* rta. on 13/2/2001). Also, with respect to the registration of the work in the National Copyrights Registry it has been said that: 'An author of a work – of any type – has rights over it as from the very same moment when it initiates its creation, this is when it is born. The registration, as it has been mentioned, is merely declarative and not attributive and consequently it does not condition the existence of the individual right aforementioned which is obviously inherent to the act of creation of the work. . .' (C.Criminal Cassation, Chamber S II, cause no. 3105 *Blaustein, D.* resolved on 23/5/2001. In the same sense see CNCrim. and Correc., Chamber IV, cause no. 18.862 *Lecouna, R.* resolved on 11/6/2002, Chamber VI, cause no. 27.953 *González A.*, resolved on 21/10/97).

In this type of registration, even if established in an obligatory manner, 'the omission does not harm the copyright' (Article 106 of the Italian law and Article 162 of the Mexican law). Sometimes a pecuniary sanction is established for cases of non-compliance.

In Argentina, law 11.723 distinguishes – although without defining them – between 'published works' and 'unpublished' for the purposes of the obligation for registration. Article 62 establishes in its second part that 'Regarding unpublished works, the author or its assignees may deposit a copy of the document with the certified signature of who performs the deposit'.

This use of the word 'may' demonstrates the *voluntary* character of the *deposit 'in custody' of an unpublished work*, an expression utilized in Article 1 of decree 31.964/39 (issue May 26, 939; B.O. of June 27, 1939). According to the latter, the deposit 'in custody' of unpublished works referred to under Article 62 (in fine) of law 11.723, is carried out in a closed envelope and wax-sealed. Once the deposit has been made accordingly, its content may only be known by court order; it may be returned, always provided that the person who carries out the devolution is the same as the one declared as author in the application of the deposit (decree 71.180/40, B.O. of September 13, 1940).

But this registration is temporary and has to be renewed within 30 days once three years have lapsed after the intitial registration. Through decree 7.616/63 (B.O. of September 12, 1963). The National Directorate of Copyrights (at the time, the Registry) was authorized to incinerate works whose unpublished deposit had not been renewed in this way. Thus, in order to maintain it in force, the deposit 'in custody' of an unpublished work shall be renewed periodically.

Many authors carry out this registration because it is easy to perform and costs little, but they frequently forget that it is temporary and do not renew it, and it is an unpleasant surprises for them to discover when they try to enforce it, that the deposit has been destroyed.

The jurisprudence has acknowledged the voluntary character of the deposit of *unpublished* works and the consequent non-applicability of the extension of the regulations regarding published work to the same.[14]

---

[14] In *Rodríguez, Aurelio v. Lowe Argentina,* CNCiv., Chamber G, May 30, 1989 (libre no. 45.176), the court took into account the voluntary character of the deposit of unpublished works and the subsequent non-applicability of the extension of the regulations of published work to these and highlighted: 'Likewise, since the copyright originates with the creation of the work and not with its registration, the guarantee of such property acknowledged in the Constitution, cannot be affected by an extensive interpretation of some regulations, which are not clearly

At other times, the voluntary character of the deposit of an unpublished work is not taken into account and hence, the tax legislation requires registration in order to have access to certain benefits.[15]

Authors of texts of dramatic works (theater, television, radio, and so on), disclosed but not edited, have attained the implementation of a registry of works *disclosed but not published*, with which they solved a practical problem of undoubted importance.

It is worth pointing out that the deposit of an unpublished work, which is facultative, does not replace that which should be carried out compulsorily pursuant to Article 57 of law 11.723 once the work is published.[16]

One of the most serious issues deriving from this type of registration lies in the fact that the declarations submitted are not always true and, by operation of the law or through the interpretation given to the effects of the registration, in the meantime, an assumption of *iuris tantum* is created against the true author, who does not have the time – or resources – required to produce the evidence that invalidates such an assumption, when the effects inherent in such an administrative act may derive solely from the registration: the subject matter of the work on the date on which the register was entered into. As previously stated, it is the administrative act that is assumed to be valid and not the content, because the latter is not examined.

---

requested in the case (Cam. Civ. Chamber B, E.D. 75-957; Cam. Com. Chamber C 28/VII/1976, *Sociedad ARGENTORES c. Dicon S.A.*)'.

15 For example, law 24.073 on taxes over profits (t.o. 1997, B.O. of 6-8-1997), Article 20, Exemptions, [. . .] j): 'Up to the sum of $ 10.000 per fiscal period, the profits originating in the exploitation of copyrights and the remaining earnings deriving from the Rights protected by law 11.723, provided that the tax applies directly on the authors or their assignees, that the respective works are duly registered in the National Directorate of Copyrights, that the benefit derives from the publication, execution, representation, exposition, alienation, translation or other form of reproduction and it does not derive from works carried out by assignment or acknowledging its origin in a location of the work or of services formalized contractually or not. This exemption shall not apply to foreign beneficiaries'.

16 *Cesani, Pedro E. v. Mortero y Cía. and/or others,* CNCom., Chamber A, October 19, 1989, LL. 1990-B-239: 'the deposit of the unpublished work does not replace the registration of the published one. Consequently, the enjoyment of the intellectual property right is subject to the formality of its registration because the lack of such formality suspends the enjoyment of the intellectual rights. Thus, the published works not registered are not protected (Emery, 'Advertising Agreements. Notions. Modern Issues', L.L. 1984-C, p. 283)'.

Id. in *Cosentino, Antonio v. La Razón S.A.*, CNCiv., Chamber F, August 22, 1977, LL 1978-B-190; the court deemed that the deposit in custody of an unpublished work 'is equivalent to an injunction destined to protect the authorship of the document foreseeing possible extractions'.

The issue was a special concern in the Treaty on the International Registration of Audiovisual Works (Geneva, April 18, 1989), for which reason Article 4, §1 (ii) established an *exception* to the evidentiary effect of the indication entered in the registry, as well as some rules with the purpose of assuring that only truthful statements would be registered.

3.4.2 Registrations referred to personal circumstances of the author, of the work or its utilization

In connection with anonymous works and works with pseudonyms, in Germany the law establishes that the duration of the right is 70 years, counted as from its publication, and in its absence, as from its creation, except when – as provided by Article 66, §2 – within these terms the true name of the author is declared for registration in the registry pursuant to the effect established in Article 138, in which case the duration shall expire 70 years *post mortem auctoris*.

In Austria, we find a similar provision in Article 61, §2.

In Hungary, the copyright law of 2005, in its second paragraph of Article 94/B, establishes voluntary registration, with the effect of assuming *iuris tantum*, of the author's name of the work in the event that it does not appear stamped in the work in the usual manner.[17]

While in Germany and Hungary the registration is in charge of the Patents Office, in Austria it is provided that the notice is made at the author's public registry (*Urheberregister*).

3.4.3 Other formalities admitted

The Berne Convention itself allows a non-registration formality in Article 10*bis* that allows national laws to allow the reproduction of certain articles published in periodicals or that have been broadcast by the written press or radio and television, if all the conditions imposed by the conventional norm have been observed. Amongst these, we find the rule that the use should not have been specifically prohibited by the rightholder.[18] We find

---

[17] See answer to the questionnaire by the Hungarian national group.

[18] The other conditions are: (a) that the national legislation authorizes it expressly; (b) that it relates to current articles; (c) that they refer to subjects of economic, political or religious discussions; (d) that have been previously published by the press or broadcasted through radio, namely, that they relate to a reproduction; (e) that its utilization has not expressly been prohibited by the right's owner. On the other hand, the minutes of Brussels, Article 9, §2, authorized the free reproduction *iure conventionis* of current articles, of economic, political or religious discussions, if the reproduction was not expressly reserved by the owner of the right, but this limitation only referred to the reproduction in the written press.

this provision for example in Austria, where the copyright law establishes in Article 44, §1 that in order to make such publication effective, it is enough to mention that the right is reserved, being attested to below the essay or in the masthead of the newspaper or magazine.

3.5 Formalities Not Related to Registration

We also find formalities not related to registration compliance which may be established or not as a requirement for exercising the right.

3.5.1 As a requirement for exercising the right

When they are established as prerequisites for the exercise of the rights, these requirements are in breach of the Berne Convention because they share the characteristics of the foregoing, as occurs in Argentina in connection with photographic and cinematographic works. The work shall bear the indication of the date, place of publication, and the name or stamp of the author or publisher, according to the third paragraph of Article 34 of law 11.723 because 'non-compliance of this requirement shall not give place to a criminal action foreseen in this Law for the case of the reproduction of such works'.[19]

If the reproduction of a photograph is carried out in a periodic publication and the registration is carried out thereby, the registration benefits the author since the newspaper includes the date and place of publication, as well as the publisher's name.

---

[19] In *Szawarski Daniel v. MTM Video Producciones* and *Szawarski Daniel v. Muñoz Rubén*, CCiv. and Com. de Mar del Plata (Buenos Aires), Chamber II, April 27, 2004, elDial – AA20F2, the court mitigated the scope of the last section of Article 34, while sustaining that the photographic work is protected by copyright and it is included as such in the equity of who acts under the terms of Articles 2, 12 and following of law 11.723 'even beyond not having been subject of registration regulated by Art. 34 (conf. C.Nac.Civ., Chamber I, 15/6/99, in *'J.A.'*, February 16/2000, N° 6181, p. 50). On one hand, the omission of such requirement only bans the criminal action and not the indemnity deriving from the common law (conf. Art. 12), and on the other hand, the perception of the copyright contained in Art. 63, shall be interpreted in a restrictive manner and only referring to, as a rule, to the works which have been subject to a publishing agreement and not to those that have been made public – as in the case of writs – due to their exposition or indiscriminate manifestation (conf. code Belluscio-Zannoni, volume 8, p. 470, N° 2)'.

3.5.2 As an obligation not having effects over the exercise of the right, but foreseeing a sanction in case of breach

On the other hand, some legislation establishes formalities not as an obligation having effects over the exercise of the right, but foreseeing a sanction in case of breach. This is the case in Mexico (a member of the Berne Convention as from 1967), where the Federal Copyright Law establishes the obligation of mentioning in a visible place the reservation 'Rights Reserved', or its abbreviation 'R.R.', followed by the symbol ©, the complete name and address of the owner of the copyright and the year of its first publication. The relevant provisions clarify that the omission of these requirements does not imply the loss of copyright, but the licensee or publisher responsible shall be subject to the sanctions established in the law.

Likewise, in the Dominican Republic – also a unionist country – Article 111 establishes that 'All publishers or any person publishing a work is obliged to indicate, in a visible place, in all counterparts published, including those eventually destined to be distributed free, the following indications: [. . .] 5) The mention to the reserve of copyright, with the symbol ©, accompanied with the owner of the copyright indicating the year of first publication. The symbol, name and year shall be indicated in such a way and in a place that clearly shows that the copyright is reserved; [. . .]'.

3.6 Registration of Acts and Agreements

In general, its purpose consists of the acts and agreements authorizing the exploitation of protected works, and those that in any way confer, modify or transmit proprietary copyrights, deeds of incorporation and by-laws of entities of collective processes of copyrights and related rights as well as their modifications; representation agreements between entities of collective processes of copyrights acting in the country and those acting abroad; general powers of copyright administration and related rights.

The conveyance of *mortis causa* copyrights as well as of injunctions is also recorded in the Registry.

The registration of acts and agreements (conferring true date and content accuracy) relates to the capacity of being opposed *erga omnes* deriving from the publicity granted to the act by the registration. The expression 'publicity', as has been well documented, in these cases does not mean advertising and disclosure, but the possibility of knowing;[20]

---

[20] Lacruz Berdejo, J. L. and Sancho Rebullida, F. de A., *Derecho inmobiliario registral*, Barcelona, 1968, p. 11, cit. by Coghlan, A. R., *Teoría general de derecho inmobiliario registral,* Buenos Aires, Abeledo-Perrot, 1991, p. 15.

'from a formal point of view relating to the disclosure of the contents of the registry, the activity of the entity results as particular and directed solely towards those who pretend the news about the registration'.[21]

Legislations differ regarding the scope of registration of acts and agreements:

Mexico 'Acts, agreements and contracts through which proprietary rights are conveyed shall be registered with the Copyrights Public Registry so that they have effect against third parties' (Article 32). After the agreement has been registered, the registration establishes a presumption of validity of the data entered onto it until proof of the contrary is established even of any registration leaves the rights of third parties unaffected. Should any controversy arise, the effect of the registration shall be suspended while the final resolution is issued by a competent authority' (Article 168), but, not withstanding, 'the acts, agreements or contracts granted or entered into by individuals entitled thereto and entered into the registry, shall not be invalidated in prejudice of a third party in good faith, even though such registration may be annulled subsequently' (Article 169);

Chile (Articles 73 and 74) establishes a similar provision to that of Article 32 of Mexican law, although only with respect to the rights of the author's co-contracting party;

Colombia provides that in order to be valid before third parties, all copyright alienation acts, whether in whole or in part, shall be registered (Article 183);

Venezuela The registration of acts and agreements is optional (Article 105: 'May be registered [. . .]');

Argentina Article 65 of law 11.723 establishes that other circumstances related to the works, such as agreements of which they form the object and the decisions of courts that concern the work, should also be registered.

In turn, Article 66 establishes: 'The Registry shall record all agreements of Edition, translation, purchase and sale, assignment, participation and any other relating to the intellectual property right provided that the works referred to have been published and not contrary to the provisions of this law'.

---

21 Coghlan, A.R., *op. cit.*, p. 14.

Because they derive from a transcribed text, these registrations are voluntary, since the provision does not establish any obligation.

In turn, law 11.723 demands registration in the cases foreseen in the last paragraph of Article 34 ('Assignments in whole or in part of temporary exploitation rights of cinematographic movies shall solely be subject to opposition by third parties as from the time of their registration with the National Registry of Intellectual Property') and in Article 53 ('The alienation or assignment of a literary, scientific or musical work, whether in whole or in part, shall be registered with the National Registry of Intellectual Property; without this requirement it shall not be valid'). It is worth remembering that, with respect to this last provision, Alberto G. Spota points out that that the law establishes that the agreement shall not be 'valid' if it is not registered, using an inadequate expression, since its intention was to refer to the fact that the assignment would not be subject to being opposed before third parties (*erga omnes*).[22]

3.7 Registrations with Authors' Associations

To fulfill their purpose, the authors' associations performing collective acts need a very considerable volume of technical documentation, generic expression that refers to the information regarding authors, publishers and works. This information is expressed in a schematic but complete manner, and refers to the association's own repertoire and to that administered by virtue of the agreement of representation (generally reciprocal, although they may also be unilateral) that concludes with their foreign equivalents.

The quantity and availability of such information have grown significantly as a consequence of the development of the Common Information System (CIS) of the International Confederation of Authors and Composers Societies (CISAC). From 1994-98, this was designed to take advantage of the enormous potential provided by the developments in information technology, such as huge electronic databases and the transmission of

---

[22] Spota, A.G., *Instituciones de derecho civil: Contratos,* Buenos Aires: Depalma, 1981, vol. VI, pp. 340–341.

In *Velich, Emilio R. v. SADAIC and other,* CNCiv., Chamber A, May 15, 1980, E.D. 89-463, the plaintiff had assigned all its rights over the tango 'Rodríguez Peña', but the assignment was not registered with the National Directorate of Copyrights. The court pointed out that 'although art. 53 does not distinguish between the parties and third parties, the requirement solely refers to the latter and not to the contracting parties for which it is valid'.

these on line. The CIS aimed to carry out in a more efficacious way both everyday administration as well as information exchanges among the CISAC associations, effectively utilizing works in a digital environment as well as in the traditional sphere.

4 SUBSISTENCE OF REGISTRATIONS WITH CONSTITUTIVE EFFECTS AND THE APPLICATION OF INTERNATIONAL CONVENTIONS (INEQUALITY 'UPSIDE DOWN')

Since the Berne Convention does not foresee its direct application in the country of origin of the work (Article 5.3) in countries where registrations with constitutive effects or with effects over the copyrights subsist, a situation of inequality 'upside down' occurs: authors of national works are less protected than the authors of foreign works. It is worth asking if this situation may be admitted. In some cases, it was deemed that it may affect the constitutional guarantee of legal equality; in other cases, it highlighted the paradoxical situation resulting from the application of the principle of assimilation of the foreigner to the national if in turn it is not translated into the inverse assimilation, namely, if a national does not enjoy such extensive rights as those accorded to a foreigner.

It has been highlighted that based on the principle of national treatment, a more ample principle has been found: that of non-discrimination between nationals and foreigners arising from the quality of the human right acknowledged to copyrights (Article 27, §2 of the Human Rights Declaration – Paris 1948 – and Article XIII of the American Declaration of Rights and Duties of Man – Bogotá 1948). In those countries whose political constitutions grant foreigners the same civil rights enjoyed by citizens, the question is if the legal consequence of this equality principle is to accord the owners of national works the best rights that apply to their counterparts that hold the title to unionist works.

The possibility that the owners of rights on national works claim the utmost protection enjoyed by authors of unionist works – and the reasons for it – depend on the Constitution of each state and on the effects acknowledged over the internal right to adherence to international treaties.

In Uruguay, motivated by the contradiction between the formalism of the constitutive registration established in Article 6 of the law and the automatic protection adopted in the Berne Convention, Romeo Grompone stated, citing the opinion of Eduardo Jiménez de Aréchaga about the primacy of the international arrangement of internal orders[23] that law no 14.910 of July, 1979, approving the Paris Minutes, had suppressed 'the demand of formalities, in accordance with the dominant criterion that states that the international provision prevails in a hierarchical manner over the internal provision', expressing that, with a general character, 'For the case of provisions that are not included in the foregoing paragraph (provisions exceeding the minimum requirement of the Berne Convention), if a contradiction exists between what has been set forth in the internal law and the provisions set forth in the Berne Convention, the latter shall prevail'.[24]

Subsequently, the Court of Appeals regarding civil matters of the third Section, through a decision dated May 13, 1987, deemed that: 'Regarding the lack of registration in the respective Registry by the author, pursuant to the requirement contained in art. 6 of law 9.739, it is worth to point out that said provision has lost its enforceability through the ratification by Uruguay of the Berne Convention for literary and artistic works by decree-law n° 14.910 dated July 19, 1979 (art. 5)'.[25]

The anomalous 'upside down' inequality motivated the adoption of Resolution 3 at the 36th Inter-American Bar Association/Federación Interamericana de Abogados Conference (Panama, June 17–23): '1. To recommend the Governments of countries of the American Continent that, in those cases where it is allowed by the Constitution, the nationals be granted the copyrights and related rights in conditions not less favorable than those granted by the treaties to foreign authors'.[26]

---

[23] *Public International Law Course*, University of Buenos Aires, vol. I, p. 213.

[24] *Uruguay and the Berne Union (Modifications to law 17 dated December 1937*, Montevideo: AGADU, 1979, pp. 10–11 and 14).

[25] Montevideo, LJU, case 1130, pp. 126–7.

[26] This Resolution adopted in 2000 by the FIA was based on the following recitals, which illustrate well what has been mentioned above: 'That in the western hemisphere, some countries adjust their domestic law to the terms of international treaties prior to or simultaneously with the entry into force of such treaties, while other countries adjust their laws long after the effective dates of the international agreements; and

That, while treaties dealing with copyrights and related rights are based on the principle of equal treatment of nationals and foreigners, frequently such treaties confer rights upon foreigners that are not enjoyed by their own nationals. The result is what might be called "reverse discrimination"'.

5 THE REGISTRATION IN THE INTER AMERICAN SYSTEM

The adherence of Latin American Spanish-speaking countries to the registration constitutive of the right was also reflected in the conventions of the Inter-American system adopted as from 1902, the year of the first diplomatic conference in Mexico, when the actions of the Pan-American bodies start. A series of conferences followed, dealing with numerous matters relating to private international law, and concluding several conventions on copyrights: Rio de Janeiro, 1906; Buenos Aires, 1910; Havana, 1928 and Washington, 1946.

With regards to formalities we find the following provisions, which illustrate the cited adherence:

- In the *Mexico Convention (January 27, 1902)*, the acknowledgement of rights over a work required an application to be submitted to the official department appointed by each government, accompanied by two counterparts; if the author or its assignees wished for the property right to be acknowledged in other signatory countries, they would also attach counterparts of the work corresponding to the number of countries. The relevant official department shall distribute among these countries the counterparts accompanied by a certificate so that the author's property is acknowledged, but the omissions shall not entitle the interested parties to file any claims with the state (Article 4).
- In the *Rio de Janeiro Convention (August 23, 1906)*, international copyright protection is regulated jointly with industrial property (literary and artistic property and patents of invention, drawings and industrial models and manufacturing and commercial trademarks) constituting a Union of the Nations of America, creating offices, under the name of the International Bureau for the Protection of Intellectual Property (BIPRI), one in Havana (for countries in North America, Central America and countries of north South America) and the other one in Rio de Janeiro (for the remaining countries of South America), in order to centralize the registration of literary and artistic works, patents, trademarks, drawings and models, and so on, registered in each of the signatory nations, in accordance with the respective treaties, and for purposes of their validity and acknowledgement in the other countries. This registration is merely optional for the interested party, who remains free to request, on its own or through an attorney, registration in each of the states in which it requests protection (Article II). The offices mentioned have

never operated, which is not odd, taking into account that only nine countries ratified the Convention.

- The *Buenos Aires Convention (August 11, 1910)* introduces the obligation to mention the reservation of the rights as a condition for maintaining the copyrights (Article 3).
- The *Havana Convention (February 18, 1928)* was destined to replace the Buenos Aires Convention (1910). It constitutes a revision of the latter, from which most of the provisions were taken, although with several important modifications. Regarding formalities, they are increased, establishing that the mention to reserve property shall include the name of the person in whose favor this reserve is registered, as well as the country of origin of the work (that or those wherein simultaneous publications have been carried out) and the year of first publication (Article 3).
- The *Washington Convention (June 22, 1946)* – destined to replace that of Buenos Aires, revised in Havana – with regard to formalities, suppresses the mention of the right's reserve (Article 9) although it promotes the use of the expression 'Rights Reserved' or its abbreviation 'D.R. (in Spanish)', clarifying that 'it shall not be interpreted as a condition for the protection of the work in accordance with the terms of the herein Convention' (Article 10)

All this international activity was characterized by several obstacles. Certainly not least important amongst these were the difficulty to make the legal systems of the Latin American countries compatible with those of the United States, and the lack of interest of the United States and other countries on the Continent to adhere to these conventions even if they often participated actively in the drafting of the conventions and in their preparatory work. Various efforts made to achieve a convention that would attain a Pan-American character succeeded each other, but they did not reach their goal.

The Buenos Aires Convention, the only one incorporating a considerable number of countries including the United States of America, suffered from the absence of Argentina and Chile until the 1950s, by which time its importance had frankly started to decline due to the advent of the Universal Convention (Geneva, 1952).

6 THE UNIVERSAL CONVENTION

These two big systems, the Berne Convention to which European countries belonged along with their colonies of Africa and Asia, and the members of the Commonwealth, and that of the Conventions of the Inter-American System coexisted separately in their respective areas of influence.

Even though, from the originating minutes of 1886, the Berne Convention had expressed its universal vocation to remain open to the adherence of all the states (Article 18) without discriminating against any political or religious expressions, it was the result of a European initiative and, for the time being, it dealt with an act that only linked European countries and its more ample extension to other continents, at least immediately, could only be achieved through the 'colonial clause'.[27] Thus, it was considered to be a treaty which was essentially European, destined for the protection of works among Europeans. Such prejudice subsisted in America until relatively recent years up to the point that, during its first 80 years of enforceability, the Convention only received the adherence of Haiti (which subsequently denounced it, so it was applicable only between 1887 and 1943), of Brazil and Canada, which have been members since 1922 and 1928, respectively.

For its part, the conventions of the Inter-American system were, on the one hand, closed to the adherence of extra-continental countries, and on the other, neither did they satisfy the American countries (until the 1950s, Argentina and Chile, with a high publishing activity, had not ratified the Buenos Aires Convention, executed in 1910).

The coexistence of the Berne Convention – which was not able to become universal – and the Inter-American Conventions determined that, at least since 1928, the idea of unification would start to be promoted.[28]

But the efforts carried out did not render positive results until 1947, when UNESCO took up the initiative of unification and universality again. It was a particularly fitting time because the Second World War had just finished and neither of the two hegemonic powers that resulted had ratified either the Berne Convention or the Conventions of the Inter-American System. The United States of America had only adhered in 1908 to the Mexico Convention and in 1911 to the Buenos Aires Convention. In turn, the freedom of the European and Asian colonies threatened to reduce the context of territorial enforceability achieved by the Berne Convention, since the new states were not deemed, in principle, to be bound by treaties in which they had been included through the 'colonial

[27] De Sanctis, Valerio, 'Development and International Enshrinement of Copyrights', translation by Juana Martínez Arretz, *RIDA*, January 1974, p. 230.

[28] During the sixth vote of the conference of revision of the Berne Convention carried out in Rome (1928), concerns about integrating both systems were officially stated.

clause' and its applicability depended on a subsequent attitude of confirmation or denouncement.

After seven years of preparation (during which expert meetings were held in 1947, 1949, 1950 and 1951), on September 6, the works of the international conference summoned by UNESCO in Geneva were completed, with the adoption of the Universal Convention.

But two great obstacles had hindered the way towards the Universal Convention: on the one hand, a fear that a massive desertion of the Berne Convention towards the new instrument would be significant – and less demanding – and on the other hand, the insistence, especially of the United States of America – a country that had been providing decisive political support for the project – on maintaining certain fundamental principles of their own legislation, among them, that referring to the compliance with formalities.

It was during the third meeting of the Expert Committee (Washington, October–November, 1950) where the proper mechanisms to overcome these two great obstacles were designed: the 'Protection Clause of the Berne Convention'[29] and the simplification of formalities through the

---

[29] Article XVII sets forth that the Universal Convention shall not affect the provisions of the Berne Convention or the fact of belonging to the Union created by the same. With such a purpose, the Convention institutes two mechanisms destined to avoid desertion, which is established in the Attached Declaration relating to Article XVII:

(1) the Universal Convention shall not apply to relations among States bound by the Berne Convention in matters referring to protection of works that, in accordance with the latter, may have as country of origin one of the countries of the Berne Union (§b), and
(2) the works that according to the Berne Convention have as country of origin a country which, after January 1, 1951 has withdrawn from the Union created by the same, shall not be protected by the Universal Convention in the countries of the Union of Berne (§a).

Consequently, based on the general principle that the Berne Convention shall not be affected by the Universal Convention, two consequences derive: the predominance of the Berne Convention in the relations among states that from part of the two Conventions and the non-application of both to works originating in countries that have withdrawn from the Berne Union subsequent to a certain date.

These provisions set forth that the Universal Convention was not created to substitute for the Berne Convention or other multi- or bilateral conventions and the purpose pursued was not either to compete with the Berne Convention, but to achieve that countries would be excluded from the international copyright protection system; for such purpose; the reluctant countries were allowed to become part of the Berne Union through their adherence, as a first stage, to a convention less

symbol ©, but not as a condition for the enjoyment of the exercise of the right but for considering the fulfillment of formalities – such as deposit, registration, mention, notarial certificates, payment of fees, manufacture or publication within the national territory – established in the national legislation.[30] The symbol © was proposed by North American experts and had the precedent the 'mention of reserve' ('copyright notice') established in Article 19 of Title 17 (regarding Copyrights) of the US Code.

Simplification of formalities meant a reciprocal sacrifice for both groups of countries: for the American republics, it meant a rupture with systems of formalities deeply rooted and long maintained (for the United States particularly, it represented leaving aside the strict requirements regarding the copyright notice, registration, deposit and manufacture clause); for the countries of the Berne Union, the acceptance of the symbol © also meant an important concession, since from the revision of Berlin (1908), not being subject to formalities (the principle of automatic protection) was an essential part of the Berne Convention System.[31]

The symbol © continues to be systematically inserted, although the

---

demanding regarding the level of protection, assuring the copyrights and more fitting to their legal traditions to reach, in the future aiming for adherence.

As pointed out by Carlos A. Villalba, 'finally, the Universal Convention pursued the purpose of harmonizing existing legislations, regardless of their level. For such purpose, all fundamental intentions for attaining a uniform legislation or any intent in search of an upgrade of the degree of protection were abandoned. It fulfilled its purpose of harmonizing different conventions, arrangements or treaties about the matter. On this basis it complies with one of the historic principles: the universality of the system.' ('Introduction to international treaties regarding', *Industrial Property*, revised edition, Buenos Aires: Depalma, 1980, pp. 331–49).

[30] In accordance with Article III, 'every contracting State that, pursuant to its internal legislation, requires as condition for the protection of the copyrights, compliance of formalities such as deposit, registration, mention, notarial certificates, payment of fees, manufacture or publication within the national territory' assumes the commitment of considering such demands satisfied with respect to any work protected by the Convention, if, as from the first publication of such work, 'all the counterparts published with the authorization of the author or any other owner of the rights, shall bear the symbol © accompanied by the name of the owner of the copyrights and the indication of the years of its first publication' (§1).

This provision shall not prevent that the contracting states demand compliance with formalities with respect to 'works published the first time in its territory or of works of its nationals wherever they are published' (§2). But none of the formalities is enforceable with respect to unpublished works included within the context of the Convention (§4).

[31] See Ricketson, Sam and Ginsburg, Jane C. (2006), *International Copyright and Neighboring Rights: The Berne Convention and Beyond*, Oxford: Oxford University Press, p. 1186, §18.23.

applicability of the Universal Convention has been reduced substantially: from the 100 countries that are members currently, nowadays the only case in force is that of those countries which are not part of the Berne Union: Burundi, Cambodia (although these two countries form part of the TRIPS Agreement of the WTO, which incorporates through reference the substantial provisions of Berne, except for Article 6*bis*) and the Lao People's Democratic Republic (known as Laos).

Even Mexico, which became a member of the Berne Union in 1967 and whose Copyright Federal Law provides that 'The acknowledgement of copyrights and related rights does not require the registration or any document of any kind, nor shall be subject to fulfillment of any formality' (Art.5), establishes ahead – as we have seen – in Article 17 the obligation of the copyright notice, even though its omission does not have effects over the existence of the copyrights. Similarly, for Dominican Republic – also a unionist country – in Article 111.

7 LEGAL DEPOSIT AND FORMALITIES: DIFFERENCES

As has been said, the majority of national legislations make the publishers of printed works and generally, the producers of the counterparts of the works – whether natural persons or private or public organizations – responsible for the obligation[32] of delivering one or more counterparts, regardless of the formats in which they are submitted,[33] to designated libraries or archives, with the main purpose of gathering and maintaining the results of the intellectual production carried out in the country, to nurture therewith certain libraries – even those of a national university – or main archives and to make them available to the community. The delivery may be made directly to such libraries or archives through a legal

---

32 Except in the Netherlands, where the legal deposit is not obligatory and the national collection of deposit has been constituted through voluntary deposit agreements between the national library (*Koninklijke Bibliotheek*) and the publishers (see http://www.ifla.org/IV/ifla64/021-141e.htm, cited by Richard Uribe and Robert Max Steenkist (2005), *The Legal Deposit in Latin American Countries in 2005. Its Regulations and Enforceability: Comparative Statistics*, Bogotá: CERLALC, p. 8).

33 Library material (books, magazines and journals, micro formats, scores, maps, leaflets, opuscules, etc.), audiovisual material (sound recordings, films, video, etc.), electronic publications (see Jules Larivière (2000), *Legislation on Legal Deposit: Guidelines, Revised Edition, Augmented and Updated as of Publication of 1981 of Jean Lunn*, Paris: UNESCO, CII-00/WS/7, p. 3).

deposit center or through the National Registry of Copyrights or another official body.

But as highlighted, even if they are included in copyright laws, and where enforceability may be imposed by administrative coercive laws or by the threat of sanctions in case of breach, these provisions about *legal deposit* are not really provisions about copyrights but prescriptions regarding the administration of culture.[34]

Provisions about legal deposit exist in the majority of countries. The International Federation of Library Associations and Institutions (IFLA)[35] identifies several models of legal provisions regarding legal deposit,[36] and it considers a special law dealing with the matter the most usual arrangement (Germany, Austria, Belgium, France, Greece, Indonesia, Norway, Peru, South Africa, Sweden). In countries such as Germany, Belgium, Canada, Japan and Nigeria, the registration of the legal deposit is contemplated within the legal provisions that govern national libraries. In other countries, the legal deposit has the form of administrative decrees or ordinances (Chile, Cuba, Nigeria).

In several countries, the legal deposit is included in legal provisions governing other matters, for example, copyrights, as in Italy and the United Kingdom, without the obligation to submit said deposit of counterparts being a condition of the origin of copyright protection, even when fulfillment of the respective provisions may be imposed by administrative coercive measures or by the threat of sanction in the event of breach. This is manifest in Article 106 of the Italian law, which expresses in its §1 the concept that the omission of the legal deposit will not affect the grant of copyright in the work or its exercise, as set out in Title I of the law (provisions on copyright). For Dietz, this is evident even more before the fact that, according to §2 of the same article, the omission of the deposit shall prevent the acquisition and exercise of copyrights over works referred to under Title II of the law (provisions on rights relating to the exercise of copyrights).[37]

Also the law of Dominican Republic foresees in Article 161 that 'compliance of the obligation of the legal deposit, pursuant to the provisions in this law, is a prior indispensable requirement for the registration of the works and phonograms that shall be deposited, which shall be evidenced with the corresponding receipts. Breach of the legal deposit obligation

---

34 Dietz, Adolf (1983), *Copyrights in the European Community*, Madrid, Ed. Ministerio de Cultura de España, pp. 75–76.

35 http://www.ifla.org

36 Uribe and Steenkist, *supra.*

37 Dietz, *supra.*

shall give place to a sum equivalent to ten (10) times the commercial value of the counterparts that were not deposited, payable jointly and severally by those persons obliged by such deposit, but it shall not limit the exercise of the rights granted in the herein law'. Previously, the same law clarifies in Article 156, subparagraph, that the legal deposit 'does not prevent the enjoyment or exercise of the author's and related rights acknowledged in the herein law'.

The legal deposit does not have any registration effects, although in some countries both obligations (legal deposit and registration) are imposed in the same provision, in a non-differentiated manner, for example in Argentina and Nicaragua.

In Costa Rica, both obligations are attested to in the same regulation (Article 106 of law 6.683 of 1982, modified by law 7.979 of January 31, 2000), but a distinction is made between the legal deposit that has to be carried out, on the one hand, in each of the eight institutions to receive a counterpart and, on the other hand, registration with the respective entity: 'All persons, physical or legal, public or private, responsible of reproducing a work through printed, magnetic, electronic, electromagnetic or any other means, shall deposit, during the eight days following the publication, a counterpart of such reproduction in the following: libraries of the Universidad Estatal a Distancia, Universidad de Costa Rica, Universidad Nacional, Asamblea Legislativa, Biblioteca Nacional, del Ministerio de Justicia y Gracia, la Dirección General del Archivo Nacional, el Instituto Tecnológico de Costa Rica and the Registro Nacional de Derechos de Autor y Derechos Conexos. The counterpart for the aforementioned registration shall be accompanied with the documents of receipt of the other institutions. Non compliance with any of these entities shall be sanctioned with a penalty equivalent to the total value of the reproduction'.

In Argentina, the intellectual property law in Article 57 provides: 'The publisher shall deposit the works included in art. 1 with the National Registry of Intellectual Property, three complete counterparts of every published work, within the three months following its appearance. If the edition is a luxury edition or if it does not exceed 100 counterparts, only one counterpart deposited shall be enough'. Decree 41.233/34 regulating the law clarifies in Article 17 that the publishers shall carry out the deposit through the submission of three complete counterparts, one for the National Library, one for the Library of the Congress of the Nation and the third one, accompanied by the receipts for the first two and for the corresponding application, in the Intellectual Property Registry. Subsequently, one more counterpart was added for the General Archive of the Nation (decree 3.079 of 1957) and it was provided that the receipt of all counterparts shall be carried out with the Copyrights National Registry.

Nevertheless, the destination of those four counterparts is different: three are destined to fulfill the obligation of the legal deposit and the remaining one is destined to comply with the registration obligation.

In other Latin American countries, the regulations on legal deposit and registration are established in different laws, as for example, in Venezuela, Bolivia and Mexico.

- In Venezuela, the law of legal deposit dated September 3, 1993 imposes an obligation on publishers, small producers (authors) and distributors to deposit with the National Library Autonomous Institute (Directorate of Collections, Legal Deposit Division) two counterparts of all books, leaflets, periodic publications, non-bibliographic and audiovisual material published in the country, a deposit that is independent from the one carried out with the registration office pursuant to Articles 103 to 107 of the law in copyrights.
- In Bolivia, supreme decree 28.598 of January 19, 2006 regulates the legal deposit regime that places an obligation to submit, gratuitously, a pre-determined number of counterparts of all publications, whether textual, graphical, sound, audiovisual, electronic or motion image documents, to be preserved, organized, served and disclosed at the central offices of legal deposits appointed for such purpose: the Archive and National Libraries in Bolivia, the Bolivian Cinematheque, the National Repository and the Military Geographical Institute. These deposits are independent of the registration established in copyrights law (Article 63 of law 1.322 for copyrights dated April 2, 1992).

  The utilization of the expression 'registration' in the regulations of legal deposit frequently causes confusion in both institutions, although the institution in charge of receiving the legal deposit shall bear a registration (an official nomination) of who receives it.

- In Mexico, the presidential decree dated July 8, 1991 sets forth an obligation on all publishers and producers of bibliographic materials and documentaries, edited and produced in the country, to contribute to the integration of the cultural patrimony of the nation, which is complied with by the delivery of counterparts of each of the editions and productions of their works, to the National Library and the Library of the Congress of the Union, of two counterparts of books, leaflets, magazines, newspapers, maps, musical scores, posters and other printed materials with cultural, scientific and technical contents, and of one counterpart of microfilms, slides,

> discs, diskettes, audio and video cassettes and of other audiovisual and electronic materials containing information with the characteristics mentioned. The materials cited shall be delivered to the libraries mentioned within 30 days following the date of their publication or production, with the exception of periodic publications, which shall be submitted as soon as they are released. The General Directorate of Copyrights shall agree with the libraries that receive the legal deposit the supervision of compliance of the same, fixing penalties in case of breach.

It is worth pointing out that the legal independent deposit of the registration corresponding to copyrights, even if it lacks registration effects, may be useful as an evidentiary mechanism in actions of plagiarism and other processes, for example, to evidence the fact of publication and the assumptions deriving therefrom pursuant to Article 15 of the Berne Convention, or the year of publication, information about the publisher and generally, whoever claims ownership of the right over the work or its publication, or to prove that the work was originally published or to prove the fact of forgery of a 'pirate' edition when comparing it with the legitimate counterpart submitted to the library or archive for purposes of legal deposits.

These proofs can also be obtained from various other sources, among them, evidence arising from the registration of acts and agreements, and also from the registers of the collecting societies.

29. Formalities in the digital era: an obstacle or opportunity?

Stef van Gompel*

1 INTRODUCTION

For a very long time in the history of copyright, the coming into existence and/or the exercise of copyright was subjected to formalities of some kind. The first modern laws on copyright, including the 1710 UK Statute of Anne, the 1790 US Federal Copyright Act and the 1791 and 1793 French *droit d'auteur* decrees, all imposed formalities. To enjoy copyright protection or to enforce the right before courts, these laws required authors or copyright owners to register their copyrights, to deposit copies of their works or to mark these copies with some kind of copyright notice.[1] These statutory formalities were maintained in later copyright acts, not only of the states just mentioned, but of nearly all countries worldwide.[2]

---

* Ph.D. candidate, Institute for Information Law, University of Amsterdam; LL.M. University of Amsterdam (2005). You are invited to direct any comments, criticism or ideas on this paper to: vangompel@ivir.nl.

[1] See secs II (registration) and V (deposit) of the Act for the Encouragement of Learning (1710), 8 Anne, c. 19 (UK); secs 1 (renewal registration), 3 (registration and publication of a copy of the record of entrance in US newspapers) and 4 (deposit) of the US Federal Copyright Act of 31 May 1790 (1st Cong., 2nd Sess., c. 15); and art. 6 of the French Decree of 19–24 July 1793 on the property rights of authors of writings of all kind, of music composers, of painters and of designers (deposit). The French Decree of 13–19 January 1791 on theatrical plays required authors who wished to retain a public performance right in their plays, to publicly announce this by a notice, which should be deposited with a notary and printed in the text of the play. The 1791 Decree, however, was repealed by the Decree of 1 September 1793 and the prescribed formality did not reappear in later acts.

[2] Examples are Germany, the Netherlands, Italy, Spain, Australia, Canada, Japan and most Latin-American countries. For a state-of-the-art overview of copyright formalities in national copyright law in the 1850s, 1900s and 1950s, see A.W. Volkmann (1855), *Zusammenstellung der gesetzlichen Bestimmungen über das Urheber- und Verlagsrecht: Aus den Bundesbeschlüssen, den deutschen Territorialgesetzgebungen und den französischen und englischen Gesetzen,*

Around the end of the nineteenth century, however, a number of states, particularly those in continental Europe, began to limit imposing formalities on authors or to soften their nature and legal effects.[3] This ultimately resulted in the complete abolition, in some states, of all formalities (for example in Germany in 1907).[4] Additionally, at the international level, the prohibition on formalities was introduced with the 1908 Berlin revision of the Berne Convention for the Protection of Literary and Artistic Works (BC). Article 4(2) BC (1908) – currently Art. 5(2) BC (1971) – reads: 'The enjoyment and the exercise of these rights shall not be subject to any formality [. . .].'[5] Since 1908, therefore, states adhering to the Berne Convention were required to automatically grant copyright to works of other contracting states. This induced most signatory countries to the Berne Convention to remove all formalities and grant unconditional protection to all works of Berne Union authors, irrespective of their origin.[6] Consequently, formalities were removed, for example in the UK in

---

Footnote 2 (*cont.*)
Leipzig: Polz, pp. 132–36; Ernst Röthlisberger (1904), *Der interne und der internationale Schutz des Urheberrechts in den verschiedenen Ländern: Mit besonderer Berücksichtigung der Schutzfristen, Bedingungen und Förmlichkeiten*, Leipzig: Börsenverein der Deutschen Buchhändler; and 'Formalities for acquisition, maintenance and transfer of copyright', in H.L. Pinner (ed) (1953–60), *World Copyright: An Encyclopedia*, 4 vols, Leyden: Sijthoff, II (1954), pp. 672–703.

[3] Stef van Gompel (2010), '*Les formalités sont mortes, vive les formalités!* Copyright formalities and the reasons for their decline in nineteenth-century Europe', in Ronan Deazley, Martin Kretschmer and Lionel Bently (eds), *Privilege and Property: Essays on the History of Copyright*, Oxford: Open Book Publishers.

[4] In Germany, all formalities were abolished, for literary and musical works, by the Act Concerning Copyright in Literary and Musical Works of 19 June 1901, *RGBl.* 1901, 227 and, for artistic works and photographs, by the Act Concerning Copyright in Artistic Works and Photographs of 9 January 1907, *RGBl.* 1907, 7.

[5] Because the Berne prohibition on formalities has been incorporated by reference in both the TRIPS Agreement (art. 9(1) TRIPS) and the WIPO Copyright Treaty (art. 1(4) WCT), it has largely become the norm at the international level. Only the Universal Copyright Convention (art. III UCC) allows contracting states to subject international protection to a prescribed notice requirement (i.e. the symbol © accompanied by the name of the copyright owner and the year of first publication).

[6] There are obvious reasons for contracting states not to just abolish formalities for foreign works, but to grant unconditional protection to all works, regardless of their origin. Besides the clear and understandable antipathy to grant foreign authors more rights than domestic authors, it would make little sense to require national authors to continue with formalities, because they could always choose to publish their works in another Berne Union country which had eliminated formalities. This would allow them to claim protection in their own country under the

1911,[7] in the Netherlands in 1912[8] and in France in 1925.[9] Other countries followed, some of them later, some of them much later. Uruguay, for instance, did away with all mandatory copyright formalities in 1979,[10] Colombia in 1982[11] and Spain in 1987.[12] The US did not abandon formalities as a prerequisite for protection until 1989.[13]

Accordingly, just around the time of the transition to the digital era, copyright formalities had been abolished in practically all countries around the globe. The digital revolution, however, caused a paradigm shift in the way copyright protected content is produced and consumed. While, in the pre-digital era, all content was locked up in physical information products and the cost of dissemination was high, the current digital networked environment allows for interactive, simultaneous and decentralized production and access. In addition, as digitization has considerably lowered the cost of production, storage and distribution, content goods have never before been made available to the public on such a large scale.[14] In view of that, there is an increased need for more legal certainty concerning the claim of copyright, for an improved rights clearance and for an enhanced free flow of information. It has been suggested that copyright formalities are able to meet these current needs. In the last decennium, this idea has encouraged several academics to call for a reintroduction of formalities in copyright law.[15]

Berne Convention without the need to comply with their own domestic formalities. See Stephen P. Ladas (1938), *The International Protection of Literary and Artistic Property*, 2 vols, New York: Macmillan, I, p. 275.

7 Copyright Act (1911), 1 and 2 Geo. V, c. 46 (UK).

8 Act of 23 September 1912 containing new regulation for copyright, *Stb.* 1912, 308 (the Netherlands).

9 Act of 19 May 1925, *Journal Officiel* of 27 May 1925 (France).

10 Law No. 14.910 of 19 July 1979 (Uruguay).

11 Law No. 23 of 28 January 1982 on Copyright (Colombia).

12 Law No. 22/1987 of 11 November 1987 on Intellectual Property, *Boletin Oficial del Estado*, no. 275, of 17 November 1987 (Spain).

13 Berne Convention Implementation Act of 31 October 1988, Pub. L. No. 100-568, 100th Cong., 2nd Sess., 102 Stat. 2853 (US). This act became effective on 1 March 1989.

14 James Gibson (2005), 'Once and Future Copyright', *Notre Dame Law Review*, 81, 167–243 (pp. 212 et seq.).

15 The reintroduction of formalities has been called for, inter alia, by Lawrence Lessig (2001), *The Future of Ideas: The Fate of the Commons in a Connected World*, New York: Random House, pp. 251–52; (2004) *Free Culture: How Big Media Uses Technology and the Law to Lock Down Culture and Control Creativity*, New York: Penguin Press, pp. 287–90; and (2008) *Remix: Making Art and Commerce Thrive in the Hybrid Economy*, New York: Penguin Press, pp. 260–65; William M. Landes and Richard A. Posner (2003), 'Indefinitely renewable Copyright', *University of*

Unsurprisingly, the recent calls for a reintroduction of formalities are surrounded by quite some controversy. Although there are surely good reasons to reconsider imposing formalities, opponents of the idea claim that formalities have not been removed for nothing.[16] This raises the question which of these reasons in the present digital age should prevail. Put differently, the question is whether the historical issues with formalities are still relevant at present and, if so, how they weigh up against the opportunities that formalities can bring in the digital era.

To examine this question, this paper first considers the new challenges for copyright that have come to the fore in the digital environment (Section 1) and scrutinizes whether formalities may help with facing these challenges (Section 2). It reaches the conclusion that formalities can fulfil a useful role in this respect. Subsequently, the legal-historical concerns that in the previous centuries caused the abolition of formalities are introduced (Section 3) and contextualized (Section 4). It will be shown that, although some of the historical concerns may still apply at present, they do not completely militate against formalities. Moreover, digital networked technologies have made it entirely feasible to establish registration and deposit schemes. Therefore, it appears that the legal-historical concerns do not impede the reintroduction of formalities altogether.

Accordingly, this paper queries whether the absence of formalities in copyright law should perhaps be perceived as a temporary phenomenon only. It proposes that it might be time to set aside some of the legal-historical objections against copyright formalities and to look ahead at how formalities could be deployed to meet the challenges that copyright faces today.

Footnote 15 (*cont.*)
Chicago Law Review, 70, 471–518; François Lévêque and Yann Ménière, *The Economics of Patents and Copyright*, Berkeley Electronic Press, p. 105; Christopher Sprigman (2004), 'Reform(aliz)ing Copyright', *Stanford Law Review*, 57, 485–568; Cecil C. Kuhne III (2004), 'The steadily shrinking public domain: inefficiencies of existing copyright law in the modern technology age', *Loyola Law Review*, 50, 549–563; Gibson (2005), *supra*; Kevin A. Goldman (2006), 'Limited times: rethinking the bounds of copyright protection', *University of Pennsylvania Law Review*, 154, 705–740; and Pamela Samuelson (2007), 'Preliminary Thoughts on Copyright Reform', *Utah Law Review*, no. 3, 551–71, at 562–63.

16 See e.g. Arthur Levine (1995), 'The End of Formalities: No More Second-Class Copyright Owners', *Cardozo Arts and Entertainment Law Journal*, 13, 553–557; Irwin Karp (1995), 'A Future Without Formalities', *Cardozo Arts and Entertainment Law Journal*, 13, 521–528; Shira Perlmutter (1995), 'Freeing Copyright From Formalities', *Cardozo Arts and Entertainment Law Journal*, 13, 565–588 and Graeme W. Austin (2005), 'Symposium: Metamorphosis of artists' rights in the digital age: Keynote address', *Columbia Journal of Law & the Arts*, 28, 397–418, at 416.

2 THE CHALLENGES FOR COPYRIGHT IN THE DIGITAL ENVIRONMENT

The calls for a reintroduction of formalities in copyright law are obviously a response to the momentous change in the production and usage of copyright protected works caused by the advent of digital technologies. While creating and commercially exploiting creative content used to be the almost exclusive province of creative industries, it has now become something that nearly anyone can undertake. The widespread availability of computers, digital recording devices and online networks as media for dissemination has allowed and, in fact, encouraged people to create and distribute works to a potentially worldwide audience. This undeniably has presented new challenges for copyright. Above all, it has increased the need to establish legal certainty concerning the claim of copyright, to improve rights clearance and to enhance the free flow of information. These challenges are considered in more detail below.

2.1 Establishing Legal Certainty Concerning the Claim of Copyright

Because of the fact that copyright arises automatically upon the creation of an original work of authorship, it is not always easy to establish *ex ante* whether a particular object is protected by copyright. Even for experienced copyright lawyers this may be difficult to determine, as the definition of what constitutes a work of authorship is very broad and open-ended and the standard of originality required for protection is uncertain.[17] A wide array of different types of creations may thus qualify for protection. In fact, in the past decades, the subject matter of copyright has been extended both by legislature and the courts. This has brought all kinds of industrial and technical creations (such as software and databases) within the realm of copyright protection. In some countries, courts have also opened the door for protecting blank forms,[18] the scent of a perfume[19] and

[17] Art. 2(1) BC (1971) defines a work of authorship as 'every production in the literary, scientific and artistic domain, whatever may be the mode or form of its expression' and gives a non-exhaustive list of examples of what this might entail. The Berne Convention contains no further definition of the requirement of originality.

[18] See e.g. the Australian case *Kalamazoo (Australia) Pty Ltd v. Compact Business Systems Pty Ltd* (1985) 5 IPR 213, where it was held that copyright could exist in a collection of blank accounting forms.

[19] Judgment of the Supreme Court of the Netherlands of 16 June 2006, *Kecofa v. Lancôme, Nederlandse Jurisprudentie* 2006, 585 (annotated by J.H. Spoor). A few days earlier, in the case of *Mme Nejla Bsiri-Barbir v Sté Haarmann et Reimer*

even transcripts of a simple conversation.[20] And these are just examples. Copyright currently seems to '[spring] up to protect nearly every creation of the human mind, be it ever so trivial'.[21]

This may cause legal uncertainty for authors, copyright owners and users alike. Unlike patents, designs and trademark rights, the property titles of which are defined by registration, the absence of copyright formalities together with the 'lack of legislative definitional closure' of copyright-protectable subject matter makes an *ex ante* definition of the claim of copyright very difficult.[22] For authors and copyright owners this may create legal uncertainty, as only *ex post* can it be established whether and to what extent they have acquired copyright over their creations. In addition, users face legal uncertainty when they use a particular object believing no copyright subsists in it, only to be informed *ex post* by the courts that it is copyright protected.[23]

With the recent expansion of the domain of copyright to industrial and technical creations (such as software), as well as 'creations' of a more obscure character (such as the scent of perfume and simple conversations), the need for a clear *ex ante* qualification of creations as protectable subject matter has become ever more pressing. The vaguer the limits of copyright-protectable subject matter are, the more ambiguous the claim of copyright is.[24] This explains why in some countries voluntary registers have been created for the registration of, for example, television formats, websites

---

Footnote 19 (*cont.*)
(Arrêt No. 1006, 13 June 2006), the French Court of Cassation declined to accord copyright protection to the scent of a perfume.

20 Judgment of the Supreme Court of the Netherlands of 30 May 2008, *Zonen Endstra v. Nieuw Amsterdam*, *Nederlandse Jurisprudentie* 2008, 556 (annotated by E.J. Dommering); *Ars Aequi* 2008, pp. 819–22 (annotated by P.B. Hugenholtz).

21 Sir Hugh Laddie (1996), 'Copyright: Over-Strength, Over-Regulated, Over-Rated', *E.I.P.R.*, 18, 253–60, at 257.

22 Kathy Bowrey (2001), 'The Outer Limits of Copyright Law: Where Law Meets Philosophy and Culture', *Law and Critique*, 12, 75–98, at 85.

23 See for example Brad Sherman and Lionel Bently (1999), *The Making of Modern Intellectual Property Law: The British Experience, 1760–1911*, Cambridge: Cambridge University Press, pp. 192–93, arguing that 'to this extent, unlike the other areas of intellectual property law, copyright law remains pre-modern.'

24 See for example A.A. Quaedvlieg in his annotation to the judgment of the Supreme Court of the Netherlands of 24 February 2006, *Technip v. Goossens*, *AMI* 2006-5, no. 13, pp. 153–61, at 156), in which he concludes that, while the boundaries of the 'objective domain' of intellectual creations (for example patent law) are fairly strict, the opposite is true for the boundaries of the 'subjective domain' of intellectual creations (for example copyright law).

and slogans.[25] Moreover, the recent calls for the establishment of registers for the registration of the source code of computer programmes can be better understood against this background.[26]

Additionally, even if it may reasonably be assumed that a creation falls within the subject matter of copyright and is sufficiently original, no property claim will exist if the term of protection has expired. The term of protection may be difficult to establish, however, if a work does not contain any information concerning the author or date of first publication.[27] For several types of works (for example photos, film footage and so on) it will not be uncommon that this information is not provided. Therefore, if it cannot be determined whether a work is still protected by copyright, this again could prove a source of legal uncertainty for prospective users.[28]

2.2 Improving Rights Clearance

Another area where the current copyright system presents real challenges involves the clearance of rights. Whereas, in the digital environment, re-utilizing creative content has become easy, inexpensive and commonplace, copyright protected works cannot be used legally without the consent of the copyright owner (unless the usage is covered by an exception or limitation). As a consequence, the copyright owner must first be identified and located. This may be difficult, as not all works carry a statement indicating the authorship or ownership of rights and, even if they do, this

---

25 See for example the UK Copyright Service's registration centre where television formats and websites can be registered: http://www.copyrightservice.co.uk/; and the Dutch *GVR/slagzinnenregister* for the registration of slogans: http://www.gvr-slagzinnenregister.nl/.

26 See for example Robert Bond (1995), 'Public registers for software programs', *Copyright World*, no. 49, pp. 35–39 and Gibson (2005), *supra*.

27 In general, the term of protection of copyright is calculated either from the date of death of the author or, in case of anonymous or pseudonymous works or works the authors of which are not a natural person (but for example public institutions or companies), from the date of creation or communication to the public of the work.

28 See Lucie Guibault, 'Wrapping Information in Contract: How Does it Affect the Public Domain', in Lucie Guibault and P. Bernt Hugenholtz (eds) (2006), *The Future of the Public Domain: Identifying the Commons in Information Law*, Information Law series no. 16, Alphen aan den Rijn: Kluwer Law International, pp. 87–104 at p. 95, questioning: 'How can an average user easily know whether a work has fallen into the public domain or whether an element of information qualifies for protection?'

information may be outdated due to a change of ownership.[29] Often, information on copyright ownership cannot be obtained from other sources either, because, in the absence of copyright formalities, adequate and up-to-date copyright registers are scarce.

Although these licensing difficulties are certainly not new, they have clearly been exacerbated in recent times. While in the pre-digital era, the production and dissemination of creative content was restricted to the relatively few authors that could exploit their works through a publishing house or media conglomerate, nowadays virtually anyone can become the creator and distributor of creative content.[30] Modern technologies allow nearly anyone to digitally record, assemble and reproduce creative content and make it available online. Thus, '[with] the rise of amateur creators and the availability of digital networked environments as media for dissemination, the volume of works to which copyright law applies and the universe of authors of whom users must keep track have exploded'.[31] Moreover, because in the online environment works are increasingly exploited across borders, reutilizing these works implies that rights might need to be cleared in potentially unknown foreign territories. Consequently, the number of occasions where the clearance of rights is a problem has grown exponentially.

Furthermore, the licensing difficulties have intensified as a result of the expansion of the traditional domain of copyright (and related rights) in recent decennia. Over the years, various new categories of rights have been introduced to adapt copyright law to the emergence of new technologies. This has added new layers of protection to existing productions and has brought new categories of right holders into the realm of copyright (including software producers, performers, producers of phonograms and films, broadcasters and database producers). As a result, a single object now may be protected by various layers of overlapping rights, each of which may potentially be held by a different right holder.[32] Moreover, as most countries have extended the term of copyright, the practical difficulties of clearing rights have increased even more.[33] Not only has this

---

29 See for example US Copyright Office, *Report on Orphan Works*, A Report of the Register of Copyrights, January 2006, http://www.copyright.gov/orphan/orphan-report-full.pdf, pp. 23 et seq., summarizing the main obstacles to identifying and locating copyright owners in current copyright law.

30 Gibson (2005), *supra*, pp. 213–14.

31 Samuelson (2007), *supra*, p. 563.

32 Stef van Gompel (2007), 'Unlocking the Potential of Pre-Existing Content: How to Address the Issue of Orphan Works in Europe?', *IIC* 38, 669–702, at 675–76.

33 Whereas the main international copyright treaties stipulate a minimum term of protection of copyright of 50 years *post mortem auctoris*, many countries have

term extension resulted in an increased number of works covered by an exclusive right, but with the passage of time, the ownership of rights may also become more obscure as a result of the transferability and divisibility of copyright.[34]

2.3 Enhancing the Free Flow of Information

A last important challenge for copyright law lies in preventing the automatic 'lock up' in the copyright system of all creative content. In the absence of copyright formalities, the threshold for obtaining copyright protection is rather low. In general, any literary or artistic work that is sufficiently original is automatically protected by copyright (some states impose an additional condition to the effect that the work is fixed in a tangible medium of expression). As a result, the vast majority of creative output that is created nowadays is propertized under copyright law.[35] Irrespective of whether or not authors want to avail themselves of protection, they enjoy exclusive copyrights in their works until at least 50 years – and in many countries 70 or more years – after their death. This allows them or their successors in title, at the exclusion of all others, to authorize or prohibit the reproduction, distribution, communication or making available to the public of their works.

In the pre-digital era, when distribution costs were high and the level of interactivity low, it may not have made such a great difference that

---

extended this copyright term. In 1993, for example, art. 1 of the Council Directive 93/98/EEC of 29 October 1993 harmonizing the term of protection of copyright and certain related rights, OJ L 290/9 of 24 November 1993 (as recently has been repealed and replaced by Directive 2006/116/EC of the European Parliament and of the Council of 12 December 2006 on the term of protection of copyright and certain related rights (codified version), OJ L 372/12 of 27 December 2006), provided for an upward harmonization by setting the copyright term for all EU Member States at 70 years *post mortem auctoris*.

[34] Over the years, information on copyright ownership may become outdated or even lost, for instance, because the copyright has been assigned to an unknown third party or because a corporate body owning the copyright has gone out of business. A longer term of protection may also lead to an exponential growth of the number of right holders in the later years of the term of protection, thereby resulting in an increased fragmentation of rights. This is particularly true in case of hereditary succession of rights upon the death of the author. See Van Gompel (2007), *supra*, pp. 674–75.

[35] See Laddie (1996), *supra*, p. 9: 'Another of the problems with copyright law is that [. . .] the requirements for qualification are so low to be virtually non-existent. Virtually any written material, any sketch and any film footage or sound recording is automatically protected.'

copyright automatically attached to all (fixed) content that was sufficiently original. Due to the high costs involved in the dissemination of content goods, it could generally be assumed that anyone engaged in exploiting a creative work desired protection against free-riding by others. The fact that virtually all creative content was protected automatically, even if it did not necessarily merit protection (for example, if it was not meant for commercial exploitation), had few detrimental effects. Most creative works that were not commercially exploited were simply not directly available for use. As all content was locked up in physical information products, it was accessible only to those few people that could obtain a copy of the work. Also, 'analogue' works did not easily lend themselves to be used as building blocks for new creative efforts. As a result, little transformative use was made of pre-existing works. The public still consisted of passive consumers of media content.[36]

All this has changed dramatically in the digital era. Modern digital networked technologies offer the capacity to produce and distribute works on a large scale and at a modest expense. Nowadays, anyone with a computer and internet access can upload content and distribute it on the world-wide-web. Therefore, creative content has never been more readily accessible to the public than it has now. This allows citizens, researchers and creative industries to take full advantage of digital content and make it usable for studies, work, leisure or as raw material for new creative efforts (for example 'user-created content'). Hence, ordinary people are now able to participate in the creation and dissemination of creative works. An important indicator is the success of various personal websites, weblogs, social networking sites, such as MySpace and Facebook, and online audio, photo or video communities, such as YouTube. Here, works are constantly uploaded, viewed, shared and reused for the creation of new derivative works. This social partaking in the creative process is clearly enriching our culture and society.

In view of this, it is highly questionable whether, in the current digital era, all works should automatically warrant copyright protection. The old maxim that 'what is worth copying is prima facie worth protecting'[37] seems to become increasingly irrelevant in the online environment. While copyright undeniably aims at protecting creators and creative industries against free-riding by others, the costs of producing and disseminating content have fallen so significantly that it is doubtful whether all works

---

[36] Gibson (2005), *supra*, pp. 212–13.

[37] Peterson J in *University of London Press Ltd v. University Tutorial Press Ltd*, [1916] 2 Ch 601, 610.

automatically merit the strong and long-term copyright protection that is presently granted.[38] In addition, the assumption that 'most of the most useful and valuable creative content' should be automatically protected by copyright law seems odd,[39] in view of the fact that more and more works are created, not for commercial purposes, but for the benefit of social sharing and remixing.

Obviously, this by no means implies that copyright law has become totally redundant. On the contrary, lots of creative content still warrants protection. 'Without the law, the incentives to produce creative work would be vastly reduced. Large-budget films could not be produced; many books would not get written.'[40] However, the fact that certain creations do deserve the protection of copyright is not the issue here. The point is that copyright law lacks the flexibility to assure that those works that do not necessarily merit protection – or at least not for the full copyright term – are not unnecessarily locked up in the copyright regime, but remain free to be used by others. From the analysis below, it will be seen that formalities may contribute significantly to achieving this goal.

3 FACING THE CHALLENGES: A NEW ROLE FOR COPYRIGHT FORMALITIES?

In addressing the above challenges, formalities may have a useful role to play.[41] However, the degree to which the problems may be overcome depends largely on the particularities of the formality employed. Before exploring the role of copyright formalities in the light of today's challenges, therefore, the various kinds and categories of formalities will be introduced and defined.

---

38 See e.g. Gibson (2005), *supra*, pp. 212 et seq.

39 Lessig (2001), *supra*, p. 107.

40 Ibid.

41 See also Samuelson (2007), *supra*, p. 563 arguing that 'copyright formalities may have a useful role in reshaping copyright norms and practices in the more complex world that has evolved in recent years', thereby referring in particular to 'the problems of too many copyrights and not enough notice of copyright claims and ownership interests', which basically are the problems that we have identified in para. 1 above.

3.1 The Different Kinds and Categories of Formalities

Copyright formalities exist in different kinds. The most prominent examples are copyright registration, recording of assignments of copyright, renewal registration, legal deposit and copyright notices (the familiar 'c-in-a-circle' and the various notices of reservation of rights). Moreover, depending on their role in the copyright system, formalities vary greatly in nature and legal effects. In this regard, four categories of formalities can be distinguished:

(1) constitutive formalities: formalities on which the coming into existence of copyright depends;
(2) renewal formalities: formalities that after a certain period must be completed to renew (and extend) copyright protection;
(3) specifying formalities: formalities that affect the enjoyment of a particular type of right, usually of a specific class of works (for example notices of reservation to retain a public performance right in musical compositions);[42] and
(4) declarative formalities: formalities on which the ability to legally enforce copyright, to recover statutory damages or to claim other – for example procedural – benefits depends.[43]

3.2 The Functions of Copyright Formalities

Formalities may perform various significant functions depending on their kind and role in the copyright system. First, constitutive and renewal formalities play an important role as filtering instruments between works for which authors desire copyright protection and those for which they do not.[44] If authors must fulfil a formality before their works are eligible for protection, they are obliged to make an initial assessment of whether or not their works are sufficiently commercially valuable to warrant

---

[42] The term 'registration as specification' was introduced by Friedemann Kawohl and Martin Kretschmer (2008), 'Abstraction and Registration: Conceptual Innovations and Supply Effects in Prussian and British Copyright (1820–50)', *Intellectual Property Quarterly*, 2, 209–28, at 221 et seq.

[43] Examples of declarative formalities can still be found in US federal copyright law, which still relies heavily on copyright formalities. For works of US origin, registration is a prerequisite for initiating an infringement action. Moreover, for works of both US and foreign origin, the recovery of statutory damages and attorney's fees is limited to instances of infringement occurring after registration. See 17 U.S.C. §§ 411 and 412.

[44] Sprigman (2004), *supra*, pp. 502 et seq.

protection, that is whether the expected revenue of royalties would exceed the costs of completing the formality.[45] The same assessment must be made if copyright is subject to a renewal formality. If this assessment appears favourable, authors are likely to fulfil the formality so as to secure protection for their works. If not, they most likely will refrain from doing so and the work will enter the public domain.[46] Thus, in their capacity as filtering instruments, formalities may greatly enhance the free flow of information.

Secondly, formalities may fulfil important signalling functions for the public. If, in a system where copyright protection relies on formalities, works for which no protection is desired are easily identifiable as being unprotected (for example if no notice is attached to the work or if the work has not been registered or deposited in a public registry), it is instantly recognizable when a work resides in the public domain and thus can be used without prior authorization. This will significantly increase legal certainty for prospective users.[47] More legal certainty will also be established if formalities provide indicators that facilitate the calculation of the duration of protection (for example if they would require authors and/or right owners to make relevant information concerning the author or date of first publication publicly available).

In the same vein, formalities may help to define and identify copyright-protectable subject matter. Constitutive formalities could provide the public with a clear indication of works for which authors claim protection. Obviously, this would not imply that these works automatically satisfy the substantive requirement(s) for protection. That will always be a matter for the courts to decide.[48] Moreover, if copyright depended on

---

45 Kawohl and Kretschmer (2003), *supra*, pp. 221–22; Sprigman (2004), *supra*, p. 514.

46 In contrast to the present situation, in which each and every original work of authorship was automatically covered by copyright, constitutive formalities and renewal formalities may substantially enlarge the number of works in the public domain. See e.g. Lessig (2001), *supra*, pp. 106–07 and 251–52; Lessig (2004), *supra*, pp. 137–38; Landes and Posner (2003), *supra*, pp. 517–18; Lévêque and Ménière (2004), *supra*, p. 105; Sprigman (2004), *supra*, pp. 502–28.

47 See for example Guibault (2006), *supra*, p. 95, who poses the question of whether a reintroduction of formalities as a precondition for copyright protection could perhaps provide an acceptable solution to remedy the lack of legal certainty as to what content is protected by copyright and what is in the public domain.

48 In other fields of intellectual property law, it is completely normal that, despite the grant of protection upon completing the prescribed formalities, the substantive requirements for protection can be tested by the court. A patent application, for example, can typically be invalidated by the court on the ground that the subject matter of the patent is not patentable within the terms of the law.

registration, it is likely that registering bodies are given the discretionary power to refuse registering creations that obviously do not qualify as 'literary or artistic works' or lack sufficient originality (which should of course be subject to appeal by the applicant). This would help in preventing all kinds of trivial works from entering the copyright arena. Likewise, it is possible that in cases of highly complex and technical works, applicants would be required to clearly indicate the elements of information for which they seek protection. Requirements of this kind are not uncommon in other fields of intellectual property law. In a patent specification, for example, the subject matter which the applicant regards as his invention must be particularly pointed out and distinctly claimed and, if necessary, be accompanied by a drawing.[49] Likewise, the registration of a design typically takes no legal effect unless the filing of a design sufficiently reveals its characteristics.[50]

Even if only declarative of the right, formalities may grant a few key benefits. In general, they fulfil important evidentiary functions. The receipt of deposit or entrance in the registers, for instance, may establish prima facie proof of initial ownership of copyright.[51] Moreover, if the law requires a compulsory recording of assignments or licences, this may produce prima facie evidence of the legal transfer of ownership of copyright.[52] This enables authors and copyright owners to easily assert their rights and claim the title of property in a work. This may be particularly useful in conflicts where the anteriority of authorship and/or the priority of a claim to the title must be resolved. In addition, even if the prima facie

---

Footnote 48 (*cont.*)
See for example Art. 138(1) under (a) of the Convention on the grant of European patents (European patent convention) and Art. 75(1) under (a) of the Dutch Patents Act 1995.

[49] §§ 112 and 113 of the US Patent Act (35 U.S.C. §§ 112 and 113). Likewise, Art. 83 of the European patent convention requires a patent application to disclose the invention in a manner sufficiently clear and complete for it to be carried out by a person skilled in the art. See also Art. 25(1) of the Dutch Patents Act 1995.

[50] See for example Art. 3:6 under (f) of the Benelux (Belgium-Netherlands-Luxembourg) Convention on Intellectual Property 2005.

[51] Under the nineteenth century French legal deposit scheme, for instance, the receipt that was given upon deposit constituted prima facie proof of the property right on the work deposited. See Art. 9 of the French Ordinance of 24 October 1814. Currently, voluntary registration schemes often provide for the same. See for example Art. 53(2) of the Canadian Copyright Act (R.S., 1985, c. C-42): 'A certificate of registration of copyright is evidence that the copyright subsists and that the person registered is the owner of the copyright.'

[52] See for example 17 U.S.C. § 205 under (c) and art. 53(2.1) and (2.2) of the Canadian Copyright Act.

status of the claim allows the recorded facts to be rebutted by other proof, formalities may facilitate the exercise of rights by providing more certainty concerning the claim of copyright ownership.

Finally, formalities may constitute an indispensable source of information relevant to the clearance of rights. If authors and copyright owners were obliged to register their copyrights in a publicly accessible register and to duly record each assignment of rights, this would increase the availability of information identifying the work, its author(s) and current right owner(s) and other valuable information (for example about the date of first publication). To a greater or lesser degree, the same information would become available if authors were obliged to mark the copies of their works with a copyright notice. As a result, formalities may contribute noticeably to lowering transaction costs,[53] to providing adequate legal certainty and to alleviating rights clearance problems, such as those of 'orphan works' (that is works the copyright owners of which cannot be identified or located).[54] Hence, formalities may perform a key role in facilitating the licensing of copyright, thereby stimulating the legitimate use of copyright protected content.

3.3 Conclusion

The above overview demonstrates that formalities may function to the benefit of the public at large. By enlarging the public domain, enabling the public to differentiate between protected subject matter and unprotected content, facilitating licensing and enhancing legal certainty for users and copyright owners alike, they may contribute significantly to facilitating the regular exercise of rights. In view of this fact, it seems safe to conclude that

---

[53] See for example Lessig (2001), *supra*, p. 252; Lessig (2004), *supra*, p. 249; Landes and Posner (2003), *supra*, pp. 477-80; Lévêque and Menière (2004), *supra*, p. 105; Sprigman (2004), *supra*, pp. 500–02; Dennis W.K. Khong (2007), 'Orphan Works, Abandonware and the Missing Market for Copyrighted Goods', *International Journal of Law and Information Technology*, 15(1), 54–89, at 61.

[54] See Khong (2007), *supra*, p. 88: 'The easiest solution to the orphanhood problem is a copyright register.' The lack of adequate rights management information resulting from the absence of formalities is seen by many as one of the structural causes of the 'orphan works' problem. See for example Jerry Brito and Bridget Dooling (2005), 'An orphan works affirmative defense to copyright infringement actions', *Michigan Telecommunications and Technology Law Review*, 12, 75–113 (pp. 82–83); Benjamin T. Hickman (2006), 'Can you find a home for this "orphan" copyright work? A statutory solution for copyright-protected works whose owners cannot be located', *Syracuse Law Review*, 57, 123-56 (pp. 129–32); and Olive Huang (2006), 'U.S. Copyright Office orphan works inquiry: Finding homes for the orphans', *Berkeley Technology Law Journal*, 21, 265–88, at 268–71.

formalities may well be fit to address the challenges that copyright is facing in the current digital environment.

But this is just one side of the coin. Although reintroducing formalities may have become something worthy of consideration, one cannot ignore the fact that, despite the fact that formalities fulfilled similar functions in the history of copyright, they were nevertheless abolished. The next sections therefore introduce and contextualize the legal-historical concerns with formalities.

4 THE OTHER SIDE OF THE COIN: THE LEGAL-HISTORICAL CONCERNS WITH COPYRIGHT FORMALITIES

As observed in the introduction, from the late nineteenth or early twentieth centuries onward, copyright formalities began to lose their significance at both the national and the international levels. The reasons for this are manifold. In general, they can be grouped into four categories, which concern the ideological foundation of copyright, the 'natural justice' legitimation of copyright, the concept of abstract-authored works and the practical implications for securing international copyright protection. These four concerns are examined in more detail here.

4.1 The Ideological Foundation of Copyright

One of the primary arguments against formalities is that they are believed to be inconsistent with the idea that copyright is not granted by the legislature, but arises 'naturally' and *ex lege* upon the creation of an original work of authorship. Under this conception, copyright is not created by law, but the law merely recognizes its existence and demarcates its legal boundaries.[55] It is generally considered that to subject the enjoyment or the exercise of copyright to formalities would be to undercut the notion that the right originates directly from the act of creation.[56]

---

[55] See for example Adolf Dietz (1978), *Copyright Law in the European Community: A Comparative Investigation of National Copyright Legislation, with Special Reference to the Provisions of the Treaty Establishing the European Economic Community*, Alphen aan den Rijn: Sijthoff & Noordhoff, p. 25 (no. 54) and Silke von Lewinski (2008), *International Copyright Law and Policy*, Oxford: Oxford University Press, p. 119 (no. 5.58).

[56] See Jane C. Ginsburg, 'A Tale of Two Copyrights: Literary Property in Revolutionary France and America', in Brad Sherman and Alain Strowel (eds),

This idea can be traced back to the continental-European property and personality rights theories of copyright (*droit d'auteur*), which developed in France and Germany during the course of the nineteenth century. In France, justification for the protection of authors' rights was increasingly found to exist in their identification as property rights. Expanding on the theory of 'intellectual property' developed in the eighteenth century under the influence of natural law,[57] and in particular on John Locke's labour theory which held that man has a natural right to property which exists in his own person and which he originally acquires by appropriating the commons through his labour,[58] the proponents of the theory of literary and artistic property stressed the inextricable bond between the work and its author.[59] By regarding the person of the creator as 'the natural law basis of literary and artistic property',[60] they believed authors' rights

---

Of Authors and Origins: Essays on Copyright Law, Oxford: Clarendon Press, pp. 131–58, at 133–34 and 147.

[57] On the evolution of the theory of intellectual property ('*geistigen Eigentum*') in eighteenth century Germany, see Ludwig Gieseke (1995), *Vom Privileg zum Urheberrecht: Die Entwicklung des Urheberrechts in Deutschland bis 1845*, Göttingen: Schwartz, pp. 115 et seq. This theory also found support in France. Already in 1725, Louis d'Héricourt pleaded that the author should be recognized as the owner of the work he created. Without questioning the ownership of the tangible work, he found that the author deserved to be accepted as a proprietor of a work because of his intellectual creation. See the text of his *Mémoire* in Éd. Laboulaye and G. Guiffrey (1859), *La propriété littéraire au XVIIIe siècle: Recueil de pièces et de documents*, Paris: L. Hachette, pp. 21–40.

[58] John Locke (1690), *Two Treatises of Government*, London, pp. 245–46 (sec. 27). Locke's labour theory appears to have been quite popular among nineteenth century liberal thinkers in France. See for example Alfred Nion (1846), *Droits civils des auteurs, artistes et inventeurs*, Paris: Joubert, pp. 127–28.

[59] For instance, during the parliamentary debates of 1839, Joseph Marie Portalis maintained that the author's right constituted a '*propriété par nature, par essence, par indivision, par indivisibilité de l'objet et du sujet*'. In 1879, Eugène Pouillet affirmed that the author's work consisted '*dans une création, c'est-à-dire dans la production d'une chose qui n'existait pas auparavant et qui est tellement personnelle qu'elle forme comme une partie [de son auteur]*'. The quotations are taken from Laurent Pfister (2005), 'La propriété littéraire est-elle une propriété? Controverses sur la nature du droit d'auteur au XIXème siècle', *Revue Internationale du Droit d'Auteur*, no. 205, 116–209, at 156–57 and 158–59.

[60] Pfister (2005), *supra*, pp. 158–59. Ibid. pp. 124–25 and 156–57: 'For the proponents of literary and artistic property, the work was all the more its creator's own as it proceeded immediately from an original and natural property of man: his person'. Authors' rights were increasingly perceived as a natural right. In a case involving the operas of Verdi, for example, the French Court of Cassation fully acknowledged that authors' rights derived from natural law. See French Court of Cassation, 14 December 1857, *Verdi et Blanchet v. Calzado*, *Dalloz* 1858, 1, 161:

to emanate directly from the quality of the authors' own intellectual creations.[61] The rights were considered to have always existed in the legal conscience of men.[62] The law was seen as merely recognizing the existence and regulating the exercise of authors' rights.[63]

This idea also became widespread among nineteenth century German intellectuals. As in France, authors' rights were progressively regarded as rights of intellectual property ('*geistigen Eigentum*').[64] In parallel, another theory evolved in Germany that gave even more prominence to the person of the author as the creator of his work. This was the personality theory, which was based largely on the philosophies of Kant, who recognized that authors have an innate right vested in their own person ('*ius personalissimum*'),[65] and Fichte, who introduced the differentiation between freely usable 'content' and the protectable 'form' of the author's thoughts and ideas (comparable to the idea/expression dichotomy).[66] This last differentiation especially

---

Footnote 60 (*cont.*)
'*Attendu que si la propriété des œuvres littéraires, musicales et artistiques dérive du droit naturel, . . .*' (p. 164). See also Étienne Blanc (1855), *Traité de la contrefaçon en tous genres et de sa poursuite en justice*, 4th edn, Paris: Plon, p. 139: '*la propriété littéraire était une création . . . du droit naturel et des gens*'.

61 See Blanc (1855), *supra*, p. 138: '*La propriété, c'est-à-dire la qualité d'auteur, . . .*'.

62 See Francis J. Kase (1967), *Copyright thought in continental Europe: Its development, legal theories and philosophy*, South Hackensack: Rothman, p. 8, who concludes that under the theory of authors' rights as intellectual property rights, '[copyright] is thus a natural right growing out of natural law'.

63 See Imperial Court of Paris, 8 December 1853, *Lecou v. Barba* in Blanc, pp. 38–39: '*Considérant que la création d'une œuvre littéraire ou artistique constitue au profit de son auteur une propriété dont le fondement se trouve dans le droit naturel et des gens, mais dont l'exploitation est réglementée par le droit civil*'.

64 German natural law and legal philosophy assumed a fairly broad concept of property, included property of physical goods, property of the human body and property of man-made commodities. See Diethelm Klippel (1993), 'Die Idee des geistiges Eigentums in Naturrecht und Rechtsphilosophie des 19. Jahrhunderts', in Elmar Wadle (ed), *Historische Studien zum Urheberrecht in Europa: Entwicklungslinien und Grundfragen*, Schriften zur europäischen Rechts- und Verfassungsgeschichte, 10, Berlin: Duncker & Humblot, pp. 121–38, at 126 et seq.. Intellectual property thus was generally accepted, as it constituted '*durch Arbeit mit der Persönlichkeit verbundene geistige Eigentum*' (ibid. p. 135). Here again, we see the influence of the labour theory of Locke.

65 I. Kant (1785), 'Von der Unrechtmäßigkeit des Büchernachdrucks', *Berlinische Monatsschrift*, 5, 403–17, in L. Bently and M. Kretschmer (eds) (2009), *Primary Sources on Copyright: 1450–1900*, www.copyrighthistory.org (accessed 1 February 2009), p. 416.

66 J.G. Fichte (1793), 'Beweis der Unrechtmäßigkeit des Büchernachdrucks: Ein Räsonnement und eine Fabel', *Berlinische Monatsschrift*, 21, 443–83, in L.

provided a strong justification for copyright to be vested in the author. By assuring protection against any taking of the personal and unique form in which the author had expressed his thoughts or ideas, this new abstract concept linked everything done to the work back to the personality of the author.[67] This laid the groundwork for a number of German scholars to develop the theory of a largely personal author's right.[68] By accentuating the personal element in the author's creation, they claimed that authors' rights arise directly from the authorship of a work.[69] Hence, they considered these rights to come into being through the very act of creation ('*die geistige Schöpfungsthat*') and through the act of creation alone.[70]

This had some important consequences for the way in which formalities were perceived. In general, the idea that copyright was born with the creation of a work did not correspond with the notion of formalities being constitutive of the right. Thus, there was a growing consensus that the existence of copyright should not be subject to formalities and that failure to comply with formalities should never be the occasion of a defeat of copyright protection.[71]

Bently and M. Kretschmer (eds) (2009), *Primary Sources on Copyright: 1450-1900*, www.copyrighthistory.org (accessed 1 February 2009), pp. 447 et seq.

[67] Friedemann Kawohl and Martin Kretschmer (2009), 'Johann Gottlieb Fichte, and the Trap of *Inhalt* (Content) and *Form*: An Information Perspective on Music Copyright', *Information, Communication & Society* (special issue on *Copyright, and the Production of Music*, ed. by Martin Kretschmer and Andy C. Pratt), 12, 41–64, at 46–52.

[68] See Johann Caspar Bluntschli (1853), *Deutsches Privatrecht*, 2 vols, Munich: Literarisch-artistische Anstalt, 1853–54, I, pp. 191–92: '*Das* Werk *als* Geistesproduct *gehört zunächst dem* Autor *an, der es erzeugt hat, . . . als eine* Offenbarung *und ein* Ausdruck seines persönlichen Geistes. *Zwischen Autor und Werk besteht ein natürlicher Zusammenhang, wie zwischen* Schöpfer *und* Geschöpf, *und jener hat ein natürliches Recht, dass* dieses Verhältnis geachtet *werde*'; and p. 186: '*Heutzutage gehört das* Autorrecht *zu den allgemein anerkannten* menschlichen *Rechten*'. See also Otto Gierke (1895), *Deutsches Privatrecht*, 3 vols, Leipzig: Duncker & Humblot, 1895–1917, I, p. 756: '*Das Urhebberecht ist ein Persönlichkeitsrecht, dessen Gegenstand ein Geisteswerk als Bestandtheil der eignen Persönlichkeitssphäre bildet*'.

[69] See Bluntschli (1853), *supra*, p. 199: '[*Das Autorrecht*] *entsteht aus der Urheberschaft. . .*'; and Gierke (1895), *supra*, p. 755: '*durch die Schöpfung eines Geisteswerkes* [*entsteht*] *in der Person seines Schöpfers ein gutes Recht*'.

[70] Gierke (1895), *supra*, pp. 766 and 787–88: '*Das Urheberrecht entsteht durch die* geistige Schöpfungsthat, . . . *wird* unmittelbar *durch die Schöpfungsthat begründet* [*und*] *wird* nur *durch geistige Schöpfungsthat begründet*'.

[71] As a consequence, at the end of the nineteenth century, there was a growing tendency, in Germany, to limit the imposition of formalities and, in France, to soften their nature and legal effects. See Van Gompel (2009), *supra*.

4.2 The 'Natural Justice' Legitimation of Copyright

Another argument still put forth today by many legal scholars is that formalities would conflict with the 'natural justice' or fairness legitimation of copyright.[72] This argument is closely connected with the assumed incompatibility between formalities and the ideological 'natural rights' underpinnings of copyright law. Because the legitimation of copyright is seen in the very nature of the author's personal creation, the supporters of this theory believe that the author should not only be properly rewarded for the creative efforts he has put into his work (economic rights), but should also be protected against acts that could damage or alter his work or that could prejudice his name or reputation (moral rights).[73] In view of that, these scholars are very sceptical about formalities. They regard it as unreasonable if authors should inadvertently and unjustly lose protection due to a failure to complete a formality, as this may unnecessarily harm their economic and personal interests.[74]

The notion of 'natural justice' again originates in the nineteenth century. In view of the personal and 'sacred' bond between the author and his work,[75] it was increasingly held to be unfair if authors could lose protection over a failure (for example an inconsistency or neglect) in the process of completing a formality. This was especially the case if the failure was ascribable to another person than the author (for example if the formality could also be legally complied with by the publisher),[76] to complicated

---

72 Von Lewinski (2008), p. 43 (no. 3.25).

73 This already came to the fore in the 1769 case of *Millar v. Taylor*, 98 *Eng. Rep.* 201, 4 *Burr.* 2303 (Court of King's Bench, 1769), where Lord Mansfield expressed the opinion that 'it is just, that an author should reap the pecuniary profits of his own ingenuity and labour. It is just, that another should not use his name, without his consent. It is fit that he should judge when to publish, or whether he ever will publish' (at 252; 2398).

74 See also H.R. Report No. 94-1476 (94th Cong., 2nd Sess. 1976), *U.S. Code Congressional and Administrative News* (1976), 5659–5809 (p. 5750), in which the US Congress noted that certain copyright formalities, the renewal registration in particular, were the 'cause of inadvertent and unjust loss of copyright'.

75 See P. Bernt Hugenholtz (2001), 'Copyright and Freedom of Expression in Europe', in Rochelle Cooper Dreyfuss, Diane Leenheer Zimmerman and Harry First (eds) *Expanding the Boundaries of Intellectual Property: Innovation for the Knowledge Society*, Oxford: Oxford University Press, pp. 343–363 (p. 344).

76 This was the case, for example, with respect to the legal deposit requirement in France. While art. 6 of the 1793 French Decree placed the duty to deposit on the author, the Decree of 5 February 1810 makes the publisher responsible for depositing. However, this must be understood correctly. In theory, the publisher's obligation was separate from that of the author. Both were equally responsible

procedure and costs involved (for example if the facilities where a formality should be accomplished were centralized and located too far away) or to mere technicalities, such as innocent mistakes or late submissions of applications.[77] In the nineteenth century, it was not uncommon for authors to lose protection as a result of any of these practicalities.

4.3 The Concept of Abstract-Authored Works

Another, more general problem is that formalities do not combine well with the abstraction implicit in works of authorship. Since formalities typically are connected with the outside appearance of a work, the distinctive features that make the work eligible for protection, that is the level of originality and subjectivity in the author's creation, are not easily captured by formalities.

This concern came to the fore when, in the nineteenth century, copyright law 'moved from the concrete to the abstract'.[78] Instead of merely granting protection against a straightforward reproduction of printed matter (books, maps, charts, journals and sheet music) or pre-fixed works of art (sculptures, engravings, drawings and paintings), protection was increasingly conferred on works *qua abstractum*. Accordingly, severed from the physical object in which literary and artistic works

---

for performing the duty imposed on them. This also manifests itself in the legal consequences of non-compliance. For authors, an omission to deposit resulted in the inadmissibility of their claims before a court. For publishers, it gave rise to a fine and confiscation of the copies that were not deposited. In practice, however, it was unnecessary for both the publisher and author to deposit. A deposit carried out by the publisher exempted the author from his obligation. See for example Eugène Pouillet (1908), *Traité théorique et pratique de la propriété littéraire et artistique et pratique et du droit de représentation*, Georges Maillard and Charles Claro (eds), 3rd edn, Paris: Marchal and Billard, pp. 465–66 (no. 425). Consequently, the deposit performed by the printer was sufficient to ensure the preservation of the author's rights. Cf. the rulings of the Court of Cassation of 1 March 1834, *Thiéry v. Marchant*, *Dalloz* 1834, 1, 113; *Sirey* (2me Sér.) 1834, 1, 65; of 20 August 1852, *Bourret et Morel v. Escriche de Ortéga*, *Dalloz* 1852, 1, 335; and of 6 November 1872, *Garnier v. Lévy*, *Dalloz* 1874, 1, 493. But see Court of Cassation, 30 June 1832, *Noël et Chapsal v. Simon*, *Dalloz* 1832, 1, 289, ruling in the opposite direction.

[77] See e.g. Henri Louis de Beaufort, *Het auteursrecht in het Nederlandsche en Internationale recht* (Utrecht: Den Boer, 1909; repr. Amsterdam: Buma, 1993), p. 263.

[78] See Sherman and Bently (1999), *supra*, pp. 55 et seq. for an account of how 'the law . . . moved from the concrete to the abstract' due to the 'shift from the surface of the text to the essence of the creation'.

were embodied or manifested, copyright protection was accorded to the personal and unique form of expression of the author's thoughts or ideas.[79]

Formalities, however, are not easily applicable to abstract work identities. In particular in the pre-digital era, it was considered difficult (if not impossible) 'to reduce the subject matter of copyright law beyond the material form in which it existed'.[80] Because a representative description or sample of the intangible property was hard to give, literary and artistic works needed to be reproduced in their full physical manifestation to be able to identify the subject matter of protection.[81] Not all works lend themselves easily to reproduction however. Artistic works and special or limited editions of literary works were particularly difficult to duplicate and, even if technically reproducible, it would be inapt to demand a deposit of replicas or copies of these works, as the cost of reproduction were often prohibitively high.[82] Moreover, formalities could not be completed unless a work was fixed in a tangible medium.[83]

Accordingly, as the identification of the subject matter of copyright protection continued to rely on the specific object in which the work existed and not, as in the case of patents, designs and trade marks rights, on a registered representation of the object,[84] formalities seemed less indispensable for an efficient protection of copyright.[85] This was even more so after the law had introduced legal presumption of authorship, stipulating that, without proof to the contrary, the person who was named as author on the

---

79 Kawohl and Kretschmer (2003), *supra*, pp. 214 et seq.

80 Sherman and Bently (1999), *supra*, p. 183.

81 Ibid. pp. 183-84.

82 See for example the remark on this point by Mr Meissonier, president of the 1878 International Conference on Artistic Property in Paris, in (1879): *Congrès International de la Propriété Artistique: Tenu à Paris du 18 au 21 septembre 1878*, Paris: Imprimerie Nationale, p. 56. Others, however, questioned the impracticability of registration for artistic works. See for example the response by Eugène Pouillet (ibid. pp. 56–57).

83 J. Heemskerk Az. (1869), *Voordragten over den eigendom van voortbrengselen van den geest*, 2nd edn, Amsterdam: Beerendonk; repr. Amsterdam: De Kloof, 2000, with introduction by R.J.Q. Klomp, pp. 81–82.

84 Sherman and Bently (1999), *supra*, pp. 191–93.

85 The possibility of proving the author's identity by means other than formalities was stressed by John Leighton, a British artist, at the 1878 International Conference on Artistic Property in Paris. He maintained that registration was redundant because the author of a work could always be recognized by experts, either by his writing, his drawing, his brushstroke, or the manner of painting. See *Congrès International de la Propriété Artistique* (1879), *supra*, p. 57.

work was deemed to be the actual author.[86] This weakened the importance of registration or deposit for establishing priority.[87] In addition, in copyright law, there was less need of avoiding difficulties of proof regarding independent creation (*Doppelschöpfung*). If compared with designs and patents law, the chances that this occurred were limited, due to the very personal nature of literary and artistic property.[88]

4.4 The International Implications of Formalities

There are significant concerns with formalities at the international level as well. In contrast to the above-mentioned ideological and legal-theoretical concerns, however, these international concerns are mostly pragmatic. In the mid-nineteenth century, when international copyright protection was first explored, the patchwork of bilateral agreements by which protection was secured laid down numerous formalities.[89] Hence, if authors sought protection in a foreign territory, they usually were required to fulfil the

---

[86] In Germany, for example, Art. 28 of the Federal Copyright Act of 1870 laid down a general presumption of authorship, stipulating that without proof to the contrary, the person who was named as author on the work was deemed to be the actual author. The Berne Convention also contained legal presumptions of authorship from its early inception. See Art. 11 BC (1886). Nowadays, similar presumptions are contained in Art. 15 BC (1971).

[87] Legal presumption of authorship were considered to give authors greater latitude for the assertion of their rights. While less onerous for authors, they were believed to generally achieve the same outcome as formalities. Since most formalities provided prima facie proof only, legal certainty could equally be established by a set of legal presumptions. Because the facts recorded by formalities usually were not verified *ex ante*, their correctness could always be contested. In principle, therefore, formalities only proved that a fact was recorded at a certain time. See for example Robert Fischer (1870), *Gesetz, betreffend das Urheberrecht an Schriftwerken, Abbildungen, musikalischen Kompositionen und dramatischen Werken vom 11 Juni 1870*, Gera: Griesbach, pp. 33–34; Otto Dambach (1871), *Die Gesetzgebung des Norddeutschen Bundes betreffend das Urheberrecht an Schriftwerken, Abbildungen, musikalischen Kompositionen und dramatischen Werken*, Berlin: Enslin, pp. 205–09.

[88] See J.J. Wijnstroom and J.L.A. Peremans (1930), *Het auteursrecht*, Zwolle: Tjeenk Willink, pp. 16–17 and Lionel Bently (1997), 'Requiem for Registration? Reflections on the History of the UK Registered Designs System', in Alison Firth (ed), *The Prehistory and Development of Intellectual Property Systems*, Perspectives on Intellectual Property Series, 1, London: Sweet & Maxwell, pp. 1–46, at 38 and 41.

[89] For a general overview of the formalities in bilateral copyright agreements prior to 1886, see Ladas (1938), *supra*, I, pp. 55–57 and Sam Ricketson and Jane C. Ginsburg (2006), *International copyright and neighbouring rights: the Berne Convention and beyond*, 2 vols, Oxford: Oxford University Press, I, at pp. 37–38.

formalities prescribed by the relevant bilateral treaty. This made it very difficult to secure international protection, especially at a multi-national level.[90]

When the issue of formalities was considered in the framework of the Berne Convention, therefore, the drafters were led by a strong desire to liberate authors from the multitude of formalities which they needed to complete to secure protection in different countries.[91] This resulted in the adoption of the rule, in 1886, that Union authors received protection under the Berne Convention once they completed the formalities in the country of origin of the work.[92] In practice, however, this rule caused problems, as it required national courts in international disputes to interpret the laws of foreign countries.[93] Moreover, some countries still continued to require that foreign authors claiming protection under the Berne Convention comply with domestic formalities.[94] Therefore, a further simplification was needed to enable authors to optimally secure international copyright protection. This was found in the independence of protection and the corresponding prohibition on formalities, which still apply at present.

---

90 See for example Ladas (1938), *supra*, I, p. 55, who speaks about formalities as being 'one of the most unsatisfactory features of the conventions on literary and artistic property prior to 1886'. Illustrative is the letter of concern which a group of French experts in the field of literary and artistic property addressed to the Committee of Organization of the1858 Brussels conference, reported in Édouard Romberg (1859), *Compte rendu des travaux du Congrès de la propriété littéraire et artistique*, 2 vols, Bruxelles/Leipzig: Flatau, I, pp. 217–238.

91 See, in this respect, the speech of Numa Droz (1884) in *Actes de la Conférence internationale pour la protection des droits d'auteur: réunie à Berne du 8 au 19 septembre 1884*, Berne: Imprimerie K.-J. Wyss, p. 21.

92 Art. 2(2) BC (1886).

93 Despite the delivery of a certificate from a foreign authority affirming that the formalities of the country of origin had been fulfilled, some courts felt the need to apply the formalities to particular cases to control whether the foreign procedures had been followed correctly and, if not, to deny protection to the author of a foreign work. See Ernst Röthlisberger (1906), *Die Berner Übereinkunft zum Schutze von Werken der Literatur und Kunst und die Zusatzabkomme: Geschichtlich und rechtlich beleuchtet und kommentiert*, Bern: Francke, pp. 110–11.

94 British courts, in particular, upheld the requirement that national formalities applied equally to alien works for which protection was sought under the Berne Convention. See for example *Fishburn v. Hollingshead*, [1891] 2 Ch. 371 (Chancery Division, 14 March 1891). But see *Hanfstaengl Art Publishing Co. v. Holloway*, [1893] 2 Q.B. 1 (Queen's Bench Division, 1893) and *Hanfstaengl v. The American Tobacco Company*, [1895] 1 Q.B. 347 (Court of Appeal, 1894) in which the *Fishburn v. Hollingshead* ruling was not followed and, in fact, overruled.

5 CONTEXTUALIZING THE LEGAL-HISTORICAL CONCERNS WITH COPYRIGHT FORMALITIES

In view of the ideological and practical concerns with copyright formalities considered above, it is not difficult to understand why copyright gradually lost its attachment to formalities in the course of the twentieth century. This is not to say, however, that the historical reasons for abolishing formalities are absolute impediments for their possible reintroduction. Upon closer inspection, it appears that neither the ideological concerns nor the pragmatic concerns mentioned above exclude the imposition of formalities completely.

First, copyright formalities do not seem to be entirely at odds with the labour theory and natural rights approach underlying the property and personality rights theories of copyright (*droit d'auteur*). These theories concentrate on the *acquisition* of rights and therefore on their enjoyment (that is the existence of rights), rather than their exercise.[95] Accordingly, they merely oppose reliance on formalities as prerequisites for the coming into being of copyright, but they do not seem to preclude formalities that affect the exercise of copyright as such.

In fact, the exercise of copyright has never been absolute and unconditional. Just as the law contains exceptions to and limitations of copyright, there appears to be no reason why, from a principled standpoint, the exercise of copyright could not be subjected to formalities of some kind.[96] At the most, it could be argued that such formalities should always be accompanied by adequate legal safeguards to accommodate the legitimate interests of authors and copyright owners.[97] Likewise, because the duration of

---

[95] For the late nineteenth century French legal terminology of the 'enjoyment' and 'exercise' of a property right, see Marcel Planiol (1908), *Traité élémentaire de droit civil: conforme au programme officiel des facultés de droit*, 5th edn, 3 vols, Paris. Pichon etc., 1908–10, I, p. 161 (no. 431): '*Avoir la jouissance du droit de propriété, c'est avoir l'aptitude nécessaire pour devenir propriétaire*' (referring basically to the acquisition of the right and thus to the title of property); and: '*en avoir l'exercice* [*du droit de propriété*], *c'est pouvoir user de son droit de propriété*' (referring to the ability to use the right, that is to legally enforce it, assign it, license it, etc.).

[96] In nineteenth century France, all limitations to copyright were considered permissible by the proponents of literary and artistic property, as long as they did not affect the author's title of ownership and thus the property rights in his work, during the statutorily prescribed terms of protection. See Pfister (2005), *supra*, pp. 166–67.

[97] It could perhaps be asserted that similar safeguards should apply as the three-step test lays down in relation to exceptions and limitations. However, it is debatable whether this would be desirable. Formalities are not one-to-one comparable to exceptions and limitations. On the one hand, formalities are less

copyright is limited but unspecified by nature, it could be asserted that, from a principled point of view, there appears to be little objection to subjecting copyright to more differentiated terms, for example renewable terms that are conditional on compliance with formalities, instead of to a fixed term after the author's death, as is currently the case. However, since the duration of copyright is directly linked to its legitimation, this should be preceded by a careful, balanced and comprehensive discussion on the optimal term of protection.[98] Such an exercise is necessary to determine to what extent differentiated terms can be introduced, given the 'natural justice' and other rationales of copyright.[99]

In summary, provided that copyright formalities leave the genesis of copyright unaffected and cause no unnecessary prejudice to the legitimate interests of copyright owners, they seem to be consistent with its ideological underpinnings and 'natural justice' legitimation.

This can also be perceived in the history of copyright. Despite the rise of 'natural' property and personality rights theories in nineteenth century continental Europe, there was common understanding that the exercise of

---

Footnote 97 (*cont.*)
far-reaching in the sense that authors and copyright owners control themselves whether or not they comply with them. Unlike exceptions and limitations, which in specific cases must simply be tolerated, they remain in command of their own rights as long as they observe the prescribed formalities. On the other hand, the legal consequences of non-compliance with formalities may be far more rigid. Where exceptions and limitations apply in specific cases only, authors and copyright owners may lose control over the exercise of their rights in case they have failed to complete formalities. This calls for additional legal safeguards, which may perhaps be found in the possibility to cure any inadvertent omission of formalities within a reasonable timeframe (see e.g. 17 U.S.C. § 405(a)(2) (1976)).

98 The optimal duration of copyright protection is directly linked to its legitimation: finding the optimal term of protection is to identify the point at which the objectives for which copyright was granted in the first place are best realized. Until today, however, the literature on law and economics has failed to identify an optimal term of protection for copyright or any other right of intellectual property. See Natali Helberger, Nicole Dufft, Stef van Gompel and Bernt Hugenholtz (2008), 'Never Forever: Why Extending the Term of Protection for Sound Recordings is a Bad Idea,' *E.I.P.R.*, 30, 174–181, at 177 and the references contained therein.

99 Obviously, there are various rationales underlying copyright protection. Apart from the ideological 'natural justice' rationale, there are utilitarian and economic rationales, free speech arguments, cultural and social rationales, pragmatic rationales and so on. See F.W. Grosheide (1986), *Auteursrecht op maat: Beschouwingen over de grondslagen van het auteursrecht in een rechtspolitieke context*, Deventer: Kluwer, pp. 127–43; and F. Willem Grosheide (1994), 'Paradigms in Copyright Law', in Brad Sherman and Alain Strowel (eds), *Of Authors and Origins: Essays on Copyright Law*, Oxford: Clarendon Press, pp. 203–33, at 207 et seq.

copyright could always be restricted if that were to be in the public interest.[100] This was equally the case for other property rights.[101] Because of its cultural importance and social utility, it was deemed completely normal that copyright at a certain moment would enter the public domain (and thus had a limited duration) and that its exercise could be subject to particular formalities.[102] This clarifies to a great extent why, despite the growing belief that copyright is born with the creation of a work, copyright formalities were nevertheless continued. In France, for example, the legal deposit was thought to fulfil a few key functions for facilitating the regular exercise of copyright.[103] Therefore, in the nineteenth century, copyright formalities were considered to have a central role in upholding the balance between safeguarding the rights of authors and the public interest.[104] This may explain why several countries continued imposing formalities until (far into) the twentieth century.

Equally, the pragmatic reasons that added to the growing irrelevance of formalities in the nineteenth and twentieth centuries do not fundamentally oppose formalities either, but must rather be understood in their historical

---

100 French Court of Cassation, 14 December 1857, *Verdi et Blanchet* v. *Calzado*, *Dalloz* 1858, 1, 161: '*Que des considérations d'ordre et d'interêt public ont dû determiner le législateur à en régler et modifier l'exercice*' (p. 164). In Germany and other states, the laws were based on a comparable 'balancing act' between the protection of authors and the interest of the public. See for example Bluntschli (1853), *supra*, p. 193, Gierke (1895), *supra*, p. 755 and Klippel (1993), *supra*, p. 135.

101 Proprietors of real property, for example, were also obliged to sacrifice a portion of their rights if the public interest so required, for example for the exploitation of (mineral) resources or for road construction. See Étienne Blanc at the 1858 International Conference in Brussels, in Romberg (1859), *supra*, I, p. 69.

102 See Resolution, part II, no. 7: '*Si des formalités particulières peuvent être utiles, soit comme mesure d'administration et d'ordre, soit comme moyen de constater et de prouver le droit de propriété, . . .*', and Resolution, part IV, no. 4: '*dans un cas comme dans l'autre, des formalités peuvent être désirables comme mesure d'ordre et pour faciliter l'exercice régulier du droit*' of the 1858 International Conference on Literary and Artistic Property in Brussels in Romberg (1859), *supra*, I, pp. 175–78.

103 At the 1858 International Conference on Literary and Artistic Property in Brussels, the importance of formalities for the exercise of rights was emphasized, inter alia, by Étienne Blanc, *avocat* at the Imperial Court in Paris. See Romberg (1859), *supra*, I, p. 210. The same was done by Jules Pataille, *avocat* at the Court of Appeals in Paris, at the 1878 International Conference on Artistic Property in Paris. See *Congrès International de la Propriété Artistique* (1879), *supra*, pp. 53 et seq. For a similar account from Germany, see the *Mémoire* of Prof. Warnkönig and Dr O. Wächter in response of the questions proposed by the 1858 Committee of Organization, in Romberg (1859), *supra*, I, 268–74, at 269.

104 See Van Gompel (2009), *supra*.

context. While the practical difficulties surely weighted heavy in the previous centuries, in the present digital age, many of the old pragmatic concerns over formalities appear to no longer exist or at least may be easier to overcome. In the online environment, registration and deposit systems can be organized quite efficiently.[105] Moreover, regardless of the abstraction implicit in works of authorship, these formalities can be made applicable to virtually any type of work (except for works that are unfixed). While in the pre-digital era, a good description of the essence of a work (for example an artistic work) may have been hard to provide, modern technologies for digital recording and reproduction, such as digital photo and video cameras, have enabled almost any type of work to easily and cost-effectively be reproduced verbatim, so as to capture its distinctive – subjective and original – features.

Lastly, the practical implications of formalities for securing international copyright seem to be fairly easy to overcome, at least from a theoretical standpoint. The success and ubiquity of the world-wide-web has enabled the creation of online registers, which would allow anyone with a computer and internet access to register and upload works.[106] At the international level, these registers could be amalgamated in a central register. Alternatively, an international (for example WIPO-administered) online register could be established. This would have great advantages, because, as we have seen, the copyright market has become increasingly international.

To avoid the historical difficulties of securing copyright in multiple countries, however, international registration schemes of this kind should be accompanied by international rules. In this respect, recourse could be made for example to the rule under the Berne Convention of 1886 stipulating that to acquire international protection, it would suffice to fulfil the formalities in the country of origin of the work. Yet, this would have the downside in that, if formalities would not be imposed in all countries worldwide, authors may circumvent the formalities of their home country by publishing their works in a country that does not prescribe

---

105 See for example Lessig (2008), *supra*, p. 265: 'Technology offers an extraordinary opportunity for making registration work efficiently'.

106 Admittedly, not all people around the world have easy access to computers and the internet. There still are major divides between the industrialized and developing world. In view of that, reintroducing copyright formalities on a worldwide scale may not yet be a realistic option. On the other hand, things should not be exaggerated. The level of computer and internet access in developing countries is growing steadily and even in the least developed countries, people are increasingly provided internet access on local public terminals.

formalities.[107] It seems that the 1886 rule cannot be successfully reinstated, therefore, without international consensus on the necessity of reintroducing formalities. On the other hand, if an international register were established, it would also be possible to provide that international protection is secured upon registering a work in this register.

However, both possibilities would require a revision of the Berne Convention and/or the other international copyright treaties that have incorporated the substantive provisions of the Berne Convention (1971) by reference.[108] This is easier said than done. To change the Berne Convention would require the unanimity of the votes cast.[109] This may be difficult to realize, given the large number of contracting states to the Berne Convention.[110]

Hence, even if, at the international level, the pragmatic objections against formalities have largely disappeared, in practice solutions may be difficult to achieve, given the requirement of international consensus on this – at least for some countries – rather delicate topic. Still, this does not mean that the idea of reintroducing formalities should be entirely abandoned. If there are legitimate reasons for doing so – and this paper has identified at least a few of these reasons – attempts at international consensus-building could certainly be further pursued.

6 CONCLUSION

By contrasting the current calls for reintroducing formalities with the legal-historical reasons for their aboloiton, this paper has identified and examined some of the main arguments in favour of and against a reintroduction of copyright formalities. Evaluating these arguments in the light of today's digital realities, it can safely be concluded that there is now sufficient reason to look upon the issue of copyright formalities with new eyes

---

107 See note 6 above.

108 These are the TRIPS Agreement (Art. 9(1) TRIPS) and the WIPO Copyright Treaty (Art. 1(4) WCT).

109 Art. 27(3) BC (1971).

110 On 1 June 2009, there were 164 contracting parties to the Berne Convention (source: WIPO). Past experience teaches that revising the Berne Convention is not always a viable option. When the international copyright framework needed adaptation to respond to the challenges of protecting copyright in the digital era, it was considered impossible to do this by introducing changes to the Berne Convention, because that would require unanimity among the contracting states. Instead, a new independent treaty was concluded, the WIPO Copyright Treaty, which is a special agreement within the meaning of Art. 20 BC (1971). See Art. 1(1) WCT.

The challenges for copyright that have emerged as a result of the increased production of digital content and its direct and ubiquitous accessibility in the online environment undeniably warrant legislative reform. The growing needs for creating more legal certainty concerning the claim of copyright, for improving copyright clearance and for enhancing the free flow of information are so pressing that it seems untenable to leave these challenges unaddressed.

Resurrecting copyright formalities may be one of the most salient ways of dealing with the current needs. Because of their inherent capacities to enlarge the public domain, to define and facilitate the recognition of copyright-protectable subject matter, to improve the licensing of copyright protected works and to enhance legal certainty for users and copyright owners alike, formalities seem fit to address the challenges that copyright is presently facing.

Moreover, from a contemporary viewpoint, the legal-historical reasons that contributed to the abolition of formalities are no absolute impediment for their reintroduction. Although some ideological concerns with formalities, particularly the claims of the *ex lege* 'natural law' existence of and 'natural justice' legitimation of copyright, still appear relevant today, they do not seem to form an impregnable barrier to the reinstitution of formalities. In addition, the practical objections to copyright formalities, which relate to their awkwardness in the context of abstract-authored works and in securing international protection, have largely disappeared or at least may be easier to overcome. From a legal-theoretical point of view, therefore, there is sufficient ground to further explore and study the possible reintroduction of formalities.

In conclusion, in questioning whether formalities in the digital era provide an obstacle or an opportunity, this paper argues in favour of the latter. Copyright has never been an absolute and unconditional right, but has always reflected a balancing of interests between authors and the public. In the history of copyright law, formalities clearly played a key role in maintaining this balance. Although, in the twentieth century, they were abolished for obvious reasons, it is reasonable to ask whether they should now be reintroduced in the light of the changes caused by the advent of digital technologies. As this paper demonstrates, there indeed is sufficient reason to believe that reviving the copyright formalities of yesterday may help to address the challenges of today, with the object of preserving copyright for tomorrow.[111]

---

[111] See Gibson (2005), *supra*, p. 173, who argues that '[reviving] the formalities of the past will preserve copyright for the future'.

30. The US experience with formalities: a love/hate relationship

Jane C. Ginsburg*

1 INTRODUCTION

Given calls, such as those expressed in Stef van Gompel's provocative contribution, *Formalities in the digital era: an obstacle or opportunity?*,[1] a reality check might be in order. The United States has had *de jure* or *de facto* mandatory copyright formalities for over 200 years: Does our experience serve as an inspiration or as a cautionary tale?

Copyright formalities – conditions precedent to the existence or enforcement of copyright, such as provision of information about works of authorship that will put the public on notice as to a work's protected status and its copyright ownership, or deposit of copies of the work for the national library or other central authority, or local manufacture of copies of works of foreign origin – have performed a variety of functions in US copyright history. First, formalities that condition the existence or enforcement of copyright on supplying information about works of authorship should enable effective title searching, thus furthering the economic interests both of copyright owners and of potential exploiters. Secondly, copyright-constitutive formalities, principally notice of copyright, but also at various times deposit, registration and renewal, erect a barrier to the existence of protection, concomitantly casting into the public domain published works that fail to comply. These formalities thus (at least in theory) have divided

* Morton L. Janklow Professor of literary and artistic property law, Columbia University School of Law. This report is based in part on a lecture given 20 April 2009 at the University of Rome 1 La Sapienza, 'Protezione del pubblico o trappola per gli autori, le formalità nella concezione e nella pratica del diritto d'autore.' Many thanks to Professors Laura Moscati and Paolo Spada for their comments. Thanks also to David Carson, Esq. and especially to Professors R. Anthony Reese and Lionel Bently.

[1] See Stef van Gompel, *Formalities in the digital era: an obstacle or opportunity?* Report to ALAI Congress, London 2009, Chapter 29 in this volume.

works of perceived economic significance worth the effort of compliance from the mass of other creations, leaving the latter free for others to exploit. Thirdly, formalities with whose compliance protection depends entail additional results, probably intended, and in any event certainly foreseeable. US manufacturing requirements, introduced when the US at last extended copyright to works of foreign origin,[2] served not only local labor interests, but consigned to the public domain foreign works whose authors were unaware that US protection for works of foreign creators required the employment of local printers and artisans. Thus, the international copyright protection that Congress belatedly gave with one hand, it may have placed substantially out of reach with the other.[3] Finally, and perhaps of most practical importance today, formalities predicate to the existence or enforcement of copyright can serve to shield large copyright owners who routinely comply with formalities from the infringement claims of smaller copyright owners, particularly individual authors, who may lack the information or resources systematically to register and deposit their works.

Confiscatory formalities, long lamented in US copyright commentary,[4] have now garnered favor in some quarters, particularly with respect to exploitations on the Internet. One hundred years after the 1908 Berlin Act of the Berne Convention confirmed the automatic vesting of international

---

[2] An act to amend title sixty, chapter three, of the Revised Statutes of the United States, relating to copyrights, 26 Stat.1106 (1891), sec.3 ('Provided that in the case of a book, photograph, chromo or lithograph, the two copies of the same required to be delivered or deposited as above shall be printed from type set within the limits of the United States, or from places made therefrom, or from negatives, or from drawings on stone made within the limits of the United States, or from transfers made therefrom').

[3] The manufacturing clause applied to all books, periodicals, lithographs and photo-engravings, including those by US authors. See 17 USC sec 15 (1909 Act, repealed). For a summary of the complexities of the 1891 and 1909 Act manufacturing clauses, starkly illustrating the many pitfalls for foreign, and even some domestic, authors, see R.R. Bowker (1912), *Copyright, Its History and Law*, pp. 153–61. See also Elizabeth K. Dunne (1960), Study No.20, 'Deposit of Copyrighted Works', reprinted in 1 *Studies on Copyright* 409, 425 (Arthur Fisher Mem. Ed., South Hackensack, NJ: FB Rothman) ('It was found almost impossible for foreign authors, writing in a foreign language, to complete negotiations for the publication of an American edition of their work (as required by the manufacturing clause) prior to publication abroad.')

[4] See, for example, Shira Perlmutter (1995), Freeing Copyright From Formalities, 13 *Cardozo Arts & Ent.L.J.* 565; Irwin Karp (1995), 'A Future Without Formalities', 13 *Cardozo Arts & Ent.L.J* 521; Arthur Levine (1995), 'The End of Formalities: No More Second-Class Copyright Owners', 13 Cardozo Arts & Ent.L.J 553.

copyright by forbidding the imposition of copyright-constitutive or enforcement-predicate formalities on foreign Berne member works, most countries have also ceased to require compliance by local authors as well. With formality-free initial protection, any work created, no matter how trivial (so long as minimally 'original'), automatically enjoys enforceable exclusive rights in every country of the Berne Union. Protection thus 'subsists'[5] even for casual communications, and even though the author may not be a professional creator and hence may be unaware of or indifferent to any copyright in her work.[6] On the other hand, the Internet has put vast amounts of formal and informal copyrighted content at the *de facto* (if not *de jure*) disposal of countless users. A clash between users disinclined, or practically unable, to clear rights, and the subsisting rights of authors may seem inevitable. The relaxation of formalities is also evoked as a cause of 'orphanage' of works: were registration required, then right holders might more easily be found.[7]

Hence the current vogue for 'reformalizing copyright',[8] to return to the author or right holder the burden of asserting claims to copyright, and thereby to enlarge the public domain with works whose authors do not 'care' sufficiently about to mark off their ownership.[9] In other words, the draconian features of US formalities, once seen as deplorable, now in some respects are celebrated. Whether or not a return to the copyright-confiscatory function of formalities is desirable, the United States' Berne obligations would forbid it from imposing a reformalized regime on

---

[5] See 17 USC sec.102(a) ('Copyright protection subsists in original works of authorship fixed . . .').

[6] One may, however, dispute the indifference of non professional authors to the subsistence of copyright in their works. To the extent that the use of Creative Commons icons serves as a guide, most users affix icons denoting a reservation of copyright control over their works, for example, with over three quarters of persons posting photographs to Flickr adopting the 'non commercial' and/or 'no derivative works' directions. See http://www.flickr.com/creativecommons/

[7] Lawrence Lessig, Op-Ed., 'Little Orphan Artworks', *N.Y. Times*, 20 May 2008, at A23; David Fagundes (2009), *Crystals in the Public Domain,* 50 *B.C.L.Rev.*139. See also, World Intellectual Property Organization, Standing Committee on Copyright and Related Rights, Thirteenth session, Survey of National Legislation on Voluntary Registration Systems for Copyright and Related Rights, Doc. SCCR/13/2 (9 November 2005) at 4–6 (discussing relationship of formalities to orphan works).

[8] See, for example, Christopher Sprigman (2004), 'Reform(aliz)ing Copyright', 57 *Stanford L.Rev.*484; James Gibson (2005), 'Once and Future Copyright', 81 *Notre Dame L.Rev.*167; David Fagundes (2009), 'Crystals in the Public Domain', 50 *B.C.L.Rev.*139.

[9] But see note 6, *supra*.

foreign works. Berne's reservation of domestic protection in the country of origin[10] would, however, permit the United States to reinstate formalities with respect to US works. While, as we will see, the US has applied a 'two-tier' approach to certain enforcement-predicate formalities, a return to conditioning the existence or persistence of copyright on compliance with formalities so significantly increases the discrimination against local creators as to be politically problematic. Moreover, given the ease in the digital era with which the country of origin can be manipulated,[11] it is not even clear that a two-tier regime will in fact burden any but the least-informed and least-affluent local creators.

This Report will first further define 'formalities', and then will consider their conceptual foundations. Next, it will examine the US experience with formalities, from the first copyright statute of 1790 to the present. Finally, it will consider whether and how the beneficial, information-providing role of formalities might be achieved, without engendering forfeitures of protection or posing practical impediments to meaningful enforcement of copyright.

2 FORMALITIES IN THEORY AND IN PRACTICE: THEORY

2.1 What are 'Formalities'?[12]

In the sense of the Berne Convention, the formalities that Art. 5.2 prohibits member States from imposing on foreign authors include 'everything which must be complied with in order to ensure that the rights of the author with regard to his work may come into existence'.[13] Thus requirements

---

[10] Berne Conv. Art. 5.3 ('Protection in the country of origin is governed by domestic law').

[11] See 17 USC sec 101 (definition of 'United States work' for purposes of section 411 – pre-suit registration requirement; if the work is first published outside the US in another Berne member State and not simultaneously published in the US, it is not a 'US work'); Berne conv. Art. 3.4.(definition of country of origin; 'simultaneous' publication occurs within 30 days of first publication).

[12] The first two paragraphs of this section have been adapted from Sam Ricketson and Jane C. Ginsburg (2006), *International Copyright and Neighbouring Rights: The Berne Convention and Beyond*, Oxford: Oxford University Press, paras. 6.102–6.105.

[13] See *Actes de la Conférence internationale pour la protection des droits d'auteur réunie à Berne du 8 au 19 Septembre 1884* 43 (1884), discussed in Sam Ricketson and Jane C. Ginsburg (2006), *International Copyright and Neighbouring Rights: The Berne Convention and Beyond*, Oxford: Oxford University Press, para. 6.102.

such as registration, the deposit or filing of copies, the payment of fees, or the making of declarations or affixing notices to copies of the work, may not be made mandatory preconditions to protection. But State-imposed preconditions on the coming-into-being of the author's rights represent only part of the Berne-targeted formalities. An author may be *vested* with copyright, but unable to *enforce* her rights unless she complies with a variety of prerequisites to suit. Hence the addition by the 1908 Berlin Act of the word 'exercise', so that then-Article 4(2) (now Art. 5.2) read: 'The enjoyment and exercise of these rights shall not be subject to any formality . . .' This wording was designed to cover any provision in Member State law that, as distinct from making the recognition of an author's rights contingent upon compliance with some formality, made the bringing of proceedings to enforce these rights subject to a formality (perhaps even the same ones as required for the existence of protection). For example, the obligation the US Copyright Act imposed on authors to register their works with the Copyright Office as a prerequisite to initiating an infringement action was deemed inconsistent with the Article 5(2) prohibition on subjecting the exercise of rights to compliance with formalities.[14]

Nonetheless, not every record-keeping or even litigation-related obligation a State imposes should be considered a Berne-banned 'formality'. For example, Berne does not require the suspension of local rules of evidence or procedure applicable to all judicial proceedings; it targets only copyright-specific measures.[15] Thus, a foreign copyright holder cannot assert that Art. 5(2) dispenses her from paying court fees that attach to the filing of any kind of claim; but she may object to payment of a fee imposed only on the bringing of a copyright action. It is also necessary to distinguish between local rules that condition the validity or scope of a grant of rights on the formalization of the agreement, and rules that limit the exercise of those rights independently of their ownership. The first class of rules, which may include such requirements as that the transfer be

[14] See (1986) Report of the Ad Hoc Working Group on US Adherence to the Berne Convention, reprinted in 10 *Columbia-VLA Journal of Law & the Arts* 513, 569–574. The 1988 Berne Convention Implementation Act accordingly lifted the requirement for non-US Berne works, but retained it for US works. See Jane C. Ginsburg and John M. Kernochan (1988), '102 Years Later: The US Joins the Berne Convention', 13 *Columbia-VLA Journal of Law & the Arts* 1, 13.

[15] See, for example, Claude Masouyé (1978), *WIPO Guide to the Berne Convention*, Geneva: WIPO, para.5.5 (1978); US Adherence to the Berne Convention: Hearings Before the Subcomm. on Patents, Copyrights, and Trademarks of the Senate Comm.on the Judiciary, 99th Cong.72 (1987) (statement of Donald C. Curran, the Assoc. Librarian of Congress and Acting Register of Copyrights, Copyright Office).

in writing, that it be signed by the author, and that the scope of the grant be clearly articulated,[16] are generally designed to protect authors from ignorant or improvident transfers. The rationale and the effect of this kind of author-protective formalism are profoundly different from public-protective formalities, such as notice or registration, or copyright-specific litigation hurdles, which seek to shield the public from authors' claims. In the former instance, the formal rules tell us *who* is entitled to enforce a copyright whose existence the rules do not call into question. In the latter instance, the formalities limit *any* copyright claimant's enforcement, and may destroy the copyright altogether.

The characterization as 'formalities' of three other copyright-pertinent obligations – recordation of transfers, deposit of copies for the Library of Congress, and conditioning certain remedies on registration – warrants examination. The US has since 1802 required that transfers of copyright ownership be recorded. Most enactments of this requirement have not made it a condition to enforcement of the copyright; rather, the penalty for failure to record is invalidity of the transfer in the event of a subsequent bona fide purchase, which the later transferee does record.[17] Because this obligation addresses who may assert copyright ownership, rather than whether the copyright exists or may be enforced, a general recordation requirement, carrying the same sanctions as those accompanying duties to record other kinds of property, for example, title to land,[18] would not seem inconsistent with Berne Art.5.2.

By contrast, making recordation a prerequisite to suit, as the US briefly did between the implementation of the 1976 Copyright Act and the enactment in 1988 of amendments to conform to Berne Convention minima,[19] presents

---

16 See, for example, 17 U.S.C.§ 204(a) (transfers of exclusive rights require a writing signed by the grantor); France, Code of intellectual property, Art. L 131-2 ('The performance, publishing and audiovisual production contracts defined in this Title shall be in writing.'), Art. L 131-3 ('Transfer of authors' rights shall be subject to each of the assigned rights being separately mentioned in the instrument of assignment and the field of exploitation of the assigned rights being defined as to its scope and purpose, as to place and as to duration.').

17 See [Acts of 1802, 1831, 1909].

18 See, for example, New York Real Property Law § 291, Recording of conveyances ('Every such conveyance [of real property] not so recorded is void as against any person who subsequently purchases . . . the same real property . . . in good faith and for a valuable consideration, from the same vendor or assignor, his distributees or devisees, and whose conveyance, contract or assignment is first duly recorded . . .'); *Miller v. Hennen*, 438 N.W.2d 366 (Minn.1989) (purchaser who first recorded the sale of real property prevails against previous purchaser who did not record).

19 See 17 USC sec 205(d) (repealed).

a more difficult question. Such a prerequisite does condition the exercise of copyright on compliance with an obligation to supply information to a government authority. But, as indicated earlier, a 'formality' is copyright-specific. If recordation of transfers of title were a prerequisite to assertion of property rights in general, then one might contend that a recordation requirement should be viewed no differently than, for example, general court costs (as opposed to special copyright litigation fees), which we have already posited are Berne-permissible. If, however, recordation of title is not generally mandated, a copyright recordation prerequisite might still survive Berne scrutiny, on the ground that the requirement concerns who may exercise the rights, rather than whether they may be enforced at all.

The obligation to deposit copies for the national library does not violate the Berne prohibition so long as the penalty for failure to deposit is not tied to the existence or enforcement of copyright. Berne does not prevent member States from requiring authors to subsidize a member State's national library by in effect taxing the local publication of foreign authors' works; thus, a member State may demand deposit and may impose fines for failure to comply, so long as any sanctions do not compromise the existence or enforceability of the copyright.

Finally, conditioning certain remedies on registration of the work[20] may be problematic. Arguably, so long as a Berne member State leaves basic claims for injunctive relief and statutory damages unencumbered by formalities, it may limit the availability of enhanced remedies, such as statutory damages, to compliance with registration or other obligations.[21] However, 'the difference between a permissible conditioning of an *enhanced* remedy, and an impermissible conditioning of an *effective* remedy may not always be apparent, thus making the distinction a delicate one in practice'.[22]

---

[20] See 17 USC sec. 412 (pre-infringement registration of work a prerequisite to obtaining statutory damages and attorneys fees), discussed *infra.*

[21] See, for example (1986), 'Report of Ad Hoc Working Group on US Adherence to the Berne Convention', reprinted in 10 *Colum.-VLA Journal of Law and the Arts* 513, 572–74. See also *Football Ass'n. Premier League Ltd. v. YouTube,* 2009 U.S. Dist. LEXIS 57438 (S.D.N.Y.3 July 2009) (exemption of foreign works from pre-suit registration obligation does not extend to prerequisites to obtaining statutory damages; the latter registration obligation does not violate the Berne Convention or the TRIPs Accord: 'The Senate Judiciary Committee concluded that Section 412 and other provisions of the Copyright Act "do not condition the availability of all meaningful relief on registration, and therefore are not inconsistent with Berne". S.Rep.No.100-352, at 14–15.'; in any event, the Berne Convention and TRIPs are not self-executing in the US).

[22] Ricketson and Ginsburg (2006) Oxford: Oxford University Press, *supra* at para.6.108.

2.2 Conceptual and Historical Underpinnings

This section will set the question of copyright formalities on the broader stage of copyright theory, if only to overturn that platform by examining the history of copyright formalities. Since at least the mid-nineteenth century, commentators have articulated two general concepts of copyright, one founded in natural property rights, the other based on a State grant of monopoly. For example, in 1838 Charles-Augustin Renouard, author of one of the first French copyright treatises, articulated two opposing philosophies of copyright. According to one, grounded in natural rights conceptions of property, authors are the absolute owners of their work, both before and after publication. Their property right is, like all other property rights, transmissible, perpetual, and inviolable. According to the other, social contract-based, system of copyright thought, authors are:

> workers and not property owners; if the laws ensure them exclusive exploitation of their works, it is by virtue of a positive grant of civil law and of a tacit contract which, at the moment of publication, intervenes between the public and the author. It is by the establishment of a privilege, created as a legitimate and fair compensation, that the full and free exploitation of a published work is forbidden to all persons composing the public.[23]

From these opposing bases for copyright different attitudes towards formalities might follow. If copyright is essentially a government grant, it might well come with conditions. For example, requiring the author to affix a notice of copyright, or to register and deposit copies of the work with a government agency before the right will be recognized or enforced, is fully consistent with a social-contractual view of copyright. Imposition of formalities thus would reflect the premise that creating the work does not alone justify protection: copyright is a quid pro quo, and it is the author's burden properly to assert her rights; should she fail to keep her end of the bargain, the innocent public should not be liable for unauthorized exploitations. Formalities thus make free copying the default position; that initial stance should not vary unless the author undertakes to warn the world of her claims. So characterized, formalities clash with a conception of copyright as springing from the creative act. If copyright is a natural property right in the fruits of the author's intellectual labor, then

---

[23] Ch.-A. Renouard (1838), *Des Droits des Auteurs Sur les Produits de Leur Intelligence*, Paris: J Renouard et Cie, 242. See also Augustine Birrell (1899), *Seven Lectures on Copyright*, South Hackensack, NJ: FB Rothman, pp. 10–15 (distinguishing between concepts of copyright as a property right, and as a 'privilege'.)

copyright is born with the work, and no further action should be necessary to confer or confirm the right. Hence, a natural property rights conception of copyright should in theory eschew formalities.[24]

Such tidy coherence may be theoretically satisfying, but it is also substantially anachronistic. In historical context, the opposition of natural rights and social contract (State-granted monopoly) concepts was much less sharp. By the same token, the role of formalities as exemplifying one or another concept reflects subsequent rationalizations more than contemporary experience. Neither at the beginning of the eighteenth century, with the Statute of Anne, nor towards its end, with the US constitution's copyright clause or the first US copyright statute, did lawmakers set out to conceptualize copyright exclusively as a natural right, or only as a conditional State grant, or for that matter to adopt any overriding theory of copyright. In the case of the Statute of Anne, the vesting of rights in authors rewarded their intellectual labor,[25] and the conditioning of an additional term of protection on the author remaining alive[26] further demonstrates the Act's focus on the rights of authorship, but the statute also adopted the regulatory framework, including registration with the Stationers' Company and deposit of copies of books with designated libraries, established under the 1662 Licensing Act.[27] Arguably, Parliament retained the bureaucratic aspects of the pre-copyright printing

---

[24] Benjamin Kaplan (1958), Study No.17, 'The Registration of Copyright' in 1 *Studies on Copyright* 325, 366 (Arthur Fisher Mem. Ed., 1960 South Hackensack, NJ: FB Rothman) ('Those for whom copyright is a "natural" right have regarded formalities as repugnant to such a right and therefore offensive in their nature; while those who think of copyright as a State-granted, limited "monopoly" have tended to look upon formalities as somehow the proper or even the necessary accompaniment of the grant.'); Silke von Lewinski (2008), *International Copyright Law and Policy*, Oxford: Oxford University Press, paras. 3.25–3.26.

[25] Laura Moscati (2003), 'Un "Memorandum" di John Locke tra Censorship e Copyright', *LXXVI Rivista di storia del diritto italiano* 69, has demonstrated a link between Locke's general theory of property rights, and his expression of literary property rights, subsequently captured in the Statute of Anne.

[26] The last sentence of the Statute of Anne (sec.11) provides: 'Provided always that after the expiration of the said term of fourteen years the sole right of printing or disposing of copies shall return to the Authors thereof if they are then living for another Term of fourteen years.'

[27] Ibid, (providing for pre-publication registration of the book's title with the Stationers' Company, 'in such manner as hath been usual'). On registration with the Stationers' Company under the 1662 Licensing Act, see, for example, Michael Treadwell (2002), 'The stationers and the printing acts at the end of the seventeenth century', in John Barnard and D.F. McKenzie, (eds), *The History of the Book in Britain*, Volume IV, Cambridge: Cambridge University Press, 1557–1695, p. 755.

privileges not because its Members carefully conceptualized the nature of copyright, but because the prior system was known and had worked.[28] In the case of the early US enactments, many pre-Constitutional State copyright statutes included preambles with ringing declarations of natural property rights,[29] but then copied the Statute of Anne almost verbatim, including its requirements of registration and deposit of copies,[30] and even including language almost certainly irrelevant to the situation of the ex-Colonies.[31] The cut-and-paste character of these statutes belies any consistent reflection on the nature of copyright.

Indeed, in the US, authorities throughout the nineteenth century conveyed highly mixed messages regarding the nature of copyright and the role of formalities. While courts (including the Supreme Court) often articulated a rigidly positivistic concept of copyright, for which strict adherence to formalities formed a cornerstone,[32] treatise writers eloquently insisted on the natural rights of authorship, generally treating

---

[28] See, for example, John Feather (1994), *Publishing, Piracy and Politics: an historical study of copyright in Britain*, London: Mansell, p. 63 (the Statute of Anne was generally consistent with past business practice: 'For the trade, the 1710 Act represented a simple continuation of legal and commercial practices which had developed since the middle of the sixteenth century, but which had been under challenge in the absence of any statutory authority since 1695.')

[29] See, for example, Massachusetts Copyright Statute (1783), L. Bently and M. Kretschmer (eds), *Primary Sources on Copyright (1450–1900)*, www.copyrighthistory.org ('. . .as such security [of the fruits of authors' study and industry] is one of the natural rights of all men, there being no property more peculiarly a man's own than that which is produced by the labour of his mind'); North Carolina Copyright Statute (1785), ibid ('Whereas nothing is more strictly a man's own than the fruit of his study . . .'). See generally Francine Crawford (1975), 'Pre-Constitutional Copyright Statutes', 23 *Bull. Copyr. Soc.* 11.

[30] Crawford, *supra*, at 23–24, states that the registration requirement was for evidentiary purposes – to prove that the claimant was the author or held rights from the author – rather than constitutive of copyright protection.

[31] See Crawford, *supra*, at 15 and n.15a.

[32] See *Wheaton v. Peters*, 33 U.S. (8 Pet.) 591 (1834) (strict compliance with all statutory formalities held a prerequisite to the vesting of federal copyright protection for published works); *Osgood v. AS Aloe Instrument Co*, 83 Fed. 470 (CC ED Mo.1897) (despite judge's 'disposition much in favor of upholding copyrights, and thus securing to authors what seems to be a natural right to the rewards of their own literary labors', holding that author 'never acquired a valid copyright' because she failed to fulfill statutory obligations to deposit copies of her book with Library of Congress before publication and to insert proper notice of copyright on the title-page). See also *Clayton v. Stone*, 5 F.Cas.999 (CCSDNY 1829) (inferring that a 'daily price quote' could not be the subject matter of federal copyright protection because its publication was too evanescent to permit compliance with full range of statutory formalities).

formalities as an administrative afterthought.[33] Similarly, the Judiciary Committee report accompanying the bill that ultimately became the 1831 copyright amendments, making registration of the work before its publication an unambiguous prerequisite to the obtaining of federal copyright protection, nonetheless extolled the author's natural entitlement to a property right: 'If labor and effort in producing what before was not possessed or known will give title, then the literary man has title, perfect and absolute, and should have his reward . . .'[34]

But formalities, and the highly restricted view of copyright they ultimately symbolized, came to dominate US landscape, particularly following the Supreme Court's 1834 decision in *Wheaton v. Peters*.[35] The first State and then Federal copyright statutes had included formalities modeled on Statute of Anne, but it was not inevitable that they be interpreted as constitutive of copyright, as opposed to predicate to special statutory remedies. Indeed, British authorities since the eighteenth century had confined the sanction for non-compliance with registration and deposit requirements to restricting the author's or rightholder's remedies for copyright infringement to those available at common law.[36] Non-compliance did

---

[33] See George Ticknor Curtis (1847), *A Treatise on the Law of Copyright* pp. 1–25 ('Introduction – Theory of the Rights of Authors; copyright founded in "general principles of justice and right"), reprinted 2005, Clark, NJ; The Lawbook Exchange, pp. 193–98 (Chapter VI: Of the Statute Requisites for a Valid Copyright'); Eaton S. Drone (1879), *A Treatise on the Law of Property in Intellectual Productions in Great Britain and the United States* pp. 1–20 ('Origin and nature of Literary Property', especially p. 13, challenging argument that author's natural rights cease upon publication: 'It is a ridiculous doctrine which recognizes a species of property, and yet pronounces its only use unlawful and self-destructive'); pp. 262–300 ('Statutory Requisites for Securing Copyright'). Stef van Gompel (2009), '*Les formalités sont mortes, vive les formalités! Copyright formalities and the reasons for their decline in nineteenth-century Europe*', in Ronan Deazley, Martin Kretschmer and Lionel Bently, (eds) *Privilege and Property: Essays on the History of Copyright*, London: Legal Classics Library has observed a similar pairing of natural rights rhetoric and formalities in 19th-century Continental European copyright systems.

[34] H.R.Rep.No.3, 21st Cong, 2d sess.(1830), available at Primary Sources on Copyright, http://www.copyrighthistory.org/cgi-bin/kleioc/0010/exec/showThumb/%22us_1831%22/start/%22yes%22 Professor Oren Bracha, in his commentary on this Committee Report, http://www.copyrighthistory.org/cgi-bin/kleioc/0010/exec/ausgabeCom/%22us_1831%22, suggests that the Committee's fulsome endorsement of authorial property rights reflected the influence of Noah Webster, a tireless advocate of copyright protection, whose son-on-law, Oliver Ellsworth, wrote the Committee Report.

[35] 33 U.S.(8 Pet.) 591 (1834).

[36] See *Beckford v. Hood* [1798] 7 TR 620, 101 Eng. Rep. 1164, and general survey of English case law on formalities in Kaplan, Study, *supra* at 327–35.

not endanger the existence of the author's copyright. By contrast, the US Supreme Court in *Wheaton v. Peters* imposed punctilious compliance, making post-publication copyright a tributary of the many statutory pre-requisites.[37]

Different explanations for the centrality of formalities to *Wheaton v. Peters*' delimitation of US copyright might be ventured. Given the Framers' suspicion of restraints on competition, statutory formalities could have been perceived as a necessary counterweight to the prospect of excessive market power that even a monopoly limited in time might engender.[38] The statutory institution and judicial requirement of strict observance of statutory formalities would suggest that Congress and the courts were far more fearful of establishing monopolies than concerned to foster authorship. The more stringent the formalities, the more works freely available in the public domain, and the smaller the universe of works over which exclusive rights could be enforced.[39] An alternative account suggests that the *Wheaton* court's embrace of a highly positivistic, formality-defined approach to copyright was a necessary corollary of the Court's federalism jurisprudence, for Henry Wheaton's assertion that non compliance with federal formalities did not bar his common law copyright claims clashed with the Court's previous rejection of residual State common law intellectual property rights whose assertion undermined Federal control of interstate commerce.[40] Formality-free copyright was thus a casualty of the

---

[37] See 33 U.S.(8 PET.) at 663–64, 'No one can deny that when the legislature are about to vest an exclusive right in an author or inventor, they have the power to prescribe the conditions on which such right shall be enjoyed; and that no one can avail himself of such right who does not substantially comply with the requisitions of the law.'

[38] See, for example, L. Ray Patterson and Craig Joyce (2003), 'Copyright in 1791: An Essay Concerning the Founders' View of the Copyright Power Granted to Congress in Article I, Section 8, Clause 8 of the U.S. Constitution, 52 *Emory L.J.* 909, 941.

[39] The extent to which the Framers and their immediate successors were in fact as monopoly-phobic as the above account implies is subject to some debate. See, for example, Thomas Nachbar (2002), 'Constructing Copyright's Mythology' 6 *Green Bag* 2d.37, 45 (modern scholars' attribution of anti-monopoly animus to the framing of early US copyright laws is overstated); Edward C. Waltersheid (1994), 'To Promote the Progress of Science and Useful Arts: The Background and Origin of the Intellectual Property Clause of the United States Constitution' 2 *J. Intell. Prop. L.* 1, 55–6 ('very few actually gave much thought to' Congress' power to grant copyright monopolies).

[40] See Jane C. Ginsburg (2006), '*Une Chose Publique?*: The Author's Domain and the Public Domain in Early British, French and US Copyright Law', 65 *Cambridge Law Journal* 636, 662–66.

Marshall Court's determination to eliminate barriers to interstate trade and to consolidate Federal power.[41] In the light of the Court's federalism jurisprudence, Justice Joseph Story's perhaps otherwise surprising alignment with the *Wheaton* majority becomes more readily understandable. Although Justice Story was an advocate of broad copyright protection,[42] and may have been sympathetic to Wheaton's common law copyright claims, he was also 'greatly concerned with the development of [the Court's] jurisprudence as a tool of national power',[43] and had joined or authored the Court's principal federalism decisions.[44]

3 US FORMALITIES IN PRACTICE

Whatever their conceptual foundation, formalities in practice dominated nineteenth and twentieth century US copyright law, their extent and complexity often proving a trap for the unwary.[45] It is important to emphasize, however, that those 'ensnared' could as well (if perhaps not as often) be exploiters as authors, at least when incompletely or incorrectly fulfilled formalities misled the user into believing the work unprotected.[46] Users might draw unreliable conclusions regarding a work's status because, notwithstanding the legacy of *Wheaton v. Peters*, some courts, particularly following enactment of the 1909 Act, endeavoring to avoid forfeitures of

---

41 See *Gibbons v. Ogden*, 22 U.S.1 (1824) (holding commerce clause prevailed over any residual State power to grant patent monopolies on steamboat traffic).

42 See, for example, Joseph Story (1839), *Commentaries on Equity Jurisprudence*, Boston: Little, Brown and Company, paras. 930–44. See generally, R. Anthony Reese (2006), 'The Story of *Folsom v. Marsh*', in Jane C. Ginsburg and Rochelle Cooper Dreyfuss, (eds), *Intellectual Property Stories* New York. Foundation Press, p. 259.

43 See Craig Joyce, The Story of *Wheaton v. Peters*: 'A Curious Chapter in the History of Judicature' in *Stories*, *supra*, at pp. 36, 41.

44 In addition to *Gibbons v. Ogden*, *supra*, see, for example, *Martin v. Hunter's Lessee*, 14 U.S.304 (1816).

45 See generally, Vincent A. Doyle, George D. Cary, Marjorie McCannon and Barbara Ringer (1957), 'Study No.7, Notice of Copyright' reprinted in *Studies on Copyright*, South Hackensack, NJ: FB Rothman, *supra*, at p. 229; Kaplan study, *supra*.

46 See *Washingtonian Pub. v. Pearson*, 98 F.2d 245, 249 (D.C.Cir.193x), rev'd, 306 U.S.30 (1939) (if failure 'promptly' to deposit work following publication does not invalidate copyright, then the formality becomes 'a mere snare for the unwary, who were foolish enough to rely upon absence of registration as showing absence of copyright'.)

copyright, interpreted (or interpolated into) the statute some tolerance for substantial, albeit imperfect, compliance.[47]

But not all courts were equally forgiving, as others persisted in requiring strict fulfilment of all statutory conditions. As a result, the legal norm became increasingly incoherent and unpredictable. The doctrine of 'limited publication' further roiled the landscape. Formalities were required for works which had been, or were about to be, published. Until the 1976 Copyright Act, an unpublished work, as a chattel, remained the object of formality-free common law rights.[48] 'Unpublished', however, did not mean unexploited or undivulged. Public performance of a work did not 'publish' it, and therefore did not subject it to formalities, even if the performed work had been widely seen.[49] Borrowing from old English decisions holding that a public performance was not a 'publication',[50] US courts elaborated a parallel universe of 'unpublished' works. The rather strained notion of publication was motivated in large part by courts' awareness that, were the work to be deemed 'published', and had the author not complied with all applicable federal statutory formalities, the work would go into the public domain, and all protection, state or federal, would be lost.[51]

---

47 See generally Study 7, *supra*, at 237–49; Study 17, *supra*, at 346–51.

48 The 1976 copyright act abolished the publication threshold for entitlement to federal copyright, which now 'subsists' as of the creation and fixation of the work, see 17 USC § 102(a).

49 See, for example, *Estate of Martin Luther King v. CBS*, 194 F.3d 1211 (11th Cir.1999) ('I Have a Dream' speech technically 'unpublished' despite delivery before live audience of thousands, and television and radio broadcast to millions); see generally, William S. Strauss, Study No. 29, 'Protection of Unpublished Works', in *Studies on Copyright*, South Hackensack, NJ: FB Rothman, *supra*, at 189.

50 See *Macklin v. Richardson*, [1770] Amb 694, 27 Eng. Rep.451; *Coleman v. Walthen*, [1793] 5 TR 245, 101 Eng. Rep.137; *Morris v. Kelly*, [1820] 1 Jac. & W.481, 37 Eng. Rep.451.

51 Courts' efforts to avoid forfeitures may also explain the somewhat tortured US case law relating to sound recordings, see Study No 29, *supra* at 202–04. In this instance, two different forfeitures loom, first of the recorded musical composition, and second of the recorded performance. Under the 1909 Act regime, if sale of phonograms constituted 'publication', and the recorded composition had not previously been published with notice or registered, then the sale of the recording would cast the composition into the public domain. With regard to the recorded performance, sound recordings were not included within federal copyright subject matter until 1972, Pub. L. No.92-140, 85 Stat. 391 (1971), as amended by Pub. L. No. 93-573, 88 Stat.1873 (1974) (federal protection for sound recordings fixed and published with notice on and after 15 February 1972). As a result, were pre-1972 recordings deemed 'published', they would have immediately gone into the public

Table 30.1 summarizes the formalities in force under various copyright laws, from the Statute of Anne and the first Copyright Act to the present.

3.1 Formalities in Practice: 1909 Act[52]

3.1.1 Threshold criterion: publication

As indicated earlier, the pivot of the 1909 law was the concept of 'publication'. This event was generally the dividing line between common law protection on the one hand and either statutory or no protection on the other. Thus publication with the prescribed copyright notice obtained statutory copyright, while publication without such notice placed a work in the public domain. This rule was anchored in the text of s. 10 of the 1909 Act, which provided: 'Any person entitled thereto by this title may secure copyright for his work by publication thereof with the notice of copyright required by this title'. The concept of 'publication' as utilized in s. 10 developed into a rather technical construct; it was not always coterminous with the general notion of 'making public', nor even with the act that divests the author of common law rights.

The 1909 Act did not expressly define 'publication'. This omission was apparently based on the assumption that a general definition of this concept was too difficult.[53] Section 26, however, provided that in the case of a work 'of which copies are reproduced for sale or distribution', 'the "date of publication" shall . . . be held to be the earliest date when copies of the first authorized edition were placed on sale, sold or publicly distributed by the proprietor of the copyright or under his authority'.[54]

Despite the need for a coherent concept of 'publication' under the 1909 Act, a number of rather arbitrary distinctions emerged. Among the most well known, and most important, was the generally accepted rule that the public performance of a spoken drama did not constitute publication.

---

domain. Hence the judicial rulings that the sale and distribution of phonograms did not 'publish' the performances, which, accordingly, remained subject to common law copyright. See *Capitol Records v. Naxos of America*, 4 N.Y.3d 540 (2005); *Capitol Records v. Mercury Records Corp.*, 221 F.2d 657 (2d Cir.1955)

52 Subsections 3.1.1 and 3.1.3 are in part adapted from Robert A Gorman and Jane C. Ginsburg (2006), *Copyright: Cases and Materials*, New York: Foundation Press, Chapters 4 and 5 (7th ed).

53 *Hearings on S.6330 and H.R.19853 Before Committee on Patents,* 59th Cong., 1st Sess.71 (June 1906).

54 As noted by the court in *Cardinal Film Corp. v. Beck,* 248 F.368 (S.D.N.Y.1918), the section was evidently intended to fix the date from which the term of copyright should begin to run for such a work, rather than to provide a general definition of what should constitute publication in all cases.

Table 30.1 Evolution of US formalities

Formality	(Brit.) Statute of Anne 1710	1790 Act	1802 Act	1831–1905 Acts	1909 Act	1976 Act	1989 (Berne) Amendments
registration	Registry of title of book in Stationers' Co. register 'in such manner as hath been usual' required pre-publication	Registry of title of book in clerk's office of local federal district court required pre-publication and for renewal term	Registry of title of book in clerk's office of local federal district court required pre-publication and for renewal term	With Librarian of Congress before publication; renewal term within 6 months of expiration of initial term	With Copyright Office, accompanying deposit	With Copyright Office, accompanying deposit; now optional (but see below)	With Copyright Office, accompanying deposit; now optional (but see below)
– sanction for non-compliance	Statutory penalties unavailable, but copyright still enforceable for remedies in equity	'no person shall be entitled to the benefit of this act'; maybe ambiguous whether non statutory remedies available without registration	Not entitled to 'benefit of [1790] Act'; construed in *Wheaton v. Peters* (US 1834) to mean no copyright protection at all without total compliance	Precondition to protection; failure to register before publication cast work into public domain	Prerequisite to infringement action (prima facie evidence of facts stated); registration within 1 year of expiration of first term required for renewal term	Prerequisite to infringement action (prima facie evidence of facts stated); registration pre-infringement requisite to statutory damages and attorneys' fees	Prerequisite to infringement action – **US works only**; registration pre-infringement requisite to statutory damages and attorneys' fees – **all works**

deposit	9 copies to designated libraries	One copy within six months of publication to Secretary of State	One copy within six months of publication to Secretary of State	2 copies to Library of Congress w/in 1 month (1846 Act)/10 days of pub. (1870 Act)	2 copies to Copyright Office 'promptly' following publication	2 copies to Copyright Office within 3 months of publication	2 copies to Copyright Office within 3 months of publication
– sanction for non-compliance	fines for non deposit; (1775 Act) Statutory penalties unavailable	Not stated	Not entitled to 'benefit of [1790] Act'; see above	Forfeiture of copyright (1846 Act); then precondition to copyright (1870 Act)	Prerequisite to infringement suit; if after demand, no deposit, fines, forfeiture of copyright	Prerequisite to infringement suit; if after demand, no deposit, fines imposed	Prerequisite to infringement suit **for US works**; if after demand, no deposit, fines imposed
notice	[implicit in registration and provision for public inspection of Stationers' Company registry]	Publication of record of registration in one or more newspapers for 4 weeks within 2 months of publication, and, for renewal term, during last 6 months of first term	Same newspaper publication requirements, **plus**: publication of full record of registration in title page of book or page immediately following	On title page of book or page immediately following; newspaper notice now required only for renewal term, to be made within 2 months of renewal date	On title page or page immediately following; newspaper notice no longer required for renewal term	Must be affixed to published copies, but omission can be cured within five years of publication	Optional

Table 30.1 (continued)

Formality	(Brit.) Statute of Anne 1710	1790 Act	1802 Act	1831–1905 Acts	1909 Act	1976 Act	1989 (Berne) Amendments
– sanction for non-compliance	[no explicit provision]	'no person shall be entitled to the benefit of this act'	Not entitled to 'benefit of [1790] Act'; see above	Precondition to protection; publication without notice cast work into public domain	Same, unless notice omitted from 'a particular copy or copies'; but no damages v. innocent infringer	Forfeiture of copyright, if omission of notice not cured by registration of work with Copyright Office	No forfeiture, but innocent infringer defense in theory possible
recordation	Entry of permission to print in Stationers' Co register	[no provision]	'Transfer or assignment of copyrights' to be recorded in clerk's office	Same, with recordation in Library of Congress	Assignments to be recorded within 3 or 6 months of execution	Any transfer of copyright or document pertaining to copyright	Any transfer of copyright or document pertaining to copyright
– sanction for non-compliance	Statutory penalties unavailable	[no provision]	If not recorded within 60 days of execution, void against subsequent good faith purchaser	If not recorded within 60 days of execution, void against subsequent good faith purchaser	Transfer void against subsequent good faith purchaser who recorded assignment	Prerequisite to suit; if not filed within a month, void against later recording good faith purchasers who record first	Same, re later purchasers, but no longer prerequisite to suit

This rule was established under the pre-1909 law,[55] and was applied by analogy to the exhibition of a motion picture,[56] the public performance of a musical composition, whether for profit or not,[57] and the oral delivery of a lecture or address,[58] all irrespective of the methods employed, including radio broadcasting.[59]

Because disclosure or communication of a work to another person did not always amount to 'publication' under the 1909 copyright law, restricted communication of the contents of a work was generally held not to be a publication of the work. Distribution with limitation by the proprietor of the persons to whom the work was communicated and of the purpose of the disclosure was long known as 'limited', 'restricted', or 'private' publication, but was, more accurately, no 'publication' at all.[60] The distinction between limited and general publication under the 1909 Act was complicated even further by the distinction between 'divestive' and 'investive' publication. The former described dissemination that lost common law copyright; the latter described dissemination, with copyright notice, that triggered statutory copyright – and, out of concern for forfeitures, courts more readily found the latter than the former.[61]

---

[55] *Ferris v. Frohman,* 223 U.S.424 (1912).

[56] See, for example, *De Mille v. Casey,* 121 Misc.78 (N.Y.Sup.Ct.1923).

[57] See, for example, *McCarthy v. White,* 259 F.364 (S.D.N.Y.1919).

[58] See, for example, *Nutt v. National Institute, Inc.*, 31 F.2d 236 (2d Cir.1929).

[59] See, for example, *Uproar Co. v. National Broadcasting Co.,* 81 F.2d 373 (1st Cir.1936).

Under the 1909 Act, considerable uncertainty was also created as to the effect of publication of a derivative work – such as a reproduction of a work of art, or the motion picture based on a novel – on the status of the underlying work on which it is based. Compare *Rushton v. Vitale,* 218 F.2d 434 (2d Cir.1955), with *Leigh v. Gerber,* 86 F.Supp.320 (S.D.N.Y.1949). In *Batjac Prods. v. GoodTimes Home Video Corp.*, 160 F.3d 1223 (9th Cir.1998), the Ninth Circuit held that 'a common law copyright in the underlying screenplay does not survive the motion picture's loss of copyright and falls into the public domain due to a failure to renew the movie's copyright'. *Accord, Shoptalk, Ltd. v. Concorde-New Horizons Corp.*, 168 F.3d 586 (2d Cir.1999) (publication of motion picture 'The Little Shop of Horrors' published as much of the film's screenplay as was disclosed in the film); *Harris Custom Builders, Inc. v. Hoffmeyer,* 92 F.3d 517, 520 (7th Cir.1996), *cert. denied,* 519 U.S.1114 (1997) (publication of architectural drawings publishes underlying plans); *Classic Film Museum, Inc. v. Warner Bros., Inc.,* 597 F.2d 13 (1st Cir.1979) (publication of motion picture publishes underlying screenplay to the extent the movie incorporates the screenplay).

[60] *See White v. Kimmell,* 193 F.2d 744 (9th Cir.), *cert. denied,* 343 U.S.957 (1952).

[61] See, for example, *Atlantic Monthly Co. v. Post Pub'g Co.,* 27 F.2d 556 (D.Mass.1928) (sale of proof copy of magazine to publisher's treasurer held investive publication 'insofar as the statutory formalities are concerned').

In sum, although publication triggered statutory formalities, the statutorily-undefined concept of 'publication' remained elusive, thus compromising the prospect of a clear dividing line between works still entitled to common law protection or qualifying for federal protection on the one hand, and works dedicated to the public on the other hand. Judicial reluctance to avoid forfeitures, while inconsistently acted-upon, undermined the efficacy of copyright-constitutive formalities in consigning to the public domain publicly-disclosed works which had not properly complied with the various statutory formalities. At the outset, then, one of the signal goals of the US system of formalities was, to say the least, imperfectly realized.

3.1.2 The notice requirement

Once a work was deemed 'published', the 1909 Act – as did all of its forebears from 1802 – s. 10 required the placement of a copyright notice in a specified location.[62] The required form of notice was set forth in s. 19, which (with some minor exceptions) provided for the word 'copyright' (or abbreviation) or the familiar copyright symbol, the name of the copyright proprietor and the year of publication.That section also mandated the location of the notice – for a book, 'upon its title page or the page immediately following'; for a periodical, 'either upon the title page or upon the first page of text of each separate number or under the title heading'; and for a musical work 'either upon its title page or the first page of music'.

Some courts were prepared to overlook minor departures from the form and location requirements of the 1909 Act, provided there was substantial compliance.This was particularly true if a technically inaccurate corporate or partnership name was used, but was close enough to the name of the true copyright proprietor (for example, a company with identical officers) such that no one could reasonably claim to have been misled. But other courts were more punctilious, operating on the theory that the copyright was a special legislative privilege that could be secured only through full compliance with formalities. Although a notice accompanying the masthead of a periodical (typically on the editorial page of a newspaper) was commonly regarded as satisfactory, it was, for example, held that it was improper to place the copyright notice on the back cover of a 28-page pamphlet; such a defect was regarded as fatal, and the work was thrust into the public domain.[63] Similarly, courts could be strict about the placement of

---

[62] On the history of the notice requirement, see generally R. Anthony Reese (2007), *Innocent Infringement in US Copyright Law: A History*, 30 *Colum Journal of Law & the Arts* 133, 148–54.

[63] See *J.A. Richards, Inc. v. New York Post,* 23 F.Supp.619 (S.D.N.Y.1938).

the notice on a journal or other collective work, holding that such notice would not protect included works that were authored by others and that did not carry a separate copyright notice.[64]

Inaccuracies in the year date placed in the notice could also be fatal to the copyright. The general rule that developed, through judicial decisions and Copyright Office regulations, was that an inaccurately *early* date was not fatal, but the beginning of the statutory term would be reckoned from that year (so as to shorten the term of protection, for the benefit of the public); while a notice that was *postdated* by more than one year (thus allowing for end-of-the-year slippage in publication schedules) was regarded as fatally defective. Of course, if the required notice was altogether omitted, that too was fatal. The statute itself, however, in s. 21, allowed of one exception: when the copyright owner had 'sought to comply' with the notice provisions but 'by accident or mistake' had omitted the notice 'from a particular copy or copies'. That oversight would not invalidate the copyright, but would 'prevent the recovery of damages against an innocent infringer who has been misled by the omission of the notice'.[65] Another issue that divided the courts was whether US copyright was lost, under the 1909 Act, when a work was first published without a notice of copyright outside of the US. The Court of Appeals for the Ninth Circuit has consistently since 1996 answered that question in the negative.[66]

In sum, while the notice formality marked the dividing line between

---

[64] For example, *Sanga Music Inc. v. EMI Blackwood Music, Inc.*, 55 F.3d 756 (2d Cir.1995).

[65] This statutory exception, however, was held not to apply if the omission of notice was through 'neglect or oversight', *Sieff v. Continental Auto Supply,* 39 F.Supp.683 (D.Minn.1941), or through a mistake of law, *Wildman v. New York Times Co.,* 42 F.Supp.412 (S.D.N.Y.1941).

[66] See, for example, *Twin Books Corp. v. Walt Disney Co.*, 83 F.3d 1162 (9th Cir.1996) In *Twin Books*, the literary work, 'Bambi, A Life in the Woods', was first published without notice in Germany in 1923, and then republished with notice in 1926 (and registered for US copyright).The copyright owner renewed the copyright in 1954, which would have been too late had the work's first publication been in 1923. The court noted some early decisions which indicated that publication abroad without notice forfeits the possibility of securing copyright through a later US publication, but the court concluded that such a view conflicted with the prevailing doctrine of 'territoriality' of the copyright law. The Ninth Circuit relied upon *Heim v. Universal Pictures Co.*, 154 F.2d 480 (2d Cir.1946), for the proposition that publication abroad without notice – in a nation that does not place the work in the public domain for that reason – will not prevent subsequently obtaining a valid US copyright. The Ninth Circuit has recently reasserted its adherence to *Twin Books*, see *Succession Guino v. Renoir*, 549 F.3d 1182 (9th Cir 2008) (sculptures published in France without copyright notice in 1917 and 1974).

protected and public domain works, inconsistencies in its application blurred the boundary. Moreover, the willingness of some courts to accept 'substantial compliance' may have achieved individually just results, but at the cost of systemic unpredictability.

3.1.3 Deposit and registration

Under the 1909 Act, registration was not a prerequisite to federal protection during the initial 28-year term of copyright, although it was necessary to have registered the work and deposited copies before bringing an infringement action.[67] On the other hand, section 13 of the Act required that copies of the work be deposited 'promptly' following publication, thus posing the question whether failure to deposit copies shortly after publication would strip the author or rightowner of the copyright that would have vested upon publication with notice. It was ultimately held, however, that failure promptly to deposit copies did not divest the copyright but would bar the right holder from bringing suit until deposit was made.[68]

While not initially constitutive of copyright, registration was a prerequisite to obtaining a second statutory term of 28 years. The renewal term could be claimed by the author if he or she survived the initial term (or at least until the date in the 28th year when renewal was sought). If the author had died, then the right to claim the renewal passed successively to three other statutory beneficiaries – the surviving spouse or children, or for lack of those the author's executor, or in the absence of a will the author's next of kin.The renewal term came into being only if an initial application for registration and then an application for renewal registration were filed with the Copyright Office. The registration prerequisite to renewal had the effect of limiting the duration of most copyrights to 28 years.[69] Most non-renewals probably reflected the right owners' determinations that the works no longer had commercial value justifying the effort and expense of renewal, but some non-renewals likely resulted from failure to keep track of when renewal was due, or from other inadvertence or ignorance.[70]

---

[67] 1909 Act, sec.12.

[68] *Washingtonian v. Pearson, supra.*

[69] See Barbara Ringer, Study No.31, 'Renewal of Copyright', in *Studies on Copyright*, South Hackensack, NJ: FB Rothman, *supra*.

[70] See, for example, statement on the floor of the House of Representatives in connection with Pub.L.102-307, 106 Stat. 264 (substituting the equivalent of a single 75-year term for the prior dual terms, by making the second term – 28 plus 19 years – vest without filing for renewal): 'The renewal requirements are highly technical and have resulted in the unintended loss of valuable copyrights. In addition to countless individuals who do not have knowledge of the requirements, even famous directors such as Frank Capra have fallen victim. Capra's "It's a

Thus, the renewal formality ensured early entry into the public domain of the bulk of works initially protected for 28 years, but at the cost of divesting those authors (most likely, individual and foreign authors) who may have wished protection but failed correctly to fulfill statutory requirements.

3.2 Interlude: 1925 Bill to Amend the US Copyright Act to Join the Berne Convention

The US stance on formalities long precluded its membership in the Berne Convention. During the 1920s, the efforts of the then-Register of Copyrights Thorvald Solberg and of the Authors League and the American Society of Composers, Authors and Publishers, led to a 1925 bill 'to amend and consolidate the acts respecting copyright and to permit the United States to enter the International Copyright Union'.[71] The cornerstone of this bill was the automatic, formality-free vesting of copyright upon creation of the work. Its advocates characterized the then-current law's obligation to comply exactly with technical requirements as a 'rather primitive situation',[72] and as 'restrictions on the fundamental rights and privileges of the author and composer which should come away'.[73] The concept of automatic copyright, however, encountered considerable skepticism from some lawmakers and fierce opposition from copyright-exploiting industries, particularly the league of motion picture theaters and the producers of phonograph records and piano rolls,[74] for whom formalities combated expansive assertions of authors' rights and formed a bulwark against

Wonderful Life", starring Jimmy Stewart and Donna Reed, went into the public domain when the film production company that owned the copyright went bankrupt and no one was around to file the renewal application.' Reprinted in Robert A. Gorman and Jane C. Ginsburg (2006), *Copyright: Cases and Materials*, New York: Foundation Press, pp. 423–24 (7th edn).

[71] HR 11258, 68th Cong., 2d sess.(1925), also known as the Perkins Bill. The 1924 Dallinger Bill proposed similar reforms.

[72] Statement of Thorvald Solberg, Register of Copyrights, Hearings Part I on HR 11258 at 14 (22 January 1925).

[73] Ibid, at 19.

[74] Ibid, at 136 et seq. (Victor Talking Machine Co.) (bill would 'create an undisclosed monopoly'); Hearings Part II on HR 11258 at 227 et seq.(3 February 1925) (Music Industries Chamber of Commerce) ('The sponsors of the proposed legislation apparently have no concern for those members of the American public who would thereby be subjected to great and unavoidable danger of infringement claims by foreigners.')

unanticipated liability. Some of the objections voiced against formality free copyright seem drearily prescient of the claims of today's 'Copyleft'. For example, Representative William Hammer, Democrat of North Carolina, exclaimed, 'Do you mean to chain human thought so that in the Free America, just by signing the author's name, an article can not be printed in a newspaper without infringing upon a copyright? Is that the kind of law you are asking us to enact?'[75] Similarly, the entrepreneurs of new technological modes of exploitation then, as now, sanctimoniously strained to equate their profits with the public interest. Thus the president of the association of Motion Picture Theater Owners declared, 'Congress should grant no copyright privilege which would have any tendency to inhibit the activities or interfere with the progress of great agencies like the motion-picture screen and the newspaper that are of such consequence to the general welfare of the people of the United States'.[76] It would take the US another 50 years to adopt and (partially) implement the Berne principle that exclusive and enforceable authors' rights arise with the creation of the work.

3.3 Formalities in Practice: the 1976 Act

The principal conceptual and practical innovation of the 1976 Act was to bring published and unpublished works under a single federal regime, thus making creation of a fixed copy of the work, rather than publication with notice, the starting point for federal protection. But, while the 1976 Act was intended to bring the US closer to the Berne Convention,[77] it did not at first fully adopt the post-Berlin system of automatic, formality-free copyright. Rather, if copyright attached upon creation and fixation of the work, it could detach, and the work fall into the public domain, if the author upon publication failed to affix a notice

---

[75] See, *Hearings I* at 68.

[76] Ibid, at 113. Some Members of Congress seemed particularly unmoved by pretensions of this kind, see, e.g., ibid, at 296, colloquy between Mr. Paine of the Victor Talking Machine Company and Rep. Hammer of N. Carolina:

> Mr. Paine. The position that we take is to come down here and urge this committee not to put copyright users at the peril of making infringements of copyrighted works when they know nothing about the copyrights.
> Mr. Hammer. From a purely humanitarian standpoint of the pubic good, not your own private interest?

[77] See, for example, H.R.Rep.No.94-1476, 94th Cong.2d sess. at 135–36 (1976).

of copyright, and failed to cure that omission within the time period allowed by the statute.

3.3.1 Publication and notice

Thus publication remained a key concept in US copyright law, but the 1976 Act, unlike its predecessors, included a definition of publication. Section 101 defined publication as:

> The distribution of copies or phonorecords of a work to the public by sale or other transfer of ownership, or by rental, lease, or lending. The offering to distribute copies or phonorecords to a group of persons for purposes of further distribution, public performance, or public display, constitutes publication. A public performance or display of a work does not itself constitute publication.

This definition resolved many of the problems that arose by virtue of the definitional vacuum in the 1909 Act, particularly by providing that a public performance or display of a work is not a 'publication' that entails a copyright notice; but that the public distribution of phonograph records does constitute publication of the recorded work (as well as of the sound recording).[78] A definition of publication clarified what acts triggered the notice obligation. For despite the US' drawing closer to Berne, the 1976 Act retained a modified version of the notice requirement. Among the issues most hotly debated during the comprehensive revision of the 1909 Copyright Act leading up to the 1976 Act was the continued imposition of a requirement to place copyright notice on 'published' works and the

---

[78] Nonetheless, the 1976 Act did not succeed in dispelling all confusion or uncertainty regarding use of the notice. For example, almost 70 years after *White-Smith Music Pub'g Co. v. Apollo Co.,* 209 U.S.1 (1908), Congress still declined to equate recordings with copies. Thus, in this definition and throughout the statute, one notes the refrain 'copies or phonorecords'. And, as will be noted below, there is no provision for use of a copyright notice on phonorecords pertaining to the underlying recorded work. (There *is* a provision for a P notice pertaining to the recorded *performance* under s. 402.) And, while the statute uses 'copies' and 'phonorecords' in the plural, the committee reports state that under this definition 'a work is "published" if *one or more* copies or phonorecords embodying it are distributed to the public'. (Emphasis added.) S. Rep. No. 94-473 at 121; H.R. Rep. No. 94-1476 at 138. But Chairman Kastenmeier of the House subcommittee stated on the House Floor that 'in the case of a work of art, such as a painting or statue, that exists in only one copy . . .[i]t is not the committee's intention that such a work should be regarded as "published" when the single existing copy is sold or offered for sale in the traditional way – for example, through an art dealer, gallery, or auction house'. 122 Cong. Rec. H10875 (22 September 1976).

sanction for a failure to do so. Congress initially decided to retain the notice requirement but to make less draconian the consequences of an error or omission, in particular allowing for a fiveyear grace period for registration of the work with the Copyright Office, and efforts to add notice to copies after the omission was discovered, as a cure for omission of notice.

The notice requirements were set forth in Sections 401 and 402 of the 1976 Act. Section 401 applied to 'copies' of published works, and Section 402 to 'phonorecords'. In 1988, in order to permit United States adherence to the Berne Convention, Congress eliminated the copyright notice as a precondition to copyright protection. Nonetheless, in part because it is difficult to break with such a longstanding practice as the use of copyright notice, and in part because Congress and the Copyright Office continued to believe that notice served useful purposes in warning unauthorized users and in conveying information, the Berne Implementation amendments to the 1976 Act continue to provide incentives to copyright owners to avail themselves of what has, since 1 March 1989, become merely a discretionary option to use the notice on published works.

After Berne adherence, the amended 1976 Act provided that, for works first published on or after 1 March 1989 – and also for copies or phonorecords distributed after that date of works that had been published previously, Sections 401(a) and 402(a) no longer require placement of notice on publicly distributed copies and phonorecords, but instead provide that the © notice 'may' be placed on copies and the P-in-a-circle notice 'may' be placed on phonorecords of sound recordings. The form and placement of the optional notice are as they were previously when the notice was mandated. The incentive provided for use of the notice was set forth in a new subsection (d) to Sections 401 and 402, which disallow an innocent infringement defense if the requisite notice 'appears on the published copy or copies to which a defendant in a copyright infringement suit had access'.[79] The incentive is, however, rather weak, because the innocent infringer defense applies only to the calculus of statutory damages; it affects neither actual damages nor the existence of liability.[80]

The question has arisen whether the copy 'to which a defendant . . . had access' means the source copy for the infringing act, or rather gener-

---

[79] As to whether continued use of the notice may be expected once no meaningful sanctions attach to its omission, see H.R. Rep. No. 100-609, 100th Cong., 2d Sess.26-67 (1988): 'It is entirely possible that elimination of the notice formality may not in the end curtail its use. Old habits die hard; it remains useful under the Universal Copyright Convention; and, it is, in all probability, the cheapest deterrent to infringement which a copyright holder may take.'

[80] See 17 USC secs.401(d), 504(c)(2).

ally available copies, whether or not such a copy was the one from which the defendant copied. In *BMG v. Gonzales*,[81] the defendant downloaded numerous recorded songs from the Internet. She sought a diminution of statutory damages on the ground that the copies from which she copied did not bear a copyright notice. Recognizing that unauthorized source copies may often lack copyright notice or other copyright-owner identifying indicia, the court rejected the defendant's contention.

> It is undisputed that BMG Music gave copyright notice as required – 'on the surface of the phonorecord, or on the phonorecord label or container' (§ 402(c)). It is likewise undisputed that Gonzalez had 'access' to records and compact discs bearing the proper notice. She downloaded data rather than discs, and the data lacked copyright notices, but the statutory question is whether 'access' to legitimate works was available rather than whether infringers earlier in the chain attached copyright notices to the pirated works. Gonzalez readily could have learned, had she inquired, that the music was under copyright.

It is important to remember that the Berne Implementation amendments concerning notice do not apply retroactively. Thus, as to copies or phonorecords first distributed before the amendments' effective date of 1 March 1989, one must still ascertain whether notice was properly affixed. With respect to copies distributed without notice between 1978 and February 1989 (inclusive), it is necessary to determine whether the omission was discovered and cured within five years of initial publication, and whether the copyright owner made reasonable efforts to add notice to afterdistributed copies.[82]

3.3.2 Deposit and registration

Sections 407 through 412 of the 1976 Act enact a modernized administrative scheme with the dual purpose of enriching the resources of the Library of Congress and providing a comprehensive record of copyright claims. The former is achieved in section 407, which prescribes a mandatory system of deposit as to published works for Library purposes with administrative flexibility as to implementation and realistic sanctions for non-compliance under section 407(d) (not including forfeiture of copyright). The latter is embodied in a 'permissive' registration provision, section 408. The Library deposit under section 407 may do double duty as the deposit required for registration under section 408. Moreover, the incentives for registration are quite strong. Accordingly, the dichotomy between these two deposit provisions may not be quite as sharp as initially thought.

---

81 430 F.3d 888 (7th Cir.2005).

82 See, for example, *Garnier v. Andin Int'l, Inc.*, 36 F.3d 1214 (1st Cir.1994).

3.3.2.1 Deposit for Library of Congress The section 407 deposit, which 'shall' be made by 'the owner of copyright or of the exclusive right of publication' within three months after publication in the United States, is to consist of 'two complete copies of the best edition' or, if the work is a sound recording, two complete phonorecords of the best edition, together with all accompanying printed material. The term 'best edition' is defined in section 101 as 'the edition, published in the United States at any time before the date of deposit, that the Library of Congress determines to be most suitable for its purposes'. The Library has issued a policy statement on what constitutes such a 'best edition', and this is now referred to in the implementing Copyright Office regulations.[83]

The material for use or disposition of the Library of Congress under section 407(b) of the 1976 Act is to be deposited in the Copyright Office. Section 407(c) gives the Register of Copyrights authority to issue regulations exempting categories of material from the deposit requirements of this section, reducing the required copies or phonorecords to one, or, in the case of certain pictorial, graphic, or sculptural works, providing for exemptions or alternative forms of deposit. The Register is also empowered, under section 408(c), to specify classes of works for purposes of deposit and to permit the deposit of 'identifying material instead of copies or phonorecords'.

3.3.2.2 Registration

- *Procedure* Registration under section 408 contrasts with the Library deposit provision under section 407 in the following respects: (1) it may be made by not only the owner of copyright but also the owner of any exclusive right thereunder rather than by the owner of the exclusive right of publication; (2) it applies to unpublished as well as published works; (3) it includes works published abroad; and (4) it may be made 'at any time' during the subsistence of copyright. If the Library deposit under section 407 is accompanied by a prescribed application for registration along with a fee (to be $35 for an electronic filing and $65 for a paper filing for most works),[84] it

---

[83] See 37 C.F.R. s.202.19(b)(1), and Appendix B. The deposit requirement was sustained against a variety of constitutional attacks in *Ladd v. Law & Technology Press*, 762 F.2d 809 (9th Cir.1985).

[84] See US Copyright Office, Analysis and Proposed Copyright Fee Adjustments to go into effect on or about 1 August 2009, http://www.copyright.gov/reports/fees2009.pdf.

may be used to satisfy the deposit requirements of registration. The deposit copy must in fact be a copy of the work in which copyright is claimed.[85]

The application for registration includes various items of information potentially required for computation of duration, for example, dates of death, year of creation, and year of publication if any, as well as the basis of ownership for persons other than authors and a brief, general statement of pre-existing and added material used in any derivative work or compilation.[86]

- *Effect of registration* Although the Berne Convention Implementation Act of 1988 had as one of its objectives the elimination of the need to comply with statutory formalities, its principal focus was upon the elimination of the *notice* requirement for published works; it made few changes in the sections on *deposit and registration* as they were written in the 1976 Act. The major change in this respect is that registration of copyright is no longer a prerequisite to an action for infringement of copyright 'in Berne Convention works whose country of origin is not the United States'. Most pertinently, this means that registration remains a prerequisite for an infringement action when the copyrighted work is first published in the United States or when the work, if unpublished, is by a United States author. The 1988 Act thus creates what is known as a two-tier registration system, with works of US origin being on the 'lower' tier for purposes of litigation. The requirement of pre-suit registration has been criticized, both because of the inferior position in which it places US authors compared to foreign authors and because it is not clear that the requirement in fact induces a substantial number of incremental registrations.[87]
- In addition to seeking to encourage registration through the pre-suit requirement, the 1976 Act provided the following incentives for

---

[85] See *Coles v. Wonder*, 283 F.3d 798 (6th Cir.2002) (1990 registration of 1982 song was invalid when the deposited copy was a 'reconstruction' of the song from memory and without direct reference to the original; defendant is therefore awarded summary judgment, for lack of jurisdiction).

[86] See s. 409.

[87] See Robert Wedgeworth and Barbara Ringer (1993), *The Library of Congress Advisory Committee on Copyright Registration and Deposit – Letter and Report of the Co-Chairs*, 17 *Colum.-VLA Journal of Law & the Arts* 271, 310 ('one thing on which all of the Members of ACCORD appeared to agree was the lack of hard evidence concerning the effect of sections 411(a) and 412(a) as inducements to registration.'); ibid, at 273 ('no empirical proof that these three sections induce registration').

timely registration: (1) registration within five years of first publication will ensure prima facie proof of validity of the copyright;[88] (2) statutory damages and attorney's fees may be awarded only if registration is made prior to the commencement of the infringement.[89] Given the high costs of litigation, the last-mentioned incentive is particularly important, and indeed, for smaller litigants, may determine whether bringing an infringement action is financially viable. It is important to emphasize that these incentives apply to all works regardless of their countries of origin. As a practical matter, then, copyright registration promptly upon publication remains key to effective enforcement of copyright, even for non-US works for which registration is not a prerequisite to suit.

Whether or not they in fact increase the numbers of works registered, the registration incentives thus achieve a gatekeeper function, forestalling the claims of litigants, many of whom are likely to be individual authors, but this filtering of small claimants may not always prove a boon to the larger economic actors who may perceive the pre-suit requirement and limitations on statutory damages and attorneys fees as a desirable screen.[90] For example, in a case involving the unauthorized digitization of the works of freelance journalists by the periodicals in which they had published their work, the Second Circuit held that the section 411 pre-suit registration requirement is 'jurisdictional', and that the court therefore did not have authority to approve a class action settlement which included compensation to authors of works whose authors had not registered them with the Copyright Office. As a result, the large newspaper and magazine publisher defendants in that case face the prospect of additional liability for copyright infringement should the excluded class members subsequently register their works and resume the litigation. The US Supreme Court has agreed to hear an appeal from the decision.[91] Treating the pre-suit registration requirement as

---

88 17 U.S.C.s. 410(c).

89 Ibid, s. 412, which makes these remedies available even as to post publication infringements that commence before registration if the latter is made within three months after first publication.

90 See, for example, ACCORD Report, *supra*, at 293 (fear that elimination of registration prerequisite to statutory damages and attorneys fees will engender a 'flood of infringement claims').

91 See *In re Literary Works in Electronic Databases Copyright Litigation*, 509 F.3d 116 (2d Cir.2007), *cert. granted*, 129 S.Ct.1523 (2009). The Second Circuit's decision appears to have inspired a particularly perverse interpretation of section 411 as barring an action for a declaration of *non* infringement if the work at issue

'jurisdictional' produces other undesirable results as well. For example, some courts have held that an author may not bring an infringement action until the registration in fact issues or is definitively refused by the Copyright Office.[92] As a result, an author who promptly *filed* an application for registration, but the determination of whose application falls prey to backlogs in the Copyright Office, may not have her claims adjudicated until the Copyright Office acts on the application.[93] Where the author has in fact sought to make the requisite public record of her claim, it is unclear what public policy such a wooden approach to registration advances.

- *Registration and renewal of copyright* While works created as of the 1 January 1978 effective date of the 1976 Copyright Act, enjoy a unitary term of the life of the author plus (since 1998) 70 years (or, for works made for hire, anonymous or pseudonymous works, now 95 years from first publication), works first published under the 1909 Act come within a transitional regime. The 1976 Act initially

---

has not been registered for copyright, see *Stuart Weitzman, LLC v. Microcomputer Res., Inc.*, 542 F.3d 859 (11th Cir.2008).

While registration is a prerequisite to a suit for copyright infringement of a US work, nonregistration or improper registration does not prevent an action alleging violation of the s. 1201 provisions prohibiting circumvention of technological measures that protect access to or prevent copying of a copyrighted work. See, for example, *I.M.S. Inquiry Mgmt. v. Berkshire Info. Sys.*, 307 F.Supp.2d 521 (S.D.N.Y.2004).

[92] See, for example, *La Resolana Architects v. Clay Realtors Angel Fire*, 416 F.3d 1195 (10th Cir.2005); *Corbis Corp.v.Amazon.com*, 351 F.Supp.2d 1090 (W.D.Wash.2004); *Strategy Source, Inc. v. Lee*, 233 F.Supp.2d 1 (D.D.C.2002); *Do Denim v. Fried Denim*, 2009 U.S. Dist. LEXIS 51512 (SDNY 2009). But see *Tri Marketing v Mainstream Marketing*, 2009 US Dist. LEXIS 42694 (D.Minn.2009) (holding jurisdictional requirement met upon submission of application).

[93] In 2005, Congress amended the registration provisions to add sec 408(f), Pub. L. No.109-9, 119 Stat. 218, 221, allowing for 'preregistration of works being prepared for commercial distribution'. The provision assists enforcement of copyright in a 'class of works that the Register determines has had a history of infringement prior to authorized commercial distribution'. This class consists of motion pictures, sound recordings, musical compositions, literary works being prepared for publication in book form, computer programs (including videogames), or advertising or marketing photographs, see 37 CFR sec 202.16 (b). The fee is $100 per work, ibid, sec. 201.3(c)(10).

While it is possible to obtain rapid resolution of an application for registration, the expedited procedure involves substantial additional expense: where the standard fee is $65 (or $35 for an online filing), the fee for 'special handling' is $760. Copyright Office Regulations, § 201.3(d), Fees for registration, recordation, and related services, special services, and services performed by the Licensing Division, Fed. Reg. vol.74, no. 103, at 32805, 32808 (9 July 2009).

preserved the renewal requirement for all works then in their first term of copyright. Thus, the author of a work first published in 1960 would have had to register the work and renew its registration in order to obtain the second term of protection. In 1992, Congress provided for the 'automatic renewal' of any work still in its first term; thus, for works first published between 1964 and 1977, the author's failure to renew would no longer cast the work into the public domain.[94]

3.3.3 Recordation of transfers

The principal purpose of the registration formality is to facilitate ascertaining the copyright status and ownership of a work of authorship. Registration will aid title-searching, however, only to the extent it also accounts for subsequent transfers of ownership. Section 205 of the Copyright Act permits recordation of properly executed documents, and accords constructive notice to the recorded facts if:

> (b)(1) the document, or material attached to it, specifically identifies the work to which it pertains so that, after the document is indexed by the Register of Copyrights, it would be revealed by a reasonable search under the title or registration number of the work; and
> (2) registration has been made for the work.

Section 205 offers a further encouragement to take measures enhancing the utility of the Copyright Office's records: in the event of a conflict of transfers, the first to record prevails. Section 205, however, no longer accompanies these carrots with a stick. In its original guise, § 205(d) of the 1976 Act made recordation a prerequisite to suit, but in the Berne-adherence amendments Congress deleted that requirement. The Berne amendments may in this instance have undermined one of the beneficial functions of formalities in a context in which the requirement may not in fact have been Berne-incompatible.[95]

4 SAVING THE BABY FROM THE BATHWATER

Formalities have benefits. If all works are protected, whether or not their authors have asserted rights in them, then an untold number of works whose authors neither maintain nor exploit them remain off limits to others' exploitation, without profit to their creators. If the creator cannot

94 See 17 USC sec.304(a)(2).
95 See discussion, *supra*.

take care enough to mark off her claims, then perhaps the public should be entitled to rely on the absence of notice to treat the work as unclaimed and free. Law and economics reasoning might reinforce this conclusion: the creator is better able to assume the costs of notification than the public is to incur the costs of tracing right holders. And those search costs can be high, particularly if the work is old, or if rights have been divided up among a variety of grantees (and their heirs). A system that requires authors first to assert rights, through notice in distributed copies, or registration in a publicly accessible record, alerts the world to the author's claims. A system that obliges all transfers of rights to be recorded on the publicly accessible record facilitates tracing right holders.

Notice, registration, and recordation of transfers thus are unquestionably beneficial and desirable; the problem, and the historical difference between the US and much of the rest of the world, lies in the consequences of failure to affix notice, register, or record a transfer of ownership. Confiscating the copyrights of the non-compliant, or barring their way to the courthouse door, may encourage adherence to formalities.[96] But not all those who fail to fulfill these obligations do so because they do not care about their works. Some lose track; some are ignorant of the obligation, particularly if they reside in foreign countries which do not impose formalities; some may find the fees prohibitive. The last point is not trivial, particularly for individual creators. Fees of $35 (for electronic filings) to $65 (for paper filings) per work may not impose a significant financial burden if the author creates relatively few works. For example, if the author produces one novel every year or two, the registration fee would seem unproblematic (and will in any event likely be paid by the publisher). But if the author creates a large volume of works, for example, in the visual arts, the fees per work quickly add up. The author who cannot afford to register all her works might wait to see which of her works attracts an audience before selecting which to register, but this strategy may prove perilous. Not only does the cost of registration increase to $760 for an eve-of-litigation registration,[97] but because statutory damages and attorneys' fees are available only with respect to works that were registered before the infringement occurred, the author who waits to see what succeeds (and infringement can be evidence of success) will have lost the opportunity to obtain statutory damages and attorneys fees, and therefore may find she cannot afford to bring the suit.[98]

---

[96] But see note 87, *supra*.

[97] See *supra* note 93.

[98] The Copyright Office regulations allow registration of certain works, for example, photographs published within 12 months of each other, as a group, see 37 CFR sec 202.3(b)(10), for which one fee will apply. But waiting till 12 months

To obtain the social benefits of formalities without disadvantaging authors, it may be desirable to look beyond the current copyright law and the Copyright Office to other alternatives to demarcating the public domain status of a work, and to establishing a traceable public record of copyright claims. With respect to the former, under the default position of the copyright law (and of the Berne Convention) an original work of authorship is automatically protected; absence of notice or of registration does not entitle members of the public to conclude that the work is freely appropriable. But if it is no longer necessary to assert rights through notice or other formalities in order to vest copyright, perhaps a formal relinquishment of rights might suffice to place a work in the public domain (or at least to enable a court to conclude that the author is stopped from enforcing her rights). Thus, an unambiguous notice, such as the Creative Commons PD icon, might shift the default as to given works away from protected status. The burden thus would not be on the author to acquire rights, but rather to *dis*claim them.

With respect to rights clearance, the copyright management information protected by section 1202 of the Copyright Act affords one source of information, although the statutory scope of protection has proved inadequate in several instances.[99] The Creative Commons icons standardize certain kinds of copyright management information, marking off the scope of rights granted or withheld. Unfortunately, these markers do not currently assist authors who would seek to be paid for the works they distribute using the icons, because Creative Commons does not currently incorporate a payment mechanism. The records of collective licensing societies, if open to the public, offer another source of information.

Footnote 98 (*cont.*)
have elapsed before registering the group may disqualify from statutory damages any photographs not registered before the infringement occurred. It also is not clear whether, when a work is registered as part of a group, the 'work' for purposes of calculating statutory damages, is the group or its individual components. If two works within a group are infringed, then the characterization of 'the work' will either double or halve the basis for calculation of damages. Cf. *Bryant v. Europadisk*, 2009 U.S. Dist. LEXIS 37082 (SDNY 2009) (statutory damages calculated on the basis of the album – one work – rather than on the number of recorded songs copied).

[99] See, for example, *Kelly v. Arriba Soft Corp.*, 77 F.Supp.2d 1116 (C.D.Cal.1999), aff'd., 336 F.3d 811 (9th Cir.2003) (declining to protect information about authorship, terms and conditions for exploiting work because plaintiff had not embedded the copyright management information in the images themselves, but had included it elsewhere on his webpages); *Gordon v. Nextel Comms.*, 345 F.3d 922 (6th Cir.2003) (failure to prove that removal of copyright notice was intentional and intended to facilitate infringement).

Finally, with respect to the Copyright Office, while a central public register ideally should be the best, most complete source of information about the existence and ownership of copyrights, problems of practical implementation caution against tying meaningful copyright enforcement to copyright registration, unless the centralized system is adequately staffed and supported by government funding. The various incentives in the 1976 Copyright Act, as amended, are intended to promote voluntary registration (though many registrants may volunteer with twisted arms). But Congressional intent to encourage registration must be implemented through efficient and low cost procedures that will enable the Copyright Office in fact to process promptly all the applications whose registration US public policy purports to favor. At the moment, when the waiting time between filing for and issuance of a registration exceeds 18 months for a paper filing,[100] and averages six months for an electronic filing, if substantially more creators of works of authorship in fact sought to register them than do now, the already backlogged Copyright Office might well be incapable of handling them. Without a smoothly-functioning registration system, the US system of de facto mandatory formalities simply penalizes authors without sufficiently advancing the public record.

100 See Lindsey Layton, '© 2009? Wishful Thinking, Perhaps, as Backlog Mounts', *Washington Post*, 19 May 2009, http://www.washingtonpost.com/wp-dyn/content/article/2009/05/18/AR2009051803171.html.

31. The scope of formalities in international copyright law in a digital context

Takeshi Hishinuma*

1 INTRODUCTION

The promotion of the use of copyrighted works is ever more prevalent in the Internet age. Non-formality, originally aiming at international protection, is sometimes considered a barrier to such use. In addition, certain formalities could be beneficial for international enforcement. Although the non-formality principle is a widely accepted international norm, the scope of this principle has not been analyzed in full accordance with the generally accepted and permissible interpretation of the treaty. Thus, the dynamic approach is mainly explored in this essay, and the textual and subjective approaches are discussed in the existing literature. In addition, this essay considers the complementary roles the non-formality principle shares with other instruments such as the limitation of and exception to copyright, the duration of copyrights and compulsory license. Finally, this essay touches upon the intrinsic difficulties with the notice function of contractually split rights both for public registration and collective societies. Another issue relating to copyrighted works beyond the treaty protection term is analyzed. This essay does not address issues relating to the right of publicity, which often hinders the use of cultural works. The right of publicity comes under the purview of national (dominantly Constitutional) laws rather than international law.

* Visiting Scholar, Institute of Intellectual Property (IIP) of Japan, Japan.

2 SCOPE OF THE NON-FORMALITY PRINCIPLE IN THE INTERNET ERA

2.1 Permissible Approaches of Treaty Interpretation under the VCLT[1]

The Vienna Convention on the Law of Treaties (VCLT) was signed but not ratified by the United States of America. Nevertheless, VCLT rules are mostly accepted as customary international law.[2] The VCLT proposes three approaches to treaty interpretation. First, the textual approach places principal emphasis on the plain language of the treaty. This is the basic rule of the VCLT, and it integrates not only the main body of the treaty but also the connecting agreements (Art. 31.1, .2 and .3c). Secondly, the subjective approach refers to the entire course of negotiations leading to the conclusion of the treaty, and seeks to investigate the actual intentions of the parties. Legislative history can encompass both 'context' (Art. 31.1), a general element of treaty interpretation, and a 'preparatory work of the treaty and the circumstances of its conclusion' (Art. 32), an element of the supplementary means of interpretation. The former 'determines' the 'ordinary meaning' if multiple possibilities are found, whereas the latter 'confirms' the meaning obtained by the application of the general rule under Art. 31. Thus, 'context' is a more decisive element of interpretation than supplementary factors. However, the distinction is not always clear cut.[3] Finally, the teleological approach seeks to interpret the treaty in the light of the objects and purposes of the parties. Individual provisions of the treaty are construed so as to give the legal effects to these objects and purposes. This approach is often called the principle of effectiveness (*ut res magis valeat quam pereat*).[4] The term 'object and purpose' (Art. 31.1) indicates the teleological element applied to treaty interpretation.

However, the distinction between the 'object and purpose' and the 'circumstances of its conclusion' is not always self-evident.[5]

The deletion of the limiting term 'in force at the time of its conclusion', found in the original 1964 draft appearing before 'the rules of international

---

[1] Jacobs, Francis G. (1969), 'Varieties of Approach to Treaty Interpretation', *International and Comparative Law Quarterly ICLQ*, 18(2), 319–325.

[2] Gardiner, K. Richard (2008), *Treaty Interpretation*, Oxford: Oxford University Press, p. 134.

[3] Ibid, p. 178 and pp. 307–310.

[4] Cassese, Antonio (2005), *International Law*, 2nd edn, Oxford: Oxford University Press, p. 179.

[5] Gardiner (2008), *supra* note 2, p.194.

law', suggests that inter-temporal law can be applied.[6] Thus, 'international law' (Art. 31.3c) arguably includes a subsequent interpretation after the conclusion.

2.2 Interpretation of Copyright Treaties under the VCLT and Customary Law

Treaty interpretation under the VCLT, though not directly applicable to the Berne Convention concluded previously, is a 'custom',[7] which can be referred to for the interpretation of the Berne Convention and the TRIPS Agreement. During WTO dispute settlement procedures, the VCLT has been cited as the 'customary rules of interpretation of public international law' (DSU, Art. 3(2)). The exact meaning of these customary rules is not clear, but case law indicates customary and procedural laws, though not expressly stipulated under the VCLT, such as the good-faith interpretation to avoid the redundancy and inutility of other provisions.[8] The effective interpretation of the provisions of the intellectual property (IP) treaty is not unprecedented. For example, WTO dispute resolution decisions, despite lacking the binding effect of case law, have recognized the principle of effectiveness as part of the general rule for treaty interpretation.[9]

The TRIPS Agreement and Berne Convention are not 'successive treaties relating to the same subject matter' (VCLT Art. 30). Nevertheless, both treaties form the overall framework for multilateral protection, and a contradictory interpretation should be avoided unless explicitly provided for.[10] Thus, the interpretation of the TRIPS Agreement requires interpreting guidance from the legislative history of IP treaties that constitute the IP system at large.[11]

---

[6] Waldock, Humphrey (1966), 'Special Rapporteur, 5th Report on the Law of Treaties', in *Yearbook of The International Law Commission*, Vol.II, United Nations, p. 97.

[7] Art. 38.1(b), Statute of the International Court of Justice. 'Custom' has two elements: state practice and the corresponding views of states. See Cassese (2005), *supra* note 4, pp. 156–160.

[8] Yamane, Hiroko (2007), '*TRIPS Ronso wo Meguru Ronso* (Disputes on the Interpretation of the TRIPS Agreement)', *Nihon Kokusai Keizaiho Nenpo* (Yearbook of International Economic Law), Vol.16, pp. 136–139.

[9] WTO (2000), *Canada–Pharmaceutical Patents, Panel Report*, WT/DS114/R, pp. 153–54; Gardiner (2008), *supra* note 2, p. 160, referring to an Appellate Body decision (1996, *Japan-Taxes on Alcoholic beverages*).

[10] WTO (2000), 'Section 110(5) of the US Copyright Act, Report of the Panel', WT/DS160/R, para.6.66.

[11] Yamane (2007), *supra* note 8, pp. 140–141.

2.3 Dominant Approaches in the Pre-Internet Era and Current National Systems

The textual and subjective approaches have been dominant.

2.3.1 Formality

'Formality' is any condition or measure without the fulfilment of which the work is not protected or loses protection.[12] The Universal Copyright Convention (Art. III.1) presents examples such as deposit and registration. Legislative history states that registration is a 'formality,' and the question of procedure or evidence such as the presumption of authorship was excluded from the formality during the Berne Diplomatic Conference (1885). Before 1911, when the United Kingdom was under the purview of the registration system, the certification issued by the Stationers' Hall was *prima facie* proof of copyright.[13] The non-formality principle concerns only copyright measures and does not regulate evidential or procedural laws.[14] Fiscor (2004) presented the notion of '*de facto* formality', such as the court practice of accepting only registered copyright cases.

However, the boundary between prohibited and permitted formality is not clear. Many countries[15] completely abolished copyright registration after joining the Berne Convention. Many American continental countries and China maintain the copyright registration system, which has supplemental legal effects, such as *prima facie* evidence of registered information. No Berne member state considers the registration system to be a condition of the exercise of foreign copyrighted works, though national laws are divided concerning domestic works. It is noted that the non-formality principle concerns only rights holders' obligations.

Some argue for the compulsory registration of users who want to use orphan works.[16] If a users' registration requirement as a condition of

---

[12] Ficsor, Mihály (2004), 'Guide to the Copyright and Related Rights Treaties Administered by WIPO and Glossary of Copyright and Related Rights Terms', WIPO, p. 41.

[13] *Hole v. Bradbury*, 1878 H. 91, 12 Ch D 886, 17 June 1879.

[14] Ricketson, Sam and Ginsburg, Jane (2006), *International Copyright and Neighbouring Rights*, 2nd edn, Oxford: Oxford University Press, pp. 326–27. The presumptive effects of registration in 13 countries were surveyed by WIPO in 2003–04.

[15] The United Kingdom is such an example. See Loi de 1911 sur le droit d'auteur (1re et 2e année Georges V, chap.46), in BIRPI (1912), 'Législation intérieure –Grande-Bretagne', *Le Droit d'Auteur*, 15 Février 1912, pp. 17–26.

[16] US Copyright Office, Library of Congress (2006), *Report on Orphan Works*, pp. 112–113.

using orphan works were actually introduced, the non-formality principle would be irrelevant.

2.3.2 Enjoyment and exercise of rights

Rights, whether subdivided or bundled, mandated by a treaty are 'rights' to which the non-formality principle is applicable. On the other hand, rights that national law voluntarily creates are not subject to the non-formality principle. 'Enjoyment' concerns the creation of rights. Only subject matter that is protected by copyright can be subject to enjoyment. 'Exercise' includes the aspect of the enforcement of rights.[17] Remedies provided by an administrative authority, except border measures, are not mandated by treaties. Unlike other countries, China's National Copyright Administration is authorized to order the suspension of infringing acts, the confiscation of illegal profits and products, and penalties and administrative penalties including the confiscation of materials, tools and facilities that were used to manufacture infringing goods.[18] The central role of the administrative enforcement seems to be explained by socialism and Confucianism traditions, that is the notion that property belongs to the state rather than the individual.[19]

Civil remedies, such as a preliminary injunction and civil damages, constitute the exercise of rights. Thus, a registration cannot be a condition for these remedies under the non-formality principle. On the other hand, registration as a condition of criminal procedures is compatible with the non-formality principle.

2.4 Scope and Possibility of the Dynamic Approach

2.4.1 Grey zone of the non-formality principle

The Stockholm Conference clarified that the non-formality principle concerned the 'basic corpus' of rights. However, the scope of basic corpus is not self-evident. For example, first, it is discussed whether the

---

[17] Ficsor (2004), *supra* note 12, p. 42.

[18] Law on the Measures for the Implementation of Copyright Administrative Penalty (2003). With regard to an urgent case, the Administration can take immediate measures to suspend illegal acts or reinstate the original situation. The alleged infringer cannot stop the administration's enforcement even by appealing to judicial courts.

[19] Thomas, Kristie (2007), 'The Fight against Piracy: Working within the Administrative Enforcement System in China', in Torremans, Paul, et al, *Intellectual Property and TRIPS Compliance in China*, Cheltenham, UK and Northampton, MA, USA: Edward Elgar, pp. 95–96.

proposed US orphan work solution, as explained below, might create *de facto* obligation to register. Rights holders would be obliged to avoid immunity for unauthorized uses. Secondly, the creation of security interests in copyright might be a kind of 'exercise'. When the creation of security interests refers to 'transfer', the non-formality principle does not apply. However, if such a creation is an encumbrance on copyright, registration concerns exploitation and thus enjoyment. UNCITRAL made the recommendation that creation, the effectiveness against third parties, and the priority over the rights of competing claimants for a security right in intangible property, be determined by registration.[20] Meanwhile, the basic principle of UNCITRAL's recommendations is the supremacy of IP law over security interest law.[21] Moreover, there is a consensus that where national law follows a copyright registration system that determines creation and third party effectiveness of security interests in copyright, the Guide does not apply. However, when IP law is silent, the Guide – a mere non-binding but soft law adopted by a UN body – applies on a voluntary basis.

Thirdly, domestic presumption is acceptable but cross-border presumption may concern the non-formality principle. National registration does not create offshore legal effects created by copyright law. For example, US statutory damages and attorney fees are given only to US-registered copyrights. On the other hand, effects given by non-copyright law, such as presumption of ownership, are not subject to the territorial principle. Where a UK case would deny the presumption of ownership to foreign registration,[22] Australian and Japanese case laws recognize such presumptions.[23]

Finally, the compulsory element of collective societies in some countries (explained below), despite its useful notice function, could be prohibited formality.

---

[20] United Nations General Assembly (2005), *Security Interests, Recommendations of the draft Legislative Guide on Secured Transactions, Note by the Secretariat*, A/CN.9/WG.IV/WP.24, para.137.

[21] UNCITRAL (2008), *Legislative Guide on Secured Transactions*, Recommendation 4(b): The Guide does not apply to '[i]ntellectual property in so far as the provisions of the law are inconsistent with national law or international agreements, to which the State is a party, relating to intellectual property'.

[22] *Columbia Picture Industries Inc. v. Robinson*, [1987] Ch 38, [1986] 3 All ER 338, 19 December 1985.

[23] The Attorney-General's Department, Copyright Law in Australia, A Short Guide, 2005, para. 14; and Tokyo District Court, 1976 (Wa), 10039, judged on 20 April 1981.

2.4.2 Effective interpretation

Effective interpretation is permissible if it promotes the object and purpose of the non-formality principle. The non-formality principle is rooted in the *jus naturale* theory, which was dominant in continental Europe in the nineteenth century. However, legislative history states that the principle did not spread globally from the basic philosophy of copyright nature. Rather, the necessity for international protection was the driving factor of the non-formality principle.[24] Due to the reciprocity of the national treatment before the Stockholm text (1967), rights holders had been obliged to survey the required formality in the country of origin. Thus, the non-formality principle was adopted by the Berlin Revision (1908) for easier international protection of copyrights.

It should be noted, however, that an effective interpretation cannot weigh the general purpose of the treaty over the statute. The object and purpose are 'modifiers of the ordinary meaning of a term which is being interpreted, in the sense that the ordinary meaning is to be identified in their light,' but do not 'introduce an alternative option for finding the meaning'.[25]

3 ADVANTAGES OF PERMITTED FORMALITIES IN THE INTERNET ERA

3.1 Disadvantages of the Static Approaches

3.1.1 Insufficient tools to confirm the copyright ownership or encumbrance

An author's name on a digital work may not put 'his name to appear on the work in the usual manner' (Article 15.1, Berne Convention). Moreover, a digitally displayed name does not create presumption of authorship, and the applicability of the presumptions depends upon the future identification customs of the Information Society.[26] The orphan work issue has become an important agenda in various countries and regions. It is evident that legislators did not expect the advent of the Internet as a vehicle for the distribution and dissemination of works. In addition, the cross-territorial presumption of municipal registration is not supported, at least not clearly, under the static approaches.

---

[24] Ricketson (2006), *supra* note 14, p. 38.

[25] Gardiner (2008), *supra* note 2, pp. 190–192.

[26] Dusollier, Severine (2003), 'Some Reflections on Copyright Management Information and Moral Rights', 25 *Colum. J.L. & Arts* 377, pp. 391–95.

The Internet has changed the legislators' assumptions. Ordinary authors can distribute contents without capital or techniques. In addition, ordinary users can access such content without any intermediary. The confirmation of copyright ownership between ordinary individual persons is not easy.

3.1.2 Prolonged process to confirm ownership without registration

3.1.2.1 Border measures An application for border measures requires 'in writing' (Art. 51, TRIPS) and 'adequate evidence' of *prima facie* infringement (Art. 52, TRIPS). The conceptualization of 'adequate evidence' is determined by municipal laws. A soft law presents a non-exhaustive list, including the certificate of copyrights registration, for adequate evidence.[27] No legislative history or other authoritative document seems to clarify whether border measures are subject to the non-formality principle. Copyright registration is not a condition of border measures in Europe[28] and Japan,[29] and registration is merely one of the tools to verify ownership. Luckily, ownership is seldom questioned. On the other hand, in the US and China,[30] registration is practically a condition for rights holders. In the US, only registered copyrights can be protected by the customs authority[31] and the enforcement of the International Trade Commission.[32]

3.1.2.2 Enforcement by an administrative authority The administrative enforcement system in China is initiated either by the administrative authority or at the request of the rights holder. Rights holders can claim without copyrights registration, but a considerable amount of documentary evidence is required to verify the copyright ownership.[33]

---

[27] World Customs Organization (2003), 'Model Provisions for National Legislation to Implement Fair and Effective Border Measures Consistent with the Agreement on Trade-Related Aspects of Intellectual Property Rights'.

[28] Essay 2, Council Regulation (EC) No 1383/2003 of 22 July 2003 concerning customs actions against goods suspected of infringing certain intellectual property rights and the measures to be taken against goods found to have infringed such rights.

[29] Customs Format C-5840.

[30] Art. 5, Decree No.54 of the Customs General Administration on 28 September 1995.

[31] 19 C.F.R. § 133.32, T.D. 87–40, 52 FR 9474, 1987, as last amended by T.D. 99-27, 64 FR 13673, 13675, 1999; and 19 C.F.R. § 133.33, T.D. 72–266, 37 FR 20678, Oct. 3, 1972, as last amended by T.D. 99–24, 64 FR 11376, 1999.

[32] 19 C.F.R. § 210.12(a)(6)(i) & (f), 53 FR 33055, 1988, as last corrected at 59 FR 64286, 1994.

[33] Japan External Trade Organization (2005), 'Case documentary'.

Currently, only Chinese registration is accepted as *prima facie* ownership of copyrights.

3.1.2.3 Judicial provisional measures The meaning of 'reasonably available evidence' (Art. 50.3, TRIPS) to confirm copyright ownership is not clear. Most countries do not consider copyright ownership as an independent condition for claiming provisional measures but rather as a natural precondition. In the US, copyright registration is *prima facie* evidence of the validity and ownership of copyright for preliminary injunctions[34] and temporary restraining orders. In Europe, the judicial authorities can order an applicant to provide 'any reasonably available evidence' that indicates 'a sufficient degree of certainty' of copyright ownership.[35] In the UK, which abolished copyright registration, the plaintiff needs to verify ownership by tracing its course, starting from the original author.[36] In France and Germany, registration is not a condition of provisional measures or a tool to verify ownership, according to the WIPO survey (2003–2004).

3.1.2.4 Damages Since damages cases are less urgent, the necessity for *prima facie* evidential value of copyright registration is less than in provisional measures cases. Thus, formal evidential procedures are more likely to be observed in damages cases.

3.1.2.5 Notice and takedown procedures by Internet service providers (ISPs) The legal consequences of not only foreign but also domestic copyright registration during the notice and takedown procedures are not clear. The non-formality principle does not hinder ISPs from recognizing the legal effects of copyright registration but simultaneously does not protect ISPs from liability.

3.1.3 Insufficient tools to discover copyright holders

Some types of works, such as photographs and ephemera, of even original authors may not be suitable for display. The subsequent transfer of or restriction on ownership is not put to notice unless it is registered. A static understanding of the non-formality principle has resulted in many countries having no registration or few legal effects.

---

34 *Donald Frederick Evans & Assocs. Inc. v. Continental Homes, Inc.*, 785 F.2d 897, 1986 U.S. App. LEXIS 23620, 31 March 1986; and *Novelty Textile Mills, Inc. v. Joan Fabrics Corp.*, 558 F.2d 1090, 1977 U.S. App. LEXIS 12494, 12 July 1977.

35 Art. 9.3, Directive 2004/48/EC of the European Parliament and of the Council of 29 April 2004 on the enforcement of intellectual property rights.

36 *Columbia Picture Industries Inc.* (1985), *supra* note 22.

3.2 Relation to the Raison d'être of the Copyright System

There are several theories or justifications for the copyright system,[37] but it can be safely generalized that the copyright system seeks to balance the stakeholders' interests. Such stakeholders, in the sense that their interests are affected by copyrights, include authors, publishers, performers, film production companies, phonogram producers, Internet service providers, and broadcasters.[38] In addition, consumers are increasingly important stakeholders. The three main stakeholders are authors and their successors, producers, and consumers.[39] The first two stakeholders are 'rights holders'.

3.2.1 Rights holders' perspectives

Without a tool to verify or obtain a presumption of ownership, prompt enforcement – in particular cross-border injunction – may be hampered. A rights holder possesses the legitimate interest to hide his/her identity and to put notice. The current system cannot accommodate the necessity of an international notice. A domestic apostille is not available for rights holders in a country without a national registration system. In addition, the use of apostille requires that it be translated into all the foreign languages of the countries of protection, which diminishes the apostille's convenience.

Registration is an effective tool of notice, and an online survey of national registrations is costless. Voluntary registration can be promoted for rights holders by highlighting the verification of ownership during enforcement procedures.

3.2.2 Users' perspectives

International law seems to indicate the primacy of human rights over IP rights.[40] The Universal Declaration of Human Rights (UDHR, 1948) and International Covenant on Civil and Political Rights (ICCPR, 1966) maintains a balance among the stakeholders' interests. UDHR recognizes the right to participate in the cultural life of the community as well as the authors' rights (Art. 27.1 and .2), and ICCPR permits the freedom to seek,

---

[37] See, for example, Dutfield, Graham and Suthersanen, Uma (2008), *Global Intellectual Property Law*, Cheltenham, UK and Northampton, MA, USA, Edward Elgar, Chapter 3.

[38] Ibid, pp. 39 and 44.

[39] Ibid, p. 51.

[40] Ibid, p. 226, referring to ECOSOC (2001), *Economic, Social and Cultural Rights*, E/CN.4/Sub.2/2001/13.

receive and impart information and ideas, which is subject to the rights or reputations of others (Art. 19.2 and .3).

The copyright system does not protect users' interests directly, for copyright law itself cannot be the cause of action for users. Nevertheless, the system incorporates the need for balance rather than maximizes the protection of copyright. The term 'as possible' in the Preamble of the Berne Convention incorporates the public interest.[41]

Users possess a legitimate interest in knowing the ownership of copyrights. Without such information, users would hesitate to use the work for fear of being sued. On the other hand, ownership is often invisible to users. In addition, derivative activities based on the original work are commonly found in digital contexts. Compound audiovisual contents, which include music, performance and art, are increasingly available on the Internet.

3.3 Contribution to the Object and Purpose of the Non-Formality Principle

In the Internet era, the immediate removal of infringing content is a must to avoid serious damages. Ownership of copyright is a precondition for the application of such a removal, but verification of ownership is not always easy, in particular regarding international cases and non-registered works. Once the ownership is disputed, the claimant will be asked to present verification, or at least to present the basis for the presumption of ownership. In countries where the registration system is abolished, a rights holder may not be able to find a tool to create such a presumption. Ironically, the non-formality principle, despite its original purpose of promoting international protection, could be harmful to international protection.

The contribution to the object and purpose of the non-formality principle is judged on the basis of the comparisons among (i) the costs and burdens associated with the compliance of formality, (ii) the benefits for rights holders when formality is voluntarily accepted, and (iii) other legitimate interests such as users' interests.

3.4 Limitation of a Vitalized Formality to the Solution

First, as long as the permitted formality is not harmonized internationally, the non-uniformity of information emanating from each country of origin reduces its utility.[42] In addition, searching for registration as

---

41 Ficsor (2004), *supra* note 12, p. 21.

42 Ricketson and Ginsburg (2006), *supra* note 14, p. 322.

an automatic immune measure to the use of orphan works is incompatible with the non-formality principle. Under this formal approach, rights holders are eventually obliged to register copyrights.[43] Thus, reference to registration is a mere, rather than decisive, factor to determine whether a 'reasonably diligent search' – a condition to be free from infringement by the use of orphan works – has been done.

Secondly, there is tension regarding rights holders' interests in privacy. In general, registered information is standardized by administrative regulations and, once registered, is subject to the public eye. Full disclosure might discourage the incentives of registration for rights holders. Partial disclosure could be a possible policy choice, if such an option would be beneficial for stakeholders. However, privacy is also in conflict with the necessity of ensuring correct information. If there were a lack of substantive examination, registration could be provided to non-rights holders by mistake.[44] The presumption of ownership is based on the rights holders' opportunities to check registered information.

Lastly, the registration of all copyrighted works created and distributed on the Internet is not realistic in view of current administrative abilities and registration costs.

4 FUTURE OF THE NON-FORMALITY PRINCIPLE

4.1 Revision, Modification or Status Quo?

Revising the Berne Convention or the TRIPS Agreement is a theoretical rather than a foreseen event. Revising the Berne Convention requires member unanimity (Art. 27.3) and has not been revised since 1979. Changing the packaged TRIPS Agreement is even more difficult. A new international custom that negates the non-formality principle requires two elements of international custom, that is, the general practice (*usus* or *diuturnitas*) and the corresponding views of States (*opinio juris* or *opinio necessitatis*); however, there are no such elements. Considering the recent reiteration of the non-formality principle under the WCT and WPPT (1996), a new treaty, international custom or even a Special Agreement (Art. 20, Berne Convention) cannot be foreseen to modify the principle.

---

43 US Copyright Office (2006), *supra* note 16, pp. 72–75.

44 An administrative decision made by the National Copyright Administration over the ownership of a famous folk song 'Oriental Serenade', http://www.newiplaw.com/html/2008-01/1329.htm (in Chinese), 25 March 2009, referred by Professor Guan Yuying, Intellectual Property Center, China Academy of Social Sciences (CASS).

A fundamental change of circumstances could terminate the treaty under the VCLT (Art. 62) and the customary international law (*rebus sic stantibus*). Besides the strong criticism that would arise against such termination, if it were permitted, there is yet no such circumstance, as evidenced by the current national laws.

4.2 Role of the Collective Administration and Other Intermediaries

Collective societies manage the database of copyright-related information, thus possessing a registration function. However, there are several limitations. First, a collective society's database is normally not provided with legal effects such as the *prima facie* evidence of ownership. Due to limited access to the private database, the accuracy of the database is not checked. In some countries, the function of collective societies is presumed even for non-trusted copyrighted works, as seen in 'legal presumption', 'extended collective licenses', or 'compulsory collective management'.[45] Such a presumption is not extended to foreign territories. Secondly, collective societies handle only limited types of copyrighted works. Finally, the geographical scope is limited.

Collective societies have been established in each country. International cooperation among collective societies is often scrutinized from the viewpoints of competition policy. It is noted that establishment of a global Internet licensing agency (GILA) by collective societies might be discussed at a future ALAI meeting. GILA administers the licensing of copyrighted materials on the Internet without territorial restriction.[46]

Collective societies and public registration seem to have complementary roles. The following Table explains the different approaches to copyright notice in several jurisdictions. Since it is difficult to provide a numerical comparison between national or regional systems, the Table might be too conceptualized. Nevertheless, it suggests that countries with strong (or weak) public registration tend to have collective societies with a limited

---

[45] Olsson, Henry (2005), 'The Importance of Collective Management of Copyright and Related Rights', WIPO/CR/KRT/05/4, pp. 3–4; Spurgeon, C. Paul (2003), 'License or Limit? On-line Educational Uses: Alternatives for Preserving the Exclusive Rights of Copyright Owners', *Copyright Bulletin of UNESCO*, pp. 12–13; and Gervais, Daniel J. (2001), 'Collective Management of Copyright and Neighbouring Rights in Canada: An International Perspective', *Department of Canadian Heritage*, pp. 35–40.

[46] Sterling, J.A.L., Morning and Afternoon Sessions Tuesday 16 June, Online Exploitation and Licensing, General Reporter's Summary and Proposals for Discussion, paper distributed at ALAI Congress (London, June 2009).

Table 31.1 Role of public administration and collective society for copyright notice

	Public registration	Collective society
China	AA	D (in most areas) C (in big cities)
US	B	B
Japan	C	B
UK	D	B
Scandinavian countries	D	A (Extended licenses)

Note: A – strong, B – intermediate, C – weak, and D – none

(or extended) function. Japan used to have a state-administered collective society but liberated the control,[47] so Table 31.1 indicates that the role of Japanese collective society is 'intermediate'.

In China, public registration plays a significant role not only in enforcement but also in private transactions. Administrative accusations are few compared to the total number of registered works,[48] but the use of civil procedures is very rare – only 1 per cent of all the administrative cases led to civil procedures in 2006. The International Copyright Trading Center (国际版权交易中心) was inaugurated in February 2009, where the Copyright Protection Center of China (CPCC) registers all types of copyrighted works, provides copyright ownership information to potential users and represents rights holders,[49] particularly with regard to all types of contents, both electronic and physical. The Center boosts the capacity to store all digital works on the Internet. Chinese future experience will tell whether public registration can provide effective notice function in the Internet era, particularly when the censorship element of formality is removed in compliance with the WTO Panel's decision.[50]

[47] Law on Management Business of Copyright and Neighboring Rights, Law No.131 (2000).

[48] Number of cases of administrative accusation is 268 in 2007, and number of registered works is 133,789 in 2007, according to National Copyright Administration of China (NCAC).

[49] This is done by Copyright Agency of China (CAC), which is managed by NCAC.

[50] WTO (2009), China – Measures Affecting Trading Rights and Distribution Services for Certain Publications and Audiovisual Entertainment Products, Report of the Panel, WT/DS362/R.

4.3 Complementary Roles with Other Systems

As explained, the dynamic approach alone does not provide any perfect solution to promote ownership notice.

4.3.1 Limitations and exceptions

Use of orphan works means using copyrighted works without the rights holder's authorization. Limitations and exceptions could reduce or eliminate the orphan works by obliging rights holders to clarify ownership. If a certain use were a limitation or an exception, the user would have a defence against future enforcement.

Guidelines for the legitimate use of an orphan work without the rights holder's authorization have been drafted in the US. The core concept of the drafts is as follows: 'if the user has performed a reasonably diligent search for the copyright owner but is unable to locate that owner, then that user should enjoy a benefit of limitations on the remedies that a copyright owner could obtain against him if the owner showed up at a later date and sued for infringement.'[51] The US Copyright Office's Report (2006) assumed that compatibility with the three-step test of this concept would be supported by dominant opinion. However, the Report was based on only three comments,[52] and there was strong opposition to such views.[53]

4.3.2 Duration of protection

Prolonged copyright protection is one of the causes of the problems associated with orphan works. The duration of copyright is controversial and there are severe conflicts of interest among stakeholders, so policy makers hesitate to combine the two issues.

4.3.3 Canadian and Japanese compulsory license systems

A compulsory license system is authorized by the Appendix of the Berne Convention and the TRIPS Agreement (Art. 9.1). Japan has a compulsory license system for orphan works, after a due diligent search has been conducted (Art. 67.1). The use of this system is stagnant[54] because of the application fee, the hurdle involved in clearing the due diligent search and

---

[51] US Copyright Office (2006), *supra* note 16, p. 95.

[52] Ibid, pp. 88–89.

[53] Goldstein, Paul and Ginsburg, Jane (2005), *Comments on 'Orphan Works' Inquiry* (Federal Register), p. 2.

[54] From 1972 to 2005 only 30 compulsory licenses were issued. See Subdivision on Copyrights, Council for Cultural Affairs at the Agency for Cultural Affairs (2005).

the difficulty of searching in newspapers and journals.[55] The compulsory license system is used slightly more in Canada than in Japan, but is still far from being used on a regular basis.[56] Canada has relatively clearer criteria for a reasonable search, but cannot be free from the substantive administrative procedures. Even the most efficient compulsory license system would not be able to handle the massive amount of copyrighted works that are daily created and distributed on the Internet, as well as the commensurate increase in the demands for use.

4.4 Possibility of Global Registration

Global registration of copyrights is a quest not only for users but also for other stakeholders such as creditors and insolvency administrators.[57] The voluntary nature of registration could avoid the non-formality issue, but theoretical and practical problems would need to be solved.

4.5 Issues for Future Discussion

4.5.1 Contractually split rights

Copyright is a bundle of rights and has subdivided rights, such as the rights of reproduction and distribution, normally prescribed by national copyright law provisions. In addition, each subdivided right can be further split by private contracts based on various elements, such as language, geographical scope and time limitation. For example, the author can split his/her right and transfer 'the right to distribute the French-language version of my paper in Tokyo between 2009 and 2010'. The validity and conditions of a contractual split are left to national legislative or judicial policy.[58] Whereas the availability of a contractual

---

[55] Subdivision on Copyrights, Council for Cultural Affairs at the Agency for Cultural Affairs (2008).

[56] From 1990 to January 2009, 232 licenses were issued by the Copyright Board of Canada.

[57] International Insolvency Institute (2007), 'Submission to UNCITRAL Working Group VI, Colloquium on Financing of Intellectual Property', EBL 1-2-7, p. 1. Information relating to copyright ownership is crucial for security interest transactions.

[58] Professor Ueno, one of the leading copyright professors in Japan, analyzes the validity based on three elements for split of copyright: (i) content splitting, (ii) geographical splitting, and (iii) splitting on a time axis. Ueno, Tatsuhiro, *The Promotion of Cross-border Exchange of Intellectual Assets-The Case of Music and Trade Secrets*, essay distributed at Geneva International Academic Network (GIAN)/Rikkyo University joint Conference (Tokyo, 8 December 2007), pp. 1–4.

split can accommodate various cultural and/or business needs, the split often complicates legal consequences, when the right is split into tiny fragments.

In addition, the legal consequences of the split become uncertain and hard to predict when the contract concerns foreign copyright, because jurisdiction and applicable law rules governing copyright contracts are not established, particularly at the international level. It is not self-evident whether contractually split rights are subject to the non-formality principle. One view is that, since contractually split rights are part of the 'right', they are subject to the non-formality principle as long as the pre-split 'right' is prescribed by a treaty. Another possible view is that the non-formality principle does not concern the contractual split itself, and the contractual split can be subject to formality such as in writing and registration. The issue is whether or not the split is non-essential for the basic corpus of copyright, like the transfer of copyright.

Neither public registration nor a collective society is likely able to accommodate the subdivision and contractually split rights, for the following reasons. First, a Copyright Office and collective society lack the technical capacity to recognize non-typical rights, which will be the case even when all processes are handled electronically. Secondly, neither a Copyright Office nor collective society has the ability to confirm the validity of a contractual split. The determination of validity is largely judged on a case-by-case basis by judicial courts. Thus, the notice function is limited for split rights. Even when the contractually split rights are registered, the presumption of foreign registration would be unlikely, since foreign courts have even more difficulties when deciding the legal consequences of the split.

4.5.2 Copyrighted works beyond the treaty protection term

In many countries, such as European countries and the US, copyright is protected for more than 50 years after the author's death. The longer protection term of copyright is compatible with the treaty obligation (Art. 7.6 of the Berne Convention). Once the minimum protection period lapses, the non-formality principle may or may not be applicable. At present, as far as the author can tell, there does not seem to be any national system where formality is imposed on copyrighted works lapsing the minimum protection term by treaty. However, this is not clear-cut. The author personally and currently supports the denial of the extension of the non-formality principle. Extended application of the non-formality principle would be sustained by a practical idea: formality after the treaty protection term would eventually oblige rights holders to comply with formality even before the lapse of the treaty protection term, because the compliance becomes difficult when supporting documents are not readily available.

However, denial of the non-formality principle would be more grounded. First, copyright, once it lapses the treaty minimum term, is no longer protected by treaty. Thus, even a foreign work would be treated like a domestic work, to which the non-formality principle does not apply. The non-formality principle concerns only rights protected by the treaty. Secondly, in substance, the necessity of notice function becomes even higher as the time lapses after creation or publication. Users would find more difficulties in finding the true author and/or rights holder in case of old works than newer ones.[59]

5 CONCLUSION

The non-formality principle, originally aimed at effective international protection, is presently not always beneficial for that purpose. The solution to emerging issues depends upon the willingness and flexibility of international and national legislators, assuming that treaty obligations will not be negated under generally accepted interpretation methodologies.

---

[59] Hishinuma, Takeshi (2009), *Chiteki Zaisanken Hogo no Kokusai Kihan –Koji Chosakubutu Mondai heno Shiza* (International Norm relating to the Protection of Intellectual Property – Perspectives for the Orphan Work Problem), *Shinzansha*, Tokyo, p. 32.

32. The graduated response and the role of intermediaries: avoiding the Apocalypse or a return to the sources?

Pierre Sirinelli*

1 INTRODUCTION

This is the final presentation of the congress. It is supposed to be part of a historical film, that of a 300-year construction! However, the law I have to tell you about is certainly not the most attractive stone. And I suppose that we will not be talking about it in 300 years. Unless, perhaps, out of curiosity and so on. It is a special law that is worth mentioning because it is indicative of trends. More a law of 'means' than content, that is to say what interests us: works and creators.

The term 'graduated response' has been used in France to describe the possible legal responses to the question of illegal 'peer-to-peer' (P2P) exchanges. It is preferable to use the phrase 'graduated response' rather than the neighbouring 'flexible response', the latter being part of military (one dares not say 'diplomatic') language, borrowed from the Cold War and evoking an attitude based on violence and nuclear response.[1]

This concept of 'graduated response' makes it possible to understand the idea of the new sanctions that the French law, voted on 13 May 2009, and entitled 'Creation and Internet', was intended to introduce in the case of breach of literary and artistic property rights. These sanctions should be proportional to the offence and appear less severe, as opposed to the

* Professor at Paris-I University (Panthéon – Sorbonne). This contribution was originally written in French. The original version, as well as a Spanish translation, can be found on the website of the British Literary and Artistic Copyright Association (BLACA): www.blaca.org.

[1] Graduated response is the basis of the MacNamara doctrine for the defence of the United States.

common law of literary and artistic property which permits criminal penalties.

In short, it allows us to envisage responses to acts of infringement which are more appropriate and realistic.

It should be added that the process is also supposed to contain an educational aspect to change behaviour for the future and so on.

The French bill envisaged the suspension of Internet access in the case of repeated violations of literary and artistic property. This cutting of Internet access was to be decided by an Independent Administrative Authority (named Hadopi). But it is the law itself that has been cut, as it has been partly censored by the French Constitutional Council, which renders my account partly obsolete!

We begin to understand already why no one else has proposed a similar response.

As the works of this congress have demonstrated, the 'author-exploiter' is an old pairing for which arbitration was made for the first time in England with the Statute of Anne:

- the rights belong to the creator;
- the publisher – who wishes to exploit the work – must obtain his authorisation, otherwise he will be regarded as infringing those rights;
- the public was, at the time, considered as 'passive' and reduced to the role of 'consumer' of works.

But three centuries later, things look a little different, notably due to the phenomenon – repeatedly studied by our association – of the rise of digital media and in particular of networks.

This digital revolution naturally presents positive aspects, both for the author and the public, in that it increases the chances of exploitation of works by offering ease of copying, storage, transmission, use and so on.

But the digital revolution also has as a consequence:

- on one hand, the arrival of new intermediaries which have imported new practices into the cultural industries sector (some from the world of computing and telecommunications) and requested the development of new rules (notably with the adoption of provisions specific to electronic commerce), giving them a status of conditional irresponsibility;
- on the other hand, a transformation of the classic roles existing within the cultural industries. Particularly from a section of the public.

At least two examples demonstrate it: peer-to-peer exchanges and the making available of works on contributory sites within the framework of what is commonly called Web 2.0.[2]

The so-called technical intermediaries, in particular the Internet Service Providers, claim a status of conditional lack of responsibility in most countries due to the existence of certain special texts.

This is the case in most of Europe due to the European Community directive of 8 June 2000 relating to electronic commerce; it is the case in the USA with the DMCA; it is also the case in other states with similar arrangements. Thanks to these texts, these intermediaries declare themselves, mainly in Europe, *a priori*, unconcerned by the opposability of copyright.

Other people who provide other means, such as the publishers of programs permitting peer-to-peer exchanges, claim the same situation.

Now, these different categories of people naturally have an economic model based on the search for creative works. To this extent is it possible to say that they use (or even, capture) the 'value' of the work. At least its power of attraction.

The problem is that copyright is essentially based on literary works and the way they are exploited. It generally relates to actual acts of use of the works (reproduction, distribution, broadcasting, performance and so on). For some, it is therefore powerless to permit opposability of the monopoly of authors to certain of these new participants who do not strictly perform such acts.

Nowadays, amongst the difficulties identified, the accent is equally put on the 'cost-free' myth which runs through the Internet. But to tell the truth, this is a false novelty. Free access to intellectual works for users has been available for a long time. One only has to think of consumption of

---

[2] In common with peer-to-peer, the phenomenon finds the Internet user at the origin of infringements. It is most often an Internet user who will make available to the public, via a contributory hosting site, a work of his choice but which he has not, most often, created himself.

But the phenomenon is distinguished from peer-to-peer in two aspects:

- firstly by its less widespread mass effect (fewer Internet users are implicated in making available works)
- secondly by the presence here of an intermediary (the contributory site which hosts the proposed videos) with which a dialogue is ultimately possible.

It is this particularity which has allowed to limit the infringement phenomenon. Thus, in the United States, the adoption of a Charter between platforms and beneficiaries, aiming at adopting fingerprinting measures has allowed the blocking of unauthorised works even before they are available on the sites.

works via television or radio, or through certain newspapers to realise that this model has been implemented for a long time without copyright being unrecognised. Gratuitousness for the public does not mean it is cost-free for exploiters and most media have come to agreements with authors to, on one hand, ensure their authorisation and, on the other, ensure their remuneration. Finally, nothing prevents any author from voluntarily making their works available cost-free.

As for Internet users, it must be appreciated that:

- they are no longer passive consumers, but take the initiative to make works available to others;
- they are spread throughout the world;
- they are not directly accessible by the beneficiaries because, to begin with, their identity is hidden behind an IP address.

How can we try to reach them, to make them aware?

Copyright exhausts itself trying to understand the behaviour of people who are manifestly, for practical or legal reasons, out of reach. It exhausts itself to the point that it loses, for many, its legitimacy.

It is exhausted to the point that one might be tempted by a radical solution consisting of the repeal of copyright, three hundred years after its creation with the Statute of Anne. Such was the electoral programme of the Pirate Party in Sweden, which has just had a representative elected to the European Parliament. But, to tell the truth, this would not be the best way to celebrate a birthday with our British friends nowadays.

The French legislator believed that he could find, for peer-to-peer, a less radical solution. This latter was not very well received.

Let us understand the debate. This is not about addressing the question of whether unauthorised uploading or downloading are or are not illegal. We will therefore take this as read,[3] to look only at the question of how to handle this mass phenomenon. The only real question here is to know how, on the facts, we can ensure the true effectiveness of the protection of works, given that the debates relating to technical protective measures, equally often discussed,[4] will not be considered here.

We could add, to reuse the image evoked yesterday by Professor Sterling of the Venetian academic, that 'the whole world is in water up to their knees' and that it is time to act rather than think. This is what the French government has done. It has 'dived in'. To the point that one could wonder whether it has drowned!

---

3 See, for example, the ALAI meetings in Budapest or Oaxaca.

4 See, for example, the New York Congress.

To continue the aquatic metaphor, two angles of approach can be envisaged. Upstream and downstream in relation to file transfers. But in each case the idea is to attempt to prevent acts rather than having to punish them, even if this solution cannot be ruled out definitively.

2 UPSTREAM: ATTEMPT TO LIMIT ACTS OF INFRINGEMENT

This targets more the intermediaries who provide the means of infringement than the Internet user.

The ideal would rather be to address people who unquestionably benefit from the infringement to the point of obtaining a profit – or, at least, a benefit – by making available to Internet users the means to carry out illegal file transfers. The measure would perhaps kill two birds with one stone: by limiting the number of tools allowing illegal file transfers, one might perhaps be able to diminish the possibilities of file transfers and thus the number of infringements.

We know that, in Sweden, those responsible for providing links – trackers – allowing file transfers were convicted ('The Pirate Bay'). The four accused individuals from the file exchange site were harshly sentenced to one year in prison for complicity in violating copyright and 30 million crowns (2.7 million euros) in damages payable to the record, cinema and video game industry.

The solution is fairly standard. All we will remember of this case is that, on the one hand, the 'pirates' have, in exchange for a tidy sum, later given up their activities, and, on the other hand these 'pirates' have questioned the impartiality of the magistrate who made this decision, on the basis that the latter belongs to an international literary and artistic association! Or how a learned society; a simple scientific community, can be presented as a lobby or a sect!

But in truth, it is decentralised exchanges which essentially pose the problem. It is not possible to declare that, on principle, the act of making available programs permitting peer-to-peer exchanges is illegal. The solution comes back to asserting that, by its very nature, peer-to-peer is contrary to copyright. Now, not only is this not the case, but it is also necessary to consider that peer-to-peer exchanges, correctly controlled, may constitute an extraordinary opportunity to legally make available these works – for the creators, the cultural industries, and the public.

Nevertheless, in certain countries, the highest courts have not hesitated to assert that making available to the public certain programs may, in certain cases, result in the liability of those individuals who were responsible for it. We know that this is the case in Australia (the *Kazaa*[5] case) or in the United States (the *Grokster*[6] case).

In France, the legislator has intervened on the occasion of the law of 1 August 2006 to remove all doubt and to permit the conviction (Article L.335-2-2 CPI – Intellectual Property Code) of the person who '*knowingly*' puts on the market a program '*manifestly destined to making available to the public non-authorised works or protected objects*'.[7]

These constructions are based on a common sense observation according to which the publishers of programs whose business model is clearly based on incitement to infringement should be held liable.

What, then, if there continue to be infringements?

3 UPSTREAM: HANDLING THE REMAINING INFRINGEMENTS

Seeking the civil or criminal liability of Internet users is neither easy nor really productive of encouraging results. While realising that the idea of dragging before the courts[8] people that we hope will become future customers is not the best marketing method, we have to appreciate that it may seem a vain attempt to try to resolve a problem concerning several million people by contemplating only a few show trials.

For this reason other solutions have been sought, relying, in a progressive approach, first on the idea of education before considering a sanction.

3.1 Education

In many countries, the educational route has been explored. Notably by sending to the pirates electronic messages explaining the breaches of copyright. This is the case, for example, in Japan, Ireland, the United States,

---

5 Federal Court of Australia, 5 September 2005. *Universal Music Australia v Sharman Licence Holdings Ltd.*

6 United States Supreme Court, 27 June 2005, *MGM v. Grokster.* In Germany, on 8 February 2006, the Hamburg High Regional Court estimated that a program provider may be considered responsible for the losses sustained by a beneficiary if his program is mainly used to commit illegal acts and that he presents his program this way. It is however difficult to consider that such would be the position of the Federal Court of Justice.

7 See also Article L.336-1 CPI (Intellectual Property Code).

8 It is estimated that over 35,000 trials have already been held in the United States.

Norway, Sweden (law which came into force on 1 April 2009), in Brazil and so on. In the United Kingdom, an agreement was signed on 27 July 2008 between the main ISPs and the cultural industries. This has led to warnings being sent on an experimental basis. The Digital Britain Report presented yesterday by the Government, planned to launch a consultation about a law which would give the power to the national regulator (OFCOM) to impose on all ISPs the requirement to send warnings, together with the conservation of data necessary to permit the beneficiaries to lead court actions against repeat offenders.

To tell the truth, this solution has never led to a reduction in the volume of infringements. Certainly in some countries significant results seem to have been achieved. The Swedish authorities have thus noted that two months after the new law came into force, a major reduction in illegal file transfers had occurred in parallel with a rise in legal sales. It is not certain that the same observation could be made in certain Latin countries. For this reason, other states have contemplated linking this educational aspect with the threat of a sanction.

3.2 'Muscular' Education

Here we enter into the domain of a more rigorous education, similar to the one practiced not so long ago in British colleges! This is what, in France, is called the 'graduated response'.

South Korea and Taiwan have recently passed laws to this effect. New Zealand contemplated doing so before postponing the law. In the United Kingdom, the Digital Britain Report presented on 16 June 2009 plans that OFCOM (the national regulator) will have the power, if measures of prevention and education prove definitively to be insufficient, to impose upon the ISPs the obligation to take more stringent measures permitting the blocking of pirate sites or protocols, the identification or filtering of content, or even the limitation of access speed for those subscribers whose line is used for illegal ends.

In France, as we have already said, the French Parliament passed in May 2009[9] a law (called 'création et Internet' – creation and Internet) allowing the creation of an independent administrative authority (Hadopi) in charge of a mission of surveillance, education, recommendations (warnings) and, in the case of failure, sanctions.

With a very 'upstream' preventative strategy, three series of measures are envisaged:

---

[9] The 'petite loi' (little law) was adopted by the senate on 13 May 2009.

1. Educational and awareness campaigns, a new kind of 'Civics', with two aspects; firstly the emphasis of the legal alternatives,[10] and secondly the presentation in schools of the dangers of downloading and the principles and virtues of intellectual property.[11]
2. The establishment of a list, a portal, of legal alternatives.
3. The obligation for ISPs to offer filtering solutions.

If, despite all this, infringements continue, French law envisaged to carry on with the educational work by targeting it more carefully, by adding fear of the Law and ultimately a penalty.

The plan passed on 13 May 2009 was the following.

Beneficiaries may, on the basis of findings made by sworn agents, refer the matter to the administrative authority to demand from the ISP the identity of the Internet user holding the IP address from which the illegal file transfers have been carried out.

The authority may then send an electronic message explaining to the subscriber that an illegal act has been committed.

In the event of a repeated offence noted as a result of the maintenance of a central file, the authority may again communicate with the subscriber via electronic message, then send him a recorded delivery letter by post.

In the event of a further offence, the law allows for the independent administrative authority to be given the power to impose upon the ISPs the obligation to suspend the subscription of the subscriber who has carried out – or who has not succeeded in preventing – illegal file transfers using his line.

A conciliation procedure is envisaged to allow the subscriber to be partly released of the penalty in exchange for implementing technical control or filtering solutions.

This legal construction was partly censored by the French Constitutional Council on 10 June 2009 on the basis that 'the liberty of communication and expression, set out in article 11 of the Declaration of the Rights of

---

[10] Several provisions reflect this concern. This task falls not only to the Hadopi but also to the beneficiaries themselves, together with the National Cinematographic Centre and the ISPs. It will also be done by means of national education.

[11] Thus article 15 of the law adds to Article L. 312 – 6 of the Education Code, a clause according to which 'in the framework of these lessons, the pupils receive information on the dangers of downloading and of illegally making available works or objects protected by copyright or a similar right for artistic creation.' This, for a teacher opens gulfs of thought. Literary and artistic property was up to now studied at postgraduate level; now these principles will be taught even before GCSE. From now on nobody will be able to claim that 'standards are falling'!

Man and of the Citizen of 1789, [. . .] today implies, given the widespread development of the Internet and its importance for participation in democratic life and the expression of ideas and opinions, the freedom to access these services of online public communication'.

This decision should be considered in parallel with the recent debate between the Community institutions (Parliament and Council). In the framework of the revision procedure of the 'Telecoms Reform Package' (co-decision), the European Parliament has, again, voted for an amendment stating that 'no restriction can be imposed on the fundamental rights and freedoms of end-users, without a prior ruling by the judicial authorities'. We thus find in France an echo of this analysis: access to the Internet is a fundamental right of end-users.

But we must not lose sight of the fact that, as we saw on Monday, copyright was founded on the idea that it represented progress and one of the means to allow freedom of expression (while the system of privileges was seen as favouring censorship, copyright was established as a guarantee of liberty).

For all that, the importance of copyright has not been denied by the Constitutional Council, as the latter has also recalled, first, the constitutional value of property rights to which intellectual property belongs, and secondly the importance of the war against copyright infringements in order to preserve this right.

This clearly signifies that the Constitutional Council recognises the possibility for the legislator to enact laws to reconcile the pursuit of the objective of the war against piracy with the free access of citizens to the Internet, which is a component of freedom of communication. But the attacks on freedom of expression and communication which are thus allowed must be necessary, appropriate and proportionate to the objective pursued.

In this context, the Constitutional Council considers that giving the power to restrict or prevent access to the Internet to an administrative authority to combat piracy is disproportionate. This power should be held by the only judicial authority which can guarantee the rights of Internet users.

What is therefore the future of the 'Création et Internet' law? And the Hadopi one?

This is not to say that the regulating authority will never see the light of day, nor even that the proposed construction will be abandoned overall. As the Constitutional Council said 'The role of the High Authority (Hadopi) is to warn the downloader that he has been noticed, but not to penalise him'; this task being assigned, if it must be carried out, to a judge.

The French government therefore committed itself to enact, on 13 June 2009, the thus truncated law rather than to pass a new law which would give a criminal judge the duty of pronouncing sentence, in other words the suspension of the subscription, see 'Epilogue' below.

The judge may act thus, the case having in some way been 'instructed' by the regulatory authority.

The educational messages will continue to be broadcast,[12] but the final judicial decision, which the judge will pronounce totally independently, in any case, without obligation to follow the line of the administrative authority, must naturally respect the presumption of innocence[13] of the subscriber.

Regarding the Internet user, it is sufficient to recall that in France a Chancellery circular of 3 January 2007 had already envisaged a 'proportionate response', distinguishing, for the pronouncement of penalties, between uploading and downloading, and also taking into account the volume, extent and gravity ('primo-upload') of the acts accomplished.

Even if the general architecture, somewhat reorganised, is on the whole retained, it is noticeable that the substitution of a judge for the administrative authority will not lead to the same effect in terms of volume. In fact, the use of the administrative authority led to an automated handling process which would permit the mass management of cases (at least a thousand cases dealt with per day).[14] This objective has very little chance of being achieved with the use of a judge, even with the creation of a specialised chamber.

Certain states were awaiting the implementation of the French solution to begin studying a similar solution. One could imagine that they will now be more circumspect.

One could also wonder whether, in spite of everything, in certain states, the cut-off cannot already happen.

Thus in the United States of America, suspension is already implemented in some universities. In addition, the DMCA (Article 512 i, 1°, clause a) makes the lack of responsibility of the ISPs subordinate to the existence, when this is possible, of a provider policy allowing an end to be put to the problem, for example by cutting access in appropriate circumstances. But

[12] The Hadopi will also have the power to deliver quality labels for the legal alternatives and to set out the 'state of the art' in terms of filtering and so on.

[13] Indeed, while the censored law envisaged that an Internet user would be presumed to have illegally downloaded as soon as his IP address was identified by the beneficiaries, for the wise men of the Constitutional Council, 'in breach of article 9 of the Declaration of 1789, the law thus instituted, in effecting a reversal of the burden of proof, a presumption of guilt which could lead to the subscriber being sentenced to custodial or restrictive penalties'.

[14] Unless there is a penal order procedure?

the most significant developments show themselves in the margins of legal status. Thus the 'RIAA' has made an agreement with the ISPs according to which the technical providers engage to transmit a notification to users suspected by the RIAA of being implicated in acts of piracy. However, to alleviate any disquiet relating to respect of privacy, the RIAA will not request the identity of the customers from the ISPs.

It is true that in certain states the suspension of the subscription as a penalty might equally be carried out but on the basis of a slightly different construction. Most often on the basis of a more consensual collaboration between ISPs and beneficiaries. Thus, the German Federal government, which seems reluctant to adopt a Hadopi type construction, recommended, in its 2008 annual report on Media and Communication, the development of cooperative approaches between the holders of rights and ISPs.

It is not impossible that in the future, providers will be more willing and involved. If only because it raises the question of 'Net neutrality'. If some have been able, wrongly or not, to suspect a certain duplicity on the part of certain technical providers who were complacent in the face of illegal downloads which brought them new subscribers, it is also true to say that saturation of the networks by illegal file transfers is not a happy solution for the ISPs either, due to the limitations of the existing bandwidth. Assuming that virtue is not in itself an incentive to dictate the behaviour of an ISP, economic analysis might be more decisive.

The lesson to draw from this brief exposé is that the responses we produce when cornered are not always the best ones. Would it not be better in the future to be inventive rather than simply defensive? Would it not be better to be active instead of just reactive?

Just like copyright was born three centuries ago in contemplation of a technical, economic and social reality, the copyright of the twenty-first century cannot ignore the evolution of these realities to propose realistic solutions; solutions naturally protective of the balances which led to its creation but also likely to be accepted by the society.

Accepted in such a way that copyright remains perceived as the fair recompense for a creative work that benefits everyone rather than just as a tax. Or even, which would be a terrible reversal of logic, an instrument of censorship or of violation of fundamental rights when, as we have seen, it was born out of exactly the opposite idea!

It is in the interest of an association like ours to be able to calmly consider together the future of our discipline. Our potential differences are also our wealth. I do not know if we are beginning a new cycle of 300 years of copyright, but we can at least, beforehand, try to reasonably write the future together.

4 EPILOGUE

As a consequence of decision no. 2009-580 DC of the Constitutional Council, the French government has prepared a new bill with a slightly different slant. This bill, related to the criminal protection of literary and artistic property on the Internet, was adopted by the Parliament on 22 September 2009 (see Figure 32.1, overleaf). It gives the judge the power to pronounce the suspension of Internet access, notably on the basis of files transmitted by the Hadopi.

As a direct consequence of the judicialisation of the graduated response process, the members of the Rights Protection Committee and its sworn and empowered public agents are given the prerogatives of the police, allowing them to uncover facts likely to lead to infringement of literary or artistic property, as soon as this is committed by means of an online public communication service.

The text adopted by the Parliament was careful to provide reinforced procedural guarantees on behalf of Internet users. Thus, those people having received a recommendation (warning) may transmit their observations to Hadopi agents and be heard at their request by the Rights Protection Committee (accompanied, if they wish, by a counsel of their choice).

Deprived of all power of sanction in terms of graduated response, the Hadopi remains however constrained by Article 40 of the Code of Criminal Procedure to advise the Public Prosecutor of any crime, particularly of infringement, of which it becomes aware. The bill also draws the outline of a class five violation penalising gross negligence of a subscriber who, having received a recorded delivery letter inviting him to implement a means of securing his Internet access, has not taken the measures necessary to do so (Art. L. 335-7-1 CPI – Intellectual Property Code).

The essentials of the plan deal with the criminal procedure (applicable penalties and procedures). Regarding infringements committed by the means of an online public communication service, use of the simplified penal order procedure becomes possible (Art. 495-6-1 of the Code of Criminal Procedure). The judge is also granted the power to pronounce against the perpetrator of these acts a suspension of access for a maximum duration of a year, together with a prohibition on signing another contract during the same period for a service of the same nature with any other operator (Art. L. 335-7 of the Intellectual Property Code). A penalty of suspension may also be pronounced, for a maximum duration of a month, in the case of gross negligence by the subscriber, determined by the Rights Protection Committee of the Hadopi. In all cases, the judge must, in ordering the suspension and determining its duration, ensure the 'reconciliation

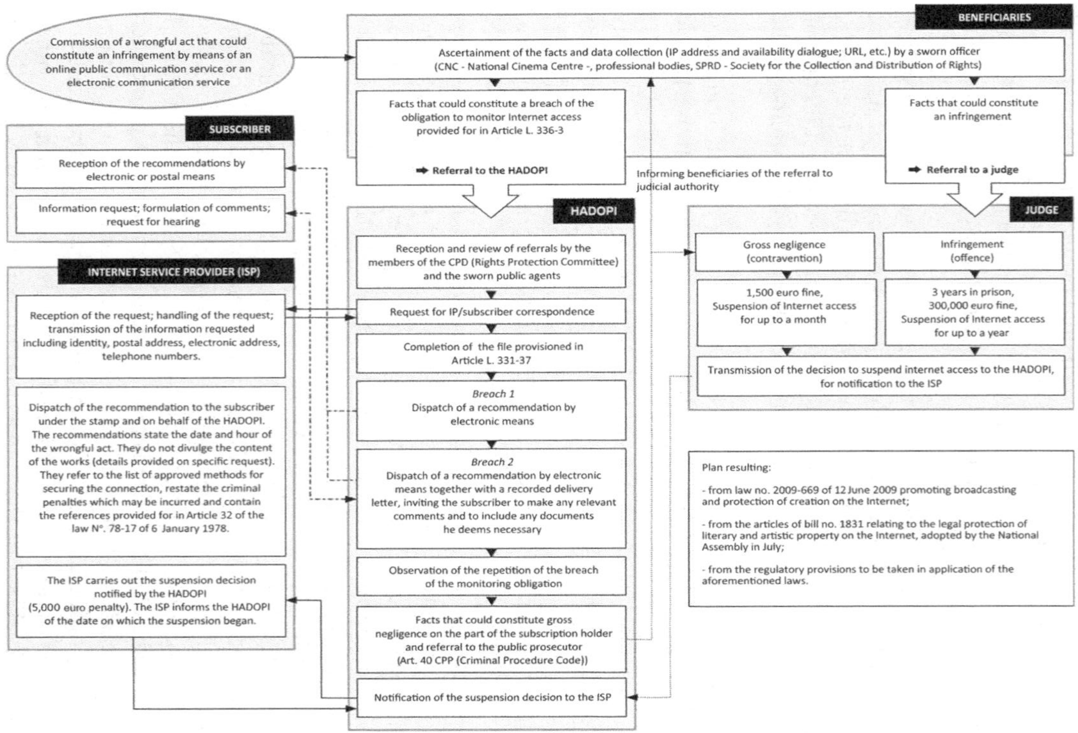

Source: ARMT (Technical Measure Regulation Authority).

Figure 32.1 Table of implementation of the solutions produced by the Hadopi 2 law of September 2009

of intellectual protection and the right to express oneself and communicate freely, particularly from one's home'.

Article L.335-7 provides that, in the case of a 'triple play' offer, the suspension must only affect Internet access and not the television and telephone services. The subscriber whose access has been suspended continues to pay for his contract (unless terminated on his part within the conditions of the contract).

The new law no longer retains the idea of the creation of a national register of those persons having had their access suspended. As a consequence, the obligation on the ISPs to verify that their new customers are not bound by a current suspension also disappears. Re-subscription, however, remains forbidden to the subscriber and may be criminally punished. In addition, the Hadopi remains charged with ensuring that the ISP carries out the decision pronounced by the judge.

A new appeal has been made with the Constitutional Council whose decision should be made public during the month of October.

Closing Speech

Victor Nabhan*

Ladies and Gentlemen,

We have now reached the end of a three-day journey. It has been an exceptional journey, which started off with the Statute of Anne and ended up with global world copyright in the digital age, let alone cosmic copyright, if one follows the path of Professor Sterling, a man of great vision.

A few days ago, I received a book sent to me by Professor Paul Torremans. It had a note attached to it which read as follows:

> Dear Victor
> You will find that reading this book is very useful and instructive before attending our Congress in London.
> Yours Truly,
> Paul

The title of the book: 'The Aliens Guide to Britain and the British'.

I went through the book and found it quite an eye opener!

I learned, among other things, that 'the English appear as one thing, and are actually another. They say one thing, and mean something else'. So much so that 'Brits never say what they mean; often it is the exact opposite, even and particularly when they are being serious'.

I find this quite troubling. In light of this quote, and if I were to behave as a Brit, which in all likelihood is what Professor Torremans expects me to do by sending me the book, I would have to come up with devastating conclusions along the following lines: 'this is one of the worst ALAI Congresses I have ever attended. If not the worst ever. It was terribly organized. The speakers were lousy, the hospitality dreadful. And the food was simply disgusting'.

The problem is that I am not a Brit.

And fortunately so, I dare say, in this very instance.

I really have a hard time understanding why on earth should one be compelled to express the very contrary of what one thinks. I gather that

* ALAI Chairman

there must be a way of stating one's mind while at the same time complying with local customs.

And this is where things get even worse! Let me quote an excerpt from the chapter entitled 'Social Customs':

> You as a foreigner have no chance. Apologise. Keep saying you're sorry. That's good manners. And good manners are what makes the British British.

So here I am confronted with a choice between two attitudes, both of which are equally unsatisfactory: either express the contrary of what I think, which I hate to do, or state my mind and apologize for it, which I equally loathe.

I am afraid the only real choice I am left with, dear Paul, and I am going to be blunt about it, is the following: to hell with your book, and to hell with British good manners as well! I am not going to apologize for what I say. Nor be sorry about it. Nor even be sorry for not being sorry.

Sorry for that.

Now that I am going to speak my mind freely, no more constrained by British rules of good behaviour, let me say in a clear and loud voice that this Congress lived up by all accounts to the historical event it was designed to celebrate.

It all started at the registration desk, with both Jacqui and Maggie, charming, efficient and all smiles. And it continued inside the conference room: excellent speakers offering challenging interventions, chairpersons performing their delicate job with the right amount of flexibility and firmness, and highly professional interpreters. Surprisingly enough, even the food, in a country not renowned for it, was, how shall I put it, extremely . . . edible. And more surprisingly the nice weather did not fail us during the three days!

But above all, one should mention the members of the organizing committee: they have been working hard, and under very difficult conditions, given the economic crisis. They all deserve to be named: Geoffrey Adams, Lionel Bently, Jack Black, Simon Clark, Gillian Davies, Alison Firth, Maria Mercedes Frabbani, Michael Freegard, Florian Koempel, Brigitte Lindner. But perhaps one should single out the three who were even more particularly and deeply involved: Tom Rivers, Paul Torremans, and Uma Suthersanen.

I think they all deserve amply our appreciation. And when I asked Lord Justice Jacob about what his ruling would be in terms of manifesting our thanks, his response was immediate and unequivocal: 'A Standing Ovation'. Consequently may I kindly ask you all to stand and 'ovate', please.

Before leaving, one should keep in mind the statement made during this meeting by Mauren Duffy: 'Let us make sure that there will be a just remuneration for the author, so that the author can continue to create'.

Were not these after all the very objectives of the Statute of Anne: to provide authors and assignees with some right of property 'in order to encourage learned men to compose and write useful books'?

These have been memorable days. So much so that I am already looking forward to the 400th anniversary. So my dear Paul, this is something you should start making plans for. You still have some time to go, but one should not drag one's feet. Except that for next time I am warning you: don't you ever dare send me this silly book again!

Closing dinner speech at Lincoln's Inn, 17 June 2009

Lord Hoffmann*

It is a great honour to address this Congress of the Association Littéraire et Artistique which has such a distinguished record of achievements in international copyright, starting with its foundation under the Presidency of no other literary giant than Victor Hugo in 1878, and playing an important role in that remarkable example of international cooperation achievement less than 10 years later, the Berne Convention.

But tonight we look back 300 years to 1709, to a very different world, in the reign of Louis Quatorze in France and Queen Anne in England. It was certainly not a world of international cooperation: later this year, on September 11, will be the 300th anniversary of the horrific battle of Malplaquet, between the armies of Louis Quatorze and the allied armies led by the Duke of Marlborough; the bloodiest battle of the eighteenth century, in which the Duke lost over 20,000 men. And yet it was a period of great elegance in which literature and the arts flourished in both England and France. Alexander Pope, the greatest English poet of the eighteenth century, had his first poems published by the enterprising publisher Joseph Tonson just 300 years ago last month; at the age of 21 he became instantly famous. The book trade was flourishing. That was the background to the Copyright Act introduced into Parliament in 1709.

The background to the Act is fascinating and I have greatly profited from reading the work of Professor Mark Rose, who addressed the Congress on Monday. There are some themes which emerge from the history which struck me as specially intriguing. The first is the close relationship, after the invention of printing, between – I won't say copyright, but the right to publish and sell books – on the one hand, and government control, or, not to put too fine a point on it, censorship, on the other. The new technology of printing, allowing mass distribution of books and pamphlets, was a threat to the control by government and church over the

* Honorary Professor in Intellectual Property Law, Queen Mary, University of London. Formerly, Lord of Appeal in Ordinary.

information which ordinary people could receive. It was the distribution of printed bibles and other religious works which fuelled the Reformation and enabled the Protestant religion to gain its hold. The reaction of the government in this country was, I think, typically English. They did a deal with the publishers. They granted to the publishers who belonged to the Stationers' Company an exclusive monopoly of printing. In return, the publishers accepted the government censorship of what they could publish, imposed in the sixteenth century through the Committee of the Privy Council which met in the Star Chamber in Whitehall Palace. The publishers made money out of what amounted to a perpetual copyright in the works, buying manuscripts outright from the authors, and the government exercised indirect control without having openly to ban or burn books.

This cosy relationship was blown apart by the English Revolution of the 1640s. The Star Chamber and its censorship was abolished. Everyone was free to set up a printing press in the kitchen and print whatever they liked. The monopoly of the Stationers was broken. For a few years, in the 1640s, England was flooded with books and pamphlets on politics and religion, by all kinds of new political and religious groups: Millenialists, Diggers, Levellers, Vegetarians, Fifth Monarchists; you name them. With the entire constitution up for grabs, Parliament at war with the King, the King executed at the end of the decade, there was a wonderful ferment of ideas about what society should be for. The Stationers were horrified and petitioned Parliament to restore government control. Of course they were not particularly interested in censorship. That was a matter for the politicians. What they wanted was money: the restoration of their monopoly of publishing and they could not think of any way to get it back except by restoring government control of the press. It was at this point in the great crisis of the 1640s that Milton published his essay, *Areopagitica*, arguing that the press should remain free. Just as the Stationers were not particularly bothered about censorship but cared very much about their monopoly of publishing, so Milton did not care very much about whether the Stationers made money but did care a great deal about censorship. If the two had to go together, he wanted none of it. The result is magnificent rhetoric in support of the freedom of the press and freedom in general. We all love it. Everyone in England who writes about the freedom of the press quotes from *Areopagitica*. I have quoted *Areopagitica* in my judgments. But what I did not realise until I looked into the background to the Copyright Act of Queen Anne was the link between politics and money in the forces which Milton was trying to oppose.

What the 1709 Act did was to break that link. It enabled the publishers to have a limited monopoly in their books without having to have a system of government control. It allowed the freedom of the press and the property rights and publishers and authors to co-exist. That was the real innovation. But that brings me to the second interesting point about the historical background. There is a certain view of history, which was popular in the nineteenth century, that things get incrementally better. We were taught that Parliamentary government began in a primitive kind of way in the thirteenth century and gradually improved until we had the fully-fledged democracy we have today. Likewise with copyright, it began as the little acorn of the Act of Queen Anne, providing rights for a relatively short period in printed matter and gradually extended itself to the magnificent oak tree we have today, with much sturdier rights over many forms of artistic and literary creations. This theory of linear development is almost always an oversimplification and certainly so in the case of copyright. Indeed, the work of Professor Rose and others seems to show that, at least in retrospect, the Act of Queen Anne might have been a setback for the publishers rather than an advance. This may seem a bit paradoxical, but there is an explanation. In the seventeenth and well into the eighteenth century, there was a strong view that publishers who bought a book for publication acquired the sole right to publish that book in perpetuity. That was said to be a matter of common law, by the custom of England, and was not dependent on the publishing monopoly they enjoyed under the system of government licensing. John Milton is famous in publishing history not only for *Areopagitica* but also because we have the contract, dated 27 April 1667, by which he sold the right to publish *Paradise Lost* to the printer Samuel Simmons. The terms were a down payment of £5, another £5 when the first edition had been sold and £5 each for a second and third edition. In return for that, Milton sold the manuscript 'with the full benefit profit & advantage thereof or which shall or may arise thereby', exactly as if it was a freehold estate in land. Clearly Simmons thought he was getting the right to publish the book in perpetuity.

However, when the licensing system finally lapsed in 1695, the publishers were nervous that a court might decide that the rights in their books were dependent on the licensing system and so they promoted the idea of a statute which would confirm their rights. What they had in mind was a statute that would give them the perpetual rights which they claimed at common law. It was only during the passage of the bill through Parliament in 1709 that the politicians objected to the idea of a perpetual monopoly and cut it down to a term of 14 years. At first the publishers shrugged this off by saying that it did not matter, they still had their perpetual rights at common law. But then, as we know, the House of Lords decided in 1774 that they had no rights at common law and were entirely dependent on the Act. I can't help feeling that if there had been no Act of 1709 and the publishers had put their common law rights to the test at that time instead, they might have won. What course would English copyright law then have taken?

The last point is the obvious analogy between the sixteenth and seventeenth century concerns of the government to maintain control over the flow of ideas and the Stationers to maintain their profits in publishing, both of which were threatened by the technology of the printing press, and the current concerns of both governments and publishers in the face of digital technology. In 1735 the London booksellers petitioning Parliament for a more effective copyright law than was given to them by the Act of Queen Anne, said 'Authors have ever had property in their works. The invention of printing did not destroy this property of authors, nor alter it in any respect, but by rendering it more easy to be invaded.' That is a complaint which still resonates in the arguments over file sharing and the like.

Looking back into history may yield lessons for today. A meeting of this Congress under the title: 'From 1710 to Cyberspace' is timely for such reflections. For those of you who have come from abroad, I hope you have enjoyed your time in London and that your discussions have not prevented you from enjoying the unusually fine weather we have been having this week.

APPENDICES

whatsoever from and after the tenth day of April One thousand seven hundred and ten within the times granted and limited by this Act as aforesaid shall print, reprint or import, or cause to be printed, reprinted or imported, any such book or books without the consent of the proprietor or proprietors thereof first had and obtained in writing signed in the presence of two or more credible witnesses, or knowing the same to be so printed or reprinted without the consent of the proprietors shall sell, publish or expose to sale, or cause to be sold, published or exposed to sale, any such book or books without such consent first had and obtained as aforesaid, then such offender or offenders shall forfeit such book or books and all and every sheet or sheets being part of such book or books to the proprietor or proprietors of the copy thereof who shall forthwith damask and make waste paper of them; and further that every such offender or offenders shall forfeit one penny for every sheet which shall be found in his, her or their custody either printed or printing, published or exposed to sale contrary to the true intent and meaning of this Act, the one Moiety thereof to the Queens Most Excellent Majesty her heirs and successors and the other Moiety thereof to any person or persons that shall sue for the same to be recovered in any of Her Majesty's Courts of Record at Westminster by action of debt, bill, plaint or information in which no wager of law, essoign, privilege or protection, or more than one imparlance shall be allowed.

s. 2 And whereas many persons may through ignorance offend against this Act unless some provision be made whereby the property in every such book as is intended by this Act to be secured to the proprietor or proprietors thereof may be ascertained as likewise the consent of such proprietor or proprietors for the printing or reprinting of such book or books may from time to time be known, be it therefore further enacted by the authority aforesaid that nothing in this Act contained shall be construed to extend to subject any bookseller, printer or other person whatsoever to the forfeitures or penalties therein mentioned for or by reason of the printing or reprinting of any book or books without such consent as aforesaid unless the title to the copy of such book or books hereafter published shall before such publication be entered in the Register Book of the Company of Stationers in such manner as hath been usual which Register Book shall at all times be kept at the Hall of the said Company, and unless such consent of the proprietor or proprietors be in like manner entered as aforesaid, for every of which several entries sixpence shall be paid and no more; which said Register

Book may at all reasonable and convenient times be resorted to and inspected by any bookseller, printer or other person for the purposes before mentioned, without any fee or reward; and the Clerk of the said Company of Stationers shall when and as often as thereunto required give a certificate under his hand of such entry or entries and for every such certificate may take a fee not exceeding six pence.

s. 3 Provided nevertheless that if the Clerk of the said Company of Stationers for the time being shall refuse or neglect to register or make such entry or entries or to give such certificate being thereunto required by the author or proprietor of such copy or copies in the presence of two or more credible witnesses, that then such person and persons so refusing, notice being first duly given of such refusal by an advertisement in the Gazette, shall have the like benefit as if such entry or entries, certificate or certificates, had been duly made and given; and that the clerks so refusing shall for any such offence forfeit to the proprietor of such copy or copies the sum of twenty pounds to be recovered in any of Her Majesty's Courts of Record at Westminster by action of debt, bill, plaint or information in which no wager of law, essoign, privilege or protection, or more than one imparlance shall be allowed.

s. 4 Provided nevertheless, and it is hereby further enacted by the authority aforesaid, that if any bookseller or booksellers, printer or printers, shall after the said Five and twentieth day of March One thousand Seven hundred and ten set a price upon or sell or expose to sale any book or books at such a price or rate as shall be conceived by any person or persons to be too high and unreasonable, it shall and may be lawful for any person or persons to make complaint thereof to the Lord Archbishop of Canterbury for the time being, the Lord Chancellor or Lord Keeper of the Great Seal of Great Britain for the time being, the Lord Bishop of London for the time being, the Lord Chief Justice of the Court of Queens Bench, the Lord Chief Justice of the Court of Common Pleas, the Lord Chief Baron of the Court of Exchequer for the time being, the Vice-Chancellors of the two Universities for the time being, in that part of Great Britain called England, the Lord President of the Sessions for the time being, the Lord Justice General for the time being, the Lord Chief Baron of the Exchequer for the time being, the Rector of the College of Edinburgh for the time being, in that part of Great Britain called Scotland, who or any one of them shall and have hereby full power and authority from time to time to send for, summon or call before him or them such bookseller or booksellers, printer or printers, and to examine and enquire of the reason of the dearness and enhancement of the price or value of such book or books by him or them so sold or exposed to sale; and if upon such enquiry and examination it shall be found that the price of such book or books is enhanced or any wise too high or unreasonable, then and in such case the said Archbishop of Canterbury, Lord Chancellor or Lord Keeper, Bishop of London, two Chief Justices, Chief Baron, Vice-Chancellors of the Universities, in that part of Great Britain called England, and the said Lord President of the Sessions, Lord Justice General, Lord Chief Baron, and Rector of the College of Edinburgh, in that part of Great Britain called Scotland, or any one or more of them so enquiring and examining have hereby full power and authority to reform and redress the same and to limit and settle the price of every such printed book and books from time to time according to the best of their judgments and as to them shall seem just and reasonable; and in case of alteration of the rate or price from what was set or demanded by such bookseller or booksellers, printer or printers, to award and order such bookseller or booksellers, printer or printers, to pay all the costs and charges that the person or persons so complaining shall be put unto by reason of such complaint and of the causing such rate or price to be so limited and settled; all which shall be done by the said Archbishop of Canterbury, Lord Chancellor or Lord Keeper, Bishop of London, two Chief Justices, Chief Baron, Vice-Chancellors of the two Universities, in that part of Great Britain called England, and the said Lord President of the Sessions, Lord Justice General, Lord Chief Baron, and Rector of the College of Edinburgh, in that part of Great Britain called Scotland, or any one of them by writing under their hands and seals, and thereof public notice shall be forthwith given by the said bookseller or booksellers, printer or printers, by an advertisement in the Gazette; and if any bookseller or booksellers, printer or printers, shall after such settlement made of the said rate and price sell or expose to sale any book or books at a higher or greater price than what shall have been so limited and settled as aforesaid, then and in every such case such bookseller and booksellers, printer or printers, shall forfeit the sum of five pounds for every such book so by him, her or them sold or exposed to sale, one Moiety thereof to the Queens Most Excellent Majesty her heirs and successors and the other Moiety to any person or persons that shall sue for the same to be recovered with costs of suit in any of her Majesty's Courts of Record at Westminster by action of debt, bill, plaint or information in which no wager of law, essoign, privilege or protection, or more than one imparlance shall be allowed.

s. 5 Provided always, and it is hereby enacted, that nine copies of each book or books upon the best paper that from and after the tenth day of April One thousand seven hundred and ten shall be printed and published as aforesaid or reprinted and published with additions shall by the printer and printers thereof be delivered to the Warehouse-Keeper of the said Company of Stationers for the time being at the hall of the said Company before such publication made for the use of the Royal Library, the Libraries of the Universities of Oxford and Cambridge, the Libraries of the four Universities in Scotland, the Library of Sion College in London, and the Library commonly called the Library belonging to the Faculty of Advocates at Edinburgh respectively; which said Warehouse-Keeper is hereby required within ten days after demand by the Keepers of the respective libraries or any person or persons by them or any of them authorised to demand the said copy to deliver the same for the use of the aforesaid libraries; and if any proprietor, bookseller or printer or the Warehouse-Keeper of the said Company of Stationers shall not observe the direction of this Act therein, that then he and they so making default in not delivering the said printed copies as aforesaid shall forfeit besides the value of the said printed copies the sum of five pounds for every copy not so delivered, as also the value of the said printed copy not so delivered the same to be recovered by the Queens Majesty her heirs and successors, and by the Chancellor, Masters and Scholars of any of the said Universities, and by the President and Fellows of Sion College, and the said Faculty of Advocates at Edinburgh with their full costs respectively.

s. 6 Provided always and be it further enacted that if any person or persons incur the penalties contained in this Act in that part of Great Britain called Scotland they shall be recoverable by any action before the Court of Session there.

s. 7 Provided that nothing in this Act contained do extend or shall be construed to extend to prohibit the importation, vending or selling of any books in Greek, Latin or any other foreign language printed beyond the seas, any thing in this Act contained to the contrary notwithstanding.

s. 8 And be it further enacted by the authority aforesaid that if any action or suit shall be commenced or brought against any person or persons whatsoever for doing or causing to be done any thing in pursuance of this Act the defendants in such action may plead the General Issue and give the special matter in evidence; and if upon such action a verdict be given for the defendant or the plaintiff become nonsuited or discontinue his action then the defendant shall have and recover his full costs for which he shall have the same remedy as a defendant in any case by law hath.

s. 9 Provided that nothing in this Act contained shall extend or be construed to extend either to prejudice or confirm any right that the said Universities or any of them or any person or persons have or claim to have to the printing or reprinting any book or copy already printed or hereafter to be printed.

s. 10 Provided nevertheless that all actions, suits, bills, indictments or informations for any offence that shall be committed against this Act, shall be brought, sued and commenced within three months next after such offence committed or else the same shall be void and of none effect.

s. 11 Provided always, that after the expiration of the said term of fourteen years the sole right of printing or disposing of copies shall return to the authors thereof if they are then living for another term of fourteen years.

Appendix 2 Further reading*

Deazley, R., *On the Origins of the Right to Copy* (Oxford, 2004)
Deazley, R., *Re-Thinking Copyright: History, Theory, Language* (Cheltenham, 2006)
Feather, J., *A History of British Publishing* (London, 1988)
Feather, J., *Publishing, Piracy and Politics: an Historical Study of Copyright in Britain* (London, 1994)
Gómez-Arostegui, H.T., 'What History Teaches Us about Copyright Injunctions and the Inadequate Remedy-at-Law Requirement' (2008) 81 *Southern California L.R.* 1197–1280
Kaplan, B., *An Unhurried View of Copyright* (New York, 1967)
McFarlane, G., *Copyright: the Development and Exercise of the Performing Right* (Eastbourne, 1980)
Myers,R. and Harris, M. (eds), *Development of the English Book Trade, 1700–1899* (Oxford, 1981)
Patry, W., *Copyright* (New York, 2007) Volume I
Raven, J., *The Business of Books: Booksellers and the English Book Trade* (New Haven, 2007)
Rose, M., *Authors and Owners: the Invention of Copyright* (Cambridge MA, 1993)
St Clair, W., *The Reading Nation in the Romantic Period* (Cambridge, 2004)
Saunders, D., *Authorship and Copyright* (London, 1992)
Sherman, B. and Strowel, A., *Of Authors and Origins* (Oxford.1994)
Seville, C.A., *Literary Copyright Reform in Early Victorian England: the Framing of the 1842 Copyright Act* (Cambridge, 1999)

* Provided by Prof. Em. William Cornish.

Index